MAKING GLOBAL TRADE GOVERNANCE WORK FOR DEVELOPMENT

Discussion of the governance of global trade and the multilateral trading system is too often dominated by developed country scholars and opinion-makers, with inadequate attention to developing country perspectives. *Making Global Trade Governance Work for Development* gathers a diversity of developing country views on how to improve the governance of global trade and the WTO to better advance sustainable development and respond to developing country priorities. With contributions by senior scholars, commentators and practitioners, the essays combine new, empirically grounded research and practical insights about the trade policy-making process. They consider the specific governance issues of interest to developing countries and acknowledge the changing dynamics in the global economy and in trade decision-making.

CAROLYN DEERE BIRKBECK is a Senior Researcher at Oxford University's Global Economic Governance Programme, where she is Director of its Global Trade Governance Project and leads its Expert Taskforce on Global Knowledge Governance.

MAKING GLOBAL TRADE GOVERNANCE WORK FOR DEVELOPMENT

Perspectives and Priorities from Developing Countries

Edited by

CAROLYN DEERE BIRKBECK

CAMBRIDGE
UNIVERSITY PRESS

CAMBRIDGE UNIVERSITY PRESS
Cambridge, New York, Melbourne, Madrid, Cape Town,
Singapore, São Paulo, Delhi, Tokyo, Mexico City

Cambridge University Press
The Edinburgh Building, Cambridge CB2 8RU, UK

Published in the United States of America by Cambridge University Press, New York

www.cambridge.org
Information on this title: www.cambridge.org/9781107007826

First published 2011

Printed in the United Kingdom at the University Press, Cambridge

A catalogue record for this publication is available from the British Library

Library of Congress Cataloguing in Publication data
Making global trade governance work for development : perspectives
and priorities from developing countries / [edited by] Carolyn Deere Birkbeck.
p. cm.
Includes bibliographical references and index.
ISBN 978-1-107-00782-6 (hardback)
1. Foreign trade regulation – Developing countries. 2. Free trade – Developing
countries. 3. World Trade Organization – Developing countries. 4. International
economic integration. 5. Globalization. I. Deere-Birkbeck, Carolyn, 1973–
II. Title.
K3943.M345 2011
343.′124087–dc23
2011017976

ISBN 978-1-107-00782-6 Hardback

CONTENTS

FIGURES

TABLES AND BOXES

Tables

Boxes

CONTRIBUTORS

LUISA BERNAL works as a Policy Specialist at the United Nations Development Program's (UNDP's) Trade and Human Development Unit in Geneva. Before joining UNDP, she was Coordinator of the Trade for Development Programme at the South Centre in Geneva where she provided technical assistance on trade negotiations to developing countries. She worked as a diplomat for the Permanent Mission of Venezuela to the World Trade Organization (WTO) and served as project manager at the Ministry of Production and Commerce of Venezuela. Some of her publications include *Agricultural Special Safeguards in the Context of the Economic Partnership Agreements in Trade Relations Between the EU and Africa* (2010) edited by Yenkong Ngangjoh-Hodu and Francis Matambalya, and *Methodology for the Identification of Special Products (SP) and Products for Eligibility under Special Safeguard Mechanism (SSM) by Developing Countries* (2005). She holds a Masters degree in International Affairs from Columbia University (New York) and a Bachelor of Arts degree from Universidad Central de Venezuela.

RICHARD L. BERNAL is the alternative Executive Director for the Caribbean in the Inter-American Development Bank. He was previously lead trade negotiator on behalf of the CARICOM and CARIFORUM countries in the Free-Trade Area of the Americas (FTAA), EU-CARIFORUM Economic Partnership agreement and the WTO. Between 2001 and 2008, he was Director-General of the Caribbean Regional Negotiating Machinery. He was Jamaica's ambassador to the USA and Permanent Representative to the Organization of American States (OAS) during 1991–2001. Earlier in his career, Ambassador Bernal was CEO of a commercial bank and previously worked in Jamaica's Central Bank and Ministry of Finance. He has taught international and development economics at the University of the West Indies. Dr Bernal holds a BSc in Economics from the University of the West Indies, an MA and PhD in Economics from the New School for Social Research and an

MIPP (international public policy) from the School for Advanced and International Studies, Johns Hopkins University.

TRINEESH BISWAS is Adviser to the Chief Executive at the International Centre for Trade and Sustainable Development (ICTSD). Prior to his current role at ICTSD, he edited *Bridges Weekly Trade News*, an electronic news bulletin covering developments at the intersection of trade and sustainable development, writing on issues ranging from the Doha Round negotiations at the WTO to food security and access to medicine. Previously, Mr Biswas worked on trade and investment issues for the International Institute for Sustainable Development (IISD). Born in Canada, Mr Biswas went to high school in New Delhi before going on to do a BA in Government from Cornell University and an MA in Political Science from the University of Toronto. A Canadian citizen, he currently lives in Geneva.

OLIVIER CATTANEO, a French national, is a Research Associate with the Groupe d'Economie Mondiale de SciencesPo, Paris, where he is also an Adjunct Professor. From 2005 to 2010, he worked in different capacities at the World Bank, including as a Senior Trade Specialist in charge of the Global Trade and Financial Architecture project. Prior to joining the Bank, he led the trade work at the Agence Française de Développement. His previous experience also includes work with the French Parliament (Finance Committee), the Ministry of Labor and Social Affairs (Minister's Private Office), the Ministry of Health (Minister's Private Office), the United Nations Office in Geneva (Director-General's Office), the WTO (Liaison Office) and the OECD (Trade Department). His most recent publications include *Effective Crisis Response and Openness: Implications for the Trading System*, co-editor with S. Evenett and B. Hoekman (2009); *The Fateful Allure of Protectionism: Taking Stock for the G8*, co-editor with S. Evenett and B. Hoekman (2009); *The WTO and Accession Countries*, two volumes, co-editor with C. A. Primo Braga (2009). Dr Cattaneo has taught WTO law at the joint LLM Program with Columbia Law School and the University of Paris I Panthéon-Sorbonne. Previously, he was a lecturer in Human Science at the Ecole Nationale des Ponts et Chaussées. Dr Cattaneo is a New York Attorney and Counselor at Law. He holds a PhD in International Law from the Graduate Institute in Geneva, and received degrees from the Georgetown University Law Center and SciencesPo, Paris. He was a World Fellow at Yale University, an IIEL Fellow at Georgetown University and a SYLFF Fellow at the Graduate Institute.

BHUPINDER CHIMNI is Chairperson of the Centre for International Legal Studies (CILS) at Jawaharlal Nehru University, New Delhi. He is the former Vice Chancellor of West Bengal National University of Juridical Sciences, Kolkata. He has been a visiting professor at Brown and Tokyo Universities and a visiting scholar/fellow at Harvard, York (Canada), Cambridge and Minnesota Universities, as well as at the Max Planck Institute for Comparative and Public International Law, Heidelberg. He has taught international economic law for over twenty-five years and is the author of *International Commodity Agreements: A Legal Study*. He has also published a number of articles on different aspects of international economic law in leading journals. Dr Chimni has delivered several prestigious lectures including the Eighth Grotius Lecture at the Centennial Meeting of the American Society of International Law in Washington (2006) and the Sir Kenneth Bailey Memorial Lecture at the Melbourne Law School (2007). He self-identifies as a Member of a group of scholars engaged in articulating a critical third world approach to international law. He is a General Editor of the *Asian Yearbook of International Law* and a Member of the Executive Council, Asian Society of International Law.

CAROLYN DEERE BIRKBECK is a Senior Researcher at the Global Economic Governance Programme (GEG) at the University of Oxford where she is Director of GEG's Global Trade Governance Project and its Expert Taskforce on Global Knowledge Governance. She is an Associate Fellow at the Royal Institute for International Affairs and was a Resident Scholar at ICTSD from 2008 to 2010. She is also the founder and Chair of the Board of Directors of Intellectual Property Watch. Dr Deere Birkbeck previously worked at the Rockefeller Foundation in New York where she was responsible for grant-making on intellectual property, trade and sustainable development. In partnership with colleagues across the Foundation, she designed and coordinated the Foundation's initiative to Promote a Fairer Course for Intellectual Property Policy and launched the Bellagio Series on Development and Intellectual Property Policy. During this time, she also co-founded the Funders Network on Trade and Globalization (FNTG) and served on its Steering Committee. Prior to moving to the Rockefeller Foundation, she worked in Washington, DC for the World Conservation Union (IUCN) and was the Manager of the Congressional Staff Forum on International Development at the Overseas Development Council (ODC). She has been a consultant to a range of non-governmental and international organizations, including the World Intellectual Property Organization, UNDP's Office of the Human Development Report, the National Wildlife

Federation, the Yale Centre for Environmental Law and Policy, the Open Society Institute and the South Centre. Among other publications, Dr Deere Birkbeck is the author of *The Implementation Game: The TRIPS Agreement and the Global Politics of Intellectual Property Reform in Developing Countries* (2008) and co-editor (with Dan Esty) of *Greening the Americas: NAFTA's Lessons for Hemispheric Trade* (2002). She holds a DPhil in International Relations (University College, Oxford), an MA (Johns Hopkins University School of Advanced International Studies) and a Bachelor of Economics (Hons I) (Political Economy) from the University of Sydney. She is an Australian and British citizen.

HENRY GAO is a tenured law professor at Singapore Management University. With law degrees from China, the UK and the USA, Dr Gao started his professional career in Geneva as the first Chinese lawyer at the WTO Secretariat with stints at the Appellate Body Secretariat and Trade in Services Division before returning to Asia to teach in 2003. Dr Gao has extensive experience in conducting WTO training programmes, including organizing and lecturing in the official WTO Regional Trade Policy Course for developing countries in the Asia-Pacific region. Over the past decade, he has also designed and delivered numerous training courses for the governments of China, Hong Kong, Singapore, Canada and Australia, as well as major international donors such as ADB, APEC and ASEAN, and has been a consultant to the World Bank. Dr Gao is a Member of the Committee on International Trade Law of the International Law Association, based in London; the Nominating Committee of the Society of International Economic Law, based in Geneva; the Board of Directors of the China WTO Law Studies Association, based in Beijing; and the Asian WTO Research Network, based in Tokyo. He is also a Member of the international Advisory Board of the WTO Chairs Programme, which was established by the WTO in 2009 to promote research, teaching and training activities on WTO issues in leading universities around the world. A frequent commentator in major international media such as the *Wall Street Journal*, CNN and Bloomberg, Dr Gao's writings have appeared as chapters in books and articles in international journals, including *Journal of International Economic Law* and *Journal of World Trade*.

ARUNABHA GHOSH is Chief Executive Officer at the Council on Energy, Environment and Water (CEEW). This research was undertaken when he was an Oxford–Princeton Global Leaders Fellow at the Woodrow Wilson School of Public and International Affairs, Princeton. He is also Associate at the Global Economic Governance Programme, Oxford, and Faculty Associate at the Smith School of Enterprise and the Environment, Oxford. He was previously a Policy Specialist at the United Nations Development Programme in New York and co-author of three Human Development Reports. Dr Ghosh led research on transboundary water basins, intellectual property and the rights of indigenous people, violent conflict and extremist movements, and has undertaken/advised research projects on aid, financial crises and trade negotiations for DFID (UK), IDRC (Canada) and the Commonwealth Secretariat. His advocacy efforts for human development span a documentary on the water crisis set out of Africa, presentations to the President of India, the Indian Parliament and other legislatures, training of ministers in Central Asia, public lectures in several countries and regular articles in the print media. He is on the editorial board of the *Journal of Human Development and Capabilities.* Dr Ghosh holds a DPhil in International Relations from the University of Oxford.

FAIZEL ISMAIL is the Permanent Representative of South Africa to the World Trade Organization, based in Geneva. He joined the new democratic government of South Africa in 1994 as it began its transition to reintegrate with the world economy and led South Africa's trade negotiations with the European Union, the Southern African Development Community, the Southern African Customs Union and the WTO. He chaired the WTO Committee on Trade and Development Special Session (CTDSS) between 2004 and 2006 and the WTO Committee on Trade and Development (CTD) in 2006/7. He has written numerous articles on trade and development and published two books: *Mainstreaming Development in the WTO: Developing Countries in the Doha Round* (2007), and *Reforming the World Trade Organization: Developing Countries in the Doha Round* (2009). He holds an MPhil degree in Development Studies from the Institute of Development Studies, University of Sussex, UK, and BA and LLB degrees from the University of Kwa-Zulu Natal, South Africa. He is an Associate Editor of the *Journal of World Trade.*

RASHID S. KAUKAB is Deputy Director and Research Coordinator, CUTS Geneva Resource Centre. From 1998 to 2008 he worked at the South Centre, an intergovernmental organization of developing countries, as coordinator of the Programme on Trade and Development, Head of Strategic Policy and Planning, and then as Acting Head of Programme and Research Coordination at the South Centre. He led the South Centre delegation to the Geneva, Seattle, Doha and Cancún Ministerial

Conferences of the WTO and the XI Ministerial Conference of the United Nations Conference on Trade and Development (UNCTAD). He also attended the X Ministerial Conference of UNCTAD and the Hong Kong WTO Ministerial Conference of the WTO as Deputy Head of the South Centre delegation. Before joining the South Centre, Mr Kaukab worked as a Pakistani delegate to the WTO from the middle of 1995 until early 1998. During this time he was actively involved in the negotiations on implementation and the built-in agenda (i.e. agriculture, services and intellectual property) of the Uruguay Round agreements, and other issues under the WTO. He was also a Member of the Pakistani delegation to the First WTO Ministerial Conference, held in Singapore in December 1996 and IX Ministerial Conference of UNCTAD, held in Midrand, South Africa. Mr Kaukab graduated from GC Lahore in Economics and English Literature and has Masters degrees in Economics (Karachi University) and Business Administration (Yale University).

ATUL KAUSHIK is currently Director (Climate Change), Ministry of Environment and Forests in India and was previously head of CUTS Geneva Resource Center. He has more than two decades of research and practitioner experience on multilateral trade and development policy, including assignments to implement the Uruguay Round commitments of India and as legal officer and trade negotiator in India's Mission to the WTO. Mr Kaushik is a science and law graduate and holds postgraduate qualifications in management. He contributed to the literature on trade and environment, intellectual property, Aid for Trade for least developed countries (LDCs) and developing countries in the WTO dispute settlement mechanism.

EDWIN LAURENT has spent much of his working life as a diplomat and is currently Head of Trade and Regional Cooperation at the Commonwealth Secretariat where he leads a team undertaking research and advocacy on interlinkages between trade and development. He also helps Commonwealth developing country Members build their trade capacity and provides policy advice. Ambassador Laurent was educated at the University of the West Indies, Manchester University and the Johns Hopkins School of Advanced International Studies in Washington, DC. His public service started in Saint Lucia's Ministry of Finance and he was subsequently appointed Permanent Secretary, Ministry of Trade, Industry and Tourism where he helped foster a constructive and collaborative relationship between the Ministry and the private sector. From 1989 he served as a diplomat first in London then as Permanent Representative to the WTO and the Food and Agriculture Organization. Subsequent postings included ambassadorships to France, Germany and Belgium. He became the first Eastern Caribbean States Ambassador to the EU. While in Brussels, he was active in the African, Caribbean and Pacific Group of States; chaired the Banana Working Group; and at times various Ambassadorial bodies, including the Caribbean Group, the Committee on Trade and Commodities and, in ACP negotiations with the EU, where he was the lead Ambassadorial negotiator on certain subjects. In 2004, Ambassador Laurent was appointed by the Windward Islands' Governments as their Special Envoy to the EU on bananas and organized a broad-based coalition campaign to safeguard the islands' banana exports. He has provided capacity-building support and lectured on Economic Partnership Agreements and WTO negotiations in West and Central Africa and written on trade and commodity issues and on international negotiations.

YONG-SHIK LEE is a scholar in international trade law and economic development. Professor Lee has taught at leading universities in the United States, Asia and Australia. He is currently the Director and Professorial Fellow of the Law and Development Institute. He graduated in economics with academic distinction from the University of California at Berkeley and studied law at the University of Cambridge. He is the author of *Reclaiming Development in the World Trading System* (Cambridge University Press, 2009), *Safeguard Measures in World Trade: The Legal Analysis* (2007) and *Economic Development through World Trade: A Developing World Perspective* (2008). He is an Associate Editor of the *Journal of World Trade* and the Founding Editor-in-Chief of the *Law and Development Review*.

DAVID LUKE is a Trade, Debt and Globalization Adviser to the UNDP, assigned to Southern African countries. His career experience encompasses policy management and analysis including trade negotiations and academic teaching and research. In particular, from 1995 to 2001, he was the Organization of African Unity (OAU) focal point on WTO issues. In this capacity, he coordinated the preparation of OAU Member States for the Singapore, Geneva, Seattle and Doha WTO Ministerial Conferences. Dr Luke's previous appointments were Senior Economist Multilateral Trade Issues at the Permanent Mission of the OAU in Geneva (1999–2001); Chief of Trade Section at OAU Headquarters, Addis Ababa (1995–9); Adviser and Consultant at the Economic Development and

Cooperation Department, OAU Headquarters and at the UN Economic Commission for Africa, respectively, Addis Ababa (1992–5); Hallsworth Fellow, Institute of Development Policy and Management, University of Manchester, UK (1990–1); and Associate Professor, Assistant Professor and Killam Postdoctoral Fellow, Dalhousie University, Halifax, Canada (1982–93). A Canadian citizen, Dr Luke was educated at the London School of Economics (BSc Honours, 1977, MSc 1978) and at the London School of Oriental and African Studies (PhD 1982).

NIALL MEAGHER has been Senior Counsel at the ACWL since September 2004. In this capacity, he has assisted ACWL Members and LDCs in several WTO dispute settlement proceedings before WTO panels, the Appellate Body and arbitrators, and has prepared numerous legal opinions on issues of WTO law. He also participates in the ACWL's training activities and is a frequent writer and speaker on issues of trade law. Prior to joining the ACWL, Mr Meagher was a partner in the international trade and dispute resolution practice of the law firms of Sidley Austin LLP, and, previously, Powell Goldstein LLP, in Washington, DC. He represented both governments and interested private parties in WTO dispute settlement proceedings, international investment disputes, and in domestic customs and trade remedy proceedings before national regulatory authorities. Mr Meagher also gained extensive experience in all aspects of domestic anti-dumping, countervailing duty and safeguards proceedings, and regularly argued trade and customs law cases before the US Court of International Trade and the US Court of Appeals. Mr Meagher holds a Bachelor of Laws (LLB) from Trinity College, Dublin, and a Master of Laws (LLM) from the Law School of the University of Chicago. Mr Meagher's recent publications include a series of articles on WTO dispute settlement in the *World Trade Review* and a chapter on the same topic in the *Princeton Encyclopedia of the World Economy* (with David Palmeter).

RICARDO MELÉNDEZ-ORTIZ is co-founder of the International Centre for Trade and Sustainable Development and has been its Chief Executive Officer since 1996. Previously, he co-founded and was Director-General of Fundación Futuro Latinoamericano (Quito). He has represented Colombia as a negotiator in several multilateral fora, including as permanent delegate of Colombia in Geneva and as a negotiator in GATT's Uruguay Round, the Rio '92 UN Conference process, UNCTAD VIII, the Climate Change Convention, the Intergovernmental Panel on Climate Change (IPCC) and the Montreal Protocol. He acted as spokesperson for the G77 in several fora and served as Chair of the UN Standing Committees on Commodities and on Trade Preferences. Earlier, he served as Principal Adviser to the Colombian Minister of Economic Development and as Chief of Administration of the Office of the President of Colombia. Since 1997, Mr Meléndez-Ortiz has been the publisher of *BRIDGES* and its sister publications. A graduate of Harvard University, he has edited, authored and published a wide range of books, articles and opinion pieces in English, French and Spanish on economic governance, trade, sustainable development and conflict management, including *Envisioning a Sustainable Development Agenda for Trade and Environment* (2007) with A. Najam and M. Halle; *Agricultural Subsidies in the WTO Green Box: Ensuring Coherence with Sustainable Development Goals* (Cambridge University Press, 2009) edited with C. Bellmann and J. Hepburn; *Intellectual Property and Sustainable Development: Agendas in a Changing World* (2009) edited with P. Roffe; and *WTO Dispute Settlement: The Developing Country Experience* (Cambridge University Press, 2010) edited with G. Shaffer.

JULIAN MUKIIBI, a Ugandan national, is a lawyer with a postgraduate degree in International Trade Law and Economics. He currently works as a Programme Officer at CUTS Geneva Resource Centre, and previously served as an Advisor on Legal and Economic Affairs in Uganda's Mission to the WTO. Prior to that worked as a research officer at the NGO CUTS Geneva Resource Centre, where he contributed to the literature on the East Africa Community trade agreements and integration process. He has also worked in private legal practice and worked for over ten years in the Uganda Revenue Authority, the revenue-collecting entity in Uganda.

ALEJANDRO NADAL is a professor at El Colegio de México, where he directed the Research Program on Science, Technology and Development (1982–2007). He has a BA in Law from the National Autonomous University and a PhD in Economics from the University of Paris X (Nanterre). He covers issues from macroeconomics, general equilibrium theory, technical change and nuclear weapons, to sustainable resource management. Dr Nadal's publications include *Rethinking Macroeconomics for Sustainability* (2010); and 'Redesigning the World's Trading System for Sustainable Development' in A. Najam, M. Halle and R. Meléndez-Ortiz (eds.) *Trade and Environment: Visions from the South* (2007). He is Member of the editorial board of *International Environmental Agreements*, the *International Journal of Technology, Management & Sustainable*

Development and *Global Environmental Politics*. He is co-Chair of the Theme on the Environment, Macroeconomics, Trade and Investment (TEMTI) as part of the Commission for Environmental, Economic and Social Policies (CEESP) of the International Union for the Conservation of Nature (IUCN). He writes a weekly column on economics and sustainability in *La Jornada*, one of Mexico's leading national newspapers.

AMRITA NARLIKAR is University Senior Lecturer at the Department of Politics and International Studies at Cambridge University, and is Official Fellow of Darwin College. Prior to joining Cambridge in 2004, Dr Narlikar held a permanent lectureship at the University of Exeter (2003–4), won a Research Fellowship at St John's College, Oxford (1999–2003) and held a Visiting Fellowship at Yale (Spring 2002). Her degrees include a Cambridge PhD (by incorporation), an Oxford DPhil and MPhil from Balliol, an MA from the School of International Studies, JNU, Delhi and a BA (Hons) in History from St Stephen's College, Delhi. Dr Narlikar is the author and editor of numerous books and papers in the areas of trade politics, multilateral negotiations and rising powers. Current projects include *The Oxford Handbook of the World Trade Organization* (which she is co-editing with Professors Martin Daunton and Robert Stern); and a co-authored book (with Professor Andrew Hurrell) entitled *Pathways to Power: Brazil and India in International Regimes*. She is Editor-in-Chief of the book series, *Studies in International Institutional Dynamics*, published with the Republic of Letters (an offshoot of Brill), and has served as a Commissioner on the First Warwick Commission on the Reform of the Multilateral Trading System.

JOSÉ ANTONIO OCAMPO is a Professor of Professional Practice in International and Public Affairs and Director of the Program in Economic and Political Development at the School of International and Public Affairs, Columbia University. He is also a Member of Columbia University's Committee on Global Thought and co-President of the Initiative for Policy Dialogue. In 2008 he won the Leontief Prize for Advancing the Frontiers of Economic Thought. Prior to his appointment, Professor Ocampo served in a number of positions in the United Nations and the Government of Colombia, most notably as United Nations Under-Secretary General for Economic and Social Affairs; Executive Secretary of the Economic Commission for Latin America and the Caribbean (ECLAC); Minister of Finance and Public Credit, Chairman of the Board of Banco del República (Central Bank of Colombia); Director, National Planning Department

(Minister of Planning); Minister of Agriculture and Rural Development, and Executive Director, FEDESARROLLO. Dr Ocampo received his BA in Economics and Sociology from the University of Notre Dame and his PhD in Economics from Yale University, 1976. He was previously a Professor in the Advanced Programme on Rethinking Development Economics at Cambridge University, a Professor of Economics at Universidad de los Andes, a Professor of Economic History at the National University of Colombia, as well as a Visiting Fellow at Yale and Oxford. Dr Ocampo is the author of numerous books and articles on macroeconomics policy and theory, economic development, international trade and economic history. His recent publications include *Growth and Policy in Developing Countries: A Structuralist Approach*, with Lance Taylor and Codrina Rada (2009), and *Time for a Visible Hand: Lessons from the 2008 World Financial Crisis*, co-edited with Stephany Griffith-Jones and Joseph E. Stiglitz (2010).

FÉLIX PEÑA is a specialist in international economic relations and negotiations, economic integration and foreign trade policy. He has a Law degree from the Universidad del Litoral Law School in Santa Fe; a Doctorate degree in Law from the Universidad de Madrid; and a European Law degree from the Catholic University of Louvain, Belgium, where he also studied economics. At present, he is Professor at Universidad Nacional de Tres de Febrero and Director of its Master's programme in International Trade Relations; Director of the Institute of International Trade-Standard Bank Foundation; Professor at EPOCA-Universidad del Salvador; Member of the Executive Board of the Consejo Argentino para las Relaciones Internacionales (CARI); Chairman of the Academic Council of Fundación Export-Ar; Member of the Group of Experts on EU-Mercosur relations at the Chaire Mercosur – SciencesPo, Paris; Member of the Evian Group Brains Trust; and an independent consultant. Dr Peña was formerly Undersecretary of Foreign Trade in Argentina's Ministry of Economics in charge of Mercosur affairs and Undersecretary of Economic Integration in the Ministry of Foreign Affairs, also in charge of Mercosur affairs. Previously, he was Deputy Manager for Integration at the Inter-American Development Bank (IADB); Undersecretary of Economic International Relations in the Ministry of Foreign Affairs; and Expert and then Director of the INTAL-IADB.

CARLOS PRIMO BRAGA, a Brazilian national, is Special Representative and Director, External Affairs, Europe of the World Bank Group. Since January 2008, he has been the Director, Economic Policy and

Debt in the Poverty Reduction and Economic Management Network (PREM). His main roles in this capacity are to provide integrated support to country programmes in the areas of debt, macro-policy and inclusive growth. He is also the Chairman of the Economic Policy Sector Board of the World Bank. He was previously Senior Adviser of the PREM Vice-Presidency, anchoring strategic relationships with key shareholder groupings (e.g. G7/8, G20, G24, APEC, ASEM) and the dialogue between the World Bank and partners such as the IMF, OECD and the Commonwealth Secretariat, among others. From 2003 to 2006, he was the Senior Adviser of the World Bank's International Trade Department. Based in Geneva, he was responsible for covering international trade issues of relevance to developing countries vis-à-vis European-based institutions, including the OECD, the European Commission, UNCTAD and the WTO. His most recent publications include *Innovation and Growth: Chasing a Moving Frontier*, co-editor with V. Chandra, D. Erocal and P. C. Padoan (2009); *Debt Relief and Beyond*, co-editor with D. Doemeland (2009); *The WTO and Accession Countries*, co-editor with O. Cattaneo (2009); and *Trade Preference Erosion: Measurement and Policy Response*, co-editor with B. Hoekman and W. Martin (2009). Prior to joining the World Bank in 1991, Dr Braga was a Fulbright Scholar (1988/9) at the Paul Nitze School of Advanced International Studies (SAIS) at the Johns Hopkins University and taught there as a visiting professor (1988–98). In the 1980s, he was an Assistant Professor of Economics, University of São Paulo and Senior Researcher at FIPE, São Paulo, Brazil. Dr Primo Braga received a degree in Mechanical Engineering (1976) from the Instituto Tecnologico de Aeronautica (Brazil) and an MSc (1980) in Economics from the University of São Paulo, Brazil. He holds a PhD (1984) in Economics from the University of Illinois, Urbana-Champaign, USA.

LAKSHMI PURI is Assistant Secretary General and Deputy Executive Secretary of UNWOMEN – the UN Entity for Gender Equality and Women's Empowerment since March 2011. She was formerly Director of the United Nations Office of the High Representatives for the Least Developed Countries, Landlocked Developing Countries and Small Island Developing States. Prior to that she was Director of UNCTAD's Division on International Trade in Goods, Services and Commodities and led the work of the Organization in making trade work for development in all its dimensions. Apart from directing research, analysis and advocacy work, she was able to mobilize a significant and unprecedented amount of resources for technical cooperation. She contributed to the revitalization of the intergovernmental policy dialogue and consensus-building aspects of UNCTAD's work and from 2007 to 2009 was Acting Deputy Secretary General. Before joining UNCTAD in 2002, Ms Puri worked for twenty-eight years in the Indian Foreign Service where she was involved in policy-making and in bilateral and multilateral economic diplomacy, with a focus on the interrelationship between trade, investment, technology and economic development policies. She managed India's premier technical cooperation programme, ITEC, which provides training in Asia, Africa and Latin America. She has also served on the boards of institutions such as Indian EXIM Bank, Export Credit and Guarantee Corporation, India Brand Equity Fund and Committee for Overseas Indian Investment. She was also in charge of the Economic and Multilateral Economic Relations Division in India's Ministry of External Affairs, where she was involved in formulating and negotiating regional and interregional economic and trade initiatives between India and Asian, African and Latin American countries and groupings including BIMSTEC, India-Sri Lanka Agreement, India-Mercosur, G15, Indian Ocean Rim Association, India-SACU, India-COMESA, India-EU and India-OECD. Her recent studies include 'Towards a New Trade "Marshall Plan" for Least Developed Countries: How to Deliver on the Doha Development Promise and Help Realize the UN Millennium Development Goals?'; 'Trade in Services, Gender, and Development – A Tale of Two Modes'; 'Globalization's Last Frontier: Labour Integration and Implications for Trade and Development Perspectives of the Global Energy Economy'; and 'Addressing the Global Food Crisis – The Trade and Development Dimensions'. Ms Puri holds the rank of Permanent Secretary of the Government of India. She was Ambassador of India to Hungary and concurrently accredited to Bosnia and Herzegovina from 1999 to 2002. In that capacity, she worked closely with the peacekeeping operation in Bosnia and Herzegovina through coordination with the Special Representative of the UN Secretary General and the Indian peacekeeping contingent. During her diplomatic postings in Geneva, including as Deputy Permanent Representative of India, she played an active role in the Commission on Human Rights and its subsidiary bodies as well as at the WHO, ILO, UNHCR and WIPO. Ms Puri's education (BA (Hons) First Division from Delhi University and post-graduate degree from Punjab University, as well as professional diplomas) has been in history, public administration, international relations, law and economic development.

MIGUEL RODRÍGUEZ MENDOZA is a Senior Fellow at ICTSD, where he focuses on Aid for Trade issues, regionalism and trade policy. From 1999 to 2002, he served as Deputy Director-General of the WTO. Between late 2002 and the end of 2004, Mr Rodríguez Mendoza led the Geneva office of Van Bael & Bellis, a Brussels-based international law firm that specializes in EU and international trade law. He has also advised several Venezuelan private companies on trade matters. He was, until March 1998, Chief Trade Advisor at the OAS, where he established that organization's Trade United, which has played an important role in the preparatory process as well as the negotiations of the FTAA. Between 1991 and 1994, he was Minister of State, President of the Institute of Foreign Trade, Venezuela's governmental body responsible for the country's trade policies. During this period he led Venezuela's trade negotiations and concluded trade and integration agreements with Colombia, Mexico, Chile and the countries of Central America and the Caribbean. He became President of the Commission of the Cartagena Agreement, the policy decision body of the Andean Community, in 1993. Between 1989 and 1991, he was Special Advisor to the President on International Economic Affairs, and was appointed as chief negotiator for Venezuela's accession to the GATT, which was completed in 1990. From 1982 to 1988, Mr Rodríguez Mendoza was Director for Consultation and Coordination at the Latin American Economic System (SELA), where he was responsible for assisting Latin America and the Caribbean countries in international economic negotiations. He has also been a member of Venezuela's Foreign Service, and served as first secretary at the Venezuelan Mission to the United Nations (1978–81). Mr Rodríguez Mendoza's publications include *Trade Rules in the Making: Challenges in Regional and Multilateral Negotiations* (1999); *The Andean Community and the United States: Trade and Investment Relations in the 1990s* (1998); *Growth or Recession: The IMF and the World Bank in Latin America* (1987); and *A Difficult Co-Existence: Latin America and U.S. Economic Policies* (1987). He has also published several articles in different books and specialized journals. Mr Rodríguez Mendoza obtained a law degree at the Central University of Venezuela. He has completed a Postgraduate Course in Economic Development at the University of Manchester (England), and attended the Ecole des Hautes Etudes en Sciences Sociales (Paris, 1975–7), where he prepared a Doctorat de 3ème Cycle in the field of political sociology.

BRENDAN VICKERS is the Chief Director of Research and Policy in the International Trade and Economic Division of South Africa's Department of Trade and Industry. He was formerly the Director of the Multilateral Programme at the Institute for Global Dialogue (IGD) in South Africa and Research Associate of the Department of Political Science at the University of Pretoria. He previously worked as a policy analyst in the Office of the President of South Africa. His main areas of research include international trade, investment, development and governance. He holds a PhD from the University of London, focusing on international trade. Dr Vickers has published extensively on South Africa's international relations and political economy, and also lectured on these subjects at several South African universities. He is the co-editor (with Amrita Narlikar) of *Leadership and Change in the Multilateral Trading System* (2009).

MARIE WILKE works at the International Centre for Trade and Sustainable Development (ICTSD) as Programme Officer for International Trade Law. She previously worked at the United Nations Conference on Trade and Development (UNCTAD) and for the German Federal Ministry of Economics and Technology, as Fellow of the German Young Expert Programme in International Affairs (Stiftungskolleg für Internationale Aufgaben). She holds an LLM in International Law from Helsinki University, and an LLB in Comparative and European Law at Hanse Law School (Cooperation of the Universities of Bremen, Oldenburg, Groningen and Sheffield).

VICENTE PAOLO B. YU III is the Programme Coordinator of the South Centre's Global Governance for Development Programme. His work includes overseeing policy research and analysis and the provision of technical and legal advice by the South Centre to developing country delegations on global political, economic, social and environmental issues, including on trade and climate change. Mr Yu obtained his political science (with honours) and law degrees from the University of the Philippines, and his LLM from Georgetown University where he was a Fulbright Scholar. Prior to joining the South Centre, he served as a WTO Programme Officer, based in Geneva, for Friends of the Earth International (FOEI) and was also a Staff Attorney and head for Research and Policy Development of the Legal Rights and Natural Resources Center (LRC) in the Philippines. He has also taught at the University of the Philippines College of Law and the University of Tulsa College of Law, and is Global Economic and Trade Governance Course Director of the Geneva Summer Program of Duke University's Terry Sanford Institute of Public Policy. Mr Yu has published papers and articles on issues relating to trade and environment, sustainable development, environmental policy, climate change policy and indigenous peoples' rights.

ACKNOWLEDGEMENTS

This book is a product of the global trade governance project at the University of Oxford's Global Economic Governance Programme (GEG). Based at University College, GEG is linked to the Department of Politics and International Relations and the newly founded Blatnavik School of Government. Launched in 2007, GEG's activities on trade include a programme of ongoing research on global economic governance and trade involving researchers and practitioners from developing countries. The project has worked to advance scholarly and policy-relevant research on global trade governance that reframes the agenda to focus on challenges of development and sustainability; strengthen dialogue among scholars and policy practitioners beyond the narrow group of trade officials and lawyers that otherwise dominate debates on the possibilities for reform; and raise the visibility of developing country voices and perspectives in debates on global trade governance.

To advance these objectives, GEG co-hosted lectures in Geneva that profiled leading thinkers from developing countries on trade, co-organized seminars in Brazil, India and China, and participated in a range of meetings on trade reform in both developed and developing country capitals. In implementing this work, GEG benefited from partnerships and interactions with a range of research centres and organizations, including the South Centre, the Centre for Trade and Economic Integration at the Graduate Institute for International and Development Studies, Institute for Governance and Sustainable Development (IGSD), the International Centre for Trade and Sustainable Development (ICTSD), the Commonwealth Secretariat, the Latin America Trade Network (LATN), the EDGE Institute, the Brazilian Centre for International Relations (CEBRI), Third World Network, China State Council's Development Research Centre, the Center for International Governance Innovation (CIGI), the Indian Council for Research on International Economic Relations (ICRIER) and International Lawyers and Economists Against Poverty (ILEAP).

At GEG, our work on trade has been supported by the Ford Foundation and the Geneva International Academic Network (GIAN), and also benefits from the financial support to GEG from the Macarthur Foundation, IDRC and the Old Members of University College. I am particularly grateful to Leonardo Burlamaqui at the Ford Foundation for his commitment to GEG's work on the governance of trade, finance and knowledge. The trade governance project has benefitted enormously from the enthusiasm and academic guidance of GEG's Director, Professor Ngaire Woods, and from a fantastic group of researchers, including Mayur Patel, Arunabha Ghosh, Matthew Eagleton-Pearce and Emily Jones. I thank all of them for their support, as well as Reija Fanous for providing the back-up vital for moving the project forward and Jeni Whalen for helping us all communicate our research more effectively.

Engagement with policymakers and experts has been a key feature of GEG's work on trade. Our work included a number of brainstorming seminars with developing country trade officials. I am grateful to staff at Geneva's Graduate Institute for co-hosting a series of Geneva lectures, which provided an opportunity to engage with Geneva's international trade and development community. At Oxford, GEG's work benefited from collaboration with Kalypso Nicolaïdis at the European Studies Centre on a project on Global Trade Ethics, supported in its early phase by the German Marshall Fund and now by the PEGGED network, which has included interaction with leading scholars on WTO reform as well as with Mr Pascal Lamy and trade officials from the European Commission. In 2009, we conducted research for the Commonwealth Secretariat on the constraints small States face in international trade negotiations. I thank Ambassador Edwin Laurent for his substantive inputs into that study and for the many opportunities that research provided to engage with policy-makers and practitioners from small developing countries. In addition, I thank the EDGE Network, the Progressive Policy Institute (London), the WTO Secretariat, the German Marshall Fund, the Evian Group, Society for International Economic Law (SIEL) and the IDEAs Centre for the opportunity to participate and learn from their events on issues related to WTO reform.

This book represents a culmination of this work, gathering contributions from scholars and researchers met in the course of the project. The scope of the book emerged from the many conversations with academics and policy-makers about the issues that matter most to developing countries.

A book of this nature draws on the support and input of many people. My thanks go to Matthew Stilwell, Cédric Dupont and Vicente Yu for their collaboration in the GIAN project, and to Ricardo Meléndez-Ortiz for sharing his advice on scholars and experts to contact for the project. In the course of planning the book and the topics it should cover, I benefitted from the insights of colleagues at ICTSD, notably Christophe Bellmann, Ahmed Abdel-Latif, Trineesh Biswas, Sergio Marchi and Adriana Verdier.

In the process of preparing the book, I had opportunities to interact not only with the contributors to this book, but with many of the leading thinkers on the global trading system, including Diana Tussie, Richard Steinberg, Debra Steger, John Odell, Robert Wolfe and Jean-Pierre Lehmann. I thank them for their encouragement and feedback. My thinking about the issues that mattered for this book was also shaped by conversations with senior trade policy-makers, including Supachai Panitchpakdi, Rob Davies, Debapriya Bhattacharya, Guillermo Valles Galmés, Alejandro Jara and Kamal Nath.

The book is the collective work of the twenty-eight contributors. I thank all of them for their commitment to this book, and for their patience with the peer-review and editorial process. With them, I thank all of the reviewers, both anonymous and those named individually by authors in their chapters. We were particularly grateful for feedback from Bernard Hoekman, Julia Lacarte, Robert Wolfe, Massimilano Cali, Bonapas Onguglo, Alejandro Jara, Nicolas Imboden, David Primack, Hugo Cameron, Sheila Page, Trineesh Biswas, Kevin Gallagher, Peter Mavroidis, Mark Halle, Emily Jones, Gregory Shaffer, Chad Bown, Mahesh Sugathan, Ambassador Servansing and several colleagues at the WTO for their anonymous input.

On my own team, I am especially grateful to Caitlin Zaino, Iveta Cherneva, Samantha Derksen, Catherine Monagle and Meg Harbourd for editorial and research assistance. Thank you especially to Meg, who stepped in and worked so efficiently in the final stages. Finally, I thank the team at Cambridge University Press, particularly Nienke van Schaverbeke, for their collaboration on this book.

My deepest thanks go to my husband, Alec, for his patience, love and support, and to our spirited little daughter, Emily, who brings light, laughter and sunshine to everything we do.

Introduction: making global trade governance work for development

CAROLYN DEERE BIRKBECK

In a world where the vast majority of nations are developing countries and a significant proportion of their population lives in poverty, ensuring that international trade supports development is one of the greatest challenges for global governance.

Over the past decade, development issues have properly emerged as a central concern of international trade negotiations. Yet, considerable dissatisfaction remains with the degree to which development concerns, and broader issues of sustainable development, are addressed in practice. This dissatisfaction has two core dimensions.

On the one hand, developing countries complain of an enduring failure of trade liberalization and trade rules to adequately reflect their development priorities. The challenge of linking trade and development has spurred a vast literature by researchers in universities, think tanks, business associations, intergovernmental organizations (IGOs) or non-governmental organizations (NGOs) around the world. Their contributions range from grand theorizing on development strategy, to assessments of the development impacts of trade, and technical briefings on development-friendly options for specific topics of trade negotiation.

On the other hand, there are persistent complaints about how the global trade agenda and the content of trade rules are forged and implemented – that is, about how the work of governing global trade is conducted. This book takes up this second challenge – how to make the *governance* of global trade work better for development.

The motivation for this edited volume is that scholarly discussion of the governance of global trade and institutional reform of the World Trade Organization (WTO) (and indeed of the global economy more broadly) is dominated by developed country scholars and opinion-makers, with too little attention to developing country perspectives.

To address this shortfall, *Making Global Trade Governance Work for Development* has a unique focus on developing country priorities and perspectives. It draws together views from twenty-eight scholars and practitioners, who offer empirical evidence, theoretical explorations and practical insights about the trade policy-making process. Whether radical or pragmatic in their critique of the trading system, four perspectives unite the contributors.

First, the contributors concur about the importance of international trade and effective trade policy for economic development. Second, they affirm that *how* global trade is governed matters for developing countries and specify key problem areas. The contributors all emphasize the need for governance and regulatory frameworks that are structured to better account for development needs and the voice of developing countries. Third, the contributors demonstrate a common willingness to provide constructive, concrete proposals for how global trade governance could work better for development. Their proposals range from a focus on incremental improvements to calls for a more fundamental overhaul. In so doing, the contributors reflect on political strategies for achieving change and what this requires of rising powers, weaker countries, social movements and developed country governments. Fourth, the volume's contributors acknowledge the changing dynamics in the global economy and in trade decision-making, and explore what this means for how developing countries should organize themselves to better influence the governance of global trade.

1 Origins of this book and methodology

This volume is an output of the project on Global Trade Governance at the Global Economic Governance Programme (GEG) at the University of Oxford.[1] The goals of the project's work on trade are to reframe the research agenda on the governance of global trade so that it better addresses development and sustainability; respond to research priorities voiced by policy-makers from developing countries; and improve the profile of developing country perspectives. Within this framework, GEG's activities have included substantive new research as well as iterative engagement with developing country experts, scholars and policy-makers through lectures held in Geneva and Oxford, research seminars, brainstorming meetings,

[1] GEG's work on trade has been supported by the Ford Foundation, the Geneva International Academic Network (GIAN), the Macarthur Foundation, the International Development Research Centre (IDRC), the Old Members of University College and the Commonwealth Secretariat.

interviews, and regional seminars co-hosted with research institutes in China, India and Brazil.[2] This book represents the culmination of an effort to identify core problems and priorities, and to build a research and policy agenda on global trade governance on that basis.

In choosing contributors for the book, the emphasis was on combining scholarly expertise and real-world knowledge of the global politics of trade policy-making. Many of the 'big names' on the political economy of trade and development devote only occasional attention to governance issues, often in favour of providing strategic guidance or practical advice on the immediate technical dimensions of negotiations. Scholars engaged in 'big-picture' conceptual discussions of global governance often lack practical understanding of the trade arena. I wanted to avoid the peculiar and irritating tendency for trade negotiators and lawyers to assume that only they are sufficiently versed in the technical minutiae of trade to offer a credible view on the challenges trade governance faces and on the desirability and possibilities of reform. Indeed, the reification of the 'complexity of trade rules' and technocratic thinking that prevails among trade experts make trade an unwelcoming terrain for many of the brightest thinkers on global governance and North–South politics.

The contributing authors to this volume include senior officials and experts from international organizations (such as the WTO, the United Nations Conference on Trade and Development (UNCTAD), the UN's regional economic commissions, the World Bank and the Commonwealth Secretariat), government (including former Ministers and Ambassadors), international NGOs and academia. Their experience includes assisting developing countries in trade negotiations, advising the private sector on trade matters, facilitating civil society engagement in trade policy-making and supporting developing country engagement in trade-related litigation. No other book on trade governance brings together such a diversity of expertise and analytical perspectives, from Marxist scholars and heterodox development economists to committed

[2] In this work, we benefitted from partnerships and informal interactions with a range of research centres and organizations, including the Center for Trade and Economic Integration at the Graduate Institute of International and Development Studies, the South Centre, the Institute for Governance and Sustainable Development (IGSD), the International Centre for Trade and Sustainable Development (ICTSD), the Commonwealth Secretariat, Third World Network (TWN), the Latin America Trade Network (LATN), China State Council's Development Research Centre (DRC), the Center for International Governance Innovation (CIGI), the Evian Group, the EDGE Network, Brazilian Centre for International Relations (CEBRI) and the Indian Council for Research on International Economic Relations (ICRIER).

free traders. A further aim was broad geographical diversity. The contributors gathered here thus hail from Latin America and the Caribbean (Colombia, Venezuela, Argentina, Brazil, Mexico, St Lucia, Jamaica), Africa (South Africa, Uganda), the Asia-Pacific region (Hong Kong/China, South Korea, the Philippines, India, Pakistan), Europe (United Kingdom, Ireland, France, Germany), North America (Canada) and Australia.

This book offers a broad definition of global trade governance as comprising the set of processes, principles, norms and institutions through which rules and practices for managing global trade are generated and implemented. The subject matter treated in this book includes multilateral, regional and bilateral trade agreements as well as their dispute settlement provisions, and the work of international institutions like the WTO and UNCTAD. Within that framework, the contributors to this volume were asked to consider the following four sets of questions:

1. What are the challenges that developing countries and sustainable development face in the governance of the global trading system? How are these linked to the broader problems of global economic governance?
2. How do the challenges and priorities in respect of global trade governance differ among and within regions, and between developing countries? What are the roles and responsibilities of rising powers in global trade governance?
3. How could the governance of the global trading system work better to address the constraints developing countries face?
4. What are the political obstacles to making global trade governance work better for development, and what strategies would progress require?

For each of these questions, I proposed specific chapter topics based on the practical concerns and proposals that emerge in policy debates on trade reform. Each chapter was peer-reviewed by at least one scholar and policy practitioner.

This book is intended for policy-makers, stakeholders, scholars and commentators engaged in debates on global economic governance, the WTO, international political economy and development. It will be of interest to students in the area of political science, global politics, international law, international development, sustainable development and geography. In the global policy community, the analysis in this book also addresses staff of international organizations, negotiators based in government missions to the WTO and the United Nations, NGOs, as well as capital-based policy-makers and stakeholders.

This introduction continues in three parts. Section 2 outlines the place of this book within scholarly and policy debates on trade governance and development (my concluding chapter provides a fuller exposition of this context and the relevant scholarly literature). Section 3 provides a brief note on the scope of the book and Section 4 introduces the book's structure and each of its chapters.

2 The state of debate on global trade governance and development

This book is published at a time of renewed interest in how the global economy is governed and the need for a greater say on the part of developing countries. The push for greater developing country influence is not novel. Interest in the relationship between trade and development – and the challenge of ensuring that the architecture and processes for global trade governance support development – has its roots in long-standing developing country efforts at the UN, the Bretton Woods Institutions and the General Agreement on Tariffs and Trade (GATT) to forge a more equitable international economic order. Developing countries have long argued that current trade arrangements are skewed toward the needs of developed countries with inadequate attention to developing country priorities. They have argued that decision-making is dominated by large powers, marginalizing the majority of developing countries, and that power asymmetries frustrate their efforts to devise rules that would help them reduce poverty and achieve the economic growth that developed countries also rely upon for their prosperity.

As global economic dynamics change, the context for debates on global trade governance is evolving. The publication of this book comes at a time when the developing country share of global trade is expanding. Collectively, developing countries contributed 50 per cent of global growth in 2010, and represented the fastest growing share of international trade, especially due to the growth rates of China, India and Brazil. Developing country demand for imports, for instance, is rising twice as fast as that of high income countries. The proportion of global trade that takes place among developing countries (i.e. South–South trade) is also growing and now accounts for one-third of global trade. The importance of trade – both imports and exports – to developing country economies means, however, that their trade interests were particularly heavily impacted by the 2008–10 global economic crisis, most notably by the worst collapse in trade in seventy years, the contraction of affordable trade finance, protectionist pressures fuelled by macroeconomic imbalances and tensions over exchange rates. And, developing countries as a group remain faced with vast challenges of poverty, income inequality and the impacts of intersecting crises in the areas of food security, energy, climate and the environment.

The growing economic significance of developing countries in global trade also has political implications. As the developing country share of trade and the degree to which their economies depend on trade increase, whether in goods, services or knowledge, their interest in shaping the rules and processes of the trade system is reinforced. The rise of the emerging trade powers and the strategic use of coalitions by developing countries has yielded new power dynamics in trade negotiations, and fuelled debates on the voice and responsibilities of emerging powers in global governance, including to poorer developing countries. For the weakest and smallest developing countries, which often rely on a narrow set of goods and services for export, preferential arrangements for market access, and/or are heavily dependent on selected imports, concerns about the representation of their interests in trade rules and negotiations persist.

The analysis offered in this book builds on a large body of literature and many years of intense broad-ranging policy debate at the UN and the WTO and among stakeholders on how to improve the global trading system. A diversity of civil society groups, scholars and governments has raised concerns about global trade governance and voice frustration with the efficiency, transparency, fairness and inclusiveness of decision-making processes. While there is considerable developing country interest in trade global governance (as we will see throughout this book and especially in its concluding chapter), the visibility of their perspectives in scholarly debates on trade governance has been relatively weak. There is, however, a growing body of research on trade governance from IGOs, NGOs, developing country research centres and a number of developing country think tanks and universities, as well as from developing country negotiators and senior international officials reflecting on their own experiences.

Importantly, the trade governance debate is far broader than development issues, which have not traditionally been the major focus of most of the literature on trade governance matters.

Beyond broad treatises on the political economy of the global trading system and international trade negotiations, the governance discussion has focused on the proliferation of bilateral and regional trade and investment agreements, and their relationship with the multilateral trading system; the interplay between the key international institutions involved in global trade governance (e.g. the WTO, UNCTAD, the International Financial Institutions (IFIs) and various UN bodies); and the complex intersections between trade agreements and a range of international legal regimes and instruments (on issues ranging from the environment to human rights and labour standards). Debates on the 'trade-and' issues have been supplemented by concerns about the transparency of trade agreements and opportunities for public participation in trade policy-making, which in turn have spawned a vast literature on the concepts of democracy, legitimacy and sovereignty in the trade arena and critical concerns about the influence of larger multinational corporations on trade policy-making. There has been focused interest on particular functions of the international trading system, including proposals for new approaches to trade negotiations; improvements to the WTO's dispute settlement system; better monitoring and transparency of national implementation of international trade rules; greater attention to assessment and evaluation of the impacts of trade agreements; and for strengthening the 'missing middle' of trade governance – those spaces for policy deliberation and strategic thinking – and for the regular work of administering international agreements. There is also interest in the appropriate scale and role of the WTO and UNCTAD Secretariats. The political salience and public attention to particular items on the 'reform' agenda have waxed and waned over time as have debates about how much and what kind of change is necessary, desirable or possible.

A considerable focus of debate on global trade governance has been the WTO, the leading multilateral institution for global trade. In the fifteen years since the WTO was established, the issue of institutional reform or 'strengthening' – whether it is needed, in what form, and through what kind of process – has been an ever-present issue for the organization and its Member States.

At the WTO, and beyond, there have been significant evolutions in how the trading system is governed (see, for instance, Box 21.1 in the concluding chapter to this book). The WTO has demonstrated that it is a dynamic institution – the approach to negotiations has changed as the political leadership of the Secretariat and of delegations has been replaced. Endeavours such as the Aid for Trade initiative have significantly altered the governance landscape as it deepens the formal engagement of UN agencies and IFIs in trade governance and strengthens what was formerly a far narrower function of the multilateral trading system. Beyond the WTO, the trade governance arena is not static. In addition to FTAs (Free Trade Agreements), regional integration efforts among countries, partnership agreements and cooperation efforts abound.

Of course, the degree of satisfaction with such changes varies widely, as do political analyses of the motivations behind and impact of these changes. As Doha fatigue and exasperation have mounted, interest in trade governance has increased. The WTO's 2009 Ministerial Conference illustrated considerable interest across the WTO's 153 members in more systematic discussion of how to strengthen the institution. Further, with the emergence of the G20 Leaders' Summits, questions about the intersection of the varying intergovernmental organizations, such as the WTO, and questions between them and smaller-group innovations, have also emerged in the trade arena.

For those interested in trade governance and development, a number of questions are on the agenda. Are we seeing a fragmentation of developing country solidarity in global trade negotiations? To what extent does the rise of developing country coalitions solve the much-maligned representation deficits? How significant are the opportunities for greater South–South cooperation and what are the governance implications? What is the role of developing country citizens in the global trading system? How far can global challenges related to the environment and social justice be addressed in the trading arena? To what extent can the WTO be a development institution? How can greater coherence between the finance, development assistance, debt and trading components of the international system be fostered around development goals?

Broadly speaking, development-oriented contributions to the governance reform debate fall into four areas. A summary of the existing literature in each of these areas is provided in the conclusion to this book. Briefly, the first emphasizes the importance of placing global trade governance in the context of broader debates on global economic governance and socioeconomic development, and ensuring a coherent approach grounded in an appreciation of development strategy. It examines opportunities for developing countries in a range of different trade arrangements, including those of the WTO and UNCTAD as well as South–South cooperation, international commodity agreements, bilateral FTAs and regional integration initiatives.

The second area of study explores expectations about roles and responsibilities of developing countries in trade governance, as well as the diversity in their priorities and strategies depending on their size and levels of development. Here, a vast number of cross-cutting issues emerge ranging from concerns about the links between trade and poverty alleviation, industrial strategy and competitiveness, to issues related to labour standards, migration, exchange rates, the food crisis, climate, fisheries, access to trade finance and capacity-building for trade.

The third theme focuses on proposals for strengthening multilateralism in global trade and priorities for WTO reform. Here, core concerns have been the operationalization of the principles guiding the WTO (such as special and differential treatment) and a review of its functions, to boost developing country engagement in negotiations and dispute settlement, as well as improve the usefulness of WTO monitoring and capacity-building to developing countries.

Fourth, considerable attention has been devoted to the vexed issue of fairness in the trade negotiating process, complaints about power asymmetries and inadequate representation of developing countries, and the difficulties poor countries face in securing benefits from their participation in the global trading system.

In each of these areas, proposals for improvement – and sometimes radical change – have been offered. A cross-cutting theme has been reflections on strategy in terms of ultimate objectives and approaches to achieving change. In addition to sometimes very detailed technical proposals for improvements to processes and institutions, pessimism among some critics about the prospects for progress in the face of overwhelming power dynamics is matched by the determined optimism of others about the potential to harness the collective political power of developing countries. For some, progress will only be possible with a substantial increase in the scope for political debate within international processes on trade governance. For others, hope lies beyond developing country governments with social movements, civil society groups, the poor and the marginalized pushing 'from the bottom up' for more radical changes.

3 Scope of this book

While the emphasis of this book is on governance rather than the rules of trade, individual topics of trade policy or negotiations under way in the Doha Round, these distinctions can be blurred. For many analysts, the question of *what* is on the global trade negotiations agenda (i.e. the scope of agreements and negotiations) is a core governance issue (in addition to questions of *how* that agenda is formed and advanced). In practice, the institutional and procedural aspects of how rules should be made, implemented and adjudicated are often difficult to separate from discussion of the substance of trade arrangements – the principles and norms they should uphold, the goals they should advance (e.g. sustainable development) and the form they should take. For instance, many authors in this book emphasize the importance of key trade principles such as SDT for developing countries – and their operationalization in trade agreements – as an integral part of trade governance. Further, some topics covered in this book are simultaneously the subject of the Doha negotiations (e.g. reform of the WTO's Dispute Settlement Understanding (DSU) and rules related to Regional Trade Agreements).

The discerning reader will find gaps in the coverage of the book and missing issues. The book is weaker on non-Anglophone and on African perspectives (despite efforts to include such contributions), and within each region perspectives or emphases may differ from those offered here. The book does not purport to capture or address comprehensively the full range of issues or perspectives that emerge in discussions of global trade governance and development. Indeed, such an endeavour would require many volumes. Rather, the intention is to offer a 'reader' that provides a taste of the diversity of developing country views and priorities and that compiles a representative spectrum of proposals on the table. In the concluding chapter, I place the contributions in the context of the broader literature, including works on several key issues and perspectives otherwise missing from this book.

4 Overview of this book

The book is divided into four parts, which follow the themes outlined in Section 2 above. A summary of the content and sequencing of the chapters follows below. The concluding chapter of the book summarizes the core recommendations that emerge from these contributions.

4.1 Enduring development challenges and new agendas for global trade governance

In Part I of this compilation, the contributors argue that the challenges of global trade governance must be considered in light of broader dynamics in the global economy and debates on its governance. They emphasize intersections between trade, finance, development assistance and debt, on the one hand, and between these economic issues and social and environmental priorities on the other. In addition, they highlight the complex intersections between the many international, regional and bilateral agreements within and beyond the trade arena, and the difficulties the international community faces in securing appropriate coordination among these to address development priorities.

In Chapter 1, José Antonio Ocampo (Colombia) places the discussion of global trade governance in the context of two core asymmetries in global economic governance, namely large income inequalities among and within countries, and the asymmetry between the rapid globalization of (some) markets and the relative weakness of the international social agenda. He emphasizes the macroeconomic vulnerability of developing countries to external shocks (particularly financial, but also trade shocks), the high concentration of technical progress in developed countries, and the contrast between the high mobility of capital and the restrictions on the international movement of labour. Lamenting the decline of the principle of special and differential treatment, Ocampo sets out recommendations in respect of international financial management, boosting development assistance, promoting technology transfer, diversifying developing country industries and devising frameworks for labour migration that protect social security benefits and human rights. On the challenges of global governance, he emphasizes the importance of democratic national processes for determining economic and social development strategies and mediating the tensions that globalization creates. He also underlines the need for developing country leadership on development strategies and for the international system to provide them policy space to that end, as well as for greater support to regional institutions on trade, finance and technological cooperation.

Chapter 2 emphasizes the dual importance of the global trading system as a global public good that can help countries solve trade-related problems through a coordinated multilateral response and also as a 'global development good', which facilitates economic, social and environmentally sustainable development for all. Lakshmi Puri (India) highlights the contribution of the UN's development agenda to the evolution of global trade governance, and the importance of the UN's Millennium Development Goals (MDGs) and values of solidarity. Her specific recommendations for improving trade governance include enhancing developing country market access, capacity to trade and competitiveness; ensuring that countries can pursue a 'development flexibility agenda', whereby they can retain and use policy space in multilateral, regional and bilateral trade agreements; supporting an enabling agenda that boosts development assistance, trade finance and Aid for Trade, addresses debt and provides incentives for investment in least developed countries (LDCs); and improving corporate responsibility; and controlling on anti-competitive practices. She calls for complementary efforts in trade, finance, monetary, environmental and technology governance systems to address demographic shifts and migration; ecological sustainability and climate; natural resource management; technology transfer; the complexity of standards and other non-tariff barriers that impact trade; the challenges of managing asymmetric bilateral and regional trade negotiations; the rise of emerging developing country economics; and the growth of South–South cooperation in trade.

The subsequent two chapters take up the sustainability dimensions of the trade and development intersection, and their implications for how analysts think about improving the governance of trade.

In Chapter 3, Alejandro Nadal (Mexico) contends that taking environmental sustainability objectives seriously demands examining global trade and its governance in light of their interaction with other components of macroeconomic policy that condition trade dynamics and how these together impact the environment and people's livelihoods. He uses examples from Latin America to demonstrate how trade is one component of a bigger policy package in which monetary and fiscal policies, financial deregulation and income policies can play a much more important role than trade in shaping the economic forces that affect the environment. On this basis, he proposes reforms to the international monetary system; stronger regulations for international finance and capital flows; a new approach to debt management and cancellation, overhauling how development and global environmental stewardship are financed; and reforms to the international trade regime. On trade, he argues for greater attention to responsible use of the balance of payments provisions in trade rules where countries face crises; a new approach to agricultural trade that addresses food security, livelihood and sustainability concerns; tackling concentrations of market power; and a new generation of international commodity agreements (ICAs) that would help stabilize commodity markets, promote value-added activities and boost the terms of trade for countries that rely on primary commodity exports.

In Chapter 4, Ricardo Meléndez-Ortiz (Colombia) and Trineesh Biswas (Canada) examine the institutional challenges of making trade governance more supportive of sustainable development. They examine how the global policy context is shaping (and being affected by) governance dynamics across the international system, and offer recommendations for how creative action within trade institutions, particularly the WTO, could help make the trading system more supportive of sustainable development; how the work of international organizations could be better coordinated; and how action taken outside the trade arena could leverage the contribution that trade governance makes to sustainable development. Their analysis incorporates discussion of topics at the intersection of trade and sustainable development governance, including climate and food security.

4.2 Roles and responsibilities in global trade governance: diversity in developing country priorities and strategies

Part II of this book explores variation in the behaviour and interests of developing countries in global trade governance. It draws attention to the implications of shifting power dynamics and the particular concerns of poor, small and vulnerable countries in how global trade is governed. The contributors highlight how these factors can yield distinct priorities for trade reform and political strategies for the ways developing countries organize themselves.

In Chapter 5, Amrita Narlikar (India) argues that the WTO's efforts to accommodate the new developing country powers – Brazil, India and China – at the heart of its decision-making have produced new inefficiencies, heightened its proclivity to deadlock and exacerbated disengagement and disillusionment among its stakeholders. She discusses the changing role of the new powers in the WTO, analyses the opportunities and challenges that these developments generate for governance and examines possible routes to reform. While she observes that very little can be done to alter the balance of power itself, she argues that appropriate institutional reform could help the multilateral trading system retain the advances it has made in terms of fairness while addressing the concerns of efficiency that are central to the crisis it faces.

China's importance as the world's largest emerging trade power makes it worthy of in-depth consideration. As China enters its tenth year of WTO Membership, Henry Gao (China) asks in Chapter 6 whether the dragon has brought a 'reign of fire' to the multilateral trading system and rocked its institutional foundations. To answer this question, his chapter reviews China's participation in two key activities of the WTO, namely trade negotiations and dispute settlement, as well as in regional trade agreements (RTAs). He argues that, overall, China has evolved from a passive 'taker' of the existing rules to a country that will 'shake' the rules for its own interests or even 'make' new rules. At the same time, the pace of China's ascent has been uneven in different areas; the most aggressive strategy has been apparent in RTA negotiations. Similarly, while China was initially reluctant to use the multilateral dispute settlement system, it has become a major player since 2007. In terms of multilateral trade negotiations, China has been sending mixed signals: while it has made many submissions on negotiating issues in the Doha Round negotiations, Gao observes that China has so far successfully resisted calls from the USA and EU for it to play a leading role or make substantial concessions in the long-stalled trade talks. After exploring the reasons for varying behavioural patterns in a range of areas, the chapter concludes by exploring China's future role in the WTO, as well as the potential ramifications of China's ascent in global trade governance.

The book's focus then shifts to the concerns that the poorest and smallest countries articulate with respect to trade governance and how it might better respond to their particular needs. Chapter 7 addresses the challenges that LDCs, most of which are in Africa, face in participating effectively in global trade governance. Atul Kaushik (India) and Julian Mukiibi (Uganda) explore the evolving role of LDCs in WTO decision-making processes and the emergence of the LDC group in the WTO. They then set out LDC priorities for improved global trade governance, emphasizing the importance of special and differential treatment and the need for LDCs to take greater ownership of efforts to integrate them into the trading system. Among their core recommendations is a call for the creation of a new institution to address LDC-specific needs in Geneva.

The next two chapters explore how the unique characteristics of small States give them trade interests that are distinct from other developing countries and consider adaptations in global trade governance structures that would afford small States greater influence in agenda-setting and rule-making. In Chapter 8, Edwin Laurent (St Lucia) argues that small States themselves have to pursue the changes, decisions and concessions in the multilateral trading system that they alone have a vested interest in securing, rather than relying on larger and more influential states to advocate on their behalf. He takes up the challenging task of determining exactly what is unique about small States in international trade, and what this means for the content of a 'smallness' agenda. Even with the growing scope for mitigating power imbalances through diplomacy and advocacy, negotiation strategies and litigation, he argues that size still impedes the effective and beneficial participation of small States in the multilateral trading system. He emphasizes the importance of strengthening the rule-based character of the multilateral system; more effective organization among small States and collaboration with others to maximize their ability to exert influence; and the importance of defining and securing specific trade measures that are favourable to their particular interests.

On a similar theme, Richard Bernal (Jamaica) observes in Chapter 9 that the vulnerability of small developing countries to external economic events and their reliance on international trade for prosperity give them a particular interest in the rules and institutions governing the multilateral trading system. In his chapter, Bernal evaluates the participation of small countries in the governance of the multilateral trading system, with a focus on the Small and Vulnerable Economies (SVE) group. He presents recommendations on how small developing countries can improve the efficacy of their participation in the WTO's decision-making process and proposes ways in which the WTO could be adapted to better integrate such countries into its governance.

4.3 Strengthening multilateralism: priorities for improving WTO governance

Part III of this book concentrates on the WTO as the central institution in global trade governance. It addresses a range of ways in which attention to governance matters could improve the responsiveness of the multilateral trading system to developing countries, focusing on the purpose and principles of the WTO, as well as on the WTO's specific functions (including, for instance, trade monitoring, dispute settlement, capacity-building and outreach to civil society). The WTO's negotiation function is addressed separately in Part IV, which focuses on trade negotiation processes.

The first two chapters examine several areas for reform of the multilateral trading system, including changes in how development issues are treated within the WTO's internal processes. In Chapter 10, Bhupinder Chimni (India) presents a radical critique of the WTO and the prospects for improved trade governance. Writing from a Marxist perspective, Chimni emphasizes the class character of the WTO and outlines the complex ways in which the power of the transnational capitalist class, mediated through states, dominates the WTO and limits the prospects for reform. Nevertheless, he presents a number of recommendations for reforming WTO processes and rules to embed greater democracy in the WTO and help achieve development for all, including subaltern states and disadvantaged communities. Among the challenges touched on are the absence of deliberative democracy in WTO negotiations, the specific problems with the consensus-based decision-making process, the problematic nature of the 'single undertaking' formula, the absence of an active role for national parliaments in WTO negotiation and ratification processes, and the ineffectiveness of the special and differential treatment principle.

In Chapter 11, Yong-Shik Lee (South Korea) reviews the WTO's governance system and disciplines, assesses whether they are structured adequately to support and facilitate the economic development of developing countries, and offers a series of proposals for closing the gaps. He argues that the current Committee on Trade and Development and the development provisions scattered throughout GATT/WTO disciplines are not sufficient to advance the interests of developing countries. He proposes both institutional reforms and new WTO disciplines to address these shortfalls, including the elevation of the CTD to a new Council for Trade and Development; the creation of an Agreement on Development Facilitation; improved assistance for developing countries to participate in WTO meetings; an expansion of the Advisory Centre on WTO Law (ACWL); and measures to improve the scale, monitoring and evaluation of trade-related development assistance.

Chapter 12 takes up the issue of developing country engagement in the WTO's dispute settlement function. Niall Meagher (Ireland) reviews the challenges developing countries face in the WTO dispute settlement system and their governance implications. He observes that the WTO has provided its Members with a successful system of third-party adjudication of intergovernmental disputes, but argues that the success of the system is not unqualified, especially with respect to the participation of developing and least developed countries. He reviews the participation of developing countries in the system since 1995 and discusses the role the ACWL has played in fostering developing and least developed country engagement. Key challenges for developing countries noted by the author include the complexity of the process, lack of resources, the limited use of public–private sector partnerships, the disuse of alternative mechanisms and the fear of retaliation. Finally, the chapter evaluates some of the alternative mechanisms and proposals to assist developing countries in utilizing the dispute-settlement system to the fullest. It concludes that improvements can be made both in streamlining the system itself and in increasing the capacity of developing countries to engage in it.

The subsequent chapters each take up other specific functions of the WTO system. In Chapter 13, David Luke (Canada) and Luisa Bernal (Venezuela) focus on the governance of Aid for Trade. Highlighting the skewed distribution of Aid for Trade across countries, they argue that its institutional arrangements are too complicated with regard to access by potential developing country beneficiaries. The authors argue that as the Aid for Trade initiative has evolved, the mutual accountability of donors and beneficiaries has emerged as the key governance principle, whereas equally important principles of access to – and predictability of – resources are much less prominent. They compare the Aid for Trade governance arrangements to those of three major initiatives similarly established to support the provision of global public goods (that is, the Global Environment Facility (GEF); the Global Fund to Fight AIDS, Tuberculosis and Malaria; and the Enhanced Integrated Framework for Trade-Related Technical Assistance to Least Developed Countries (EIF)). The chapter makes the case for 'empowering' regional economic communities (RECs) already engaged in implementing regional trade agreements and other cross-border integration initiatives by adding regional financial facilities to the Aid for Trade governance structure.

In Chapter 14, Arunabha Ghosh (India) examines the WTO's monitoring function, which accounts for half of the Secretariat's budget. He examines the mandate of the WTO's Trade Policy Review Mechanism (TPRM) and presents empirical evidence on deficiencies in the TPR reports and in review meetings. While acknowledging that notifications and discussions within individual WTO Committees are an important part of the WTO's monitoring activities, Ghosh focuses primarily on the TPRM and the WTO's new monitoring mechanisms (such as in the area of sanitary and phytosanitary measures, and regional trade agreements). These are among the most institutionalized parts of the WTO's information system, are extensive in the scope of countries and issues covered, and have dedicated budgets for conducting their monitoring tasks. He critically examines the TPRM's mandate, as well as the content- and process-related challenges that it has faced so far, with particular consideration of the needs and interests of developing countries and the gaps in institutionalized capacity for monitoring at the domestic level. The chapter reviews the minimal reforms that have been made to the TPRM thus far and explores why developing countries have not pushed for further changes, despite suffering from persistent information gaps.

In Chapter 15, Félix Peña (Argentina) emphasizes the importance of transparency, accountability and civil society engagement in the WTO's work to enhance its legitimacy, shorten the distance between international rule-making and local realities, and to ensure that the outcomes of international trade agreements properly advance the WTO's mandate for sustainable development. To this end he outlines an initial proposal for adding an Ombudsperson role to the WTO's institutional structure to investigate citizens' concerns about the impact of trade agreements on sustainable development and provide non-mandatory technically based opinions on the complaints. He proposes that the Ombudsperson's role should be elaborated through broad worldwide multi-stakeholder consultations.

4.4 Making WTO negotiations and decision-making processes fairer

Part IV of this book focuses on the much-debated processes for negotiation and decision-making in the WTO.

In Chapter 16, Faizel Ismail (South Africa) and Brendan Vickers (South Africa) argue that many proposals for reform of the WTO negotiation process place too much emphasis on the formal processes of decision-making and privilege efficiency over other principles, such as inclusiveness and legitimacy. They argue that processes of multilateral decision-making must promote learning and the empowerment of developing countries in the WTO. In their view, too few proposals address the representation problem in the WTO, namely the inclusion of developing countries at the 'High Table' of the negotiations. The authors make three core recommendations to this end, namely strengthening the WTO's consensus principle and culture, avoiding decision-making through informal small groups and adopting a code of conduct for WTO chairs.

In Chapter 17, Miguel Rodríguez Mendoza (Venezuela) and Marie Wilke (Germany) argue that a more balanced approach to WTO negotiations demands setting aside the 'single undertaking'. They argue that the single undertaking artificially limits the flexibilities of WTO Members in their negotiations, and too often serves as a tool for those who aim to block negotiations until certain concessions in their favour have been made. The authors contend that it is the divergence of interests of Member States, rather than the single undertaking, that brought about the deadlock in the Doha Round of negotiations. But they argue that the single undertaking helps those countries that hold negotiations hostage, at disproportionate cost to developing countries. Together, they call for a move away from all-encompassing 'rounds' of negotiations on an ever increasing number of subjects to a more à la carte approach, with negotiations on subjects that are more likely to produce significant and faster results. They present recommendations for how such negotiations might be pursued.

Since the collapse of the WTO Ministerial Conference in Cancún and throughout the Doha Round, the increased use of coalitions and groups by developing countries to advance their interests in WTO negotiations has spurred considerable reflection on their implications for trade governance. In Chapter 18, Vicente Yu (the Philippines) explores the potential for South–South coalitions to enhance developing country participation in global trade governance, with a focus on the WTO. He argues that the marked improvement in the overall extent of developing country participation in WTO negotiations in the Doha Round has been in large part due to developing country efforts to work in a more coordinated fashion through groups or coalitions. He reviews the lessons learned for future collective action by developing countries, providing suggestions on how developing countries can be more consistent and united in promoting their views and interests.

In Chapter 19, Rashid Kaukab (Pakistan) reflects on the challenges of making trade governance more inclusive, drawing on his practical experience working with governments and stakeholders from developing countries to build their capacity for trade negotiations. He argues that instruments of trade governance at the national and international level must be developed through an inclusive process that ensures the participation of all relevant stakeholders, from trade unions to export industries. Noting that greater inclusiveness improves the accountability of governments to their citizens and contributes to the 'legitimization' and public acceptance of the outcomes of trade policy, he argues that inclusiveness can also lead to better policies and outcomes that are more aligned with national development objectives. He presents new evidence on the role of stakeholders in trade policy-making at the national level in a number of developing countries, particularly in Africa, juxtaposing the varying degrees of participation and influence by different stakeholder groups in trade-related consultations and decision-making.

In a final chapter on negotiations at the WTO, Carlos Primo Braga (Brazil) and Olivier Cattaneo (France) critically review the WTO accession process. In Chapter 20, they observe that as all the remaining candidates for WTO accession are developing or transition countries (except Andorra), accession is de facto a development issue. They argue that the reform of the WTO accession process is not only a North–South debate, but also an issue between incumbent and acceding Members. Using evidence of the twenty-five WTO accessions that occurred between January 1996 and July 2010 as the basis for evaluating the functioning – and dysfunction – of the accession process, they conclude that newly acceded countries have rarely been offered the same benefits as incumbent Members with comparable levels of development. From a governance angle, they argue that the price for WTO accession has become too high and pays insufficient attention to the specific needs of developing countries, leading to accession protocols that create a 'second class' of citizens in the WTO and contradict core WTO principles. They explore how the negotiating process for accession influences these outcomes and review options for reform.

5 Conclusion

Does global trade governance matter for development? Is there still a need for reform? This book's response to both questions is an emphatic 'yes'. Improved governance of the global trade system and global economic governance more broadly continue to be critical priorities for developing countries, even as the dynamics of global trade, their roles in its governance and their political strategies evolve. The contributors to this book also show that while there are commonalities, the scope and focus of the governance agendas that officials, experts and scholars from developing countries advance diverge from those of developed countries and place accent on different challenges.

In this book's final chapter, I bring together the core recommendations emerging from the contributors. These are gathered under four headings: 1) Putting Global Trade Governance in Context: Sustainable Development Challenges in the Global Economy; 2) Improving How Developing Countries Participate in Global Trade Governance; 3) Strengthening WTO Governance to Respond to Developing Countries; 4) Improving Trade Negotiation Processes. In so doing, I place the contributions in the context of existing scholarship, noting where and how they add value or emphasize specific problems and proposals. I also outline what the contributors recommend in terms of political strategy for achieving their proposed changes. A basic requirement for progress is for developing country and development-oriented voices to have a more central influence on how the trade governance discussion is framed, both in the scholarly literature and in the policy arena. On that front, this book represents a positive step in the right direction.

PART I

Global trade governance: components and context

1

Globalization, development and democracy

JOSÉ ANTONIO OCAMPO

'We believe that the central challenge we face today is to ensure that globalization becomes a positive force for all the world's people', reads the fifth paragraph of the United Nations Millennium Declaration (United Nations 2000). Although globalization reflects technological advances and economic forces, it can be moulded by society and, particularly, by democratic political institutions. In fact, the form that globalization has been taking has been largely determined by explicit policy decisions.

In this sense, the most disturbing aspect has been the uneven and unbalanced character of the current phase of globalization and of the international policy agenda that accompanies it. The latter has both reproduced the traditional asymmetries in the world economy and created new ones. There are four issues that have dominated the economic agenda: free trade, intellectual property rights, investment protection, and financial and capital account liberalization. In the latter case, the condition that it should be subject to strong regulatory frameworks has been superimposed as a result of recent crises, particularly in the developing world by the 1997 Asian financial crisis and in the industrial world by the most recent 2008–9 global financial crisis. Moreover, in the area of international trade, liberalization is incomplete and asymmetric: various goods of special interest to developing countries are subject to the highest levels of protection and, in the case of agriculture, to subsidies in industrialized countries.

On the other hand, major issues have been left out of the international economic agenda: the mobility of labour, particularly unskilled labour;

José Antonio Ocampo is Professor of Professional Practice at the School of International and Public Affairs and a Member of the Committee on Global Thought at Columbia University.
The chapter draws on a paper with the same title published in 2005 by the Social Science Research Council, with permission. The author is grateful to Giovanni Andrea Cornia and Carolyn Deere Birkbeck for comments on the previous version.

international norms regarding taxation, especially on capital, which is essential to guarantee an adequate contribution of this highly mobile factor to public sector financing; the formulation of truly international norms on competition and codes of conduct applicable to multinational corporations; the design of effective instruments to ensure adequate technology transfer to developing countries; and compensatory financing to assure the inclusion of those countries and social groups that tend to fall behind in the process of globalization.

The preceding reflects, in turn, the most important asymmetry: that which exists between the rapid globalization of (some) markets and the relative weakness of the international social agenda. The international social agenda has its best expression in the UN Development Agenda that has emerged out of the United Nations Conferences and Summits of the past two decades (United Nations 2007), and aims to set some global social norms and standards, guaranteeing the provision of minimum living standards and basic social services to all world citizens. The social agenda has to cope, in turn, with weak accountability and enforcement mechanisms, the limited supply of Official Development Assistance (ODA), and the conditionality that characterizes international financial support.

In broader terms, it is increasingly recognized that globalization has made more evident the need to enhance international cooperation. One crucial area of such cooperation should be the provision of political, social, economic and environmental 'global public goods' (Kaul *et al.* 2003; International Task Force on Global Public Goods 2006; Barrett 2007), in view of the fact that, with the growing interdependence of nations, many areas of public interest that were previously national (and, in some cases, local) have become spheres of global attention. Existing efforts at international cooperation, and the UN Development Agenda, in particular, have defined, in turn, two other objectives of international cooperation: that are, as pointed out above, setting an international social agenda, which can be understood as covering a set of 'goods of social value' that complement 'global public goods';[1] and international cooperation to overcome

[1] The concept of 'goods of social value' captures what in the literature on welfare economics have been called 'merit goods'. Thus, 'public goods' focus on the interdependence among consumers and economic agents in general (in the case of pure public goods, on the fact that consumption has some collective features), whereas 'goods of social value' emphasize the decision of society to provide certain goods and services to all citizens, and is thus akin to the concept of economic and social rights. It should also be recognized that, although this distinction makes sense in the context of welfare economics, the sense in which the term 'public goods' is used in common social and political, as well as legal discourse, usually encompasses both.

the asymmetries of the international economic order that affects developing countries. In broad terms, global economic and social cooperation responds, therefore, to three distinct objectives: managing interdependence; furthering the development of societies; and gradually overcoming the asymmetries that characterize the world economic system (Ocampo 2010a). Nevertheless, there is an undisputable contrast between the recognition of the importance of these objectives and the weakness of international governance structures, as well as limited resources allocated to further them and political will to address these issues.

This chapter provides a succinct analysis of some of the challenges faced in building a more balanced globalization. It is divided into four sections. The first summarizes the facts about global inequalities. The second focuses on the asymmetries of the international economic system and the international schemes and national policies needed to overcome them. The third deals with the broader relations between globalization and social equity, and between globalization and democracy as core challenges on the long road to better global governance. The last draws some brief conclusions.

1 Global inequalities

The extensive literature on economic growth makes it clear that the world has experienced a long-term *divergence* in the levels of per capita incomes among countries over the past two centuries – 'divergence, big time' to use Pritchett's (1997) terminology. This trend was particularly strong in the nineteenth century and the first half of the twentieth century. Measured as the ratio of the average per capita income of developing to that of industrial countries, divergence continued to increase during the second half of the twentieth century, experiencing sharp upward trends during the major crises in the developing world: that is, the 'lost decade' of the 1980s in large parts of the developing world and the broad-based financial crisis, which had erupted in 1997 out of the East Asian financial crisis and spread to other developing country regions (see Figure 1.1). Divergence was stronger if we focus on the ratio between per capita income of the industrialized countries and the region with the largest number of the poorest countries – Africa. Trends are more favourable over the last two decades of the twentieth century if population-weighted averages are used, but this reflects primarily the rapid growth of China (with growing disparities within it) and, secondarily, India (Milanovic 2005). It was only during the 2003–7 world economic boom that all indicators of relative per capita incomes

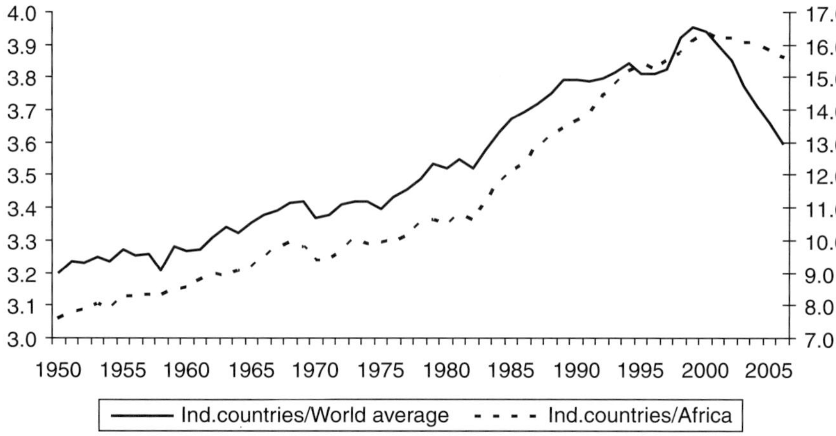

Figure 1.1 Disparities in per capita GDP among countries
Source: Maddison (2006) and online update of the database.

experienced a reduction. This trend may continue in the next few years due to the recent crisis, which engulfed all industrial countries but had generally weaker effects on the developing world (see below).

An analysis of the same data source brings to light another and equally important phenomenon: the marked and growing dispersion of the rates of growth *among* developing countries. Ocampo and Parra (2007) have referred to the combination of both trends as a 'dual divergence': between the industrial and the developing countries, and within the developing world. In fact, for the same sample, the standard deviation of the rates of growth of per capita Gross Domestic Product (GDP) of developing countries increased sharply from the 1950s to the 1970s and has remained very high since then, in sharp contrast to the falling and low standard deviation of the rates of growth among industrial countries (Figure 1.2).

The divergence in per capita incomes has, finally, been accompanied by a fairly broad trend towards increasing inequality *within* countries. According to Cornia (2010; see also Cornia 2004), fifty-nine out of eighty-five countries for which information is available experienced a deterioration of income distribution during the last decades of the twentieth century. These fifty-nine countries contain 76 per cent of the population of those eighty-five countries. In contrast, only nine countries, with 5 per cent of the population, experienced an improvement in income distribution and, in the rest, income distribution remained essentially stable.

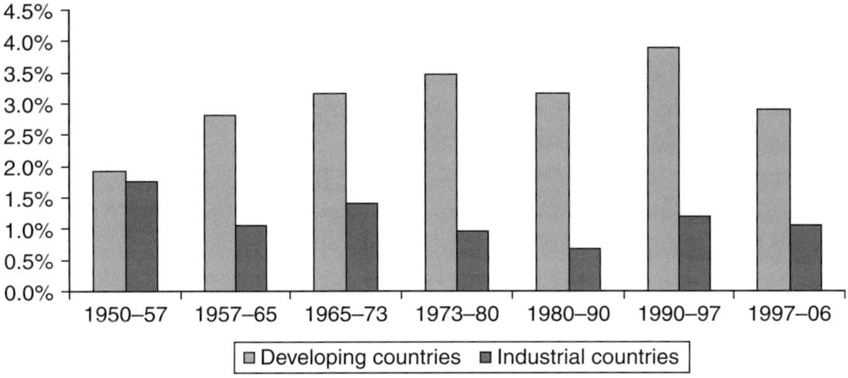

Figure 1.2 Standard deviation of annual per capita GDP growth rates
Source: Maddison (2006) and online update of the database. Excludes Eastern Europe and Central Asia.

According to this study, inequality tended to increase, sometimes markedly, in a large group of industrial countries, in the transition economies of Central and Eastern Europe, Central Asia, and in developing countries in Asia and Latin America. Africa and the Middle East and North Africa (MENA) were the only regions where the majority of countries did not experience deterioration in income distribution. Data for the first decade of the twenty-first century is more favourable, where the number of countries experiencing improvements in income distribution is similar to those showing deterioration. From a regional perspective, Latin America experienced the most widespread improvements in income distribution (Gasparini *et al.* 2009), with several African countries in a similar condition (Cornia 2010).

The reasons for the broad-based worsening of income distribution within countries that has been experienced during the last two decades of the twentieth century continue to be a subject of heated debate. The combination of the adverse distributive effects of market reforms (or, at least, of some of them) and the simultaneous weakening of the institutions of social protection, including the growing difficulties experienced by governments in providing effective social protection in a globalized world economy, offers the best explanation (Cornia 2004). The effects of biases associated with technological change on differentials in labour income according to skill levels provide a complementary explanation, and one that enjoys broader consensus among analysts. A third force, which has been subject to less attention, is the increasing asymmetry between the international mobility of some factors of production (capital and highly skilled labour) and the restrictions on the mobility of other factors (unskilled labour), which generate forces that distribute income at the disadvantage of the latter (see below).

Since the 1980s, these two forces – the divergence in per capita income levels among countries and the growing inequality in income distribution within countries – have been counterbalanced by rapid economic growth in China and, to a lesser degree, India – the two most populous poor countries of the world. The trend in the distribution of income among the world's citizens thus depends on the statistical methodologies used to aggregate individual country distributions in order to estimate a world income distribution.[2] Accordingly, various studies have reached different conclusions about the nature of that trend over the last decades of the twentieth century.[3]

Nonetheless, three conclusions can be drawn from this literature. The first and most important is that world inequality is appalling and remains at or very close to its historical peak. The second is that if there has been deterioration in the world distribution of income since the mid twentieth century, it has been slower than that which characterized the nineteenth century and the first half of the twentieth century, during which the gap between per capita income of developed countries and developing countries increased markedly (Bourguignon and Morrison 2002; Milanovic 2005). The third is that any estimated improvement in world income distribution during the last two decades of the twentieth century was exclusively due to the rapid growth of China and, to a lesser extent, India. Indeed, according to Berry and Serieux (2007), if the effect of the rapid growth of these two countries is excluded, there was a sharp augmentation in world

[2] There are two issues that are critical in this regard: (i) the use of market prices versus purchasing power estimates of national income (as well as the specific PPP estimates used); and (ii) whether the information provided by household surveys is exclusively used or, alternatively, if it is combined with that provided by the national accounts on national income and consumption.

[3] Among the studies that claim that there was a deterioration in world income distribution in recent decades, we could include Dikhanov and Ward (2001) for the period 1970–99, Bourguignon and Morrison (2002) for 1970–92 using the Theil inequality index (the other two indexes used by these authors show no clear trend during that period) and Galbraith and Kum (2004). The opposite conclusion is reached by Bhalla (2002) and, more reliably, by Berry and Serieux (2007) and Sutcliffe (2007). The most comprehensive study, that of Milanovic (2005), indicates that different effects essentially compensated each other, in such a way as to generate a global income distribution that was probably trendless.

inequality, due to the joint effect of increased intra-country inequalities and the adverse distributive effect of fast population growth in poorer countries.[4]

Taken as a whole, these studies also indicate that there has been a major redistribution of world income since 1980. China and India (or, to be precise, some regions and sectors within these two large economies), as well as the relatively rich households of industrial countries, have gained in world income distribution, while the poor from sub-Saharan Africa and most poor and middle-income recipients from the less successful middle-income countries and transition economies have clearly lost. Given the critical importance of China and India in global estimates, it is important to emphasize that their rapid economic growth should not be understood as the result of the ability of globalization processes to redistribute world income more equitably. These two experiences, as well as those of other Asian Newly Industrialized Countries (NICs), certainly reflect the fact that greater participation in world trade has opened opportunities to developing countries, particularly to exporters of manufactures and services. However, they also indicate that these successful stories of integration into the global economy have been matched by several failures.

In summary, existing studies underscore the widespread increase of inequality within countries that characterizes the current global order, as well as the fact that the opportunities that it provides to different countries are distributed very unevenly. Thus, 'virtuous' and 'vicious' circles have been put in place in the world over the past decades, resulting in major 'winners' but also in a large set of 'losers'. Several factors may be at work here, particularly the differential effects of major international shocks on different economies, and agglomeration forces, which tend to concentrate economic activity in certain locations. As we have seen, the two major crises of the late twentieth century generated a sharp increase in international inequalities. Given the large number of developing countries that remain commodity-dependent, we must add to this list the strong downward trend of commodity prices that characterized the

[4] Also, and independently of the trend in the overall indicator of world income distribution, the richest 10 per cent of the world population may have increased its share in world income. Berry and Serieux (2007, Table 4.3), who estimate that world income distribution improved in 1980–2000, also calculate that the share of the richest decile in world income increased from 46.6 to 49.3 per cent during the same period. This is also the conclusion of the estimates of Bourguignon and Morrison for 1980–92, which indicates that the share of the richest decile in world income increased from 51.6 to 53.4 per cent over that period.

quarter century or so since 1980, which was, in fact, one of the major determinants of the 'lost decade' (Ocampo and Parra 2010).

The rapid growth of China generated a recovery of commodity prices in the early twenty-first century,[5] and the quick bounce-back of this country during the recent global financial crises also helped maintain surprisingly high commodity prices, in open contrast with all previous world crises. In turn, although thanks to this and the greater 'policy space' that developing countries enjoyed, the recent global financial crisis made a lesser impact in the developing than the industrial world. Nonetheless, some developing countries were strongly hit, particularly the transition economies and, to a lesser extent, Latin America. East Asia (China aside) was also hit hard, but recovered rapidly thanks to expansionary macroeconomic policies and trade links to China (Ocampo *et al.* 2010).

2 The asymmetries of the global economic order

2.1 World economic asymmetries

The growing disparities in the levels of development among countries indicates that, although domestic economic, social and institutional factors are obviously important, economic opportunities are significantly affected by the position that countries occupy within the global hierarchy and that rising up on this international ladder is a rather difficult task. Fundamental international asymmetries largely explain why the global economy is essentially *not* a 'level playing field' and thus contribute to the generation of significant inequalities.

These asymmetries are of three kinds (Ocampo and Martin 2003). The first is associated with the *macroeconomic vulnerability of developing countries to external shocks*, which has tended to increase with the tighter integration of the world economy. Importantly, the nature of this vulnerability has been changing in recent decades. Although the transmission of external shocks through trade remains important – as made evident by both sharp commodity price volatility over the past few decades and the collapse of world trade and trade finance during the most recent global economic crisis – financial shocks have come to play a more

[5] Nonetheless, and although trends were strongly positive in the first decade of the twenty-first century, particularly in 2003–8, largely due to the effects of the rapid growth of China on the price of minerals, it is still unclear whether this episode represented a reversal of the long-term trend in commodity prices, which fell strongly, in a stepwise fashion, through the twentieth century. See Ocampo and Parra (2010).

prominent role, revisiting patterns that have been observed in the past in many developing countries, especially during the world financial boom-bust cycle of the 1920s and 1930s.

In this sense, macroeconomic asymmetries are associated with the fact that the global monetary system is centred on the United States (US) dollar and, secondarily, other currencies from industrial countries,[6] as well as with the asymmetric features of global capital flows and their relationship to macroeconomic policies in the industrial and developing world. Capital flows are pro-cyclical in most countries, but the volatility experienced by flows to developing countries is more marked, as the recent global crisis confirmed once again. Also, whereas certain types of financial meltdowns tend to affect industrial and developing countries alike (particularly banking crises), other forms of crises are more typical of developing countries (external debt and currency crises and associated sovereign defaults) (Reinhart and Rogoff 2009).

As a result of pressures coming from world financial markets, industrial countries have more room to manoeuvre when adopting counter-cyclical macroeconomic policies. This is particularly true of the United States, which issues the major international currency, and experiences counter-cyclical capital flows during periods of global 'flight to quality', as the September 2008 world financial meltdown and the crisis of the Eurozone during the second quarter of 2010 have once again revealed. In contrast, developing countries generally lack that room for manoeuvre. Thus, in these countries, pro-cyclical macroeconomic policies frequently amplify rather than smooth out the capital account cycle.[7] Market agents furthermore expect and evaluate authorities on their ability to adopt such pro-cyclical policies – particularly, the adoption of austerity policies during crises.

As a result of past crises, since the 1990s, 'self-insurance' in the form of accumulation of large amounts of foreign exchange reserves has become a broad-based pattern in the developing world. During the recent global

[6] This gives rise to the general incapacity of developing countries to issue debt in international markets in their own currencies (the phenomenon that Eichengreen *et al.* 2003 have called the 'original sin'), and the fact that 'flight to quality' during crises benefits the issuer of the major global currency.

[7] See Kaminsky *et al.* (2004), who call this feature of developing countries the 'when-it-rains-it-pours syndrome'. Interestingly, the crisis experienced by the Eurozone in the second quarter of 2010 has revealed similar trends within the European Union, with the peripheral countries facing pro-cyclical financial shocks and forced to adopt pro-cyclical macroeconomic policies.

economic crisis, greater room was provided for counter-cyclical macroeconomic policies, though in quite a diverse way (see Ocampo *et al.* 2010). In any case, this trend still reflected the asymmetries that characterize the world economy, as it forced developing countries to accumulate large amounts of foreign exchange reserves to manage the pro-cyclical capital flows they faced. It must be underscored that reserve accumulation represents lending to the richest countries of the world (particularly the USA) at very low interest rates, that it has costs for developing countries and that it tends to amplify global payments imbalances.[8]

The second asymmetry is derived from the *high concentration of technical progress in developed countries*. The diffusion of technical progress from source countries to the rest of the world remains 'relatively slow and uneven', affirming Prebisch's (1950) classical predicament. This concentration reflects the costs of entry into more dynamic technological activities, including the obstacles that developing countries face in technologically mature sectors, where opportunities for them may be largely confined to attracting multinationals that control the technology, global production and distribution networks. For many developing countries, opportunities are further limited to the low-skilled part of the value-added chain (assembly operations). In turn, technology transfer is subject to the payment of innovation rents, which have been rising due to the generalization and strengthening of intellectual property (IP) rights, particularly through the incorporation of IP standards and enforcing requirements into the World Trade Organization (WTO) and bilateral trade agreements.

The combined effect of these factors explains why, at the global level, the productive structure has exhibited a high and persistent concentration of technical progress in the industrialized countries, which thus maintain their dominant position in the most dynamic sectors of international trade and their hegemony in the establishment of large transnational enterprises. A few developing countries have been able to make inroads into the world of technological innovation though active research and development (R&D) policies, though this remains a secondary phenomenon so far. There has also been a rise of transnational enterprises from the developing world but, due to these forces, they tend to be concentrated in technologically standardized sectors.

The third asymmetry is associated with the *contrast between the high mobility of capital and the restrictions on the international movement of*

[8] See Ocampo (2010b). See also Rodrik (2006) for the estimation of the costs of reserve accumulation.

labour, particularly of unskilled labour.[9] This also remains, as noticed, an area where international cooperation is generally absent, as reflected in the fact that it has been ignored in most international economic agreements; in the WTO, for example, though it is included as one of the modes of service provision, its development has been essentially circumscribed to skilled labour.

It should be emphasized that this asymmetry is a characteristic of the present phase of globalization, since it was not manifested in the nineteenth and early twentieth centuries (a period characterized by large mobility of both capital and labour), nor in the first twenty-five years following the Second World War (a period in which both factors exhibited very little mobility). As has been pointed out by Rodrik (1997), these asymmetries in the international mobility of the factors of production generate biases in the distribution of income in favour of the more mobile factors (capital and skilled labour) and against the less mobile factors (less skilled labour). This, in turn, affects relations between developed and developing countries in as much as the latter have a relative abundance of less skilled labour.

2.2 *Global asymmetries and international economic structures*

Since the creation of the United Nations Conference on Trade and Development (UNCTAD),[10] the need to correct the asymmetries that characterize the international economic system has been explicitly recognized by the international community. The commitments concerning the flow of Official Development Assistance and 'special and differential treatment' for developing countries in trade issues were some of the partial, although relatively frustrating, results of this effort to build a 'new international economic order' aimed at redressing the large inequalities between industrial and developing countries. In addition, it is important to underline that in areas of sustainable development, new principles were agreed to at the start of the 1990s, notably principle seven of the Declaration of the Conference on the Environment and Development that took place in Rio de Janeiro in 1992 (commonly known as the Earth Summit), regarding the 'common but differentiated responsibilities' of developed and developing countries.

[9] See an extensive analysis of this issue in United Nations (2004).

[10] See, for example, the report of Raúl Prebisch as the first Secretary-General of UNCTAD (Prebisch 1964).

This vision has been radically eroded in the last few decades and substituted by an alternative paradigm according to which the basic objective of the international economic system should be to ensure a uniform set of rules to facilitate the efficient functioning of free market forces, thus ignoring the essential asymmetries that continue to characterize the world economic system.

According to this vision, the essential gains for developing countries lie in the eventual dismantling of the protection of 'sensitive' sectors in industrialized countries, and in the stability that export sectors derive from an international trading system with clear and stable rules. Acknowledgement of the need to correct international asymmetries is confined to the recognition of international responsibility towards *least* developed countries, replicating at an international level the vision of social policy as a strategy that targets State support to the poorest segments of the population.

Even though all these actions are desirable, would they be sufficient in themselves to generate a greater convergence in levels of development? The answer is probably 'no'. The application of the same measures in very different situations can even aggravate existing inequalities. Moreover, 'levelling the playing field' implies restrictions on developing countries that the industrial countries themselves never faced in previous periods of their history (Chang 2002). Examples of such restrictions are standards of intellectual property protection that are those of countries that generate technology, rather than those that were adopted in the past by countries that copied technology, and limitations on policy options for promoting new production sectors for either the domestic or the external markets.

The concept of 'common but differentiated responsibilities' of the 1992 Rio Declaration and the already classic principle of special and differential treatment incorporated in international trade agreements are thus more appropriate guidelines for building an equitable global order, rather than that of a 'level playing field'. In recent decades, however, the latter has been the norm that has guided efforts to reform the international economic system.

These considerations outline the essential elements that should guide international economic reform in order to address the asymmetries developing countries face. First, in the financial arena, the essential function of the international financial institutions, from the perspective of developing countries, is to compensate for the pro-cyclical impact of financial markets, smoothing financial boom and bust at its source through adequate regulation, and providing a larger degree of freedom for countries to adopt counter-cyclical macroeconomic policies. This implies, in turn, adequate surveillance during boom periods, avoiding the accumulation of excessive macroeconomic and financial risks, and adequate financing during crises to smooth the required adjustment in the face of 'sudden stops' of external financing. An additional function, which is equally essential, is to make resources available to countries and economic agents that have limited access to private international capital markets through multilateral development banks or bilateral financing.

With respect to the second asymmetry, the multilateral trade system must facilitate the smooth transfer to developing countries of heavily protected and subsidized agricultural goods, processed primary commodities, technologically mature manufacturing activities and standardized services. It should, therefore, avoid erecting obstacles to such transfers through protection or subsidies. Moreover, this system must accelerate developing countries' access to technology and ensure their increasing participation in the generation of technology and in the production of goods and services with high technological content.

In light of the problems that developing countries face in ensuring dynamic transformation of their productive structures, special and differential treatment is required, particularly in two critical areas. First, regimes for intellectual property protection should avoid creating excessive costs for developing countries or limit the modalities through which the transfer can be made. These schemes must also provide clear incentives for the transfer of technology towards them. Second, instruments are needed to promote new economic activities, including new exports (infant export industries), which foster diversification and increase their value added. All of this requires a search for the appropriate instruments that are able to avoid a sterile competition among countries in order to attract footloose industries.

Finally, to overcome the third asymmetry, labour migration must be fully included in the international agenda through a globally agreed framework for migration policies and through the strict protection of human and labour rights of migrants. This should be complemented with regional and bilateral frameworks and negotiations. In the area of trade, service provision through labour mobility should be facilitated, including low-skilled services and the mobility of low-skilled workers in all service sectors. Moreover, such agreements must envisage complementary mechanisms to facilitate migration, such as the recognition of educational, professional and labour credentials; the transferability of social security benefits; and low cost for transferring remittances.

While progress towards a 'development friendly' international system will require work to address these basic asymmetries that exist within the current global system, we cannot ignore the fact that the responsibility for development resides first and foremost with the countries themselves. This has been reiterated in numerous international declarations, particularly in the Monterrey Consensus adopted by the United Nations Conference on Financing for Development (United Nations 2002). This principle also responds to an old postulate of development literature: that institutional development, the creation of mechanisms of social cohesion, and the accumulation of human capital and technological capacities ('knowledge capital') are essentially *endogenous* processes. To use a term coined by Latin American structuralism, in all these cases development can only come 'from within' (Sunkel 1993). There are no universal models and there is, therefore, vast scope for institutional learning and diversity and, as we will see below, for the exercise of democracy.

This implies, in turn, that such a development-friendly international system must provide enough room for the adoption of development strategies that developing countries consider adequate to their economic circumstances: that is, 'policy space', to use the term that became common after the UNCTAD XI in June 2004 in São Paulo.[11] Such policy space is particularly critical in the design of policies and strategies in three areas: 1) macroeconomic policies that reduce external vulnerability and facilitate productive investment; 2) active productive development strategies aimed at diversifying economic structures and developing system-wide competitiveness; and 3) ambitious social policies designed to increase equity and guarantee social inclusion.[12]

3 A more balanced globalization

3.1 *The long road to better global governance*

As the World Commission on the Social Dimension of Globalization (2004) has indicated, the road to a balanced globalization inevitably lies in better global governance. However, this road is long and rocky, since the

[11] See www.unctadxi.org/templates/Startpage____4.aspx [accessed in November 2010].

[12] For a longer analysis of the issues raised in this section, see Ocampo (2002) and Ocampo and Martin (2003), chapter 5.

asymmetries that characterize the present globalization and the resulting distributive tensions reflect the intrinsic characteristics of politics and the political economy of the world today.

In fact, the imbalance of the current globalization agenda reflects the greater influence that is exerted by more powerful states and large multinational firms. It is also the result of the disorganization of other actors, particularly developing countries, in international debates. This behaviour is linked not only to the weakening of historical mechanisms of collective action of developing countries (such as the Group of 77),[13] but also to 'policy competition' that globalization itself has created: the incentive for each country to show its attractiveness to investors in an era of capital mobility and greater susceptibility to relocation of production.

This situation is also affected by the resistance of most countries to give up their economic sovereignty to international organizations. Under the strong market forces that characterize globalization and the unilateral liberalization processes simultaneously undertaken by countries, market regulations have weakened worldwide. Many analysts see this as progress, but it is also a source of serious distortion and risk, as the recent global financial crisis made patently clear in the area of finance. In addition, although open regionalism is one of the traits of the current globalization process and it has led to integration efforts in many regions of the developing world (such as in Latin America, South East Asia and, more recently, Africa), these efforts have not resulted so far in strong coalitions among developing countries. In fact, the European Union aside, countries are not ready to give up their sovereignty even to regional organizations (and, in the case of the EU, only in a limited way).

These characteristics of politics and political economy have had important consequences for reforms aimed at improving global governance. The most obvious is that efforts towards a substantial reform are weak. Furthermore, global reform efforts have prevented a more balanced negotiation process, thus undermining or even ignoring the interests of some actors. Thus, for example, the recent G20 excludes most countries of the world even from indirect representation, and its agenda seems to be highly driven by that of the major industrial countries that launched this process in the first place. Hence, the asymmetries in global power

[13] A development in the first decade of the twenty-first century was, however, the rise of new groupings of developing countries that cross regions, and have had an important influence on trade negotiations (e.g. the G20 led by Brazil, the group of African cotton exporters and the coalition of ACP countries and LDCs).

relations and the high cost of establishing international coalitions to compensate for them have taken on greater importance.

Limitations in global governance structures imply that the institutions thus far created at the national level will not exist at the global level or will only have limited functions. Given the likelihood of incomplete international arrangements, developing countries should continue to claim autonomy in areas of critical importance, particularly in the definition of strategies of economic and social development. Moreover, as we will see below, national autonomy in this area is the only system coherent with the promotion of democracy at the global level.

A final implication of the aforementioned analysis is that no international architecture is neutral in terms of the balance of power in international relations. In this regard, an international system that depends exclusively on a few global institutions will be less balanced than one that relies also on regional institutions – in particular, for the issues analysed here (regional financial and trade institutions), as well as regional technological cooperation. The positions of countries lacking power at the international level will improve if they actively participate in such regional schemes. In fact, these schemes offer levels of autonomy and mutual assistance that countries would otherwise not be able to obtain in isolation. Therefore, the international order should offer ample room for the functioning of strong regional institutions respectful of a rules-based global order; in other words, a system of 'open regionalism'. In fact, building a strong network of regional institutions could be the best way to gradually build a better international order.

3.2 Globalization and democracy

Despite the biases of the current global economic agenda, the current phase of globalization is a multidimensional phenomenon that has also included the gradual spread of common principles and international social objectives. These principles have been sanctioned in international declarations and agreements on human rights, and in the UN Development Agenda that has emerged out of declarations and plans of action from the sequence of United Nations Conferences and Summits, including in particular the Millennium Declaration (United Nations 2000) and the associated Millennium Development Goals, which constitute a subset of that broader UN Agenda. These principles and international social objectives represent, in a deep sense, the 'social dimensions of globalization'. These processes are also rooted in the long historical struggle by international civil society for human rights, social equity, gender equality, protection of the environment and, more recently, globalization of solidarity and the 'right to be different' (cultural diversity), which indeed represents one of the most positive aspects of globalization.

These UN-centred ideas and civil society processes have also been instrumental in spreading democratic principles and a broad vision of citizenship, based on the spread of both civil and political rights, as well as economic, social and cultural rights – i.e. a 'rights-based' approach to the design of political, as well as economic and social institutions. However, the simultaneity of this process with the liberalization of market forces has generated tensions without creating mechanisms to attenuate them. The main reason for this is the duality that characterized globalization in this area: while supporting the recent spread of democracy and the establishment of international social objectives, it has also eroded the capacity for action by nation-states. It has kept the complex task of sustaining social cohesion in the hands of nation-states, but has constrained at the same time their room for manoeuvre. Moreover, the necessary space required by democracy to engender diversity has been reduced as a result of the homogeneity of norms and the strong weight of conditionality in international financial assistance.

In this sense, the absence of a true internationalization of politics is the major paradox of the current globalization process. In other words, the simultaneous growth of democratic forces and distributive tensions has not been accompanied by the strengthening of the political institutions that would reduce the tension between them. Although there are incipient instances of global citizenship that take place in the form of struggles by international civil society, their capacity to affect the course of globalization still depends on their influence on national political processes.

This has deep implications for the international order. In the first place, it implies that it is necessary to create democratic spaces of a global character. However, this process will be necessarily slow and incomplete. Therefore, as long as the nation-state remains the main space for the expression of political citizenry, the promotion of democracy as a universal value will only make sense if national processes of representation and participation are allowed to determine economic and social development strategies and to mediate the tensions created by globalization. This coincides with the idea that institutional development, social cohesion and the accumulation of human and knowledge capital are endogenous processes (see section 2.2).

The support for these endogenous processes, the respect for diversity and the formulation of norms that would facilitate it are essential for a development-friendly international democratic order. This means, therefore, that *the international order should be strongly respectful of diversity*, obviously within the limits of interdependence. It also implies that an essential function of international organizations is to support national strategies that contribute to reducing, through political citizenry, the strong tensions that exist today between the principle of equality and the functioning of globalized markets.

3.3 International social goals and global social cohesion funds

The construction of a global social agenda should recognize that all members of global society are citizens and, as such, are bearers of economic, social and cultural rights. The international declaration and covenants of human rights, as well as international agreements adopted at United Nations Conferences and Summits, should thus be considered as defining the foundations of the concept of global citizenship where all world citizens share common rights.

However, in this rights-based approach to global development, there has not been a full transition from domestic to international responsibilities. In fact, the respect for economic and social rights and the responsibility for achieving social objectives still remain at the national level. Moreover, the execution of these obligations and commitments still lies with the nation-state and does not explicitly include other social actors. Finally, as of now, there are few effective enforcement mechanisms for guaranteeing that these rights and international commitments are respected by nation-states. The European Social Charter,[14] signed by members of the Council of Europe in 1961 and revised in 1996, provides the major exception in the international institutional structure, by allowing citizens to judicially demand the fulfilment of the social rights guaranteed by the Charter.

One essential activity in this field is the production, dissemination and analysis of information on the situation of economic, social and cultural rights, and on the provision of both 'global public goods' and 'goods of social value', as part of stronger accountability of objectives already agreed upon at world conferences and summits. These periodic evalu-

[14] See www.coe.int/T/DGHL/Monitoring/SocialCharter/ [accessed in November 2010].

ations should be discussed at representative national fora, with active participation by parliaments and civil society. A process of this type would contribute to creating a culture of responsibility for meeting international objectives and commitments, and to adjusting domestic public policies accordingly. It would thus help build strong *political accountability* for international commitments.

The political visibility and the mechanism designed to evaluate progress towards the United Nations Millennium Development Goals represent major progress in this regard. It is important to build upon this experience and to create new and broader mechanisms to promote accountability that would eventually lead to an integrated evaluation that covers the internationally agreed social rights (e.g. the principles and fundamental rights to employment, agreed upon at the International Labour Organization, and the rights of children, women and ethnic groups), and the closely related commitments reached at global UN Conferences and Summits.

This political accountability could in turn gradually make room for the possibility of citizens being able to *judicially demand* the fulfilment of their economic, social and cultural rights and of other international social commitments in competent national and international courts, possibly following the model of the Council of Europe. The obligations of States must in all cases correspond to the degree of development of countries and, in particular, with their ability to reach goals that can indeed benefit *all* citizens within those countries. This would avoid both voluntarism – whose more ambitious social goals may exceed the means of achieving them and generate frustration – as well as populism, whose efforts to satisfy popular demands beyond fiscal means can generate adverse macroeconomic effects.

Finally, the existence of significant global inequalities and asymmetries means that economic globalization will succeed in achieving convergence in the levels of development between countries only if accompanied by resource flows explicitly aimed at that objective. The European Union, through its policy of 'social cohesion', has undoubtedly provided the institutional mechanisms through which this principle has been applied most clearly. It is indicative of the underlying political philosophy of these arrangements that the deepening of economic integration in the last decade of the twentieth century was accompanied by the strengthening of its cohesion policy. There is, however, no similar experience outside the European context. For this reason, as some analysts have argued, it would be desirable to extend this experience to other regional arrangements.[15] Indeed, the final objective should be to design an explicit global redistributive mechanism that serves as a global cohesion fund, which could build upon the European experience but also upon the regional redistribution mechanisms that most countries have developed through time.

However, at the global level, the only instrument for the achievement of social goals has been, and will continue for some time to be, ODA. Such assistance should be provided in accordance with international commitments agreed at the United Nations (to allocate ODA equivalent to 0.7 per cent of the Gross National Income of developed countries) and with the basic criteria agreed by the international community in the 2002 Monterrey Conference on Financing for Development: that is, to give priority to the fight against poverty and to the ownership of socio-economic development policies by the countries that adopt them (United Nations 2002). The negative trends of the fiscal crises of industrial countries on ODA, which has broken the positive trend experienced since Monterrey, will be one of the major costs of the recent global financial crisis.

4 Conclusions

The major argument of this chapter is that building a better global economic governance necessarily involves overcoming two basic sets of asymmetries that characterize the current global order and that have been reflected in rising inequalities, both among and within countries. The first are the inequalities and asymmetries that characterize the global economic system and that largely determine divergence of income levels among countries. The second is the asymmetry between the rapid globalization of (some) markets and the relative weakness of the international social agenda, which is essential to overcome the strong trends towards worsening inequalities within countries. As long as the nation-state remains the main space for the expression of political citizenry, the promotion of democracy as a universal value will only make sense if national processes of representation and participation are allowed to determine

[15] See, for example, Bustillo and Ocampo (2004) in relation to the application of this framework to a possible Free Trade Area of the Americas – an idea that, since that paper was written, is essentially defunct, but a similar idea could be extended to many other processes.

economic and social development strategies and to mediate the tensions that globalization tends to create in the face of these strong international asymmetries.

References

Barrett, S. 2007. *Why Cooperate? The Incentive to Supply Global Public Goods*, New York: Oxford University Press.

Berry, A. and Serieux, J. 2007. 'World Economic Growth and Income Distribution, 1980–2000', in Jomo, K. S. and Baudot, J. (eds.), *Flat World, Big Gaps: Economic Liberalization, Globalization, Poverty and Inequality*, Himayatnagar, London and Penang: Orient Longman, Zed Books and Third World Network, in association with the United Nations, chapter 4.

Bhalla, S. S. 2002. *Imagine There's No Country: Poverty, Inequality, and Growth in the Era of Globalization*, Washington, DC: Institute for International Economics.

Bourguignon, F. and Morrison, C. 2002. 'Inequality Among World Citizens: 1820–1992', *American Economic Review* 92(4) September.

Bustillo, I. and Ocampo, J. A. 2004. 'Asymmetries and Cooperation in the FTAA', in *Integrating the Americas: FTAA and Beyond*, Estevadeordal, A. *et al.* (eds.), The David Rockefeller Center Series on Latin American Studies, Cambridge: Harvard University.

Chang, H. J. 2002. *Kicking Away the Ladder: Development Strategy in Historical Perspective*, London: Anthem Press.

Cornia, G. A. (ed.) 2004. *Inequality, Growth, and Poverty in an Era of Liberalization and Globalization*, Oxford University Press/United Nations University: World Institute for Development Economics Research.

2010. 'Economic Integration, Inequality and Growth: Theory and Comparative Assessment', background paper for the United Nations World Economic and Social Survey 2010. www.un.org/esa/policy/publications/wess_background_papers.htm [Accessed in September 2010].

Dikhanov, Y. and Ward, M. 2001. 'Evolution of the Global Distribution of Income in 1970–99', Document prepared for the 53rd Session of the International Statistical Institute, Seoul: Republic of Korea.

Eichengreen, B., Hausman, R. and Panizza, U. 2003. 'Currency Mismatches, Debt Intolerance and Original Sin: Why They Are Not the Same and Why They Matter', *NBER Working Paper 10036*, October.

Galbraith, J. K. and Kum, H. 2004. 'Estimating the Inequality of Household Incomes: A Statistical Approach to the Creation of a Dense and Consistent Global Data Set', University of Texas Inequality Project, *Working Paper No. 22*: rev. edn, December, University of Texas at Austin.

Gasparini, L., Cruces, G., Tornarolli, L. and Marchionni, M. 2009. 'A Turning Point? Recent Developments on Inequality in Latin America and the Caribbean', *Research for Public Policy, Human Development, HD-02-2009*. New York: UNDP Regional Bureau for Latin America and the Caribbean.

International Task Force on Global Public Goods. 2006. *Meeting Global Challenges: International Cooperation and the National Interest*. Final Report, Stockholm.

Kaminsky, G. L., Reinhart, C. M. and Végh, C. A. (2004). 'When It Rains, It Pours: Procyclical Capital Flows and Macroeconomic Policies', *NBER Working Paper 10780*, September.

Kaul, I., Conceição, P., Le Goulven, K. and Mendoza, R. U. (eds.) 2003. *Providing Global Public Goods: Managing Globalization*. New York: Oxford University Press.

Maddison, A. 2006. *The World Economy, vol. II: Historical Statistics*, Paris: Development Centre, Organization for Economic Co-operation and Development (OECD).

Milanovic, B. 2005. *Worlds Apart: Global and International Inequality, 1950–2000*, Princeton University Press.

Ocampo, J. A. 2002. 'Rethinking the Development Agenda', *Cambridge Journal of Economics* 26(3) May.

2010a. 'Rethinking Global Economic and Social Governance', *Journal of Globalization and Development* 1(1) Article 6.

2010b. 'Reforming the Global Reserve System', in Griffith-Jones, S., Ocampo, J. A. and Stiglitz, J. E. (eds.), *Time for a Visible Hand: Lessons from the 2008 World Financial Crisis*. New York: Oxford University Press.

Ocampo, J. A. and Martin, J. 2003. *Globalization and Development: A Latin American and Caribbean Perspective*, Palo Alto: Stanford University Press and ECLAC.

Ocampo, J. A. and Parra, M. A. 2007. 'The Dual Divergence: Growth Successes and Collapses in the Developing World Since 1980', in Ffrench-Davis, R. and Machinea, J. L. (eds.), *Economic Growth with Equity: Challenges for Latin America*. Houndmills, Hampshire: Palgrave Macmillan and ECLAC.

2010. 'The Terms of Trade for Commodities since the mid-Nineteenth Century', *Revista de Historia Económica/ Journal of Iberian and Latin American Economic History* 28(1): 11–43.

Ocampo, J. A., Griffith-Jones, S., Noman, A. *et al.* 2010. 'The Great Recession and the Developing World', Document prepared by the Initiative for Policy Dialogue of Columbia University for the Spanish Presidency of the European Union. www0.gsb.columbia.edu/ipd/programs/item.cfm?ptid=4&prid=132&iyid=13&itid=2022 [Accessed in September 2010].

Prebisch, R. 1950. 'Crecimiento, desequilibrio y disparidades: interpretación del proceso de desarrollo', *Estudio Económico de América Latina 1949*. New York: United Nations.

1964. *Nueva política comercial para el desarrollo*. Mexico: Fondo de Cultura Económica.

Pritchett, L. 1997. 'Divergence, Big Time', *Journal of Economic Perspectives* 11(3) Summer: 3–17.

Reinhart, C. M. and Rogoff, K. 2009. *This Time is Different: Eight Centuries of Financial Folly*. Princeton University Press.

Rodrik, D. 1997. *Has Globalization Gone Too Far?* Washington, DC: Institute for International Economics (IIE).

2006. 'The Social Costs of Foreign Exchange Reserves', *International Economic Journal* 20(3) September.

Sunkel, O. (ed.) 1993. *Development from Within: Toward a new Neostructuralist Approach for Latin America*. Boulder and London: Lynne Rienner Publishers.

Sutcliffe, B. 2007. 'A Converging or Diverging World?', in Jomo, K.S. and Baudot, J. (eds.), *Flat World, Big Gaps: Economic Liberalization, Globalization, Poverty and Inequality*. Himayatnagar, London and Penang: Orient Longman, Zed Books and Third World Network, in association with the United Nations.

United Nations. 2000. *The Millennium Declaration*, New York: General Assembly, Millennium Summit.

2002. *The Monterrey Consensus*, International Conference on Financing for Development. Monterrey: Mexico.

2004. *World Economic and Social Survey 2004: International Migration*, New York, November.

2007. *The United Nations Development Agenda: Development for All*. New York, ST/ESA/316.

World Commission on the Social Dimension of Globalization 2004. *A Fair Globalization: Creating Opportunities for All*. Geneva: International Labour Organization.

2

Trade, development and the UN Millennium Development Goals: the United Nations in the governance of world trade

LAKSHMI PURI

> We, the People of the United Nations ... are determined to promote social progress and better standards of life in larger freedoms ... [and] to employ international machinery for the promotion of the economic and social advancement of all peoples.
>
> Charter of the United Nations, 1945

> Ministers affirm that the establishment of the World Trade Organization ushers in a new era of global economic cooperation, reflecting the widespread desire to operate in a fairer and more open multilateral trading system for the benefit and welfare of their peoples.
>
> Marrakesh Declaration of 15 April 1994, establishing the WTO

One of the greatest challenges, and opportunities, facing the international community today is how to remould global trade governance to ensure greater coherence between the systems for international trade, financial, monetary and technology governance so that they support development and, specifically, to advance the achievement of the United Nations' Millennium Development Goals (MDGs). A critical part of this challenge is how to more overtly foster global solidarity and integrate development principles and equity considerations into how the global economy is governed. This chapter emphasizes the dual importance of the global trading system as a global public good that can help all nations solve trade-related problems through a coordinated multilateral response, and also as a 'global development good', which facilitates economic, social and environmentally sustainable development for all.

Lakshmi Puri is Assistant Secretary General and Deputy Executive Secretary of UNWOMEN – the UN Entity for Gender Equality and Women's Empowerment. The views expressed here are those of the author and do not necessarily represent those of the United Nations Secretariat nor its Member States.

This chapter traces the evolution of the United Nations' (UN's) development ideas, initiatives and goals as related to trade, including the MDGs. It demonstrates how the UN, through its research, analysis and strategic monitoring as well as the advocacy and support for developing country causes, policy-makers and negotiators, has contributed to remould the global trade governance system towards a greater focus on development. It recognizes that despite the best efforts of the UN Secretariat and Member States, progress has been limited, however, and that there are new and emerging issues, or 'game changers', to reckon with. It reaffirms the need for a strong UN role and partnership with the World Trade Organization (WTO), as well as other existing and emerging economic governance systems, if development goals and principles of sustainable development are to be realized and to harness the new game changers as a positive force for development.

The chapter begins by tracing the evolution of the UN's development agenda, highlighting the importance of the MDGs, and the intersections that have emerged between that agenda and global trade arrangements. Section 2 analyses international trade and its contribution to the achievement of the MDGs, as well as increased advocacy for development gains by developing countries. Section 3 outlines a 'responsive' or 'enabling' development agenda in world trade governance that would be critical to permitting developing countries to effectively use trade as an engine of development in the background of major changes and evolution in the global economy and trading system. Finally the conclusion emphasizes that while global trade governance faces great challenges it has several opportunities to reinvent itself as a 'global development good' to meet the expectations of countries and peoples for a better world.

1 Evolution of the UN's development agenda for global trade

1.1 From economic growth to MDGs: evolution of the UN's development agenda

Since its founding in 1945, the United Nations has sought to make economic and social development an ethical, moral and practical imperative for global economic governance in all its dimensions – discourse, institution-building and norm-setting. The UN has linked development to the realization of other humanitarian goals, namely peace, security and the promotion and protection of human rights. In the UN's vision, development is a holistic concept based on accelerated and sustained economic growth, employment generation and poverty eradication, which embraces environmentally sustainable and socially just outcomes. There has been a close connection between the UN's development agenda, and how the development dimension of global trade governance has evolved.

In the 1960s, the UN's development effort began in earnest and was signalled by the launch of the first of four 'UN development decades' proposed by former US President J. F. Kennedy,[1] and coincided with the creation of the UN Conference on the least developed countries (LDCs).[2] In the 1970s, a 'basic needs' development strategy, which aimed at promoting universal access in developing countries to food, clothing, housing and such public services like education, health and transportation was conceptualized and promoted.[3] In 1995, the UN's Copenhagen Conference on Social Development brought into focus the key elements of social development – namely poverty eradication, social integration and protection and employment generation – as both means and objectives of development (UN 1995a). In the same year, the UN's Beijing Conference on Women emphasized issues of gender equity and welfare as integral to development (UN 1995b). Concepts of human development and people-centred economic growth and development policies further enriched the UN's panoply of ideas for promoting development. Moreover, the human development concept and successive Human Development Reports, published by the United Nations Development Programme (UNDP), highlighted the importance of acquiring, inter alia, access to the resources needed to build human capabilities and improve the availability of essential choices for a decent standard of living.[4]

In the year 2000, 147 Heads of State met in New York at the United Nations Millennium Summit to adopt the Millennium Declaration (UN 2000). In the declaration, UN Members identified the following fundamental values as essential to international relations in the twenty-first century: freedom, equality, solidarity, tolerance, respect for nature and shared responsibility. To translate these values into reality, the Millennium

[1] See www.un.org/observances/decades.shtml [accessed in November 2010].

[2] See www.un.org/en/development/devagenda/ldc.shtml [accessed in November 2010].

[3] See, for example, International Development Strategy for the Second United Nations Development Decade (A/RES/25/2626).

[4] Such ideas were developed into a systemic approach in the UNDP Human Development Report by its first author Dr Mahbub ul Haq. The intellectual foundations for a human development approach are provided in writings of eminent development economists and experts, including Professor Amartya Sen, Sir Richard Jolly and Professor Sakiko Fukuda-Parr.

Declaration included a number of key objectives in the areas of peace, security and disarmament; development and poverty eradication; environmental protection; human rights, democracy and good governance; protecting vulnerable populations; meeting the special needs of Africa; and strengthening the United Nations. From among these main objectives, eight development goals (known as the Millennium Development Goals) were singled out as deserving particular attention, with the aim of attainment by 2015. The eight MDGs are to: 1) eradicate extreme poverty and hunger; 2) achieve universal primary education; 3) promote gender equality and empower women; 4) reduce child mortality; 5) improve maternal health; 6) combat HIV/AIDS, malaria and other diseases; 7) ensure environmental sustainability; and 8) develop a Global Partnership for Development.

The MDGs are particularly focused on poverty, hunger reduction and sustainable development as global undertakings. They set health, education, environment, water and sanitation-related goals and give particular attention to vulnerable populations and disadvantaged groups, like women and children, especially in the world's poorest, most vulnerable countries. In a single package, the MDGs put together commitments made at different conferences and set time-bound and measurable targets and indicators for monitoring progress.

Encapsulated in the eighth MDG is the notion of a 'Global Partnership for Development' based on the shared responsibilities of both developing and developed countries to work multilaterally to promote economic and social development worldwide. The targets set under Goal 8 include attaining an open, rule-based, non-discriminatory and predictable multilateral trading and financial system; addressing the special needs of LDCs, Landlocked Developing Countries (LLDCs) and Small Island Developing States (SIDS); comprehensively dealing with the debt challenges facing developing countries to ensure long-term debt sustainability; providing access to affordable essential drugs in developing countries; and making the benefits of new technologies available to developing countries, especially information and communication technologies.

MDG 8 is underpinned by the principle of global solidarity with the weakest and most vulnerable countries through trade, finance, technology-related support and access to medicine. Indeed, the principle of global solidarity becomes a guidepost for good global economic governance. 'Global challenges must be managed in a way that distributes the costs and burdens fairly in accordance with the principle of equity and social justice. Those who suffer or those who benefit least deserve help from those who benefit the most' (UN 2000: para. 6). The values of equality (that is, the equal right to development within and among nations), freedom, tolerance and respect for the environment are other values also encapsulated by the MDGs. This environmental dimension of the Declaration is especially relevant given the current struggle to agree on improved measures to respond to climate change and to boost environmental governance. 'Prudence must be shown in the management of all living species and natural resources in accordance with the precepts of sustainable development ... Our current unsustainable patterns of production and consumption must be changed in the interest of our future welfare and that of our descendants' (UN 2000). Thus the MDGs focus both on improving the livelihoods of people today, as well as strengthening the well-being of the planet for future generations.

The MDGs have prompted considerable debate among development experts. There are debates, for instance, about whether or not the MDGs are too specific, limited and incomplete. There are concerns too about the measurability of different goals and targets, and the usefulness of the indicators adopted. Some analysts express concerns that the MDGs' call for a Global Partnership for Development is vague and too narrow, and that the specific roles of the international community and economic governance systems in helping achieve the MDGs are inadequately defined. There are also fears that the MDGs could become shorthand caricatures of much more comprehensive, inclusive and sophisticated development agendas within the UN, which have been elaborated and adapted over sixty-five years. However, limitations aside, the MDGs represent a significant contribution to the UN's efforts to promote development cooperation. They highlight a number of core and urgent development imperatives, and provide a focal point for developing countries and their development partners to rally around and work together on. Progress in attaining the MDGs, even with all the statistical constraints in developing countries, is indeed measurable. Moreover, the MDGs have become the moral and ethical basis for development cooperation, without seeking to limit its scope.

1.2 The UN development agenda and world trade governance: converging issues

Within the UN system, ideas on strategies for development have been nurtured with a purpose. The UN has, at different times and in various ways, tried either to play a stronger role in global economic governance itself, or to influence world economic governance in favour of a global development agenda that advances the goals promulgated under its auspices. This is particularly true in the area of global trade governance. Indeed, the early efforts to establish a multilateral trading system were hosted by the United Nations. From November 1947 to March 1948, the United Nations Conference on Trade and Employment[5] met in Havana to establish an international trade organization. However, the effort to establish a system of multilateral rules consistent with development and full employment goals failed. Instead, as an interim arrangement, a truncated global trade governance system (the General Agreement on Tariffs and Trade (GATT)) with limited developing country participation, and a focus on trade liberalization and rule-making for trade, was established in 1947. Subsequently, developing countries organized themselves into the Group of 77 and worked to create a development-oriented alternative to the GATT system in the form of the UN Conference on Trade and Development (UNCTAD), established by the UN General Assembly in 1964.

In the subsequent four and a half decades, however, UNCTAD far from replaced the GATT as the central pillar of the world trade governance system. In fact, with the founding of the WTO in 1995, the GATT itself has been transformed into an increasingly universal and all-encompassing world trade governance structure and permanent negotiating forum. Nevertheless, UNCTAD, against all odds, has managed to exert a powerful, often unsung, influence on global trade governance through its work to insert the development dimension and the UN's evolving development agenda and goals into negotiations at the WTO and elsewhere. Through consistent monitoring and review of the international trading system, UNCTAD has played the role of a development watchdog, pointing to shortcomings and gaps from the developing country perspective, albeit often at the cost of developed country accusations of a development bias.[6] In addition, while emphasizing the importance of international trade and its governance, UNCTAD has also advocated greater consideration of linkages between trade and other aspects of global governance, such as for finance, monetary policy, technology and the environment. In light of the growing interdependence of countries, UNCTAD has also

[5] United Nations Conference on Trade and Employment, Havana Charter for an International Trade Organization, in the Final Act of the United Nations Conference on Trade and Employment, adopted on 24 March 1948 [never entered into force].

[6] For more discussion see, for example, South Centre 2006.

argued that such an integrated approach to global economic governance is necessary for achieving positive-sum development outcomes for all countries.

1.3 The UN's intellectual case for a development-oriented trading system

The UN's approach to examining the international trade governance paradigm from a development perspective was built on the work of experts, such as Folke Hilgerdt (League of Nations 1942), Hans Singer (Singer 1950) and Raul Prebisch (ECLAC 1950), who worked in organizations such as the UN Statistical Organization, the UN Economic Commission for Latin America and the Caribbean (ECLAC) and UNCTAD (UNCTAD 2004). They argued that developing countries in Latin America and those emerging from colonialism in Asia and Africa were inherently disadvantaged in international production and trade. They were commodity-dependent and suffered from a secular decline in their terms of trade. They would need to pursue targeted trade and development strategies to build up their industrial and technological base and competitiveness. To derive maximum benefit from their own resources and from international trade, they argued that developed countries needed to recognize these historical, structural, socio-economic and technological handicaps facing developing countries and accord them differential and more favourable treatment in trade. In addition, developed countries should, they purported, follow aid, debt, monetary, financial and technology policies conducive for countries on the periphery of the global economy to move to the centre. These ideas were not posited as charity. The development of the periphery was presented as being in the economic and wider interest of the centre as well – prosperity in the periphery would result in greater prosperity in the centre.

These and successive generations of idea-entrepreneurs at UNCTAD, the UN Development Programme (UNDP), the UN Department of Economic and Social Affairs (DESA) and elsewhere in the United Nations (Jolly *et al.* 2009), sought continuously to draw linkages between international trade, monetary and financial governance, and how they could better support achievement of internationally agreed development goals, including the MDGs. Importantly, this agenda continued to be underpinned by an emphasis on values – equity, fair play, altruism, humanism, the common good and making trade work for societies everywhere. Additionally, it was argued that interdependence among countries, policy areas and issues, as well as beneficial and inclusive globalization, required dialogue and cooperation between developed and developing countries, as well as economies in transition. In addition, pragmatic arguments were advanced that contended that it would serve the enlightened self-interest of developed countries to provide a ladder for developing countries to increase their production, export capacity and purchasing power so as to become major markets with exponential future growth prospects. Progress on development and poverty eradication on the only planet we share have also been presented as insurance against conflict, terrorism, unregulated migration and environmental degradation. More recently, a more development-friendly global trade system has been conceptualized as a global public good,[7] and as a mechanism realizing the international community's human rights agenda.[8]

Equally important has been the UN's insistence, both through its Secretariat's policy analysis and through various intergovernmental deliberations and consensus (e.g. including the declarations that emerged from the regular UNCTAD Conferences held every four years since 1964, the 2002 Monterrey Consensus on Financing for Development,[9] and the 2002 World Summit on Sustainable Development[10]), that trade is not an end in itself but a means to sustainable development and poverty reduction, and that the trading system must thus be structured and managed so as to ensure development gains from trade. The logical extension of this idea is that when governments establish rules for liberalizing and regulating the cross-border flow of goods, services, capital and labour, these rules should be consciously 'weighted' in favour of developing countries, especially the poorest among them. It has also been widely affirmed by governments and experts that the world trade governance structures – the WTO, in particular – should themselves be

[7] Global public goods are those goods that benefit the global community, individually and collectively, as nations and peoples within and between nations without discrimination. Examples of global public goods include a clean environment and education. A distinguishing feature of such goods tends to be that they cannot be produced by the marketplace alone, but rely on collective public action. For a discussion of global public goods, see Kaul *et al.* 1999.

[8] This concept perceives human rights (such as right to work, education or development) as a global good, available to all countries and peoples without discrimination. See United Nations. 1948. *The Universal Declaration of Human Rights*. General Assembly resolution 217 A (III), adopted on 10 December 1948.

[9] See 'Report of the International Conference on Financing for Development' (A/CONF. 198/11).

[10] See 'Report of the World Summit on Sustainable Development' (A/CONF.199/20).

considered a global public good that serves a development-promotion purpose. That is, they should become what I call a 'development public good'. For this to occur, both the openness agenda and fairness agenda from the developing country perspective have to be incorporated. Towards this end, as emphasized by the Millennium Declaration and also by the declarations from both the UNCTAD XI and XII, the international community must establish and uphold a more open, rule-based, non-discriminatory, predictable and equitable multilateral trading system.

1.4 The UN's role in world trade governance: norm-setting

UN organizations have played important roles in shaping world trade governance. UNCTAD, the UN Economic and Social Council, and the Second Committee of the United Nations General Assembly have each engaged in norm-setting through the adoption of resolutions and decisions that lay down principles, set goals and specify commitments by Member States to conduct trade and development policies in a mutually supportive way.[11] Although these outcomes may not have had the force of legal contracts, they have constituted an important body of international soft-law. Moreover, many of these norms have been translated into national, regional and global policies and measures. Within the UN system, UNCTAD has played the leading role in such efforts.

The general principles adopted at the first UNCTAD Conference in 1964,[12] for example, included the right of countries to dispose freely of their natural resources. They also recognized international trade as one of the most important factors in development, which should be made mutually advantageous based on the most favoured nation (MFN) treatment. The 1964 principles also stated that developed countries should grant developing countries both tariff and non-tariff preferences in trade, on a non-reciprocal basis, and that developed countries should cooperate

[11] ECOSOC (the UN Economic and Social Council), for example, decides on admitting into or graduating countries from the status of least developed countries. The second committee, for example, monitors, each year, the state of international trade and adopts a resolution suggesting key areas in which Member States could take policy decisions and measures to enhance the participation of developing countries in global trade. Since 2002, special attention was given to the WTO Doha negotiations and in 2009, deliberations focused on the impact of the global crisis.

[12] The Final Act of UNCTAD I, adopted by the Conference at its thirty-fifth plenary meeting held on 15 June 1964 in Geneva (UN documents, 1964.II.B.II).

with developing countries to set targets for the expansion of trade.[13] In addition, it was noted that developing countries should have the right to protect their infant industries and that there must be a universal commitment to correct and compensate for the deterioration in the terms of trade of developing countries.

Subsequent UNCTAD conferences built on these concepts and over the years contributed to the mainstreaming of development into the GATT and later WTO processes, as well as to consideration of development dimensions in regional trade and economic integration agreements. In 1968, for example, the UNCTAD II Conference[14] adopted a resolution calling for tariff preferences for developing countries to foster industrialization. The UNCTAD III Conference[15] in 1972 was marked by the adoption of the Charter of Rights and Duties of States, deemed by developing countries to be an effective instrument towards a New International Economic Order that would, among other goals, promote more equal world trade. In the 1980s, UNCTAD Conferences signalled a major shift in thinking on the relationship between development and trade. These Conferences emphasized that developed countries should pursue structural adjustment of their economies, eschew protectionism in terms of both tariff and non-tariff barriers, and vacate their sunset industries to enable developing countries to move into economic activities involving higher levels of technology and production. The Conferences emphasize the importance of endogenous agricultural, industrial and technological revolutions in developing countries where exports would play a major role.

1.5 *The UN's research and analytical role*

UNCTAD and other UN organizations have acted as think tanks on world trade governance through their empirical and normative research and analysis of trade and development issues. They have made a strong intellectual case for eschewing purely mercantilist and pro-big business approaches to global trade liberalization and regulation or deregulation.

[13] The Final Act of UNCTAD I contained fifteen general and thirteen special principles agreed by Member States, with the objective of strengthening the participation of developing countries in global trade on a beneficial basis and promoting trade on the basis of fairer trading measures.

[14] Report of the United Nations Conference on Trade and Development on its second session (UN documents, 1968.II.D.14).

[15] Report of the United Nations Conference on Trade and Development on its third session (UN documents, 1973.II.D.4).

They have argued for considering the special needs, interests and capacities of developing countries in general, and for least developed countries and other more disadvantaged nations like SIDS and LLDCs in particular. They have tried to keep a specific focus on public interest and public goods issues as well. Their analysis has presented matters from the developing country perspective and has tended to be independent and innovative. They have often identified alternatives that go beyond conventional wisdom and prevailing, sometimes misguided, orthodoxy, particularly which was put forward under the so-called Washington Consensus and the Bretton Woods institutions, including structural adjustment programmes.

UNCTAD's research and analysis reoriented the discourse in the negotiations on trade in services in the run-up to the WTO's General Agreement on Trade in Services (GATS) towards a more development-friendly direction while contributing to breaking the North–South negotiating impasse. Its studies made seminal contributions by advancing the idea of modes of delivery (later to be adopted in GATS as the four modes of supply of services[16]), the positive list approach to making commitments, the separation of market access and national treatment commitments, and the Telecommunications Annex. Further, UNCTAD's studies on Trade Related Intellectual Property Rights (TRIPs) and Trade Related Investment Measures (TRIMs) sought to promote greater balance between the rights and freedoms of Intellectual Property Rights (IPR) holders and foreign investors on one hand, and, on the other, the rights and duties of governments to take certain measures to curb these rights for the public interest.

1.6 The UN as a source of proposals and schemes for development weighting in GATT–WTO

The UN has been the source of specific proposals and schemes, which have succeeded in incorporating a development dimension into world trade governance structures and rules, as well as ideas such as 'trade justice' – a term coined by development non-governmental organizations (NGOs) and used by developed country leaders like Gordon Brown of the United

[16] The WTO's General Agreement on Trade in Services has the following four modes of delivery of services: Mode 1 is cross-border supply of services; Mode 2 is consumption abroad of services; Mode 3 is supply of services through commercial presence; and Mode 4 is presence of natural persons supplying services.

Kingdom. A seminal UN contribution to the trading system has been the concept of 'special and differential treatment' for developing countries in international trade, that is, that developing countries should be given non-reciprocal preferential market access, policy flexibility and what was later called policy space in undertaking certain commitments in keeping with their trade, financial and development needs. These principles of special and differential treatment were postulated not as exceptions, but as fundamental principles of the multilateral trading system.

While many of the concrete UN proposals that now feature as part of global trade governance officially emerged from UNCTAD, many of the ideas, policy dialogues and consensus-building activities took place throughout the UN system and its agencies. Following are some of the key concrete measures for differential and favourable treatment that are now part of global trade governance that originated at UNCTAD, or to which UNCTAD made substantive contributions:

- Part IV of the GATT on Trade and Development (WTO 1994a);
- 1979 'Enabling Clause' (Decision on Differential and More Favourable Treatment, Reciprocity and Fuller Participation of Developing Countries) (GATT 1979);
- Generalized System of Preferences (GSP)[17];
- Global System of Trade Preferences among Developing Countries (GSTP) schemes for trade preferences to and among developing countries[18];
- The progressive liberalization and positive list approach to GATS commitments in the WTO negotiations (WTO 1994b Articles IV, XIX, XVI, XVII) and the GATS Annex on Mode 4 (Annex on Movement of Natural Persons Supplying Services under the Agreement) (WTO 1994c));
- Provisions on special and differential treatment in the various WTO Agreements (WTO 1994d and in the 2001 Doha Declaration on TRIPS and Public Health (WTO 2001a)).

The affirmation in the WTO 1994 Marrakech Declaration that global economic policy-making at the WTO should make a contribution to greater coherence among macroeconomic, trade, financial and monetary policies also owes its origin to UNCTAD's proposals.

[17] The legal basis for the GSP is the 1979 'Enabling Clause'.

[18] The legal basis for the GSTP schemes is the 1979 'Enabling Clause'.

1.7 UN assistance to developing country negotiators

As a growing number of developing countries have joined the GATT-WTO system over the last sixty years, they have been challenged to engage and negotiate in eight rounds of multilateral trade negotiations. In so doing, they have worked to fashion the trade governance to better serve their interests. At the same time, they have needed to grapple with the complexity and development implications of new, beyond-the-border measures such as environment-related measures, a plethora of standards and so-called trade-related issues – like trade-related investment, intellectual property rights and services sector liberalization – which have been progressively imported into the WTO and also into the proliferating number of Regional Trade Agreements (RTAs) and Bilateral Trade Agreements (BTAs). In addition, developing countries have had to meet the challenges of labour rights-related conditionality, which while successfully resisted in the WTO, has emerged in RTAs, BTAs as well as in practical dealings with global enterprises and negotiations on trade preferences.

In this context, organizations like UNCTAD, UNDP and the UN Regional Commissions have played a significant role in helping developing countries to not only understand the implications of these new and emerging issues, but also to formulate and substantiate their negotiating strategies and proposals to cater to their development interests through capacity-building and technical cooperation. This is especially so with regard to the GATT-WTO. For instance, in the run-up to one of the most important rounds of negotiations, the Uruguay Round (1986–94), developing countries submitted a record 50 per cent of all negotiating proposals with support from UNCTAD. These included proposals to make special and differential treatment binding instead of just 'best-endeavour' type provisions; to emphasize the need for transfer of technology commitments in return for higher intellectual property rights protection; and to compensate developing countries for their implementation difficulties.

UNCTAD and UN Regional Commissions have also provided technical support to developing countries in the negotiation of Economic Partnership Agreements (EPAs) between the EU and the African, Caribbean and Pacific (ACP) countries; Free Trade Agreements (FTAs) between the USA and Latin American countries; and on South–South agreements for free trade and deeper economic integration (UNCTAD 2005, 2007). However, it must be admitted that due to the country and subregion specific political sensitivity of EPAs with the EU, as well as FTAs with the USA, the UN's advice based on substantive cost-benefit analysis has not been heeded to the same degree as in the case of the multilateral trade negotiations. In the EPA negotiations, for instance, some individual countries and arbitrarily demarcated subregions within the ACP group have broken rank and signed interim EPAs based on reciprocity with the EU, despite the fact that such reciprocity among vastly unequal partners further disadvantages weaker ACP countries. In these interim EPAs, ACP states have undertaken WTO-plus commitments in areas such as competition, investment, intellectual property rights, services and tariff liberalization without necessarily receiving, as collectively demanded by the ACP countries, a substantial development assistance package to meet the cost of implementation and build-up productive capacity.[19]

2 The trading system and its development vocation

2.1 The trading system as a 'development public good' and the Doha Development Round

The notion that trade must serve a development purpose and that developing countries have a positive interest and agenda found formal expression in the Doha Declaration of 2001. Launching the latest Round of WTO negotiations (WTO 2001b) and issued on the heels of the adoption of the MDGs the year before, the Declaration vowed to put development at the heart of the negotiations. It was hence labelled the Doha Development Round or Doha Development Agenda (DDA). Whether it was genuinely meant to be so or was given a development garb by developed country proponents, as a means to get buy-in from developing countries wary of negotiations and additional commitments, may never be known and it is not material. What is important is that resurgent and increasingly influential groups of developing countries with both the strength of numbers and market power, made it their clarion cry to demand reform in the WTO to better reflect their offensive

[19] The TRIPS-plus intellectual property provisions of the US–Andean Free Trade Agreement provide a further example. Despite advice from the UN and the NGO community about the risks, many developing countries have vied to sign agreements in the hope that these will enable them to retain previously granted preferential access in these major markets and also to gain some WTO-plus concessions from partners as a bonus. The expectation also seems to have been that these agreements will enable them to attract increased foreign direct investment (FDI) from partner countries, as well as third countries seeking special access to the EU or US markets. It is too early to present a cost-benefit analysis of some of these agreements and their derogations from the special and differential provisions of the WTO in terms of their development impact, but early indications are that their impact will be mixed.

(positive agenda), defensive (policy space and flexibility agenda) and responsive (enabling agenda) interests. For the first time, developing countries were able to spell out their own development agenda and, despite differential capacities and interests, unite as issue-based coalitions like the G20, G33, G90 and G110,[20] thereby dramatically changing negotiating dynamics.

That the Doha Round is still stalling after nearly nine years is a reflection of this dynamic struggle. Developing countries want their developed country partners to deliver on the development promise of the Doha Round and rebalance the trading system. The developed countries' dilemma is that they do not seem to be in a position or mood to do so. On the contrary, they want to reinterpret the DDA's *raison d'ệtre* and they are seeking ever more market access concessions from developing countries themselves. But unlike in the pre-WTO era, developed countries are not able to go ahead and conclude multilateral trade agreements with an à la carte approach on selective issues without the major developing countries and their groupings being involved; they are targeting these very markets. Apart from this change in the balance of trading power, the 'single undertaking' aspect of the WTO architecture and its consensus nature of decision-making dictates carrying all developing countries along on the negotiating areas, or risking paralysis. Moreover, the recent global financial and economic downturn led many developed countries to institute crisis mitigation measures, including domestic support measures for affected industries such as automotive and financial sectors that are contrary to the liberalization agenda. Attention has also been diverted from the DDA to critical national economic agendas.

2.2 MDGs and the trading system reform agenda

Despite the considerable efforts of the UN and developing countries, many of which have now become forces to reckon with in international

[20] The G20 is a group of over twenty developing countries from Latin America, Asia and Africa that are important exporters of agricultural products and seek more competitive trade in agriculture in the Doha negotiations through the removal of export subsidies and trade-distorting agricultural subsidies by developed countries, as well as improved agricultural market access conditions. The G33 is the group of developing countries at the WTO, led by Indonesia, which is championing the concept of special products and special safeguard mechanisms for developing countries in the Doha agriculture negotiations. The G90 is a coalition of developing country members of the African, Caribbean and Pacific Group (ACP), the African Union and the LDCs, as well as other developing countries. The G110 was formed by 110 developing countries with the common goal of ensuring that the development content of the Doha Development Round is realized.

trade and trade negotiations, the system of global trade governance has not yet been sufficiently reformed to provide an ideal trading environment for developing countries. The 2005 MDG Project Report on Trade for Development, prepared by the Millennium Task Force (UN 2005) – of which this author was a member – concluded, inter alia, that the trading system is stacked against developing countries and that in order for them to use trade as a means to achieve poverty reduction and other MDGs, the trading system needs to be rebalanced in their favour. Coherence between trade and development policies nationally and internationally is key. This report also emphasized that in respect of LDCs and countries in special need, such as the SIDS and LLDCs identified in MDG 8, progress towards greater solidarity, policy coherence and development-conducive global governance and policy is as critical, if not more so, than market access and rules agendas being pursued in RTAs, BTAs and the DDA negotiations.

3 Trade and development governance reform: the way forward

3.1 A positive developing country agenda

From the MDGs, especially Goal 8 on a Global Partnership for Development, the Millennium Report and other UN studies linking trade to MDGs (including this author's study on a New Trade Marshall Plan for LDCs (Puri 2005)), the messages are clear: for the trading system to contribute to the realization of MDGs, a combination of policies and measures aimed at enhancing market access and fairness quotient are necessary prerequisites, as are strengthened capacity to trade and cost-quality competitiveness. Vital pro-development reforms also include giving enhanced and preferential market access to developing country goods and services (duty-free, quota-free market access for LDCs, for example) and levelling the playing field by disciplining developed country subsidies (e.g. in agriculture and industry under various programmes). There is also a need to discipline and improve the transparency of developed country standards (whether Sanitary and Phytosanitary (SPS), Technical Barriers to Trade (TBT), environmental and other standards) that constitute Non-tariff Barriers to Trade (NTBs). In this regard, developing countries need to be involved in global standards setting and help to establish national and regional standards-related infrastructure and capacity.

3.2 *The development flexibility agenda*

Many studies and even intergovernmental policy outcomes have come to emphasize that developing countries need to revisit their trade and development strategies. They argue that developing countries should take on a proactive role in fostering productive and export supply capacities and related entrepreneurship much as developed countries, and some developing countries in East and South East Asia, China, India and Brazil, have done successfully. This is not just in reaction to the partial failure of the free market and to the Washington Consensus view that the state should get out of production and trade, which many poor countries followed in exchange for loans from the Bretton Woods Institutions in the 1970s, 1980s, 1990s and even in the first decade of the twenty-first century. But there is widespread realization that one size does not suit all. Each country must be able to achieve efficiency and make welfare gains, attain rapid economic growth, and spur agricultural and industrial revolutions through policy mixes at least in part dictated by each country's unique circumstances, baseline scenarios and resource endowments. Ideally, each country must be able to set its own terms of engagement with the global trading system and a globalizing economy. At the same time, such policy space should not be a licence to diverge totally from the rules of global trade nor from following the norms of good governance at the national level. Institutional and regulatory soundness and rule of law are indispensable for the developmental State and for developmental governance to work.

Developing countries need, and should therefore be allowed, to pursue their 'development flexibility agenda' to retain and use policy space in the public interest vis-à-vis the trade governance regimes in place or under negotiation in the WTO, and in RTAs and BTAs. For example, such flexibilities could be used towards ensuring universal access to medicines and other essential goods and services for the poor vis-à-vis the WTO TRIPs, TRIMs and GATS-related commitments. Such flexibilities could also be used to support efforts to reduce hunger, ensure food security and promote an agricultural renaissance in developing countries vis-à-vis the WTO Agreement on Agriculture and the WTO Agreement on Subsidies and Countervailing Measures-related commitments. There needs to be a prioritization of generating employment, reducing poverty, creating sustainable and green industrialization, and inducing technological and capacity-building of human resources. This should happen vis-à-vis some of the WTO commitments to liberalize access to their own markets, protect intellectual property rights, and reduce and eliminate performance requirements for FDI and limitations on Mode 3 of services supply, for example. It must be recognized that the LDCs, except the ones who were made to pay a heavy entry fee for WTO accession, enjoy greater flexibility in terms of such commitments.

3.3 *A responsive and enabling development agenda*

What I have called a 'responsive' or 'enabling' development agenda in world trade governance is critical to permit developing countries to effectively use trade as an engine of sustainable development, income, decent work, employment generation, gender equity and the reduction of hunger and poverty. Going beyond trade liberalization and rules, it is at the same time the surest way to help achieve the MDGs through trade. MDG 8 most directly refers to the connection between the trading system and the achievement of MDGs and rightly emphasizes the importance of a Global Partnership for Development. Such a partnership envisages not only an MDG-conducive multilateral trading and financial system that gives preferential market access to developing countries, but also one that honours commitments to enhance Official Development Assistance (ODA) and deal comprehensively with developing country debt. Other targets under this goal include addressing the special needs of the LDCs, LLDCs and SIDS.

Most developing countries, especially the poorest and most vulnerable among them, need technical cooperation and financial support in order to structurally and institutionally adjust to new trading regimes and more competitive markets at home and abroad. Moreover, a strong dose of highly concessional, complementary, targeted, predictable and additional Aid for Trade to create and strengthen trade-related infrastructure and institutional capacity is essential. Considerably scaled-up and concessional aid for development directed towards building a critical mass of productive capacity in agriculture, manufacturing and services, as well as physical and social infrastructure, especially for the poorest and most vulnerable countries, is equally an imperative. The MDGs and the basic needs and universal access to essential services agendas and goals, particularly of least developed, small and vulnerable developing countries, would thus be best served if preferential and effectively enhanced market access for their goods and services is combined with a supportive ODA package targeted at trade development.

Perhaps the greatest challenge for developing countries is the financing of trade and development needs, such as meeting the cost of adjustment to implementation, benefitting from liberalization agreements, building and strengthening trade-related infrastructure, and cost-quality competitive supply capacity. Domestic resource mobilization, ODA, foreign direct investment, trade finance and special drawing rights (SDRs) are just some of the international development finance-related support measures that need to be significantly enhanced, and linked to trade capacity and export revenue generation. There is also a need for a reflection on how to make the Aid for Trade initiative, as well as the special and differential treatment provisions in WTO Agreements, binding. Special purpose trade and development funds for developing countries, especially for the weakest among them, could be developed on a priority basis. Proposals in this respect include proposals for a Commodity Stabilisation Fund; a Diversification and Productive Capacity Fund; a Climate Change Adaptation Fund; a Technology Bank; and a Skills Development Initiative.[21]

Home country measures by developed country partners to provide incentives and risk assurance to their enterprises to invest in LDCs' productive capacity, for example, can be another complementary plank. Stimulating FDI in productive sectors, including infrastructure rather than just enclave mineral and fuel sectors in LDCs, would bring these countries into global production and distribution networks and generate sustained employment and incomes. Infrastructure will improve the transfer of technology and know-how will be affected. FDI that enhances the local content, value addition and value retention in the host country for processing natural resources, particularly in LDCs, will bring further development and MDG dividends.

The UN has been emphasizing that developing countries' indebtedness needs to be dealt with in positive coherence with trade, aid and

[21] The special purpose funds have been proposed mainly by developing countries under a variety of forms during trade and development negotiations, arguing either that implementation of new commitments from new agreements requires funding or that taking advantage of the new agreement requires funding to build productive and other capacities. For example, the commodity fund has been suggested under WTO negotiations on commodities by African countries; production funds have been advocated by developing countries in the context of the WTO Aid for Trade initiative, negotiations of North–South trade agreements like EPAs and by LDCs in the framework of making the duty-free, quota-free treatment meaningful; and funds for skill and technology development have been advanced under MDG 8 commitments and WTO deliberations on transfer of technology commitments. The climate change adaption fund was proposed ten years ago under the Kyoto Protocol and first became operational in September 2010.

development policies and norms at the national and international levels. For the most indebted and poorest countries in particular it has urged and prompted the international community to come forward with comprehensive debt relief and debt forgiveness packages. The objective is to enable these countries to achieve long-term debt sustainability. The idea is that increased revenues and precious resources from trade and ODA should not be diverted to debt repayment but rather deployed for development expenditure-productive capacity creation, infrastructure building and the promotion of universal access to essential services. It is also necessary to prevent several developing countries from experiencing net reverse flows of resources and falling into a debt distress situation due to reduced export revenues arising from global economic crises, terms of trade shocks and costly access to external public and private borrowing (UNCTAD 2008). Although to some extent the Heavily Indebted Poor Countries (HIPC) and Multilateral Debt Relief Initiatives have succeeded in this objective, debt relief efforts would need to be continuously pursued by the international community to redress debt-sustainability of indebted developing countries, costly access to external public borrowing and the impact of the global economic and attendant crises mitigation measures.[22] In respect of the most vulnerable countries, debt moratorium has been advocated.

3.4 *Corporate responsibility in trade governance*

The trade governance system has traditionally been a vehicle for freeing up corporate space for cross-border trade and investment; the transnational corporations have particularly benefitted from this. It has also commensurately involved governments getting out of business. Through the Global Compact,[23] the Code of Conduct for Trans-National Corporations (TNCs),[24] and more recently the elaboration of the ideas

[22] See, for example, 'Heavily Indebted Poor Countries (HIPC) Initiative and Multilateral Debt Relief Initiative (MDRI) – Status of Implementation'. IMF/World Bank Report, 15 September 2009.

[23] The UN Global Compact is a strategic policy initiative for businesses that are committed to aligning their operations and strategies with ten universally accepted principles in the areas of human rights, labour, environment and anti-corruption (www.unglobalcompact.org) [accessed in November 2010].

[24] Following UN Economic and Social Council resolution 1982/68 of 27 October 1982, further reiterated by UN General Assembly resolution (A/RES/45/186) of 21 December 1990, the UN facilitated consultation in the 1980s and 1990s on the creation of an international

and norms of Corporate Responsibility for Development and Corporate Social Responsibility, the UN has tried to stimulate a pro-development corporate behaviour that would maintain a proper place in the trade governance system. The logic is that just as governments assume rights and obligations in the WTO and under RTAs, the bigger and most resourced corporations that profit most and gain progressively more rights must also assume certain obligations, including on good corporate governance, development and MDG sensitivity of their operations in developing countries in general and LDCs in particular. There is also the issue of bringing certain practices that affect developing countries' market entry and capacity to trade into the fold of world trade governance, such as private or voluntary technical standards that corporations implement.

Similarly, over the years, the UN has drawn attention and tried to legislate on curbing the anti-competitive practices of global enterprises and on mitigating their impact on the ability of developing country enterprises to compete fairly in their own markets, as well as internationally. The UN Set of Multilaterally Agreed Rules and Principles for the Control of Restrictive Business Practices, under the auspices of UNCTAD, is the only soft-law international agreement aimed at disciplining the anti-competitive practices of global enterprises, such as abuse of dominance, collusive tendering and cartels. It has specific provisions for special and differential treatment vis-à-vis developing countries, as well as multilateral consultations to resolve problems faced by developing countries.

Problematically, efforts to actively apply this soft-law and transpose these disciplines in the WTO in a development-friendly way have not been successful. In fact, they have backfired. Developing countries have rejected the introduction of competition policy issues into the WTO; they saw this as an attempt to expand developed country market access and to constrain the policy space of developing countries to support and grow their enterprises. Competition provisions are, however, appearing in different forms in North–South RTAs, such as EPAs, and South–South agreements. In addition, UNCTAD is supporting capacity-building in developing countries – institutional and regulatory – to deter, detect and take action against enterprises that engage in anti-competitive practices. The institution is also working to protect domestic enterprises from adverse impacts, especially small and medium-sized businesses. International cooperation focused on controlling anti-competitive practices, coupled with a sound

code of conduct for transnational corporations. The code was drafted, with mandatory and voluntary requirements, but was never adopted.

competition policy framework, is also conducive to poverty reduction, consumer protection and universal access to essential goods and services. These elements must be appropriately mainstreamed into world trade governance.

3.5 Global trade governance and development: the emerging game changers

The WTO is truly at a crossroads. It has ceded more than half its space to RTAs. Moreover, its perpetual negotiating role, the comprehensiveness of its mandate and its development credibility are all in question due to the DDA deadlock. Indeed, it will be an uphill task to recapture momentum at the multilateral level. In order for the WTO and multilateral governance systems to regain the initiative, Member States need to invest political capital and to align themselves more closely and symbiotically with the longstanding and evolving development agenda. It is this cooperation and collaboration between the UN, WTO and other organizations – whose positive interplay at the axis of trade, development and globalization is vital – that can best enable all institutions to deal with what I deem the 'game changers' of this century. Throughout such cooperative endeavours, the positive market access and fairness agenda, the policy space and development flexibility agenda, and the responsive and development support agendas of developing countries, as elaborated earlier in this chapter, need to be fully reflected.

The first set of these game changers are demographic shifts in labour markets, mobility and migration within and among countries. Aging and declining populations in developed countries where skills and labour shortages are rapidly growing are coming up against young populations and increasingly skilled and cost-quality competitive labour forces in developing countries, creating tectonic and complementary shifts in demand and supply patterns and push and pull factors for increased skills, trade and cross-border labour mobility. The anomalous situation whereby Mode 4 of GATS – the temporary movement of natural workers – is the only window for utilizing this factor with exponential trade and development potential means that in any twenty-first century world trade governance structure, a bigger role needs to be given to the liberalization of labour mobility, in which almost all developing countries have a distinct comparative advantage. Mode 1 or outsourcing for IT-enabled services also has shown a tremendous development impact and must not be restricted. The challenge is that there will be shortsighted resistance to this, ignoring the welfare gains and win-win outcomes for all, especially in view of the economic crisis-related jobs-protectionism that we are witnessing today. There could also be demands in developed countries for offsetting the low-cost labour advantage of developing countries by inserting a labour standards-related conditionality into the trade governance system.

The second game changer is the imperative of environmental protection, ecological sustainability and combating and adapting to climate change and its implications for triple-win outcomes at the interface between environmental, trade and developmental governance: win for environment, win for trade and win for development. The WTO's Doha Round is seeking to deal with some of these governance issues, including by removing tariff and non-tariff measures on environmental goods and services. Doha is also examining the relationship between the special trade provisions in Multilateral Environment Agreements (MEAs) and WTO Agreements, including issues of environmental standards and eco-labelling. However, much still needs to be done to make further progress on capturing coherence between the three policy areas. The addition of climate change mitigation and adaptation-related challenges to the agenda is still a matter of contention as developing countries weigh the relative merits of allowing climate protectionism to be unilaterally determined by trading partners or multilaterally disciplined in the WTO or in other fora such as the United Nations Framework Convention on Climate Change (UNFCCC). There is also the task of linking any climate governance deal-setting emission control targets under UN auspices to trade regimes and translating them into some rule-based, predictable and equitable multilateral systems of standards, verification and trade measures in a way that does not further disadvantage developing countries. Significant financial and technology transfer packages for development sustaining climate change mitigation and adaptation by developing countries is another major requirement.

The third game changer is the urgent need to improve management of natural resources such as land, water, energy resources, minerals, metals and marine and coastal resources, to meet the burgeoning needs of development, such as by providing food and energy security, shelter and basic infrastructure, and expanding access to, and benefits from, these resources to developing country producers and consumers. As both major producers and consumers of natural resources, developing countries face internal pressures to derive higher value from their natural resources and for their products to be more inclusively distributed among their populations. On the other hand, developing countries depend on foreign trade and investment to meet their capital, technology and entrepreneurial needs and to optimally exploit these resources for development. Catering to these development needs will need to be balanced with environmental possibilities, especially considering the many factors threatening the depletion of natural resources. Prevention of such depletion is essential to the management of natural resources for future generations. The recent food and energy crises have shown that there may be a need for governance compacts in the areas of food and agriculture, as well as energy, that have both trade and non-trade elements. Improved global governance norms also need to be in place for mineral resources and water.

The fourth game-changing issue is the need for more effective governance of research and development (R&D) resources and the upgrading and innovation of technology in a way that ensures creativity is adequately rewarded. At the same time, as called for in MDG 8, developing countries, and especially the poor within them, must be assured access to the benefits of critical technologies, processes and know-how on a concessional and affordable basis in order to leapfrog into building more environmentally sustainable, less carbon and materials intensive, pro-poor productive capacity, essential infrastructure, and services, while keeping in mind the legitimate profit-oriented interests of private enterprises that hold much of this technology. Further FDI, which is a major vehicle of transfer of technology, may not flow in sufficient quantity and quality to vulnerable countries with little bargaining power. There is a need for innovative thinking on ways for governments to support the transfer of technologies, especially to LDCs and other vulnerable countries, and to help build their endogenous technological and R&D capacities. The Development Agenda currently being implemented at the World Intellectual Property Organization (WIPO) as a counter to the upward harmonization of the strength of international IPR regimes is also relevant in this regard, as is putting into operation TRIPs provisions on technology transfer, compulsory licensing and control of anti-competitive practices.

The fifth game changer is the emergence of what has been called the new geography of international trade, whereby some large and dynamic developing country economies are growing rapidly and moving beyond the comparative advantage of natural resources and low-cost labour to wield technological and financial market power. Their rise, led by China and followed by India, Brazil and South Africa, has meant the emergence of new regional and global demands and production dynamics both in respect of North–South and South–South trade and investments. These emerging economies are spawning their own global enterprises with operations around the world, their share of global trade has grown significantly, and there has been a spectacular rise in South–South trade and investment (as well as South–South aid). This expansion has also been driven by South–South trade liberalization – at the regional and inter-regional level. Emerging developing countries have also made progress in granting duty-free, quota-free treatment to LDCs, for example in the third round of GSTP negotiations.[25] How these countries and their relationships with other developing countries are accommodated in global trade governance will be crucial to the development prospects of developing countries.

The sixth game-changing element is the need to make sense of and address the great maze of regulatory requirements and standards and other non-tariff barriers that affect more than 90 per cent of all developing country exports. These NTBs remain elusive in terms of definition, classification and quantification that could provide the basic data and information on the basis of which to enter into negotiations to address them and thus have so far eluded efforts to devise horizontal disciplines cutting across conventional trade agreements. Developed country governments unilaterally determine most SPS, TBT, health, environmental and safety standards. The proliferation of private sector standards in goods and services further adds to the complexity. Their variation between markets and changing goals set from year to year makes it ever more difficult for developing country exporters, including the SMEs, to overcome market entry barriers. In the Doha Round, WTO Members must find ways to discipline standards and regulations and other NTBs that affect developing country market access and entry, working with UNCTAD and others to come up with suitable and credible modalities. Moreover, developing country capacities to set and conform to global standards must be strengthened.

The epochal confluence of financial, economic, public debt, jobs-related crises and the Great Depression in the metropole economies of the world have given rise to fundamental issues about the laissez-faire capitalist system on which world trade governance has been based for the last sixty years. It has also raised questions about the relative roles of the State and markets in delivering social justice, welfare and public goods. Scepticism about free trade, cross-border investment and globalization as well as

[25] China provides tariff preferences to thirty African LDCs; India launched a duty-free quota-free scheme for all LDCs in 2008, and Brazil in 2009. The third round of GSTP negotiations is taking place among participating countries in Geneva with the support of UNCTAD, and was completed at the end of 2010.

protectionist sentiments are spreading among both producers and consumers in the developed world, and political elites are pandering to their concerns. Even some of the global corporate champions of freer trade are on the defensive. How this crisis of confidence is overcome will depend on how quickly and effectively global financial market and exchange rate systems are overhauled to better allocate capital, manage risk and rein in speculation, including in commodity markets. As UNCTAD, which has played Cassandra in warning about systemic risks, has long advocated, the international community will have to go beyond national prudential regulation and supervision of major financial players to establish global financial and monetary governance systems that complement the global trading system. Elements of such governance could include effective capital account management, changing the currency reserve system, and strengthening the role of SDRs for development financing and global liquidity (UNCTAD 2009).

4 Conclusion

Global trade governance faces great challenges and yet has several opportunities to reinvent itself as a 'global development good'. For these challenges to be met and opportunities seized, Member States at the UN, the WTO, the International Monetary Fund (IMF) and the World Bank, as well as participants in emerging global economic fora such as the G20, need to take a holistic view that integrates the development perspective into trade, financial, monetary, environmental and technology governance systems. They need to balance the needs of liberalization with those of transparency, good regulation and oversight, while increasing the voice and participation of developing countries in decision-making. Greater coherence, less fragmentation and the elimination of asymmetries, including in the trading system, are critical. The principle of global solidarity and equity considerations must more overtly animate all institutions of global governance. In this respect, the UN must be given greater recognition as the repository of development-focused knowledge and experience, and more effective cooperation and collaboration must be forged between the UN, the WTO and other institutions to enable their Member States to deal more effectively, coherently, and in a development-enhancing way with the series of 'game changers' we face this century, namely the need to address demographic shifts within and among countries in labour markets, mobility and migration; environmental protection, ecological sustainability and combating and adapting to climate change; the management of natural resources such as land, water, energy resources, minerals and metals; the governance of R&D resources, technological upgradation and innovation; the emergence of the new geography of international trade; and the great maze of regulatory requirements and standards, as well as other NTBs impacting trade. Only by addressing the interplay of these factors at the axis of trade, development and globalization will the governance of global trade be able to contribute effectively to improving the livelihoods of people everywhere and promoting a better and safer world for all.

References

Economic Commission for Latin America and the Caribbean (ECLAC). 1950. *The Economic Development of Latin America and its Principal Problems* (E/CN. 12/89/rev. 1). Lake Success, New York: United Nations Department of Economic Affairs.

General Agreement on Tariffs and Trade (GATT). 1979. GATT CONTRACTING PARTIES. Differential and More Favourable Treatment, Reciprocity and Fuller Participation of Developing Countries. Decision of 28 November 1979. L/4903.

Jolly, R., Emmerij, L. and Weiss, T. G. 2009. *UN Ideas that Changed the World*. Bloomington: Indiana University Press.

Kaul, I., Grunberg, I. and Stern, M. A. (eds.) 1999. *Global Public Goods: International Cooperation in the 21st Century*. Oxford University Press.

League of Nations (Folke Hilgerdt). 1942. *The Network of World Trade: A Companion Volume to Europe's Trade*. Geneva: League of Nations.

Puri, L. 2005. *Towards a New Trade 'Marshall Plan' for Least Developed Countries; How to Deliver on the Doha Development Promise and Help Realize the UN Millennium Development Goals?* UNCTAD/DITC/TAB/POV/2005/. New York and Geneva: United Nations.

Singer, H. 1950. 'The Distribution of Gains between Investing and Borrowing Countries', *American Economic Review: Papers and Proceedings* 40(May): 473–85.

South Centre. 2006. *Reinventing UNCTAD*, Submitted to the Panel of Eminent Persons on Enhancing UNCTAD's Impact by Boutros Boutros-Ghali former Secretary-General of the United Nations, Chairman of the South Centre Board, Research Papers 7. July.

UNCTAD. 2004. *Beyond Conventional Wisdom in Development Policy – An Intellectual History of UNCTAD (1964–2004)*. (UNCTAD/EDM/2004/4). New York and Geneva: United Nations.

2005. *Multilateralism and Regionalism: The New Interface*. UNCTAD/DITC/TNCD/2004/7. New York and Geneva: United Nations.

2007. *Trade And Development Report 2007: Regional Cooperation for Development*. UNCTAD/TDR/2007. New York and Geneva: United Nations.

2008. *Trade And Development Report 2008: Commodity Prices, Capital Flows and the Financing of Investment*. UNCTAD/TDR/2008. New York and Geneva: United Nations.

2009. *Trade and Development Report 2009*. Geneva: UNCTAD.

United Nations Economic Commission for Latin America (ECLAC). 1950. *The Economic Development of Latin America and its Principal Problems* (E/CN. 12/89/rev. 1). Lake Success, New York: United Nations Department of Economic Affairs.

United Nations (UN). 1995a. United Nations World Summit for Social Development. *Report of the World Summit of Social Development (Copenhagen, 6–12 March)*. A/CONF.166/9.

1995b. United Nations Fourth World Conference on Women. *Beijing Declaration and Platform for Action*. Beijing, China. 4–15 September.

2000. United Nations General Assembly, United Nations Millennium Declaration (A/RES/55/2), adopted on 8 September.

2005. UN Millennium Project. *Trade for Development*. Task Force on Trade. London: Earthscan.

World Trade Organization (WTO). 1994a *'Part IV Trade and Development' in General Agreement on Tariffs and Trade* (Annex 1A of the WTO Agreement). (1867 U.N.T.S.187, 33 I.L.M. 1153) adopted on 15 April 1994 and entered into force on 1 January 1995. Geneva: WTO.

1994b. *General Agreement on Trade in Services* (Annex 1B of the WTO Agreement). (1869 U.N.T.S. 183, 33 I.L.M. 1167) adopted on 15 April 1994 and entered into force on 1 January 1995. Geneva: WTO.

1994c. *'Annex on Movement of Natural Persons Supplying Services under the Agreement' in General Agreement on Trade in Services* (Annex 1B of the WTO Agreement). (1869 U.N.T.S. 183, 33 I.L.M. 1167) adopted on 15 April 1994 and entered into force on 1 January 1995. Geneva: WTO.

1994d. *Agreement in Trade-Related Aspects of Intellectual Property Rights* (Annex 1C of the WTO Agreement). (1869 U.N.T.S. 299, 33 I.L.M. 1197) adopted on 15 April 1994 and entered into force on 1 January 1995. Geneva: WTO.

2001a. *Declaration on the TRIPS Agreement and Public Health*. Geneva: WTO.

2001b. *Doha Ministerial Declaration*. WT/MIN(01)/DEC/1. 20 November. Geneva: WTO.

3

The interactions of trade, macroeconomic policies and sustainability: implications for global trade governance

ALEJANDRO NADAL

The relation between trade liberalization and the environment has been the object of many studies, both in the academic and the policy-making communities. Myriad research projects have been carried out at the sector level or at the economy-wide level, using applied general equilibrium models. A great variety of environmental dimensions have been covered by these studies (Khan 2002; UNEP-IISD 2005; Gallagher 2008). However, one crucial theme has escaped most of these analyses. It is the fact that trade liberalization is but one component of a bigger policy package in which monetary and fiscal policies, financial deregulation and income policies play a much more important role in determining and shaping the economic forces that affect the environment. Trade and environment studies are too often carried out as if the other macroeconomic policies did not matter. Even themes such as subsidies and exchange rate manipulation are seen through the lens of trade policy, not as key components of fiscal and monetary policies. This is unfortunate because it is difficult to interpret the impact of trade and trade liberalization on the environment (and on people's livelihoods) without an analysis of the entire set of macroeconomic policies that condition trade dynamics.

This chapter makes the argument that taking sustainability objectives seriously demands that we examine global trade, and its governance, not in isolation but in light of their interaction with the other components of macroeconomic policies and governance systems.

Alejandro Nadal is a professor at El Colegio de México. The author is grateful to Alan Cibils, Sergio Schlesinger, Pablo Samaniego, Carlos Murillo and Marcos Chávez for their participation in the project on Macroeconomic Policies and the Environment in Latin America. The project was designed by the author and carried out with the support of the International Union for the Conservation of Nature (IUCN). The author thanks Carolyn Deere Birkbeck and two anonymous reviewers for their feedback.

The first section of this chapter briefly reviews how trade liberalization is related to macroeconomic policies in general. The second section describes the results of a project on macroeconomic policies and the environment in Latin America. The final section examines some of the key implications of the analysis for global trade governance and proposes reforms.

1 Trade liberalization and macroeconomic policies

There are good reasons why the study of how trade liberalization impacts the environment needs to take into account the larger picture of macroeconomic policies. While agreements to liberalize trade play an important role, trends in trade liberalization are also driven by other, often more significant components of macroeconomic policy. Even the UN Conference on Trade and Development (UNCTAD) and the World Trade Organization (WTO) have recognized the fact that trade policies need to be coherent with other components of macroeconomic policy-making (WTO 2004; UNCTAD 2009). The remainder of this section introduces some of the key linkages between trade policies and broader macroeconomic policies, examining finance, monetary and fiscal policies in turn. Failure to take these linkages into account can lead to erroneous conclusions on the dynamics and course of trade policies and their impact on the environment.

Perhaps the most important example of the close relationship between trade and macroeconomics is that exports provide a mechanism to meet the challenges of deficiencies in effective aggregate demand and employment. Gaining competitive advantages to penetrate foreign markets can be attained through currency manipulation, the containment of real wages in exporting sectors or through a combination of these mechanisms. Subsidies and unfair trade practices, like dumping, can also be used to attain this goal. China has kept its currency undervalued in order to gain additional competitiveness in international markets. Germany has used income policies to repress the growth of real wages, which is reflected in low unit labour costs of its exports. Part of the current crisis in Europe is related to the fact that Germany has gained a strong competitive base by maintaining the growth rate of wages well below that of its trading partners in the European Union. The debates on the flexibility of labour markets are closely related to the issue of competitiveness.

Trade liberalization and cheap imported goods have also been used as an instrument to control inflationary pressures. This is frequently accompanied by overvalued exchange rates, high interest rates and tight credit policies that accompany trade and financial liberalization. All of this creates an uneven playing field for domestic investors. The ensuing lack of competitiveness and weak export performance are more related to macroeconomic policies than to inherent weaknesses of the domestic producers.

Financial deregulation has been a driver of trade liberalization because finance drives trade. International capital flows have become one of the most important features of the world economy. Under the Bretton Woods regime of fixed exchange rates, currency trading closely followed the needs of international trade. When floating exchange rates became the norm, exchange risk was privatized (Eatwell and Taylor 2000) and currency trading became an independent activity with little connection to the requirements of international trade. The need to hedge against the costs of fluctuating exchange rates brought about new incentives to deregulate international capital flows. Since then, capital flows have expanded enormously and have reached astronomical proportions. Capital flows help finance current account deficits, leading governments to deregulate the capital account. In the case of a persistent trade deficit, capital flows contribute to the appreciation of the exchange rate precisely when an adjustment should be taking place. Moreover, trade driven by these current account deficits can dismantle entire branches of economic activity through negative multiplier effects (Bhaduri 1998). Capital flows may intensify the negative effects of trade flows (Nadal 2004).

In the past twenty years, the need for balanced budgets has been the main priority of fiscal policies in developed and developing economies. In this context, generating a surplus on the primary balance (the difference between income and expenditures net of financial charges) has been critical. Because governments have been reluctant to increase taxes, the only way in which a primary surplus can be generated is through reductions in expenditures. In many developing countries, the curtailment of expenditures has affected social expenditures (health and education) as well as investments in environmental stewardship (natural protected areas or the payment of environmental services).

To summarize, trade liberalization and its impacts on the environment cannot be understood unless analysed in the context of the macroeconomic policy package to which it belongs. The analysis of the environmental implications of macroeconomic policies and trade has to take into account their compound effects and not only their isolated impacts.

2 Perspectives from Latin America

During the period following the Second World War, most Latin American economies followed an import substitution strategy. This scheme met with some success until the 1970s, when internal and external tensions slowed down growth rates. The debt crisis of the 1980s spelled the demise of the import substitution strategy and weakened the industrialization process. Eventually, import substitution gave way to the establishment of an open economy model along the lines of the Washington Consensus. The economic performance of the Latin American economies under this new strategic approach presents a mixed picture, but in general, average growth rates were lower than in the post-war years. The old contradictions and tensions did not disappear and in the 1990s several financial crises struck the region, bringing about important changes in the policy outlook of countries like Argentina, Bolivia, Brazil and Ecuador.

This section summarizes a study carried out in Latin American countries in 2008. The four case studies considered here focus on the interactions between trade liberalization and macroeconomic policies, and their impact on the environment.

2.1 Argentina

In the 1970s Argentina embarked on a process of economic transformation resulting in widespread de-industrialization and a re-primarization of the economy; accumulation of a large and periodically unsustainable public debt; and extensive privatizations and deregulation. During this period, the military dictatorship sought to radically alter the policy framework that had dominated in Argentina since the 1940s and to do away with the welfare state and the policies that were a part of the import substitution industrialization (ISI) strategy. Subsequently, under military dictatorship (1976–83), Argentina's public debt quintupled.

The new policy framework was based on trade and financial liberalization, and extensive privatization and deregulation, issuing in an era of 'speculation-led development' and massive public debt accumulation. The return to democratic rule in 1983 did not change the policy framework and in 1989 President Carlos Menem adopted an extreme neoliberal economic programme with a currency board system pegging the Argentine peso to the US dollar on a one-to-one exchange rate, and a requirement that all pesos in circulation be backed by dollars in the Central Bank's reserves. By the time Menem left power, Argentina's debt had more than doubled (from US$58 billion to US$143 billion).

Large capital inflows fuelled a boom in consumer credit, but the 1994 Mexican crisis led to capital flight, driving the Argentine economy into a deep recession in 1995. Poverty and inequality increased steadily, reaching unprecedented levels at the end of the century. Fiscal spending remained fairly constant as a percentage of Gross Domestic Product (GDP), but debt service payments spiralled out of control due to the fiscal revenue gap left by the 1994 privatization of social security (which was covered by debt) and interest rate hikes.

In 1999, as the recession deepened, Argentina's fiscal policy acted procyclically. The country was caught in a downward spiral of falling growth, larger deficits and more austerity. In 2001 capital flight intensified and the government was no longer able to borrow to cover its fiscal gap. In 2002 Argentina defaulted on roughly US$80 billion of debt, making it the largest sovereign default in history. The fixed exchange rate regime was abandoned with a very substantial devaluation and GDP contracted by 20 per cent.

Spurred by the devaluation the economy began to grow in 2002, leading to several years of expansion. As a result, the International Monetary Fund (IMF) and defaulted creditors increased pressure on Argentina for a solution to its US$100 billion default debt. A debt swap was opened and concluded in February 2005, with a 76 per cent acceptance rate. The debt-to-GDP ratio dropped from 113 per cent at the time of default in December 2001 to 87 per cent after the restructuring. Despite this reduction, Argentina was left with a heavy debt service burden.

Following the 2001–2 crisis and peso devaluation, soya bean production and exports became the key component of Argentina's macroeconomic balance. Soya bean exports have grown considerably and now account for approximately 25 per cent of total exports. Export taxes now represent 15–20 per cent of total fiscal revenue and between 1.6 and 3 per cent of GDP – roughly equivalent to half of Argentina's public debt service burden. Soya bean cultivation has significant impacts on the environment in terms of soil degradation, loss of biodiversity and deforestation (Pengue 2005; Giarracca and Teubal 2006). Social and economic vulnerability of small-scale producers has increased, diminishing their capacity for environmental stewardship.

The last thirty years has brought about a radical restructuring process of Argentina's economy and society. Abrupt trade liberalization and restrictive credit policies bankrupted much of the domestic industry and production, turning Argentina into a primary product and service economy. As a result, 're-primarization' has intensified during the last two decades. This change in the output mix has critical environmental impacts because it implies greater pressure on the natural resource base. The 're-primarization' process has turned out to be crucial for macroeconomic balances.

2.2 *Brazil*

Brazil started on a path to industrialization through import substitution in the 1930s, but the main priorities after the 1980s responded to debt service, external imbalances and inflationary pressures. After 1983, Brazil accepted the supervision of the IMF and introduced drastic cuts in public spending, a tight monetary policy and high interest rates, as well as financial and trade liberalization. Repressing aggregate demand was enforced through high interest rates, the contraction of public expenditures and the containment of real wages. In spite of these policies, stabilization remained an elusive goal.

In 1994 the *Plano Real* introduced a new currency, the *real*, pegged to the US dollar to stabilize inflationary expectations. The new plan included a mandatory balanced budget and succeeded in bringing stability and putting a lid on inflationary pressures. However, the reduction of inflation was not instantaneous and the new currency became overvaluated, further deteriorating the trade balance. The currency gap had to be covered through capital flows, but the high interest rates affected investment and caused unemployment rates to increase. Investors and speculators alike started to doubt the country's capacity to sustain the *real* and, as a result, a reversal of capital flows took place in 1999, bringing about a massive devaluation.

To summarize, Brazil's macroeconomic policies have been shaped by its debt burden. Its fiscal policy is dominated by the short-term objective of generating a primary surplus. This process has shifted resources from the real sectors of the economy (and from needs in education, health, housing, transportation, infrastructure, research and development, and the environment) to the financial sector. Between 2000 and 2007, federal investment and expenditures in education and health represented only 43 per cent of the total amount allocated to financing the interest over the public debt.

In 1992 Brazil deregulated capital flows and profit remittances by foreigners and liberalized the financial sector. Because of price stabilization policies, credit was scarce and the banks of large corporations started to fill the gap of commercial credit. In agriculture the withdrawal of State support had already left a huge vacuum, as the operations of development banks were severely curtailed. Loans provided by these corporate banks led to various forms of commercial agriculture in which the key decisions on output and technology were taken away from producers.

In 2000 the Cargill Bank, as well as other banks belonging to multinational corporations (MNCs), initiated business in Brazil in order to achieve deeper market penetration and gain control over primary production. As a result, soya bean production underwent a dramatic expansion; between 1991 and 2005, the surface devoted to soya bean tripled and by 2006 occupied more than 22 million hectares. Total output of soya beans reached 58 million tonnes, approximately 25 per cent of world production.

This process has several important environmental impacts. The first is the loss of agro-biodiversity, due to the expansion of monoculture and the use of chemical inputs. The second type of damage comes from the destruction of the biodiversity-rich *cerrado* – a two million square kilometre savannah in West Central Brazil with 12,000 plant species and 2,000 animal species, many of which are endemic. The region also hosts forty ethnic groups, several of which face the threat of extinction. Today, rates of destruction of the *cerrado* remain at very high levels.

Soya bean expansion also contributes indirectly to the destruction of the Amazon forest, as deforested areas previously used for ranching are converted into soya bean production. Monoculture crops are displacing cattle production in the regions of Legal Amazonia; between 1995 and 2005, cattle increased from 74 million to more than 110 million in the North and Central-West of Brazil, precisely where the Amazon rainforest is located. Ranching is, and will continue to be, the main driver of deforestation in Amazonia, representing 80 per cent of total deforested land. This deforestation is being further intensified by the reallocation of land for soya bean and sugar cane production.

Macroeconomic policies have set the stage for this process; in the context of intense inflationary pressures, high indebtedness, a restrictive monetary policy, financial liberalization and a fiscal policy preoccupied solely with generating a primary surplus, the vacuum left by the withdrawal of support for small-scale agricultural activities has been occupied by large consortia. This has brought about a radical transformation of the rural landscape in Brazil, with deep and longlasting environmental consequences.

2.3 *Ecuador*

Ecuador is a megadiverse country with a varied landscape and a rich tapestry of ecosystems; from tropical rainforests and inter-mountain valleys to the famed marine ecosystems of the Galápagos Islands.[1] However, Ecuador is also experiencing its highest deforestation rates in decades, with a tremendous impact on biodiversity.

The discovery of oil in the 1970s opened the door to an industrialization strategy, but the exchange rate became rapidly overvalued and international loans rose from US$300 million in 1971 to US$8,000 million in 1985. In 1982, with the international debt crisis, Ecuador started implementing a neoliberal policy package.

After 1986 a growth model based on extractive practices was implemented. Production was intensified in the old commercial crops and in new sectors such as shrimp, fisheries, flowers and African palm trees. As industrial activities declined during this period, the re-primarization of the economy became evident; the economic structure of Ecuador in 1995 resembled the one it had in 1970.

During the 1980s and 1990s, a suite of privatizations followed, banking activities were deregulated and, most importantly, Ecuador's capital account was liberalized. The macroeconomic policy objective of price stabilization spurred further trade liberalization in an effort to align domestic prices with lower international prices. While some progress was made with respect to the external accounts and public finance, inflation and interest rates remained at very high levels. Thus, financial charges could only be met in those economic sectors with highly profitable activities, leading to a greater weakening of the real sectors of the economy.

In 2000, after another crisis, Ecuador adopted the US dollar as its national currency and lost control over its monetary policy. The price level and interest rates now depended on the net balance of the current account. Monetary policy could no longer be used in a counter-cyclical manner and interest rates remained at a very high level, with highly negative consequences for productive investments. Declining productivity was

[1] Megadiverse countries harbour the majority of the world's species and are therefore defined as extremely rich in biodiversity. According to the World Conservation Monitoring Centre, an executive branch of the United Nations Environment Programme, there are seventeen megadiverse countries, most of them in the tropics. See www.unep.ch [accessed in November 2010].

compensated by increased pressure on natural resources and the environment. Land use patterns changed and agricultural practices intensified pressure on soils and biodiversity. The dollarization led to a greater re-primarization of the economy and of exports in order to increase the monetary base.

Dollarization was accompanied by legislation setting ceilings on the growth of public expenditures so as to achieve a reduction of the public sector's external debt. The external and fiscal accounts improved, but this was due to oil prices, remittances of migrant workers, the depreciation of the US dollar vis-à-vis other currencies and foreign investment flows. Ecuador may have fallen into the trap of low productivity and static comparative advantages that lead to environmental degradation. Abandoning dollarization entails political and economic costs, but if Ecuador maintains the dollar as its domestic currency, it will need to intensify exports of agricultural products and extractive industries. An innovative project designed to pave a way out of this dilemma is the Yasuní project.[2] This bold project aims to set aside plans to develop significant oil reserves located in a megadiverse region covered by pristine tropical rainforest that is home to several indigenous peoples. In so doing, Ecuador would contribute to cultural and biodiversity conservation, as well as the reduction of Carbon dioxide (CO_2) emissions. In exchange for this effort, the Yasuní initiative proposes to compensate Ecuador with funds disbursed by international donors, governments and the private sector. This would allow Ecuador to reap the economic benefits of both its natural resource endowment and its contribution to environmental sustainability.[3] If implemented correctly, the Yasuní initiative could not only provide momentum to a structural transformation of Ecuador's economy, but also provide a solution to the dilemma imposed by dollarization.

2.4 Mexico

Mexico is a megadiverse country with a rich tapestry of varied ecosystems covering its landscapes, including tropical rainforests, temperate forested areas, cloud forests, semi-arid and arid environments. This wealth of

[2] For more information on the Yasuní-ITT Initiative, see www.yasuni-itt.gob.ec/ [accessed in November 2010].

[3] On 3 August 2010, Ecuador and the United Nations Development Programme (UNDP) signed the Memorandum of Agreement for the Yasuní-ITT Initiative to leave this oil underground in exchange for an international contribution equivalent to at least half of the resources that would be received if Ecuador exploited its oil in this area. See www.yasuni-itt.gob.ec/ [accessed in November 2010].

environmental diversity is at risk and there are alarming signs in almost every environmental dimension.

In 1982 high interest rates and collapsing oil prices led Mexico to default on its international financial obligations. The stabilization plans of the 1980s gave way to structural reforms and the adoption of a neo-liberal policy package. Fiscal policy was redefined in order to generate a permanent primary surplus directed to debt service. This led to cuts in public spending, affecting several environmentally sensitive sectors from small-scale agricultural production to natural protected areas. Monetary policy was radically transformed and price stability became its main objective. Maintaining exchange rate stability in order to control inflation and attract foreign direct investment and capital flows also became a priority. After 1988 Mexico underwent an intense process of privatization and deregulation that culminated with the completion of the North American Free Trade Agreement (NAFTA) in 1994.

To control inflation, Mexico's aggregate demand was repressed through high interest rates, which attracted capital flows and led to an overvalued exchange rate. The trade balance continued to deteriorate and Mexico found itself relying increasingly on capital inflows to sustain its growing trade deficit. The adjustment of the current account to combat the trade deficit was postponed until the financial community had serious doubts about Mexico's ability to maintain exchange rate stability. In December 1994 the crisis exploded, a macro-devaluation took place, the temporary gains of the struggle against inflation were eliminated, and the economy went into a tailspin.

Economic performance has been marked by slow growth, high unemployment and a chronic external deficit. The surplus observed with the United States is not enough to cover the deficit in Mexico's trade with Europe and Asia (especially China). In addition, the balance of payments is sustained by the remittances of migratory workers; since 1994 Mexico has expelled an average of 400,000 migrant workers annually to the United States. These remittances play an important role, but their abundance is a testimony of the failure of the Mexican economy to provide adequate job opportunities for its people.

On Mexico's fiscal account the primary surplus has been achieved through pro-cyclical measures such as the increase of value-added taxes and the curtailment of expenditures in real terms. Due to past bailout operations the financial requirements of the public sector double the normal public balance deficit. Servicing this deficit is an unsolved problem that hinders the capacity to invest in environmental stewardship. Fiscal revenues from Mexico's regressive tax system are siphoned to cover the debt that resulted from past corruption and mismanagement. Social expenditures have been drastically affected by this approach to fiscal policy and resources for environmental stewardship have also been cut.

Mexico's system of satellite (environmental) accounts shows that its economy has been eating away resources from the environment as a result of macroeconomic priorities that respond to the needs of financial capital. The future of Mexico's economy will continue to be compromised by this high environmental burden. Today deforestation proceeds unabated, with an estimated one million hectares being lost every year to illegal logging and the expansion of the agricultural frontier. Soil erosion, loss of topsoil and the reduction of soil fertility continue to haunt the rural landscape. More than 35 per cent of the country's underground aquifers are being exploited at rates higher than natural replenishment. Most commercial fisheries are over-exploited and some are on the verge of collapse. Pollution of soils and water bodies is progressing rapidly as toxic waste accumulates. If the current macroeconomic framework is maintained, these negative trends will not only subsist, but may even worsen.

3 Implications for global trade governance

To meet sustainability objectives, global trade governance issues need to be integrated with macroeconomic policy-making. In this section, I present a set of reforms to global economic governance, including trade governance as well as the governance of finance, monetary systems and aid. The overarching message is that the full employment objectives of macroeconomic policy are closely related to sustainability, and the outcomes of the international trade regime are closely linked to macroeconomic dynamics. Keynes (1973: 383) famously captured these intersections when he observed that international trade should not be a desperate expedient to maintain employment at home by forcing sales on foreign markets, shifting the problem of unemployment to neighbours. Moreover, improving the sustainable development impact of trade cannot be properly advanced without attention to improved global environmental governance. The proposals presented here are not intended to give a complete blueprint, but rather highlight that neither international trade, nor its governance, can be addressed in isolation, and to present some of the key issues that need to be taken into account to achieve meaningful improvements. I begin with reforms to the international monetary system, and then turn to reforms of international financial regulation and debt relief.

I continue by highlighting key complementary reforms needed in the area of environmental governance and conclude with some key specific reforms needed in the area of global trade governance.

3.1 *Changing the international monetary system*

The world's monetary system needs to undergo a deep transformation if sustainability objectives are to be attained. An international monetary system catering to sustainability should have three main objectives: to guarantee sufficient liquidity and prevent deficiencies in aggregate demand, to avoid structural imbalances between deficit and surplus countries and, finally, to ensure that adequate financial resources be allocated to global environmental stewardship. Two levels of reform are needed to meet these objectives. The first requires a deep transformation of the world's monetary system and involves a new international reserve currency. The second implies a strong overhaul of existing institutions and of their role in money creation. Both approaches would need a strong regulatory regime for international finance.

There have been several proposals in this direction (Davidson 1999; United Nations Financial Reform Commission 2009). Among the most important of these proposals is the call for a new unit of account and ultimate reserve asset for international liquidity (such as a scheme described in Davidson (1999)). The international system would be endowed with a trigger mechanism to encourage creditor nations to spend 'excessive' credit balances accumulated by running current account surpluses. These excessive credits could be spent on the products of any other member of the international system, on new foreign direct investment projects, or on unilateral transfers to deficit members. In such a new system, surplus countries would have considerable freedom to adjust and the system would be oriented towards investments that ensure environmental sustainability. Deficit countries would no longer have to adjust painfully, as they would be able to remedy their imbalances through increased exports.

This scheme could still allow for export-import imbalances, but in the case of poor nations with persistent current account deficits due to heavy debt service obligations, clearing union officials would foster negotiations for debt restructuring, as well as partial or total debt cancellation. This scheme needs a strong regulatory regime for international capital movements, but could at the same time be compatible with blocks of nations that would like to permit free capital flows.

At present, the US dollar will only continue to be a reserve currency if others are willing to hold it as such, but as risk increases, doubts about the dollar will intensify. The USA has responded to the crisis with large injections of liquidity with unpredictable implications for the international reserve system. Thus, both the United States and foreign exchange reserve holding countries may actually find it acceptable to introduce a new system. The former would be able to take policy decisions with less concern about their global impact, and the latter would be less concerned about the impact of US policies on their reserve holdings. This is a solution to the conundrum of holding huge reserves in US dollars while at the same time offering the opportunity to channel significant resources to environmental stewardship.

Interestingly, with a supranational reserve currency, the United States would regain full control over its monetary policy. Everyone would benefit from the reduction of global risks associated to aggregate demand deficiencies. Failure to carry out this transformation will impede stable growth and will continue to promote instability, weighing heavily on our ability to attain sustainable development.

3.2 Capital flows and regulations for international finance

The global financial crisis of 2008 showed the time has come to seriously debate and put in place a robust regulatory system for international finance, and for capital flows in particular. Capital controls can contribute to smooth cycles in the capital account, reducing overall economic vulnerability (Furman and Stiglitz 1998). In Chile, unremunerated reserve requirements shielded the economy from overabundance of short-term capital at times of surges and helped attain higher growth rates (French-Davis and Tapia 2004). In Colombia, capital controls also allowed for better handling of maturity periods of external debt (Ocampo and Tovar 2003). In both cases, capital controls allowed policy-makers to regain some autonomy to implement a counter-cyclical monetary policy. This is also consistent with the historical record of developed countries, which shows long periods of capital controls and only gradual liberalization of capital flows (Eichengreen 1996).

Capital controls can smooth the cycles of the capital account, enhance stability and allow for a greater degree of independence of monetary policies. This objective can also be attained with the use of balance of payments provisions within the WTO framework. Such provisions, introduced in the original text of the General Agreements on Tariffs and

Trade (GATT) (Article 12), could provide a constructive response to current account crises (Nadal 1996) and should be recovered as an important tool at the intersection of trade and financial flows.[4] The international trade regime needs to be revised in order to make it compatible with country-level counter-cyclical policies and with regulations directed to crisis prevention. In addition, trade agreements such as the WTO General Agreement on Trade in Services (GATS) need to be reviewed in terms of their balance of payments effects, their impacts on macroeconomic stability and the scope they provide for financial regulation.

Regulations for the world's banking sector are another critical aspect of this problem. The Bank for International Settlements (BIS) in Basel has thus far been unable to prevent crises. The BIS's Basel I and II accords aimed to regulate capitalization and risk management, but were unable to function as early warning signposts. The 2010 Basel III accords aimed to rectify some of these challenges but remain weak in key areas.[5] Further, and in addition to the Basel accords, the Basel Committee on Banking Supervision could help identify and design new policies that would bring the banking sector closer to the needs of social and environmental sustainability. One way to get started in this area would be to establish a Working Group within the Policy Development Group charged with the tasks of identifying and reviewing emerging supervisory issues, and proposing and developing policies that promote a sound banking system.

Several initiatives involving self-regulation in the banking system offer important lessons and have generated intense debates. For example, the Wolfsberg Group, an association of twelve large banks with global operations, developed a set of anti-laundering principles, albeit the motivation

[4] Balance of payments provisions are important tools for adjustment in a world of fixed exchange rates. Recognizing the need for exceptional measures to meet balance of payments crises, GATT Article 12 opened the possibility for temporary exceptions to GATT obligations and established the required disciplines to avoid abuses. These provisions are included in the Marrakesh Agreements establishing the World Trade Organization. See the WTO's 1994 Understanding on the Balance of Payments Provisions of the GATT at www.wto.org [accessed in November 2010].

[5] The Basel III accord (approved on 12 September 2010, see www.bis.org [accessed in November 2010]) strengthened capital requirements, raising the minimum common equity requirement from 2 per cent to 4.5 per cent, plus another 2.5 per cent to be phased in by 2019. This is a step in the right direction, but the accord has several weak spots. The first is that much of the shadow banking system and its operations are ignored, leaving the volatile and risky business of this subsector without regulation. The second is that capital ratio can be meaningless if assets are overvalued and the Basel III accord does not include binding guidelines for valuation. Finally, Basel III does not have a strong chapter on enforcement.

was primarily one of reducing legal risks for banks.[6] However, several of the banks subscribing to these principles have engaged in loans to African countries that entail serious environmental damages.[7] The Equator Principles are another voluntary initiative focusing on project finance, whereby signatories agree to only provide loans to projects that align with the nine principles, which cover matters such as social and environmental assessments.[8] Unfortunately, there have been allegations that the Equator Principles have not been very effective. In 2010, for instance, a campaign launched by more than a hundred non-governmental organizations (NGOs) and several think tanks challenged several of the signatory banks and projects as environmentally unsound and socially irresponsible.[9] The campaign pointed out the deficiencies of this self-regulatory scheme in terms of transparency, accountability mechanisms, and specific implementation requirements.[10]

3.3 *Solving the debt predicament*

The world lacks a system to deal with the ongoing international debt problem inherited from the debt crisis in the 1980s. Past negotiations on debt relief for developing countries were dominated by creditors and led to unfair and inefficient risk-sharing schemes that only provided temporary relief to countries. Typically, debt negotiations have emphasized the notion that strong pressure is needed so that debtor countries do not feel tempted to default. Needless to say, the emerging solutions have not been in the general interest. Debt rescheduling and relief cannot continue to depend on the negotiating capacity of individual debtor countries.

As long as developing countries are weighed down by their debt burden, sustainable development will be an elusive goal. Every year, developing countries in all regions are forced to generate a primary surplus to cover their financial charges, a significant part of which is related to the original or 'old' debt. This is why resources have been siphoned from the developing world for more than fifty years, with terrible social costs and highly negative environmental consequences worldwide. The recent global financial crisis puts even more pressure on indebted countries.

6 See www.wolfsberg-principles.com [accessed in November 2010].
7 See www.globalwitness.org [accessed in November 2010].
8 See www.equator-principles.com [accessed in November 2010].
9 See www.banktrack.org [accessed in November 2010].
10 For discussion of the challenges of self-regulation and governance in this and other contexts, see Conzelmann and Wolf (2005) and Mattli and Woods (2009).

A different approach to debt management is required. It needs to go beyond the simple notion that fiscal policy has to generate funds for debt service. A concerted effort to help debtors and creditors reach common ground must be launched by the relevant international organizations, based on the premise that effective debt relief is essential. In the past, real debt relief has been extremely weak and has usually been linked to rather optimistic projections about future economic performance. Another round of simple rescheduling of obligations is clearly not desirable.

In the context of today's crisis, the recovery of debtor nations will demand a redefinition of what constitutes sustainable debt. The urgency arises from the fact that the poorest and most vulnerable countries already face difficulties in meeting external debt service and these will surely increase. For the poorest and most vulnerable countries, a debt moratorium and, where appropriate, debt cancellation must be considered (United Nations Financial Reform Commission 2009), together with provision of concessional funds to engage in counter-cyclical policies. For other countries, negotiations over debt must also recognize the suite of economic, social and environmental objectives that countries are struggling to meet, and not just the right of creditors to recover. Public and private creditors should recognize that a rapid solution to the problem of debt overhang will improve recovery prospects.

To date, the Heavily Indebted Poor Countries (HIPC) initiative has been insufficient to solve the debt problem.[11] In 2005, a new Multilateral Debt Relief Initiative, providing 100 per cent relief on eligible debt to low-income countries, was launched under the auspices of the International Monetary Fund.[12] However, this initiative has been designed and implemented without due consideration to the macroeconomic policy regime in the debtor countries and the debt relief packages are embedded in a pro-cyclical policy framework. This aggravates inequality, poverty and impedes the allocation of adequate resources for environmental stewardship. Total and unconditional debt cancellation for the poorest countries would liberate resources for social and environmental sustainability in countries rich in biodiversity.

Major debt negotiations today take place under the informal and imperfect coordination of the debtor and its creditors at the IMF, under

[11] For more information on the HIPC Initiative, see www.imf.org/external/np/exr/facts/hipc.htm [accessed in November 2010].

[12] For more information on the Multilateral Debt Relief Initiative, see www.imf.org/external/np/exr/facts/mdri.htm [accessed in November 2010].

the guidance of the major industrialized countries, which set the policy directions for the IMF and other fora, such as the Paris Club, where debts are restructured.[13] This system has failed to solve the debt problem.

The institutional architecture governing international debt needs to be fundamentally overhauled so that debtors and creditors are placed on an equal footing. The priorities of social and environmental sustainability should be the guiding principles when solving debt problems. International civil society organizations, as well as several UN commissions, have proposed the creation of a new International Debt Court that would be able to address cases of international insolvency in fair and more efficient terms. It would adjudicate debt issues between sovereign debtors and their creditors. This Court would also serve as an international bankruptcy court, prioritizing the claims of debtors, debt cancellation and overall debt relief along previously agreed criteria that ensure equity and sustainability (Krueger 2002; Rogoff and Zettelmeyer 2002). Most importantly, this Court would differentiate between countries and between types of indebtedness. In particular, it would be able to distinguish between good faith inability to cover debt service, odious debt and *force majeure* (cases of extraordinary circumstances preventing compliance with contractual obligations).

3.4 Overhauling how we finance development and global environmental stewardship

To complement improvements in how we govern global trade and macroeconomic dynamics, a new credit facility must be established to ensure adequate resources for long-term programmes for social welfare and environmental sustainability. Resources currently available bilaterally and through the World Bank and multilateral efforts such as the Global Environment Facility (GEF) are inadequate in the face of the mounting challenges and the current economic crisis. Official Development Assistance (ODA) resources have been insufficient and very few countries have met their international commitments (Easterly 2006). Developing countries will need access to additional sources of finance to ensure that environmental stewardship is not pushed to the back burner in favour of urgent post-crisis economy recovery prices.

[13] The Paris Club is an informal group of official creditors whose role is to find coordinated and sustainable solutions to the payment difficulties experienced by debtor countries. See www.clubdeparis.org [accessed in November 2010].

In recent years, the challenges of climate change, of deforestation, biodiversity loss and the deterioration of oceanic ecosystems, have spurred several proposals for a new facility to guarantee a stable and trustworthy flow of resources to finance environmental stewardship. The priorities of the facility could draw from those already set out through initiatives such as the UN's Millennium Development Goals[14] and the 'Stamp Out Poverty' campaign (Hillman *et al.* 2006), which include the provision of clean drinking water, basic sanitation and human health. Other dimensions of sustainable development that could also be added to the work of the new facility could be housing, education and support for small-scale agriculture.

There are at least three sources of finance that could be tapped for this new entity. The first source would be the mechanism described above for the international reserve currency of creditor/surplus countries. The new fund could use the 'excessive credit balances' resources from creditor/surplus countries that have accumulated large international non-borrowed reserves.

The second source could be a tax on the currency transactions market. The volume of trade in the currency markets of the world has expanded from about US$4 trillion in 1973 (when the Bretton Woods system collapsed) to more than US$450 trillion in 2007 (Hillman *et al.* 2006). The Stamp Out Poverty initiative proposes a Currency Transaction Development Levy (CTDL) at a very low level (0.005 per cent) and shows this can generate a significant and stable amount of resources (Hillman *et al.* 2006). In contrast to the original Tobin tax proposal, the purpose of the new CTDL proposal would be to raise funds for global sustainable development projects.[15]

The third potential source of finance would be a tax on transactions in the stock exchanges of the most important financial centres (Hillman *et al.* 2006). World equity markets have registered a very rapid increase in turnover during the past two decades. A tax on currency transactions markets and financial operations such as share trading, bond trading and operations with derivatives could generate significant revenues. Over-the-counter (OTC) operations could also offer a new source of revenues if they were to become the object of new regulations.

[14] For more information on, and a listing of, the UN Millennium Development Goals, visit www.un.org/millenniumgoals/ [accessed in November 2010].

[15] For a detailed analysis of these differences, see United Nations Financial Reform Commission (2009).

3.5 *Reforming the international trade regime*

The dynamics of trade negotiations should no longer be dominated by the fallacious premise that reducing trade barriers is an end in itself. The goals must be sustainability and development, not freer trade per se. To advance these goals, at least five key reforms are necessary to the rules and principles governing global trade.

3.5.1 Balance of payments provisions

Greater recognition must be given to balance of payments provisions as a tool for economic adjustment; in today's world of flexible exchange rates these balance of payments provisions (BOPs) are not redundant (Nadal 1996). Recognizing the need for exceptional measures to meet balance of payments crises, the original GATT provided contracting parties with temporary exceptions from GATT obligations. Article II established the central principle that in case of balance of payments difficulties, countries could restrict the quantity or value of imports subject to certain disciplines. Temporary restrictions on trade flows may be less damaging than macro-devaluations and draconian fiscal adjustment measures. Responsible use of BOPs entails inferior social and environmental costs in case of balance of payments difficulties.

Reinforcing coherence among trade and monetary policies must go hand in hand with changes in the role and operations of the IMF (United Nations Financial Reform Commission 2009).

3.5.2 Agriculture

To date, the international community has been unable to reconcile the need for adequate food production and distribution systems, improved living standards and environmental sustainability of the agricultural system. Although global agricultural production has continued to outstrip total population, the rate of growth of yields has been slowing down and it is expected that gains in yield per unit area will remain lower than historical yields (International Assessment of Agricultural Knowledge, Science and Technology for Development (IAASTD) 2009). The per capita surface of cultivated land has begun to contract, indicating that we have reached the limits of the agricultural frontier in many key areas of the world. Usage consumption rates of irrigation have spelled over-exploitation of aquifers, and heavy use of chemical inputs contributes to pollution of underground and surface water bodies. All of this coincides with a situation in which close to a billion human beings do not have enough to eat (United Nations World Food Programme 2010). The WTO's Agreement on Agriculture contributed to trade liberalization but left untouched the capacity of developed countries to channel resources to the agricultural sector and failed to create adequate market access for the products of developing countries, while global agricultural commodity prices suffered severe reductions and volatility increased.

An institutional and legal framework that blends sound supply-management policy measures with adequate support mechanisms in developing countries is needed. The world needs adequate crop prices that contribute to a healthy worldwide agricultural sector. A new institutional arrangement, perhaps a new framework convention, needs to tackle the issues of sustainable agriculture, small-scale producers, biodiversity, food security and access to genetic resources, not on a piecemeal basis, but as part of a single undertaking. The new convention should restate the fundamental right of nations to defend themselves from unfair business practices and from the distortions brought about by the concentration of market power.

3.5.3 Special and differential treatment

Special and differential treatment (SDT) is based on the idea that fairness is an important guiding principle in international economic relations, and linked to the recognition of existing international asymmetries in the functioning of markets and generators of inefficiencies. In the context of the WTO, the principle of SDT articulates the idea that developing countries are not obligated to (fully) reciprocate trade concessions made by developed countries because they need more time to adjust to the economic forces unleashed by trade liberalization.

But SDT has been a failure in establishing a level playing field. SDT provisions such as extended transition periods and concessions of a few tariff points below those of developed countries have not been sufficient to redress asymmetries that took decades or even centuries to crystallize. Moreover, SDT has been accompanied by a severe contraction of the policy space of developing countries. As a result of structural adjustment policies, several WTO agreements, and some regional and bilateral trade agreements, national control over macroeconomic and sector level policies has been drastically reduced. This has to be revised and changed in order to recover the original objectives of SDT.

3.5.4 Foreign investment

The WTO Agreement on Trade-Related Aspects of Investment Measures (TRIMs) forces developing countries to forego the use of important industrial policy instruments. It inhibits, for instance, the ability of WTO Members to impose performance requirements (such as on the proportion of domestic value added in exports). Without these instruments, developing countries may be condemned to remain in a low productivity trap and to rely on exports of primary and raw materials that have a greater ecological footprint. Instead of protecting against the effects of market concentration, TRIMs shields foreign investors against public policies in host countries. In addition to allowing performance requirements, a revised TRIMs Agreement should incorporate the need for greater market transparency through the monitoring of operations of multinational corporations, especially where market concentration is present.

3.5.5 International Commodity Agreements

International Commodity Agreements (ICAs) are an important component of the road to greater market transparency and less volatility (Gilbert 2007). In the past, the facilitation of such commodity agreements was part of UNCTAD's mandate, with the aim of arresting the deterioration of developing countries' terms of trade and stabilizing commodity markets in the face of large price fluctuations. Several agreements were established, but ICAs were largely set aside in the aftermath of the debt crisis in the 1980s.[16] Despite consistent calls from UNCTAD for renewed attention to ICAs, their use has never subsequently been restored.

The vulnerability of developing countries relying on basic products for exports puts undue pressure on people and the environment. ICAs could help change this situation. Market failures caused by price volatility and long-term trends of declining prices for many primary commodities provide the rationale for a second generation of ICAs (Ocampo and Parra 2003). ICAs could also help reduce distortions due to market concentration and reinstate more transparency in trade through the supervision of multinational corporations. In addition, a new generation of ICAs could explore ways and means to increase the value added of raw commodities, creating forward and backward industrial linkages that generate more employment opportunities and have healthy multiplier effects in commodity production chains. A range of national and international policies

[16] For a balanced account of the multiple causes behind the decline of ICAs during this period, see Gilbert (2007).

covering issues from credit, land, technology and transportation to tariff protection and access to markets, are essential if agricultural production is to bring a better future for farmers.

4 Concluding remarks

Most of the reforms discussed in this chapter do not entail radical transformations of the way the international trade regime works today. While this chapter advocates changes that would increase the policy space available to developing countries, it emphasizes that there is still a role for the WTO. However, trade liberalization would not be its overarching objective. Rather, the members of the WTO need to make their commitment to sustainable development in the first paragraph of the Agreement Establishing the WTO a reality.[17] This in turn demands a broader macroeconomic model that appropriately addresses both the environment and sustainability considerations more directly, which is not an easy task. A preliminary step in the right direction is to better integrate debates on global trade governance with the analysis of how macroeconomic strategies and policy packages operate in the real world.

References

Bhaduri, A. 1998. 'Implications of Globalization for Macroeconomic Theory and Policy in Developing Countries', in Baker, D., Epstein, G. and Pollin, R. (eds.), *Globalization and Progressive Economic Policy*. Cambridge University Press, pp. 149–59.

Conzelmann, T. and Wolf, K. 2005. 'Governance by Private Codes of Conduct', paper presented at the Annual Meeting of the International Studies Association, Honolulu, Hawaii (March).

Davidson, P. 1999. 'Global Employment in Open Economy Macroeconomics', in Deprez, J. and Harvey, J. (eds.), *Foundations of International Economics: Post-Keynesian Perspectives*. London and New York: Routledge, pp. 9–35.

Easterly, W. 2006. *The White Man's Burden: Why the West's Efforts to Aid the Rest Have Done So Much Ill and So Little Good*. New York: Penguin Books.

Eatwell, J. and Taylor, L. 2000. *Global Finance at Risk. The Case for International Regulation*. New York: The New Press.

17 The Agreement recognizes the importance of 'allowing for the optimal use of the world's resources in accordance with the objective of sustainable development'. The legal text is available at www.wto.org [accessed in November 2010].

Eichengreen, B. 1996. *Globalizing Capital. A History of the International Monetary System*. Princeton University Press.

Ffrench-Davis, R. and Tapia, H. 2004. 'The Chilean Style of Capital Controls: An Empirical Assessment'. Paper prepared for the ECLAC project 'Management of Volatility, Financial Liberalization and Growth', presented at the Latin American Studies Association meeting, Las Vegas, October.

Furman, J. and Stiglitz, J. 1998. 'Economic Crises: Evidence and Insights from East Asia', *Brookings Papers on Economic Activity* No. 2. Washington, DC: The Brookings Institution.

Gallagher, K. 2008. *Handbook on Trade and the Environment*. Cheltenham, UK: Edward Elgar.

Giarracca, N. and Teubal, M. 2006. 'Democracia y neoliberalismo en el campo argentino: Una convivencia difícil', in *La construcción de la democracia en el campo latinoamericano*, Hubert, G. (ed.). Buenos Aires: CLACSO.

Gilbert, C. 2007. 'International Commodity Agreements', in *Handbook on International Trade Policy*, Kerr, W. and Gaisford, J. (eds.). Cheltenham, UK: Edward Elgar.

Hillman, D., Kapoor, S. and Spratt, S. 2006. *Taking the Next Step. Implementing a Currency Transactions Development Levy*, Report commissioned by the Norwegian Ministry of Foreign Affairs. www.stampoutpoverty.org [Accessed in November 2010].

International Assessment of Agricultural Knowledge, Science and Technology for Development (IAASTD). 2009. *Agriculture at the Crossroads. Global Report*. Washington: Island Press.

Keynes, J. M. 1973. *The General Theory of Employment, Interest and Money*. Cambridge, UK: Macmillan and Cambridge University Press for the Royal Economic Society.

Khan, S. (ed.) 2002. *Trade and Environment. Difficult Policy Choices at the Interface*. London: Zed Books.

Krueger, A. 2002. *A New Approach to Sovereign Debt Restructuring*. Washington, DC: International Monetary Fund.

Mattli, W. and Woods, N. (eds.) 2009. *The Politics of Global Regulation*. Oxford University Press.

Nadal, A. 1996. 'Balance-of-Payments Provisions in the GATT and NAFTA', *Journal of World Trade* 30(4): 5–24.

2004. 'Contradictions of the Open Economy Model as Applied in Mexico', in Ackerman, F. and Nadal, A. (eds.), *The Flawed Foundations of General Equilibrium. Critical Essays on Economic Theory*. London: Routledge.

Ocampo, J. and Tovar, C. 2003. 'La experiencia colombiana con los encajes a los flujos de capital', *Revista de la CEPAL* 81: 7–32.

Ocampo, J. and Parra, M. 2003. 'Los términos de intercambio de los productos básicos en el siglo XX', *Revista de la CEPAL* 79: 7–35.

Pengue, W. 2005. 'Transgenic Crops in Argentina: The Ecological and Social Debt', *Bulletin of Science, Technology and Society* 25(4): 314–22.

Rogoff, K. and Zettelmeyer, J. 2002. 'Early Ideas on Sovereign Bankruptcy Reorganization: A Survey', *IMF Working Paper* No. 02/57 March. Washington, DC: IMF.

UNCTAD. 2009. *The Global Economic Crisis: Systemic Failures and Multilateral Remedies*. Report by the UNCTAD Secretariat Task Force on Systemic Issues and Economic Cooperation. UNCTAD/GDS/2009/1. ISBN 978–92–1–112765–2. www.unctad.org [Accessed in November 2010].

UNEP-IISD. 2005. *Environment and Trade. A Handbook*. Geneva and Winnipeg: United Nations Environmental Programme (UNEP) and International Institute for Sustainable Development (IISD).

United Nations Financial Reform Commission. 2009. *Report of the Commission of Experts of the President of the United Nations General Assembly on Reforms of the International Monetary and Financial System*. New York: United Nations General Assembly.

United Nations World Food Programme. 2010. *Fighting Hunger Worldwide*. Annual Report 2010. www.wfp.org [Accessed in November 2010].

World Trade Organization (WTO). 2004. *World Trade Report 2004: Coherence*. www.wto.org/english/res_e/publications_e/wtr04_e.htm [Accessed in November 2010].

4

Trade governance and sustainable development

RICARDO MELÉNDEZ-ORTIZ AND
TRINEESH BISWAS

The fact that we need not go into great detail about what sustainable development *is* speaks volumes about how widespread the notion has become in policy-making and scholarly circles over the past two decades. Nor is it novel any longer to draw links between sustainable development and trade governance. It is now well understood that as international arrangements on trade expanded their reach 'behind the border' to establish contractual obligations covering non-tariff measures such as health and safety regulations, environmental policies, intellectual property protections and practices related to investment, they took on greater significance in national governments' efforts to convert the opportunities presented by the globalized economy into sustainable development. The trade system has been transformed from a market-opening device into a rules-focused regime (Barton *et al.* 2008). Regulations for the global economy determine today the way resources are allocated and how they may be used, and thus define sustainable development possibilities.

But how do we get from where we are today to the 'sustainability' aspiration? Fortunately, we are not tasked with answering this. We focus our attention on the 'trading system' – a term that encompasses the multilateral regime embodied in the World Trade Organization (WTO) together with the growing landscape of bilateral and regional trade agreements and other preferential arrangements for economic integration. It is clear that new policies for governing investment, finance, energy and knowledge will be necessary to harness economic activity into modes of production that favour conserving resources over exhausting them. How

Ricardo Meléndez-Ortiz is co-founder of the International Centre for Trade and Sustainable Development (ICTSD) and has been its Chief Executive Officer since 1996. Trineesh Biswas is Adviser to the Chief Executive at ICTSD. The authors thank Ahmed Abdel-Latif, Christophe Bellmann, Hugo Cameron, Carolyn Deere Birkbeck and David Primack for input and comments.

is the trading system equipped to help steer economic activity towards the necessary pathways of change?

In this chapter, we examine how trade governance could be made more supportive of sustainable development. In section 1, we examine the global policy context that is shaping (and being affected by) governance efforts on trade and sustainable development. In section 2, we make a few specific recommendations for how creative action taken within trade institutions, particularly the WTO, could help make the trading system more supportive of sustainable development. In section 3, we examine how the work of international organizations could be better aligned. Finally, in section 4, we provide some examples of how action taken outside the trade arena could leverage trade governance's contribution to sustainable development.

1 The global policy context

Policy recommendations, in order to be realistic, must take into consideration the environment in which policy is made. In this section, we examine that context, looking first at the importance of institutions in making trade work for development, before turning to the challenges facing the pursuit of sustainable development.

1.1 The critical importance of institutions

Export-led growth has underpinned unprecedented poverty reduction, particularly in East Asia. But openness does not automatically lead to growth, poverty reduction or better resource management, or else Haiti would be richer, greener and more equitable than Vietnam (taking from Rodrik 2001). What made the difference? Institutions.

Though we do not pretend that institutions are the only factor in growth, domestic and international institutions, including macroeconomic, social and environmental policies, play a critical role in translating trade liberalization into economic growth and increased opportunities for individuals. The old view that property rights, regulatory structures, independent judiciaries and bureaucratic capacity are an effortless by-product of growth has been turned on its head; institutions are now viewed as important determinants of long-term growth (Rodrik 2003: 8). One function of institutions that is particularly relevant to our analysis is to 'align economic incentives with social costs and benefits' (Rodrik 2003: 10). This 'alignment' is a key determinant of how increased trade and economic activity will impact social fabrics and the environment. Getting the alignment right is a function of economic, social and environmental policies. These policies in turn depend on processes for policy-making: whether they reflect all concerned voices and not just traditional privileged actors, and whether they ensure that social and environmental costs are internalized into markets and prices.

Maximizing global trade governance's contribution to the pursuit of sustainable development will also hinge on institutions. Too often, domestic and international institutions act at cross-purposes. Governments need to ensure that they pursue sustainable development goals and that they interact constructively. To do this, governments will need to work innovatively within and across trade and other institutions. Crucial sustainable development policies – carbon pricing, to take one example – need to be decided outside the trading system. Several of these policies will – if serious action is ever taken – have ramifications for commercial exchange. Shaping and managing that intersection is the governance challenge. While national governments can establish sustainability directives for ministries, this is not an option available at the multilateral level. There is no 'global government' – no formal worldwide authority that operates within defined laws. The distinction between 'global government' and 'global governance' is useful here. 'Global governance' recognizes that the international system operates under various formal and informal rules and practices arising from multiple sources, and that it is accountable to multiple groups of stakeholders. Getting the multiplicity of rules affecting trade and sustainable development to reinforce each other and work together coherently is the task (Petersmann 2007a, 2007b).

The relationship between governments and international economic institutions has changed dramatically over the past forty years. As the post-war economic order's 'embedded liberalism' – multilateral rules for international trade and capital movement, predicated upon domestic interventionism to preserve social stability (Ruggie 1982) – fractured in the 1970s, global economic rules and pressures, especially from capital flows, began to loom ever larger in domestic policy and politics (Kirshner 1999). The General Agreement on Tariffs and Trade (GATT)/WTO system's attack on trade-distorting policies moved from tariffs to non-tariff policies, touching upon areas traditionally reserved for sovereign management.

The blurring of the line between domestic and international regimes has been accompanied by the rise of new transnational actors attempting to influence policy outcomes in international economic institutions (Keohane and Nye 1972; Petersmann 2007b). Traditional mercantilist players like farm lobbies may now find themselves at odds with activists calling for changes to domestic agriculture policy and positions taken at the WTO in the interest of reducing hunger abroad. Other key stakeholders remain all too marginalized, often due to insufficient capacity – notably poorer countries, and especially health and environmental interests within them. Building capacity and setting up processes at the domestic and international levels to give voice to a wider range of stakeholders would help global governance become more supportive of sustainable development (see, for instance, Halle and Wolfe 2007).

We caution that a focus on improved policy processes must not become a substitute for attention to results. Simply talking about trade and climate change at the WTO would mean little if the discussion did nothing to soften potential clashes between the trading system and measures taken by individual governments in the name of climate protection. 'Legitimacy may derive from performance as well as process', aptly observes the international relations scholar Robert Keohane (2002: 239). The WTO's Doha Round negotiations have been marked by a substantially more inclusive process than in previous GATT/WTO negotiations – the talks are assuredly no longer dominated by a small group of rich countries – but with little in the way of results.

1.2 *The rise and stall of sustainable development in global policy-making*

Having spared readers a lengthy exposition on how environmental and developmental considerations came to be seen as inextricably linked, we must make two definitional observations about sustainable development because of their salience to ongoing international economic governance processes.

First, sustainable development's conceptual flexibility helped the attractive, holistic notion of a balanced coexistence among humanity's economic, social and ecological aspirations find acceptability as an overarching objective of a wide range of policy endeavours. The WTO's preamble speaks of expanding trade in goods and services 'in accordance with the objective of sustainable development'[1]; WTO Members repeated

[1] The Preamble to the Marrakesh Agreement Establishing the World Trade Organization opens with 'The Parties to this Agreement, *recognizing* that their relations in the field of trade and economic endeavour should be conducted with a view to raising standards of living, ensuring full employment and a large and steadily growing volume of real income and effective demand, and expanding the production of and trade in goods and services,

this commitment when launching the Doha Development Round negotiations in 2001 (WTO 1994a, 2001).[2] The text of the Kyoto Protocol clearly establishes sustainable development as its goal. Since the Group of 20 leading industrialized and developing nations came together as the global financial crisis deepened in late 2008, their declarations have stressed 'sustainable growth and development', 'green recovery' and the removal of environmentally harmful subsidies encouraging the use of fossil fuels (G20 2008, 2010).

It is easy to dismiss these references as rhetoric. But they can have concrete value – best illustrated in the trade context by the WTO Appellate Body, which has cited the organization's preambular commitment to sustainable development in key rulings finding that unilateral trade restrictions to promote the conservation of exhaustible natural resources can, if appropriately constructed, be justifiable under multilateral trade rules (Howse 2002).[3]

Our second observation is that the very suppleness of the concept of sustainable development allows it to mean different things to different people, and to different governments.

Consider the negotiations under the United Nations Framework Convention on Climate Change (UNFCCC). Rich countries invoke

while allowing for the optimal use of the world's resources *in accordance with the objective of sustainable development*, seeking both to protect and preserve the environment and to enhance the means for doing so in a manner consistent with their respective needs and concerns at different levels of economic development…' [italics added]. (See WTO 1994b).

[2] See WTO 2001: para. 6. 'We strongly reaffirm our commitment to the objective of sustainable development, as stated in the Preamble to the Marrakesh Agreement. We are convinced that the aims of upholding and safeguarding an open and non-discriminatory multilateral trading system, and acting for the protection of the environment and the promotion of sustainable development can and must be mutually supportive.'

[3] See WTO 1998: para. 12. 'An environmental purpose is fundamental to the application of Article 20', and such a purpose cannot be ignored, especially since the Preamble to the Marrakesh Agreement Establishing the WTO (WTO 1994b) acknowledges that the rules of trade should be 'in accordance with the objective of sustainable development', and should seek to 'protect and preserve the environment'. As per Howse (2002), the Appellate Body used the Marrakesh Agreement's reference to sustainable development to justify interpreting the notion of 'exhaustible natural resources' in light of evolving international environmental law. In the case, the Appellate Body found that a US import ban on shrimp harvested by techniques that might harm turtles was justified in principle, except for the fact that it was applied in a discriminatory fashion. Howse argued that the Appellate Body's acceptance that unilateral measures conditioning market access on exporters' practices could be justifiable under the general exceptions to standard trade obligations set out in GATT Article 20 represented a rejection of 'the traditional approach to environmental trade measures in the GATT/WTO system', thus establishing a new legal baseline for the trade and environment debate.

sustainable development to observe that global emissions cannot be blunted and reduced without action from large developing countries. China, India and others counter that Northern nations, with their higher per capita emissions and historical responsibility for the overwhelming share of anthropogenic greenhouse gases already in the atmosphere, should lead efforts on mitigation, foot the bill for adaptation and provide the means for decarbonizing the global economy. They see Northern demands for binding emissions limits as constraints on their own prospects for growth and the pursuit of sustainable development. Neither camp is fundamentally wrong, but the differences have brought the climate talks to an impasse.[4]

This has been mirrored in the trade realm by the contested meaning of the word 'development' in the WTO's Doha Round talks (Petersmann 2007a; Ismail 2009). 'Market access is the key to the development impact of the round', top US trade officials have said, arguing that in light of the relative openness of Northern markets, the 'development content' of the WTO talks hinges on market-opening by large developing countries (Schwab 2007). South Africa and other developing countries have made roughly the opposite argument, arguing that delivering on development in this round would require rich countries to remove persisting trade-distorting policies such as farm subsidies and high tariffs on products that developing countries produce competitively (NAMA-11 2006). For good measure, sustainable development is also invoked by countries seeking tariff liberalization for environmental goods – but the goods concerned tend to overlap with their advocates' export interests, and there is no agreed upon benchmark for goods to qualify as environmental (ICTSD 2007). The WTO negotiations, too, are at an impasse.

The sustainable development construct was crafted through a long and complex process involving myriad stakeholders.[5] The product was a compromise – but a very rich one nonetheless, one that expresses a clear vision and possibilities for application. The WTO Appellate Body had no trouble

[4] There is an enormous literature examining this debate. A prolific analyst of the politics and economics of climate is Stanford professor David Victor who offers a balanced synthesis in Victor (2006) and more recently in Victor and Yueh (2010). A classic and powerful argumentation can be found in Agarwal and Narain (1991). Complementary analysis is offered in Stanton and Ackerman (2009) and Aldy and Stavins (2009).

[5] As with the debate on climate, literature is abundant on the genesis of the sustainable development construct. A synthesis can be found in Najam *et al.* (2005). On the economics see for example Munasinghe (1993); and on the evolution of the corpus of international law stemming from it, see Gehring and Cordonier-Segger (2005).

coming up with a legal *interpretation* of the demands entailed by an overarching commitment to sustainable development (see footnote 3). But as a guide to governments' attempts to *negotiate* economic rules, it often seems that the concept of sustainable development is so all-encompassing that it points in no specific direction.[6]

Trade negotiations have suffered from governments' attempts to apply mercantilist logics that may have worked for negotiating reciprocal tariff concessions to the more complicated business of devising rules. The traditional GATT concern of tariff bargaining was underpinned by longstanding economic theory predicting mutual benefits among clearly identifiable actors. This clarity of purpose – and clarity about perceived benefits – was lost amidst the shift towards domestic policies and the negotiation of rules to harness them to international trade (all in pursuit of the ultimate goal of sustainable development). In the new game, the stakes are broader, and different participants have diverse goals and interests: some prioritize economic growth while others emphasize environmental outcomes, social agendas or the preservation of 'policy space'. In this more complex context, mercantilism and the logic of reciprocal bargaining seem out of place. Expectations grow for the delivery of mutual benefits, of welfare-enhancing outcomes rather than simply commercial gains, of greater benefits for the poor and disadvantaged. One might hope that a highly diverse range of stakeholders would dilute the relative influence of narrow commercial agendas in favour of the public interest, for reasons of fairness and legitimacy. Yet it takes only a quick look at current negotiations to demonstrate that the adoption of sustainable development as an objective remains elusive and seems to have thus far failed to jolt governments out of short-term thinking.

This victory for myopic policy-making is particularly frustrating because the end goals of sustainable development are so clear: high human development based on sustainable use of the earth's capacity, a world of available nourishment, shelter, healthcare and opportunities, all within the planet's capacity to replenish resources. Only such a world can offer to current *and* future generations what Amartya Sen has identified as the heart of development: the ability to pursue that which they have cause to value (Sen 1999).

Knowing where we need to go has not helped us get there. The United Nations Earth Summit in Rio de Janeiro in 1992 adopted Agenda 21, a

[6] One partial exception is the Doha Round fisheries subsidy negotiations, where many WTO Members accept that sustainable development dictates curbing government payments that encourage overfishing. But even there, consensus is absent (see Chang 2003).

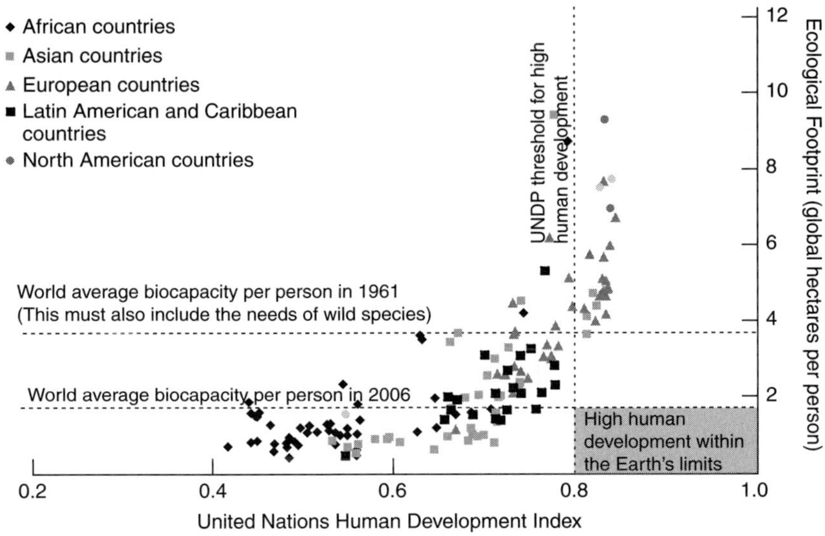

Figure 4.1 Human Development Index and Ecological Footprint, 2006

detailed implementation-oriented framework for the pursuit of sustainable development, covering issues such as poverty reduction, resource management and governance arrangements.[7] But none of the Rio commitments have been fulfilled, and despite considerable poverty reduction (thanks mainly to China and India), the challenges to development, equity and the environment remain severe (Marglin *et al.* 2010).

1.3 Goals clear: but how to get there?

While some countries have done better than others at decoupling economic progress from resource use and pollution, virtually none has reached the ideal, that is, that their healthy, educated and well-nourished populations are supported by an employment of resources such that the prospects for maintaining or improving future living standards are not impaired, as illustrated powerfully by the Global Footprint Network (GFN) in Figure 4.1.[8]

[7] For more details about Agenda 21, see www.un.org/esa/dsd/agenda21/ [accessed in November 2010].

[8] Graph reproduced with permission from the GFN. Footprint data was compiled from the Global Footprint Network 2009 National Footprint Accounts and the United Nations Development Programme's (UNDP's) Human Development Index Data from the 2009 Human Development Report.

Sustainable development means bringing all of those dots into the graph's small grey area that signifies 'high human development within the Earth's limits'.[9] We know a few things about what such a world would look like. It would be characterized by market prices that internalize environmental costs, particularly in terms of energy and water. Ecosystem services would be duly rewarded, so that turning a rainforest into charcoal would not earn more money than protecting it. It would be marked by innovation enabling radically more efficient resource and energy use.

The challenges are manifold. We are currently on track to venture into the unknown – from a plentiful world affluent in resources to an impoverished world, compromised in its biophysical capacity to sustain our routines. The world's population is projected to grow to around 9 billion by 2050. Much of the increase will come from the poorest countries, where meeting basic human development needs – let alone aspirations – would already entail increased resource use by much of the population (at least based on current technologies).

Consider two of humanity's most fundamental needs – food and water. The growing world population will need more of both. Increasing wealth in the developing world – a good thing – is changing diets, boosting demand for resource-intensive meat, putting more pressure on food resources. As if this were not enough, climate change is complicating the picture even more. The International Food Policy Research Institute (IFPRI) estimates that by 2050, climate change will push calorie availability in the developing world below 2000 levels, eliminating much of the projected progress on child malnourishment (IFPRI 2009). IFPRI estimates that the developing world will need some US$7.3 billion a year in investments in agricultural productivity just to offset the nutritional consequences of climate change (IFPRI 2009).

[9] In the Global Footprint Network's own words: 'Sustainable human development will occur when all humans can have fulfilling lives without degrading the planet. Two leading indicators have identified how we can get there. Ecological Footprint data tells us that, given current population and available land area, an Ecological Footprint [the vertical axis] of less than 2.1 global hectares per person makes a country's resource demands globally replicable. The United Nations' Human Development Index (HDI) [on the horizontal axis] – which measures a country's average achievements in the areas of health, knowledge, and standard of living – tells us that an HDI higher than 0.8 is considered "high human development".' Detailed information on the GFN and the calculation of the indicators used above can be found at www.footprintnetwork.org/en/index.php/GFN/page/fighting_poverty_our_human_development_initiative/ [accessed in November 2010].

Let us be under no illusions about the trading system's capacity to play a driving role in addressing these challenges. Many, indeed, most of the domestic and international policy decisions necessary to set the planet on a course to sustainability will not be taken in the trading system. But virtually all of them – from the internalization of environmental costs to policies to encourage innovation – will have ramifications that impinge directly on trade: what we produce, where we produce it, how we exchange it. Some will overlap with issues now dealt with by international trade rules, such as intellectual property, standards and protections for foreign investors. In today's globalized world, trade and investment policies help determine the allocation and use of resources, from minerals and labour to knowledge and soil. Individual societies' ability to manage these policies is affected by global and international regulatory systems for trade and investment – systems that they in turn can influence. Thus, there is ample scope for policy-makers and influencers to respond proactively in the trading system to bolster sustainable development policy: by building a supporting environment where possible, anticipating and moving to defang potential discord, and ensuring that trade-related policies do not detract from the pursuit of sustainable development goals. At the same time, the trading system must remain true to its own principles, and not allow environmental policy to become a pretext for governments to engage in discriminatory practices or pander to influential domestic economic actors.

The idea is simple enough, but governments have a solid track record of taking away with one hand what they have given with the other. By conflating development policy with development *aid*, they have too often ignored the developmental effects of their trade, investment, immigration and environmental policies. The classic example is levying high tariffs on goods exported by aid recipients. A more complex narrative, which we will return to below, comes from the incoherence of governments' pursuit of a fundamental global developmental goal: food security. Assuring physical and economic access to food has been an international policy objective for decades. The Food and Agriculture Organization (FAO) was founded in 1945, following the allies' recognition that defeating hunger would be essential to building a peaceful post-war world. Despite the nascent Green Revolution, the early 1970s were marked by food shortages and sharp increases in prices for food and fuel. This gave rise to new institutions and initiatives to boost food production and accessibility. In 1974, Henry Kissinger famously told a World Food Conference that within a decade, no child would go to bed hungry. For all this action, today nearly one human in six does still not get enough food to lead a healthy and active life (United Nations World Food Programme 2010). What happened? One problem was intimately linked to trade governance: rich country farm subsidies and tariffs pushed down prices and weakened incentives for developing country governments or the private sector to invest in agricultural production, and to build roads and the other rural infrastructure necessary to support it. The Uruguay Round trade talks, which brought agricultural tariffs and subsidies firmly into the scope of multilateral trade rules, failed to correct these practices. Decades of low productivity and low farm prices pushed many small farmers in developing countries to look for other sources of income. In the process, they became net buyers of food. So when food prices rose in 2007–8, driven by high fuel costs, demand growth, supply shocks, export bans and the diversion of crops into biofuel production, these farmers were caught in the middle (ICTSD 2008a).

Before elaborating some principles that could help guide more effective institutional policy-making and coordination, two points about global governance in general bear examination.

First, global governance is viscerally linked to domestic policies. One of the looming threats to trade harmony comes from global financial imbalances, which owe much to national policies in surplus and deficit countries. A political climate in the United States supportive of strong action on climate change would have been hugely beneficial to the UNFCCC talks. Leadership and political courage is vital. But public attitudes too need to shift. Jean-Claude Juncker, a politician from Luxembourg, has summed up the lawmakers' dilemma: 'We all know what to do, but we don't know how to get re-elected once we have done it' (The Economist 2010a).

Second, we cannot pretend to look at trade governance processes in clinical isolation from the broader challenges facing multilateral governance. Modern international institutions must operate in circumstances they have never had to confront: an increasingly multipolar world. The Doha Round would have been far easier to conclude had one group of countries been able to impose its will upon the others (although the terms of such an agreement might have left much to be desired). In addition, the worst financial and economic crisis in decades has devastated some of our core assumptions about the global economy, thus further complicating multilateral coordination. Scholars have identified how 'dominant ideas' can shape states' behaviours, with the belief in Keynesian macroeconomics and later in monetarist principles affecting the creation of international economic institutions and then the way states coordinated policies within them (Milner 1998). Today, with a generation's orthodoxies discredited, major powers disagree on fundamental aspects of how economies should be organized. *Foreign Affairs* runs headlines such as 'State Capitalism Comes of Age: The End of the Free Market?' (Bremmer 2009). International regimes are hard to develop when actors' expectations do not converge.

'Policy coherence' is a phrase that is used too much and followed too little, at least in terms of making sure that the full suite of a government's policies support sustainable development. But it is a concept to which we must return. Our collective failure, over the past decade, to produce global public goods such as updated multilateral trade rules that respond better to poor countries' needs, or curbed greenhouse gas emissions, has been due at least in part to an inadequacy of what some have called 'cosmopolitics' – 'global political action transcending a strict state-to-state, or multilateral, basis' (Charnovitz 2002: 299). Despite the glimmers of cosmopolitics visible in the emerging global civil society, the dismal state of global cooperation suggests that 'cosmopolitical institutionalism' may be a lot to hope for at this juncture, notwithstanding the existence of proposals for formally linking trade and environmental institutions. We therefore focus on more modest suggestions, starting with policy coherence.

1.4 The government leadership gap

The rules and practices embodied in the multilateral trading system offer governments ample potential to take helpful action on current and future challenges linked to sustainable development – it is just that they have not yet taken advantage of it.

Making trade governance more supportive of sustainable development will require the behaviour of individual governments to change. We do not pretend that governance is the sole province of governments, and that citizens and transnational communities affected by cross-border policymaking deserve no say in how those policies are shaped. Global public policy networks bringing together civil society, business, international organizations and governments have done sterling work on several global challenges, from public health to environmental protection and corruption. But trade institutions remain a largely intergovernmental enterprise. Moreover, the 'legislative' or rule-making function of the WTO and other trade institutions is likely to remain that way. On the other hand, outside input into their 'ideational' function – identifying which issues to discuss, and potential solutions – would be desirable, especially from non-traditional sources (i.e. those other than business). But here too, governments will play a central role. Even if a 'trisectoral network' analogous to the World Commission on Dams[10] were created to bring governmental, business and civil society together to think through problems facing the trading system, an idea raised by Keohane, any eventual recommendations would have trouble getting heard at the WTO unless the initiative had received member governments' blessing (Keohane 2002: 239).

As we have seen, the stances governments take domestically and in different international institutions are already influenced by the institutions themselves. But they will also be shaped by how governments formulate them, the partnerships they build to incorporate input from relevant stakeholders in business and civil society, and the alliances they strike among each other. It may be useful for governments to set up mechanisms with representation from all relevant ministries and civil society for regularly evaluating the coherence of positions taken in different trade-related international fora. Some governments already do this via regular interdepartmental consultations (Halle and Wolfe 2007).

A continuing black mark for the trading system is the vast inequality in the capacity of governments to assess their own needs and fully engage in the WTO and other trade institutions. While there are no quick and easy solutions to this, making the system more inclusive would help enhance its legitimacy.

The following three sections set out our proposals for making trade governance more supportive of sustainable development. Section 2 looks at action that governments could take within trade institutions, particularly the WTO. Section 3 considers how international institutions might be made to interact more constructively, in a manner less taxing for developing countries. In section 4, we propose some steps governments could take outside trade institutions to boost the trading system's contribution to sustainable development.

2 Proposals: creative action within trade institutions

In this section, we focus our suggestions primarily on the WTO, but make some observations about bilateral and regional trade agreements

[10] Information on the World Commission on Dams can be found at www.dams.org/ [accessed in November 2010].

as well. We believe that some existing WTO mechanisms could be fairly easily modified to identify sustainable development concerns and boost accountability to the public (section 2.1). Beyond that, we think WTO Members would do well to build on existing provisions – such as those for subsidies or for special and differential treatment for developing countries – to make them more effective and supportive of environmental and developmental goals (section 2.2). Looking ahead, WTO Members could act within the framework of the multilateral system to anticipate potential challenges to trade governance that might arise from governments' pursuit of sustainable development, enabling a nimble response (section 2.3).

2.1 *Modify existing mechanisms and practices*

2.1.1 The WTO Trade Policy Review Mechanism

The WTO's Trade Policy Review Mechanism (TPRM) provides a detailed examination of each member's trade policies and practices, and the opportunity for other governments to provide feedback to them. Reviews include a report prepared by WTO secretariat economists, including their views on trade policy reforms that could better contribute to the member's growth and development.[11]

The WTO Trade Policy Review Mechanism's mandate, set out in Annex 3 of the Marrakesh Agreement, is to contribute to 'the smoother functioning of the multilateral trading system' (WTO 1994b). But the reviews are also supposed to take place 'to the extent relevant, against the background of the wider economic and developmental needs, policies and objectives of the Member concerned, as well as of its external environment'.

Tweaking the Trade Policy Reviews to consider environmental and developmental factors in its assessment would make the mechanism a useful tool for sustainable development policy-making.[12] Currently, reviews mention environmental considerations primarily in the context of trade measures justified on environmental grounds, such as import and export restrictions or taxes. Robert Wolfe (2007) has suggested that the Trade Policy Review Mechanism could receive input from the United

[11] Information on the Trade Policy Review Mechanisms, its origins, terms of reference and the library of its reports since inception, can be found at www.wto.org/english/tratop_e/tpr_e/tpr_e.htm [accessed in November 2010].

[12] For a critical review of the TPRM and its functioning, see Ghosh (2010).

Nations Environment Programme (UNEP) and the International Labour Organization (ILO), and look at how trade is affecting employment and the environment, and suggest potential complementary policy measures that could help offset any negative effects. For instance, if increased farm exports are driving deforestation, the report could note this and suggest that the government re-examine land use laws. Members would have little to fear: the Trade Policy Review Mechanism's advice is non-binding, anyway. An alternative would be to set up an independent body to subject countries' environmental policies and needs to a review process comparable to that for trade. Sylvia Ostry (2004) has proposed modifying the Trade Policy Review Mechanism to consider countries' domestic trade policy-making processes.

2.1.2 Dispute settlement

Public participation in the dispute settlement process has evolved greatly since the WTO's creation. A number of dispute panel proceedings have been opened to the public, at the behest of participating countries. The Appellate Body has said that panels have the choice, though not the obligation, to accept and consider unsolicited *amicus curiae* 'friends of the court' briefs from outside groups with expertise on the public interest implications of the case at issue. The original WTO dispute settlement rules did not even contemplate the possibility of such briefs (Petersmann 2007b).

One option might be for WTO Members to adopt open panel proceedings as the default option, unless vetoed by a party to the dispute. Panels could be empowered to invite input from the secretariats of multilateral environmental agreements (MEAs) if relevant environmental issues in a trade dispute are the subject of an MEA. A formal agreement, however, might actually turn out to be less open than the informal status quo as it has evolved.

Even if WTO Members stick to the (acceptable) status quo, they would do well to reach understandings about potential trade disputes arising from specific high-profile issues. WTO meetings are no longer besieged by turtle-costumed demonstrators. But a dispute over the WTO-compliance of 'border carbon adjustments' introduced by one member to offset the presumed climate inaction of others would bring the protesters back with a vengeance. All countries who wish the WTO system well should recognize that allowing critics to doze off while watching panel meetings would be better for the institution than forcing them to fulminate outside closed doors.

2.2 *Build on existing rules*

2.2.1 Subsidies

The WTO Agreement on Subsidies and Countervailing Measures (SCM) sets out a detailed framework regulating governments' use of non-agricultural subsidies. It prohibits several types of subsidies, such as those linked to export performance or the use of domestic inputs instead of imported ones. Other subsidies are permitted unless another country can show that the subsidy has an adverse effect on its interests. The agreement defines subsidies, and provides rules for determining whether they are causing 'injury' elsewhere.

The mandate for the Doha Round negotiations called on members to 'clarify and improve' subsidy rules for agriculture, services and fisheries support. WTO Members could do the same for energy subsidies. The Global Subsidies Initiative (GSI) of the International Institute for Sustainable Development (IISD) estimates subsidies to fossil fuels at around US$600 billion per year, of which about US$100 billion goes to producers. Many of these payments damage the environment, entailing considerable economic costs down the road. Cutting the subsidies would help reduce greenhouse gas emissions and free up taxpayers' money (based on GSI 2010). The absence of an international framework for regularly monitoring these subsidies makes precise figures impossible to know. Creating a framework for identifying and quantifying subsidies, and classifying them based on environmental and social impacts (some of these subsidies are aimed at making fuel consumption affordable for the poor), would be a good start.

Sadeq Bigdeli has argued that provisions in the SCM Agreement could be interpreted to already require WTO Members to notify energy subsidies.[13] The problem is the fact that governments have not been good about meeting notification requirements (Bigdeli 2008: 85–6). He calls for the establishment of a 'subsidy watch' subcommittee that would work with organizations such as the International Energy Agency (IEA), the UNEP and the UNFCCC to examine whether members' energy subsidy notifications accurately represent the real level of support provided. Bigdeli notes

[13] Article 2.1 of the SCM Agreement says that subsidies are 'specific' if they are provided to 'an enterprise or industry or group of enterprises or industries (referred to in this Agreement as "certain enterprises") within their jurisdiction of the granting authority', but not to others. Article 25.2 requires members to, inter alia, 'notify any subsidy as defined in paragraph 1 of Article 1, which is specific within the meaning of Article 2, granted or maintained within their territories'.

that the SCM Agreement already empowers members to create such a body. Article 24.2 authorizes the Committee on Subsidies and Countervailing Measures to 'set up subsidiary bodies as appropriate'. Article 24.5 specifies that 'the Committee and any subsidiary bodies may consult with and seek information from any source they deem appropriate'.

A WTO initiative on energy subsidies would do well to have a component on transparency in government support to the clean energy industry. The billions of dollars that governments are spending on attempts to create 'green jobs' are welcome. But neither taxpayers nor the atmosphere would be well served if the wave of largesse produces bloated companies that compete less on their own merits than on their success at tapping into the public dole. Transparency can only help.

In addition, WTO Members could reinvent the 'Permanent Group of Experts' (PGE) set up by the SCM Agreement to look at energy subsidies. The PGE, 'composed of five independent persons, highly qualified in the fields of subsidies and trade relations', is supposed to be available to assist dispute panels, and to provide the committee or individual members with an 'advisory opinion on the existence and nature of any subsidy'. However, the PGE has never been called upon to do any of those tasks (Vis-Dunbar 2006).

Governments could transform the PGE into a 'Permanent Group of Experts on Energy Subsidies and Sustainable Development' composed of independent experts highly qualified in the fields of subsidies, environmental protection, social welfare and trade relations. One issue that should be high on its agenda is the subsidy implications of free emissions allowances granted to some sections of industry under cap-and-trade schemes. Further, environmental non-governmental organizations (NGOs) have in the past played a crucial role in drawing public and policy-makers' attention to the negative effects of various subsidies (Steenblik 1998). They could play a constructive role in turning the spotlight onto energy subsidies, which would in turn feed into a WTO discussion. The GSI has already been doing yeoman work at drawing attention to the amounts of public money that support unclean energy.

2.2.2 Special and differential treatment: modulated rules

The first few years of the Doha Round negotiations on making WTO provisions for special and differential treatment (SDT) 'more precise, effective and operational' were bedevilled by arguments about 'differentiation' among the developing country beneficiaries. Developed countries were wary of granting a country such as Kenya greater policy flexibility within WTO rules if it meant doing the same for Brazil or even Korea. This resistance held back the necessary task of re-imagining SDT within the WTO system, which had hitherto been limited to ineffective time-based extensions for poorer countries to implement obligations (Meléndez-Ortiz and Delhavi 2000).

But now, de facto differentiation among non-LDC (least developed countries) developing countries has clearly emerged in the Doha Round. The negotiations on industrial goods and agriculture foresee gentler tariff cuts for small and vulnerable economies (SVEs) and some other categories of non-LDCs (see, for example, WTO 2008).[14] This is a sort of enhanced SDT, to be sure, but there have been no corresponding moves to explore how WTO strictures on investment, subsidies, tariffs and intellectual property might be relaxed for this de facto new class of poorer or small developing countries (there has been some movement on doing so for LDCs; see Annex F of the Hong Kong Ministerial Declaration, WTO 2005).

Whether this de facto subgroup of non-LDCs should be seen as limited to SVEs, which account for less than 0.1 per cent of world trade, or to include some other countries, such as the fairly poor WTO Members with binding caps on a low number of tariff lines, is an open question. But WTO Members could use the emergence of developing country subgroups to experiment with new, deepened SDT provisions that would restore to beneficiaries an expanded policy toolkit through which to pursue sustainable development goals like food security and the creation of productive industrial capacity.

Developing countries have long resisted attempts to classify them into subgroups at the WTO, fearing a 'divide and rule' outcome that would weaken their ability to make common cause. But there are good reasons to alter this stance. Most of the SVEs are countries that have struggled to take advantage of opportunities presented by the multilateral trading system. They are too small to trigger subsidy competition or have any great effect on world markets. Countries like Brazil, India and China can in any case hardly argue that their existing WTO commitments have been a straitjacket on growth. These countries have become necessary pillars of a predictable, rules-based trading system. More understandable opposition

[14] The NAMA text, which also provides for special tariff treatment for some recently acceded members and the generally poorer countries with binding caps on a low number of tariff lines, defines SVEs as those accounting for less than '0.1 per cent of world NAMA trade for the reference period of 1999 to 2001'. A WTO Document issued in 2005 (WTO, TN/MA,/S/18, 2005) lists WTO Members' shares in world trade. Countries like Kenya, Jordan, Mauritius fall below the 0.1 per cent threshold for the period from 1999 to 2001, while the Philippines, Costa Rica, Colombia, Peru and Tunisia exceed it.

to differentiating among developing countries would come from countries just big enough not to qualify for the subgroup, especially those reliant on exports of a single primary commodity. They would fear a loss of competitiveness vis-à-vis countries at comparable wealth levels relieved of obligations to which they would still have to adhere.

An alternative approach would be to develop indicators for measuring WTO Members' integration into the global economy, and make deepened SDT available to countries that have failed to break into world markets for manufactured exports, the traditional first step out of poverty (Meléndez-Ortiz and Delhavi 2000; Collier 2007).[15] Graduation criteria could be developed to progressively withdraw enhanced policy flexibility if and when a member gains a foothold in international markets. Eligible countries could notify the WTO about whether or not they want to take advantage of these provisions. Some may choose not to for fear that signs of policy uncertainty will discourage foreign or domestic investment. Conditioning WTO treatment on the basis of objective criteria has a precedent in the Doha Round negotiations, where developing countries will slate some farm products for lower-than-normal tariff cuts on the basis of food and livelihood security and rural development concerns. A controversial innovation in the trade system aimed at addressing particular situations may well prove to be effective as a response to sustainability requirements.

We do not pretend that picking winners, raising tariffs, subsidizing exports or imposing performance requirements on foreign investors will automatically lead to industrial development. Economists continue to disagree on the medium-term and welfare effects of such policies. Alex Keck and Patrick Low, for instance, demonstrate that these classic measures of the interventionist developmental state can have the opposite of the intended effect (Keck and Low 2004). And even supporters of industrial policy recognize that picking winners needs a particular set of conditions to be successful – conditions that are hardly available to all countries at

[15] While he may be horrified by it, this suggestion owes much to Paul Collier (2007). Collier observes that Asia's success at breaking into world markets has ironically made it harder for Africa to do so, since the gap in the cost of production between Africa and Asia is much smaller than the gap was between Asia and the West when manufacturing first started setting up in Asia. As a remedy, he calls for OECD countries to grant temporary duty-free access for exports from all African countries, not just LDCs. The whole point, he says, is to get some African countries a foothold in global export markets – and the non-LDCs like Kenya and Ghana would have the best shot. We think this would be worth trying, and borrow the logic to argue that it is countries that lack a presence in the global market for manufactures that might benefit from increased policy space.

all times. This is why instances of successful interventionist states, like South Korea, have been the exception rather than the rule (Keck and Low 2004; Chang 2010). Yet it is also clear that the status quo has not helped a significant number of developing country WTO Members spur the development of competitive industries. Giving developing countries the option of greater freedom to chart and change their own policy course, whether laissez-faire or interventionist, could lead to many policy disasters, with investors scared or confused, nascent industries that are coddled and inefficient, and agricultural policies that are thoroughly botched. But it might lead to some successes. Policy space is like rope: you can use it to escape from prison or to hang yourself.[16]

2.3 Create spaces within institutions to address future challenges

After over a decade of either trying to launch a trade round or conclude one, WTO Members have developed the bad habit of only forging agreements on any issue in the context of trade-offs arising from a comprehensive negotiation. Governments have not made full use of the WTO's institutional apparatus to discuss and try to defuse irritants. This is a dangerous symptom: if countries are unwilling to act nimbly to respond to new challenges within economic governance institutions, those institutions will eventually drift towards irrelevance.

The trade and the environment relationship underlines the opportunities missed. The WTO's early years were marked by considerable anxiety about the relationship between multilateral trade rules and environmental goals. (The Doha Round negotiations on the issue have been inconclusive, although as we saw above, the Appellate Body has gone some way to assuage those concerns.) Today, new fears have arisen: many trade observers worry that, having avoided protectionism during the worst of the financial crisis, the world could blunder into tit-for-tat retaliation as a result of unilateral trade restrictions imposed in the name of fighting climate change (Levi 2009). Less apocalyptically, things like carbon labelling and 'food miles' have considerable ramifications for developing countries' export prospects (ICTSD 2008b). Intellectual property rights have become the subject of a polarized debate over the need to promote the widespread diffusion of new green technologies (ICTSD 2008c).

But WTO Members have a forum and indeed a mandate to address such challenges – they just fail to use it. The April 1994 Ministerial Decision

[16] Original thinking on the notion of policy space can be found in Corrales-Leal (2007).

on Trade and Environment instructed the WTO General Council to establish a Committee on Trade and Environment (CTE) with terms of reference that included 'identify[ing] the relationship between trade measures and environmental measures in order to promote sustainable development' and 'mak[ing] appropriate recommendations on whether any modifications of the provisions of the multilateral trading system are required' to encourage 'positive interaction' between trade and environmental measures, to avoid protectionism, to ensure the responsiveness of the multilateral trading system to environmental objectives set forth in Agenda 21 and the Rio Declaration, and to monitor trade measures used for environmental purposes (WTO 1994a).

The CTE was directed to start work on the following issues, a list that deserves to be quoted at length:

> the relationship between the provisions of the multilateral trading system and trade measures for environmental purposes, including those pursuant to multilateral environmental agreements;
>
> the relationship between environmental policies relevant to trade and environmental measures with significant trade effects and the provisions of the multilateral trading system;
>
> the relationship between the provisions of the multilateral trading system and:
>
> 1) charges and taxes for environmental purposes;
> 2) requirements for environmental purposes relating to products, including standards and technical regulations, packaging, labelling and recycling;
>
> the provisions of the multilateral trading system with respect to the transparency of trade measures used for environmental purposes and environmental measures and requirements which have significant trade effects;
>
> the relationship between the dispute settlement mechanisms in the multilateral trading system and those found in multilateral environmental agreements;
>
> the effect of environmental measures on market access, especially in relation to developing countries, in particular to the least developed among them, and environmental benefits of removing trade restrictions and distortions ...

Another 'integral part' of the committee's work was to examine trade in services and the relevant provisions of the Agreement on Trade-Related Aspects of Intellectual Property Rights (TRIPS).

The language in the CTE's original mandate covers virtually every aspect of the trade and climate change debate. But instead of addressing the matter inside the WTO, governments have preferred to throw around threats of tariffs and litigation. This is unfortunate. Former WTO Appellate Body chair James Bacchus has warned that 'the world does not have the time to await judgments on disputes about the potential conflicts between trade and climate change on a case-by-case basis … [and] leaving WTO jurists to judge such disputes on a case-by-case basis may result in a perilous political overload of the WTO dispute settlement system' (Bacchus 2010).

2.4 Create a WTO subcommittee on trade and climate change

With prospects weak for a multilateral climate deal, global policy action on curbing greenhouse gas emissions has shifted to the national level. In many industrialized countries, fears are growing that unilateral emissions cuts could compromise industrial competitiveness and simply drive polluting industries to flee to less regulated jurisdictions (a phenomenon called 'carbon leakage'). These concerns have led to calls for border carbon adjustments (BCA) – taxes or other charges on imports from carbon-unrestrained countries – to 'level the carbon playing field'.[17] As the presumed target of unilateral border carbon adjustments, it would be in developing countries' interest to start a conversation on trade and climate change at the WTO.

An open-ended conversation about climate-related trade measures would not automatically legitimize them. It might even help defang the issue in political discourse in the United States, by enabling lawmakers clamouring for tariffs to offset perceived competitiveness losses to be told 'Hold your horses, they're working on this at the WTO'.[18] More seriously, a subcommittee of the CTE dedicated to trade and climate change would afford developing countries an opportunity to define the terms of the debate and to try to ensure that it stays evidence-based. The 'carbon leakage' debate is already showing dangerous signs of being captured by protectionist sections of industry. The European Commission has deemed no less than 164 industrial sectors and subsectors to be exposed to a 'significant risk of carbon leakage', including the production of wine, bicycles and underwear. Not only does this go well beyond the trade-exposed, energy-intensive sectors identified by most experts, namely steel, glass,

[17] A trade policy analysis of the claims is provided by Hufbauer *et al.* (2009). On the claims by European industry see Burniaux *et al.* (2010).

[18] See an analysis of the debate in the USA in Stavins (2010).

cement, aluminium, paper, pulp and chemicals, the Commission's list largely matches the list of Europe's main users of WTO trade remedies (Messerlin 2010).

In this subcommittee, WTO Members could discuss the latest research on the trade-climate change interface. For instance, while the political economy in favour of BCAs is clear, the economic and environmental rationale remains unproven. A recent OECD study suggests that BCAs would not restrain the output losses incurred by domestic energy-intensive industries as a result of carbon curbs, because they rely to a significant extent on carbon-intensive intermediates produced elsewhere in the world (Burniaux *et al.* 2010). Depending on how they are structured, border tax regimes on carbon-intensive products could lead to a fall-off in trade comparable to that at the worst of the global financial and economic crisis of 2008–9, according to some projections (Messerlin 2010).

Members may also review the growing number of ideas for how to address the relationship in a rules-based manner consistent with the WTO's core principle of non-discrimination. Options countries might choose to examine could include: 1) negotiating a plurilateral code delineating rules for a policy space in which participating countries could take emissions curbing measures, without fear of becoming the target of disputes (Hufbauer *et al.* 2009); 2) allowing members to offset carbon taxes at the border the way value-added taxes have been for decades, but prohibiting tariffs levied on selected countries on the basis of their carbon policies (Messerlin 2010); Daniel Esty has suggested a graduated move towards a common global carbon price over the next few decades (rich countries get there first, followed by large developing countries), with the possibility of eventual trade sanctions for countries that do not comply (Esty 2010); 3) a 'waiver' to depart from WTO obligations for specified actions to deal with the threat of climate change (Bacchus 2010); 4) a moratorium on border carbon adjustments while national and international climate policies take shape; 5) the subsidy effects of free allocation allowances (see above); 6) whether special rules for intellectual property are needed to best promote the innovation and diffusion of green technologies; or 7) whether WTO Members could work together on standards harmonization for such technologies. In theory, members could use this subcommittee to negotiate shared understandings and interpretive agreements about WTO rules and their relationship to climate policy, thus reducing the potential for damaging uncooperative action.

2.5 *Create a 'Functioning of the WTO System' group*

WTO Members could create a standing body to review the functioning of the multilateral trading system, in effect institutionalizing the process of thinking about the WTO's functioning as an institution. A key priority of such a body would be to assess the trading system's functioning through the prism of sustainable development.

Commenting on the shortcomings of the Uruguay Round's 'Functioning of the GATT System' (FOGS) negotiating set-up, Thomas Cottier said the group was 'neither appropriate nor sufficient to discuss innovation'. Building on research conducted under the auspices of the International Law Association (ILA), he suggests that a new version at the WTO have a two-tier structure: the first would operate 'as a think tank, a forum of expertise, information-exchange and non-hierarchical deliberation between government and academia', while the second would be 'mandated to negotiate and prepare political decisions in the field' (Cottier 2007).[19] Such a system could conceivably provide a valuable opening for civil society to participate in the 'ideational' agenda-setting aspect of the WTO's work.[20]

Bilateral and regional trade agreements would also benefit from an analogous process – a periodic review, involving government and non-governmental actors, of the functioning of each accord and its provisions. The reviews could identify rules that were not delivering on sustainable development, and recommend re-negotiation.[21] If intellectual property protections in the agreement were found to be harming public health, they could be relaxed. Parties to comprehensive bilateral trade agreements

[19] Gary Sampson called for creating a 'functioning of the WTO system group' in Petersmann (2004: 233–48; 282–96).

[20] 'Ideational' as discussed in Section 1.4.

[21] This idea of reviewing the performance of rules and trade arrangements against explicitly proclaimed or shared public policy goals is not new – what's novel is the notion of actually modifying provisions or agreements in light of review, which is hardly ever done. On this question, several of the Uruguay Round Agreements as well as various regional trade agreements include provisions and mechanisms for review. From a sustainability perspective, the late 1990s saw a heated debate on the inclusion of mandatory provisions to undertake sustainability impact assessment (SIA) of trade agreements and of trade negotiations. The 2001 Doha Ministerial failed to agree to hard-wired language on it but still mandated something vague in this regard as an exercise to be undertaken prior to conclusion. (See WTO 2001: para. 51 that reads: '51. The Committee on Trade and Development and the Committee on Trade and Environment shall, within their respective mandates, each act as a forum to identify and debate developmental and environmental aspects of the negotiations, in order to help achieve the objective of having

could alter the investment provisions so that they cannot be used as a sword against legitimate health and environmental negotiations.

2.6 Build quid pro quos to meet northern priorities, southern needs

Developing countries should work with developed ones to build pro-sustainable development quid pro quos into trade agreements. For instance, a poor nation might agree to certain environmental provisions in a bilateral trade deal with a northern one – with a proviso that it would only be obliged to enforce those provisions once its richer partner provided it with the funds, technical assistance and capacity to do so (Halle and Meléndez-Ortiz 2007). This could prove doubly beneficial in cases where the developing country's key exports are associated with heavy local pollution.

Services trade is another area that offers potential for pro-development quid pro quos. Regulation is critical to realizing the benefits of open services markets, as well as for managing impacts that arise from liberalization. Yet building regulatory capacity is expensive and particularly intricate; virtually all countries organize governance of their services economy on a sectoral basis. Many have historically delegated normalization and regulation to private associations and most developing countries lack institutional infrastructure in the form of regulatory and supervisory bodies. Yet, the services economy has become for many the main segment of economic activity. Linking openness of services sectors to trade-related technical assistance and capacity-building that focuses on institutions could help exporters access new markets while helping people in developing countries benefit from open, yet well-regulated services markets (Sauvé 2008). The WTO has a clear precedent for such quid pro quos. The mandate for the Doha Round negotiations

sustainable development appropriately reflected.') In the context of the North America Free Trade Agreement (NAFTA) the environmental side arrangements established a trilateral mechanism, the Commission for Environmental Cooperation, which has been performing environmental assessment of various aspects of the implementation of the NAFTA and is currently now embarked in its post-NAFTA phase; see www.cec.org/Page.asp?PageID=924&SiteNodeID=588 [accessed in November 2010]. And the European Commission has adopted an ambitious and far-extended exercise to carry out SIAs of all trade negotiations in which it engages. A critical and fascinating review of the origin, methodological musings and the experience in implementing such an approach can be found in Kirkpatrick and George (2007).

on trade facilitation would not require developing and least developed countries to implement some commitments if they did not receive the aid they needed to do so (WTO 2004).

3 Institutional discipline for sustainable development policy

Complementing the policy incoherence of individual governments is a collective tendency to deal with the same issue in different international fora in a varying, uncoordinated manner.

It is natural, indeed desirable, for issues to receive attention in a variety of relevant institutions. But governments should be clear about what they wish to achieve within each forum. A failure to do so leads to forum shopping and a sort of 'pass the parcel' in which opponents of a particular policy goal try to shunt it off to be dealt with in a different institution. Developing countries, with their more limited negotiating capacity and hence ability to participate actively in different institutions, are automatically disadvantaged by forum shifting.

A case in point is international policy action to regulate the use of genetic resources and traditional knowledge, a key aspect of building incentives for the protection of biodiversity. In negotiations at the WTO, a large majority of developing countries have argued that fighting biopiracy demands nothing less than amending the WTO's TRIPS Agreement to require patent applicants to disclose any genetic resources or traditional knowledge used in their invention, along with evidence of prior consent and benefit-sharing. For years, many developed countries said that the issue should be addressed in the World Intellectual Property Organization (WIPO), which had its own mandate to discuss traditional knowledge, folklore and genetic resources (ICTSD 2006).[22] For good measure, governments have been negotiating a binding international regime on 'access and benefit sharing' – the terms under which genetic resources, whether plant, animal or microorganism, are accessed in countries of origin, and the benefits that result from their use by academics or private companies are shared with the people or countries that provide them – under the Convention on Biological Diversity (CBD).

[22] The EU and Switzerland came around to the TRIPS amendment camp in summer 2008, in return for support from the developing country backers of that proposal for extending special 'geographical indication' protections beyond wines and spirits to cover foods with place-linked names, like Parma ham (WTO 2008).

Daniel Bradlow, a law professor, recently argued that '[i]nternational economic governance cannot function efficiently unless its various institutions have a limited and specialised mandate' (Bradlow 2010). He reiterated long-standing calls for the establishment of a mechanism for facilitating coordination between international economic governance institutions and other organizations and arrangements involved in global governance. Such coordination is a worthy goal, but in the short run, governments should at least work with each other to arrive at a sort of 'institutional subsidiarity'. By subsidiarity, we mean that issues should be discussed wherever relevant, but with specific decisions to be negotiated in the institution most appropriate to do so. But the utility of such subsidiarity is contingent on sustainable development-friendly outcomes in each forum. Subsidiarity for its own sake could even be counterproductive. Developing countries have raised intellectual property issues at the World Health Organization (WHO) in part because they were not confident that satisfactory outcomes would come out of WIPO, the UN system's specialized body for dealing with intellectual property. WIPO, they have felt, was beholden to the patent-holders that fund it. Moreover, it had stayed disengaged during the heated debate over the links between TRIPS and public health. In addition, many were dissatisfied with WIPO's technical assistance on TRIPS implementation, and felt that it did not adequately address how to take advantage of flexibilities in the rules for the public interest.[23]

In the case of genetic resources and traditional knowledge, governments could act at the WTO to amend the TRIPS Agreement, which provides the global baseline for patent rules, to include a genetic resources disclosure requirement for patent applicants. At the CBD, they could finalize a protocol spelling out the rules guiding access to those genetic resources, as well as the sharing of benefits that arise from them. WIPO could focus on an instrument to protect folklore and traditional cultural expressions, while also serving as a repository for best practices on the protection of genetic resources.

4 Leverage other arenas to help trade governance support sustainable development

Issue-specific cooperation outside trade-related institutions could amplify the contribution that trade governance could make to sustainable

[23] Interview with former Egyptian negotiator, ICTSD, 4 October 2010, record on file with authors. For a comprehensive critical review of the developing countries' evolving stance on intellectual property, see Deere (2008).

development. We have already said that governments should take a wide range of views into consideration when formulating positions to take in trade institutions. At the same time, they should ask themselves 'What is the ultimate goal of this? What policy action elsewhere might help us reach that goal?' Some examples follow, focusing on issues of food security and environmental goods.

When discussing food security above, we highlighted the deleterious effects of rich country farm subsidies on incentives for rural investment in poor nations, and pointed to the need in upcoming decades for the world to produce much more food from much less soil, water and air. While continuing the slow process of disciplining and reducing subsidies inside the WTO, OECD governments could act outside it to agree to a sort of 'tax' on farm subsidies, with the proceeds directed at funding agricultural research and development and extension services in developing countries (Biswas 2010). Calculations could be based on OECD estimates of producer support – some US$252.5 billion in 2009 (OECD 2010). An alternative baseline could be the bound limit for trade-distorting support committed to by rich WTO Members (Meléndez-Ortiz *et al.* 2009).

Money thus raised could go to existing international and national research bodies, as well as to government and non-governmental extension services programmes. One option for funding agricultural extension services would be to contribute part of the farm subsidy tax to the new Global Agriculture and Food Security Program (GAFSP), which was set up in April 2010 with funding from some governments and the Gates Foundation with the goal of targeting poor farmers and assisting them in improving the efficiency of their farming techniques.[24] Another alternative would be to establish a Global Fund for Food on the model of the existing fund for HIV/AIDS, tuberculosis and malaria: part of the subsidy tax could go into this pot (open to other donors), which would be used to finance projects proposed by developing countries and validated as useful by scientific experts. Having to pay extra for the privilege of subsidizing would hopefully make governments think twice about lavish farm programmes (and their international consequences). Investing a share of subsidy money directly in boosting agricultural productivity in developing countries would amplify the effects of the WTO's subsidy reform process. A farm subsidy tax may be wishful thinking. But a different trade issue with direct ramifications for food security – agricultural export bans – will be impossible to address without serious complementary policies.

[24] For more information on the GAFSP, please see its website at www.gafspfund.org/gafsp/ [accessed in November 2010].

The WTO is the appropriate forum for governments to negotiate disciplines on the use of agricultural export bans (although Russia, a major wheat exporter, is not yet a WTO Member). Sudden bans of farm exports are not good policy-making: not only do they 'starve your neighbour', in the phrase of Joachim von Braun, a former IFPRI director, they discourage investment to raise future production (Reuters 2008). But export bans do make a lot of sense to a government faced with rioters demanding cheaper food. Similarly, growing rice in solar-powered greenhouses, fed by groundwater and cooled with seawater, seems preposterous from both a cost standpoint and an environmental one. But Djibouti started doing it when it felt that it could no longer trust world markets for its food supply (Martin 2008). For farm exporters to even consider curtailing their ability to cut off exports, they would need to be confident that funding would be available to them to buy food on world markets even in the event of a major spike in prices. Sanctimoniously scolding farm exporters about scaring away investors will not help. One potential vehicle for such a funding mechanism would be the World Bank.

Action outside the WTO could enhance the sustainable development effects of the Doha Round talks to liberalize trade in environmental goods and services. Empirical research in the renewable energy sector suggests that tariffs are just one in many factors determining whether companies choose to invest in green technology (Jha 2009). Other policies, such as 'feed-in tariffs' guaranteeing a price for renewable electricity, subsidies for components and the use of renewable energy tax breaks, matter at least as much. If a group of governments got together and cooperated on these other factors – for instance, by harmonizing standards or making them interoperable, and establishing incentives for the sharing of trade secrets linked to green technology – it would substantially expand the market for environmental goods.

5 Closing remarks: the imperative of political will

No international policy process can replace the apparent unwillingness or inability of governments to pursue sustainable development policies at home, and to cooperate with each other to promote sustainable development globally. Creating new committees at the WTO will not help if they turn into empty talk shops in which countries do not even try to reach shared understandings. The Doha Round talks remind us that starting development-oriented negotiations is not the same as concluding them.

Multilateral deadlock has revived hopes for plurilateral action to reanimate cooperation on trade and environmental issues. But simply moving to smaller, more exclusive fora will not solve the problem that bedevils the multilateral arena: disagreement among major governments. Global sustainability challenges require coalitions of the relevant, not just coalitions of the willing. In the end, process matters, but results matter more. The trading system can help the pursuit of sustainable development, but only if governments want it to, and publics compel them to do so. The proof of the pudding, when it comes to sustainable development, is not just in the eating. It is in whether there is enough left for our grandchildren.

References

Agarwal, A. and Narain, S. 1991. *Global Warming in an Unequal World: A Case of Environmental Colonialism*. New Delhi: Centre for Science and the Environment.

Aldy, J. and Stavins, R. (eds.) 2009. *Post-Kyoto International Climate Policy: Summary for Policymakers*. Cambridge University Press.

Bacchus, J. 2010. *Questions in Search of Answers: Trade, Climate Change, and the Rule of Law*. Keynote address to conference on 'Climate Change, Trade and Competitiveness: Issues for the WTO' at the WTO, Geneva, 16 June.

Barton, J., Goldstein, J., Josling, T. and Steinberg, R. 2008. *The Evolution of the Trade Regime: Politics, Law, and Economics of the GATT and the WTO*. Princeton University Press.

Bigdeli, S. 2008. 'Will the "Friends of Climate" Emerge in the WTO? The Prospects of Applying the "Fisheries Subsidies" Model to Energy Subsidies', *The Carbon and Climate Law Review* 2(1): 78–88.

Biswas, T. 2010. 'Let's counter the damage of subsidies', letter to the *Financial Times*, 8 September.

Bradlow, D. 2010. 'Reforming Global Economic Governance: A Strategy for Middle Powers in the G20', Voxeu.org, 13 August. www.voxeu.org/index.php?q=node/5403 [Accessed in November 2010].

Bremmer, I. 2009. 'State Capitalism Comes of Age: The End of the Free Market?' *Foreign Affairs*, May/June.

Burniaux, J.-M., Château, J. and Duval, R. 2010. *Is There a Case for Carbon-based Border Tax Adjustment? An Applied General Equilibrium Analysis*. OECD Economics Department Working Paper No. 794. Paris: Organisation of Economic Cooperation and Development (OECD).

Chang, H.-J. 2010. *Twenty-Three Things They Don't Tell You About Capitalism*. London: Allen Lane, Penguin Press.

Chang, S. 2003. 'WTO Disciplines on Fisheries Subsidies: A Historic Step Towards Sustainability?' *Journal of International Economic Law* 6(4): 879–921.

Charnovitz, S. 2002. 'WTO Cosmopolitics', *New York University Journal of International Law and Politics* 34: 299–354.

Collier, P. 2007. *The Bottom Billion: Why the Poorest Countries are Failing and What Can Be Done About It*. Oxford University Press.

Corrales-Leal, W. 2007. *Basic Concepts and Proposals on the Use of Policy Spaces in Trade-supported Strategies for Sustainable Development*. ICTSD Programme on Competitiveness and Sustainable Development Series Issue Paper No. 1. Geneva: International Centre for Trade and Sustainable Development.

Cottier, T. 2007. 'Preparing for Structural Reform in the WTO', *Journal of International Economic Law* 10(3): 497–508.

Deere, C. 2008. *The Implementation Game: The TRIPS Agreement and the Global Politics of Intellectual Property Reform in Developing Countries*. Oxford University Press.

Deere Birkbeck, C. and Meléndez-Ortiz, R. (eds.) 2009. *Rebuilding Global Trade: Proposals for a Fairer, More Sustainable Future*. Oxford and Geneva: Global Economic Governance Programme and the International Centre for Trade and Sustainable Development.

Deere Birkbeck, C. and Monagle, C. 2009. *Strengthening Multilateralism: A Mapping of Proposals on WTO Reform and Global Trade Governance*. Oxford and Geneva: Global Economic Governance Programme and the International Centre for Trade and Sustainable Development.

Esty, D. 2010. Conference Paper. Economic Series Seminar: Reassessing the Trade-Environment Relationship. Held at the WTO, Geneva, 3 June.

G20. 2008. Declaration of the Summit on Financial Markets and the World Economy, Washington, 15 November. http://georgewbush-whitehouse.archives.gov/news/releases/2008/11/20081115-1.html [Accessed in November 2010].

2010. The G20 Toronto Summit Declaration. 26–7 June 2010. www.g20.org/Documents/g20_declaration_en.pdf [Accessed in November 2010].

Gehring, M. and Cordonier-Segger, M.-C. 2005. *Sustainable Development in World Trade Law*. The Hague: Kluwer Law International.

Ghosh, A. 2010. 'Developing Countries in the WTO Trade Policy Review Mechanism', *World Trade Review* 9(3): 419–55.

Global Subsidies Initiative (GSI). 2010. 'Defining Fossil-Fuel Subsidies for the G-20: Which Approach is Best?', *GSI Policy Brief*, March, Geneva: Global Subsidies Initiative and International Institute for Sustainable Development (IISD).

Halle, M. and Meléndez-Ortiz, R. 2007. 'The Case for a Positive Southern Agenda', in Najam, A., Halle, M. and Meléndez-Ortiz, R. (eds.) *Envisioning a Sustainable Development Agenda for Trade and Environment*, pp. 9–28. New York and Hampshire: Palgrave Macmillan.

Halle, M. and Wolfe, R. (eds.) 2007. *Process Matters: Sustainable Development and Domestic Trade Transparency*. Winnipeg: International Institute for Sustainable Development.

Howse, R. 2002. 'The Appellate Body Rulings in the Shrimp/Turtle Case: A New Legal Baseline for the Trade and Environment Debate', *Columbia Journal of Environmental Law* 27(2): 491.

Hufbauer, G., Charnovitz, C. and Kim, J. 2009. *Global Warming and the World Trading System*. Washington, DC: Peterson Institute of International Economics.

ICTSD. 2006. 'Discussions on CBD-TRIPS Gain Momentum with New Proposals', *Bridges Trade BioRes* 6(11). http://ictsd.org/i/news/biores/9044/ [Accessed in November 2010].

2007. 'A Doha Round Deliverable for Climate Change?', *Bridges Trade BioRes Review* 1(2). http://ictsd.org/i/news/bioresreview/10631/ [Accessed in November 2010].

2008a. 'High Food Prices Leave Developing Countries Struggling to Cope', *Bridges Weekly Trade News* 12(14). http://ictsd.org/i/news/bridgesweekly/11073/ [Accessed in November 2010].

2008b. 'Sticky Sticker Situation: Food Miles, Carbon Labelling and Development', *Bridges Trade BioRes Review* 2(2). http://ictsd.org/i/news/bioresreview/12095/ [Accessed in November 2010].

2008c. *Climate Change, Technology Transfer and Intellectual Property Rights*, prepared for Trade and Climate Change Seminar in Copenhagen, 18–20 June. Geneva: International Centre for Trade and Sustainable Development.

IISD. 2001. *Private Rights, Public Problems: A guide to NAFTA's controversial chapter on investor rights*. International Institute for Sustainable Development and WWF-United States.

International Food Policy Research Institute (IFPRI). 2009. *Climate Change: Impact on Agriculture and Costs of Adaptation*. Washington, DC: International Food Policy Research Institute.

Ismail, F. 2009. *Reforming the World Trade Organization: Developing Countries in the Doha Round*. Geneva and Jaipur: Friedrich Ebert Stiftung and CUTS International.

Jha, V. 2009. 'Trade Flows, Barriers and Market Drivers in Renewable Energy Supply Goods: The Need To Level The Playing Field', *Bridges Trade BioRes Review* 3(3). Geneva: International Centre for Trade and Sustainable Development. http://ictsd.org/i/news/bioresreview/64027/ [Accessed in November 2010].

Keck, A. and Low, P. 2004. *Special and Differential Treatment in the WTO: Why, When and How?* WTO Staff Working Paper. Geneva: WTO.

Keohane, R. 2002. *Power and Governance in a Partially Globalized World*. London: Routledge.

Keohane, R. and Nye, J . (eds.) 1972. *Transnational Relations and World Politics*, Cambridge : Harvard University Press.

Kirkpatrick, C. and George, C. 2007. *Impact Assessment and Sustainable Development: European Policy and Experience*. Cheltenham: Edward Elgar.

Kirshner, J. 1999. 'Keynes, Capital Mobility and the Crisis of Embedded Liberalism', *Review of International Political Economy* 6(3): 313–37.

Levi, M. 2009. 'The Dangers of a Carbon Trade War', *Boston Globe*, 12 August.

Marglin, S. *et al.* 2010. From a statement reflecting discussions that took place during the workshop 'The challenge of sustainability: towards Rio+20', organized by the United Nations Division for Sustainable Development on 8–10 May in New York.

Martin, A. 2008. 'Mideast Facing Choice Between Crops and Water', *New York Times*, 21 July.

Meléndez-Ortiz, R. and Delhavi, A. 2000. 'Sustainable Development and Environmental Policy Objectives', in Konz, P. (ed.) *Trade, Environment and Sustainable Development: Views From Sub-Saharan Africa and Latin America: A Reader.* Geneva and Tokyo: ICTSD and United Nations University.

Meléndez-Ortiz, R ., Bellmann, C . and Hepburn, J . (eds.). 2009. *Agricultural Subsidies in the WTO Green Box: Ensuring Coherence with Sustainable Development Goals.* Cambridge University Press.

Messerlin, P. 2010. *Climate Change and Trade Policy: From Mutual Destruction to Mutual Support*, World Bank Policy Research Working Paper 5378. Washington, DC: World Bank.

Milner, H. 1998. 'International Political Economy: Beyond Hegemonic Stability Theory', *Foreign Policy* 110: 112–23.

Munasinghe, M. 1993. *Environmental Economics and Sustainable Development.* World Bank Environment Paper No.3. Washington, DC: The World Bank.

Najam, A., Lee, B. and Meléndez-Ortiz, R. 2005. 'Desarrollo Sostenible: Cómo superar las carencias de gobernanza de la globalización', in Torrent Macau, R., Millet Abbd, A. and Arce Suárez, A. (eds.). *Diálogo sobre Gobernabilidad, Globalización y Desarrollo.* Barcelona: Universitat de Barcelona. (English version available as *Sustainable Development: Filling the Governance Gap for Globalisation* at www.ub.edu/obsglob/DialogoMelen.html) [Accessed in May 2011]

NAMA-11. 2006. NAMA 11 Ministerial Communiqué, 29 June. www.philippineswto.org/Alli/NAMA11_Ministerial_Comm.htm [Accessed in November 2010].

OECD. 2010. *Agricultural Policies in OECD Countries.* Paris: Organisation for Economic Cooperation and Development (OECD).

Ostry, S. 2004. 'External Transparency: The Policy Process at the National Level of the Two Level Game', in Moore. M. (ed.) *Doha and Beyond: The Future of the Multilateral Trading System.* Cambridge University Press.

Petersmann, E.-U. (ed) 2004. *Preparing the Doha Development Round: Challenges to the Legitimacy and Efficiency of the World Trading System.* Florence: European University Institute.

2007a. *Constitutions and Global Markets: How to Define the Development Objectives of the World Trading System*. European University Institute: Max Weber Conference, Florence, 14 June.

2007b. 'Multilevel Judicial Governance of International Trade Requires a Common Conception of Rule of Law and Justice', *Journal of International Economic Law* 10(3): 529–51.

Reinicke, W., Witte, J. and Benner, T. 2003. *Global Public Policy Networks: Lessons Learned and Challenges Ahead*. Washington, DC: Brookings Institution.

Reuters 2008. *'Starve Your Neighbor' Policy Roils Food Trade*, by Missy Ryan, 5 March.

2010. *Carbon Tariffs on Imports Risk Trade War: EU Study*, by Pete Harrison, 30 April.

Rodrik, D. 2001. *The Global Governance of Trade – As if Development Really Mattered*. UNDP Background Paper. www.wcfia.harvard.edu/node/587 [Accessed in November 2010].

2003. 'Introduction' in Rodrik, D. (ed.), *In Search of Prosperity: Analytic Narratives on Economic Growth*. Princeton University Press.

Ruggie, J. 1982. 'International Regimes, Transactions, and Change: Embedded Liberalism in the Postwar Economic Order', *International Organization* 36(2): 379–415.

Sauvé, P. 2008. 'Services-Related Projects in Aid for Trade', in Njinkeu, D. and Cameron, H. (eds.), *Aid for Trade and Development*. Cambridge University Press, pp. 293–99.

Schwab, S. 2007. Remarks by the United States Trade Representative at a luncheon hosted by the Confederation of Indian Industry (CII), New Delhi, 13 April. http://newdelhi.usembassy.gov/pr041307.html [Accessed in November 2010].

Sen, A. 1999. *Development as Freedom*. Oxford University Press.

Stanton, E. and Ackerman, F. 2009. 'Climate and Development Economics: Balancing Science, Politics and Equity', *Natural Resources Forum* 33(4): 262–73.

Stavins, R. 2010. 'In Defense of Markets', in the Belfer Center's blog *An Economic View of the Environment*. http://belfercenter.ksg.harvard.edu/analysis/stavins/?p=775 [Accessed in November 2010].

Steenblik, R. 1998. *Previous Multilateral Efforts to Discipline Subsidies to Natural Resource Based Industries*. Paper prepared for the Workshop on the Impact of Government Financial Transfers on Fisheries Management, Resource Sustainability, and International Trade, organized by the Fisheries Development and Co-operation Task Force of the Pacific Economic Co-operation Council (PECC). 17–19 August, Manila, Philippines.

Stiglitz, J. 2010. 'Needed: A New Economic Paradigm', *Financial Times*, 20 August.

The Economist. 2010a. 'Can Anything Perk up Europe?', *The Economist*, 8 July.
2010b. 'Picking Winners, Saving Losers', *The Economist*, 5 August.

United Nations World Food Programme. 2010. *Fighting Hunger Worldwide: Annual Report 2010*. Rome: United Nations World Food Programme.

Victor, D. 2006. 'Toward Effective International Cooperation on Climate Change: Numbers, Interests and Institutions', *Global Environmental Politics* 6(3): 90–103.

Victor, D. and Yueh, L. 2010. 'The New Energy Order: Managing Insecurities in the Twenty-First Century', *Foreign Affairs*, January/February.

Vis-Dunbar, D. 2006. 'A New Role for the Permanent Group of Experts on Subsidies?', *Subsidy Watch*. www.globalsubsidies.org/en/subsidy-watch/a-new-role-permanent-group-experts-subsidies [Accessed in November 2010].

Wolfe, R. 2007. *Can the Trading System be Governed? Institutional Implications of the WTO's Suspended Animation*. CIGI Working Paper No.30. Ottawa: Centre for International Governance Innovation.

World Trade Organization (WTO). 1994a. *Decision on Trade and Environment*. Adopted by ministers at the meeting of the Uruguay Round Trade Negotiations Committee on 14 April. www.wto.org/english/tratop_e/envir_e/issu5_e.htm. Geneva: WTO [Accessed in November 2010].

1994b. *Marrakesh Agreement Establishing the World Trade Organization*. Adopted on 15 April 1994 and entered into force on 1 January 1995. Geneva: WTO.

1998. *U.S. – Import Prohibition of Certain Shrimp and Shrimp Products*, WT/DS58/AB/R, Appellate Body, October. Geneva: WTO.

2001. *Ministerial Declaration*, Doha Ministerial Conference, WT/MIN(01)/DEC/1, 20 November. Geneva: WTO.

2004. *Text of the 'July package' – the General Council's post-Cancún Decision*, adopted by the General Council on 1 August, WT/L/579. Geneva: WTO.

2005. *Ministerial Declaration*, Hong Kong Ministerial Conference. WT/MIN(05)/DEC, December. Geneva: WTO.

2008. *Fourth Revision of Draft Modalities for Non-Agricultural Market Access*. Negotiating Group on Market Access. TN/MA/W/103/Rev.3. Geneva: WTO.

PART II

Roles and responsibilities in global trade governance: diversity in developing country priorities and strategies

5

New powers in the club: the challenges of global trade governance

AMRITA NARLIKAR

The Doha Development Agenda (DDA) – the first trade round to be negotiated under the umbrella of the World Trade Organization (WTO), and the ninth in the post-war multilateral trading system – has been dogged by recurrent deadlock. But the stasis surrounding the Doha negotiations should not be mistaken for stasis in the WTO. The world that the WTO was created to govern has been changing rapidly, and, unlike many other international organizations, the WTO has proved unusually responsive to these changes. The most important has been the shift in the economic balance of power, with the emergence of the new powers that have come to be popularly known as the BRICs.[1] Unlike other organizations, such as the International Monetary Fund (IMF), the World Bank or the United Nations (UN) Security Council, that have been slow to adapt their decision-making structures to reflect these ground-level changes, the WTO has welcomed Brazil, India and China (the BICs) into the core of its decision-making. Moreover, many of these institutional changes within the organization are not a knee-jerk reaction to the financial and economic crisis, but predate it. As a result, the WTO today looks quite different from the 'rich man's club' of the General Agreement on Tariffs and Trade (GATT), which was dominated by the old Quad (the European Union (EU), the United States (USA), Canada and Japan). Interestingly,

Dr Amrita Narlikar is University Senior Lecturer at the Department of Politics and International Studies at Cambridge University and Official Fellow of Darwin College. For helpful comments and suggestions on an earlier draft of this article the author is grateful to Paola Subacchi, Andrew Cooper, Diana Tussie, Denise Gregory, Wang Yong, Peter Draper and Paolo Guerrieri. The usual caveats apply. This article first appeared in *International Affairs* and is reprinted here with permission. See Narlikar 2010c.

[1] The acronym was coined by Goldman Sachs (2003). Note, however, that the inclusion of Russia is contested, see e.g. Hurrell (2006). Moreover, given that Russia is not a Member of the WTO, I focus in this article only on Brazil, India and China, i.e. the BICs.

however, this ability of the WTO to adapt to changing external imperatives has generated mixed results. In this article, I address the question: What impact has the emergence of the new powers of the BICs had on the WTO?

The article proceeds in four parts. In the first section, I provide a brief account of the changing role of the new powers in the WTO. The second section analyses the opportunities that these developments generate, while the third investigates the challenges they pose. The fourth and concluding section explores possible solutions, both within the organization and in parallel institutions such as the G8 and the G20, which may improve both the fairness and efficiency of global trade governance.

1 New powers in the WTO

There are at least three indicators of the growing importance of the BICs in global trade governance: their large and growing trade shares, their concerted activism in the WTO and their growing presence in key decision-making fora within and beyond the WTO.

The figures, to start with, speak for themselves. China, despite the downturn in the world economy precipitated by the financial crisis, remained the world's second-largest exporter of merchandise, accounting for 11.3 per cent of the world's exports (excluding intra-EU trade) in 2008. Brazil and India, though further behind at sixteenth and nineteenth positions in the export table, accounting for 1.6 per cent and 1.5 per cent of the world's export market respectively, still featured in the list of top twenty leading exporters of merchandise. In services, too, the BICs have cornered a large chunk of the market: in 2009, China ranked as the third-largest exporter of commercial services, with a 5.3 per cent share of the market; India was the fifth largest, with 3.7 per cent of the market; and Brazil ranked eighteenth but still occupied a significant 1 per cent of the market. Compare these figures against the position of the BICs just over a decade ago. China in 1997 ranked as the tenth-largest exporter of merchandise, with 3.3 per cent of world exports, and as the sixteenth-largest exporter of commercial services, with 1.9 per cent of world exports (which at the time included intra-EU trade). Brazil and India did not even feature in the list of the top twenty-five leading merchandise or services exporters. In other words, the rise of the BICs as major trading nations has been dramatic.[2] All three economies have shown far greater resilience to the havoc wrought by

[2] International trade statistics. Accessed at www.wto.org [accessed in November 2010].

the financial crisis than Western markets. Add to this the still untapped potential of their vast markets, and other power indicators (including military prowess), and we would expect them to have a major role in most aspects of global governance.

But cornering a large share of the world's export markets and showing resilience to economic downturns do not automatically lead to greater voice in the WTO. The inertia of, and entrenched interests in, most international organizations make them slow to respond to external changes. The WTO, which is driven by its Members, is less prone to bureaucratic inertia than organizations led by their staffs, but even in the WTO market power does not immediately translate into institutional power. Not all the twenty to twenty-five leading traders in the WTO enjoy regular invitations to the 'High Table' of multilateral negotiations or other small-group meetings. Insofar as exercising voice in any international organization is a function of the agency and activism that particular countries are able and willing to invest, the BICs stand out in comparison to most Members of the WTO, developed and developing.

Brazil and India have a long history of activism in both GATT and the WTO. One of the means through which they have exercised this activism is by forming and leading coalitions of developing countries (Narlikar 2003). Both as a result of their increasing economic power and through institutional learning and adaptation within the organization, these two countries have shown increasing willingness and ability to provide the 'club good' of coalition unity (by bearing the burdens of research and information-sharing, and allowing considerable free-riding by smaller Members of the coalition) (Narlikar and Tussie 2004; Hurrell and Narlikar 2006; Tussie 2009). China, joining the WTO in 2001, started off by adopting a lower profile than Brazil or India. For instance, though it was a founding member of the G20 coalition, it occupied itself with work behind the scenes in contrast to the front-line leadership exercised by Brazil and India (Chin 2009; Narlikar 2010a). But in the July 2008 talks it adopted a much more prominent role, and joined India in blocking the deal that was on offer. All three countries now show a much greater sophistication in the proposals they present, and also greater confidence in negotiating with their coalition allies as well as with other parties (Ismail 2009).

The third indicator of the growing importance of the BICs in the global trading system is the extent to which WTO decision-making processes have been adapted and reformed to accommodate them. The old Quad has been replaced by new groupings that have taken the shape of the 'New Quad' or G4, the Five Interested Parties (FIPs), the G6 and the G7. These groupings represent the high tables of decision-making, where the first steps are taken towards building consensus, and Brazil and India (along with the EU and the USA) are invited to all of them. At the July 2008 talks, the grouping was extended to seven, including China (besides the EU, USA, Brazil, India, Australia and Japan). Nor is this inclusiveness a form of tokenism. As the EU and the USA have seen repeatedly since 2003 (when the first major deadlock of the DDA occurred at the Cancún ministerial), the BICs, individually or in coalition, are not shy of using their veto power.

It is perhaps also worth noting that parallel institutions with some remit in trade matters have also shown some responsiveness to the rise of the BICs. In part this predates the crisis: for instance, the attempts to expand the G8 by according a greater voice to these countries goes back to the creation of the Outreach Group (Cooper 2007). In global attempts to deal with the financial and economic crisis, their importance has only risen. For example, the three are also key members of the G20 (to be distinguished from the trade coalition of the G20 within the WTO, which will be referred to for the purposes of this article as the Trade G20), which has come into the limelight since 2008 in its attempt to provide coordinated leadership to solve the financial crisis. The impact of the growing role of the BICs on global trade governance, and particularly the WTO, is analysed in the next two sections.

2 The opportunities of greater inclusiveness

The inclusion of the new powers into the core of global trade governance brings with it several benefits and opportunities. The first and most important of these is that the WTO presents a much more accurate reflection of the global balance of power outside it than most other formal organizations (or indeed, even the G8, where the new powers have at best acquired the status of an 'outreach group' and do not figure as fully fledged members). Decisions arrived at in an organization that offers a relatively realistic representation of political power are likely to have greater efficacy and durability than those emerging from smaller 'elite' bodies. For example, one of the crucial problems with the IMF and the World Bank is that their governance structures no longer reflect existing power realities, which reduces both the efficiency and the legitimacy of their decision-making; the WTO's willingness to evolve with the changing times helps the organization to avoid some of these problems. A necessary (though not sufficient) condition for any properly functioning government or governance system is that the major players buy into it; by giving them a bigger say in the decision-making, the WTO can potentially secure greater buy-in from the BICs.

Second, it is important to bear in mind that the BICs, despite their rising economic trajectories, continue to maintain close links with the global South. Having these countries at the heart of decision-making is very different from including Canada, Australia or even Japan. As Andrew Hurrell (2006) rightly argues, these three countries, plus Russia, lie outside or on the margins of the liberal 'Greater West' formation. In contrast to Australia, Canada, Japan and the European countries, they are not closely integrated in alliances with the USA. Their visions of international order, moreover, have presented a challenge to those espoused by the liberal West (Hurrell 2006: 1–9). The continued association of the BICs with Third Worldist coalitions as well as with ideas of distributive justice and developmentalism means that their inclusion at the core allows for the possibility of the creation of a more pluralist trading system. As such, the benefits that can follow are not only those of efficiency (deriving from a better representation of the altered balance of power) but also those of fairness (deriving from the BICs' association with, and indeed membership of, the developing world).

Third, insofar as the BICs operate in coalitions, their increasing prominence in the WTO has the potential to offer greater representation to their smaller coalition partners. Of course, the ability of the BICs to truly 'represent' other developing countries is contested, and rumblings of discontent came to the fore, particularly in the discussions of July 2008. But equally, a close examination of coalition dynamics (particularly the refusal of Members to be bought off through side deals) reveals that coalition unity is not a factor that can be easily disregarded (Ismail 2009; Narlikar 2009). It also, by implication, offers at least some representativeness for the smallest players through their coalition leaders.

Finally, greater weight and voice for the BICs in trade governance have given development concerns unprecedented importance in trade negotiations. It is difficult to imagine that a trade round in the GATT days would have been named the Doha Development Agenda; it is even more difficult to imagine that development would have continued to form the main theme of the negotiations after token goodwill gestures had been made towards the concept at the start of the process. That development remains central to the DDA can partly be explained by the fact that the WTO has major developing countries at its helm rather than just the old Quad.

The list of opportunities provided here would suggest that the rise of the BICs in the WTO augurs well for the organization: an organization that is fairer, more efficient, more pluralist and more development-friendly is likely to enjoy greater ownership among its stakeholders (including non-governmental organizations (NGOs)). Unfortunately, however, power transitions are seldom easy, and the rise of the BICs has also thrown up new and unanticipated challenges for the organization as well as parallel mechanisms of governance.

3 New powers in old clubs: challenges and problems

Flexibility and adaptability to new balances of power should have resulted in the WTO functioning more smoothly. Instead, however, we see disengagement by the EU and the USA (and domestic political constituencies within them), dissatisfaction from the BICs (which have shown considerable reluctance to compromise and have held up agreement) and discontent from the rest of the developing world (which complains of marginalization despite improvements in inclusiveness and transparency). Permanent deadlock at the WTO is one significant indication of how poorly the organization is functioning: the DDA was scheduled for completion in 2005, but is nowhere near conclusion over five years past the deadline. The turn to bilateralism and regionalism is a reaction on the part of States disillusioned with multilateralism and seeking market access through other means.

Recurrent deadlock within the organization not only delays the promised benefits of trade liberalization under the DDA, but also undermines the credibility of the WTO, and further heightens the risk that countries will return to protectionism when the going gets tough. This is indeed the outcome that we have seen as governments grapple with the financial crisis and its aftermath. The third Global Trade Alert Report, for instance, points out:

> Since the first G-20 crisis-related summit in November 2008, the governments of the world have together implemented 297 beggar-thy-neighbour policy measures; that is, more than one for every working day of the year. Add in another 56 implemented measures that are likely to have harmed some foreign commercial interests, and the total reaches 353. Moreover, since the Global Trade Alert's (GTA's) last report was published in September 2009, the number of beggar-thy-neighbour measures discovered (105) was more than 8 times the number of benign or liberalizing measures (12). Looking back on all of the measures implemented since

> November 2008, the ratio of blatantly discriminatory measures to liberalizing measures stands at nearly six to one.
>
> (Evenett 2009)

The fourth Global Trade Alert Report goes on to note that despite stabilization since the third report, protectionist pressures have persisted (Evenett 2010). The WTO has been able to do very little to slow down the juggernaut of protectionism, regionalism and bilateralism. Why is this?

In the very strengths of the WTO – its adaptability to altered balances of power, reinforced by its Member-driven character – also lie its weaknesses. There are four important reasons why the multilateral trading system, which had ensured the provision of the public good of freer trade since the end of the Second World War, is failing us today. All four reasons are related in one way or another to the changed balance of power that the WTO has tried to accommodate.

First, the inclusion of the BICs at the core of decision-making places a more diverse group of countries in the driving seat. The old Quad displayed far greater homogeneity than its newer incarnation has done, whether it takes the shape of the smaller G4 or the bigger G7. Not only are the BICs at considerably different stages of development, with very different domestic political economies from the EU and the USA (which makes it harder for them to make concessions on certain areas such as agriculture), but they also bring very different negotiating cultures and ideas of fairness and distributive justice to the negotiating table. To this variable of cultural diversity must be added the additional factor of multipolarity. After all, power in the WTO today is more evenly distributed among the leading players, in contrast to the monopoly of power that was enjoyed by the USA when the GATT was created, or indeed the duopoly that emerged with Europe's post-war recovery. And the more equal the power distribution, the harder it is to reach agreement.[3]

A multipolar system with several diverse powers in leading positions may still manage to function adequately if there are institutional mechanisms in place that can help overcome the problem of deadlock. But this brings us to the second problem with the WTO: even though it has accommodated the BICs, the process by which it functions remains unchanged. Consensus-based decision-making worked in the 'Rich Man's Club' because the great majority of the contracting parties to GATT were willing

[3] In a recent study on deadlocks in multilateral negotiations, the hypothesis that deadlocks are a function of the balance of power was the most popular hypothesis of six that were analysed, and was confirmed by all the case studies. See Narlikar 2010b.

to forgo their right to veto an agreement; the 'principal supplier principle' allowed the major powers to reach an agreement first and then multilateralize its benefits via the Most Favoured Nation clause to all GATT signatories. But consensus-based decision-making makes it impossible to reach agreements today, even among the diverse group of countries at the helm, let alone the rest of the membership. In other words, limitations of institutional process are holding up the WTO, but these limitations arise fundamentally because of the altered balance of power that the organization now reflects.

Third, one of the sources of the strength in the WTO of Brazil and India particularly, and to a lesser extent of China, lies in the coalitions they have formed and led. Their recent successes in leading coalitions, particularly the Trade G20 formed at Cancún in 2003 (of which Brazil, China and India were founding members) and also the G33 (also originating in Cancún, and comprising China and India), are a source of empowerment for their allies as well as themselves. In any international organization, irrespective of whether it works on the basis of majority voting or not, the support of large numbers strengthens and legitimizes one's claims at the agenda-setting stage. The Doha coalitions of the South, including the Trade G20 and the G33, go a step further than that by remaining united in the negotiation phase. As such, these coalitions are a far cry from previous developing country coalitions that were firm in making their demands but would usually collapse in the endgame, thereby not only destroying the collective negotiation position but also undermining the negotiation positions of individual members. While the emergence of such strong coalitions is a positive development in terms of the bargaining positions of the BICs and their allies, it generates an important cost: countries operating in strong coalitions find it particularly difficult to make concessions. This is so for two reasons. First, coalition allies may see any attempts by the leaders to initiate concessions as a sign of defection. Second, the outside party (in this case, the EU or the USA) can interpret any concession as a sign of weakness, especially if it is aware of dissensions within the coalition (Narlikar and Houten 2003).[4] Effectively, multilateral diplomacy that is founded on strong coalitions may empower some of the weakest members, but it is also prone to deadlock and usually

[4] Bernard Hoekman (2003) makes a related point: 'The move towards the creation of negotiating coalitions of groups of countries may reduce the number of "principals" but possibly at the cost of greater inflexibility and a higher risk of breakdown, especially in a setting where there is little time to consult.'

decreases the efficiency of the system. And coalitions of the South are here to stay. Even if the BICs were to stop leading them, alternative leaders of new coalitions would emerge, and would produce another change in the balance of power of the organization.

Finally, while there is no question that a system that includes the BICs at its core is more representative than one without – and especially so insofar as the BICs further offer indirect representation for members of coalitions that they lead – the impact of their inclusion on the general legitimacy of the system is questionable. Exactly what constitutes legitimacy is subject to debate, but Allen Buchanan and Robert Keohane offer a simple and useful definition, where the legitimacy of global governance institutions is 'the right to rule, understood to mean both that institutional agents are morally justified in making rules and attempting to secure compliance with them and that people subject to those rules have moral, content-independent reasons to follow them and/or to not interfere with others' compliance with them' (Buchanan and Keohane 2006). It is obvious that an institution that is deemed fundamentally 'unfair' is likely to have its legitimacy challenged (as the Seattle demonstrations, for instance, highlighted in the case of the WTO). But it is also highly unlikely that an institution will be accorded the 'right to rule' if it is seen to be fundamentally inefficient. Even if an institution manages to acquire a reputation for ensuring fair process and outcomes, its members would find it very difficult to legitimize their commitment to it if the time and resources spent on reaching these goals were disproportionate to the accrued benefits.[5]

While the WTO has gone far in improving its transparency and inclusiveness, thereby correcting some of its fairness deficit, it has been less successful in addressing its efficiency deficit. In fact, recent developments in the WTO reveal the trade-off between fairness and efficiency considerations. Though the WTO assures developing countries of a fairer process than the GATT, its negotiation and decision-making processes have become considerably more laborious (as highlighted in the previous paragraphs). Moreover, the success of developing countries in managing to bring development to the fore, sometimes at the expense of other issues prioritized by the developed countries (such as the Singapore issues), has created considerable apathy towards the multilateral trading system in the North. The private sector, which so successfully created pressures on

[5] For a conceptual treatment of legitimacy in terms of its fairness and efficiency components, see Narlikar 2009.

developed country governments to get a deal in the Uruguay Round, has chosen to invest its energies elsewhere. Unsurprisingly, when faced with interminably long rounds and no political support for them at home, politicians are turning to the more populist, cheaper and quicker alternatives of bilateralism, regionalism and protectionism.[6]

No good deed goes unpunished: the WTO's timely responsiveness in accommodating the new powers at the heart of its decision-making has produced new inefficiencies, has heightened its proclivity to deadlock, and has exacerbated disengagement and disillusionment among all its stakeholders. Particularly in the context of a major economic crisis, a reliable international institution is necessary to ensure the continued provision of freer trade (well recognized as the route to recovery). With the WTO's recent record to provide these necessary public goods in doubt, where do the solutions lie?

4 Reforming global trade governance

The problems of the WTO stem fundamentally from changes in the balance of power, both within and outside the organization. The financial crisis, by diffusing power further away from the USA and the EU and towards the new powers, further tilts the balance of power away from the old Quad, shifting the organization towards greater multipolarity. As the WTO is the central institution responsible for the liberalization and regulation of international trade, its problems are also problems for global trade governance as a whole. There is very little by way of reform that can realistically be done – or indeed should be done – to alter the balance of power itself. A more productive line of reform would be to build on the gains in fairness and inclusiveness that the system has already achieved, while further addressing considerations of efficiency. I address two sets of proposals below: reform external to the WTO through the G20, and internal institutional reform within the organization.

[6] On the disengagement of interest groups and lack of leadership, see the Warwick Commission (2007); and Narlikar and Vickers (2009). Note that a vicious cycle links declining political will and institutional stasis in the WTO: constant deadlock and other inefficiencies make politicians reluctant to offer concessions in the DDA, and this declining political will further embeds the stalemate within the organization. Note further that the financial crisis exacerbates this vicious cycle. If politicians were finding it hard to legitimize their commitment to an inefficient organization before the crisis, they are hardly likely to embrace the idea of making concessions to preserve multilateralism in difficult economic times at home.

4.1 *The role of the G20*

The G20 neither is nor can be (nor indeed should it be) a substitute for a multilateral trade organization or some of the decision-making processes of the WTO.[7] For example, any attempts to build preliminary consensus through a G20-level mini-ministerial are unlikely to enjoy ownership by the rest of the WTO Membership. Moreover, as was argued in the previous section, one of the problems with the WTO today is that it brings together at the helm multiple and diverse powers among which it is difficult to reach consensus; attempting to build consensus in an even larger and more diverse group such as the G20 is going to be more difficult still. In other words, bypassing some of the processes of the WTO and taking them to the G20 level is unlikely to address the inefficiency problem. Such a strategy also risks reversing the significant advances that the WTO has made in ensuring fairer processes, not only by including the BICs in the new Quad but also through improved internal transparency mechanisms that allow considerably more access to smaller countries than the G20 does. This is not to say that mini-ministerials and other forms of small-group consultations among a subset of the membership do not happen or should not happen; especially in conditions of stalemate, such meetings are and will remain an important mechanism in finding the pathway to agreement. But to institutionalize such meetings in a forum outside the WTO, from which the great majority of the membership of the organization is systematically and institutionally excluded, will not improve the legitimacy or ownership of the multilateral trade regime.

What role, then, can the G20 play in the preservation and improvement of the multilateral trading system? A particularly important and constructive role for the G20 would be not as a substitute for the WTO but as its supporter. At a time when leadership has been lacking in the organization, the commitment of the world's leading economies to uphold the norms and rules of the WTO via the G20 could be just the boost that the system needs. To some extent, this is what the G20 has attempted to do. The London communiqué, for instance, declared:

> World trade growth has underpinned rising prosperity for half a century. But it is now falling for the first time in 25 years. Falling demand is exacerbated by growing protectionist pressures and a withdrawal of trade

[7] Discussions of this possibility predate the current debates by at least six years: in 2004, CIGI sponsored a conference in Oxford to discuss the implications of Paul Martin's idea of the leaders' level G20 with responsibilities for trade negotiations.

> credit. Reinvigorating world trade and investment is essential for restoring global growth. We will not repeat the historic mistakes of protectionism of previous eras.
>
> (Group of Twenty 2009)

To this end, it made all the right noises in terms of pledging commitment to the 'ambitious and balanced completion' of the DDA, and also pledging 'to refrain from raising new barriers to investment or to trade in goods and services, imposing new export restrictions, or implementing WTO inconsistent measures to stimulate exports'. In practice, however, these 'commitments' have so far shown themselves to be little more than what game theorists call 'cheap talk'. First, the commitment to resist protectionism is simply not borne out in reality; in fact, the third Global Trade Alert Report points out that, of the 297 beggar-thy-neighbour policy measures that were implemented from November 2008 to December 2009, 'G20 governments were responsible for imposing 184 of these protectionist measures' (Evenett 2009). Second, Geoff Pigman rightly argues that, in contrast to the attention accorded to the IMF, 'the WTO was the ghost at this feast of multilateral cooperation and compromise, with conclusion of multilateral negotiations to complete the DDA far from prominent on the London G-20 agenda' (Pigman 2009).

More costly signals will be needed to show its commitment to multilateral trade if the G20 is to play a useful role in both facilitating and sustaining economic recovery. Some of these were outlined by Paola Subacchi and Alexei Monsarrat, including a twelve-month freeze on new protectionist measures and a rollback on existing measures, and commitment to complete the DDA as not just an empty promise but with specific milestones (Subacchi and Monsarrat 2009). A freeze on protectionist measures by the G20 that is binding (perhaps even linked to the WTO via the Dispute Settlement Mechanism) would not only help slow down spiralling protectionism in the system, but would also serve as the necessary costly signal to other WTO Members. Overall, such steps would not only serve the immediate purpose of facilitating economic recovery, but would also help to address the longer-standing problem of absent leadership that the DDA was facing even prior to the crisis.

4.2 *Internal reform within the WTO*

Supportive measures from the G20, along the lines spelt out above, would still come to naught if the WTO itself were to retain institutional processes that are out of sync with altered power realities. The most seriously flawed of these processes is the pursuit of decision-making by consensus in a context of multipolarity and increased diversity at the core. There are several different routes to reforming consensus-based decision-making, which can be broadly grouped into two categories: delegation of powers to an executive board, and altering the voting rules.

The first set of solutions – the creation of an executive/consultative/advisory board – has been explored more thoroughly (Schott and Watal 2002; Blackhurst and Hartridge 2004). This may address the issue of efficiency, but will create serious new problems associated with fairness. Delegation of power to an executive board – even of limited advisory capacity – would prompt complaints of disenfranchisement from a great majority of the members. In some ways, an executive board solution would take the WTO even further behind GATT in formalizing the exclusion of the greater part of its membership. Parallel examples in other international organizations (the IMF, the World Bank, the UN Security Council) and the criticisms that they have attracted on grounds of inclusiveness and representativeness warn against importing similar institutional flaws into the WTO.

The limitations of the first set of proposals, in terms of both their normative implications and their political feasibility, have led many scholars recently to explore ideas of alternative forms of voting through 'critical mass' approaches (Cottier and Takenoshita 2003; Lawrence 2006; Warwick Commission 2007; Elsig 2010). A discussion of the details of these proposals lies beyond the scope of this paper (Narlikar 2011 (forthcoming)). But it is worth mentioning briefly that one of the biggest problems with a critical mass approach on its own is that it can be seen as little more than a return to the 'principal supplier principle', with all the associated problems of marginalization and exclusion. This is why I argue elsewhere that any revision of the voting system would have to involve two thresholds: one that would buy in the commitment of the major players by improving the efficiency of the system, but another that would ensure that the great majority of the membership also had a meaningful say in the decision-making process. One combination of this would be a critical mass approach combined with a second threshold of voting system that required a super-majority (Narlikar (in press)). Such a system of voting would remove the inefficiencies inherent in a consensus-based system that accords effective veto power to the entire membership. Its dual benefits would lie in bringing back the commitment of the major markets to the system and simultaneously ensuring that the majority of the membership preserves a sense of ownership of the decisions. The improved democratic credentials of the organization would be retained, but its efficiency would also be enhanced.

Though power transitions represent a challenge to any international institution, they also provide a great opportunity to reform and rebuild. The entry of the BICs into the WTO as veto players has certainly created new problems, as analysed in this chapter. But it also offers a new opportunity to reform the WTO and related institutions, thereby contributing to the creation of a fairer, more efficient and, overall, more legitimate system of global trade governance. The context of urgency provided by the financial crisis could be further exploited to this end. If there were ever a need and an opportunity to strengthen the multilateral trading system, they are here now.

References

Blackhurst, R. and Hartridge, D. 2004. 'Improving the Capacity of WTO Institutions to Fulfil their Mandate', *Journal of International Economic Law* 7(3): 705–16.

Buchanan, A. and Keohane, R. 2006. 'The Legitimacy of Global Governance Institutions', *Ethics and International Affairs* 20(4): 412.

Chin, G. 2009. 'Reforming the WTO: China, the Doha Round and Beyond', in Narlikar and Vickers (eds.), *Leadership Change in the Multilateral Trading System*. Republic of Letters: Dordrecht.

Cooper, A. 2007. 'The Logic of the B(R)ICSAM Model for G8 Reform', *CIGI Policy Brief* in International Governance No. 1 (May). Ontario: Centre for International Governance Innovation (CIGI).

Cottier, T. and Takenoshita, S. 2003. 'The Balance of Power in WTO Decision Making: Towards Weighted Voting in Legislative Response', *Aussenwirtschaft* 58(2): 171–214.

Eagleton-Pierce, M., Jones, E. and Nicolaidis, K. (eds.). 2009. *Building Blocks for a Global Trade Ethics: A Compendium of the Oxford Programme on Global Trade Ethics*. University of Oxford and German Marshall Fund.

Elsig, M. 2010. 'Towards Weighted Voting: Can We Get a Little Help From the Secretariat and Critical Mass?', in Steger (ed.), *Redesigning the World Trade Organization for the 21st Century*. Ontario: Wilfred Laurier Press/CIGI/International Development Research Centre.

Evenett, S. (ed.). 2009. *The Unrelenting Pressure of Protectionism: The 3rd Global Trade Alert Report* (7 December): p.3. http://globaltradealert.org/gta-analysis/unrelenting-pressure-protectionism-3rd-gta-report [Accessed in February 2010].

2010. *Will Stabilisation Limit Protectionism? The 4th Global Trade Alert Report* (15 February). http://globaltradealert.org/gta-analysis/will-stabilisation-limit-protectionism-4th-gta-report [Accessed in February 2010].

Goldman Sachs. 2003. *Dreaming with the BRICs: The Path to 2050*, Global Economics Paper No. 99. New York: Goldman Sachs.

Group of Twenty. 2009. 'Global Plan for Recovery and Reform: The Communiqué from the London Summit'. 2 April. www.g20.org/Documents/final-communique.pdf/ [Accessed in June 2011].

Hoekman, B. 2003. 'Cancún: Crisis or Catharsis?', 20 September. http://siteresources.worldbank.org/INTRANETTRADE/Resources/Hoekman-CancunCatharsis-092003.pdf [Accessed in February 2010].

Hurrell, A. 2006. 'Hegemony, Liberalism and Global Order: What Space for Would-be Great Powers?', *International Affairs* 82(1) (January): 1–19.

Hurrell, A. and Narlikar, A. 2006. 'The New Politics of Confrontation? Developing Countries at Cancún and Beyond', *Global Society* 20(4) (October): 415–33.

Ismail, F. 2009. 'Reflections on the WTO July 2008 Collapse: Lessons for Developing Country Coalitions', in Narlikar, A. and Vickers, B. (eds.), *Leadership and Change in the Multilateral Trading System*. Republic of Letters: Dordrecht.

Lawrence, R. 2006. 'Rulemaking Amidst Growing Diversity: A Club-of-clubs Approach to WTO Reform and New Issue Selection', *Journal of International Economic Law* 9(4): 825–33.

Narlikar, A. 2003. *International Trade and Developing Countries: Bargaining Coalitions in the GATT and WTO*. London: Routledge.

2009. 'Moving Beyond Fairness: Improving the Legitimacy of the WTO', in Eagleton-Pierce, M., Jones, E. and Nicolaidis, K. (eds.), *Building Blocks for a Global Trade Ethics: A Compendium of the Oxford Programme on Global Trade Ethics*. University of Oxford and German Marshall Fund. http://cis.politics.ox.ac.uk/materials/gte_compendiumOct09.pdf [Accessed in February 2010].

(ed.) 2010a. *Deadlocks in Multilateral Negotiations: Causes and Solutions*. Cambridge University Press.

2010b. *New Powers: How to Become One and How to Manage Them*. London and New York: Hurst / Columbia University Press.

2010c. 'New Powers in the Club: The Challenges of Global Trade Governance', *International Affairs* 86(3): 717–28.

(in press). 'Adapting to New Power Balances: Institutional Reform in the WTO', in Cottier, T. and Elsig, M. (eds.), *Governing the WTO: Past, Present, and Beyond Doha*.

Narlikar, A. and Houten, P. 2003. 'Know the Enemy: Uncertainty and Deadlock in the WTO', in Narlikar, A. (2010), *Deadlocks in Multilateral Negotiations: Causes and Solutions*. Cambridge University Press.

Narlikar, A. and Tussie, D. 2004. 'The G20 at the Cancún Ministerial: Developing Countries and their Evolving Coalitions', *The World Economy* 27(7) (July): 947–66.

Narlikar, A. and Vickers, B. (eds.) 2009. *Leadership and Change in the Multilateral Trading System*, Republic of Letters: Dordrecht.

Pigman, G. A. 2009. 'US Trade Policy and the Rise of the Big Emerging Economies', in Narlikar, A. and Vickers, B. (eds.), *Leadership and Change in the Multilateral Trading System*. Republic of Letters: Dordrecht.

Schott, J. and Watal, J. 2002. 'Decision-making in the WTO', *International Economic Policy Briefs 00–2*. Washington, DC: Institute for International Economics.

Steger, D. (ed.) 2010. *Redesigning the World Trade Organization for the 21st Century*. Ontario: Wilfred Laurier Press/CIGI/International Development Research Centre.

Subacchi, P. and Monsarrat, A. 2009. 'New Ideas for the London Summit: Recommendations to the G20 Leaders', *A Chatham House and Atlantic Council Report*. www.chathamhouse.org.uk/files/13733_r0409_g20.pdf [Accessed in February 2010].

Tussie, D. (ed.) 2009. *The Politics of Trade: The Role of Research in Trade Policy and Negotiation*. Leiden: Martinus Nijhoff.

Warwick Commission. 2007. 'The Multilateral Trade Regime: Which Way Forward?', *Report of the First Warwick Commission*. Coventry: University of Warwick.

6

China's ascent in global trade governance: from rule taker to rule shaker and maybe rule maker?

HENRY GAO

Since China's accession to the World Trade Organization (WTO) in late 2001, one of the most intriguing questions for trade analysts has been how the 'new kid on the block' would behave once it became a formal Member of the multilateral trading system. The question is twofold. First, will China faithfully implement its WTO accession commitments? Second, will China seek to upset the existing power structure in the WTO?

Of the two issues, the first has received the most attention. In addition to abundant media coverage, official statements and academic commentaries, the concern is well illustrated by the following passages from the Working Party Report of China's WTO Accession (WTO 2001a: para. 9):

> Some members of the Working Party indicated that *because of the significant size, rapid growth and transitional nature of the Chinese economy, a pragmatic approach should be taken in determining China's need for recourse to transitional periods and other special provisions in the WTO Agreement available to developing country WTO Members.* Each agreement and China's situation should be carefully considered and specifically addressed. In this regard it was stressed that this pragmatic approach would be tailored to fit the specific cases of China's accession in a few areas, which were reflected in the relevant provisions set forth in China's Draft Protocol and Working Party Report. Noting the preceding statements, Members reiterated that *all commitments taken by China in her accession process were solely those of China and would prejudice neither existing rights and obligations of Members under the WTO*

Henry Gao is Associate Professor of Law, Singapore Management University (on leave from the University of Hong Kong). Some of the initial findings in this paper were presented at the Annual Meeting of the American Society of International Law in Washington, DC in March 2010. The author wishes to thank the participants at that meeting for their most helpful comments. The author is also most grateful to Carolyn Deere Birkbeck, Samantha Derksen, and the two anonymous reviewers for their most helpful comments. All errors remain the author's own.

Agreement nor on-going and future WTO negotiations and any other process of accession ...

(Emphasis, in italics, added)

As a precaution against potential problems post-accession, the accession package includes many special rules tailor-made for China. These include substantive obligations such as the grant of national treatment to foreign persons and firms, as well as foreign products (while the normal WTO national treatment obligation applies to products only) (WTO 2001b: section 3). It also includes the commitment to treat subsidies provided to state-owned enterprises as specific subsidies (which otherwise would not be deemed illegal under the normal WTO rules on subsidies) (WTO 2001b: section 10.2). There are also procedural obligations, such as the establishment of a Transitional Review Mechanism for China in addition to the normal Trade Policy Review cycle for WTO Members (WTO 2001b: section 18), and the requirement to translate all foreign trade laws and regulations into one of the official languages of the WTO beyond the normal WTO transparency requirement (WTO 2001a: para. 334).

Moreover, concerns that China might fall short of its WTO obligations have been shared not only among WTO Memberships as a whole but have been a particular concern for the most powerful player in the WTO: the United States. For example, in the US–China Relations Act of 2000, which was enacted by the US government to grant China Permanent Normal Trade Relationship (PNTR) ahead of China's accession to the WTO, the US noted the following:[1]

> The record of the People's Republic of China in implementing trade-related commitments has been mixed. While the People's Republic of China has generally met the requirements of the 1992 market access memorandum of understanding and the 1992 and 1995 agreements on intellectual property rights protection, other measures remain in place or have been put into place which tend to diminish the benefit to United States businesses, farmers, and workers from the People's Republic of China's implementation of those earlier commitments.[2]

In light of these concerns, the US government established a complex mechanism under the same Act to monitor 'compliance by China with its commitments under the WTO' involving the Departments of Commerce,

[1] US–China Relations Act of 2000.

[2] Ibid, para. 6901 (10).

State and Agriculture, as well as the United States Trade Representative (USTR).[3]

In the view of the author, however, the second issue, while relatively neglected, is more important. At the end of the day, the first issue is only about the market access commitments made by a particular WTO Member. No matter how important the underlying commercial interests or the market of the Member might be, the implementation of such commitments is still unlikely to have a major impact on the institutional foundations of the multilateral trading system as a whole. In contrast, if China were to take an uncooperative approach in the WTO, this could well affect the smooth functioning or even viability of the multilateral trading system. Will China, a long-time outsider to the international system, be a 'good citizen' in the WTO, an institution that has evolved from a club-like group into an organization with great diversity and vast differences among its Members? Here again, the opinions are divided. In the lead-up to China's accession, some commentators believed that China could weaken both the WTO dispute settlement system[4] and the decision-making process,[5] while others countered that, judging by China's relatively uneventful track record in the United Nations (UN) and other international organizations that it has participated in, China's entry to the WTO would not be so disruptive to the status quo (Abbott 1998; Feinerman 1995; Lardy 1996, 1999, 2002).

As China enters its tenth year of WTO Membership, has the dragon brought a 'reign of fire' to the multilateral trading system and rocked its institutional foundations? This chapter will answer this question by reviewing China's participation in two key activities of the WTO – i.e. trade negotiations and dispute settlement – as well as another important component of global trade governance: regional trade agreements (RTAs). I will argue that, overall, China has evolved from a passive 'taker' of the existing rules to a country that will 'shake' the rules for its own interests or even 'make' new rules. At the same time, the pace of China's ascent has been uneven in different areas. The most aggressive strategy

[3] Ibid, paras. 6943 and 6951.

[4] For views that China's accession will overburden the WTO dispute settlement system, see Ostry (1998: 9, 2003: 263).

[5] For views that China's accession will weaken the effectiveness of the WTO decision-making mechanism, see e.g. Steinberg (1999). According to Steinberg, the unique political-economic system of China and the sheer size of its economy will cause 'political frictions' in the WTO upon its accession. However, due to its ineffective consensus decision-making process, it is unlikely that the WTO will be able to adopt new rules to deal with such problems. This will in turn further weaken the WTO decision-making mechanism.

has been apparent in RTA negotiations, where China has been on a frantic shopping spree since its accession to the WTO. Similarly, while China was initially reluctant to use the multilateral dispute settlement system, it has become a major player since 2007. In terms of multilateral trade negotiations, China has sent mixed signals: while it has made many submissions on negotiating issues in the Doha Round of WTO negotiations, China has so far successfully resisted calls from the United States (USA) and the European Union (EU) for it to play a leading role in the long-stalled trade talks. After exploring the reasons for varying behavioural patterns in a range of areas, this chapter concludes by exploring China's future role in the WTO, as well as the potential ramifications of China's ascent in global trade governance.

1 Multilateral trade negotiations

As the world's third-largest economy (in terms of nominal GDP) and trader (World Bank 2010c; WTO 2009a), China has considerable economic clout. The growing economic muscle of China has been gradually translated into elevated standings in key international institutions. While China has been a permanent Member of the UN Security Council ever since it resumed its UN Membership in 1971, it only recently gained more voting rights in both the International Monetary Fund (IMF) and the World Bank (BBC 2006; World Bank 2010a, 2010b; Xinhuanet 2010). However, the transition seems yet to happen at the WTO, where many key players keep complaining about China's alleged 'back-seat' role. Indeed, as recently as early 2008, both the USA and the EU were still reportedly frustrated over China's passive approach to the Doha Round of negotiations and the WTO's management more broadly (Otteman 2008). Even senior Chinese officials openly acknowledge this. For example, in late 2006, Dr Zhang Xiangchen, then Director-General of the Department of WTO Affairs of the Ministry of Commerce of the People's Republic of China (MOFCOM) and the current Deputy Permanent Representative of China's WTO Mission, conceded in an interview that China is only playing a 'preliminary constructive role'.[6]

[6] See Beijing Youth Daily, Shangwubu Shimao Zuzhi Si Sizhang Tan Rushi: Cheng Shimao Tixi Yifenzi (Director-General of Department of WTO Affairs on China's WTO Accession: Becoming Part of the WTO System). Available at http://finance.people.com.cn/GB/70392/5146335.html [accessed in November 2010].

While China has indeed taken a low-profile approach, this does not necessarily mean that China has made no contribution to the Doha Round. In fact, judging from the number of negotiating proposals submitted since the launch of the Round, China is one of the most active WTO Members in the negotiations. According to a study based on the official records of the WTO in 2003, China made a total of twenty-nine written submissions to the Trade Negotiations Committee and its subsidiary bodies, the Ministerial Conference at Doha, and the working groups on the four Singapore issues. On this measure, China is the most active developing country participant and the fourth most active among all WTO Members in the Doha Round (Nordström 2002: 28–30). As of July 2008, China has submitted more than one hundred proposals in the Doha Development Agenda (DDA) (Zhang 2008). These proposals are quite comprehensive and cover virtually all issues in the DDA, ranging from agriculture and non-agricultural market access (NAMA) to rules and services.

Given such active participation in the actual negotiation process, why then did China choose to take a low profile in public? In the author's view, the reasons include the following, elaborated in the forthcoming text.

1.1 *The 'Recently Acceded Member' argument* RAM!

Having been under the spotlight for fifteen years in one of the longest accession negotiations[7] in the history of the General Agreement on Tariffs and Trade (GATT)/WTO, the first explanation for China's low profile in public in the DDA is that the Chinese government wanted some quiet breathing space to digest and implement its heavy accession commitments. Indeed, China's concessions on both trade in goods and services greatly exceeded those of other WTO Members, most of which have not changed since the conclusion of the Uruguay Round. As argued by Shi Miaomiao, Deputy Director-General of the Department of WTO Affairs of MOFCOM (M. Shi 2005: 28–9):

> In terms of industrial products, if applying the Uruguay Round modality for tariff-reduction, China would only be required to reduce its tariff from a base point of 42.7% to the final bound tariff of 32.4% in year 2004, with an average reduction by 24.1%. According to its accession commitments,

[7] China's dubious honour of being the WTO Member with the longest accession process has been overtaken by Russia, which is in its seventeenth year of accession negotiation as of 2010.

> however, China's tariff reduction level is much greater. In 2004, China's average tariff rate on industrial products was reduced to 9.5%. After China's fulfillment of its commitments on accession into WTO, it has reduced its tariff rate by as much as 78.9%, which is much bigger than the 33% tariff reduction commitment made by other countries during the Uruguay Round. Moreover, even if the new round of Doha negotiation concludes with a reduction rate of as much as 68.5%, the total tariff cut of China would still exceed the total tariff cut of other countries during the Uruguay Round and Doha Round combined.
>
> ...
>
> In terms of agriculture products, if applying the Uruguay Round modality for tariff-reduction, China would only be required to reduce its tariff from the base point of 54% to a final bound tariff of 37.9%. Instead, during its WTO Accession negotiations, China made greater concessions on reduction of agricultural tariffs. Pursuant to China's commitments, the agricultural tariff fell in 2002 to 18.5%, in 2004 to 15.6%, and by the year 2008 it will be further reduced to 15.1%. Such reductions would amount to an overall tariff reduction rate by 67.1%, which far exceeds the concession made by other members (36% for the developed Members, and 24% for the developing Members). Even if the new Doha Round concludes with a reduction rate on agricultural products of as high as 48%, the total tariff cut of China would still exceed the total tariff cut of other countries during the Uruguay and Doha Round combined.

literature review

Independent experts affirm this view. For example, Mattoo notes that China's services commitments are generally higher than other WTO Members in terms of both the width of coverage and the depth of market-opening. Indeed, he praises China's commitments under the General Agreement on Trade in Services (GATS) as 'the most radical services reform program negotiated in the WTO' (Mattoo 2003: 300). This observation is shared by Lardy, who noted in his study of China's accession package that the country's commitments 'far surpass those made by founding members of the WTO and, in some cases, go beyond those made by countries that have joined the organization since its founding in 1995' (Lardy 2002: 104–5).

Because of its substantial accession commitments, China has been arguing that it, along with other 'Recently Acceded Members' (RAMs), should not be required to make the same level of concessions as the founding WTO Members (WTO 2003).

To be fair, many WTO Members were initially sympathetic to the call for special treatment for RAMs. For this reason, the Hong Kong Ministerial Declaration explicitly states that '[w]e recognize the special situation of recently-acceded Members who have undertaken extensive market access commitments at the time of accession. This situation will be taken into account in the negotiations' (WTO 2005: para. 58). Indeed, had the DDA been concluded according to the original schedule, it is not unlikely that China could have avoided making substantial concessions on agriculture or NAMA by hiding under the 'RAM' label. Unfortunately, however, as the Doha Round drags on, fewer Members are willing to give a 'free ride' to Members such as China that acceded a decade ago.

Moreover, the USA and the EU face increasing pressures: on the one hand, their negotiating partners ask them to make more concessions; on the other hand, vocal domestic constituencies (such as labour and farmers' groups) have been calling for the government to seek more inroads into foreign markets while avoiding having to provide access to their own domestic markets. Thus, they need to find another scapegoat to divert part of the attention. What could be a better target than China – the economic superpower on rapid rise? Thus, since 2006, the USA and the EU have been pushing China from both sides. For example, the USA has repeatedly urged China, as the biggest beneficiary of the multilateral trading system, to take more responsibilities at the WTO (Schwab 2006). Similarly, the EU has argued that China should be required to make contributions just like other WTO Members (Khor 2007). While the USA and EU use ambiguous terms such as 'leadership' to describe such 'responsibilities' and 'contributions', a careful reading between the lines of their messages reveals that what the USA and the EU really have in mind is asking China to provide more concessions in key areas such as agriculture, NAMA and services so that they can have a better report card to show to their domestic stakeholders.

While China fought hard to avoid making new concessions by being recognized as a RAM, it seems that it has lost the battle. According to the latest negotiating drafts, the prevailing consensus seems to be that flexibility will be extended mostly to small, low-income RAMs and 'very recently acceded Members', i.e. those that acceded to the WTO after the Doha Round was launched.

1.2 *Lack of expertise*

Even if China wishes to participate more fully in the WTO, as a new Member China lacks familiarity with the rules of the game and cannot participate effectively. This is the case for both substantive WTO rules as well as for procedural rules.

Regarding substantive rules, while the most important of them have been compiled in the Secretariat publication, *The Legal Texts: The Results of the Uruguay Round of Multilateral Trade Negotiations* (WTO 1999), there are also numerous GATT protocols, decisions and other legal instruments that are not available in a readily accessible format (WTO 1994: Article 1(a)–(c)). Moreover, as noted by the Appellate Body in *Japan – Alcoholic Beverages II*, there are many panel reports adopted during the GATT era, which, as 'an important part of the GATT acquis … create legitimate expectations among WTO Members, and, therefore, should be taken into account where they are relevant to any dispute' (WTO 1996: 18). In addition, in line with the tradition of 'constructive ambiguity', many WTO rules are drafted in such a way that they are difficult to interpret for any Member, let alone newer ones. This is especially the case for rules that provide for flexibilities, which are often too technical for developing countries to master, as Deere demonstrated in her excellent study on the use of flexibilities in the Trade-related Aspects of Intellectual Property Right (TRIPS) agreement (Deere 2009). For new Members in particular, it is a major challenge to grasp these legal rules.

"constructive ambiguity"

Compared with substantive rules, the procedural rules of the WTO are even more difficult for new Members to decipher. While Articles 9 and 10 of the Marrakesh Agreement Establishing the WTO (WTO Agreement) provide a set of elaborate rules for voting requirements for various decisions, formal voting has been rare in the history of the GATT and WTO.[8] In practice, most if not all decisions are made by 'consensus'. What is 'consensus' then? According to the footnote to Article 9.1 of the WTO Agreement, consensus is defined as the situation where 'no Member, present at the meeting when the decision is taken, formally objects to the proposed decision'. However, such cryptic explanation offers little help to the uninitiated. Ironically, that is probably the reason why the consensus rule is preferred over the clearly defined and easily understood rules, such as two-thirds or three-quarters majority. To make it even more hopeless, even the consensus rule itself is of little use in reality as it applies to decision-making in formal meetings, which unfortunately is not where most decisions are made at the WTO. As acknowledged by the WTO Secretariat, '[i]mportant breakthroughs are rarely made in formal meetings of [WTO] bodies, least of all in the higher level councils. Since decisions are made by consensus, without voting, informal consultations

[8] For a review of the problems with the GATT/WTO decision-making rules, see Ehlermann and Ehring (2005).

within the WTO play a vital role in bringing a vastly diverse membership round to an agreement'.[9] Thus, the only way to acquire essential negotiating skills such as agenda-setting and coalition-building is through actual participation in the real work of the WTO. Unfortunately, as China did not join the WTO as a formal Member until six years after the WTO was formed, it faced a rather steep learning curve.

In this regard, the thirty years of experience China had already acquired as a Member of the UN at the time it joined the WTO were not of much help either, for two reasons. First, the nature of trade negotiations is very different from the political grandstanding at the UN. As one WTO official observed: 'The UN is a talk-shop; the WTO is for getting real business done.'[10] Second, at the UN, China has been a Member of its key decision-making body – the Security Council – from the very beginning. In contrast, there is no such formal institutional arrangement at the WTO. Also, the key players in the global trade arena have been rather reluctant to grant China a seat at the table of the informal negotiating groupings for fear of diluting their own power.[11] While China has substantial trade volume, this by itself has not guaranteed China a position as a key player in WTO negotiations.

Given the substantial obstacles China has faced since its accession to the WTO, its performance in trade negotiations to date has been quite satisfactory. While no indicator can accurately quantify a country's negotiating prowess, the number of submissions made in the negotiations can serve as a useful proxy (Nordström 2002: 12). China did not make any submission in the Doha Round until 20 June 2002, when it made a proposal on fisheries subsidies.[12] By February 2005, China made more than ten submissions (G. Shi 2005: 21). The number jumped to sixty-seven by December 2007. By the time of the July 2008 meeting, China had made more than one hundred submissions concerning the Doha Round.

[9] WTO. *Understanding The WTO: The Organization, Whose WTO is it Anyway?* Available at www.wto.org/english/thewto_e/whatis_e/tif_e/org1_e.htm#top [accessed in November 2010].

[10] The author's interview with a senior WTO diplomat.

[11] As I will note below, due to China's unique position as both a developing country and a major trader, neither the developed countries nor the major developing countries regard China as one of their own and both view China more as a threat rather than a potential ally.

[12] Ministry of Commerce of China, 'Zhongguo Canyu Duoha Huihe Tanpan Dashiji (Major Milestones in China's Participation in Doha Round Negotiations'. Available at http://cwto.mofcom.gov.cn/aarticle/c/200910/20091006574682.html?1126026260=872534836 [accessed in November 2010].

Judging from the rapidly increasing number of submissions, China has been learning very fast.

1.3 *The mismatch between the China-specific provisions and the normal WTO framework*

In addition to the extensive market access commitments in both goods and services, China also reluctantly accepted many discriminatory clauses that are tailor-made for itself as part of its accession agreement. By their nature, these China-specific provisions are beyond the normal WTO framework. Thus, even if China acquired expertise in normal WTO negotiations, this would not solve the main problems facing China.

These provisions can be further divided into two categories: WTO-plus obligations, i.e. obligations that are beyond those normally required of WTO Members; and WTO-minus rights, i.e. rights that are less than those usually enjoyed by WTO Members.

The WTO-plus obligations include, for example:[13]

- The obligation to translate all foreign trade laws into one of the official languages of the WTO, while the normal transparency obligation in the WTO agreements only requires Members to publish trade laws and regulations in their own national languages (GATT Article X).
- A special transitional review mechanism. Under this mechanism, China shall be reviewed annually by the WTO since its accession. There will be a total of nine such reviews, with the first to the eighth of such reviews conducted every year after 2001 and a final review no later than the tenth anniversary after China's accession. This obligation is in addition to the normal periodic review as mandated by the Agreement on Trade Policy Review Mechanism (TPRM), under which China would only need to be reviewed once every four years at the time of its accession.[14]
- The obligation to provide national treatment to both foreign products and persons, while the WTO national treatment clauses only cover measures applicable to products.

[13] For a detailed discussion of the WTO-plus obligations, see Qin 2003.

[14] Section C of the Trade Policy Review Mechanism, Annex 3 to the Agreement Establishing the World Trade Organization. Available at www.wto.org/english/docs_e/legal_e/legal_e.htm#annex3 [accessed in November 2010]. The frequency of review is determined according to the trade share of the Member under review. At the time of its accession, China was the sixth-largest trader in the world. With its growing trade share, China is now reviewed on a biennial basis.

As to the WTO-minus rights, they include the following:[15]

- Designation of China as a 'non-market economy' in anti-dumping investigations for the first fifteen years after its accession, which makes it easier for investigating authorities to find the existence of dumping.
- The inclusion of an 'alternative benchmark' methodology in subsidy and countervailing measures (SCM) investigations, which also creates biases in favour of a positive finding on subsidies, all else being equal.
- A special textile safeguard mechanism (until the end of 2008), and a transitional product-specific safeguard mechanism (until the end of 2013). Both safeguard mechanisms considerably lowered the substantive and procedural safeguards in GATT Article XIX and the Safeguards Agreement, making it much easier for other countries to invoke safeguard measures against China while at the same time making it more difficult for China to challenge such measures.

As these provisions were specifically designed to soften the impact of China's WTO accession on other Members, they have a much more direct impact on Chinese exports than WTO rules applicable to other Members, at least during the transitional period. While the exact relationship between China's special provisions and the normal WTO rules is still subject to debate,[16] most commentators would agree that the China-specific provisions would take precedence pursuant to the principle of *lex specialis derogat legi generali* (a special rule prevails over a general rule). Thus, at least until 2017 – i.e. before the expiration of these China-specific provisions – China would regard the revision of these special provisions as a task more urgent than the revision of the general WTO rules. Unfortunately, revising the China-specific accession provisions through the WTO negotiations will be extremely hard, if not impossible. To start with, the WTO is ill-equipped for this task. Among the WTO Agreements, none contain explicit rules on how to revise the accession protocol. In practice, other than a few isolated cases of minor revisions of accession commitments,[17] there has been no precedent of comprehensive

15 For a detailed discussion of the WTO-minus rights, see Gao 2007a.

16 For the legal problems raised by these provisions, see Gao 2007a: 56–7.

17 For example, when Mongolia acceded to the WTO in 1997, it committed to phase out and eliminate its export duty on raw cashmere within ten years. Due to both economic and environmental concerns, however, Mongolia found itself unable to eliminate the export duty. It requested the Council for Trade in Goods (CTG) for a five-year waiver on its accession commitment on cashmere, which was approved by the CTG on 9 July 2007. Available at www.wto.org/english/news_e/news07_e/good_counc_9july07_e.htm [accessed in November 2010]. The background of this case can be found in Tsogtbaatar 2005.

revisions of accession terms for particular countries. Thus, if China were to insist on revising its accession provisions, the default consensus rule would probably apply. As we have seen from the history of the WTO, consensus among all WTO Members is extremely hard to come by; indeed, it is one of the reasons why the Doha Round is taking so long. More importantly, most other WTO Members are not interested in the idea of revising China's terms of accessions. Furthermore, even if assuming, *arguendo*, that China could somehow persuade other Members to accept its request to revise its accession commitments, it probably will have to provide compensation to other Members as per the current rules on the renegotiation and modification of schedules.[18] Such compensation will have to take the form of additional concessions to other Members beyond the commitments China made upon accession. However, as I explained earlier, it is very unlikely that China will be willing to provide such additional concessions. As will be elaborated below, this factor also partly explains why China chose to take a relatively high profile in WTO disputes and RTA negotiations.

Against this context, the recent calls by the USA and the EU for China to shoulder more responsibility and make more concessions in the Doha Round are rather ironic. On the one hand, the USA and the EU imposed harsh conditions on China in the accession negotiations and effectively denied China the normal Membership status.[19] Yet, on the other hand, the USA and the EU now want China to behave like a 'normal' WTO Member, or even to go beyond what normal WTO Members would offer by taking up 'leadership responsibility'. Until the USA and the EU abandon such double standards and instead treat China on a non-discriminatory basis, why should China be expected to contribute to the Round above and beyond what is expected of a normal Member? Indeed, as eloquently explained by Sun Zhenyu, China's Ambassador to the WTO, China has made more contributions to the Round than even major developed countries. According to Sun's statement at the Informal Trade Negotiations Committee Meeting held on 11 August 2008, which is a kind of post-mortem session after the failure of the Members to reach major breakthrough during the previous week:

[18] See e.g. GATT Article 28 and GATS Article 21.

[19] As noted by Cattaneo and Braga (2009) in their comprehensive study on WTO accessions, while many other WTO Members that acceded to the WTO recently were also asked to assume obligations beyond the normal WTO disciplines, none of them are as onerous as those imposed on China, which remain a 'particularly challenging and atypical case'.

> We have tried very hard to contribute to the success of the Round. It is a little bit surprising that at this time the US started this finger pointing. I am surprised because they are now talking about cotton, sugar, rice of China as seems that we are not going to make any efforts in the Round. Let me explain what China has contributed in the round.
>
> Because of our accession negotiations, our tariff in agriculture on average is 15.2% and now bound at this level, which is lower than the average of European Union, lower than Canada, lower than Japan, lower than quite a number of other developed countries on average. But on that basis, we are committed in this round to cut further down our tariffs, the applied tariffs deeply. And in NAMA, our average is 9%, bound at that level. And in this round, we will cut about 30% in applied level. So we are making contributions of 50% of the total developing countries in terms of applied rate cut.
>
> ...
>
> If you consider what the contributions that developed countries are going to make, in OTDS (Overall Trade-Distorting Domestic Support) the US is spending $7 to 8 billion this year or last year, maybe a little bit more to 10 billion, but they are offering $14.5 billion with a lot of policy space for themselves. And in their tariff cut in agriculture, they are protecting their sensitivities through sensitive products while they are saying 'well even if we have sensitive products for 5 or 4% of our tariff lines, we will have TRQ (Tariff Rate Quota) expansions'. But they can never expand their TRQ to the level of China's TRQ quantities. In our case, our TRQ is 9 million tons for wheat, 7 million tons for corn, 5 million tons for rice. How about your quota, even after the expansion they will never pass half a million tons. Where is the new market access to the developed countries?
>
> (Sun 2008)

1.4 *Awkward position on other issues*

Among the diversity of WTO Members, China is notable for not only the size of its economy but also its multifaceted interests. This in turn results in different or even conflicting demands in the formulation of its trade policy. Here are two examples of such conflicts.

The first is the conflict between China's self-designated political position as a developing country and its economic standing as a major trader. For political reasons, China has always labelled itself as a developing country and joined several major developing country groups in the WTO, such as the G20.[20] On the other hand, however, the fact remains

[20] The G20 is a coalition of developing countries pressing for ambitious reforms of agriculture in developed countries with some flexibility for developing countries (not to be

that China is one of the most important traders in the world along with major developed countries such as the USA, the EU and Japan. Thus, on many issues, China's true interests actually lie closer to those of developed countries rather than those of developing countries. Take agriculture, for example. One of the major demands of developing countries is the elimination of export subsidies and reduction of domestic support. However, as one of the largest importers of many agricultural commodities, such as wheat, cotton and soya beans, China would probably find itself becoming the primary victim of the hike in world commodity prices that would accompany the end of subsidies by developed countries. Also, in the area of NAMA, major developed countries have been pressing developing countries to reduce tariffs. As the 'factory of the world', China stands to gain tremendously from the reduction of industrial tariffs. However, China finds it politically difficult to request that developing countries lower their tariffs on industrial goods. Another example is trade facilitation. While many developing countries argued against inclusion of this issue in the Doha negotiating agenda – particularly early in the Round – China's position as one of the top exporters in the world gives it a strong incentive to push for the inclusion of trade facilitation in the WTO framework, thereby making the customs process more efficient and cheaper. On all of these issues, due to the difference between China's political position and economic interests, it would be politically awkward for China to openly deviate from the developing country 'party line'. Thus, the best strategy seems to be to keep a low profile.

The second conflict is in the area of the WTO's rules related to trade remedies, where China is both the biggest victim and a major user. Take anti-dumping measures, for example. China has been the favourite target of anti-dumping investigations and actions for many years. According to a study by Bown, from 1995 to 2008 China was subject to 295 new anti-dumping measures, which was double that against Korea – the second most frequent anti-dumping target (Bown 2009: 82). Bearing in mind that Bown's figure for China only starts from its WTO accession while the numbers for other countries date back to 1995, the contrast is even more

confused with the G20 group of finance ministers and central bank governors, and its recent summit meetings). It currently has twenty-three Members: Argentina, Bolivarian Republic of Venezuela, Bolivia, Brazil, Chile, China, Cuba, Ecuador, Egypt, Guatemala, India, Indonesia, Mexico, Nigeria, Pakistan, Paraguay, Peru, Philippines, South Africa, Tanzania, Thailand, Uruguay and Zimbabwe. See www.wto.org/english/tratop_e/agric_e/negoti_groups_e.htm [accessed in November 2010].

stark. Thus, one would think that China has reason to push for stricter disciplines on the use of anti-dumping in the Doha Round negotiations. At the same time, however, as one of the major users of anti-dumping actions in recent years, it also seems to make sense for China to argue that more discretion be given to the investigating authorities. Two other factors further complicate the picture. First, as noted by Messerlin, China is targeted more by developing countries than developed countries, especially if the number of anti-dumping actions is adjusted for trade size. For example, let's say that the EU imposes one anti-dumping measure against a certain dollar amount of imports from China. According to Messerlin's study, India will adopt ten anti-dumping measures while Mexico will adopt sixty such measures (Messerlin 2004: 32). However, for fears of endangering the solidarity among developing countries and undermining the support of China by other developing countries on key political issues such as the Taiwan problem, at least in the eyes of the Chinese leadership, it would not be a good idea for China to openly confront developing countries.

Second, because China is not treated as a market economy in anti-dumping investigations, it does not matter much if the general rules under the Anti-dumping Agreement are improved or not, unless, of course, China argues for the clarification of the rules on the treatment of non-market economies. Acquiring clarification on the latter would be a difficult task for two reasons. First, as very few countries are in the non-market economy club, most WTO Members would not be sympathetic to China's request. Second, even if the relevant rules in the main Anti-dumping Agreement were revised, it is unclear whether or not China would ultimately benefit from this as the China-specific 'non-market economy' provision is regulated by the Accession Protocol, which, legally speaking, is an entirely different agreement to anti-dumping.

As the discussions above have illustrated, China's decision to keep a low profile in the current Round actually makes great sense. Unless there are substantial changes in the factors discussed above, it is unlikely that China will voluntarily assume a leading role in the talks.

2 Multilateral dispute settlement

In contrast to its reticence in WTO negotiations, China has transformed itself from being a reluctant player into an aggressive litigant in WTO dispute settlement activities. Its roles have shifted through three stages, outlined below.

2.1 *Rule taker*

From the time of its accession, China has taken a cautious approach towards WTO litigation. As a newcomer unfamiliar with WTO legal rules, China put more emphasis on learning them than on winning specific disputes. In an effort to discourage litigation, China usually settled disputes quickly with the complainant once a case was filed or threatened, even if it might have had strong arguments to defend its actions.[21] For example, in a matter concerning value-added tax rebates on integrated circuits, the USA made a request for consultations in March 2004, and the dispute was settled just four months later. The same period also saw China cave in only two months after the EU threatened to bring a formal WTO complaint against China's export quota regime on coke, an essential raw material for the production of steel. The climax of this approach was reached in the Kraft Linerboard case, in which the United States complained of inconsistencies with the Anti-dumping Agreement when MOFCOM imposed anti-dumping duties on US Kraft Linerboard imports in September 2005. On Friday, 6 January 2006, the USA finally threatened with a formal WTO complaint. On the next working day – i.e. Monday, 9 January 2006 – the Chinese government made an announcement to scrap the anti-dumping duties in this case.

2.2 *Rule shaker*[22]

To build a better understanding of the dispute settlement process, China actively participated as a third party in real WTO cases during the first few years after its accession. From August 2003 to 2006, for example, China joined almost every panel established during the period as a third party. Through its participation as a third party, China gained invaluable understanding of the WTO dispute settlement system and boosted its confidence in participating in the system as a main player. Such enhanced confidence was well illustrated by the remarks of Minister Bo Xilai of MOFCOM in May 2005. When asked whether China would bring complaints in the WTO against the countries that imposed restrictions against textile exports, Minister Bo Xilai responded (Xinhuanet 2005):

[21] For a review of China's approach towards WTO dispute settlement in this period, see Gao 2005.

[22] For a review of China's shift in strategy, see Gao 2007b.

> First, China has the right to resort to WTO dispute settlement mechanism. We should not hesitate to use this right when needed. Second, while bilateral consultation has its own benefits, if each side sticks to its own view, the problem won't be solved as there is no neutral arbiter. Thus, in addition to one-to-one consultations, sometimes it's more effective to have the disputes reviewed in the multilateral setting. Third, the restrictions against Chinese products are inconsistent with WTO rules and discriminatory. We strongly oppose such measures. Of course, it's up to us to decide whether to take any legal action against such measures and when to do so.

Some of the thinking that informed China's more aggressive new strategy in WTO litigation is revealed in the following analysis of Mexico's litigation strategy in the Soft Drinks case (WTO 2006) by Dr Ji Wenhua, an official in charge of dispute settlement activities at China's WTO Mission in Geneva. In the article he published in the July 2006 issue of the *China WTO Tribune*, a monthly journal on trade policy published by MOFCOM and edited by Dr Zhang Xiangchen – then Director-General of the Treaty and Law Department of MOFCOM – Ji noted that Mexico fought an uphill battle in the case brought against it by the USA, but made a good effort defending its case. According to Ji:

> In this case, Mexico's legal position was rather *weak*, but it has made an *unrelenting* effort by raising many arguments which are *tenuous at best* and *fighting a losing battle*.
>
> While we should not publicly *praise* such litigation strategy and attitude, this case still offers us some worthy lessons: under certain circumstances, we should try to employ some strategies, including resorting to *sophistry* and *delay tactics*.
>
> As a respondent, we should try to come up with as many factual and legal arguments as possible. Even if such arguments are mere sophistry, or made for purposes such as creating artificial difficulties for the panel, gaining sympathies, diverting the attention of other parties, or delaying the progress of the case, they are justified so long as they serve to protect our own interest.
>
> (Original emphasis. Original in Chinese. Translated by the author.)

Equipped with this enlightened new attitude towards the WTO dispute settlement mechanism, China has taken a markedly different approach since then. The turning point came in March 2006, when the USA, EU and Canada brought a joint complaint against China in the Auto Parts case (WTO 2009e). The complainants accused China of violating WTO obligations by treating some imported automobile parts as whole-car imports and imposing additional charges equivalent to the difference between the higher tariff for whole-car imports and the lower tariff applicable to automobile parts. Technically speaking, this is a rather simple case as the illegality of the Chinese measure seems to be quite obvious, especially as China has made specific commitments to impose no more than a 10 per cent tariff on automobile parts imports in its accession package. However, rather than continuing the old practice of settling the disputes privately, China decided not to concede defeat without a good fight. Over the next two and a half years, the case went all the way from the Panel to the Appellate Body until the Appellate Body finally issued its report in December 2008.

The same aggressive approach was taken in several other cases, especially the TRIPS case (WTO 2009d) and the Publications and Audiovisual Products case (WTO 2010b). In both these instances, China tried to shake or even bend the existing rules by aggressively making legal arguments that put its position in a better light. This strategy was reflected not only in the extensive substantive legal arguments China made, but also in its sophisticated use of procedural objections. As all good lawyers know, while procedural matters may seem mundane, they are of no less importance than substantive claims; if used well, they can even save a hopeless case. Judging from its performance in these cases, China has mastered the 'sophistries' very well. In the TRIPS case, for example, China attacked the complainants on such procedural grounds as the admissibility of certain evidence (WTO 2009d: paras. 6.14–6.37) and the correct scope of the measures at issue (WTO 2009d: paras. 7.1–7.19). Similarly, in the Publications case, China's procedural arguments included the failure of the USA to establish a prima facie case (WTO 2010b: paras. 7.458–7.460), the evidentiary standards (WTO 2010b: paras. 7.620–7.632) and the appropriate scope of the Panel's terms of reference (WTO 2010b: para. 7.63).

2.3 *Rule maker*

As observed above, while China accepted some rather harsh terms as the price for its WTO accession, it will likely be difficult for China to change them through the multilateral negotiation process. This has left the country with only one option: trying to challenge the terms and soften their negative impacts through creative interpretation in WTO dispute settlement proceedings.

Among the five cases filed by China since September 2008, four (US – Anti-Dumping and Countervailing Duties (WTO 2008a); EU – Steel Fasteners (WTO 2009b); US – Tyres (WTO 2009c); and EU – Footwear

(WTO 2010a)) were aimed at changing the rules, especially the provisions in China's Accession Protocol. For example, in the United States – Anti-Dumping and Countervailing Duties case, China challenged the decision by the US authorities to impose both anti-dumping and countervailing duties against several products imported from China. In addition to the usual claims under the GATT, the Anti-dumping (AD) Agreement, and the Subsidies and Countervailing Measures (SCM) Agreements, two claims made by China are particularly interesting. These are described in more detail below.

The first claim is that the United States violated China's Accession Protocol by failing to follow the proper methodology for determining the existence and amount of subsidy benefits. Under Section 15(b) of China's Accession Protocol, in subsidy investigations, other WTO Members could 'use methodologies for identifying and measuring the subsidy benefit, which take into account the possibility that prevailing terms and conditions in China may not always be available as appropriate benchmarks'. Similar to subparagraph (a) of the same Section, which allows other WTO Members to use surrogate prices in anti-dumping investigations against Chinese firms, this provision was introduced to address the concern that prices in China do not reflect the true cost as China is not yet a full market economy. However, unlike the non-market economy (NME) status in anti-dumping investigations, which is scheduled to expire fifteen years after China's accession, the alternative benchmark methodology does not have an expiration date. Thus, theoretically speaking, the alternative benchmark methodology could be invoked even one hundred years after China's accession to the WTO. As discussed above, it would have been very hard for China to change this provision in its accession terms through negotiations in the WTO. Instead, China decided to limit the applicability of the provision by giving teeth to some seemingly innocuous terms in the provision. First, the USA failed to make a finding that there were 'special difficulties' in applying the prevailing terms and conditions in China as the basis for the determination of the existence of benefits. Second, the USA failed to notify the SCM Committee of the methodologies it used. This is a very clever way to reduce the utility of the provision. It remains to be seen how the Panel would rule in this case as it has not issued its report at the time of the completion of this chapter. However, if the Panel chooses to give a strict interpretation of the term 'special difficulties', this might greatly reduce the attractiveness of the provision and even effectively render it void.

The second claim is that the United States violated the relevant provisions in the Anti-dumping and Safeguards Agreements through its dual application of both anti-dumping and countervailing duties against the same products. The WTO rules on this matter as they currently stand are unclear. While it is possible for the same product to be subject to both anti-dumping and SCM *investigations* at the same time, under GATT Article VI.5, WTO Members are prohibited from the application of both anti-dumping and countervailing duties to the same identical products in the same case, but non-market economies do not receive the same treatment and may be subject to both anti-dumping and countervailing duties. However, this provision also states that the prohibition of dual application only applies to cases of export subsidies and does not include actionable domestic subsidies; thus it is not applicable to the alleged subsidies to Chinese products. On the other hand, one may also argue that to the extent that the dual application leads to overcompensation, this might result in inconsistencies with the 'lesser duty rule' under both the Anti-dumping and SCM Agreements. In summary, therefore, China hopes to clarify or even make new rules through this case. As the expiration date for non-market economy status in anti-dumping investigations draws closer, subsidy investigations will become the main issue facing Chinese firms. Hopefully, through the clarification of these terms in dispute settlement activities, China will be able to change the rules in its favour so that its firms will have an easier time when this issue arises.

Similarly, both the tyres safeguard case against the United States and the two anti-dumping cases against the EU involve claims of violation of the individual clauses authorizing the respective trade remedy measures in China's Accession Protocol. Given that the Panel and Appellate Body have not been particularly fond of trade remedy measures, there is a good chance that the ambiguous terms used in the Accession Protocol will be interpreted in a way that would restrict the utility of these provisions in the future. Should this be the case, China would have effectively changed the rules through the WTO dispute settlement process.

3 Regional trade agreements

Strictly speaking, RTAs exist in their own universe parallel to the multilateral trading system. However, as they cover increasingly more global trade,[23] they have become an important component to global trade

[23] For example, according to Carpenter, more than half of world trade is conducted under the preferential tariff regimes under RTAs rather than the most favoured nation (MFN) regime under the WTO. See Carpenter (2009: 25).

governance. Moreover, for most WTO Members, the WTO and RTAs are two alternative tracks that they will pursue at different times. Thus, in order to have a complete picture of China's position in global trade governance, I will also briefly discuss China's RTA approach here.

While China is now an active player in WTO dispute settlement, it still took more than five years for it to initially 'warm up'. In contrast, China did not waste any time in negotiating RTAs. Starting with the 2002 Free Trade Agreement (FTA) between China and the Association of Southeast Asian Nations (ASEAN), China has been busy negotiating RTAs covering both trade in goods and services. The subsequent years witnessed the signing of two Closer Economic Partnership Arrangements with Hong Kong, China[24] (June 2003) and Macau, China[25] (October 2003), respectively; the FTAs with Chile[26] (November 2005), Pakistan (November 2006), New Zealand (April 2008), Singapore (October 2008), Peru (April 2009), Costa Rica (April 2010); the launch of FTA negotiations with the Gulf Cooperation Council[27] (April 2005), Australia[28] (May 2005), Iceland[29] (April 2008) and Norway[30] (September 2008); and with negotiations soon to begin with the South African Customs Union (SACU).[31]

While political considerations seem to override economic benefits in many of these RTAs, China has also been trying to make new rules through them.[32] These rule-making efforts cover both the structural aspects and the substantive rules of RTAs.

[24] The full text of the Arrangement is available at www.tid.gov.hk/english/cepa/legaltext/cepa_legaltext.html [accessed in November 2010].

[25] The full text of the Arrangement is available at www.http://bo.io.gov.mo/edicoes/en/dse/cepa/ [accessed in November 2010].

[26] The full text of the Agreement is available at: www.direcon.cl/documentos/China2/tlc_chile_china_ing_junio_2006.pdf [accessed in November 2010].

[27] See 'China Completed First Round of FTA Negotiations with Six Gulf States'. Available at http://gjs.mofcom.gov.cn/aarticle/af/ak/200505/20050500088391.html [accessed in November 2010].

[28] Australia–China FTA Negotiations, Subscriber Update, 26 May 2005. Available at: www.dfat.gov.au/geo/china/fta/050526_subscriber_update.html [accessed in November 2010].

[29] See http://fta.mofcom.gov.cn/article/iceland/200809/49_1.html [accessed in November 2010].

[30] See http://fta.mofcom.gov.cn/ article/southafrica/200809/48_1.html [accessed in November 2010].

[31] See http://fta.mofcom.gov.cn/ topic/ensacu.shtml [accessed in November 2010].

[32] For a detailed discussion of China's FTA strategy, see Gao (2008: 55–6).

First, in terms of the structure, China's RTAs tend to have a narrower coverage than those used by other major players, such as the USA, EU or Japan. Normally, China would start with an agreement on trade in goods alone and would expand to services only after commitments on goods have been substantially implemented. Take the FTA with Pakistan, for example. While the liberalization of trade in goods dates back to the signing of the agreement on the Early Harvest Program in April 2005, the agreement on trade in services was only signed in February 2009. Similarly, in the FTA with ASEAN, the agreement on trade in goods was signed in November 2004, while the agreement on services was only signed in January 2007. A reverse example is the FTA negotiation with Australia, which has languished for years partly due to the fact that Australia insists on dealing with services liberalization first, while China wishes to proceed with the usual 'goods and then services' order. With regard to the issues that are not traditionally trade-related, such as environmental protection, competition policy and labour standards, China has been reluctant to include them as part of the FTA package, though recently it has shown some willingness to incorporate them. Nonetheless, in line with its cautious approach, China has largely preferred to address these in stand-alone side agreements or Memorandums of Understanding (MoUs), rather than through FTAs.

Second, with regard to substantive rules, China has insisted on the recognition of its market economy status by potential RTA partners as a precondition for virtually every RTA that it has signed. As mentioned earlier, in its accession package, China has agreed to be treated as a non-market economy. This makes it easier for other countries to find the existence of dumping in anti-dumping investigations against China. Given the structural problems in the WTO decision-making process, it is difficult for China to change its non-market economy status in the multilateral trading system. The remaining option is for China to negotiate with each of its trade partners to recognize China's market economy status. Because it has much more bargaining power at the bilateral/regional level, this strategy seems to be working. As of the end of 2009, seventy-nine economies have recognized the market economy status of China.[33] As such recognition increases, there will be mounting pressures on those who still deem

[33] Online interview with Zhou Xiaoyan, Director-General of the Bureau of Fair Trade, MOFCOM, 31 December 2009. Available at http://gzly.mofcom.gov.cn/website/face/www_face_history.jsp?desc=&p_page=2&sche_no=1515 [accessed in November 2010].

China as a non-market economy to accept its market economy status as an established precedent.

4 What lies ahead?

As we can see from the discussions above, China has gradually emerged on the central stage of the multilateral trading system. Looking to the future, it is very likely that China will become an increasingly active player in global trade governance. At the same time, given its diverse interests, China's degree and style of engagement on different aspects of global trade governance will likely vary.

First, in WTO negotiations, if the Doha Round ever concludes and a new round is launched, we will probably see a more active China at work. This will not only be the result of China's rising economic clout, but will also reflect its growing prowess in international diplomacy. Moreover, China itself will be more willing to participate in new multilateral trade negotiations as by then most of its discriminatory WTO accession provisions will already have expired. Will China's more active participation pose a challenge to the existing power balance in the WTO? Judging from China's past record in the UN and the WTO, it is unlikely that China will propose any sweeping changes to the governing structure of the institution. Instead, China will most likely focus on refining the technical rules that fine-tune the system.

Second, in WTO dispute settlement, we should expect more cases involving China as either respondent or complainant. In part, this will simply continue established patterns in the WTO: over the history of the GATT/WTO, it is rare to find cases where the two largest Members – i.e. the USA and the EU – are not involved in some capacity. It is only natural that we would find China, the next big trader, pursuing and/or receiving the same treatment. On the other hand, as some of the past cases illustrate – such as the audiovisual case, the subsidies case and the ongoing debate on China's currency policy[34] – many of China's trade disputes are not just the old-fashioned clash between the giants that we have seen in disputes between the USA and the EU. Instead, they reflect the inherent tension between the economic and political systems of China and the fundamental principles of the WTO, which were designed by and

[34] For the complicated issues raised by the currency dispute, see e.g. Evenett (2010), especially section 5: Does the crisis-era Renminbi regime violate WTO rules? Is the threat of WTO litigation credible?

for economies that operate in vastly different environments. Will China work to change the existing rules in its favour through the WTO dispute settlement mechanism? This seems unlikely. As illustrated in the previous discussion, while China has been trying to change some of the rules, the focus has been almost exclusively on rules that it finds discriminatory against itself, rather than general WTO rules.

Third, in the short- to medium-term future, we will probably see China's RTA frenzy waning down for several reasons. First, the non-market economy status clause in China's Accession Protocol will expire in 2016, leaving China with no need to reward countries with RTAs just for the sake of recognizing its market economy status. Second, if one looks around, it is evident that most countries that are willing to negotiate RTAs with China have already done so, making it harder to find new candidates. Third, as the recent protests against China in Malaysia and Indonesia[35] have shown, there might be a backlash against China when the RTA commitments kick in. The complicated political consequences of its RTAs, whose full implications remain to be seen, will probably make China more cautious in pursuing future regional agreements.

As history has shown, no international institutions can survive for long without the support of key players. As the biggest emerging power in the world today, China deserves a seat at the big-boys' table. While the other major powers, such as the USA, EU and India, might feel uneasy, they have to realize that recognizing a larger role for China in global trade governance also suits their own interests and those of the multilateral trading system as a whole. While the WTO, unlike its sister institutions, does not have any formal 'high table', it is an open secret that many key decisions are made in informal processes, such as the 'Green Room', which extends invitations only to key players. If China were denied the chance to join in the game that the major powers have been playing, it might well decide to make its own. Of course, one might have doubts as to whether the 'golden straitjacket' of multilateral trade rules, initially made for the medium-sized average WTO Members, could constrain an XXXL-size country like China. But such concerns are probably unwarranted as China has largely been a system maintainer in the WTO. In short, while China's ascent in global trade governance might raise some feelings of uneasiness, the best way to ease such concerns is by greeting it with more mutual understanding and accommodation, rather than reacting with fear and suspicion.

[35] See NAM NEWS NETWORK (2010) and Suwarni (2010).

References

Abbott, F. M. 1998. 'China's Accession to the WTO', *American Society of International Law Insights* January. www.asil.org/insigh13.cfm [Accessed in August 2010].

BBC. 2006. 'IMF Reforms Give China More Power', *BBC News* [online] 18 September. http://news.bbc.co.uk/2/hi/business/5358520.stm [Accessed in August 2010].

Bown, C. 2009. *Self-enforcing Trade: Developing Countries and WTO Dispute Settlement.* Washington, DC: Brookings Institution Press.

Carpenter, T. 2009. 'A Historical Perspective on Regionalism', in Baldwin, R. and Low, P. (eds.) *Multilateralizing Regionalism: Challenges for the Global Trading System.* Cambridge University Press, pp. 13–27.

Cattaneo, O. and Braga, A. P. 2009. *Everything You Always Wanted to Know about WTO Accession (But Were Afraid to Ask).* Policy Research Working Paper Series 5116. Washington, DC: The World Bank.

Deere, C. 2009. *The Implementation Game: The TRIPS Agreement and the Global Politics of Intellectual Property Reform in Developing Countries.* Oxford University Press.

Ehlermann, C. D. and Ehring, L. 2005. 'Are WTO Decision-Making Procedures Adequate for Making, Revising and Implementing Worldwide and "Plurilateral" Rules?', in Petersmann, E.U. (ed.), *Reforming the World Trading System: Legitimacy, Efficiency, and Democratic Governance.* Oxford University Press, pp. 497–522.

Evenett, S. J. (ed.) 2010. *The US-Sino Currency Dispute: New Insights from Economics, Politics, and Law.* London: Centre for Economic Policy Research (CEPR).

Feinerman, J. V. 1995. 'Chinese Participation in the International Legal Order: Rogue Elephant or Team Player?' *The China Quarterly* 141: 186–210.

Gao, H. 2005. 'Aggressive Legalism: The East Asian Experience and Lessons for China', in Gao, H. and Lewis, D. (eds.), *China's Participation in the WTO.* London: Cameron May, pp. 315–51.

2007a. 'China's Participation in the WTO: A Lawyer's Perspective', *Singapore Year Book of International Law* 11: 41–74.

2007b. 'Taming the Dragon: China's Experience in the WTO Dispute Settlement System', *Legal Issues of Economic Integration* 34(4): 369–92.

2008. 'The RTA Strategy of China: A Critical Visit', in Buckley, R., Lo, V. I. and Boulle, L., *Challenges to Multilateral Trade: The Impact of Bilateral, Preferential and Regional Agreements.* The Netherlands: Kluwer Law International, pp. 55–66.

Khor, M. 2007. 'Trade: China and EU Clash over RAMs at NAMA Meeting', *SUNS* 6362, 9 November. www.twnside.org.sg/title2/wto.info/twninfo110719.htm [Accessed in August 2010].

Lardy, N. R. 1996. *China and the WTO*. Brookings Policy Brief Series #9. Washington, DC: The Brookings Institute.

1999. *China's WTO Membership*. Brookings Policy Brief Series #47, Washington, DC: The Brookings Institute.

2002. *Integrating China into the Global Economy*. Washington, DC: The Brookings Institute.

Mattoo, A. 2003. 'China's Accession to the WTO: The Services Dimension', *Journal of International Economic Law* 6(2): 299–339.

Messerlin, P. 2004. 'China in the WTO: Antidumping and Safeguards', in Bhattasali, D., Li, S. and Martin, W. (eds.) *China and the WTO: Accession, Policy Reform, and Poverty Reduction Strategies*. Washington, DC: World Bank, pp. 29–47.

NAM NEWS NETWORK. 2010. 'Malaysia Government Will Address Concerns over Surge in Imports from China'. 12 February. http://bilaterals.org/spip.php?article16786 [Accessed in November 2010].

Nordström, H. 2002. 'Participation of Developing Countries in the WTO: New Evidence Based on the 2003 Official Records', Sweden: National Board of Trade.

Ostry, S. 1998. 'China and the WTO: The Transparency Issue', *UCLA Journal of International Law and Foreign Affairs* 3(1): 1–22.

2003. 'WTO Membership for China: To Be or Not to Be: Is That the Answer?' in Cass, D. Z., Williams, B. G. and Barker, G. (eds.) *China and the World Trading System: Entering the New Millennium*. Cambridge University Press, pp. 257–65.

Otteman, S. 2008. 'Low-Key Chinese Role in Doha Trade Talks Frustrates U.S., EU', *Inside US-China Trade* 8(1). 2 January.

Qin, J. Y. 2003. '"WTO-Plus" Obligations and Their Implications for the World Trade Organization Legal System: An Appraisal of the China Accession Protocol', *Journal of World Trade* 491: 37(3).

Schwab, S. 2006. *Remarks at the 40th Anniversary Gala Dinner of the National Committee on US–China Relations*. New York, USA. 12 October 2006. www.ncuscr.org/files/2006Gala_SusanSchwab.pdf [Accessed in August 2010].

Shi, G. 2005. 'Working Together for a Better Future Based on Mutual Benefit', in Gao, H. and Lewis, D. (eds.), *China's Participation in the WTO*. London: Cameron May, pp. 15–22.

Shi, M. 2005. 'China's Participation in the Doha Negotiations and Implementation of its Accession Commitments', in Gao, H. and Lewis, D. (eds.), *China's Participation in the WTO*. London: Cameron May, pp. 23–33.

Steinberg, R. 1999. *Institutional Implications of WTO Accession for China*. IGCC Working Paper No. 4. La Jolla: University of California Institute on Global Conflict and Cooperation.

Sun, Z. 2008. *Statement by H.E. Ambassador Sun Zhenyu at the Informal Trade Negotiations Committee Meeting.* 11 August 2008. http://wto2.mofcom.gov.cn/aarticle/inbrief/200808/20080805717988.html [Accessed in August 2010].

Suwarni, Y. 2010. 'Thousands Rally to Demand Delay of ASEAN-China FTA', *Jakarta Post*, 7 January. http://bilaterals.org/spip.php?article16567 [Accessed in November 2010].

Tsogtbaatar, D. 2005. 'Mongolia's WTO Accession: Expectations and Realities of WTO Membership', in Gallagher, P., Low, P. and Stoler, A. L. (eds.) *Managing the Challenges of WTO Participation: 45 Case Studies.* Cambridge University Press, pp. 409–19.

US–China Relations Act of 2000: Pub. L. 106–286, 22 U.S.C. 6901 et seq., 10 October 2000.

World Bank. 2010a. *World Bank Reforms Voting Power, Gets $86 Billion Boost.* [press release], 25 April 2010. http://go.worldbank.org/WDRT2IZSE0 [Accessed in August 2010].

2010b. *World Bank Group Voice Reform: Enhancing Voice and Participation in Developing and Transition Countries in 2010 and Beyond* [online], 25 April 2010. http://siteresources.worldbank.org/NEWS/Resources/IBRD2010VotingPowerRealignmentFINAL.pdf [Accessed in August 2010].

2010c. *World Development Indicators.* Washington, DC: The World Bank.

World Trade Organization (WTO). 1994. *General Agreement on Tariffs and Trade.* Geneva: WTO.

1996. Appellate Body Report, Japan – Taxes on Alcoholic Beverages. WT/DS8/AB/R, WT/DS10/AB/R, WT/DS11/AB/R. Adopted 1 November 1996, DSR 1996:I, 97. Geneva: WTO.

1999. *The Legal Texts: The Results of the Uruguay Round of Multilateral Trade Negotiations.* Geneva: WTO.

2001a. *Report of the Working Party on the Accession of China.* WT/MIN(01)/3. 10 November. Geneva: WTO.

2001b. *Protocol on the Accession of The People's Republic of China.* WT/L/432. 23 November. Geneva: WTO.

2003. *Statement by H.E. Mr Lu Fuyuan, Minister of Commerce of China. At the Ministerial Conference, Fifth Session, Cancún*, WT/MIN(03)/ST/12. 10–14 September. Geneva: WTO.

2005. *Doha Work Programme: Ministerial Declaration.* WT/MIN(05)/DEC. 22 December. Geneva: WTO.

2006. *Panel Report, Mexico – Tax Measures on Soft Drinks and Other Beverages.* WT/DS308/R. Adopted 24 March 2006, as modified by Appellate Body Report WT/DS308/AB/R, DSR 2006. Geneva: WTO.

2008a. *United States–Definitive Anti-Dumping and Countervailing Duties on Certain Products from China*. DS379, Request for Consultations received on 19 September. Geneva: WTO.

2008b. *United States–Definitive Anti-Dumping and Countervailing Duties on Certain Products from China*. DS379. Request for Consultations received on 19 September 2008. Geneva: WTO.

2009a. *Trade Profiles 2009*. Geneva: WTO.

2009b. *European Communities – Definitive Anti-Dumping Measures on Certain Iron or Steel Fasteners from China*. DS397. Request for Consultations received on 31 July. Geneva: WTO.

2009c. *United States – Measures Affecting Imports of Certain Passenger Vehicle and Light Truck Tyres from China*. DS399. Request for Consultations received on 14 September. Geneva: WTO.

2009d. *Panel Report, China – Measures Affecting the Protection and Enforcement of Intellectual Property Rights*. WT/DS362/R. Adopted 20 March 2009. Geneva: WTO.

2009e. *Panel Reports, China – Measures Affecting Imports of Automobile Parts*. WT/DS339/R, WT/DS340/R, WT/DS342/R and Add.1 and Add.2. Adopted 12 January 2009, upheld (WT/DS339/R) and as modified (WT/DS340/R, WT/DS342/R) by Appellate Body Reports WT/DS339/AB/R, WT/DS340/AB/R, WT/DS342/AB/R. Geneva: WTO.

2010a. *European Union – Anti-Dumping Measures on Certain Footwear from China*, DS405, Request for Consultations received on 4 February. Geneva: WTO.

2010b. *Panel Report, China – Measures Affecting Trading Rights and Distribution Services for Certain Publications and Audiovisual Entertainment Products*. WT/DS363/R and Corr.1. Adopted 19 January 2010, as modified by Appellate Body Report WT/DS363/AB/R. Geneva: WTO.

Xinhuanet. 2005. 'Bo Xilai: Decisions of the EC and US to Impose Restrictions on Chinese Textiles Totally Groundless', *Xinhuanet News* [online] 30 May. http://news.xinhuanet.com/fortune/2005-05/30/content_3022500.htm [Accessed in August 2010].

2010. 'China's Voting Power in World Bank Ascends to Third Place', *Xinhuanet News* [online] 26 April. http://news.xinhuanet.com/english2010/china/2010-04/26/c_13266890.htm [Accessed in August 2010].

Zhang, X. 2008. 'Wuzi lide Daxiang (Elephant in the Room)', *China WTO Tribune* 7.

7

LDC priorities for improved global trade governance

ATUL KAUSHIK AND JULIAN MUKIIBI

Least developed countries (LDCs) are faced with a suite of challenges to their effective participation in global trade governance. Global trade governance includes bilateral, regional and multilateral trade agreements, and intergovernmental institutions like the World Trade Organization (WTO) and United Nations Conference on Trade and Development (UNCTAD). This chapter focuses on the multilateral trading system and specifically the WTO. It explores the emerging role of LDCs in WTO decision-making processes for negotiating the rules of the multilateral trading system and makes concrete proposals for advancing their priorities.

After a brief background on LDCs in WTO decision-making processes, this chapter reviews the historical role of developing countries in decision-making related to the General Agreement on Tariffs and Trade (GATT), the emergence of developing country coalitions in multilateral trade negotiations and the development of the LDC coalition in the WTO. It then sets out LDC priorities for improved global trade governance, emphasizing the role of Special and Differential Treatment (SDT) and the need for LDCs to take greater ownership of efforts to integrate them into the trading system. It continues by making the case for the creation of an institution for LDC-specific needs in Geneva. The chapter concludes with a summary of recommendations.

Atul Kaushik is Director (Climate Change), Ministry of Environment and Forests in India and was previous head of CUTS Geneva Resource Centre. Julian Mukiibi is a Programme Officer at CUTS Geneva Resource Centre and previously served as an Advisor in Legal and Economic Affairs at the Ugandan Mission to the WTO. The authors acknowledge with gratitude the discussions they had with various LDC negotiators in Geneva, and valuable comments by an anonymous expert and Carolyn Deere Birkbeck. All errors and omissions are solely of the authors.

1 Background

Of the forty-nine countries currently recognized as LDCs by the United Nations (UN), none was a founding Member of the GATT in 1947. Today, thirty-two LDCs are WTO Members and ten more are negotiating accession to the WTO. LDCs therefore constitute a significant and important constituency in the WTO's 153-country Membership.

In principle, the practice of decision-making by consensus in the WTO gives each Member an equal right to be heard and to have its concerns addressed before rules are agreed. Equally, the consensus practice requires Members keen to see their negotiating proposals advance to devote the considerable effort needed to gain every Member's support – or at least to ensure they do not oppose. Given their limited economic clout, most developing countries face particular challenges in building such support. The strategy of introducing proposals and positions as a group rather than as individual countries can make the task easier.

In the WTO's Doha Round of multilateral trade negotiations, many coalitions have emerged as a tool for building consensus. While it is not clear whether and when the ongoing Doha Round of negotiations will conclude, these emerging coalitions have added a new dimension to WTO decision-making processes (Narlikar 2004; Odell 2006; Prieur and Serrano 2006; Rolland 2007). The rise of coalitions has also generated considerable literature on the impact of these developments on global trade governance and their implications for institutional reforms at the WTO (Patel 2007; Ismail 2009; Steger 2009).

LDCs have not been active in the decision-making process in the GATT and WTO for very long. Indeed, developing countries more generally only acquired a significant role in multilateral trade negotiations during the Uruguay Round of GATT negotiations (1986–94). However, the situation changed markedly in the Doha Round, launched in 2001. LDCs began to get a seat in some of the 'inner group' consultative processes in the Doha Round negotiations. LDCs have also made proposals, on their own as well as by joining larger coalitions, to achieve their negotiating objectives.

2 Decision-making in the WTO

2.1 The process and the practice

This section explores the existing decision-making processes and practices in the WTO, highlighting that despite the existence of voting procedures, consensus is the rule. It then examines the role expected of and played by developing countries in various earlier rounds of GATT negotiations. It goes on to explore the evolution of developing country coalitions and their use to leverage the strength in numbers and collective weight of developing countries in global trade negotiations, focusing on the partnerships formed during the Doha Round. It concludes with the role of the LDCs as a coalition in the Doha Round.

The Agreement Establishing the World Trade Organization ('the WTO Agreement') prescribes the consensus method as the primary approach to decision-making, and voting as a secondary method in circumstances where a consensus cannot be reached (WTO 1994: Article 9.1). Each Member is allocated one vote. In practice, however, voting has been used sparingly in the GATT and the WTO, most notably for decisions involving waivers, accessions and some amendments to agreements. The last recorded decision by vote in the GATT occurred in 1959 (it concerned a recommendation on Freedom of Contract in Transport Insurance).[1] Following the creation of the WTO in 1995, the practice of decision-making by consensus continued. With the exception of a vote taken to approve the accession of Ecuador (WTO 1995a), the first country to accede to the WTO, subsequent accession decisions have all been taken by consensus. Similarly, decisions to waive obligations imposed on a Member by the provisions of the WTO Agreement or any of the multilateral trade agreements governed by it, though requiring only a three-quarters majority for approval (WTO 1994: Article 9.3), have also been taken by consensus.

Indeed, even where issues have proven highly contentious among WTO Members, they have abstained from voting. In 1999, WTO Members preferred a tedious and long-winded debate, rather than a vote, with regard to appointing a successor to WTO Director-General Renato Ruggiero.[2] In 2000, for instance, although an overwhelming majority of WTO Members criticized the WTO Appellate Body for its decision to allow *amicus curiae* briefs, the WTO Members did not press for a formal vote on the issue (WTO 2001).[3] In addition, the decision taken at the 2001 Doha WTO Ministerial

[1] It was reported by SUNS that the decision to call a special session of the contracting parties in 1985 to discuss the launch of the Uruguay Round also involved voting. However, it is not a vote recorded in the GATT records (SUNS Online 1985).

[2] To break the stalemate without having to vote it was agreed to split the post among Mike Moore and Supachai Pantchpakdi as successive Director-Generals with a truncated three-year term each. See Van den Bossche (2005: 136).

[3] In the General Council Meeting in November 2000, all but one delegation that spoke criticized the Appellate Body for having drawn up procedures for consideration of *amicus*

Conference to implement paragraph 6 of the Declaration on the Trade-related Aspects of Intellectual Property rights (TRIPS) Agreement and Public Health by the end of 2002 was not implemented even though only one Member (the United States) objected; Members persevered in their efforts to achieve a consensus, which was finally reached in August 2003 and resulted in an amendment to the TRIPS Agreement in 2005 (WTO 2003e, 2005). A further example concerns the WTO dispute between the USA and Brazil on cotton subsidies, where a procedural issue regarding the appointment of a facilitator to gather information was never resolved due to the absence of consensus (WTO 2003a, 2003b, 2003c, 2003d).[4]

Given the tendency of WTO Members to insist on a consensus approach to decision-making, talk of improvements to voting procedures may be of only academic value as the focus of Members will remain on options for facilitating their efforts to achieve consensus.

2.2 *The role of developing countries*

Throughout its first five rounds of negotiations,[5] the GATT functioned primarily as a forum for developed countries to lower their tariff barriers. The sixth round of negotiations (the Kennedy Round, concluded in 1967) produced rules on anti-dumping measures, and the seventh round (the Tokyo Round, concluded in 1979) added voluntary 'codes' on anti-dumping and other non-tariff barriers. Even though some developing countries were founding Members of the GATT, neither they, nor developing countries that had joined the GATT system later, were expected to make any concessions in these rounds. Instead, it was developed countries, led by the United States and the European Community, which decided the agenda for each round and negotiated among themselves to

curiae briefs, stating that that was a legislative action which only Members could take. Upon the Chairman stating that these views would be conveyed to the Appellate Body with a request to exercise caution, the Members did not press for a vote.

[4] Annex V of the WTO Agreement on Subsidies and Countervailing Measures requires that upon request of a party to a dispute the Dispute Settlement Body (DSB) shall initiate procedures to obtain information relating to alleged serious prejudice caused by subsidization and designate a facilitator. A decision on Brazil's request was never taken, even though only one Member (the United States) objected. The DSB Chairman refused to put the item on the agenda until his informal consultations showed existence of a consensus. The dispute was never resolved and Brazil itself obtained relevant information from other WTO Members, which it submitted to the Panel.

[5] The Rounds of trade negotiations in GATT/WTO are generally named after the city where they are launched. The first five rounds were Geneva (1947), Annecy (1949), Torquay (1951), Geneva (1956) and Dillon (1961).

arrive at concessions, which were then applied on a most favoured nation (MFN)[6] basis to all GATT Members.

The Tokyo Round marked the first attempt to tackle both tariff and non-tariff barriers systemically. Concessions exchanged on products of interest to developing countries, particularly agriculture and textile products, were naturally fewer as they were far less involved in the negotiations than developed countries. Developing countries never blocked any decisions because no concessions were expected from them and because they benefitted from the MFN principle. A secure and predictable multilateral trading system with binding rules and an effective dispute settlement mechanism represented a fairer application of the rules, as opposed to market-determined trade policies. For developing countries with little political muscle and an uphill challenge to derive economic benefits from trade liberalization, this was the preferred option. Negotiating individual treaties with their trading partners – the alternative – would prove onerous not only in terms of resources required, but also because their main trading partners, the developed countries, had a better capacity to negotiate deals that favoured themselves. Also, compliance with such bilateral treaties was fraught with uncertainties.

The focus of the negotiating overtures of most developed countries was on the more advanced of the developing countries having larger markets and better opportunities for their businesses. However, given the benefits of the MFN clause, it was politically difficult to discriminate among developing countries.[7]

In 1971, LDCs were identified as a well-defined subgroup of developing countries under the United Nations. And in 1979, the incorporation of the Enabling Clause[8] to the GATT provided special benefits to LDCs. It thus became possible, for instance, to give LDCs more flexibility in terms of the tariff bindings, transition periods and technical assistance. LDCs were subsequently considered a formal group eligible for more benefits than other developing countries.

[6] This principle, enshrined in Article I of GATT, means that any advantage, favour, privilege or immunity granted by any Member to any products originating in or destined for any other country has to be accorded immediately and unconditionally to the like product of all Members.

[7] All developing countries were characterized as 'less developed countries' in Part IV of GATT negotiated in 1964.

[8] GATT. 1979. Differential and More Favourable Treatment, Reciprocity and Fuller Participation on Developing Countries. Decision of 28 November 1979. L/4903. Hereinafter referred to as the Enabling Clause.

The last round of negotiations under the GATT, the Uruguay Round (1986–94), was different. Not only were developing countries expected to make tariff concessions, new areas of business, like services and intellectual property rights, were introduced as topics for negotiation. Over the seven years of negotiations, it became evident that developed countries had substantive demands of developing countries. For developing countries, joining a consensus no longer meant just MFN benefits; it also involved tariff reduction commitments, adherence to new or better elaborated standards for the trade in goods, and rules in new areas of trade. At this point, decision-making processes became a critical issue for developing countries.

Developing country tariffs were generally very high, rendering it feasible for them to agree to formulas that bound their tariffs to levels that still allowed some tariff policy space. However, negotiations in the Uruguay Round also involved new areas like services and intellectual property rights. The concept of single undertaking[9] was added to the rubric, thus making their cost-benefit analysis even more complicated.[10] This was a far cry from the earlier rounds of negotiations when discussions focused on the extent to which developed countries provided special and differential treatment to developing countries to enable their participation in the multilateral trading system, not the extent to which developing countries offered commitments to lower their tariffs. Developing countries, thus, were not required to calculate the loss of policy space through commitments offered. In 1964, for example, a new chapter on Trade and Development was added as a new Part 4 of the GATT, and the UNCTAD was established as a UN body specifically devoted to promoting development through trade.

Although developing countries had used coalitions in other intergovernmental settings, for example through the G77 and China,[11] they did not use them as effectively in the Uruguay Round for various reasons, including the diversity of their trade interests and inadequate capacity to

[9] As negotiations progressed in the Uruguay Round it was decided that every item of the negotiation was part of a whole and indivisible package and could not be agreed separately. A further aspect of the single undertaking was that nothing would be agreed until everything was agreed. This meant that negotiators had to weigh potential losses in one area of negotiation with possible gains in another.

[10] This was further complicated by inadequate capacity of their negotiators to undertake such a cost-benefit analysis as compared with their developed country compatriots.

[11] This coalition is active in the United Nations system, and was active once in the GATT during negotiation of the Enabling Clause in 1979.

organize themselves. Where similar concerns emerged,[12] some developing countries collaborated to submit joint proposals (Narlikar 2004). These tended to be issue-based coalitions, rather than any formal groupings intended to represent their common interests. The Doha Round, on the other hand, has seen a major increase in developing country coalitions.

2.3 *The role of coalitions in the Doha Round*

Given the prominence of consensus, as the preferred approach to decision-making at the WTO, the role played by informal processes to arrive at decisions cannot be understated.

New rounds of GATT negotiations were historically launched when the main players decided to undertake further tariff reductions or establish new trade rules. The GATT Secretariat provided a forum for these main players to undertake informal discussions in what became known as the 'Green Room' (based simply on the colour of the walls in the room). Until the Tokyo Round, the Green Room comprised up to eight countries. As broader and systemic rule-making issues arose during the Uruguay Round, a full Green Room had as many as thirty countries participating. The WTO has continued this GATT practice of conducting trade negotiations informally among the main players in the Green Room and then building consensus around those decisions in concentric circles of consultative processes. The innermost circle of the main players (the Quad), which represented the core of the Green Room, was comprised of the United States (USA), the European Union (EU), Japan and Canada. This group often met before an issue even reached the Green Room. Other developed countries in the room included Australia, New Zealand, Norway and Switzerland. Developing countries in the room included Argentina, Brazil, Chile, China, Egypt, Hong Kong, India, Korea, Mexico, Pakistan, South Africa, Thailand, Indonesia and the Philippines. LDCs were not generally present in the Green Room.

In previous rounds, some small countries not on the high table of GATT decision-making used coalitions to force recognition of their collective interests. The Nordic countries, for example, negotiated as a group

[12] The 'Like-Minded Group' was one such configuration active during that Round: a developing country coalition that put forward a number of detailed proposals that would have shifted value from North to South and denied any negotiating gain to the North until the North had first granted the group's demands (Narlikar and Odell 2004).

during the Uruguay Round. A group of agriculture exporters (the Cairns group) similarly formed a coalition in the Uruguay Round. The plethora of issues under negotiation in the Doha Round and the diversity of interests among WTO Members has inspired the formation of many more coalitions (see Table 7.1). After the G20 came into existence in the run-up to the 2003 Cancún Ministerial Conference, a new quad of the USA, EU, Brazil and India emerged.

The success of these coalitions, particularly in influencing draft negotiating texts, has provided another challenge: their need to retain their unity in the wake of opposing overtures from the outside. Issues that were not initially a part of common positions are increasingly discussed as part of an effort to arrive at broader common positions on the part of coalitions. Many epitaphs have been written on these coalitions since their creation, but their numbers continue to flourish, at least for the time being. That said, this is no guarantee that such coalitions will remain intact in the end game of the Doha negotiations. Though of a different and less concrete character, few coalitions and group arrangements that were active formally and informally during the Uruguay round survived until the end game.

An important contribution of developing country coalitions has been their role in ensuring wider consultation during the Doha Round negotiations. This has added a new dimension to the Green Room discussions as well. While previously the WTO Director-General would most likely constitute the Green Room based on the degree of interest expressed by individual Members through proposals or interventions, now he has the option of calling in coordinators of these coalitions and leaving it to them to consult with their members. It has also become more relevant to involve the coordinators of coalitions because of the systemic nature of many issues before the Green Room, and especially given that grouping-based formulas and flexibilities are often part of draft texts.

Both the WTO Director-General and WTO Members find it convenient to use coalitions as a way to manage pressures that emerge from the concentric circle model of decision-making referred to earlier. The inclusion of coalitions in such decision-making processes enables more flexibility for Members to reshape their alliances as negotiations progress and the focus of the negotiation shifts. The continued use of coalitions will largely depend upon their durability. It may become increasingly important for individual Members of the coalitions to search for a 'best fit' between their individual interests and broader group positions; a negotiation process in itself. It is no wonder, therefore, that the WTO

Table 7.1. *Examples of active country groupings in the Doha negotiations*[13]

Grouping	Composition	Coverage
ACP	Fifty-six developing countries from Africa, Caribbean and the Pacific	All issues
Africa Group	All African WTO Members	All issues
LDCs	All least developed countries	All issues
RAMs	Albania, Armenia, Bulgaria, China, Croatia, Ecuador, Macedonia, Jordan, Kyrgyz Rep., Moldova, Mongolia, Oman, Panama, Saudi Arabia, Chinese Taipei, Ukraine	Uruguay Round plus concessions
Small, Vulnerable Economies (SVEs)	Barbados, Bolivia, Cuba, Dominican Republic, El Salvador, Fiji, Guatemala, Honduras, Mauritius, Mongolia, Nicaragua, Papua New Guinea, Paraguay, Trinidad & Tobago	All issues (mainly Ag. and NAMA)
Cairns Group	Argentina, Australia, Bolivia, Brazil, Canada, Chile, Colombia, Costa Rica, Guatemala, Indonesia, Malaysia, New Zealand, Pakistan, Paraguay, Peru, Philippines, South Africa, Thailand, Uruguay	Agriculture
Tropical Products Group	Bolivia, Venezuela, Colombia, Costa Rica, Ecuador, El Salvador, Honduras, Guatemala, Nicaragua, Panama, Peru	Agriculture
G20	Argentina, Bolivia, Brazil, Chile, China, Cuba, Ecuador, Egypt, Guatemala, India, Indonesia, Mexico, Nigeria, Pakistan, Paraguay, Peru, Philippines, South Africa, Tanzania, Thailand, Uruguay, Venezuela, Zimbabwe	Agriculture
G33	Antigua & Barbuda, Barbados, Belize, Benin, Bolivia, Botswana, China, Congo, Côte d'Ivoire, Cuba, Dominica, Dominican Republic, El Salvador, Grenada, Guatemala, Guyana, Haiti, Honduras, India, Indonesia, Jamaica, Kenya, Korea, Mauritius, Madagascar, Mongolia,	Agriculture

[13] A complete list of developing country coalitions active in the GATT/WTO from 1973 to 2007 can be found in Patel (2007).

Table 7.1. *(cont.)*

Grouping	Composition	Coverage
	Mozambique, Nicaragua, Nigeria, Pakistan, Panama, Peru, Philippines, St Kitts & Nevis, St Lucia, St Vincent & the Grenadines, Senegal, Sri Lanka, Suriname, Tanzania, Trinidad & Tobago, Turkey, Uganda, Venezuela, Zambia, Zimbabwe	
G10	Chinese Taipei, Rep. of Korea, Iceland, Israel, Japan, Liechtenstein, Mauritius, Norway, Switzerland	Agriculture
NAMA 11	Argentina, Bolivarian Republic of Venezuela, Brazil, Egypt, India, Indonesia, Namibia, Philippines, South Africa, Tunisia	Industrial market access
C4	Benin, Burkina Faso, Chad, Mali	Cotton
Friends of Fish	Select developed and developing countries	Fisheries

Director-General in his capacity as Chairman of the Trade Negotiations Committee, as well as the Chairs of the respective negotiating groups, have started to underline the need for Members to better negotiate within their groups and coalitions.[14]

Such efforts have sometimes become a way to arrive at compromises on specific topics of negotiation, which in turn helps reduce some of the divergences that thwart a broader consensus among the WTO Membership.

2.4 *The role of LDCs in the Doha Round*

LDCs constitute a significant group in the WTO. Given the push to arrive at a consensus in WTO decision-making, their number counts, particularly when they act collectively. From an LDC perspective, a core priority is that their coalition has a seat at the high table of WTO negotiations. Already, their collective efforts have enabled them to secure some interim

[14] This practice should be differentiated from the other and more recent call by some countries that bilateral processes should go in parallel with the multilateral processes of negotiations. This latter issue is beyond the scope of this paper and has therefore not been dealt with.

decisions to their benefit. Two in particular deserve mention: first, the decision on duty-free quota-free market access (DFQF) in the 2005 Hong Kong WTO Ministerial Conference,[15] and second, the agreement that cotton should receive more ambitious treatment in terms of elimination of export subsidies, reduction of trade distorting domestic support, and DFQF access for cotton exports from LDCs.[16] An example of a pending priority issue for the LDC group is the provision of a waiver that would give preferential market access for services of export interest to LDCs.

Bolstered by the decision on DFQF at Hong Kong, the LDCs have subsequently coordinated more closely on issues of collective interest. At the Sixth Trade Ministers' Meeting of LDCs at Dar Es Salaam (WTO 2009), held in the run up to the Seventh WTO Ministerial Conference, LDCs agreed to a number of their specific demands. First, they asked for implementation of the decision on DFQF already taken in Hong Kong by 2010. Second, they requested a waiver for preferential and more favourable treatment to services and service suppliers of LDCs. Third, they called for an ambitious, expeditious and specific outcome for cotton trade-related aspects, in particular the elimination of trade-distorting domestic support measures and export subsidies, and the granting of DFQF market access for cotton and cotton by-products originating from LDCs. They also requested an 'early harvest'[17] on these issues. Further, the eighty-four paragraph Dar Es Salaam Declaration urged WTO Members to take a number of specific LDC-friendly decisions across all areas of negotiations.

Through their negotiations for the Dar Es Salaam Declaration, LDCs arrived at compromises on some issues that were contentious within the group. This required some Members to give up more ambitious demands. For example, the Declaration does not mention requests articulated by some LDCs during informal negotiations in Geneva relating to product coverage of DFQF.[18] Nor does the Declaration mention that some WTO Members are likely to be disproportionally affected by the

[15] See paragraph 47 of the Hong Kong Ministerial Declaration and its Annex F.

[16] See paragraph 11 of the Hong Kong Ministerial Declaration.

[17] Paragraph 47 of the Doha Ministerial Declaration provided for provisional or definitive implementation of any agreements arrived at earlier than the proposed end date of conclusion of the round, or early harvest.

[18] The Hong Kong decision called upon developed countries to provide duty-free access to LDCs on 97 per cent of their tariff lines. While some LDCs already had duty-free access on almost all tariff lines under existing preference schemes of the EU and the USA, some others who did not felt it more important to emphasize increase of DFQF coverage to 100 per cent, or at least secure access for goods of export interest to them.

proposed non-reciprocal preferences in the non-agricultural market access (NAMA) negotiations (WTO 2008). It is equally pertinent that the LDCs appeared to recognize that there was no consensus within their group on making a formal request for an agenda item at the 2009 WTO Ministerial Conference for Ministers to agree to the early harvest they sought in the Declaration. Such compromises indicate that LDCs may have preferred realism rather than ambition in order to reap the benefit of taking common positions and to provide a valuable input into the concentric circles of negotiations conducted in the Doha Round.

In short, LDCs have started leveraging their numerical strength to negotiate fairer rules in the multilateral trading system and they have learnt the art of making compromises within their own group.

3 LDC priorities in global trade governance

3.1 The challenges

Although LDCs are classified according to common criteria such as low income, human assets weakness and economic vulnerability, their priorities are varied due to different conditions prevailing among them. For instance, only seven of the forty-nine LDCs account for 74 per cent of total LDC exports.[19] The recent financial and economic crisis has greatly affected LDC economies; their export value in 2009 declined by 43 per cent and the number of poor was expected to increase by six million in African LDCs and one million in Asian LDCs by the end of 2010.[20] An improved global trade governance system is critical to enable the effective participation of LDCs in the global trading system and its benefits for them. For this to happen, it is imperative to ensure that the core principles of good governance are enshrined in the global trading system. These include participation, fairness, decency, accountability, transparency and efficiency (Court 2006).

It is well understood that LDCs face supply-side constraints that weaken their participation in global trade. These constraints include lack of linkages between productive services and infrastructural sectors, insufficiently developed human resources, poor physical infrastructure and

[19] Presentation by Debapriya Bhattacharya, Special Adviser on LDCs in the Office of the Secretary General of UNCTAD at Ad Hoc Expert Group Meeting on LDC IV, 18–19 February 2010.

[20] Ibid.

production technologies, dependence on a few commodities for trade, and a lack of resources to address these shortcomings (UNCTAD 1999).

LDCs are signatories to a number of trade agreements, including the WTO Agreement, some Economic Partnership Agreements (EPAs) initialled with the European Commission and Regional Trade Agreements (RTAs) in their respective regions.[21] LDCs are also the intended beneficiaries of several market access initiatives, such as the Everything But Arms (EBA) initiative of the EU, the African Growth and Opportunity Act (AGOA) of the USA, and other unilateral initiatives by both developed and developing countries offering them duty-free access. However, to harness the potential benefits of improved market access that these initiatives promise, the supply-side constraints they face need to be overcome. Participation by LDCs in such a complex suite of trade arrangements brings with it challenges. Each trade agreement requires a careful assessment of opportunities and the constraints in realizing market access outcomes from them. It also brings the challenges of absorbing these opportunities in the national development policies of LDCs.

Further, such agreements have complexities that require different approaches and necessitate careful preparation and ability to negotiate the country's core interests into them. With limited human resources, the capacity of LDCs to advance their interests in negotiations to ensure benefits from trade agreements is constrained. LDCs also usually lack the institutional capacities to comply with the commitments assumed under these agreements and initiatives.

Effective and beneficial participation by LDCs in trade agreements is also limited by their dependency on primary commodity exports. The Ugandan President Yoweri K. Museveni has aptly referred to LDCs as the world's biggest donors for continuously exporting primary products that fetch very low prices. Value addition in LDC exports is impeded by tariff escalation in developed country markets. Even initiatives intended to benefit LDCs, such as EBA and AGOA, come with conditions such as strict rules of origin and other non-tariff barriers that frustrate access to markets. Greater efforts to address the challenges are a key priority for LDCs in global trade governance.

[21] Examples of RTAs that have a significant number of LDC parties are the Economic Community of West African States (ECOWAS), the Common Market for Eastern and Southern Africa (COMESA) and the South Asian Free Trade Agreement (SAFTA).

For LDCs to ensure that their interests are catered for in the various agreements, a further governance priority is effective involvement of all stakeholders in the formulation of their respective country positions. This requires the existence of well-organized and informed private sector associations and civil society to ensure that government policies serve public interest.

Technical assistance is another issue that requires attention in discussions of improved trade governance. The WTO, UNCTAD and International Trade Centre (ITC), among others, offer trade-related technical assistance to LDCs. The Netherlands funds a programme that enables officials from LDCs to take internships at the WTO to build national capacity to better participate in the multilateral trade system. However, these programmes are usually targeted at junior officials whose role in their countries' trade policy formulation is limited. Also, given the short nature of the programmes and limited number of participants, they may not be very effective in addressing the overall technical and other assistance commensurate with the LDCs' needs. A better approach would be to ensure that trade policy is included in the national university curricula, coupled with the provision of financial assistance to enable LDCs to comply with various requirements, such as product standards.

The LDC's 2009 Dar Es Salaam Declaration called inter alia for concretizing the SDT provisions in the various WTO agreements and trade facilitation. The extent to which implementation of these measures would improve global trade governance and thereby result in better integration of LDCs in the multilateral trading system is discussed below.

3.2 Special and Differential Treatment

Special and Differential Treatment provisions were introduced in the GATT to address the inequality of trade opportunities available to developed and developing countries. They are aimed at increasing trade opportunities through market access, safeguarding the interests of developing countries, allowing flexibility to developing countries in rules and disciplines governing trade measures, and enabling longer transitional periods and technical assistance (WTO 2004). The so-called Enabling Clause provides legal cover for special trade concessions granted to developing countries.

Most of the SDT provisions in WTO rules are couched in 'best endeavour' language, making them legally unenforceable. The 2001

WTO Ministerial Declaration that launched the Doha Round called for making the WTO's SDT provisions more precise, effective and operational. For this aim to be realized, there is a need to ensure that they are included in the schedules of commitments to which WTO Members agree; a mere change of phrasing of SDT provisions will not make them enforceable.

To date, LDCs have made limited use of SDT provisions. This is due both to the best endeavour nature of the provisions, as well as the inability of the LDCs to make the decisions necessary at the national level for implementation. For instance, the WTO Agreement on Subsidies and Countervailing Measures exempts LDCs from the prohibition on subsidies that are contingent upon export performance. However, not many LDCs are in a position to use this exemption and thereby to use subsidies to stimulate growth in relevant sectors.

Another feature of WTO SDT provisions is that many of them are transitional, providing the beneficiaries time within which to adjust their situation and start complying with trade rules. These transition periods often come to an end before the prevailing conditions for which they were granted can be improved. Even further extensions are no guarantee that transition periods will provide countries effective relief. A case in point is the WTO Agreement on TRIPS, which provided LDCs up to ten years for the implementation of TRIPS obligations. There was also a call for WTO Members to provide incentives that would encourage technology transfer to LDCs. Despite the needs assessment studies conducted in some LDCs, the funding requirements identified could not be met, necessitating an extension by another ten years. To overcome this handicap, there is a need to make transition periods contingent upon an assessment of the prevailing situation and to establish whether the beneficiary countries are ready to implement the new rules.

SDT measures are not a panacea for converting trade opportunities into market access. LDCs need to take the initiative to carry out their own needs assessment and mobilize resources to address their needs from within. Over-reliance on donors and philanthropists is a major demotivator and has contributed to economic and social stagnation in many LDCs (Collier 2007). The success of the East Asian states is instructive. Countries in this region embarked on their own developmental process irrespective of the fact that their technical capacities were not, at the outset, well advanced (Evans 1998: 71; UNCTAD 2009: 40).

Alongside the Doha Round of trade negotiations, almost all WTO Members are engaged in RTAs. For some WTO Members, these RTAs represent over 90 per cent of total trade (Crawford and Fiorentino 2005: 1). RTAs rarely, however, include SDT provisions and where they do they are quite weak. RTAs also cover issues not included in the WTO rules, such as labour and environmental standards, and require additional disciplines on investment and government procurement. This raises the question as to why there is such a contradiction between regional and multilateral agreements when both are negotiated by the same players. Some studies have pointed out that there will be no real benefits from the SDT proposed under the Doha Round in the form of DFQF market access for LDCs on 97 per cent of tariff lines by the developed countries. The remaining 3 per cent entails the bulk of the products of export interest to LDCs and if they remain protected there would be no real benefit of DFQF (Laborde 2008: 13).

Although SDT provisions are largely absent in RTAs, other measures have been put into place in order to support better participation by LDCs in the negotiation and implementation of RTAs. An example is the technical support given by the European Commission (EC) to African, Caribbean and Pacific states (ACP) as part of the European Development Fund for the negotiation of the EU-ACP EPAs. Many LDCs are known to have used such support to identify their needs and negotiation priorities in the EPA negotiations. Where LDCs are able to effectively use such upfront assistance for negotiating RTAs, such initiatives may be more beneficial than non-enforceable SDT provisions in the multilateral trading system.

3.3 *Taking ownership of efforts to integrate LDCs in international trade*

At the 1996 WTO Ministerial Conference in Singapore, WTO Members recognized that LDCs would require support in assessing trade-related technical assistance needs at the country level. To address these needs and better integrate LDCs into the multilateral trading system, the Integrated Framework (IF) was established in 1997. The IF aimed to improve the capacity of LDCs to formulate, negotiate and implement trade policy. Diagnostic Trade Integration Studies (DTISs) were initiated to identify country priorities, for which funding was then sought. In 2007 the Enhanced Integrated Framework (EIF) expanded the IF to support LDCs to build better in-country institutions and structures, carry out and/or update DTISs, and facilitate the implementation of projects thus identified. The EIF emphasizes country ownership in integration of trade into national development plans.[22]

The in-country institutions and processes developed under the EIF aim to bring all stakeholders on board in appraising national needs, contributing to trade policy and creating much-needed awareness about the opportunities provided by international trade agreements. The inclusion of the private sector and civil society ensures that their specific sectoral needs are addressed. This may also lead to strengthening lobbying groups aiming to influence their government's policies.

Although the EIF and related initiatives are positive steps, there are too often insufficient funds to implement the recommendations arising from such endeavours. Most LDCs await donor intervention to implement these recommendations. This scenario needs to be reversed; LDCs should take the initiative to fund identified projects and the donor community should be approached for complementary support. The challenge, however, is for LDC governments to find the funds to implement such recommendations.

If trade mainstreaming efforts through the EIF are fully owned by the LDC governments, the recommendations would be mainstreamed in their national development plans. These plans are implemented through government funding, albeit including the budgetary support available through bilateral and multilateral donors. Also, recent trends indicate that LDCs' revenue collections are increasing. This should form the main source of funding. With better management of the collection and utilization of revenues, they can fund priority projects, leading to enhanced trade performance and hence integration in the global trade system.

The mobilization of domestic resources should therefore be an LDC priority. For this to happen, the challenges faced in this regard need to be addressed. For instance, LDC economies are characterized by a large informal sector that does not keep business records, making it difficult for governments to tax them and raise the necessary revenue. Table 7.2 indicates the revenue trends in African LDCs.

Most LDC governments are not transparent in the expenditure of public funds, which discourages citizens from complying with their tax obligations. Poor public amenities, such as roads, hospitals and schools, are another major de-motivator. Reviews of the taxation and revenue

[22] For more information on the Integrated Framework and the Enhanced Integrated Framework, see www.enhancedif.org/ [accessed in November 2010].

Table 7.2. *Trends in tax components in African LDCs, 1990–2006 (per cent of GDP)*

Type of tax/period	1990–4	1995–9	2000–6
Direct taxes	2.67	2.75	3.50
Taxes on goods and services	2.83	3.67	4.79
Trade taxes	3.88	3.67	3.79

Source: Mckinley 2009. Based on data from the IMF (adapted from UNCTAD 2009: 65).

collection systems of LDCs to increase transparency and reduce corruption could motivate the informal sector to contribute revenue. If LDC governments become more accountable, there is real potential for raising substantial revenue to fund the projects identified through the EIF and related initiatives.

While the international support provided to assist LDCs to identify their development needs is much appreciated, LDCs need to shift the development paradigm by relying less on donor aid and hand-holding and the uncertainties attached with it. The recent financial and economic crisis is an illustration of such uncertainties. Major developed country donors now face difficulties sustaining the support to identified projects or honouring their pledges. In this light, the UN LDC Conferences (such as in Turkey in 2011) should focus more on what the LDCs can do by themselves.

4 Pro-LDC institutional reforms

4.1 The case for an LDC-specific institution

The reforms required to address LDC priorities in global trade governance need to go beyond the WTO's current trade-related technical assistance, which is oriented primarily towards negotiations and meeting WTO obligations. Improving the capacity of LDCs to assert their rights and meaningfully contribute to policy formulation in the multilateral trade system is of paramount importance. This calls for a re-examination of both their capacity and their role.

LDC delegations in Geneva are small and mandated to cover all international organizations to which their countries are affiliated. This severely limits their ability to participate in multiple meetings and to meaningfully digest the often bulky reports that are considered in the various committees before reaching decisions. Of the WTO Members and observers not having Missions in Geneva, nine of the twenty Members and four of the ten observers are LDCs. Most LDCs also lack the technical capacity to effectively participate in committees such as those dealing with technical barriers to trade (TBT) and sanitary and phytosanitary measures (SPS), despite their great need for information to assist in addressing the non-tariff barriers in these areas that hinder their access to markets of interest.

The WTO Secretariat could do more to assist LDCs on such issues. At present it provides assistance upon request. To make such a request, LDCs are first required to assess their specific needs, an exercise they may not have the competence or time to undertake given human resource constraints. The provision of adequate legal advice is rare as experts can only offer advice in a manner that ensures the continued impartiality of the Secretariat (WTO 1995b). The real challenges this presents are illustrated by the scant use of the legal experts available through the WTO, and an increased use of resources such as the Advisory Centre on WTO Law, whose legal officers are mandated to provide country-specific and issue-specific legal advice that would advance the interests of their clients. For more general capacity-building of their Missions and capital-based officials, many LDCs depend upon services provided by organizations such as UNCTAD, Commonwealth Secretariat, Consumer Unity & Trust Society (CUTS) and the South Centre, among others. Given the limited resources and reach of these organizations, however, such services are available on an ad hoc basis rather than a systemic long-term basis.

These shortcomings could be overcome by supporting an institution in Geneva to cater to the specific capacity-building needs of LDCs. Such an institution should be established by LDCs themselves and have a mandate to serve LDCs collectively, at least initially. There is a wealth of former WTO delegates from LDCs whose skills could be tapped for such an institution. The institution could start as a small office staffed by LDC resource persons charged with ensuring urgent issues for attention are correctly identified, bolstered by non-LDC personnel where specific technical expertise is required.

The support provided by the EIF to LDCs for the purpose of establishing national institutional structures to help them mainstream trade into their national development plans is a good model that could be replicated in Geneva. The priorities established at the national level could be discussed in Geneva and areas for learning through better participation in the WTO Committees could be identified. The LDC institution could link those priority needs identified nationally to the regular committee work in the WTO, examine the WTO reports and notifications relevant to such needs, and summarize them into easy-to-understand short papers for LDC delegations. These papers would enable time-starved LDC delegates to effectively participate in WTO discussions and put forward specific questions related to their interest. The lessons learned from their participation could be fed back into the national institutional processes, which could in turn inform the policy-makers, as well as entrepreneurs, of the trade opportunities available and potential challenges.

The proposed Geneva-based institution could also help decipher the increasing number of research reports that the WTO Secretariat, in particular the economic research division, now produces. Voluminous reports on important issues such as trade and labour standards, trade and climate change, globalization and informal jobs in developing countries are emerging. The proposed LDC institution could not only summarize the research already done but suggest issues of greater priority to LDCs for future research. Such outputs could then be discussed by the LDC Group in the WTO, ensuring more informed, cohesive and productive participation in the broader WTO debates and governance processes.

4.2 Leveraging the LDC political position

In keeping with trends in the WTO's consensus-building processes, LDCs have started actively participating as a group in the development and sharpening of their own negotiating positions and those of other coalitions in the Doha Round. These efforts feed into the concentric circles of negotiations expected to lead to a successful conclusion of the Doha Round (when the missing political will returns to the negotiating table).

LDCs should intensify their work as a group in pursuing their negotiating objectives. They have human and material resource constraints, no doubt, but assistance and facilitation by development partners can help address these challenges. More importantly, as the Doha Round proceeds toward conclusions, there is a need for LDCs to continue building collective knowledge and awareness of their priority issues and to seek LDC-wide convergences. As stated above, the Declaration at the Sixth LDC Trade Ministers' Meeting at Dar Es Salaam in October 2009 was a good starting point in this respect (WTO 2009).

5 Conclusion and the way forward

LDC issues need to take centre stage at the global level. The Millennium Development Goals and the 2001 WTO Ministerial Declaration recognize the critical need to address the situation of LDCs and to enable their better integration into global trade governance. In 2011, the UN LDC IV Conference will address LDC challenges at the broader level. However, to make their voice better heard, LDCs themselves need to play the leading role.

The common positions taken by LDCs in the WTO are a positive step towards achieving this objective. To reinforce this effort, a Geneva-based institution must be created to address their human resource limitations and ensure their interests are adequately fed into the ongoing debate on global trade governance.

Supply-side constraints remain a major roadblock for LDCs to convert market access opportunities into actual market access. Initiatives such as the EIF are useful in identifying constraints, in bringing in-country stakeholders on board and mainstreaming trade in national development plans. The focus now should be on making these efforts more country driven rather than dependent on donor funding. This will require formalizing the informal sector and better revenue collection (which will demand greater accountability and transparency in public expenditure) and ensuring priority needs are met. National institutions supported through the proposed Geneva-based institution could create a critical mass of local skills and expertise in the area and gradually reduce dependence on external experts. Also, trade and development policies should be built into university curricula in LDCs. LDCs should use upfront assistance available through initiatives like the European Development Fund, EIF and Aid for Trade to more clearly identify their best interests and address their constraints before taking on new commitments in trade agreements. Financial assistance windows available for meeting product standards should be utilized in a more focused manner to translate trade opportunities into actual market access. Also, preferences and SDT extended to LDCs need to be locked into the schedules of WTO Members to make them legally enforceable, predictable and therefore more beneficial to the LDCs.

References

Collier, P. 2007. *The Bottom Billion: Why the Poorest Countries are Failing and What Can Be Done About It*. Oxford University Press.

Court, J. 2006. *Governance, Development and Aid Effectiveness: A Quick Guide to Complex Relationships*. Briefing paper. London: Overseas Development Institute.

Crawford, J. A. and Fiorentino, R. V. 2005. *The Changing Landscape of Regional Trade Agreements*, Discussion Paper No. 8. Geneva: World Trade Organization.

Evans, P. 1998. 'On Institutional Prerequisites of East Asian Economic Policies', *Journal of Development Studies* 34(6): 66–86.

Ismail, F. 2009. *Reforming the World Trade Organization: Developing Countries in the Doha Round*, Geneva: CUTS International and Fredrich Ebert Stiftung (FES).

Laborde, D. 2008. *On a Meaningful Duty Free Quota Free Market Access Initiative in the Doha Development Agenda*, Issue Paper 4 ICTSD Competitiveness and Sustainable Development Series. Geneva: International Centre for Trade and Sustainable Development.

McKinley, T. 2009. *Meeting the Macroeconomic Challenges of LDCs*. Study prepared for UNCTAD as a background paper for the Least Developed Countries Report 2009. New York and Geneva: UNCTAD.

Michalopoulos, C. 2000. *Trade and Development in the GATT & WTO: The Role of S&DT for Developing Countries*. World Bank Policy Research Working Paper 2388. Washington, DC: World Bank.

Narlikar, A. 2004. *International Trade and Developing Countries: Bargaining Coalitions in the GATT & WTO*. London: Routledge.

Narlikar A. and Odell, J. 2004. *The Strict Distributive Strategy for a Bargaining Coalition: The Like Minded Group in the World Trade Organization*. Paper presented at the annual meeting of the International Studies Association, Montreal. www.allacademic.com/meta/p73418_index.html [Accessed in November 2010].

Odell, J. (ed.) 2006. *Negotiating Trade: Developing Countries in the WTO and NAFTA*. Cambridge University Press.

Patel, M. 2007. *New Faces in the Green Room: Developing Country Coalitions and Decision-Making in the WTO*, GEG Working Paper Series, 2007/WP33.

Prieur, J. and Serrano, O. R. 2006. 'Coalitions of Developing Countries in the WTO: Why Regionalism Matters'. http://hei.unige.ch/sections/sp/agenda/wto/wto2006/Developing%20Countries%20Coalitions%20in%20the%20WTO%20vrai.pdf [Accessed in April 2010].

Rolland, S. A. 2007. 'Developing Country Coalitions at the WTO: In Search of Legal Support', *Harvard International Law Journal* 48(2): 483–551.

Steger, D. P. 2009. 'The Future of the WTO: The Case for Institutional Reforms', *Journal of International Economic Law* 12(4): 803–33.

SUNS Online. 1985. *Uncertainty over GATT CPS Special Session*. www.sunsonline.org/trade/process/during/8485/cparties/09280085.htm [Accessed in April 2010].

UNCTAD. 1999. *Overview of the UNCTAD Least Developed Countries Report 1999*. Geneva: UNCTAD.

2009. *The Least Developing Countries Report*. Geneva: UNCTAD.

Van den Bossche, P. 2005. *The Law and Policy of the World Trade Organization: Text, Cases and Materials*. Cambridge University Press.

World Trade Organization (WTO). 1994. *Marrakesh Agreement Establishing the World Trade Organization*, adopted on 15 April 1994 and entered into force on 1 January 1995. Geneva: WTO.

1995a. *Accession of Ecuador. Decision of 16 August 1995*, WT/ACC/ECU/5, 22 August 1995. Geneva: WTO.

1995b. *Article 27.2 of the Understanding on Rules and Procedures Governing the Settlement of Disputes* (Annex 2 of the WTO Agreement) (1869 U.N.T.S. 401, 33 I.L.M. 1226), adopted on 15 April 1994 and entered into force on 1 January 1995. Geneva: WTO.

2001. *General Council. Minutes of Meeting*. Held in Centre William Rappard on 22 November 2000, WT/GC/M/60, 23 January 2001. Geneva: WTO.

2003a. *Dispute Settlement Body. Minutes of Meeting*. Held in Centre William Rappard on 18 March 2003, WT/DSB/M/145, 7 May 2003. Geneva: WTO.

2003b. *Dispute Settlement Body. Minutes of Meeting*. Held in Centre William Rappard on 31 March 2003, WT/DSB/M/146, 19 May 2003. Geneva: WTO.

2003c. *Dispute Settlement Body. Minutes of Meeting*. Held in Centre William Rappard on 15 April 2003, WT/DSB/M/147, 1 July 2003. Geneva: WTO.

2003d. *Dispute Settlement Body. Minutes of Meeting*. Held in Centre William Rappard on 19 May 2003, WT/DSB/M/150, 22 July 2003. Geneva: WTO.

2003e. *General Council. Implementation of Paragraph 6 of the Doha Declaration on the TRIPS Agreement and Public Health*. Decision of the General Council of 20 August 2003, WT/L/540, 1 September 2003. Geneva: WTO.

2004. *Committee on Trade and Development. Special and Differential Treatment for Least-Developed Countries. Note by the Secretariat*. WT/COMTD/W/135, 5 October 2004. Geneva: WTO.

2005. *General Council. Amendment of the TRIPS Agreement*. Decision of 6 December 2005, WT/L/641, 8 December 2005. Geneva: WTO.

2008. *Negotiating Group on Market Access. Fourth Revision of Draft Modalities for Non-Agricultural Market Access. Revision*, TN/MA/W/103.Rev 3, 6 December 2008. Geneva: WTO.

2009. *Ministerial Conference. Sixth LDC Trade Ministers' Meeting. Dar Es Salaam, Tanzania*. 14–16 October 2009. Dar Es Salaam Declaration, WT/MIN(09)/2, 21 October 2009. Geneva: WTO.

8

Priorities for small States in global trade governance

EDWIN LAURENT

To make their participation in the multilateral trading system more effective and beneficial, small States are becoming increasingly vocal in their advocacy of their special interests as 'small countries'. These efforts are attracting growing international attention. The extent to which one can make a compelling claim that systems for global trade governance should address the needs of small States, depends on whether one can establish the specificity of their interests. If the economic circumstances and needs of small States in the trading system were similar to those of other developing countries, they could simply rely on larger and more influential States to help advocate on their behalf. However, the 'smallness' of small States gives them unique characteristics, which in turn means that their trade interests are distinct from other countries. This chapter argues that to achieve the goals that they alone have a vested interest in securing in the multilateral trading system, small States themselves will have to secure the relevant changes, decisions and concessions.

The growing openness and democratization of global trade governance structures have eroded the decisive influence of commercial and political interests. This trend, along with the rise of new economic powers, has shifted patterns of influence on international decision- and rule-making, with many developing countries becoming more influential. However, the same cannot be said for small and weak developing States. They complain that their size impedes their effective and beneficial participation in the multilateral trading system. This chapter considers why this is so, despite the fact that the dominance of power as the key determinant of trade relations is being increasingly mitigated by greater scope for diplomacy, negotiation, advocacy and litigation. This chapter analyses why this is the case. It further suggests that achieving a more favourable economic

Edwin Laurent is currently Head of Trade and Regional Cooperation at the Commonwealth Secretariat. The author thanks Carolyn Deere Birkbeck, Massimiano Cali, Emily Jones and an anonymous reviewer for their input.

and trade environment for small States will require appropriate and supportive decisions in the international trading system. Consequently, a key strategic objective of small States in the management of the trading system has been to increase their influence in agenda-setting and rule- and decision-making. For this to occur, they need to secure adaptations to the trade governance structures themselves. To extrapolate the goals that small States have in terms of making the multilateral system more supportive of their economic interests, this chapter examines their policies and positions. These goals are presented under three headings. First, small States aim to strengthen the rule-based character of the multilateral system. Here the goal is to emphasize power, with which these countries are not well endowed, as a major determinant of the outcomes of engagement in the system. Second, small States aim to organize themselves and manage their collaboration with each other as well as with other players in the system so as to maximize their ability to exert influence and increase their effective power. Third, they seek adoption of specific policies and measures that are favourable to their interests. That is, they view recognition for their unique challenges as a prerequisite for securing concrete and practical measures to counteract the negative impacts of their smallness and to make it possible for them to compete on a more even basis with other countries.

This chapter begins with a review of what we mean by global trade governance. Section 2 continues by analysing the smallness of States and their consequent unique interests. It examines those characteristics that impose special and additional impediments to their beneficial participation in international trade. Section 3 examines how small States function in the trade governance structure, with a specific focus on diplomacy, advocacy, negotiation and litigation. Section 4 offers a brief overview of regional trade agreements (RTAs) and how small States can meet the challenges associated with RTAs. Finally, section 5 goes on to identify the priorities that small States need to pursue in order for trade governance structures, and hence the system itself, to better reflect and support their economic priorities and needs. Here, various instruments that can be used to secure their objectives are outlined and the challenges they face in utilizing them effectively are assessed.

1 The governance of world trade

Global trade governance structures can be viewed as the set of institutions, entities and arrangements that direct, define or exercise control over the conduct of international trade. Their reach is increasingly expanding to encompass additional aspects of economic relations among States as well as domestic production and commerce. The structures include principles, processes and procedures that set the rules according to which trade takes place. They might have enforceability provisions and scope for sanctions, but their essential characteristic is that they provide direction and guidance for States and define acceptable norms of trade conduct.

The entity at the heart of trade governance structures is the World Trade Organization (WTO). Many of its principles were inherited from the General Agreement on Tariffs and Trade (GATT) (WTO 1994a). This includes the most favoured nation (MFN) principle and the principle of national treatment, which together provide the ideological foundations for international trade regulation. Other relevant regulatory institutions include the World Intellectual Property Organization (WIPO), International Maritime Organization (IMO), International Civil Aviation Organization (ICAO) and the Organization for the Prohibition of Chemical Weapons. Some institutions such as the International Monetary Fund (IMF), World Bank, United Nations Conference on Trade and Development (UNCTAD) and the International Labour Organization (ILO) do not possess direct trade authority but can exercise influence and authority over trading arrangements and institutions.

While recognizing that several other institutions play a role in trade governance, this chapter focuses principally on the WTO, the leading multilateral trade institution. The WTO lies at the heart of the trade governance structure and is overwhelmingly dominant in terms of its reach and influence in defining and determining the rules, policies and basis on which trade takes place among countries. The WTO monitors performance of Members and has enforcement power, notably through the Dispute Settlement provisions (WTO 1994b). Countries view it as the core institutional structure for pursuing overall international trade objectives and regulating their trading environment.

In addition to the multilateral institutions and governance structures, bilateral and regional systems exert additional control over trade among countries and groupings that are often formalized in regional trading arrangements (RTAs). Small States seek greater influence in the governance and regulation of not just multilateral trade, but also of regional trade arrangements that include large developed countries.

2 The unique interests of small States

2.1 The meaning of smallness

The definition of small States is essential but difficult. No universally agreed definition exists and the concept of smallness is relative rather than absolute. Whether in terms of geographic or economic indices, countries differ in size, and thus naturally some are small relative to others. Therefore, setting objective parameters that distinguish smallness in the absolute seems almost impossible. Despite these challenges, there have been several attempts at a definition. The UN definition focuses instead on Small Island Developing States (SIDS), which operate in a formal alliance with small low-lying coastal states: Belize, Guinea-Bissau, Guyana and Suriname. A Commonwealth Secretariat/World Bank Joint Task Force on Small States (Sutherland *et al.* 2000) set the population threshold for a small State at one and a half million. Despite larger populations, Jamaica, Lesotho, Namibia and Papua New Guinea were included as they were considered to share similar characteristics to those States deemed to be small.

The WTO has its own grouping, the small and vulnerable economies (SVEs), for which Membership is by self-selection. All WTO Members that meet the Commonwealth Secretariat/World Bank criteria for smallness are included, but so are other countries, like Bolivia, El Salvador, Honduras, Nicaragua, Paraguay and even Cuba with a population of over eleven million, Dominican Republic with a population of almost ten million and Guatemala with thirteen and a half million.

The lack of consensus on what constitutes an acceptable index of smallness, and the tremendous diversity of States that deem themselves to be small, should not detract from the consideration of whether a country faces obstacles and disadvantages that can be directly attributed to its smallness.[1] To this end, this chapter explores the implications of smallness for participation in international trade. It will identify those unique features of smallness that can have adverse economic consequences, and which are not shared by larger countries.

[1] Not all current literature is convinced that smallness imposes a net disadvantage (see Spolaore 2004). This chapter does not address that debate; rather it examines whether the economic circumstances of small States are unique, and the consequences for their trade and negotiating interests.

An early analysis of the nature and consequences of smallness was undertaken by a nine-Member Commonwealth Advisory Group led by Dame Eugenia Charles (Commonwealth Advisory Group 1997). This Group found that small size itself poses obstacles to development regardless of the level of income or economic structure. Further, analysis pursued by Brigulio, Persaud and Stern (Brigulio *et al.* 2006) cited specific impediments, three of which might not be unique to small States. The first is susceptibility to natural disasters. It is true that a major disaster affecting small countries can damage the whole country, or a large part of it, since the limited geographic area of small States means that a disaster is likely to leave less of the territory unscathed. Being affected by natural disasters is also, however, a function of location, although damage might be magnified by other factors like poverty, low levels of governance, poor infrastructure and a lack of effective planning for post-disaster relief and recovery. The experience of Haiti, whose capital was devastated by a massive earthquake in 2010 and had endured a succession of destructive hurricanes, underlines the significance of location. The second factor identified by Brigulio *et al.* (2006) is inadequate access to capital. They argue that private markets tend to see small States as riskier than larger ones. However, many developing countries, small or not, have severe problems accessing capital and as Brigulio *et al.* (2006) acknowledge, the flow of capital to many small States is relatively high. The third claim is that small States suffer from poverty, which is true, but is not a unique feature of smallness. Small States do not suffer from poverty more than other developing countries, particularly least developed countries (LDCs).

A further feature of small States that Brigulio *et al.* correctly identify is trade openness. Here again, however, this feature is not unique. Openness is not exclusive to small States and is not necessarily harmful. Indeed, to the extent that it enables exploitation of comparative advantage, specialization and unimpeded sourcing of consumer goods and services from the lowest cost suppliers, it can facilitate optimal allocation of resources and hence development. The danger of openness arises when it is accompanied by a limited production base and markets. This magnifies the economic impact of price fluctuations in targeted export markets, where commodity prices are often in long-term decline. Instability, though less severe, also results if the single export on which the State relies is a service, such as tourism, financial services and migrant workers who send remittances home. Volatility and shocks are due, not only to domestic circumstances, but to exogenous factors, which the small State has little or no control over and from which it might not be able to shield itself.

For instance, small States were disproportionately affected by the global financial and subsequent economic crisis that began in late 2008, which reduced foreign investment flows, tourism and remittances. Even if openness is not harmful, when combined with dependence on the export of a single or very narrow range of goods or services, the small State becomes more vulnerable to external shocks.

Remoteness from major markets is cited as a feature of small States as well (Brigulio *et al.* 2006). Though remoteness is a particularly severe problem of Pacific islands, there is no simple correlation between a small size and a distant location of a country. By definition small States have small domestic markets and are forced to specialize in order to benefit from economies of scale. They will thus inevitably produce a limited range of products and must therefore export. For many commodity-and service-dependent small States, their export markets are in advanced industrial countries, which happen to be distant. Where goods are to be locally processed utilizing imported inputs, the distance from sources of supply is relevant and transportation costs become a significant factor. Small States generally trade in small volumes and hence the unit costs of freights are higher, which increases the cost of both their exports and imports, naturally affecting their competitiveness. For instance, in 2005 St Vincent's banana exports to Europe were 17,239 tonnes, and, in that same year, Ecuador shipped 1,026,345 tonnes to Europe. Due to bulk freighting, even though Ecuador is further away from Europe and its vessels traverse the Panama Canal, its unit shipping costs are much lower than those of St Vincent.

A variant of this problem also exists in services. In tourism, for instance, the cost of travel to small tourist destinations, because of the limited number of visitors, can be higher than to more popular and larger destinations that attract more tourists. Both the scale economies resulting from higher passenger volumes and the stronger competition among air-carriers can drive down ticket prices. For instance, travel to Gambia, Guyana and the Seychelles is generally more costly for a European tourist than a journey to New York or Thailand. Higher airfares reduce the competitiveness of a country as a tourist destination.

Reliance on a narrow range of traditional exports can limit the scope for exploiting comparative advantages. Historically, however, such reliance has been a feature of many developing countries, which were required to supply specific products to the colonial powers. When an economy relies on a variety of productive activities for its income (i.e. it is diversified), its economic progress can be facilitated. Diversification lessens the adverse impacts on the wider domestic economy of instability, slowdowns or shocks in one sector. Hence, in a diversified economy, overall progress can be possible despite a slowdown in one particular sector. While the export baskets of larger developing countries are more varied now than forty years ago, many small countries continue to rely on a single or very narrow range of export(s).

For small countries, switching to an extensive range of export activities is not an option. Due to their size, such countries suffer from diseconomies in investment, transportation and in the provision of government services, and limited government resources. In addition, their per capita costs for basic infrastructure are higher due to indivisibilities. To be able to produce the minimum volume of a particular good or service needed to trade internationally, small States are obliged to pool available national resources, devoting a considerable portion, or even the bulk of resources, to that particular activity. Doing so permits them to benefit from whatever economies of scale are possible, or to at least minimize the negative impact of diseconomies of scale. Consequently, the number of productive activities that they might reasonably undertake will be few, and in the case of the smallest States, there could be just one product that can be supplied in sufficient volume to be traded internationally. While historical circumstances might have selected the export specialization, subsequent persistence of a single or narrow range of productive activities is a consequence of small size.

A further consequence of the interplay of high trade dependence, a lack of economic diversification, extreme openness, a narrow resource base and the small size of the domestic market that characterize small States, is that their trade and economic performance is more susceptible than large States to changes in the environment in which they operate. The cumulative result of the various features identified, along with a limited scope for benefitting from economies of scale, and high per capita institutional, infrastructure and transaction costs, is a severe constraint of the ability of small States to achieve international competitiveness and a limit of the potential range and volume of the production of goods and services.

Other constraints that some small States face, which are also faced by countries at a similar level of development, include challenges mobilizing adequate domestic investment, inadequate foreign investment, unfavourable terms of trade and high indebtedness. In addition, small States are diverse among themselves with distinct economic features, structures and circumstances; some are landlocked, coastal or island; service- or commodity-dependent; LDC or non-LDC. All of these features affect their interests and therefore small States do not pursue a pure 'smallness' agenda. During negotiations they thus ally themselves to others with shared interests, not only those related to smallness.

2.2 *Why do the trade interests of small States differ from those of other developing countries?*

The preambles to the Marrakesh Declaration of 15 April 1994 and the Doha Declaration of 14 November 2001 recognize the broad objective of the WTO as one of raising living standards. The premise on which the system operates is that markets should be free and competitive, with barriers to trade removed on a non-discriminatory basis. Within this trading system, the unique characteristics of small States determine their interests and the changes they seek to pursue. Are the special provisions and flexibilities that the multilateral trading system extends to developing countries in general sufficient to meet the specific needs of small States?

Importantly, there is already a precedent in the WTO for granting flexibilities to certain categories of WTO Members, such as long implementation periods for some WTO obligations and some options for shielding domestic markets from foreign competition and for supporting domestic production. Further, the Enabling Clause, for instance, permits WTO Members to provide preferential market access to developing countries. In addition, LDCs, which constitute a distinct category, are eligible for trading advantages including duty-free, quota-free market access. Finally, the Doha Declaration accepts the need to address trade-related issues of SVEs, although specifically states that the purpose is 'not to create a sub-category of WTO Members' (WTO 2001: para. 35).

Given what we know about the limited international competitiveness and volume of exports from undiversified small State economies, is market liberalization, the premise on which the multilateral system operates, adequate to address the development needs of small States? If not, could increased flexibilities in global trade rules enable small States to protect the domestic market (a key objective of SVEs in current trade negotiations) enough to compensate for these challenges? Given the limited size of the domestic markets in small States, there seems little economic benefit to be gained from protecting them. Further, the range of goods and services that can be supplied domestically is very narrow. Although they rely on imports, small States often seek to maintain high import tariffs. Their motivation here is generally to raise government revenue rather than the protection of domestic production.

The benefits of efforts to safeguard or expand domestic production in small States depends on the terms of access to foreign markets. For this reason, the trade concessions that will benefit small States are fundamentally different from those sought by large developing countries whose production for their domestic markets is significant. A clear illustration of this principle is the position of small States on trade in preference-dependent products. Many small States have sought, through the SVE and the African, Caribbean and Pacific (ACP) groupings, to safeguard their exports via measures that permit their traditional trading partners to provide the small State exporters with protection or advantageous access. The national application of trade measures by small States would not meaningfully increase the competitive position of their producers[2] as their target market is neither domestic nor under their control. By contrast, bigger developing countries, with large internal markets that can absorb domestic production, can gain from concessions that provide greater policy flexibilities in the form of longer grace or implementation periods over market openings and the provision of production support. The diverging interests between small developing countries emphasizing benefits in their target export markets, and larger developing countries seeking policy flexibilities for their domestic markets, are reflected in their different stances in regional and multilateral trade negotiations.

Another difference in interests, resulting from smallness, relates to the extent to which expansion of market access is a priority. Although access and competition in target markets will always be important to export-oriented economies, the limited supply capacities of small States permit the export of only a modest volume and narrow range of goods and services. Small States have no real need to secure substantially expanded market access whether in terms of volume or range of products. Large countries, by contrast, do not necessarily face similar geographically imposed constraints and can have greater ambitions for penetrating foreign markets.

To deduce the specific interests of small States in the multilateral trading system, one might be tempted to review the negotiating agenda presented by the SVE group in the context of the WTO's Doha Round. SVEs have not presented their negotiating objectives in one comprehensive document. However, they have presented a number of submissions to various WTO negotiating bodies (Table 8.2 summarizes the key negotiating proposals advanced to date by the SVE group in the context of

[2] On the contrary, some measures can reduce competiveness, e.g. taxation of imported inputs necessary for production can increase the cost of exports.

the Doha Round). A brief review of these proposals, however, shows that the negotiating agenda of the SVE group in the WTO should not be seen as constituting exactly, or as limited to advocating, those measures that address or mitigate the adverse impact of *smallness* in particular. The agenda of the SVE seeks to address various concerns and priorities reflecting the diversity of its composition and its interests, which do not all stem from smallness. Rather, the countries that form the SVE group have a multiplicity of goals. Indeed, the SVE group includes some States that are not particularly small (Table 8.1 illustrates the diversity of a selected number of small States and SVEs). Since the consequences of smallness impact these larger States less severely, their Membership in the group can result in less prioritization of measures that seek to address concerns stemming entirely from extreme smallness. This is particularly so if these larger, better equipped countries exert more influence on the agenda of the group itself. Notably, of the twenty-seven countries with populations of less than half a million, several are not WTO Members, most are not directly active in the SVE group, and only two, Barbados and Brunei, have WTO Permanent Representatives resident in Geneva.[3]

Any separate significant and advantageous treatment that provides a real trading benefit would demand a special category that clearly identifies small WTO Members, but this is not likely to be feasible as it would infringe the WTO's principle of non-discrimination. Despite the merit of the proposals and achievements of the SVE group, the efforts thus far are not enough to overcome the underlying impediments faced by the small States or to enable their effective and beneficial participation in international trade. The primary need of small States is to secure international recognition of the validity and uniqueness of the impediments to beneficial participation in the trading system caused by smallness, and the formulation of concrete measures to address these impediments. As this distinct 'smallness' agenda can not be derived from the SVE group itself, the following section aims to deduce what smallness yields in terms of unique economic interests and trade agendas by exploring how small States function in the trade system.

3 How small States function in the trade governance system

This section examines how small States function in global trade, focusing on those particular challenges, interests and objectives that derive from

[3] The Secretariats of the Organization of Eastern Caribbean States (OECS) and the Pacific Islands Forum (PIF) have technical offices in Geneva.

Table 8.1. *Economic and social data for small States and SVEs (estimates for the last year available, all financial figures in US$m)*

Country	Population	GDP	Government expenditure	Imports	Exports
Tuvalu	10,472	14.94	12.82	12.91	1.00
Nauru	14,264	26.32	16.75	26.69	3.78
St Kitts and Nevis	49,190	543.35	103.53	387.99	222.44
Dominica	73,193	357.39	65.61	248.48	143.74
Seychelles	86,956	833.02	123.57	1,270.51	1,090.56
Tonga	103,566	278.24	60.46	196.46	39.16
St Vincent and the Grenadines	109,117	597.94	116.41	398.09	257.19
Sao Tome and Principe	160,174	174.61	57.53	73.00	8.00
St Lucia	170,205	996.44	188.47	755.03	513.35
Samoa	178,869	523.38	88.59	289.79	175.54
Vanuatu	233,866	589.60	161.01	343.08	263.70
Barbados	255,203	3,681.50	886.00	2,363.37	2,210.72
Maldives	305,027	1,261.27	873.00	1,388.14	1,053.06
Belize	322,100	1,358.70	215.20	951.70	843.55
Brunei Darussalam	392,280	14,780.00	4,000.00	2,610.00	10,670.00
Solomon Islands	510,672	644.88	130.34	285.00	158.50
Suriname	515,124	3,033.10	425.90	1,304.30	1,743.40
Comoros	643,571	530.11	64.04	195.85	67.65
Equatorial Guinea	659,197	18,525.10	490.70	5,952.72	14,498.33
Guyana	763,437	1,155.33	295.80	1,183.43	789.03
Fiji	844,046	3,589.71	582.25	1,779.70	745.70
Djibouti	849,245	874.69	182.00	644.00	100.00
Timor-Leste	1,098,386	497.92	309.00	101.60	43.50
Swaziland	1,167,834	2,837	604	2,289	1,947
Mauritius	1,268,854	9,319.73	1,227.30	6,308.72	4,941.80
Qatar	1,280,862	113,984.00	28,280.00	27,900.00	54,912.10
Trinidad and Tobago	1,333,388	24,145.27	2,645.27	10,210.16	17,728.27
Gabon	1,448,159	14,534.67	1,190.09	4,652.09	9,675.32

Table 8.1. *(cont.)*

Country	Population	GDP	Government expenditure	Imports	Exports
The Gambia	1,660,200	811.15	127.88	396.87	243.61
Botswana	1,921,122	13,413.67	2,674.22	5,210.59	6,197.07
Lesotho	2,049,429	1,622.06	434.40	1,796.50	767.41
Jamaica	2,687,200	14,614.27	155,308.60	8,465.40	2,438.80
Papua New Guinea	6,576,822	8,238.95	824.19	4,953.14	5,973.10
Bolivia	9,694,113	16,674	2,214	6,330	7,488
Dominican Republic	9,952,711	45,540.64	3,477.61	17,827.70	11,795.48
Cuba	11,204,735	62,705.00	50,340.00	10,173.60	2,980.20
Guatemala	13,686,128	38,983.13	3,604.51	15,434.97	9,640.49

Sources: World Bank Database 2010, CIA World Factbook 2010, UN Database 2010, US Department of States, Asian Development Bank and National Statistics Offices of the States.

their 'smallness'. I turn first to the particular issue of preferences, and then examine the issue of participation in WTO decision-making.

Given the cumulative negative impact of smallness on a country's ability to compete internationally, a further priority of small States is to secure measures that facilitate exports despite prices that are generally higher than world prices. In practice, this has meant that securing or safeguarding adequate preferences in their target markets has often been an immediate aim in trade negotiations. The differential between the zero or reduced tariff that they face and the higher levy borne by competitors can be sufficient to make their otherwise too expensive product competitive and make trade possible that may not have taken place.[4] Regardless of the size of the beneficiary country, dependence on preferences can distort

[4] The experience of the Windward Islands exemplifies the correlation between preferences and trade performance. When the EU banana market was unified by the Common Organisation of the Market in 1993, they lost the benefit of the high 20 per cent tariff and stringent quantitative restrictions on lower-cost MFN bananas on the British market. Over the next fifteen years, the EU steadily liberalized the market following successful challenges in the WTO. With the declining margins of preference, the islands faced greater competition from MFN and ACP suppliers, and prices slumped, eroding farmers' confidence and resulting in disinvestment and a steady exodus from the industry.

Table 8.2. *Development interests of SVEs in the Doha Round*

Negotiating area	Offensive interests	Defensive interests
Agriculture	Special priority for products of export interest	Need for special flexibilities
NAMA	Special priority for products of export interest	Need for special flexibilities
Services	Special priority for services of export interest Special efforts to facilitate the full range of services exports	Need for flexibilities, particularly in the area of domestic regulations
Trade rules		Fisheries subsidies: Need for flexibilities to grant subsidies to their fisheries sectors Subsidies and countervailing measures: Allow SVEs to provide certain prohibited subsidies to respond to the needs of their small business sector RTAs: Allow certain non-reciprocity in RTAs between SVEs and developed countries to take into account the special problems and characteristics of SVEs
Trade facilitation	Special consideration for the provision of technical assistance and capacity-building Address specific needs of land-locked SVEs bearing in mind that they have no seaports and have inherently high transit and other costs	
Dispute settlement	Assistance for countries to make use of the provisions of the Understanding on Rules and Procedures Governing the Settlement of Disputes and to enforce the decisions	

Table 8.2. *(cont.)*

Negotiating area	Offensive interests	Defensive interests
Technical assistance and capacity-building	Greater support to build supply-side capacity-building and human and institutional resources development Recognition of the role of regional bodies as inquiry points and technical assistance (related to SPS, TBT and TRIPS)	

Source: Kaukab 2009.

comparative advantages so that production does not necessarily take place in the sectors with the greatest international competitiveness, but rather in those that benefit from the artificial advantage provided by the preference. This is a disincentive to diversification and causes production patterns to ossify. Even where adjustment is recognized as necessary, the transition poses particular challenges in small States because the export industry to be replaced is often a dominant contributor to income and employment while the range of alternative competitive productive activities tends to be limited. That said, preferences are in long-term decline and it is clear that small States should diversify and restructure their economies in order to maximize the benefits of more optimal allocation of national resources. Small States have no option but to reduce their reliance on preferences. However, their circumstances make the process more difficult, painful and time-consuming.

Considerable progress has been made in greater openness and equality in decision-making at the WTO; debate among Members is more transparent, committees are open to all Members, and binding decisions are not taken in restricted groupings.[5] An extensive body of rules exists that governs and constrains action by Members who can face sanctions

[5] On occasion, however, conclusions reached in the 'Green Room' may seem to be binding because they are not challenged by a plenary body; however, formally this restricted group has no decision-making authority.

for violation. Consensus is required for most decision-making, which permits even the smallest Member to block progress.

However, to understand the prospect of greater influence by small States, and the extent to which influence can secure change, it is important to appreciate the role of power. The WTO system is a component of the real world of commercial, economic and political asymmetric relations among States, where power plays a major role in determining the outcomes of conflict, agenda-setting and decision-making. Despite its ostensible democratic and rule-based character, and its formal provisions restraining power, the WTO is not insulated from the consequences of the power imbalances among its Members.

Possessing power makes a country more influential in negotiations as it can support its positions with the prospect of negative and/or positive consequences for others. Therefore, WTO Members take into account not only the merits of the case or the arguments put forward, but also factor in what they could gain or lose by accepting or opposing the position that is advocated. The perception of a Member's ability to offer inducements or impose sanctions can therefore influence other representatives' receptiveness to its case. Small States generally have less power in this sense.

The differential in power between WTO Members affects most aspects of the WTO's decision-making, including the application of the consensus principle. The formal rule is that any Member can prevent the adoption of a decision by maintaining an explicit objection. However, it is the powerful Members that can withstand external pressure and continue to block a decision. A small State might initially block a consensus but is generally unable to maintain 'defiance' over a protracted period. Pressure is likely to be asserted by other WTO representatives, who will urge reconsideration, resorting to a variety of arguments and ploys. Their political authorities might also pressure the country's Ministers. While it is difficult to provide concrete evidence of countries being threatened with reprisals because of their recalcitrance in the WTO, small States are well aware of their vulnerability to sanctions, even if they are not overtly threatened. Large developed countries that have important relations with small States can exercise discretion in a number of areas, such as, among others, over the volume and terms of provision of development assistance, the degree to which they facilitate foreign investment, political support and their policies with respect to migration.

A key means by which the international community could facilitate greater effectiveness and influence of small States in global trade governance would be to address the power asymmetries that work against them. WTO Members could, for instance, take measures that would de-emphasize power in decision-making. Small States have a vested interest in institutional review that identifies and implements the precise measures that could reduce the importance of power. Moreover, by being active in the campaign for greater democratization and fairness, small States can contribute moral and political credibility to the WTO and bolster perceptions of its inclusiveness.

Imaginative and creative arrangements are needed. For instance, the ability of a single country to indefinitely block a consensus on certain types of decisions could be prevented by automatic referral to voting after a specified number of failed attempts or a prescribed passage of time. However, the Members that currently possess the most influence would not campaign for, or be enthusiastic supporters of, changes designed to neutralize their power and influence.

De-emphasizing power would not only directly increase the potential influence of small States, it would also enhance the effectiveness of the other instruments available to them – namely diplomacy, advocacy, negotiation and litigation – which could also help bring about further change. The difficulty is that the effectiveness of these instruments is subject to the availability of adequate financial, human and institutional resources and capacity. Small States seek to mitigate these constraints in a variety of ways, including through donor funding, working in coalitions, and using technical input from outside advisors. However, can their use of diplomacy and advocacy, negotiation and litigation be enough to secure change?

3.1 *Diplomacy and advocacy*

Trade representatives and diplomats engage with target countries and institutions to advance national commercial interests. However, various factors such as weak institutional structures, inadequate policy coherence and concerted political engagement can inhibit small States from succeeding in diplomacy. Small States generally lack the financial and human resources to properly staff and fund the required embassies and missions. These shortages can also affect their ability to attend negotiations. States without resident diplomatic presence in key capitals can find it more difficult to get their messages across and advance their interests. Very few small States have resident missions in Geneva; in fact, most of the WTO

Members that are non-resident are small States with populations of less than one million.

The media has a central role in shaping public attitudes and, in modern democratic societies, it exerts an important, albeit indirect, influence in policy formulation. Compared to larger, more powerful states, small States are at a disadvantage in attracting and sustaining the attention of the international press. For instance, during the 2009 WTO Ministerial Conference in Geneva, US press briefings with the United States Trade Representative Ron Kirk were well attended, while Caribbean Community and Common Market (CARICOM) press briefings were not, even though Ministers and all delegation leaders were present. Poor access to the media limits the scope both of diplomacy and advocacy. But there is still value in small States' engagement with the press on a more concerted and long-term basis.

To win support or secure favourable decisions in target States, small States need to navigate complex parliamentary and governmental structures. In Brussels or Washington, for instance, just knowing whom to contact, getting through and delivering a convincing and appropriate message can be a challenge. Not surprisingly, professional lobbying has become a major industry. Small States occasionally engage lobbyists and public relations advisors. Although the Ambassadors of small States can generally secure access to Ministers, legislators and senior government officials, lobbyists can be useful where small States do not have permanent or effective diplomatic presence in the target city and, even where they do, these experts can help them organize professional information and conduct outreach campaigns.

There are difficulties, though, in using lobbyists. For one, they are expensive, which means small States with limited financial means are at a disadvantage when competing with companies or other governments to engage the best lobbyists. As small States often lack clarity with regard to precise strategic and policy objectives, lobbyists might not be adequately briefed on the mandate, tasks and precise outputs required. Further, due to institutional capacity constraints, their oversight and accountability can be inadequate. The fact that lobbyists are often appointed by government ministers compounds these problems, as the minister is unlikely to have time to devote to detailed management and supervision. For these reasons, when engaging lobbyists, it is important that their terms of reference are defined precisely with measurable and clearly identifiable outputs and results specified, and that contracts incorporate adequate provisions for effective oversight by designated government representatives. Most importantly, the small State should view the lobbyist not as a substitute for its own diplomatic engagement, but as a supplement to its diplomatic outreach and representation to host governments, media, non-governmental organizations (NGOs) and other centres of influence.

3.2 *Negotiation*

In the WTO, and in major regional arrangements like the Economic Partnership Agreements (EPAs), negotiation is the most obvious instrument for a State to harness to advance its objectives, whether these relate to winning support or concessions from other parties, or resisting change that it would consider disadvantageous. However, there is a perception in the international community and among small States themselves that they are not able to be effective in negotiations. In 2010, the outcomes of a survey of officials from small States showed that such officials often consider themselves unable to achieve their aims in negotiations with major players (Jones *et al.* 2010). Just 3.5 per cent of officials thought that their countries could have a large influence when dealing with major players like the USA or the EU, whereas over 30 per cent considered that their influence was high when dealing with countries of similar economic size. In accordance with this perception, various segments of the donor community have provided 'capacity-building' to developing countries, especially LDCs and small States. The rationale has been that technical and financial assistance helps them become more effective and presumably successful in negotiations.

In negotiations among States, a country's diplomatic representatives intervene both directly and indirectly to try to secure predetermined outcomes. Negotiators seek to bring about changes to the position of the opposing party through deliberate argument, persuasion and bargaining, among other actions. As such, an indicator of success is when the 'opposing' party changes its position and adopts one that is more satisfactory. Alternatively, in certain circumstances, success can be achieved where the negotiator has resisted the temptation or pressure to capitulate or make concessions that are not in the State's interest.

There is no doubt that asymmetrical power relations predispose negotiations to particular outcomes. But a recent study on the constraints facing small States in international trade negotiations also suggested that if a range of obstacles are overcome, small States could increase their influence in negotiations, albeit at the margins (Jones *et al.* 2010). The study found that additional factors, such as the inadequacy of institutional, human and financial resources (Jones *et al.* 2010: 9), as well as a lack of adequate and good quality information (Jones *et al.* 2010: 26), also influence the performance of small States and impacted negotiation outcomes. The research found evidence of insufficient strategic and policy coordination within small States (Jones *et al.* 2010: 29) and, most significantly, a lack of clearly defined priorities (Jones *et al.* 2010: 36). In the survey conducted, just under one-third of respondents saw themselves as having clear short-term objectives related to specific negotiating texts, but lacking clarity on precise long-term goals and interests. The tactics used in negotiations were also examined. The study found that small States do not employ the full range of tactics available to enhance their political weight and leverage their power, whether to exert influence in favour of a proactive agenda or to defensively resist pressure in negotiations.

3.3 Litigation

The prospect of dispute settlement and the interpretation of ambiguous provisions in trade agreements on the basis of a quasi-juridical process with clear rules and operational principles would appear, at first glance, to offer a fair opportunity for small States. In practice, however, small States are disadvantaged in the WTO's Dispute Settlement Mechanism. One part of the explanation for their disadvantaged position is the high cost of mounting a case or maintaining an effective defence when challenged in a dispute. The only small State that has successfully initiated and concluded a WTO dispute was Antigua (WTO 2003), which benefitted from private sector financial backing. Even participation as a third party in a WTO dispute can be daunting. To prepare legal submissions of the appropriately high standard and appear before a WTO Panel or the Appellate Body requires specialized expertise in trade law that small States are unlikely to have in their permanent establishment. Financial constraints mean that they cannot afford to permanently employ specialized experts on the chance that they might, at some point, be required for dispute proceedings. By contrast, a large country with more abundant resources that expects to be involved in several disputes, whether as plaintiff, respondent or third party, could find it cost effective to retain the ongoing services of the required legal experts. The WTO Secretariat offers the possibility of a part-time advisor to a developing country involved in a dispute. However, this does not satisfy the range of technical expertise that a country needs should it be a plaintiff or respondent. Where the country is a third party and its interests are minimal, or the case to be presented and argued is relatively simple, that facility could be adequate. However, if it is a plaintiff, respondent or third party in a substantial and complex dispute, the support will not be enough. When small States need expertise they are obliged to purchase high-cost services on a temporary basis, or to seek the support of the Advisory Centre on WTO Law (ACWL). Established in 2001, the ACWL provides free legal support and advice to its Members, but the subscription fee is high and most small States, who unlike LDCs are not exempted from the membership fee, have not joined. Their calculation is likely that the remote probability of requiring the services of the Centre does not justify the initial outlay.

Not only is a small State less able than a large, better-resourced country to present and argue its case before a WTO Dispute Panel, it is also in a weaker position to enforce decisions and obtain redress, should it win. The instrument for enforcing compliance with a WTO dispute ruling is the application of an authorized trade sanction against the loser by the winning party. This punishment both serves as a deterrent and provides compensation. By permitting the 'winner' to withdraw a concession or impose additional duties on imports from the 'loser', the former can enjoy additional protection for local production from competition from the losing party's goods or services. While this ingenious arrangement might work for developed and advanced developing countries, a smaller country may not be able to impose trade sanctions on a major industrialized country, particularly a key trading partner.[6] In this case, additional tariffs imposed by the small State would simply result in trade diversion to a third country and/or in increased domestic prices. Were a small State to secure a ruling against a large powerful country, it would have to decide whether to risk causing offence by punishing a country on which it might rely for benefits in other areas, such as financial, military or political assistance. The small State might fear that these benefits could be withheld in counter-retaliation or that it could suffer deliberate punitive measures to which it might not successfully object since such measures are discretionary and beyond the realm of trade rules.

The extent to which such concerns are likely to deter a small State from taking action to enforce a favourable Panel ruling against a major developed country are difficult to quantify, particularly as the only relevant case to date has been Antigua winning an internet gambling case against the United States. In Antigua's case, not only is the United States

[6] This also applies if the developing country was large but did not have substantial internal productive capacity that could benefit from the trade sanctions imposed on competing imports.

its main trading partner, but it also depends heavily on US tourism (its major earner) and financial services. In the non-trade sphere, the United States is an important donor for Antigua, has a major military facility in the country, and is the dominant political power in the region. Given its size, Antigua would find it difficult to invoke meaningful sanctions against the United States that would secure compliance and is extremely vulnerable to countermeasures. Although in December 2007 Antigua secured an Arbitral award authorizing suspension of concessions under the WTO's Agreement on Trade-Related Aspects of Intellectual Property Rights (TRIPS) up to the amount of US$21 million, it tried to reach a settlement through negotiations and, to date, has not actually imposed the authorized sanctions.

Despite the limited experience of small States in the WTO's dispute settlement system, it can be surmised that the right to impose sanctions is more likely to be used by larger and more powerful States than by small States. Nonetheless, while it may not be a trump card, the authority to invoke sanctions does provide backing to an adopted and legally binding Panel decision, which could at least help a small State bring a powerful Party into serious negotiations.

In sum, small States cannot be viewed as fully equal in the WTO's dispute settlement system. Their shortage of skills and lack of financial resources mean that they are limited in the ability to adequately prepare, present and defend cases and, even if they win, they are likely to be reticent about invoking sanctions against a more powerful respondent. In a system that is based on enforcement of the ruling by the winner, it is inevitable that weaker and more vulnerable States would not feel as secure or comfortable implementing sanctions as larger and stronger States.

4 Meeting the challenges of Regional Trade Agreements

At the regional level just as at the multilateral, both power imbalances and unequal capacities and resources among trading partners influence the outcomes of negotiations and trade agreements. Small States have been involved in negotiating regional trade agreements (RTAs) with major advanced developed countries for many years. The most notable recent examples are the EPAs between the EU and ACP regions. Others include negotiations for a Pacific Agreement on Closer Economic Relations (PACER Plus) (which were launched in 2009 and engage Australia, New Zealand and most of the island states of the South Pacific) and the Canada-CARICOM Agreement. The significance of the power imbalance in RTA negotiations between small States and advanced industrialized countries can be more pronounced than in multilateral negotiations. At the bilateral and regional level, small countries might consider themselves vulnerable and with no leverage. Many non-LDC ACP countries, for instance, felt obliged to conclude EPAs due to fears, reinforced by European Commission negotiators, that preferential access for their exports to EU markets would otherwise cease. Compounding the lack of leverage is the existence of the aid donor-recipient relationship, which greatly enhances the influence of the developed country partner in negotiations. Both sides know that the issues at stake are not only those being formally negotiated, but also other aspects of the bilateral relationship on which the small State is generally more dependent.

The other key consideration relates to the relative impact of an RTA on the small State as opposed to the large developed country partner. Due to geographic and resource constraints, the small State cannot be a major overall supplier of goods and services (although of course it could be important in a particular product or service, e.g. sugar or tourism). The large country partner can, by contrast, be a substantial supplier of an extensive range of goods and services to the small State. Trade policy changes by the large powerful country can have a great impact on the small developing country partner, whereas the reverse does not necessarily apply. With respect to EPAs, for instance, the European Union is a major trading partner and source of investment and financial aid for many ACP countries. This asymmetry means that the economic impact of potential agreements is quite significant for ACP countries. The same does not, however, apply to the EU, for whom an agreement with relatively small countries, though sometimes important, would not have major overall economic consequences. This imbalance in impact means that the small State has relatively more to gain or lose from the negotiations. This disadvantage means that, in addition to the diplomatic and negotiating constraints outlined above, small States cannot as readily employ the range of valuable negotiating tactics, including bluff, brinkmanship and ultimately the threat of abandoning talks.

5 Looking ahead: proposals for change

Given that their economic circumstances give rise to needs and interests that are quite different from those of other WTO Members, small States face the major task of ensuring their interests are better understood, accommodated and supported within the global trading system.

However, the reality is that power, with which small States are not particularly well endowed, plays a decisive role in the management of the global trading system. While small States aim to bring about changes that de-emphasize power, the instruments available to them to advance such goals – diplomacy, advocacy, negotiation and litigation – rely on power and the availability of skilled human and adequate financial resources. That said, measures could be taken by the international community as a whole to reduce the role of power in determining influence and outcomes in WTO decision-making. Further, small States themselves can do a lot to maximize their individual and collective power and influence.

5.1 *Decision-making structures*

The effort to de-emphasize the role of power in decision-making in the WTO is already under way, principally due to the use of the consensus principle and to the growing openness and transparency of WTO proceedings. However, shortcomings remain and require creative solutions. For instance, while decision-making by consensus rather than voting has often been portrayed as strengthening the influence of small States and conferring equality by giving them veto power, the reality is far less clear-cut. Any WTO Member who opposes everyone else will come under pressure to concede, but a small State is likely to submit more readily than larger and more powerful States. Indeed, it would likely be very hesitant to continue defying the entire Membership even when vital interests are at stake. Thus, the consensus rule permits a veto, but does not guarantee equality since, in practice, veto is more likely to be successfully exercised by the powerful.

Another area for attention is the system of restricted consultations as part of the WTO process. There is no doubt that progress is difficult where the agenda is complex and decisions require 153 Members to agree. As such, restricted consultations are used to bring key players together as a way to organize, prepare and pursue negotiations more efficiently. The logic, and assumption, of this approach is that a Member selected from a particular group articulates the views and interests of those being represented and can later help sell any consensus reached in the smaller group to the larger group. With time, there have been efforts to include more groupings and interests in restricted consultations. Nonetheless, 'Green Room' processes continue to be portrayed by critics as reinforcing power imbalances since they increase the influence of those Members participating. In groups with active Members, there is the potential for unified positions and accountability of representatives to the group as a whole. However, in the case of small States that lack clarity over common interests, where many Members are inactive or even absent from group deliberations, and where there are no explicit arrangements for the accountability of the representative, neither group arrangements nor the 'enlightened' Green Room model work as intended. Indeed, small countries express concern that their 'representatives' in such restricted consultations might prioritize their own national interests over those of group members (Jones *et al.* 2010: 52).

One strategy for overcoming this constraint would be for Members to more strategically select and rotate the representative of their groups themselves (and for the WTO Secretariat to respect the group's decision regarding the appropriate representative rather than, for instance, choosing itself who to invite whether or not they have any formal representative authority from a larger group). This approach would reinforce the accountability of representatives to the group and increase the formal authority with which the representative speaks on behalf of the larger group. In parallel, small States could ensure better representation of their interests by adequately briefing the representative before any restricted consultations or meetings and insisting on accountability to the wider group. This in turn would require more active participation by all small States. Similarly, when spokespersons are used in RTA negotiations, fuller accountability to the broader group is also needed.

5.2 Capacity-building

To address the constraints small States face in participating effectively in trade negotiations, the international community provides a range of support, including technical advice, training of personnel, funding research, and travel to – and participation in – consultation and negotiation sessions. Given the fact that small States are not yet successful in securing the outcomes they pursue in international negotiations, it can be argued that the assistance has not been entirely successful. To improve the effectiveness of capacity-building efforts, existing programmes need to be critically reviewed and made more results-orientated. Moreover, beneficiaries themselves need to be granted a fuller role in the planning and management of capacity-building programmes. This is particularly the case where donors are party to trade negotiations. In such cases, they should avoid direct involvement in the actual management and delivery of capacity-building support. Various alternative devices could be considered, including funding intermediaries to operate capacity-building programmes. Such devices would avoid situations where the powerful party directly funds research to inform the negotiating position of its adversary or the cost of travel by officials to negotiations. Even if the motivation for such support is benign and the powerful party does not seek to use it to gain an advantage, there can be the perception among the recipient country negotiators that their position and room for negotiation is being weakened.

5.3 *Measures and actions required of small States*

The governments of small States frequently assert their expectation that systems of trade governance should deliver a range of concessions, facilities and benefits to mitigate or compensate for the challenges that small States face, and to enable them to engage in international trade on a sustainable basis. However, a comprehensive agenda that sets out specific measures needed to achieve these aims has yet to be devised by small States. An agenda that focuses specifically on addressing the impediments caused by smallness is unlikely to be pursued by the SVE group in the WTO, given that its membership is based on self-selection and that considerable influence is exercised in that group by countries that are less adversely affected by smallness. Two ways in which very small States' concerns could be prioritized would, first, be the establishment of clear criteria for membership for the SVE group, and, second, for States that manifest the extreme problems of smallness to become more active in the SVE group and more directly involved in setting its agenda.

In addition, small States should take steps to strengthen their ability to negotiate successfully. Jones *et al.* (2010: 74–6) highlight that giving sufficient priority to trade policy is a critical step. Currently, trade ministries are often understaffed and there is inadequate participation in trade negotiations both on an ongoing basis and at major encounters.

Individual small States can use diplomacy, lobbying and coalition-building more effectively, but they need to be clear on their interests and be willing to pursue them. When in coalitions, small States need to ensure that their unique interests (those linked to addressing the impediments resulting from their smallness) are appropriately incorporated into the overall agenda of the group. They also need to maintain an effective presence in negotiating fora, more fully mobilize their resources and capabilities, and tactically apply their influence in those domains that advance their objectives. Coalitions and allies, whose support can be enlisted, comprise not only States, but also NGOs and the press. Small States can and should also use campaigners or lobbyists as a helpful supplement to their own outreach, though not as a substitute for diplomatic engagement.

6 Conclusion

Smallness imposes additional challenges to the ability of developing countries to benefit from, and successfully participate in, the global trading system that larger countries do not face. Small States must themselves take responsibility for ensuring that their concerns are adequately addressed.

The problems caused by small size include a narrow resource base; small domestic markets; the inability to benefit from economies of scale; and high transaction costs. These constraints combine to limit the ability of small countries to be internationally competitive in producing and marketing goods and services. Currently, the structures governing both international and regional trade are based on principles of market opening and liberalization. However, because extreme smallness can constitute a structural impediment to competitiveness, a small State might not perceive the benefits from liberalization and market opening. Indeed, it is unlikely to be able to substantially expand its exports due to geographically imposed supply constraints. As a consequence of this, small States have negotiating interests that are distinct and additional to those of other developing countries.

As noted throughout this chapter, small States do not strongly influence the current agenda or structures for the governance of global trade, which derive heavily from power relations. Yet, small States are seeking to expand their own power by better using the tools of diplomacy, advocacy, negotiation and litigation to help achieve specific policy and operational changes that advance their interests.

At present, there is no exclusive and well-defined 'small' agenda for global trade governance reform, in part because the full economic impact of smallness and the constraints that it imposes on States are not yet fully appreciated and explicitly reflected in the multilateral negotiating agenda. This chapter has thus attempted to deduce what small States would need in order to be able to more effectively define, articulate and advance their interests in global trade governance structures, and to ensure that these structures are more supportive of, and responsive to, their needs.

References

Brigulio, L., Persaud, B. and Stern, R. 2006. *Towards an Outward-Oriented Development Strategy for Small States: Issues, Opportunities and Resilience Building*. London: Commonwealth Secretariat.

Commonwealth Advisory Group. 1997. *A Future for Small States: Overcoming Vulnerability*. London: Commonwealth Secretariat.

Cooper, A. and Shaw, T. (eds.) 2009. *The Diplomacies of Small States: Between Vulnerability and Resilience*. International Political Series. United Kingdom: Palgrave Macmillan.

Jones, E., Deere Birkbeck, C. and Woods, N. 2010. *Manoeuvring at the Margins: The Constraints Faced by Small States in International Trade Negotiations*. London: Commonwealth Secretariat.

Kaukab, R. S. 2009. *Development Effects of the Doha Round on SVEs*. (Unpublished). London: Commonwealth Secretariat.

Laurent, E. 2007. *Understanding International Trade: A CARICOM Perspective*. Jamaica: Ian Randle.

Spolaore, E. 2004. 'Is Small Really So Ugly?', *World Trade Review* 3(3): 447–52.

Sutherland, V., Faruqi, R., Masood, A. *et al.* 2000. *Small States: Meeting the Challenges in the Global Economy*. London: Commonwealth Secretariat.

World Trade Organization (WTO). 1994a. *General Agreement on Tariffs and Trade*. Geneva: WTO.

1994b. *Understanding on Rules and Procedures Governing the Settlement of Disputes*. Geneva: WTO.

2001. *Doha Ministerial Declaration adopted at the 4th WTO Ministerial Conference November 2001*. WT/MIN(01). Geneva: WTO.

2003. *WTO, US – Measures Affecting Cross Border Supply of Gambling and Betting Services*. WTO Report WT/DS285/23. Geneva: WTO.

9

Improving the participation of small developing countries in the governance of the multilateral trading system

RICHARD L. BERNAL

Given the overriding importance of international trade to the performance of small developing economies (SDEs) and their acute vulnerability to external economic events, these countries are vitally concerned with their place in the world economy and the nature of the rules and institutions governing the global economy.

For SDEs to achieve sustainable economic development, they need to reposition themselves in a strategic global sense. This repositioning will demand both changes in their internal development policies and the exertion of as much influence as possible to reshape the multilateral trading system, in particular as represented by the World Trade Organization (WTO) (Bernal 1996, 2000). As the core institution responsible for the creation and revision of the rules that govern multilateral trade, and for the adjudication of disputes arising from differences in interpretation or application of those rules, SDEs should seek more effective participation and influence in the WTO governance. It is through changes in the decision-making processes and operations of the WTO that the multilateral trading system will respond more effectively to the interests, concerns and objectives of the SDEs. Notably, the importance of the effective participation of SDEs in global governance goes beyond the ambit of international trade to encompass governance in other multilateral institutions, including the United Nations (UN),

Ambassador Richard Bernal is the Executive Director for the Caribbean at the Inter-American Development Bank and was formerly the Director-General of the Caribbean Regional Negotiating Machinery (CRNM). The views are those of the author and not those of the Inter-American Development Bank or the CRNM or their Member States. An earlier version of this chapter was published by the Canadian Centre for International Governance Innovation (CIGI). The author thanks Carolyn Deere Birkbeck and any anonymous reviewers for their input on this chapter.

the International Monetary Fund (IMF) and the World Bank (Buria 2003; Portugal 2005: 2; Woodward 2005: 5; Woods and Lombardi 2005; and Truman 2006), but the focus of this chapter is on the international trade regime.

This chapter has several objectives. The first is to review and evaluate the participation of SDEs in the governance of the multilateral trading system, with a particular focus on the WTO. The second objective is to suggest ways to improve the efficacy of the participation of SDEs in the WTO's decision-making processes. The third objective is to propose ways in which the WTO could be adapted to facilitate improved participation by SDEs in its governance. These objectives assume, of course, the need for SDEs to participate in the multilateral trading system – and, hence, in the WTO – in the first instance, despite the minute share of world trade for which they account. Indeed, there are persons, in both the public and private sectors in SDEs, who do not understand the relevance of participation in the multilateral trading system or who argue that participation might even be inimical to the interests of SDEs. Accordingly, the discussion is preceded by an explanation of why SDEs must participate and why their involvement is, in turn, important to the multilateral trading system.

This chapter proceeds in four sections. Section 1 sets out the reason why participation in the WTO matters for SDEs. Section 2 then explores the ways in which the multilateral trading system benefits from SDE participation. The chapter continues in section 3 to examine how to make SDE participation at the WTO more effective and section 4 follows with proposals for how to adapt the WTO and its governance to SDEs.

1 The participation of SDEs in the multilateral trading system

Two questions must be answered about the participation of SDEs in the multilateral trading system. First, should they participate at all? If the answer is in the affirmative, what are the compelling arguments to justify their participation? Second, given their minute share of world trade, is the participation of SDEs of any importance to the WTO?

Despite the costs and difficulties involved in participating in multilateral trade negotiations, there are five compelling reasons why small States must remain engaged in the WTO and participate as fully as possible in current and future trade negotiations.

1.1 *The importance of international trade to SDEs*

The highly open economic structure of SDEs means that, compared to larger and more developed economies, they have a high ratio of trade to gross domestic product (GDP) – in many instances, the ratio of trade to GDP is over 100 per cent (Commonwealth Secretariat/World Bank 2000: 9). For SDEs, imports are of critical importance to domestic production and consumption, both quantitatively and qualitatively. Growth is therefore extremely dependent on imports and, consequently, on import capacity, which, in turn, is a function of the quantum of foreign-exchange inflows. These inflows are determined by export earnings and net capital inflows – that is, foreign investment, development assistance, loans and remittances.

SDEs also have greater need for access to external markets than do larger economies due to the small size of their domestic market and limited resource base. Unfavourable external developments in either imports or exports, including changes in trade arrangements, can lead to a collapse in earnings or a surge in economy-wide prices, precipitating prolonged periods of severe contraction in the wider economy and rapid changes in employment.

1.2 *The vulnerability of SDEs to external developments*

A second reason SDEs need to participate in the WTO is that their exports tend to be concentrated in a small number of primary products and/or agricultural commodities that are exported with minimal processing (Briguglio 1999; Gonzales 2000). This vulnerability becomes acute when export concentration is compounded by exporting to a single overseas market and, in extreme cases, through one company. A dramatic example is the implosion of the economy of Dominica, which depended solely on exports of bananas to the United Kingdom through one company until the banana regime of the European Union (EU) was changed (Bernal 2004). Indeed, acute vulnerability is the structural characteristic that distinguishes SDEs from other types of economies; the United Nations Conference on Trade and Development (UNCTAD) has observed that small island developing states are 34 per cent more vulnerable than other developing countries (UNCTAD 2004: 6).[1] Another study reveals

[1] As an explanation, UNCTAD states that '[p]artly because of their exposure to natural disasters, their agricultural production was more unstable than that of other developing

that twenty-six of the twenty-eight most vulnerable economies are small countries (Commonwealth Secretariat/World Bank 2000: 20).[2]

1.3 *The uniqueness of SDE interests*

A third justification for the participation of SDEs in the WTO is that although the trade interests of SDEs and other developing countries have much in common, the concerns and objectives of the former are distinct, and, in some cases, unique. Accordingly, their participation in trade negotiations is necessary to ensure that their particular interests and concerns are recognized and appropriate treatment is accorded. As noted above, the uniqueness of some aspects of the international trade agenda of SDEs derives from their structural and institutional features (Bernal 2003).

In international trade negotiations, SDEs are struggling to retain existing preferences in key markets and to establish the principle that small size is an additional constraint on development and that SDEs should be accorded 'special and differential treatment' (Bernal 2006). This challenge is illustrated by the situation confronting Caribbean Community (CARICOM) countries. These states enjoy preferential market access for trade in goods with Canada through the 1986 CARIBCAN,[3] with the European Union under the Cotonou Agreement, and with the United States through the *Caribbean Basin Economic Recovery Act* and associated legislation. All three trading partners have signalled that reciprocity will be the basis of future trade agreements. Even in such arrangements, however, there is room for special and differential treatment, and CARICOM has and continues to argue the case for such treatment in these arrangements and at the WTO (Bernal 1998).

In the WTO's Doha Development Agenda and, to some extent, in the context of the Cotonou Agreement between the European Union and the African, Caribbean and Pacific countries, there is increasing recognition that small States, or 'smaller economies', require a special dispensation in the international trade regime. The 2001 Declaration of the WTO Ministerial Meeting in Doha, for example, established a work programme on small economies (WTO 2001: para. 35). In addition, in the

countries by 31%, and their exports of goods and services were more unstable by 10%' (2004: 6).

[2] These findings are confirmed by Atkins *et al.* (2001: 63).

[3] The Caribbean–Canada Trade Agreement (also known as the CARIBCAN) came into effect in June 1986. http://ctrc.sice.oas.org/Trade/caribcan/Caribcan_e.asp [accessed in November 2010].

now-abandoned Free Trade Area of the Americas (FTAA) process, there was explicit acknowledgement in several Ministerial Declarations of the need to reflect 'differences in size of economies and levels of development' as a basic principle in the negotiations. Moreover, Article 35.2 of the Cotonou Agreement states that the Economic Partnership Agreements, which replace it, shall 'take account of different needs and levels of development … ensuring special and differential treatment … and taking due account of the vulnerabilities of small, landlocked and island countries' (Cotonou Agreement 2006: 29).

The growing recognition of the validity of SDE claims for additional special and differential treatment for SDEs is a reflection of persistent advocacy and the availability of research and policy analysis on small, vulnerable economies. The next step in consolidating the empirical and analytical foundation for special and differential treatment of SDEs is to demonstrate the direct link between structural and institutional characteristics of this type of economy and the specific measures of special treatment proposed (Bernal 2006). While SDEs should pursue their particular interests in all trade negotiations, they should give special attention to deliberations in the WTO, as these establish a template that underpins other trade agreements and are the focal point for the formation of the rules that regulate international trade (in addition to agreements on liberalization).

1.4 Enhancing the negotiating leverage of SDEs

A fourth reason SDEs need to participate in the WTO is that a rules-based regime for the conduct of international trade and the resolution of disputes is arguably of more importance to small countries than to large ones. Moreover the multilateral context is where small States can best enhance their limited leverage through the use of strategic alliances and by taking advantage of the opportunities that consensus-based decision-making presents. Multilateral negotiations provide an opportunity for small countries to have a measure of countervailing power against the overwhelming power of large entities such as the United States, the European Union, Brazil, India and China. Large countries, particularly highly developed ones, wield near-dominant influence due to their market size, share of world trade and political power. The mere threat of trade action by a large country can disrupt global markets, impede market access and unsettle production and investment. They can also profoundly influence the course of trade negotiations.

Small countries, by contrast, have limited influence on trade negotiations because their small national markets and insignificant share of world trade give them little or no leverage in bargaining. Participation in the multilateral trading system gives them access to a transparent, democratic decision-making process based on consensus to temper differences in national power and economic size, and helps support a strong rules-based framework for global trade as an alternative to more coercive bilateral negotiations where opportunities for alliances are weak. Outside of a multilateral framework, the results of trade negotiations between countries that differ in size, power and development are invariably asymmetrical to the disadvantage of the smaller, less-developed country. Patrick Messerlin has described these outcomes as 'reverse' special and differential treatment (2006: 226).

1.5 The protection of the rights of SDEs

Finally, SDE participation in the WTO is important because, by establishing clear disciplines applicable to all WTO Member States, multilateral trade rules prevent, or at least limit, arbitrary behaviour by large governments and ensure greater predictability in trade relations. Multilateral negotiations curtail the abuse of power that can occur between countries that are vastly different in size, level of development and power. Through participation in multilateral institutions such as the WTO, small States are more likely to be insulated, at least partially, from the hegemony and pressure that larger and more powerful countries can exert.

Attaining rights in a multilateral trade system is one thing, but ensuring that these rights are respected, or at least not disregarded, is another hurdle altogether. The most propitious circumstances for small States to protect their rights is when there is a rules-based system with a built-in enforcement mechanism. Small States can have recourse to the WTO dispute settlement mechanism to vindicate their rights free of the disparity of power that would likely exist in a bilateral situation. For example, tiny Antigua and Barbuda, with a population of only 90,000 and an economy dependent on services (tourism and financial services) for approximately 90 per cent of its GDP and exports, took on the mighty United States in a WTO dispute over internet gaming, and won.[4] This ruling demonstrated not only that

[4] *United States – Measures Affecting the Cross-Border Supply of Gambling and Betting Services*, DS285. Antigua and Barbuda requested consultations on 13 March 2003. The Panel Report was circulated on 10 November 2004 and the Appellate Body Report on 7 April 2005.

the smallest of trading partners can have their grievances adjudicated in the WTO, but also that they can have their rights enforced and that larger countries can be compelled to adhere to multilateral rules.[5]

Given the importance of trade to SDEs, their acute vulnerability and the ever-expanding coverage of trade agreements, SDEs need to participate actively in trade negotiations in order to shape the rules, the pace of implementation and the extent of adjustment. The already high exposure of SDEs to external economic events will only increase as trade liberalization proceeds and globalization intensifies the interconnectedness of the world's economies. For SDEs, a core challenge is to mobilize sufficient human and financial resources to cover adequately the plethora of trade negotiations that are conducted bilaterally, regionally and multilaterally.

Despite such instances of success, however, small countries generally have insufficient administrative capacity and resources to use the provisions of the WTO's Dispute Settlement Understanding as often as they would like. The cost of participating in such proceedings is high, and SDEs have limited capacity either to initiate cases or to defend themselves when challenged. Current negotiations in the Doha Round seek to address some of the challenges that have emerged in the operation of the DSU (WTO 2001: para 30).[6] While little of this discussion has directly addressed issues related to the capacity of small and developing countries to use the DSU, it remains important for small States to participate actively in these discussions to ensure that their interests are reflected and advanced in any changes to the current dispute resolution regime

[5] However, the story continued after adoption of the Appellate Body Report. Arbitration under Article 21.3(b) of the WTO Dispute Settlement Understanding (DSU) determined that the USA had to implement the Dispute Settlement Body's (DSB's) recommendations by 3 April 2006. As there was disagreement as to the existence or consistency of measures taken by the United States to implement these recommendations, in May 2006, consultations were started and a Panel was established under Article 21.5 of the DSU. The Panel Report circulated on 30 March 2007 concluded that the United States had failed to comply with the recommendations and rulings of the DSB. Consequently, Antigua and Barbuda requested authorization for suspension of concessions and related obligations under the General Agreement on Trade in Services (GATS) and Trade-Related Aspects of Intellectual Property Rights (TRIPS) Agreement, for which arbitration procedures had to be started under Article 22.6. The Arbitration Report that was circulated in December 2007 determined that Antigua and Barbuda may request authorization from the DSB to suspend obligations under the TRIPS Agreement at a level not exceeding US$21 million annually.

[6] With respect to the progress of the Doha negotiations on the DSU, the Chairman reports '[o]verall, we have achieved only limited concrete progress over the past year in reaching further convergence on the various issues under discussion' (WTO 2010: para. 3.).

and to set the foundations for more direct future discussions on capacity challenges.[7]

2 The importance of SDE participation to the multilateral trading system

While the volume and value of SDEs' trade constitute a very small share of total world trade, there are some important reasons why their participation is important to the multilateral trading system.

One reason is the sheer number of SDEs. Although there is no single definition of an SDE, population size is often suggested as a criterion. If the figure of ten million people is employed, there would be 134 SDEs, meaning that the majority of states in the world are categorized as small. If a population of five million is used as the upper limit, there would be eighty-nine small countries. According to the criterion of one and a half million used by the Commonwealth Secretariat and the World Bank, then there are forty-nine small States.[8] Another definition that has emerged in WTO discussions is that of a small, vulnerable economy (SVE), that is, an economy whose share of world trade is less than 0.05 per cent. This threshold would encompass eighty-six WTO Members (Grynberg and Remy 2003: 275). Whatever definition is chosen, however, most WTO Members are small, and of those, most are SDEs.

Another reason SDE participation at the WTO is important is that the creation and operation of a seamless global economy are not possible unless all States, regardless of size and level of development, are full participants in regimes of multilateral rules. An SDE that allows activities not permitted under a rules-based multilateral trading system or whose national regime diverges significantly from those of most States, even under the threat of retaliation, could disrupt the functioning of global markets. For example, a deficient anti-money-laundering regime could undermine the efforts of other countries to prevent this illegal activity. Similarly, the absence of a comprehensive intellectual property rights

[7] The WTO's decision-making process, while far from perfect, is in stark contrast to other, less representative and transparent bodies. This is graphically illustrated by the establishment by the Organisation for Economic Co-Operation and Development (OECD) of the Financial Action Task Force, which formulated multilateral standards and regulations without inputs from many SDEs that could be affected by their application.

[8] For discussions of various population sizes as definitions of SDEs, see Kuznets (1960: 5); Demas (1965: 2); Chenery and Syrquin (1975); Streeten (1993: 197); Commonwealth Secretariat (1999: 8–10); and Commonwealth Secretariat/World Bank (2000).

regime would deprive creative industries of earnings to which they are entitled. The most dramatic illustration is the existence of offshore financial centres. The Cayman Islands is the best known of these, but several other SDEs are of growing importance in the rapidly expanding area of international financial transactions.

3 How to make SDE participation at the WTO more effective

The participation of SDEs in WTO decision-making has not been as effective as it could be. This is indicated by the failure of WTO Members to make adequate progress on the work programme on small economies mandated by the 2001 Doha WTO Ministerial Declaration and the failure of SDEs to organize a cohesive caucus. Indeed, on the latter point, one could make a similar diagnosis about the performance of most developing countries, which grapple with many of the same problems and constraints (Page 2003). There have been some areas of progress. For instance, in September 2006 the Committee on Trade and Development in Dedicated Session adopted a report to the General Council on Measures to Assist Small Economies in Meeting their Obligations under the Agreements on SPS Measures, TBT and TRIPS (WTO 2006). In October that year, the General Council took note of the report and agreed to the recommendations made therein.[9]

SDEs often find the cost of participating in the negotiation and adjudication of rules in the multilateral trading system to be onerous, even prohibitive. The involvement of ministries of trade is hampered both by fiscal constraints and the failure of cabinet colleagues – in particular, finance ministers – to appreciate fully the immediate and long-term repercussions of changes in WTO rules and provisions. Unfortunately, in many cases, small countries must limit their participation to a few ministerial-level meetings, and even then, their participation is heavily dependent on funding from multilateral financial institutions and bilateral donor agencies in developed countries, whose interests, ironically, may be diametrically opposed.

Three areas in which there is an urgent need for improvement in order for SDEs to participate more effectively are representation in Geneva;

[9] See www.wto.org/english/tratop_e/devel_e/dev_wkprog_smalleco_e.htm [accessed in November 2010].

institutional capacity; and cooperation with each other to improve their ability to advocate collectively.

3.1 Representation

An important limitation on the effective participation of developing countries is their lack of representation in the WTO. At present seventeen WTO Members[10] do not have representation based in Geneva, and attend meetings only periodically by way of their diplomatic missions in such cities as Brussels, Paris and London. This problem is illustrated by the fourteen countries of CARICOM, only three of which – Barbados, Jamaica and Trinidad and Tobago – have WTO representation at the ambassadorial level; the others have accredited their ambassadors in London and Brussels, and in the case of Antigua and Barbuda, its ambassador to the United Nations in New York. The smallest CARICOM countries, which form the Organisation of Eastern Caribbean States (OECS), are jointly represented by a technical mission funded by international donors.[11]

Even when an SDE has representation in Geneva, it typically consists of just one or two people, far too few to cover adequately the myriad issues that constitute the subject matter of the WTO – let alone to attend the 1,200 or so meetings of WTO bodies that take place every year (Michalopoulos 1998; Hoekman and Kostecki 2001). In some weeks, as many as fifty meetings are scheduled, not including numerous informal consultations. Clearly, one- or two-person missions make it impractical for representatives of most SDEs to serve as chairs of bodies and committees of the WTO, which further diminishes their influence.

The remedy would be to mobilize and deploy more financial resources to allow SDEs greater scope to attend relevant meetings; to improve the understanding of the importance of trade negotiations beyond the ministries responsible for trade; and to insert trade policy in the mainstream

[10] These are Antigua and Barbuda, Belize, Dominica, Fiji, Gambia, Grenada, Guinea-Bissau, Guyana, Solomon Islands, Malawi, Papua New Guinea, Saint Lucia, Saint Kitts and Nevis, Saint Vincent and the Grenadines, Sierra Leone, Suriname and Tonga. This list includes those countries that are represented in Geneva only by regional organizations such as the Pacific Islands Forum and the Organization of Eastern Caribbean States.

[11] Similarly, the establishment in March 2004 of the WTO mission of the Pacific Island Forum – consisting of Papua New Guinea, the Solomon Islands, Samoa, Vanuatu and Tonga – with five years of funding from the European Union has enabled these countries to participate more effectively in WTO negotiations through shared representation (Bowman 2005).

of public policy in SDEs. Additional funding for such purposes might be difficult to obtain, however, given competing claims on scarce resources for more palpable, immediate and politically sensitive demands such as schools, roads and hospitals. Local resources could be supplemented by development assistance from bilateral donor agencies, international organizations and multilateral financial institutions. However, such potential sources of assistance often have a strong aversion to funding travel, preferring to finance training, external consultants to provide technical expertise, and capacity-building.

3.2 Institutional capacity

The limited institutional capacity of SDEs severely constrains their ability to conduct technical work, to formulate negotiating positions that reflect their interests and to increase and maintain the capacity for trade policy formulation and negotiating strategies. In some small States, the ministry responsible for trade, or the department for international trade in a ministry responsible for several subjects, has a staff as small as three officials. Apart from inadequately staffed trade ministries, SDEs also may lack computer and communications equipment, as well as the resources required to conduct systematic outreach to stakeholders. In addition, they may suffer limited capabilities for information-gathering and dissemination, and insufficient access to training and research (Jones *et al.* 2010).

The solution to limited institutional capacity is more collaboration, sharing and rationalization of resource use among SDEs. This cooperation could take a variety of forms, including setting up common entities to undertake technical work, formulating shared positions, coordinating negotiating strategies and pursuing joint representation in negotiations.

Collaborative institutions and joint representation are easier for countries that are in close physical proximity, as in the case of the CARICOM countries. For example, faced with the unprecedented task of simultaneous negotiations in the WTO and with the EU, as well as several bilateral initiatives, the CARICOM countries decided to establish a single regional organization, the Caribbean Regional Negotiating Machinery (CRNM). The purpose of the CRNM is to 'assist member states in maximizing the benefits of participation in global trade negotiations by providing sound, high-quality advice, facilitating the generation of national positions, coordinating the formulation of a unified negotiating strategy for the region and undertaking/leading negotiations where appropriate' (CRNM n.d.: 5).

The CRNM fulfils the functions of giving technical advice, monitoring, analysing, reporting, coordinating common positions and negotiating (where appropriate) on behalf of Member States. It has offices in Jamaica and Barbados, deploys representatives in Brussels and Geneva, and provides technical support staff to some Member States and subregional organizations. The CRNM office in Brussels has given CARICOM countries a base for their interaction with EU officials and negotiators, and has also helped complement the diplomatic efforts of CARICOM ambassadors with those of trade negotiators, resulting in the successful completion of an Economic Partnership Agreement (EPA) between the EU and CARIFORUM (that is, CARICOM and the Dominican Republic).

The CRNM's Geneva-based team of two technicians provides day-to-day support to CARIFORUM missions, including attending meetings with the Permanent Representatives from the region, and preparing reports for staff in the CRNM offices in Jamaica and Barbados. These form valuable inputs into the papers and reports that guide the formulation of negotiating positions in the WTO. The work of the technicians in Geneva is supplemented by technical experts based in CRNM offices in the Caribbean specializing in specific subject areas such as services, agriculture and intellectual property rights. The CRNM also provides an officer to accompany ministers who attend meetings in such widely dispersed locations as Seattle, Doha, Cancún, Hong Kong, New Delhi, Cairo, Paris and Geneva.

Since the costs of the CRNM's activities are beyond the scarce financial resources of its small Member States, slightly more than half its budget comes from grants from bilateral donor development assistance agencies and multilateral financial institutions. Additional funding is provided by the Commonwealth Secretariat and the Caribbean Development Bank. These funds help to defray expenses such as salaries, travel, accommodation, studies and call-down expertise. During the negotiations with the European Union, resources from various European development agencies and institutions were indispensable to meeting the expense of conducting more than thirty technical working groups over a three-year period.

The advantages to CARICOM of the operation of the CRNM include pooling limited human resources to allow each country to undertake the necessary technical work; reducing the cost of undertaking external trade negotiations by permitting Member States to share the cost of the technical preparations of negotiating positions; reducing the cost of representation at meetings; and strengthening the negotiating positions of Member States by helping them to agree on common negotiating positions and the articulation of joint statements. A further advantage is that the CRNM can provide technical assistance to Member States through technical studies, consultations, briefings and training on matters ranging from how to fashion national trade policy, use dispute settlement mechanisms, access donor resources and improve institutional capacity.

3.3 Cooperation for collective advocacy

There is an urgent need to create a more cohesive and effective strategic alliance among SDEs in the WTO. Indeed, such a caucus could operate in all the international fora and institutions in which these states have vital interests. In some international fora where SDEs have established formal associations to advocate their cause, they have been successful. For example, an Alliance of Small Developing States (AOSIS) was formed in November 1990 as a negotiating body for the first meeting of the Intergovernmental Negotiating Committee for a Framework Convention on Climate Change in February 1991. As a direct result, language on Small Island Developing States was included in the final text of the United Nations Framework Convention on Climate Change (Ashe *et al.* 1999; von Tigerstrom 2005). AOSIS now has forty-three Members and observers, thirty-seven of which are Members of the United Nations, accounting for twenty per cent of the UN's total Membership.

Until relatively recently, cooperation among SDEs in the WTO was limited to the margins of Ministerial meetings. At the 2003 WTO Ministerial Conference in Cancún, for instance, the CARICOM countries drafted and, after consultation with other interested parties, amended and then presented a statement on issues relevant to small economies (WTO 2003). This limited approach stood in contrast to the now moribund FTAA negotiations, where a consultative Group on Smaller Economies was an integral component of the structure of negotiations (Bernal 1998).

While SDEs are attempting to enhance their role and influence in WTO governance, this has proven difficult. Progress at forming and operating as a concrete group has been inhibited by their nascent awareness of themselves as a distinct interest group and complicated by cultural, linguistic and economic differences, which are characteristic of any group of disparate countries. The coalescing of solidarity has also been seriously hampered by the lack of formal recognition at the WTO of small economies. Indeed, there is no single agreed definition of small, vulnerable economies.

Post-Cancún, a group of WTO Members who self-define themselves as small vulnerable developing countries began to meet in Geneva. Their work culminated in the inclusion of paragraph 35 in the Doha WTO Ministerial Declaration which states:

> We agree to a work programme, under the auspices of the General council, to examine issues relating to the trade of small economies. The objective of this work is to frame responses to the trade-related issues identified for the fuller integration of small, vulnerable economies into the multilateral trading system, and not to create a sub-category of WTO Members.
>
> (WTO 2001)

Similarly, paragraph 41 of the 2005 WTO Hong Kong Ministerial Declaration states:

> We reaffirm our commitment to the Work Programme on Small Economies and urge Members to adopt specific measures that would facilitate the fuller integration of small, vulnerable economies into the multilateral trading system, without creating a sub-category of WTO Members.
>
> (WTO 2005)

To date, twenty-two countries have participated regularly in the WTO's Small and Vulnerable Economies Work Programme.[12] Yet their involvement in the work programme is an act of faith given the obvious contradiction of forging measures for a type of economy that the WTO does not formally recognize. Consistent with the mandate of the Doha Ministerial Declaration, the privileges, if any, to be conferred onto SVEs will not lead to the creation of a new category of membership. The WTO will continue to recognize the traditional designations, namely developed, developing, least developed and transitional economies. Moreover, the ability of those countries involved to arrive at specific recommendations is undermined by the fact that participation in the work programme is open to all Member States – both large developing countries and developed countries sometimes attend its meetings, with the result that perspectives aired in the deliberations vary widely.

This issue of the definition of SVEs has been discussed by the WTO membership for several years without any definitive resolution. In

[12] These countries are Antigua and Barbuda, Barbados, Bolivia, Cuba, Dominica, the Dominican Republic, El Salvador, Fiji, Grenada, Guatemala, Honduras, Jamaica, Mauritius, Mongolia, Nicaragua, Papua New Guinea, Paraguay, the Solomon Islands, St Kitts and Nevis, St Lucia, St Vincent and the Grenadines and Trinidad and Tobago.

practice, the definition varies according to the topic of Doha Round negotiations. For example, in agriculture, SVEs are defined in para. 157 of the December 2008 modalities as: 'economies that, in the period 1999 to 2004, had an average share of (a) world merchandise trade of no more than 0.16 per cent or less, and (b) world trade in non-agricultural products of no more than 0.1 per cent and (c) world trade in agricultural products of no more than 0.4 per cent'.[13] In negotiations on non-agricultural market access (NAMA), SVEs are defined in para. 13 of the December 2009 modalities as: 'With the exception of developed Members, those Members having a share of less than 0.1 per cent of world NAMA trade for the reference period of 1999 to 2001.'

At the same time, a group of SVEs have organized themselves as a negotiating coalition within Doha Development Agenda (DDA) negotiations, alongside other coalitions ranging from the G20, G33, Recently Acceding Members and least developed countries (LDCs) to regional blocs that sometimes present collective positions, such as ASEAN, the African Group, the Arab Group and CARICOM. There is some confusion about the participants in the SVEs group. For example, there is a difference between members of the group and those that are eligible under the different WTO criteria. For example, in Agriculture, Sri Lanka is deemed an SVE member but does not participate in the deliberations of the group. Similarly, Paraguay rarely participates in SVE consultations, although it is eligible for benefits conferred to members of that group. Some countries in the SVE group may or may not choose to support any particular position of the SVEs group. This occurred in the cases of Jamaica and Mauritius – two countries that have consistently advocated special treatment for small economies. No joint statement was made by the SVEs group at the 2009 WTO Ministerial Conference in Geneva. Instead, individual SVE members made statements on their own behalf. That said, the Caribbean Group made a statement in support of SVEs.

4 Adapting the WTO and its governance to SDEs

Reforming the governance process of the WTO to make it more responsive to SDEs must be pragmatic if it is to have any chance of success. Therefore, proposals to effect change cannot be part of a grand design, say, to bring all the principal economic multilateral institutions – the International

[13] The 2008 Draft modalities can be consulted at www.wto.org/english/tratop_e/agric_e/chair_texts08_e.htm [accessed in November 2010].

Monetary Fund (IMF), the World Bank and the WTO – under the umbrella supervision of the Economic and Social Council of the UN General Assembly, as advocated, for example, by Cavanagh and Mander (2004: 314–15). The prospects of this happening are remote, as are even more far-reaching schemes of an entirely new global governance structure such as a global parliament (Archibugi and Held 1995; Monbiot 2003). While it may be true that many attempts to improve the WTO process have been 'palliatives and do not come close to addressing the core problem of how to resource sufficiently the smaller, weaker, poorer countries so that they too can work the WTO's relatively representative procedures to their advantage' (Payne 2005: 119), it is still worth calling for further improvements. The changes proposed in this paper are, at most, reformist, based on the recognition that countries that exercise a dominant influence in the WTO are unlikely to yield willingly to ideas and actions designed to diminish their position. In that sense, the proposals here have a more realistic chance of success than those advocating a more radical overhaul.

SDEs need to redouble their efforts to participate more effectively in the WTO by improving their representation, enhancing their institutional capacity and creating a cohesive SDE caucus. However, at the same time, the WTO itself should complement the efforts of SDEs by becoming more inclusive and supportive, democratizing decision-making, adjusting the procedures and schedules of meetings, and expanding the provision of technical assistance. Such an adaptation of the WTO to SDEs would help make the institution more user-friendly for these Member States by reducing the costs and difficulties of their involvement, and thus strengthening their participation.

4.1 Democratizing decision-making in the WTO

The WTO's decision-making process, while formally based on consensus, is in reality dominated by a small number of developed countries and some of the larger emerging economies (Jawara and Kwa 2003; Wallach and Woodall 2004). 'Consensus' does not mean unanimity; rather, it means that no country present in a meeting strongly objects to the proposed decision and that one or a few Member States cannot block decisions 'unless it happened to one of the major trading nations' (Hoekman and Kostecki 1995: 40). In other words, the power exerted by the developed countries overwhelms the formal decision-making rules. In addition, informal consultations characterized by lack of transparency and by restrictive participation have always and will likely always be part of

WTO negotiations – indeed more powerful countries use informality precisely to facilitate the deal-making process. Developing countries that do not acquiesce to the position of the most powerful countries are 'subjected to special persuasion or are marginalized or isolated' (Khor 2003: 533). The operation of this power asymmetry among Member States is an important contributor to what has been described as the 'deficit of democracy' and, therefore, a cause of the WTO's so-called legitimacy crisis (see Esty 2002).

Criticism of the current decision-making process is widespread and especially strident among developing countries and non-governmental organizations.[14] The growing importance of countries such as China, India, and, to a lesser extent, Brazil and South Africa, is also prompting them to demand a greater voice in WTO decision-making. Little attempt has been made, however, to reform the formal WTO decision-making processes. Symptomatic of the inertia is the failure of a report to the Director-General, *The Future of the WTO*, to forcefully make any specific significant proposals for formal reform of the decision-making process, although it does concede that 'consensus favours Members that can afford to be present at all meetings, since absence – or abstention – does not itself defeat a consensus' (Consultative Board 2004: 63).

From the perspective of SDEs, reform of the WTO decision-making system must ensure greater transparency and break the hegemony of developed countries, notably the United States, the European Union and Japan. Obviously, their traditional dominance reflects the reality of their political and economic power, and their commanding shares of world trade. Their pre-eminence has been institutionalized, however, in what is known as the 'Green Room' process. It is true that what was exclusively a 'club' of rich and powerful countries has been broadened in recent years to include some key developing countries and others representing various groups of countries such as the least developed ones (Patel 2008). Nonetheless, the Green Room process is still a point of contention for many Members, as it deprives the WTO of the transparency and, ultimately, legitimacy that can be established only by an inclusive, transparent democratic system.

If the voice of the SDEs is to be heard and their issues made 'visible', decision-making in the WTO must become meaningfully transparent, open, participatory and democratic. One way to correct deficiencies in the formal decision-making process and to avert at least some of the tendency

[14] See, for example, Third World Network (1999).

towards informality in negotiations would be to establish some kind of executive committee. Notably, the idea of an executive committee was contemplated as early as the Havana Charter of the International Trade Organization. It later resurfaced in the form of a proposal for a management board during the Uruguay Round and has subsequently been proposed by several scholars (see, for example, Steger and Shpilkovskaya 2010: 138–44). Among these, a compelling proposal is for an executive committee proposed of, say, twenty-five countries, consisting of the ten countries with the largest share of global trade and fifteen other countries elected by a democratic process to represent the rest of the Membership (Sutherland *et al.* 2001: 99–100), with candidates selected to ensure representation of all regions or categories of economies (Bernal 1999; Schott and Watal 2000). The creation of such a committee would help the WTO's Membership avoid the difficulties of trying to make decisions with all Members in attendance. The function of the committee would be to consult the Membership, advise the Director-General and negotiate.

Decisions made would have to be ratified by the full Membership. While the committee would not be directly representative of all Members, the alternative, we must recall, is the far less transparent Green Room process.

A similar proposal calls for a twenty-four Member Advisory Council with permanent seats for major trading countries and the remaining seats shared among the rest of the Membership by rotation (Blackhurst 2001). Others have emphasized flexibility, arguing, for example, that 'the variable geometry of trade issues suggests that the composition of the board for any given topic should be issue driven, with grouped seats determined by agreed-upon proxies of the various interests involved and assigned to a representative country' (Jones 2004: 163–4).

SDEs are also concerned about the conduct of Ministerial Conferences, which, in recent times, have witnessed the non-application of Rules of Procedure of the Ministerial Conference (WTO 1995), the expanded role of chairs of the Ministerial meetings and the proliferation of covert, informal meetings. Chairs of Ministerial Conferences are supported by other chairs who oversee important negotiating committees at Ministerials. The method of their selection is a mystery, suggesting there are no objective criteria for the decision. From personal observation, however, it is likely that the selection emerges from discussions between the chairing minister and the WTO Director-General, with the tacit approval of the United States and the European Union. Generally, ministers of the major countries opt not to chair, leaving themselves free of long, tedious and often meaningless meetings to engage where the real action is, which takes place among themselves and in the Green Room process.

4.2 Increasing technical work on SDE issues

WTO staff, particularly senior officials, are custodians of the principles and rules of the WTO. They influence the technical work that informs options discussed by Member States and, when the Membership is divided over an issue, they are called upon to devise solutions and proposals for compromise. Technical staff also draft the position papers underpinning reports by committee chairs, which are circulated as the basis of negotiation. They are particularly influential because they are specialists, often with many years of experience in advising ambassadors and officials who serve only temporarily at WTO Missions and who lack comparable technical knowledge and experience.

Despite the WTO's large number of SDE Members, they are under-represented in the WTO Secretariat, especially at the senior technical and managerial levels. The consequence of this lack of presence is the relative neglect of issues of importance to them and of the perspective they can bring to bear for the resolution of such issues. Accordingly, the establishment of a WTO unit dedicated to SDEs is warranted, even if it requires additional staff and financial resources. In this regard, George Soros is correct when he points out that 'under-resourcing' of the WTO prevents it from protecting the least developed countries (Soros 2002: 53–4).

4.3 Financial support for SDE representation

Another way in which the WTO could help SDEs participate more effectively is to provide financial and other forms of assistance to offset or substantially reduce the cost of maintaining adequate staff missions in Geneva. Financial assistance could be drawn from the WTO regular budget or from a specially arranged fund contributed to by the Organisation for Economic Co-operation and Development (OECD) countries and multilateral financial institutions such as the World Bank.[15] In-kind support could also be provided in the form of rent-free office space[16] and covering the costs for senior officials to travel to key meetings.

15 Blackhurst (1997) makes a similar proposal, but does not confine it to SDEs.

16 Condor (1999: 3) suggests the establishment of an international house in Geneva for countries with fragile economies and financial constraints.

An example of such support is the establishment and operation of a joint technical support mission in Geneva for six SDEs from the English-speaking Caribbean that comprise the OECS.[17] These countries currently have non-resident ambassadors responsible for WTO matters based in Brussels, London and New York, and in St George's, Grenada. Given that these countries are in the process of integrating their economies, it would be prudent for them to have a single ambassador resident in Geneva on behalf of all six countries. The European Union also provides funding to support the operations of the Geneva offices of the OECS (along with other donors such as the Commonwealth Secretariat) as well as the Pacific Islands Forum (PIF); it also provides expert technical advice to these missions. The physical presence of officials in Geneva allows these countries to participate in more WTO meetings, enabling them to improve the extent and quality of their reporting to officials back home. Their more active involvement has also strengthened their influence and bolstered support among WTO Members for work on issues of concern to them.

The participation of these small States in WTO processes has other beneficial spillover effects. It has raised the awareness of the importance of the WTO both in these countries and among countries that have not previously been able to contemplate the benefits of WTO Membership. The experience of working in the WTO milieu has also been superb training for technicians and negotiators, thereby directly improving their national capacity on international trade issues and the formulation of trade policy. As their technical capability has improved, these countries are in a better position to identify and articulate issues peculiar to their circumstances. It has also allowed SDEs to allocate scarce resources more effectively in various WTO fora and to gain access to technical assistance from Geneva-based institutions including non-governamental organizations (NGOs), think tanks and intergovernmental organizations (IGOs) such as UNCTAD and the International Trade Centre (ITC) to help them implement their WTO commitments.

[17] The Mission is for these countries from the OECS: Antigua and Barbuda, Dominica, Grenada, Saint Kitts and Nevis, Saint Lucia, and Saint Vincent and the Grenadines. For more information, see www.stlucia.gov.lc/pr2005/july/oecs_geneva_technical_mission_getting_down_to_business.html [accessed in November 2010].

4.4 *Expanding technical assistance*

Among SDEs, the continuing need for technical assistance – to improve their institutional capacity for trade policy analysis and to participate in negotiations – is acute (Salicrup and Vergara 2000). Yet the WTO allocates less than one per cent of its budget to technical cooperation, relying on trust funds provided by a handful of bilateral donors (Stiglitz and Charlton 2005: 170). The WTO's dispute settlement mechanism, for example, is so costly in terms of time, money and technical expertise that most SDEs are unable to make efficient and continuous use of it or to pursue cases effectively. Sometimes, SDEs have been able to participate in the process only if private-sector interests, including foreign firms, have provided financial resources for legal services, travel, accommodation and public relations. Such support, however, is not necessarily desirable if there is pressure to advance positions that reflect the interests of a particular firm or industry rather than those of the SDE.

To address these challenges, some WTO Members established an Advisory Centre on WTO Law[18] to provide legal advice to developing countries in dispute settlement proceedings, but this support is not enough. What is needed is a consortium of international development institutions and bilateral development agencies to provide technical assistance specifically to SDEs, whether or not they are currently Members of the WTO, and that would also provide strategic input for negotiations. There is also some movement towards greater cooperation among donors to support trade-related technical assistance, but much more needs to be done. The Integrated Framework for Trade-Related Technical Assistance, a cooperative venture of the WTO, IMF, World Bank, UNCTAD, the United Nations Development Programme and the ITC, was slow to become operational and had a limited mandate. While the Integrated Framework (IF) has been reformed to address the many criticisms it faced (in the process becoming the 'Enhanced' Integrated Framework[19]), long-standing criticisms of the failure to adequately

[18] The Advisory Centre on WTO Law (ACWL) provides free legal advice and training on WTO law, and support in WTO dispute settlement proceedings at discounted rates. These services are available to the developing country Members of the ACWL (thirty at present) and to LDCs that are Members of the WTO or are in the process of acceding to the WTO (forty-four at present). For more information, see www.acwl.ch/e/index.html [accessed in November 2010].

[19] For more information, see www.integratedframework.org/enhanced_if.htm [accessed in November 2010].

insert trade policy into national development strategies and linking trade policy to poverty-reduction strategies remain relevant (see UNDP 2003: 338–9).

4.5 *Countervailing measures*

The WTO could become far more amenable to the interests and capacities of SDEs if measures were introduced to countervail the effects of disparities in size and development among WTO Members. For example, the operations of the dispute settlement mechanism should ensure that special and differential treatment is applied in disputes between developed countries and SDEs (see Ewart 2007). Also, in many instances, it is not feasible for an SDE to apply effective sanctions on larger, more developed countries to force their compliance with dispute settlement rulings. In such cases, the injured party should be able to apply for the imposition of a countervailing measure. In the case of Antigua's WTO dispute with the United States over internet gambling, the WTO Panel granted Antigua the right to suspend obligations under the WTO's TRIPS Agreement up to the level of the damages awarded. The panel justified this dispensation on the basis that the 'extremely unbalanced nature of the trading relations between the parties makes it … difficult for Antigua to find a way of ensuring the effectiveness or other obligations against the United States' under the GATS (ICTSD 2008). Finally, in order to encourage compliance with a ruling in their favour, SDEs should be authorized to suspend concessions and obligations to the non-compliant Member (see Sarooshi 2003).

5 Conclusion

To break or dilute the stranglehold of the developed countries and large emerging economies on WTO governance, the various streams of disenchantment will have to coalesce into a sufficient critical political mass to press for change. Such a coalition would consist predominantly of developing countries that share many of the disabilities of SDEs. The cohesiveness of such an alliance would be difficult to maintain, however, especially if a few large developing countries are admitted to the 'club'. Already, the protracted negotiations of the Doha Development Agenda and the increasing assertiveness of developing countries in WTO Ministerial Conferences have led to a new power configuration, with Brazil and India now constituting a power quartet with the United States and the European Union. The new prominence of such countries is indicative of their weight in world trade, the centrality of agricultural issues in trade negotiations, and the assumption that they are the logical and accepted spokespersons of developing countries. But reform of the governance system of the WTO has not been a priority for these newly arrived club Members, and it would be unfortunate if their recently achieved status at the WTO's 'High Table' has made governance reform less urgent and relevant to the attainment of their interests. The elevation of such developing countries to leadership positions should not be mistaken for change in the governance process, and is no substitute for a concerted and persistently prosecuted campaign by SDEs to reform governance in a way that allows for their adequate participation. In their quest for changes aimed specifically at their particular needs, the SDEs cannot take for granted the support of other developing countries (Grynberg and Remy 2003).

Given the importance of international trade to SDEs, it is imperative for their future growth and development that they have more influence in the formation, application and enforcement of the rules of the WTO. For SDEs, a rules-based multilateral trading system offers the best possibility for protecting and advancing their interests and rights. More influence, however, will require more effective participation, starting with consistent attendance at WTO meetings, and a strengthened institutional capacity to participate (Jones *et al.* 2010). Since such improvements demand resources beyond those available to individual SDEs, political cooperation and technical collaboration among them will be necessary for efficacious collective advocacy. The efforts of SDEs to participate effectively in the WTO must be complemented by democratization of the process of WTO decision-making and greater support to assist SDEs to boost their representation and participation.

References

Archibugi, D. and Held, D. (eds.) 1995. *Cosmopolitan Democracy: Agenda for a New World Order*. Cambridge: Polity.

Ashe, J., Van Lierop, R. and Cherian, A. 1999. 'The Role of the Alliance of Small Island Developing States in the Negotiation of the United Nations Framework on Climate Change', *Natural Resources Forum* 23(3): 209–20.

Atkins, J., Mazzi, S. and Easter, C. 2001. 'Small States: A Composite Vulnerability Index', in Peretz, R. and Kisaga, E. (eds.), *Small States in the Global Economy*. London: Commonwealth Secretariat, pp. 53–92.

Bernal, R. 1996. 'Strategic Global Repositioning and the Future Economic Development of Jamaica', *North–South Agenda Paper 18*. Miami: University of Miami, North–South Center.

1998. 'The Integration of Small Developing Economies in the Free Trade Area of the Americas', *CSIS Policy Paper on the Americas* 9(1). Washington, DC: Center for Strategic and International Studies.

1999. 'Sleepless in Seattle: The WTO Ministerial of 1999', *Social and Economic Studies* 48(3): 61–84.

2000. 'Globalization and Small Developing Countries: The Imperative for Repositioning', in Benn, D. and Hall, K. (eds.), *Globalization: A Calculus of Inequality*. Kingston, Jamaica: Ian Randle.

2003. 'Small Developing Economies in the World Trade Organization', in Ingco, M. (ed.), *Agriculture, Trade and the WTO*. Washington, DC: World Bank.

2004. 'Small Developing Countries and the Multilateral Trading System: A Caribbean Perspective', Christchurch, Barbados: Commonwealth Regional Negotiating Machinery.

2006. 'Special and Differential Treatment for Small Developing Economies', in Grynberg, R. (ed.), *WTO at the Margins: Small States and the Multilateral Trading System*. Cambridge University Press.

Blackhurst, R. 1997. 'The Capacity of the WTO to Fulfil its Mandate', in Krueger, A. (ed.), *The WTO As An International Organization*, Chicago: University of Chicago Press.

2001. 'Reforming WTO Decision-Making: Lessons from Singapore and Seattle', in Deutsch, K. and Speyer, B. (eds.), *The World Trade Organization Millennium Round: Freer Trade in the Twenty-First Century*, London: Routledge, pp. 295–311.

Bowman, C. 2005. 'The Pacific Island Nations: Towards Shared Representation', in Gallagher, P., Low, P. and Stoler, A. (eds.), *Managing the Challenges of WTO Participation: 45 Case Studies*. Washington, DC: World Trade Organization.

Briguglio, L. 1999. 'Small Island Developing States and Their Vulnerabilities', *World Development* 23(9): 1615–32.

Buria, A. 2003. 'The Governance of the International Monetary Fund', in Kaul, I., Conceicao, P., Le Goulven, K. and Mendoza, R. (eds.), *Providing Global Public Goods: Managing Globalization*. Oxford University Press.

Cavanagh, J. and Mander, J. (eds.) 2004. *Alternatives to Economic Globalization: A Better World Is Possible*. San Francisco: Berrett-Koehler.

Chenery, H. B. and Syrquin, M. 1975. *Patterns of Development, 1950–1970*. London: Oxford University Press.

Commonwealth Secretariat. 1999. *A Future for Small States: Overcoming Vulnerability*. London: Commonwealth Secretariat.

Commonwealth Secretariat/World Bank. 2000. 'Joint Task Force on Small States', *Small States: Meeting Challenges in the Global Economy*. London: Commonwealth Secretariat/Washington, DC: Commonwealth Secretariat and World Bank.

Condor, T. 1999. Statement by the Deputy Prime Minister and Minister of Trade and Industry, St Kitts and Nevis to the WTO Ministerial Conference, Seattle, 30 November–3 December. WT/Min(99)/ST/123. Geneva: World Trade Organization.

Consultative Board 2004. *The Future of the WTO – Addressing Institutional Changes in the New Millennium*. Geneva: WTO.

Cotonou Agreement. 2006. Partnership Agreement ACP-EC, Signed in Cotonou on 23 June 2000. Brussels: European Commission, Directorate-General for Development and Relations with African, Caribbean and Pacific States.

CRNM (Caribbean Regional Negotiating Machinery) n.d. *Caribbean Regional Negotiating Machinery: Phase II. Five Year Strategic Plan 2003/04–2007/08*. Washington, DC: Organization of American States, Caribbean Trade Reference Centre.

Demas, W. G. 1965. *The Economics of Development in Small Countries with Special Reference to the Caribbean*. Montreal: McGill University Press.

Esty, D. 2002. 'The World Trade Organization's Legitimacy Crisis', *World Trade Review* 1(1): 7–22.

Ewart, A. M. 2007. 'Small Developing States in the WTO: A Procedural Approach to Special and Differential Treatment Through Reforms to Dispute Settlement', *Syracuse Journal of International Law and Commerce* 35(1): 27–76.

Gonzales, A. 2000. *Policy Implications of Smallness As a Factor in the Lomé, FTAA and WTO Negotiations*. Christ Church, Barbados: Caribbean Regional Negotiating Machinery.

Grynberg, R. and Remy, J. 2003. 'Small Vulnerable Economy Issues and the WTO', in Mbirimi, I., Chilala, B. and Grynberg, R. (eds.), *From Doha to Cancún: Delivering a Development Round*. London: Commonwealth Secretariat.

Hoekman, B. and Kostecki, M. 1995. *The Political Economy of the World Trading System: From GATT to WTO*. Oxford University Press.

2001. *The Political Economy of the World Trading System: The WTO and Beyond*. Oxford University Press.

ICTSD (International Centre for Trade and Sustainable Development). 2008. *WTO to Determine Worth of Gambling Concession*, BRIDGES, February, p. 12.

Jawara, F. and Kwa, A. 2003. *Behind the Scenes at the WTO: The Real World of International Trade Negotiations*. London: Zed Books.

Jones, E., Deere Birkbeck, C. and Woods, N. 2010. *Manoeuvring at the Margins: Constraints Faced by Small States in International Trade Negotiations*. London: Commonwealth Secretariat.

Jones, K. 2004. *Who's Afraid of the WTO?* Oxford University Press.

Keohane, R. and Nye, J., Jr. 2001. 'The Club Model of Multilateral Cooperation and Problems of Democratic Legitimacy', in Porter, R., Sauvé, P., Subramanian, A. and Beviglia Zampetti, A. (eds.), *Efficiency, Equity and Legitimacy: The Multilateral Trading System at the Millennium*, Washington, DC: Brookings Institution Press, pp. 264–308.

Khor, M. 2003. 'Globalization, Global Governance and the Dilemmas of Development', in Chang, H. (ed.), *Rethinking Development Economics*. London: Anthem.

Kuznets, S. 1960. 'Economic Growth of Small Nations', in Robinson, E.A.G. (ed.), *Economic Consequences of the Size of Nations*. London: Macmillan.

Messerlin, P. 2006. 'Comment: Reflections on the Trade Reforms and Policy Implications', in Laird, S. and Fernandez de Cordoba, S. (eds.), *Coping with Trade Reforms: A Developing Country Perspective on the WTO Industrial Tariff Negotiations*. London and New York: Palgrave Macmillan.

Michalopoulos, C. 1998. 'Developing Countries' Participation in the World Trade Organization', *Policy Research Working Paper 1906*. Washington, DC: World Bank.

Monbiot, G. 2003. *The Age of Content: A Manifesto for a New World Order*. London: Harper Collins.

Page, S. 2003. *Developing Countries: Victims or Participants? Their Changing Role in International Negotiations*. London: Overseas Development Institute.

Patel, M. 2008. 'New Faces in the Green Room: Developing Country Coalitions and Decision-Making in the WTO', GEG Working Paper 2007/33 (updated), Global Economic Governance Programme, University College.

Payne, A. 2005. *The Global Politics of Unequal Development*. London: Palgrave Macmillan.

Portugal, M. 2005. 'Improving IMF Governance and Increasing the Influence of the Developing Countries in IMF Decision-Making'. Paper presented at the G24 Technical Group Meeting, Manila, Philippines, 17–18 March.

Salicrup, L. and Vergara, G. 2000. *Trade Policy Education Resources in the Western Hemisphere: An Assessment of Demand and Supply*. Washington, DC: USAID and the Organization of American States.

Sarooshi, D. 2003. 'Reform of the WTO Dispute Settlement Understanding', in Mbirimi, I., Chilala, B. and Grynberg, R. (eds.), *From Doha to Cancún: Delivering a Development Round*. London: Commonwealth Secretariat.

Schott, J. and Watal, J. 2000. 'Decision Making in the WTO', in Schott, J. (ed.), *The WTO After Seattle*. Washington, DC: Institute for International Economics.

Soros, G. 2002. *On Globalization*. Cambridge: Public Affairs.

Steger, D. and Shpilkovkaya, N. 2010. 'Internal Management of the WTO: Room for Improvement', in Steger, D. (ed.), *Redesigning the World Trade Organization for the Twenty-first Century*. Waterloo, Ont.: Wilfrid Laurier University Press.

Stiglitz, J. and Charlton, A. 2005. *Fair Trade for All: How Trade Can Promote Development*. Oxford University Press.

Streeten, P. 1993. 'The Special Problems of Small Countries', *World Development* 21(2): 197–202.

Sutherland, P., Sewell, J. and Weiner, D. 2001. 'Challenges Facing the WTO and Policies to Address Global Governance', in Sampson, G. (ed.), *The Role of the World Trade Organization in Global Governance*. New York: United Nations University Press.

Third World Network. 1999. 'Transparency, Participation and Legitimacy of the WTO'. Statement at the WTO Symposia on Trade and Environment and Trade and Development, Geneva, 15–18 March.

Truman, E. 2006. 'Rearranging IMF Chairs and Shares: The Sine Qua Non', in Truman, E. (ed.), *Reforming the IMF for the 21st Century*. Washington, DC: Institute for international Economics.

Tulloch, P. 2001. 'Small Economies in the WTO', in Peretz, D., Faruqi, R. and Kisanga, E. (eds.), *Small States in the World Economy*. London: Commonwealth Secretariat.

UNCTAD (United Nations Conference on Trade and Development). 2004. *Development and Globalization: Facts and Figures*. New York and Geneva: UNCTAD.

UNDP (United Nations Development Programme). 2003. *Making Global Trade Work for People*. London: Earthscan Publications.

von Tigerstrom, B. 2005. 'Small Island Developing States and International Trade: Special Challenges in the Global Partnership for Development', *Melbourne Journal of International Law* 6(2): 402–36.

Wallach, L. and Woodall, P. 2004. *Whose Trade Organization?* New York: The New Press.

Woods, N. and Lombardi, D. 2005. *Effective Representation and the Role of Coalitions Within the IMF*. Working Paper. Oxford: Global Economic Governance.

Woodward, D. 2005. *The IMF and the World Bank in the 21st Century: The Need for Change*. Submission to the European Parliament on 'Strategic Reforms of the IMF', London, 9 May.

World Trade Organization (WTO). 1995. *Rules of Procedure for Sessions of the Ministerial Conference and Meetings of the General Council*. WT/L/28. Adopted by the General Council on 31 January 1995. Geneva: WTO.

2001. *Doha Ministerial Declaration*. WT/Min(01)/Dec/1. 20 November. Geneva: WTO.

2003. *Recommendation for Action by the General Council – Draft Decision on the Small Economies – Communication from Barbados, Belize, Bolivia, Cuba, Dominican Republic, Fiji Islands, Mauritius, Solomon Islands, Sri Lanka, Tonga and Trinidad and Tobago*. WT/COMTD/SE/W/8. 5 March. Geneva: WTO.

2005. *Hong Kong Ministerial Declaration*. WT/Min(05)/Dec. 22 December. Geneva: WTO.

2006. *Committee on Trade and Development. Report to the General Council on Measures to Assist Small Economies in Meeting their Obligations under the Agreements on SPS Measures, TBT and TRIPS*. WT/COMTD/SE/5. Geneva: WTO.

2010. *Special Session of the Dispute Settlement Body – Report by the Chairman, Ambassador Ronald Saborio Soto, to the Trade Negotiations Committee for the purpose of the TNC stocktaking exercise*. TN/DS/24. 22 March 2010.

PART III

Strengthening multilateralism: priorities for improving WTO governance

10

The WTO, democracy and development: a view from the South

BHUPINDER CHIMNI

The World Trade Organization (WTO) as an institution is the subject of critique from diverse perspectives. Thus, on the issue of democracy, mainstream international relations thinkers such as Joseph Nye are concerned with the democracy deficit that characterizes the WTO as an advocate of cosmopolitan democracy (Esty 2002: 7–22; Nye *et al.* 2003: 437–73). States are as unhappy with the WTO as non-governmental organizations are in terms of both process and outcome. Even the corporate actor, often seen as the driving force behind WTO agreements, is not fully satisfied with the architecture of the WTO for, inter alia, it is denied direct access to WTO fora, in particular its dispute settlement system. A principal reason why nearly every actor is unhappy with the WTO is that it covers so much ground, and has put in place such a complex and legalized institutional structure, that it cannot but leave all actors dissatisfied in one way or another.

With every actor unhappy, it would appear that the WTO is the work of a transcendental force. Far from it – the creation of the WTO, its rules and organization, is the work of powerful social forces and States. It has emerged as a key institution to sustain the global capitalist order to the advantage of an emerging transnational capitalist class (TCC) whose interests are articulated by powerful States. To put it differently, the fact that all actors have grievances does not mean that all grievances are of equal weight and concern.[1] It is therefore necessary to sift the grievances

Bhupinder Chimni is currently Chairperson of the Centre for International Legal Studies (CILS) at Jawaharlal Nehru University, New Delhi and formerly Vice Chancellor, West Bengal National University of Juridical Sciences, Kolkata. The author would like to thank Gregory Shaffer and Yong-Shik Lee for their comments on the draft of this chapter. The usual caveat applies. This text was previously published in the *Journal of World Trade*.

[1] The TCC and powerful States are more concerned with (i) introducing some marginal reforms that can address the legitimacy crisis; and (ii) finding ways of avoiding some of the constraints that the very existence of a multilateral institution imposes.

in terms of both process and outcome to determine the global population that is seriously hurt by the operation of the WTO and what can be done in terms of reform of the WTO rules, identifying the assistance needed from the international community, and outlining the role national parliaments and social movements must play to realize set goals. Such an exercise in social audit would allow the prioritization of reforms that should visit the WTO.

It will be the argument of this chapter that the influence the TCC exercises on the WTO rules seriously limits its reform, the objective of which should be the welfare of the global poor and disadvantaged sections (Lundberg and Squire 1999; tran-Nguyen and Zampetti 2004: 362). Nevertheless, it proceeds to make a number of recommendations in terms of reforming process and rules to embed greater democracy in WTO and help achieve development for all, including subaltern States and classes.

The chapter proceeds in the following way. In section 2 the class character of WTO is briefly discussed.[2] The complex process through which TCC influence is mediated through States is touched upon. It is clarified that the fact the TCC exercises dominant influence in shaping WTO rules does not mean the principle of free trade needs to be rejected. Instead, the historically contingent character of the principle of free trade is stressed along with the need to prevent the linkage of trade and non-trade issues. It is also contended that for a proper perspective on WTO it should not be analysed in isolation from other international institutions as these collectively impinge on the ability of the Third World to pursue independent economic and social policies. Finally, the section emphasizes that the concepts of democracy are conceptually and operationally interrelated.

In section 3, the theme of 'WTO and democracy', its different facets and the particular concern of Third World States and the subaltern classes are examined.[3] Among matters touched on are the absence of deliberative democracy in WTO negotiations, the specific problems with the consensus-based decision-making process, the problematic nature of the 'single undertaking' formula, the absence of an active role of national

[2] While I write from a Marxist perspective, I believe that the analysis offered in the chapter can be sustained even if a Marxist approach is not adopted. On the other hand, the missing Marxist perspective from the extant WTO literature helps enrich our understanding of the WTO through explicitly stressing structural capital-labour-State linkages.

[3] For a justification of the continued use of the category 'Third World' see 'Third World Approaches to International Law: A Manifesto', in Anghie *et al.* 2003: 47. In this article, however, I use both terms 'Third World' and the 'developing world'. Likewise I use the 'Third World State', 'developing country' and 'subaltern state' interchangeably.

parliaments in the negotiation and ratification process, the need for mass mobilization and resistance to compel national parliaments to respond to the concerns of the subaltern classes, the requirement for a different standard of review for developing countries (and more generally the need to strengthen hermeneutic democracy) in the dispute settlement process, and the indispensability of greater participation of developing countries in WTO and WTO-related bodies.

In section 4, the subject of 'WTO and development' is addressed. It begins by noting the emergence of a right to development in international law. The concept of 'development' like that of 'democracy' is an essentially contested concept. It therefore calls for clarifying the idea of 'development'. In this context, the section proceeds to critique four kinds of positions: the idea of 'development as a trap'; the argument that the goal of sustainable development should involve the rejection of the process/product distinction; the understanding that the special and differential treatment principles achieve little; and, finally, that development is equal to the grant of greater market access to products of developing countries. The section then touches on some other concerns that need to be addressed if development for all is to be realized.

The concluding section recapitulates some of the recommendations advanced in the chapter on the theme of 'WTO, democracy and development'. Many of these proposals would be unacceptable to powerful States as the interests of the global capitalist class (TCC plus other factions of the national capitalist class) clash with them. If they are to be even seriously considered, active peaceful resistance has to be mobilized against the WTO by both old and new social movements.

1 The character of the WTO

1.1 The WTO and the TCC

The WTO is a multilateral institution whose rules and organizational structure have been negotiated between States. While this portrayal is correct and captures a vital aspect of the creation and continuance of the WTO, it does not tell us sufficiently about the global social forces that called for a new trade institution to replace the General Agreement on Tariffs and Trade (GATT). It is also customary to think of the WTO in terms of the North–South divide. While thinking in terms of a rich and powerful North and a poor and powerless South is useful, particularly in analysing the democracy and development deficit in the WTO, the imagery does not allow the insight that certain classes in the developing world are beneficiaries of the WTO regime. In other words, the language of the North–South divide can be bewildering as it seems to suggest that there are no sections within the South that can support the cause of the WTO. The reality is that even with respect to the generally condemned Agreement on Trade-Related Intellectual Property Rights (TRIPS), there are supporting voices in the poor world.[4] Indeed, today the Third World State is often one with the neo-liberal globalization discourse that is articulated by powerful States even as it protests this or that policy. In short, there is a need to think about the WTO in the language of social forces and classes. International institutions, as the French Marxist Poulantzas acutely noted, do not have powers of their own but 'crystallize class powers' (Poulantzas 1975: 70).

The class that exercises the dominant influence on the creation and sustenance of international institutions, including the WTO, is the emerging TCC.[5] The TCC is the class that benefits from the accelerated globalization of trade finance and production and has used an opportune moment in the history of international relations, manifested in the absence of an effective counter power to the Organisation of Economic Co-operation

[4] We however do not wish to deny the often 'irreducible simultaneity' of the geographical and class divides. See Saul (2004: 223).

[5] The emergence of the TCC, its nature, character and strategies are the subject of much debate: see Robinson and Harris (2000); Sklair (2000); Bereroglu (2003); Harris (2003); Stokes 2005. My own conclusion that a TCC is emerging comes from the study of international legal materials that show how a new international legal architecture has emerged in the last quarter century (Chimni 1999, 2004). This understanding is buttressed at the economic and ideological levels by the work of Robinson, Sklair and others. At the ideological level what is striking is the degree of convergence in the thinking of the ruling elites. It would be a mistake to underestimate the role of ideas in shaping the globalization process. To illustrate the integration of economic and ideological developments at the local level one can take the example of the growing software industry in India which has given rise to 'a new kind of capitalist class': the IT business class. This class and the IT industry is, according to Upadhya: '… distinguished by its close integration into the global economy and its relative autonomy from the "old" Indian economy dominated by the public sector and a nationalist capitalist class. For this reason, the IT elite differ sharply in their ideological orientation from the established business class, many of whom (represented by the "Bombay Club") oppose unbridled globalization. In contrast to the old bourgeoisie, the IT business class emerged within the global economy and a liberalized environment [and]… is already highly transnational in its composition. The entry of multinationals in the IT industry, far from posing unwelcome competition to domestic firms … has produced synergies that have helped it to grow. For these reasons, members of the transnational IT business class are, for the most part, outspoken votaries of globalization… [and have had] a disproportionate impact on public policy, both directly by forging links with the state, and indirectly as icons of a "resurgent India" ' (2004: 5148).

and Development (OECD) countries, to codify its interests in, inter alia, WTO agreements.[6] The two central features of the interests of the TCC in WTO are internationalization and expansion of property rights (as in TRIPs, TRIMs (The Agreement on Trade-Related Investment Measures) and GATS (General Agreement on Trade in Services) texts) and the access to global markets (both in the goods and service sector) (Braithwate and Drahos 2000: 63; Hilary 2002; ICC 2003, 2005).[7] The TCC of course seeks to, like all dominant classes, represent its interests as universal ones.[8]

The emerging TCC, however, cannot carry alone the burden of creating, sustaining or redefining international institutions to realize its interests. In order to seek broader support for its larger globalization agenda, a coalition with the national bourgeoisie is often found necessary. In concrete terms it means, for example, that the TCC seeks a harder and effectively enforced intellectual property rights (IPR) regime and global market access for goods protected through tariff (e.g. against processed goods) and non-tariff barriers (often disguised as environmental protection measures). The effectiveness with which the interests of the national bourgeoisie are protected depends on the nature and character of the States, its role in international trade, and the coalition strategy it can evolve and sustain to

[6] 'Large private corporations purchase influence within all so-called democratic societies. As all Geneva trade diplomats know, their influence over ostensibly international negotiations is also considerable; witness the role of the pharmaceuticals industry in intellectual property debates and the banking and financial sector in those over capital account regimes and trade in financial services' (Helleiner 2000: 9). Ostry notes that 'without the new issues [viz. TRIPs, GATS and TRIMs] it is doubtful that the American business community or American politicians would have supported a multilateral negotiation' (2002: 268). Of TRIPs she writes: 'the TRIPs agreement was a top priority for American multinationals in the pharmaceutical, software, and entertainment industries who wanted it in the GATT rather than the UN agency WIPO (World Intellectual Property Organization), which had no enforcement mechanism' (Ostry 2002: 296).

[7] On the ICC position on non-agricultural market access, see www.iccwbo.org/policy/trade/id2877/index.html [accessed in November 2010].

[8] This representation is done through bodies such as the International Chamber of Commerce (ICC) and the World Economic Forum (WEF). Thus, e,g., the Secretary General of the ICC (formerly the Managing Director of the WEF) states: 'The ICC is convinced that the emergence of a global market economy, a process that has only just begun, *will bring unprecedented prosperity to millions*. This is why, through its website, and other means, the ICC is intensifying its efforts to better communicate this message on behalf of world business' (Cattaui 2001: 265, emphasis added). Another document of the ICC states: 'World business, as represented by ICC, firmly believes that the global economy of today offers an unparalleled opportunity to raise living standards across the world. Indeed, *the evidence is that it has already helped bring unprecedented improvements in material welfare to billions of people*' (ICC 2003, emphasis added).

realize given interests. Therefore this option is not easily available to the Third World as it lacks the power to successfully protect its national bourgeoisie against the demands of greater market access by hegemonic States.

While the defence of the interests of the national bourgeoisie is not always an unfair demand (it may go some way to prevent de-industrialization) it does not necessarily go to meet the concerns of the subaltern classes (e.g. of rising prices of essential life-giving drugs).[9] However, in view of the fact that the Third World State cannot often effectively protect the interests of the national bourgeoisie, a section of the latter may align itself with the subaltern classes. The constraints of electoral politics mean that the developing country State cannot dismiss concerns of this coalition. It is these tensions and political coordinates that explain the approach of, for example, the Indian State to WTO negotiations.

But is the underlying assumption that WTO rules negatively impact subaltern classes sustainable? On the one hand, there is growing concern, reflected in the anti-globalization and anti-WTO protests, that the condition of subaltern classes is worsening.[10] On the other hand, there is also evidence that shows that free trade does not hit the interests of the global poor (Cattaui 2001: 264; Bhagwati 2004: 51–67; WTO 2004: 11–12). In many ways this debate is misplaced. A core issue is not whether free trade is good or bad but whether it automatically translates into welfare for the subaltern class. Thus, there is sufficient evidence to show that free trade does not necessarily mean poverty alleviation.[11] For this to happen a range of national economic and social policies and institutions need to

[9] I define the subaltern class perspective to be inclusive of the inequities generated by gender, race and caste divides; WTO rules have implications for all these sections. However, I also agree that this diversity should not be allowed to 'obscure the crucial importance of a class-based comprehension of agency, actual, and potential, including the key role that Southern workers and their trade unions have continued to play in keeping anti-capitalist and anti-imperialist themes firmly in the mix of global resistance' (Saul 2004: 237).

[10] 'Whereas the relatively better-off have been doing quite well in the recent bursts of both globalization and liberalization, there is growing anxiety about the fate of the poorer, the more marginalized, the vulnerable and the powerless' (Helleiner 2000: 5).

[11] One report on the subject puts the matter as follows: 'No doubt increased foreign trade bears the potential to contribute to poverty alleviation, but there is no automatism in this respect. Obviously, one can only assume that increased foreign trade will have a positive effect on poverty alleviation if certain conditions are fulfilled in advance. These conditions relate to three levels: 1) to necessary prerequisites in developing countries, 2) to the policy of the industrialized countries and 3) to the WTO and its set of regulations. The basic prerequisites on the part of developing countries include a minimum level of economic efficiency and infrastructure in the respective country (e.g. transport and communications routes, level of technological development). Also, stabilizing and functioning

be put in place that are in turn supported by international development institutions in the matrix of an international right to development.

1.2 *Understanding the WTO: the need for a holistic approach*

However, this is not always possible, for the emerging TCC is not merely defining the rules of the WTO but also the policies of other international institutions such as, for instance, the international financial institutions. Therefore, unless the WTO regime is located and given meaning in the matrix of the rapid changes that are visiting international law and institutions in the era of globalization at the behest of the TCC, and more generally, in the matrix of colonialism and neo-colonialism, the horizon of critique tends to be limited.[12] It excludes from view developments either around WTO agreements (e.g. the TRIPs plus agreements) or outside it through policies enforced by institutions like the World Bank and the International Monetary Fund (IMF) which, inter alia, go to sustain and strengthen the WTO regime for realizing TCC interests and limit the options for Third World countries to pursue welfare-generating policies.[13] A holistic approach also allows us to appreciate the diplomatic strategy of the TCC: it often accommodates friendly interest in the WTO in pursuit of the larger goal of realizing its global interests in the realm of international finance and production.[14] It is the reason that increasingly, in the words of Panitch and Gindin, 'the globalization of capitalism has left

institutions are of importance. Furthermore, the course and speed of reforms are crucial to the impact of trade liberalization on poor sections of the population. While an all too hasty opening up of the market will affect poor and poorest sections of the population in particular, careful opening up geared to the potential and limits of a country's economy appears to have a positive impact on employment and income. Other factors crucial to poverty-reducing effects of trade include fair allocation within society, the scope for democratic participation, the setting up of social safety nets and education and health systems that are accessible to poor people' (VENRO 2004: 6).

[12] For the story of continuity in the history and technology of colonialism and neo-colonialism, see Anghie (2004).

[13] In the latter context, Howse puts it this way: 'many of the problems with neo-liberal structural economic reforms that have caused increasing doubts about the basic idea that trade brings growth, and that growth makes people better off, need to be addressed at least in part by systemic changes elsewhere, particularly in the international financial architecture and the practice of development banks' (Howse 2002: 434).

[14] In an essay on 'Finance and American Empire', Panitch and Gindin note the link between international finance and production: 'the expansion of finance has not been something apart from, but rather integral to the deepening of accumulation, as seen in both the continued internationalization of production networks and – as part and parcel of this – the continuing strength of the American economy' (Panitch and Gindin 2005: 47).

virtually no national bourgeoisie for labour to ally with, and few divisions to exploit between finance and industry' (2005: 75).

1.3 Subaltern classes not against free trade

It is implicit in the argument advanced that the critique is not of free trade or the WTO per se; neither is it the argument that the WTO can do no good.[15] The abstract principle of free trade is therefore not the target of the historically contingent subaltern critique. The critique is of the shape the principle of free trade assumes in the real world. The historically contingent subaltern critique is rooted in, first, the historical fact that neither Great Britain not the United States practised free trade as they were developing.[16] Thus, 'the US industries were literally the most protected in the world until 1945' (Chang 2003: 6). Second, the critique notes that even today the principles of free trade are not allowed to prevail when they impinge on the interests of powerful social classes, the subsidies regime sustained by the Agreement on Agriculture (AOA) being a good example. Third, it contends that the principle of free trade is being deployed without serious justification to realize non-trade values such as environmental protection or core labour standards (Krajewski 2001: 186). Fourth, more specifically, the critique suggests that the promotion of free trade has little to do with the creation and enforcement of international property rights such as IPRs; indeed IPRs are a form of protection if anything. Fifth, in contract, the WTO does not concern itself with significant trade problems such as those related to primary commodity trade. The World Commission on the Social Dimension of Globalization (hereafter

[15] 'I know of few reputable developing country analysts of governments who question the positive potential roles of international trade or capital inflow in economic growth and overall development' (Helleiner 2000: 5).

[16] Chang notes '[W]hen they were developing countries themselves, virtually all of today's developed countries did not practice free trade (and *laissez-faire* industrial policy as its domestic counterpart). Rather, they promoted their national industries through tariffs, subsidies, and other measures. Particularly notable is the fact that the gap between "real" and "imagined" histories of trade policy is the greatest in relation to Britain and the United States, which are conventionally believed to have reached the top of the world's economic hierarchy by adopting free trade, when the other countries were struck with outdated mercantilist policies. These two countries were, in fact, often the pioneers and frequently the most ardent users of *interventionist* trade and industrial policy measures in their early stages of development' (2003: 1).

World Commission) notes that, 'from 1980 to 2000 world prices for 18 major export commodities fell by 25 per cent in real terms. This fall was particularly significant in the case of cotton (47 percent), coffee (64 percent), rice (60.8 percent), tin (73 percent), cocoa (71.1 percent) and sugar (76.6 percent)' (ILO 2004: 83). Yet the WTO does not address this issue (Helleiner 2000: 16). Sixth, a point already made but worth reiteration, free trade does not automatically translate into welfare for the subaltern classes and the policies necessary to ensure this cannot often be followed because of the need to adhere to the conditionalities imposed by the international financial institutions. Finally, the WTO does not look at the whole issue of migration as consistent free traders argue. Thus, Bhagwati's suggestion that there be free movement of labour is rarely cited in the arguments for the promotion of free trade through the WTO (Bhagwati 2004: 208–21). In sum, often a false opposition is set up between the defenders and critics of free trade. The real issue is what has been the historic role of free trade, whether the norms of free trade are selectively adhered to, should non-trade values be sought to be realized through the instrument of trade, and whether the principle of free trade can afford to neglect the fact that countries entering into free trade are at different stages of development.

1.4 The complex scenario

Before proceeding further it needs to be stressed that while the TCC exercises a dominant influence over the shaping of the WTO, the process of arriving at WTO rules is a highly complex and mediated one. The complexity that informs the negotiation of 'trade' policies and their social implications are a function of a range of factors: 1) the extent of dominance of the TCC over the shaping of global economic policies in important states (both developed and developing countries); 2) the strength of the national bourgeoisie and its interests at stake in these States; 3) the nature of resistance mounted by the old and new social movements against particular trade rules; 4) the expertise available and deployed by developing country States in the negotiations; 5) the pressure that can be brought on important developing countries (India, Brazil, South Africa, Nigeria, China, Venezuela, Argentina, etc.) by powerful developed States; and 6) the ability of developing States to build and maintain coalitions in particular issue areas. It is a combination of these factors that makes the WTO negotiations such a contentious process.

1.5 Integral relationship between democracy and development

The final introductory point that needs to be made is to stress the integral relationship between the themes 'WTO and democracy' and 'WTO and development'. The concepts are entangled in two fundamental senses. First, unless the agreements of the WTO are negotiated respecting the principles of deliberative democracy, and also in a way that addresses the democracy deficit that characterizes the functioning of the WTO, the outcome cannot translate into development for developing countries. Thus, agreements arrived at in the shadow of economic and diplomatic coercion is unlikely to mean development for Third World peoples. Second, there is an internal link between democracy and development in terms of the realization of human rights. As the Vienna Declaration adopted in 1993 by 171 States at the World Conference on Human Rights states: 'democracy, development and respect for human rights and fundamental freedoms are interdependent and reinforcing'. This understanding is, as we will see later, the essence of the Declaration of the Right to Development adopted by the UN General Assembly in 1986.

2 The WTO and democracy

2.1 The WTO and democracy: different facets

Democracy is an essentially contested concept. Its meaning and implications are actively debated, especially at the global level (Marks 2000; Archibugi 2004). Its use in the context of the WTO therefore calls for clarification. Much of the debate revolves around the ideas of deliberative democracy and democracy deficit, ideas that can be addressed at several levels.

First, a key issue is about democratic principles informing the negotiation process. The general demand of Third World States and social movements is that the principles of deliberative democracy be respected, viz. good argument and not allowing power to prevail (Habermas 1987). In this respect, there is no need to see whether the consensus-building process in the WTO is not a facade behind which power rather than argument triumphs (South Centre 2001: 7).

Second, there is the question of internal democracy in States that are Members of the WTO. The idea of 'internal democracy' covers a cluster of issues including the process through which negotiating positions are arrived at, whether a State has a research and information base to effectively participate in the decision-making process, and the role national parliament should play in the negotiation and ratification of WTO agreements (South Centre 2001; ILO 2004: 15). There is also the significant question as to what processes can justify and legitimate tying the hands of future generations. Exit, as is known, is not possible from specific WTO agreements but only from the WTO.

Third, it may be asked as to whether the voices of resistance embodied in old and new social movements are heeded and accommodated in the functioning of the WTO. The general tendency has been to ignore (even in the physical sense by calling meetings in places that cannot easily be reached by protesters) social movements. It raises issues related to ways in which the WTO can become a more inclusive forum. Thus, for instance, a debate has raged over whether the submission of *amicus curiae* briefs to dispute settlement panels by non-governmental organizations (NGOs) makes it more inclusive or merely goes to reinforce the North–South divide in the WTO.

Fourth, the reference to democracy may reflect the concern to advance the cause of transparent and accountable functioning of existing WTO bodies (e.g. the WTO Appellate Body (AB) or other bodies to which reference is made in WTO texts such as the Codex Alimentarius Commission); this may involve the evolution and application of the principles of what has been called 'global administrative law' (GAL).

Finally, there is the question of hermeneutic democracy that involves issues relating to the standard of review in dispute settlement and cognizance of Third World views and scholarship by WTO dispute settlement panels and the AB in framing issues and interpreting texts. This is a necessary step in creating a level interpretative playing field in giving meaning to the ambiguities and gaps that riddle the WTO agreements.

These are some overlapping but distinct aspects of the democratizing WTO debate. In the following, each of these aspects is the subject of brief comment and recommendations. The essential argument advanced is that the democratic reform of the WTO is constrained by the interests of the global capitalist class. The question of what the possible democratic reforms can be call for collective reflection by the international community of States and scholars and this chapter is merely a modest contribution to that cause.

2.2 WTO negotiations and deliberative democracy: amend Vienna Convention on the Law of Treaties

Among the concerns that undermine the legitimacy of the WTO is the fact that its negotiations do not respect the basic principles of deliberative democracy. Krajewski, borrowing from the writings of Habermas, summarizes for us the meaning of deliberative democracy:

> Deliberation requires a dialogue among equal subjects in an open, transparent and participatory way. However, dialogue by itself is not enough. Democratic deliberation is the exchange of information and arguments by advancing, supporting and criticizing different proposals and offering reasons for the positions taken. Deliberation is arguing and not bargaining.
>
> (Krajewski 2001: 172–3)

The essence of deliberative democracy is thus the prescription that the only authority that is respected in international negotiations is that of a good argument, and following it, all disagreements are resolved by equal subjects through the force of a better argument rather than power. The criticisms of the WTO negotiation process in terms of the violation of the principles of deliberative democracy stand even if the Habermasian ideal is given a practical interpretation. In other words, even accepting the fact that international negotiations cannot entirely be purged of a variety of diplomatic and political pressures, or exclude bargaining, the WTO negotiation process is seriously flawed. The negotiations are, first, marked by the absence of a transparent and informed dialogue between all participants. Second, the text of particular agreements is often concluded in the face of intense diplomatic and political pressure from powerful states in the international system.

A South Centre paper (2001) lists the widely known problems with the consensus-based negotiation and decision-making process of the WTO. First, many Third World countries lack the research and information base to effectively participate in the negotiation of complex agreements (South Centre 2001: 7–8; ILO 2004: 15). They often do not even have sufficient staff and presence in Geneva to participate in ever-increasing meetings (Helleiner 2000: 17; South Centre 2001: ix). Second, the different agreements are essentially negotiated by a small club of countries to the exclusion of most Third World countries; for example, the infamous 'Green Room' meetings (Krajewski 2001: 169–70; South Centre 2001: 9). This was the cause of protests by a majority of African States at the Seattle ministerial meeting.[17] Despite the protest there has been little change in the

[17] While democratic in theory, 'oligarchy comes closer than democracy to describing decision-making at the WTO' (Weiss 2002: 76).

negotiation process.[18] Third, 'the informal component of WTO decision-making and diplomacy' has had 'an adverse impact on the coalitions of developing countries' (South Centre 2001: 10). While developed countries closely coordinate their positions (other than on issues where there is active disagreement) Third World countries are, given the absence of appropriate convention (they never negotiated as Group 77 in GATT) and material and human resources, unable to do so. Further, the culture of informal meetings is so alien to many a participating delegate from the Third World that it results in lack of effective participation (South Centre 2001: 11). Fourth, so far as seeking technical and other assistance from the WTO secretariat is concerned there is the absence of staff parity from the developed and Third World countries allowing some to believe that certain ideologies come to prevail (South Centre 2001: 11).[19] Fifth, developing countries 'fear the consequences of expressing their objections publicly, and hence choose the alternative option of remaining silent' (South Centre 2001: 7). A variety of threats and pressures are also used by powerful States to ensure that their positions are accepted.[20] Finally, the technique of 'single undertaking' is used to ensure that Third World countries cannot opt out of agreements that are not in their national interests.[21]

[18] For some improvements in the system, see South Centre (2001: 9). However, as the South Centre report notes, 'problems remain'. For a detailed analysis, see Weiss (2002: 9–11).

[19] 'A classic example of the Secretariat's bias that is cited is the active promotion of the new round [viz. Doha Round] by the Director-General (DG). Many developing countries assert that such an open advocacy by the Secretariat of a position on which there is no consensus among the majority of the members themselves considerably undermines the status of the WTO secretariat as a neutral broker' (South Centre 2001: 12).

[20] An Action Aid document lists some: The threat of aid budgets being cut or essential loans being blocked if a country maintains its opposition to the richer countries or, conversely, the promise of extra aid, loans, or debt relief if the country will drop that opposition. The threat of a loss of trade preferences by countries opposing the 'consensus' position, especially the cancellation of market access preferences for key exports from developing countries – a powerful weapon against countries which rely on the EU or USA as their principal export markets. Personal attacks on delegates who defend their own country's position in opposition to that of the richer countries. There are instances of strong developing country negotiators being removed from their posts at the WTO after phone calls to their governments complaining of their opposition, with threats of more widespread retaliation (Action Aid 2003: 3). Also see Shaffer (2005).

[21] 'Another casualty must be the concept of the "single undertaking" (originating in the Uruguay Round) in which member countries are required to agree on (and abide by) an entire set of rules, multilaterally negotiated within the WTO. More flexible arrangements for joining and/or opting out of particular sub-agreements within the overall organization, while maintaining a "fundamental core" of tenets and practices to which all subscribe – arrangements analogous to those in the later stages of the GATT – would

But despite many of these problems, developing countries believe that the consensus-based system 'is both necessary and non-negotiable' (South Centre 2001: 14). This position is based on 'practical consideration that Members who find themselves in a minority position would never accept the deep and legally binding obligations of the WTO' (South Centre 2001: 14). The 'tyranny of the majority' argument has played itself out before in the context of the resolutions concerning the new international economic order. Another deadlock would, it is felt, be unhelpful; it would encourage unilateralism and regionalism. One reason for developing countries not protesting too much the violation of the principles of deliberative democracy is that the ruling class in the Third World are comfortable with the ideology of the WTO. The opposition often is about 1) realizing greater benefits for the nationalist capitalist class, and 2) retaining a certain flexibility that allows it to respond to local resistance that may have a serious impact in terms of electoral politics. These objectives, it is believed, can be secured (by marginal developing countries) even with marginal improvement in the negotiation system.

Be that as it may, what can be done to strengthen deliberative democracy in multilateral negotiations and institutions? A significantly difficult but practical step that can be taken in the direction of establishing deliberative democracy is to amend the Vienna Convention on the Law of Treaties 1969 in two ways. First, it should (at present it does not) cover all aspects and phases of the process of negotiations including pre-negotiations and agenda-setting.[22] Second, it must be amended to expressly rule out the use of economic or political coercion in negotiations. Article 52 of the Vienna Convention entitled 'Coercion of a State by the threat or use of force' states: 'A treaty is void if its conclusion has been procured by the threat or use of force in violation of the principles of international law embodied in the Charter of the United Nations.'

The meaning of 'threat or use of force' is not elaborated in the Vienna Convention. The Vienna Treaty Conference however did issue a Declaration on the Prohibition of Military, Political or Economic Coercion in the Conclusion of Treaties. The Declaration:

be more conducive to future agreements among so large and so varied a membership; and are therefore also likely to be a requirement for the restoration of confidence, and for further progress, in the WTO system' (Helleiner 2000: 18).

[22] According to the World Commission 'it is essential to reform the working methods and negotiation procedures to ensure full and effective participation in agenda-setting and negotiations by all member states' (ILO 2004: 117).

> *[s]olemnly condemns the* threat or use of pressure in any form, whether military, political or economic by any State in order to coerce another State to perform any act relating to the conclusion of a treaty in violation of the principles of the sovereign equality of States and freedom of consent.[23]

This non-binding Declaration needs to be made an integral part of the Convention by suitably amending Article 52.

The implementation of the new provisions could vest with the International Court of Justice (ICJ). This is not a novel proposal. The Vienna Convention gives precisely such an authority with regard to peremptory norms of international law.[24] The proposal has in the past also had the support of eminent scholars like Sir Hersch Lauterpacht who in his report to the International Law Commission (ILC) in 1953 suggested the following provision:

> Treaties imposed by or as the result of the use of force or threats of force against a State in violation of the principles of the Charter of the United Nations are invalid if so declared by the International Court of Justice at the request of any State.
>
> (Lauterpacht 1978: 273)

[23] For the text of the Vienna Convention on the Law of Treaties, see Vienna Convention on the Law of Treaties, 1155 U.N.T.S. 331, 8 I.L.M. 679, or http://untreaty.un.org/cod/avl/ha/vclt/vclt.html [accessed in November 2010]. The Convention entered into force on 27 January 1980. For the text of the Declaration on the Prohibition of Military, Political or Economic Coercion in the Conclusion of the Treaties, see Vienna Convention on the Law of Treaties, 1155 U.N.T.S. 331, 8 I.L.M. 733. A separate resolution entitled 'Resolution relating to the Declaration on the Prohibition of Military, Political, or Economic Coercion in the Conclusion of Treaties' was also adopted. It requested Member States to give the Declaration the widest possible publicity and dissemination. The UN Secretary General was also asked to draw attention of Member States and organs of the United Nations to the Declaration. Developing countries have long argued that the definition of force included economic and political coercion. According to the Friendly Relations Declaration, 'No State may use or encourage the use of economic, political or any other type of measures to coerce another State in order to obtain from it the subordination of the exercise of its sovereign rights and to secure from it advantages of any kind'. See Declaration on Principles of International Law Concerning Friendly Relations and Cooperation Among States in Accordance with the Charter of the United Nations, UN General Assembly Resolution 2625 (25), 24 October 1970. Article 32 of the Charter of Economic Rights and Duties of States, 1974 reads: 'No State may use or encourage the use of economic, political or any other type of measures to coerce another State in order to obtain from it the subordination of the exercise of its sovereign rights.' GA Res.3281 (xxix), UN GAOR, 29th Sess., Supp. No. 31 (1974) 50. See also UNGA A/Res/42/173, 11 December 1987: 'Economic measures as a means of political and economic coercion against developing countries', at www.un.org/documents/ga/res/42/a42r173.htm [accessed in November 2010].

[24] Article 53 of the Vienna Convention on the Law of Treaties 1969.

At present, the Vienna Convention provides for a conciliation commission to make proposals to reach an amicable settlement of, among other things, a dispute concerning the invalidity of a treaty.[25] A reference to such a commission could be included if States refuse to accept the compulsory jurisdiction of the International Commission of Jurists.

What are the other practical steps that can be taken to embed deliberative democracy in WTO negotiations? One is to improve the consensus system directed towards transforming the 'passive consensus' into an 'active consensus'. Reform along such lines, 'while still minor in that it works within the perimeter of the consensus principle, would involve a re-definition of consensus such that it requires an active endorsement of the proposal under discussion, rather than simply the lack of objection' (South Centre 2001: 15). Second, there is a need to build domestic capacity of Third World countries so that they possess the research and informational base to effectively participate in the negotiations (Ostry 2002: 294). Third, developing countries should stress coalition-building, a suggestion that has been repeatedly made and to which Third World countries have eventually woken up (Chimni 1992).[26] Finally, there is a need to rethink the 'single undertaking' formula. In the words of Howse, we need a WTO 'that is not only somewhat à la carte but also one that (far more than what is allowed under existing special arrangements for developing countries) is genuinely a multiple vitesses' (Howse 2002: 434; ILO 2004: 85).[27]

[25] The grounds for the invalidity of a treaty listed in Part V of the Vienna Convention on the Law of Treaties 1969 include error, fraud, corruption or coercion of a representative of a state and coercion of state by threat or use of force.

[26] 'Developing countries can forge alliances with constituencies within the global powers. By harnessing domestic political pressure and legal expertise within the United States and Europe, developing countries can curtail, at least somewhat, great power coercion and otherwise offset some of the resource imbalances that they face…' As noted by Shaffer: 'International negotiations involve a two-level game in which national constituencies compete in the formation of national positions and those national positions are then advanced in international negotiations. If developing countries cannot neutralize the clout of US and European firms in the formation of US and European positions, then developing countries will face the full brunt of US and European pressure in regards to pharmaceutical patents and other WTO claims. In a world of asymmetric power, developing countries enhance the prospects of their success if other US and European constituencies can offset industry pressure on US and European trade authorities. Developing countries need to work with these constituencies to alter the domestic political playing fields of the other side' (2005).

[27] 'A simple starting point would be to allow flexibility to these countries (viz. developing countries) for joining in, or opting out of proposed disciplines or new issues in the WTO to permit greater policy space for them to pursue national development policies' (ILO 2004: 85).

2.3 *Negotiation and ratification of WTO agreements: greater role for national parliaments*

It has been aptly remarked that, 'WTO law not only needs to meet standards of legitimacy of international law but also national democratic constitutional standards, because WTO law defines binding guidelines for national economic and social policies' (Krajewski 2001: 167–8).[28] But as Krajewski points out:

> Parliamentary participation in the Uruguay Round and WTO negotiation process was and continues to be almost non-existent, with the notable exception of the US Congress. National parliaments are mostly faced with the negotiations only after they are finished. The results are presented to them as a *fait accompli*. It is well known that many national parliaments were not able or not willing to invest much time in the study and discussion of the Uruguay Round Agreements before they agreed to the package of treaties.
>
> (Krajewski 2001: 176)

The World Commission has therefore 'urge[d] national parliaments to strengthen their role and capacity to provide adequate checks and balances over their governments' positions at international fora' (ILO 2004: 120).

The principal reason that the consent of the people's representatives should be sought before becoming a party to WTO agreements is that it involves severe constraints on future governments on the very exercise of sovereignty in relation to core aspects of national economic decision-making (Chimni 1999, 2004). In this context Howse and Nicolaides, citing the work of Jon Elster, aptly note that:

> at the level of domestic constitution-making, an important hedge against the antidemocratic feature of hands tying is to require extraordinary levels of democratic consent in the first place to the rules that will tie the hands of future governments. Examples include referenda, super-majority votes, and elected constitutional assemblies. But judging hand tying through WTO law against this standard puts into high relief the questionable democratic *bona fides* of WTO rules. Domestic deliberation on these rules is often perfunctory and constrained by information and agency costs. This process produces a mass of general and often ambiguous rules. Their effects cannot easily be debated intelligently *ex ante* in

[28] On the policy aspects of the relationship between international agreements and municipal legal systems, see Jackson (1992).

> national legislatures, and they must be accepted or rejected as a single package.
>
> (Howse and Nicolaidis 2003: 11)

Therefore, as a first measure, national parliaments should consider passing a law requiring prior consultation and consent as a precondition to ratification of significant agreements like the WTO agreements (WTO 2004: 45–6). Provision should also be made for expert hearings so that the parliament can take an informed view. The increased role of national parliaments is at least one way of ensuring that the views of poor and marginal sections find a voice in the negotiation and ratification process.

2.4 *The WTO, low intensity democracies and resistance*

However, at the same time it is important to understand the limits of the role that national parliaments can play given the dominance of the TCC and the absence in Third World countries of sufficient expertise with civil society organizations. Arguably 'low intensity democracies' are the best shell for the adoption and legitimization of neo-liberal policies by Third World States in an era when the politics of the cold war can no longer be used to support predatory and authoritarian regimes to create conditions hospitable for transnational capital. But as Susan Marks has argued, the institutions and procedures of representative government cannot be allowed to exhaust the meaning of democracy. She rightly notes that 'the indeterminacy of the central concept of democracy' and 'the norm's potential to serve as an agent of neo-colonialism' (Marks 2000: 140–1) often result in the norm of democratic governance being 'too easily turned against redistributive claims and towards hegemonic agenda' (Marks 2000). This critique acquires an edge when it is noted that sovereign powers of states are being relocated in international institutions without commensurate benefits accruing to the vast majority of peoples of the Third World (Chimni 1999, 2004).

The role of the national parliament can only be effective if it is compelled by social movements to ensure that the WTO delivers development to all. Old social movements (OSMs) – i.e. trade unions, peasant and student movements – with their capacity for mass mobilization have a particularly crucial role to play here. Increasingly however, the space for democratic protest is colonized by NGOs (with States facilitating this) who do not represent these sections. In any case, as Rajagopal rightly notes, we must avoid analysis that 'confuses social movements with NGOs or conflate NGOs with civil society' (Rajagopal 2003: 409). However, OSMs could do well to learn from NGOs and use modern forms of resistance (e.g. e-resistance) in order to take their protest to the wider section of national and global populations.

2.5 *Need for hermeneutic democracy: differential standard of review for developing countries*

One aspect of democracy deficit in the WTO that has not received adequate attention is that of hermeneutic (i.e. interpretative) democracy. The WTO agreements are being interpreted by the WTO dispute settlement panels and the AB without, other than in specific contexts, taking into account the unique concerns of developing countries. One way of ensuring hermeneutic democracy is to invoke the special and differential treatment principle and apply the national deference principle, as contained in Article 17.6 of the Agreement on Anti-Dumping, to all disputes relating to the implementation of WTO obligations by developing countries.[29]

Since developing countries are compelled to accede to a number of agreements through the technology of a 'single undertaking' it only stands to reason that a certain flexibility be allowed in the enforcement of those obligations beyond providing for a period of transition. The adoption of a national deference principle will allow Third World countries to pass implementing legislation that keeps their special needs in view. The ongoing review of the Dispute Settlement Undertaking provides a unique opportunity to go down this road.[30] It is worth mentioning that the possibility of universalizing the national deference principle was kept open by a ministerial decision while adopting the Final Act of the Uruguay Round of Trade Negotiations (WTO 1994: 453).[31] The suggestion here is to

[29] The crucial para. (ii) of Article 17.6 states: 'the panel shall interpret the relevant provisions of the Agreement in accordance with customary rules of interpretation of public international law. Where the panel finds that a relevant provision of the Agreement admits of more than one permissible interpretation, the panel shall find the authorities' measure to be in conformity with the Agreement if it rests upon one of those permissible interpretations.'

[30] 'DSU review started already in 1997. However, it could not be concluded so far as several deadlines lapsed without tangible achievements. The last deadline missed so-far had been set for May 2004. As part of the so-called "July package" adopted on 1 August 2004, the mandate to continue the negotiations has been renewed, however, without a new deadline being set' (Zimmerman 2005: 40). For a brief review of ongoing negotiations, see Zimmerman 2005: 46–52.

[31] The Ministers decided: 'The standard of review in paragraph 6 of Article 17 of the Agreement on the Implementation of Article VI of GATT 1994 shall be reviewed after

universalize the application of the national deference principle only with respect to developing countries.

2.6 Need for hermeneutic democracy: the role of academic scholarship

Widespread ambiguities characterize the WTO agreements. The interpretative gaps are today being filled with the aid of scholarship emerging from the developed world that frames issues in specific ways of advance interpretations of texts that further the cause of particular interests and values.[32] These understandings and interpretations often find their way into the panel and AB reports as eventually the scholarship in the field does influence the manner in which certain issues are perceived (Shaffer and Apea 2005: 977). This gap of course calls for both the production of good scholarship in the Third World and concerted attempts at making it more widely available.[33] There is therefore an urgent need for investment by Third World States, industry and universities into the research of WTO law so as to be in a position to seriously contest understandings and interpretations that only further the interests of the developed world. A journal exclusively devoted to publishing Third World writings on the WTO is also called for. The WTO Secretariat can perhaps be asked to help in this regard. But above all the observation of hermeneutic democracy requires WTO panels and the AB to take cognizance of Third World scholarship.

a period of three years with a view to considering the question of whether it is capable of general application.'

[32] In debates in the First World law journals, the standpoint of developing countries is rarely taken into account. To give one example, in a symposium on 'The Boundaries of the WTO' in the *American Journal of International Law*, no representative of the developing countries or scholars were invited to write. In his reactions to the contributions to the symposium, Jackson regretted 'the absence of certain important viewpoints … particularly the absence of a developing country, or least-developed country' (2002: 118). Likewise, Bhagwati noted that 'almost none of the papers come to terms with the important North-South divide' (2002: 126).

[33] The creation of the WTO Advisory Centre on World Trade Law (ACWL) has simply 'remedied some of the resource constraints that developing countries face in the more sophisticated settings of the new dispute settlement system' through providing 'legal training, support and advice on WTO Law and dispute settlement procedures to developing countries, in particular LDCs' (Zimmerman 2005: 51).

2.7 *Need for hermeneutic democracy: the issue of amicus curiae briefs*

The issue of hermeneutic democracy assumed a controversial dimension in the context of the submission of *amicus curiae* briefs to the WTO dispute settlement panels. In the *Shrimp Turtle* case (1998), the AB rejected the panel view that non-requested information could not be accepted from non-governmental sources. It distinguished between a legal right to make a submission before a WTO tribunal and what a tribunal was authorized to do under the Dispute Settlement Understanding (DSU). While the legal right to make a submission only vested with the Members of the WTO, Article 13 of the DSU entitled the 'Right to Seek Information' gave, according to the AB, comprehensive authority to a panel to ' "seek" information and technical advice from "any individual or body" it may consider appropriate, or from "any relevant source" ' (WTO 1998: para. 104). That right was subsequently confirmed in further disputes, 'causing outrage among many developing country Members who feared undue interference from NGOs' (Zimmerman 2005: 42–3). The reasons for feeling exasperated are not far to seek.

First, the negotiating history appears to show that the idea of allowing NGOs access to the dispute settlement process had been proposed but rejected. Second, the likely beneficiaries of the AB ruling would be those with capacity in terms of human and material resources. These entities would mainly come from the developed world. Third, the AB decision would create an 'impossible burden' for any developing country Member who may wish to comment on or respond to the *amicus* briefs. If a number of briefs are received it could mean a large number of texts to go through and legal arguments to be responded to in a few days' time. Perhaps in response to the concerns of the developing world the AB has, as Zimmerman notes, 'de facto developed a very pragmatic approach':

> On the one hand, the Appellate Body displays a general openness towards the acceptance of *amicus curiae* briefs. On the other hand, it does not appear to accord decisive weight to these submissions in its decisions – at least not explicitly. This approach gives adjudicating bodies a maximum of flexibility while it respects the concerns of Members who are against such briefs.
>
> (Zimmerman 2005: 50–1)

But there is, in addition, a need to ensure, first that an NGO does not have greater access to a panel to the AB than a WTO Member State and second, that certain guidelines should be adopted to determine which NGOs can submit *amicus curiae* briefs. For example, there should be a clear proven interest in the matter on which the *amicus* brief is being submitted. Third, an NGO should have no financial or other links with business interests at stake or be funded by governments. Towards this end the NGO must make available all the necessary documentation that can be scrutinized by the WTO Secretariat or panel/AB with the assistance of Member States involved in the particular dispute.[34] For their part, the developing countries must remember that the international NGO community is not necessarily hostile to their interests.

2.8 Develop global administrative law (GAL)

A significant way in which to address the issue of democracy deficit in the WTO is, as Kingsbury, Stewart and Krisch note in a seminar paper, to develop 'global administrative law' (GAL) (Kingsbury *et al.* 2004). They identify global administrative action as 'all rule making and adjudications or other decisions of particular matter that are neither treaty-making nor simple dispute settlement between disputing parties' (Kingsbury *et al.* 2004: 6). In other words, GAL is not about 'the specific content of substantive rules, but rather the operation of existing or possible principles, procedural rules and reviewing and other mechanisms relating to accountability, participation and assurance of legality in global governance' (Kingsbury *et al.* 2004: 16).

From a Third World perspective it could be argued that in the absence of a simultaneous critique of substantive law GAL goes to legitimize unjust laws through taking the focus away from their reform and instead talking of the democratization of the administrative decision-making process. Surely, the norms relating to transparency, accountability and participation that comprise the building blocks of administrative law cannot be viewed in strict isolation from the substantive rules. The agencies/mechanisms that are to be made the subject of GAL are an integral part of substantive law. If the substantive law has an imperial character (i.e. it essentially codifies the interests of the dominant classes and States in the international system) the potential that GAL holds for democratizing international laws is rather circumscribed.[35]

[34] Similar suggestions have been made in the EU proposal on the subject. See *New Article* EU/TN/DS/W/1:*13bis: Amicus Curiae Submissions*, at www.law.georgetown.edu/iiel/research/projects/dsureview/synopsis.html [accessed in November 2010].

[35] For a detailed critique, see Chimni (2005).

On the other hand, where there is administrative decision-making involved, directly or indirectly in the WTO, the principles of GAL need to be brought into play. Two examples may help illustrate the importance of developing GAL. It is generally agreed that developing countries should participate more actively in the work of the Codex Alimentarius Commission mentioned in Article 3.4 of the Agreement on Sanitary and Phyto-Sanitary Measures (SPS) to set international standards for food safety.[36] For this, financial and technical assistance has to be made available for developing countries (Steinberg and Mazarr 2003: 78). A Codex Trust Fund has already been set up in this respect.[37] However, it suffers from the problem of a wide mandate that accentuates inadequate resources; the mandate of the Codex Trust Fund goes a long way beyond facilitating the participation of the developing countries in the work of the Codex Alimentarus Commission. It, among other things, seeks to enhance 'their capacity to establish effective food safety and quality standards and fair trade practices in food trade, both in the framework of Codex and in their own countries'.[38] On a different level there is a need for greater transparency in the process through which WTO AB Members are selected. Since the WTO AB plays a role in the interpretation and enforcement of WTO rules, the process through which its Members are selected should be more transparent and call for wider consultations with States.

3 The WTO and development

Helleiner has observed that 'even though the WTO charter formally commits it to poverty alleviation' it is not seen by anyone as a primary WTO objective (Helleiner 2000: 18). There is no process of social audit in place to see if, inter alia, there is poverty alleviation, employment generation

[36] For detailed recommendations, see Steinberg and Mazarr (2003).

[37] Codex Trust Fund at www.who.int/foodsafety/codex/trustfund/en/index1.html [accessed in November 2010]. For a detailed statement see FAO/WHO Cooperative Programme Multi-donor Project, Project Document, 17 June 2003, FAO/WHO Project and Fund for Enhanced Participation in Codex, at www.who.int/foodsafety/codex/trustfund/en/index2.html [accessed in November 2010].

[38] Agenda Item 4 CX/MPH 03/4 Add…, Joint FAO/WHO Food Standards Programme, Executive Committee of the Codex Alimentarius Commission, 51st (Extraordinary) Session Geneva, Switzerland, 13–15 February 2003, India's Comments: Trust Fund for Participation of Developing Countries and Countries in Transition in the Work of the Codex Alimentarius Commission at http://codexindia.nic.in/ipcac.htm# [accessed in November 2010]. On the terms of reference of the National Codex Committee, see *Codex India* at http://codexindia.nic.in/comm.htm [accessed in November 2010].

and gender equality promoted through trade (Chimni 2000: 1752–61; Chimni 2002). It may, however, be contended that the WTO is not after all a development organization. But, as has been pointed out, the 'argument is true but irrelevant, because trade is not trade today' (Ostry 2002: 294). It goes far beyond to regulate domestic policy in a range of non-trade areas: intellectual property rights, investment, environment and services. The fact that the Doha Round of trade negotiations has been dubbed the 'Development Round' clearly shows that WTO Members accept that development is a key objective of WTO agreements.[39]

But the problem does not end there. There are those who argue 1) that the concept of development is an imperial construction to ensnare the developing countries into a self-created trap; 2) that since development means 'sustainable development', the process/product distinction contained in WTO rules is 'too thin and formalistic of a conceptual device' to address policy issues relating to consumer choice (read in the developed world); 3) that the special and differential treatment (SDT) principle does not seriously aid development of Third World countries; and 4) that the promotion of development of Third World countries through the WTO is essentially about providing greater access to their products to the markets of developed countries. This section critiques these positions after first establishing that the right to development is a fundamental norm of international human rights law. It is important to establish this because development should be perceived as a right of every individual and not as a charity to be received from the developed world. The critique of the four positions is followed by a brief discussion of the way forward in securing development for all.

3.1 The right to development in international law

In international law the right to development (RTD) has its basis in Article 55 and 56 of the UN Charter and a range of international human rights documents.[40] Together these texts call upon the international community to facilitate the development of all nations and peoples. In its General Comment No. 3, the Committee on Economic, Social and Cultural Rights

[39] 'The majority of WTO Members are developing countries. We seek to place their needs and interests at the heart of the Work Programme adopted in this Declaration', para. 2, Doha Ministerial Declaration. The text can be accessed at www.wto.org/english/theWTO_e/minist_e/min01_e/mindecl_e.htm [accessed in November 2010].

[40] For a detailed exposition, see Marks (2004); and Chimni (2003: 255–68).

(CESCR) has stated that international cooperation for development and thus the realization of economic, social and cultural rights is an obligation placed upon all States:

> The Committee wishes to emphasize that in accordance with Articles 55 and 56 of the Charter of the United Nations, with well-established principles of international law, and with the provisions of the Covenant itself, *international cooperation for development and thus for the realization of economic, social and cultural rights is an obligation of all States*. It is particularly incumbent upon those States which are in a position to assist others in this regard.[41]

Without a doubt, however, the most relevant and significant text is the Declaration of the Right to Development (DRD) adopted by the UN General Assembly in 1986 by a vote of 146 to 1 (United States) with eight abstentions (Denmark, Federal Republic of Germany, Finland, Iceland, Israel, Japan, Sweden and the UK); the vote against and the abstentions reveal the anxiety of the global capitalist classes regarding a generalized right to development as it is seen as a challenge to the existing global capitalist order.[42]

Article 1(1) of the DRD states that, 'The right to development is an inalienable human right by virtue of which every human person and all peoples are entitled to participate in, contribute to, and enjoy economic, social, cultural and political development, in which all human rights and fundamental freedoms can be fully realized'. Article 2(1) further emphasizes that it is the 'human person' who is the central subject of development. The issue whether RTD is a human right can be said to have been effectively settled by the Vienna Declaration and Program Action 1993 (VDPA) which reaffirmed 'the right to development, as established in the Declaration on the Right to Development, as a universal and inalienable right and an integral part of fundamental human rights'. How is RTD to be realized? Article 3(3) of the DRD states: 'States have the duty to co-operate with each other in ensuring development and eliminating obstacles to development. States should realize their rights and fulfil their duties in

41 CESCR General Comment No.3 HRI/GEN/1/Rev.1 (1990). pp. 48, 52 (emphasis added).

42 For a detailed review of the US objections to DRD, see Marks (2004: 143–51). On the identity and difference between the Millennium Challenge Corporation launched by President Bush in 2004 to increase development aid on the one hand and RTD on the other hand, see Marks (2004: 156–60). According to Marks, 'it is likely that the implementation of the MCA [Millennium Challenge Account] will follow the Washington consensus and link free markets and economic growth with political freedom, rather than the Vienna consensus on the RTD' (2004: 168).

such a manner as to promote a new international economic order … as well as to encourage the observance and realization of human rights.'

Article 4 goes further and states:

> 1. States have the duty to take steps, individually and collectively, to formulate international development policies with a view to facilitating the full realization of the right to development.
> 2. Sustained action is required to promote more rapid development of developing countries. As a complement to the efforts of developing countries, effective international co-operation is essential in providing these countries with appropriate means and facilities to foster their comprehensive development.

Finally, Article 10 states:

> Steps should be taken to ensure the full exercise and progressive enhancement of the right to development, including the formulation, adoption and implementation of policy, legislative and other measures at the national and *international* levels. [Emphasis added]

The right to development has been affirmed in a range of international law instruments and is arguably a norm of customary international law.[43] It is also to be recalled that the United Nations Human Rights Commission (UNHCR) has adopted a resolution that subjects all international economic laws to the test of international human rights laws.[44] In 1998 the UN Commission on Human Rights appointed an independent expert, Dr Arjun Sengupta, to study the implementation of RTD; by 2004 he had submitted eight reports (Sengupta 2000; Marks 2004: 139). But little has come out of these reports.

The TCC does not take RTD and international human rights law seriously in as much as its norms seek to empower the subaltern classes. It has instead mobilized the language of rights to entrench international property rights. Thus, for example, the preamble to the TRIPs agreement declares 'intellectual property rights to be private rights' without seriously considering its implications for competing human rights and values. The Doha Declaration on the TRIPs Agreement and Public Health has been an attempt by the Third World countries to restore the balance. However, the TCC seeks to bypass it on the one hand with advancing interpretations

[43] For details, see Chimni (2003: 260–2).

[44] E/CN.4/sub.2/2000/7, Sub-Commission on Protection and Promotion of Human Rights – Intellectual Property Rights and Human Rights. The resolution, inter alia, 'reminds all Governments of the primacy of human rights obligations over economic policies and agreements'.

that clash with the Third World understanding of the Declaration (by declaring the Declaration as non-binding) and on the other hand signing 'TRIPs plus' agreements that negate it in other ways.[45]

3.2 Deconstruction and development as trap thesis

The RTD and DRD assume that there is no consensus over the pursuit of the goal of development. However, there are those who argue that the Third World is captive to the Western political and cultural imagination in as much as it has embraced the idea of 'development' (Escobar 1997; Gordon and Sylvester 2004). At the other end of the spectrum is the view that critics who contend that development is a trap are hoping 'to save the people of developing countries from development' (Cattaui 2001: 263). Both the critics of the concept of 'development' and its unreflective defenders often do not ponder over the fact that 1) development is understood differently in different places and by different classes – it is the imperialist notion of capitalist development that should not be universalized as it produces underdevelopment in its wake; 2) at a time when development in the Third World can, given the imperatives of sustainable development, only come at the expense of First World standards of life the very critique of 'development' has an imperial connotation; and 3) it is not correct to suggest that embracing the idea of development is to somehow believe that the self-worth of Third World societies is only judged by the criteria of development; these societies have asserted their distinctive cultural traditions to show how the absence or presence of material progress does not necessarily mean the lack of self-worth.

Therefore what should be explored in Third World countries are alternative forms of development rather than 'post-development' models. As Sutcliffe puts it:

> Development and globalization are experienced in practice in conditions of profound inequality of wealth and power between nations (imperialism) as well as between classes and sexes (capitalist class exploitation and patriarchy). It is necessary to distinguish which of the rejected aspects of

[45] Chakravarti Raghavan, '"No!" to "TRIPS-plus" IP standards' at www.twnside.org.sg/title2/twr171d.htm [accessed in November 2010]; Mohammed 2005, available online at www.twnside.org.sg/title2/twr171d.htm [accessed in November 2010]. The text of the Doha Declaration on the TRIPs Agreement and Public Health is available online at www.wto.org/english/thewto_e/minist_e/min01_e/mindecl_trips_e.htm [accessed in November 2010].

> development and globalization are inherent in these concepts and which come about because of the unequal circumstances in which we experience them. If we reject them completely because of the form in which they arrive we will always be struggling against the wrong enemy.
>
> (Sutcliffe, cited by Saul 2004: 229–230)

What we need to do is to articulate alternative forms of 'left developmentalism' that step out of the framework of a global capitalist order (Saul 2004: 230). Such an understanding does not reject the principle of free trade but recognizes the historical contexts and exceptions that it needs to come to terms with in order to generate development for all.

3.3 Sustainable development: need for sustaining process/product distinction

Even when the goal of 'left developmentalism' is accepted there is a need to interpret the prescribed practices in the light of the overwhelming consensus today that development means 'sustainable development'. The phrase 'sustainable development' also appears in the preamble to the Agreement establishing the WTO. It has been invoked by the WTO AB to interpret WTO texts, in particular Article XX of GATT (1994) and the Agreement on Sanitary and Phytosanitary Measures. Indeed, through a process of small interpretative steps, the AB has gone further and brought, even if indirectly, environmental regulation into the WTO (Chimni 1999, 2002). The AB has gone to the extent of holding that, subject to the conduct of good faith bilateral/multilateral negotiation, unilateral measures may be used by a state to uphold national environmental measures (Chimni 1999, 2002). It has raised legitimate fears that the goal of 'sustainable development' will translate into non-tariff barriers against the exports of Third World countries.

However, it has been contended that the process/product distinction that informs WTO rules 'is too thin and formalistic of a conceptual device' to address policy issues relating to the exercise of consumer choice (Kysar 2004: 533). For today, according to Kysar, 'private consumption takes on a self-consciously political dimension: consumer behaviour is directed not merely at satisfying personal needs or desires, *but at shaping the way in which goods are produced*' (2004: 531, emphasis added). Consumer choice must be seen as an ethical or an expressive act that seeks to determine 'the outcome of important policy disputes by revealing – again through private market behaviour – their true level of human safety, the environment and host of public goods' (2004: 533). The eventual goal is to create 'a novel political economy' (2004: 533). In fact, Kysar sees that 'consumption communities organized around process-related issues appear destined to become some of the most active and visible citizen's groups of global civil society' (2004: 534). He goes on to recommend that, 'if individuals come to perceive their civic role as primarily one of consumer purchase, then the state should not simultaneously deprive them of the information that is needed to express political values through their consumption of choices' (2004: 535).

In the context of the WTO, Kysar takes note that 'the Appellate Body of the WTO appears to have rejected the view that the process/product distinction gives rise to a per se ban on process-based trade measures' (2004: 547). However, according to Kysar 'the process/product distinction still poses a serious obstacle to process-based trade measures, even if they are not per se impermissible following the Shrimp/Turtle rulings' (2004: 548). In his view, 'process preferences present an unlikely but promising candidate' to close ' "democracy deficits" created by the forces of globalization' (2004: 580). The WTO should therefore take into account 'non-technical meanings of risk', which have their basis in particular cultural contexts that give significance to moral and distributional consumer choices (2004: 589 and 595). 'The process/product distinction, in short, should be discarded as a conceptual device within law and policy' (2004: 624).

But what kind of policy is it that allows consumers in one part of the world to determine the fate of producers in another part of the world? Individualized politics cannot pose as a panacea for 'problems' of a globalized world unless its victims have a voice in the politics of the country whose consumers seek to exercise certain choices. In this regard one needs to say nothing further than to observe with Archibugi the 'dangerous double standards' that 'mark even the intellectual debate on democracy': 'The most tenacious defenders of democracy within states often become sceptics, even cynics, when confronted with the hypothesis of a global democracy' (Archibugi: 2004: 438). In other words, few States or scholars are willing to endorse the idea of some form of direct democracy or global citizenship at the international level.[46] In the circumstances consumers in the developed world cannot be given a veto over process and production methods used in the Third World.

[46] For one such proposal see Falk and Strauss (1999); and Strauss (2005).

3.4 *The special and differential treatment principle: some issues and concerns*

Any discussion of the theme 'WTO and development' cannot but focus on the SDT principle. The Doha Ministerial Declaration accords SDT a central place in the current round of trade negotiations. It states that: 'provisions for special differential treatment are an integral part of the WTO Agreements … We therefore agree that all special and differential treatment provisions shall be reviewed with a view to strengthening them and making them more *precise, effective and operational*'[47] (emphasis added).

The nature of SDT obligations that would work to take advantage of the developing countries is a matter of continuous debate. Thus, for example, Kol and Winters talk of 're-inventing Special and Differential Treatment' (Kol and Winters 2004: 8). In their view 'much of what is advanced as SDT is of little positive use and serves mainly to undermine non-discrimination' (2004: 1). In their opinion schemes such as the Generalized Systems of Preferences (GSP) and the Lome Convention are of 'limited value' in terms of expanding exports because of:

- Supply side constraints, which are typically not addressed because political and entrepreneurial attention is shifted towards diplomacy to safeguard and improve the preferences;
- The administrative complexities of the schemes, including rules of origin;
- The potential instability of the schemes, which are purely unilateral and not bound by the WTO;
- The threat of safeguards if preferential exports grow too fast; and
- The many exceptions for products of greater interest to developing countries, so that they have to develop exports outside their comparative advantage.

(Kol and Winters 2004: 7)

Therefore, Kol and Winters believe that 'SDT could be given a more constructive role and be genuinely pro-development' (2004: 7). In short, they argue that there is a need to 'recast SDT' (2004: 8).

Kol and Winters offer many suggestions in this direction but the core one is reform of EU's Common Agricultural Policy (CAP) (2004: 15). It is estimated that EU agriculture import barriers 'deprive developing countries of annual export earnings of three times total development

[47] See generally, Subedi (2003).

aid' (ILO 2004: 82; Kol and Winters 2004: 12). Furthermore, the processing industries are protected through tariff escalation (Kol and Winters 2004: 12). Finally, EU surpluses are dumped in Third World markets affecting the producer in the poor world and threatening its food security.

While the reform of CAP (and US subsidies) is an urgent necessity, it is difficult to endorse the general argument that the SDT principle brings few advantages to the developing world. One reason that it does not bring sufficient advantages is that either it manifests itself as transition periods to comply with obligations (as in the TRIPs text) or the concerned obligations are cast in soft law language (e.g. Article 15 of the agreement on dumping). What is also worrisome is that the WTO AB has now legitimized the use of schemes such as the GSP as a tool of foreign policy by permitting differentiation between groups of developing countries (albeit through transparent and objective criteria) and attaching positive conditionalities thereby linking trade and non-trade issues (WTO 2004).[48] In sum, the SDT principle needs to be strengthened, and not discarded, through adopting appropriate legal provisions.

3.5 *Limits of market access and SDT reforms*

Be that as it may, simple market access (whether in the agriculture or textiles sector) and better formulation and implementation of SDT treatment will not turn the WTO into an organization that promotes the development of the Third World. It is important to remember that the WTO agreements entrench a regime of international property rights through TRIPs, TRIMs and GATS (manifested in IPRs and investor rights). These agreements, inter alia, open up developing economies to transnational financial institutions in ways that limit their autonomy to pursue independent economic policies. The process is accentuated by conditionalities prescribed by the IMF and the World Bank. The end result can be serious limits on pursuing an independent and self-reliant path of development.

In response to such an argument it is often suggested that critics of the WTO are in favour of some version of absolute sovereignty and further are unable to appreciate that cooperative arrangements are to the advantage of all. This is somewhat a baseless charge. The relocation of sovereignty from Third World State to international institutions would not be a problem if only 1) principles of deliberative democracy informed the

[48] For comment, see Bartels (2003).

negotiation of the WTO agreement; 2) reasonable benefits accrued to the developing world; and 3) the subaltern class did not bear the burden of the adjustment process necessitated by the WTO agreements. Indeed, even the vocal votaries of the contemporary globalization process (such as Bhagwati) are aware of the problems with a global international law that does not put in place rules that check the 'abuse of power' by global companies and powerful states (Bhagwati 2004: 194). In short, the demand of critics is not for rejecting multilateralism but for fair and just multilateralism.

3.6 *Which way forward? meeting adjustment costs*

What then is the way forward to realize development for all? The launch of the Doha Round as 'Development Round' is at least admission that the Uruguay Round did not deliver the promised benefits to the developing countries.[49] This has led Third World countries to stress implementation issues and demand serious concessions so far as market access for agricultural and textile products is concerned. However, few major concessions seemed to be forthcoming in the ongoing negotiations leading up to the Ministerial Conference in Hong Kong in December 2005; there is in addition the threat of the use of non-tariff barriers for protectionist ends.[50] But even greater market access for agricultural and textile products from developing countries is not, welcome as it would be, a panacea for development.[51]

There is a need to ensure space for domestic policies that help realize the objectives stated in the Preamble to the Agreement establishing the WTO; that is, 'raising standards of living, ensuring full employment and a large and steadily growing volume of real income … '. What these

[49] See 'The Multilateral Trading System: A Development Perspective: A Third World Network Report produced for the UNDP' at www.twnside.org.sg/pos.htm [accessed in November 2010].

[50] For a rosier picture on agricultural negotiations, see www.wto.org/english/tratop_e/agric_e/negoti_e.htm [accessed in November 2010]. See, however, for a realist view, WTO TN/C/5, 28 July, 2005: Report by the Chairman of the Trade Negotiations Committee to the General Council. The Chairman states that, 'I regret that the negative side of the ledger outweighs the positive', p.3. On textiles, see CUTS (2005).

[51] The results of greater market access itself may be exaggerated. As Bhagwati cautions: 'I consider many of the estimates of trade expansion and of gains from trade – produced at great expense by number crunching institutions such as the World Bank with aid of huge computable models, and then fed into the public policy domain with the aid of earnest journalists – as little more than flights of fancy in contriving flying machines' (2004: 230).

policies are will of course differ between groups of developing countries. But the focus on employment assumes particular importance because of the threat of de-industrialization that may result from the demand for greater non-agricultural market access (NAMA) to goods from developed countries (Hilary 2002; Akyuz 2005).[52] In the context of NAMA, Akyuz (2005: 2) aptly writes:

> For developing countries what matters is not one-off welfare gains or losses resulting from reallocation of existing resources, but the longer-term implications of proposed tariff cuts for capital accumulation, technical progress and productivity growth which hold the key to narrowing income gaps and catching up with richer countries. Even if there could be an instantaneous, costless adjustment to a new set of incentives allowing developing countries to fully realize the benefits of their comparative advantages as determined by their existing endowments and capabilities, an irreversible commitment to low tariffs across a whole range of sectors would carry the risk of locking them into the prevailing international division of labour.

A possible way of dealing with problems arising from 'an irreversible commitment to low tariffs' is to make a provision in WTO rules for 'developing facilitation tariff' (Lee 2004). Lee persuasively argues that WTO rules in the areas of binding tariffs need to be changed so as to allow developing countries a certain degree of flexibility. Thus, for example, a developing country should be allowed to impose additional tariffs beyond scheduled commitments to provide infant industry protection (Lee 2004: 944).[53] Even so, in other cases there is no escape from adjustment costs for which 'special programs and policies have to be considered' to, inter alia, meet problems such as 'malnourishment' and 'transitions to new jobs' (Bhagwati 2004: 234). In this regard, 'international development agencies and rich-country donors also have a role to play, particularly in financing cash-strapped governments when these policies require disbursements of funds and in ensuring that institutional support to manage the downside of openness is rapidly created' (Bhagwati 2004: 239).

[52] The text is available at www.twnside.org.sg/pos.htm [accessed in November 2010]; The Colombo Declaration. 'Ten Years is Enough – No Deal at the WTO Hong Kong Ministerial Meeting', Declaration of the Organizations, Movements and Individuals Gathered for the Asian Strategy Meeting on the World Trade Organization, Colombo, Sri Lanka, 6–7 June 2005, at http://focusweb.org/the-colombo-declaration-10-years-is-enough-no-deal-at-the-wto-hong-kong-ministerial-mee.html?Itemid=36 [accessed in November 2010]. Also see Khor (2005).

[53] For details regarding how such a rule can be made operational and stopped from being abused, see Lee 2004: 944–8.

Adjustment costs have a gender dimension that needs to be paid specific attention; gender equality, it hardly needs to be stressed, is also a fundamental norm of international law. We need to know 'as to how the costs and benefits of trade can be evenly distributed by gender, and whether trade rules and policies deepen, or, on the contrary, reduce existing gender inequalities' (tran-Nguyen and Zampetti 2004: iii). If the WTO regime does not promote gender equality then measures need to be put in place to ensure that trade promotes development of a kind that helps realize the norm of gender equality. A United Nations Conference on Trade and Development (UNCTAD) report argues that 'gender trade impact assessments (GTIA) can be used as a tool to ensure that trade policy formulation is responsive to the reality of poor women's lives' (tran-Nguyen and Zampetti 2004: 362). The GTIA is a good suggestion as long as it is not used for protectionist purposes.[54] For, after all, it is no different from the argument that, 'it is no longer possible to separate trade policy from issues such as progress on international worker's rights, economic development, and social progress' (Jordan 2001: 245).

Finally, there should not be further insistence on the liberalization of the investment and service sectors of developing countries. It is important that the developing countries do not undertake any obligations whose consequences are uncertain in terms of their development objectives. Indeed, there should be a general 'go slow' in asking developing countries to assume new obligations. It is at least one lesson that can be drawn from the outcome of the Uruguay Round.

4 Conclusions

While the subject of 'the WTO, democracy and development' is increasingly being addressed, what are mostly proposed are reforms that do not come to grips with the structural defects flowing, inter alia, from the absence of deliberative democracy in the negotiation of agreements; the entrenchment of international property rights without considering its impact on human rights; the possibility of de-industrialization of Third World countries given lowering or removal of developing country barriers; the denial of market access to export products from the developing world; the non concern with the issue of primary commodity trade; the lack of serious commitment to the SDT principle; and the absence

[54] Perhaps there is a need to provide for greater representation for women in WTO bodies and in the State-negotiating teams so that the gender issue is not neglected during the course of the negotiations and the subsequent implementation of trade agreements.

of effective participation by developing countries in the functioning of WTO or WTO-related bodies (for example, the Codex Alimentarius Commission). The reason for this state of affairs is that the maximum impact on the WTO is that of 'those countries, firms and organizations that are economically (and, it must be add, militarily) the strongest' (Helleiner 2000: 9). It is then assumed that what is good for the global capitalist class, in particular the TCC, is necessarily good for the vast majority of peoples of the developing and developed world.

To rectify the structural problems the recommendations made in this chapter to WTO Member States and civil society on the subject of 'the WTO, democracy and development' are worthy of consideration. These include:

4.1 *On the WTO and democracy*

- Amend the Vienna Convention on the Law of Treaties to eliminate the use of economic and political coercion in multilateral negotiations;
- Change the composition of negotiating teams (more women delegates and representation for old and new social movements);
- Assign a greater mandatory role to national parliaments in the negotiation and ratification of WTO agreements;
- Civil society should organize resistance to ensure that national parliaments, presently dominated by TCC factions, respond to concerns of the subaltern classes;
- Explore alternatives to the 'single undertaking' formula;
- Adopt the national deference principle as the standard of review in disputes relating to developing countries;
- The panels and AB advance hermeneutic democracy by, inter alia, taking cognizance of Third World scholarship, and in this regard the WTO secretariat supports a journal primarily devoted to publishing Third World writings on the WTO;
- Increase participation of developing countries in WTO and WTO related bodies; and
- Develop global administrative law to increase transparency and accountability in the functioning of the WTO and WTO-related bodies.

4.2 *On the WTO and development*

- Conduct a social audit of WTO agreements to map the impact on subaltern classes;

- Review the negative impact of WTO agreements on developing countries in the background of IMF and World Bank conditionalities;
- Address the problems facing developing countries' primary commodity trade;
- Ensure that international trade is not used as a tool for pursuing non-trade values;
- Take concrete steps to implement the right to development in international law;
- Recast the special and differential treatment principle in the language of 'hard law';
- Provide greater market access to the goods (agriculture, textiles, etc.) of developing countries;
- Respect the process/product distinction until some form of global democracy is embedded in the international system;
- Allow for greater movement of natural persons;
- Make employment a key goal of the WTO and provide for adjustment assistance when unemployment results from reducing trade barriers;
- Allow the imposition of a 'development facilitation tariff' aimed at infant industry protection; and
- Review and reform TRIPs, TRIMs and GATS agreements so that international property rights are balanced along with the human rights of the global poor and disadvantaged sections.

References

Action Aid. 2003. *WTO Democracy and Reform*. www.actionaid.org [Accessed in November 2010].

Akyuz, Y. 2005. *The WTO Negotiations on Industrial Tariffs: What is at Stake for Developing Countries*. Geneva: Third World Network.

Anghie, A. 2004. *Imperialism, Sovereignty and the Making of International Law*. Cambridge University Press.

Anghie, A., Chimni, B., Okafor, O. and Mickelson, K. (eds.) 2003. *The Third World and International Order: Law, Politics and Globalization*. Leiden: Martinus Nijhoff.

Archibugi, D. 2004. 'Cosmopolitan Democracy and its Critics: A Review', *European Journal of International Relations* 10(3): 437–73.

Bartels, L. 2003. 'The WTO Enabling Clause and Positive Conditionality in the European Community's GSP Program', *Journal of International Economic Law* 6: 507–32.

Bereroglu, B. 2003. *Globalization of Capital and the Nation-State*. London: Rowman & Littlefield.

Bhagwati, J. 2002. 'Afterword: The Question of Linkage', *American Journal of International Law* 96(1): 126–34.

2004. *In Defense of Globalization*. Oxford University Press.

Braithwate, J. and Drahos, P. 2000. *Global Business Regulation*. Cambridge University Press.

Cattaui, M. 2001. 'Trade Rules after Seattle: A Business Perspective', in Sampson, G. P. (ed.), *The Role of the World Trade Organization in Global Governance*. Tokyo: United Nations University Press.

Chang, H. 2003. 'Kicking Away the Ladder: The "Real" History of Free Trade', *Foreign Policy In Focus Special Report* (December).

Chimni, B. 1992. 'Political Economy of the Uruguay Round of Negotiations: A Perspective', *International Studies* April 29(2): 135–58.

1999. 'Marxism and International Law: A Contemporary Analysis', *Economic and Political Weekly* 34(6): 337–49.

2000. 'WTO and Environment: The Shrimp-Turtle and EC-Hormone Case', *Economic and Political Weekly* 35(20): 1752–61.

2002. 'WTO and Environment: The Legitimization of Unilateral Trade Sanctions', *Economic and Political Weekly* (12 January): 133–40.

2003. 'Third World Approaches to International Law: A Manifesto', in Anghie, A., Chimni, B., Mickelson, K. and Okafor, O. (eds.), *The Third World and International Order: Law, Politics and Globalization*. Dordrecht: Martinus Nijhoff Publishers.

2004. 'International Institutions Today: An Imperial Global State in the Making', *European Journal of International Law* 15(1): 1–37.

2005. 'Cooption and Resistance: Two Sides of Global Administrative Law', *IILJ Paper 2005/16*. www.iilj.org/papers/2005-16Chimni.htm [Accessed in November 2010].

Consultative Board. 2004. *The Future of the WTO: Addressing Institutional Challenges in the New Millennium*. Geneva: WTO.

CUTS. 2005. *Trade in Textiles and Clothing: Likely Problems in the New Regime*, 3/2005, New Delhi: Consumer Unity and Trust Society (CUTS).

Escobar, A. 1997. 'Anthropology and Development', *International Social Science Journal* 154: 497–515.

Esty, D. 2002. 'The World Trade Organization's Legitimacy Crisis', *World Trade Review* 1(1): 7–22.

Falk, R. and Strauss, A. 1999. 'Globalization Needs a Dose of Democracy', *International Herald Tribune*, 8 October.

Gordon, R. and Sylvester, J. 2004. 'Demonstrating Development', *Villanova University School of Law Working Paper Series No. 4*, location: Villanova University.

Habermas, J. 1987. *Theory of Communicative Action*. Vol. I. Cambridge: Polity Press.

Harris, J. 2003.'The Conflict for Power in Transnational Class Theory', *Science and Society* 67: 329–39.

Helleiner, G. 2000. *Markets, Politics and Globalization: Can the Global Economy be Civilized?* 10th Raul Prebisch Lecture, 11 December. Geneva: UNCTAD.

Hilary, J. 2002. *The Doha De-industrialization Agenda: Non-Agricultural Market Access at the WTO*. London: War on Want.

Howse, R. 2002. 'Comment: Trade Negotiations and High Politics: Drawing the Right Lessons from Seattle', in Kennedy, D. and Southwick, J. (eds.), *The Political Economy of International Trade Law: Essays in Honor of Robert E. Hudec*. Cambridge University Press.

Howse, R. and Nicolaidis, K. 2003. 'Enhancing WTO Legitimacy: Constitutionalization or Global Subsidiarity?', in Verweij, M. and Josling, T. (eds.), *Deliberately Democratizing Multilateral Organization. A Special Issue of Governance*, 16(1): 73–94.

ICC (International Chamber of Commerce). 2003. *Business and the Global Economy: ICC statement on behalf of World Business to the Heads of State and Government attending the Sea Island Islamic Summit*, 8–10 June.

2005. *World Business and Multilateral Trading System: ICC Policy Recommendations for Sixth Ministerial Conference of the World Trade Organization*, Hong Kong, 13–18 December.

ILO (International Labour Organization). 2004. *A Fair Globalization: Creating Opportunities for All*. Geneva: ILO.

Jackson, J. 1992. 'States of Treaties in Domestic Legal Systems: A Policy Analysis', *American Journal of International Law* 86(2): 310–40.

2002. 'Afterword: The Question of Linkage – Comments on Five Texts', *American Journal of International Law* 96(1): 118–25.

Jordan, B. 2001. 'Building a WTO that Can Contribute Effectively to Economic and Social Development Worldwide', in Sampson, G. (ed.), *The Role of the World Trade Organization in Global Governance*. Tokyo: United Nations University Press.

Khor, M. 2005. 'Our Industrial Future Hinges on WTO Talks', *Global Trends*. www.twnside.org.sg/title2/gtrends47.htm [Accessed in November 2010].

Kingsbury, B., Krisch, N. and Stewart, R. 2004. 'The Emergence of Global Administrative Law', *IILJ Working Paper 2004/1*. www.iilj.org/papers/2004/2004.1.htm [Accessed in November 2010].

Kol, J. and Winters, A. 2004. 'The EU after Cancún: Can the Leopard Change its Spots?' *European Foreign Affairs Review* 9: 1–25.

Krajewski, M. 2001. 'Democratic Legitimacy and Constitutional Perspectives of WTO Law', *Journal of World Trade* 35(1): 167–86.

Kysar, D. 2004. 'Preferences for Process: The Process/Product Distinction and the Regulation of Consumer Choice', *Harvard Law Review* 118(3): 525–624.

Lauterpacht, H. 1978. *International Law: Being the Collected Papers of Hersch Lauterpacht*. Vol. IV. Cambridge University Press.

Lee, Y. 2004. 'Facilitating Development in the World Trading System: A Proposal for Development Facilitation Tariff (DTF) and Development Facilitation Subsidy (DFS)', *Journal of World Trade* 38: 935–54.

Lundberg, M. and Squire, L. 1999. *The Simultaneous Evolution of Growth and Inequality*. Washington, DC: World Bank.

Marks, S. 2000. *The Riddle of All Constitutions: International Law Democracy, and the Critique of Ideology*. Oxford University Press.

2004. 'The Human Right to Development: Between Rhetoric and Reality', *Harvard Human Rights Journal* (Spring) 17: 137–68.

Mohammed, E. 2005. 'The Road from TRIPs-Minus to TRIPs, to TRIPs-Plus Implications of IPRs for the Arab World', *Journal of World Intellectual Property* 8(1): 53–65.

Nye Jr., J., Einhorn, J. and Kadar, B. 2003. *The Democracy Deficit in the Global Economy: Enhancing the Legitimacy and Accountability of Global Institutions*. Washington, DC: The Trilateral Commission.

Ostry, S. 2002. 'The Uruguay Round North-South Grand Bargain: Implications for Future Negotiations', in Kennedy, D. L. and Southwick, J. (eds.), *The Political Economy of International Trade Law: Essays in Honor of Robert E. Hudec*. Cambridge University Press.

Panitch, L. and Gindin, S. 2005. 'Finance and American Empire', *Socialist Register* 2005, London: Merlin Press, pp: 46–81.

Poulantzas, N. 1975. *Classes in Contemporary Capitalism*. London: New Left Books.

Rajagopal, B. 2003. 'International Law and Social Movements: Challenges of Theorizing Resistance', *Columbia Journal of Transnational Law* 41(2): 409.

Robinson, W. and Harris, J. 2000. 'Towards a Global Ruling Class? Globalization and the Transnational Capitalist Class', *Science and Society* 64(1): 11–54.

Saul, J. 2004. 'Globalization, Imperialism, Development: False Binaries and Radical Resolutions', in Panitch, L. and Leys, C. (eds.), *Socialist Register: The New Imperial Challenge*. London: The Merlin Press, Monthly Review Press, Fernwood Publishing, pp. 203–44.

Sengupta, A. 2000. 'Realizing the Right to Development', *Development and Change* 31(3): 553–78.

Shaffer, G. 2005. 'Power, Governance and the WTO: A Comparative Institutional Approach', in Barnett, M. and Duvall, B. (eds.), *Power and Global Governance*. Cambridge University Press, pp. 130–61.

2006. 'The Challenge of WTO Law: Strategies for Developing Country Adaptation', *World Trade Review* 5(2): 177–98.

Shaffer, G. and Apea, Y. 2005. 'Institutional Choice in the Generalized System of Preferences Case: Who Decides the Conditions for Trade Preferences? The Law and Politics of Right', *Journal of World Trade* 39(5): 977–1008.

Sklair, L. 2000. *The Transnational Capitalist Class*. Oxford: Blackwell.

South Centre. 2001. *WTO Decision-Making and Developing Countries*. Working Paper 11. Geneva: South Centre.

Steinberg, J. and Mazarr, M. 2003. *Developing Country Participation in Transnational Decision Making: Lessons for IT Governance*. www.goodgovernancebd.org/link/Good%20governance%20studies/Articles%20from%20Internet/Governance%20in%20developing%20countries%206/lessons_it_governance.pdf [Accessed in November 2010].

Stokes, D. 2005. 'The Heart of Empire? Theorising US Empire in an Era of Transnational Capitalism', *Third World Quarterly* 26(2): 217–36.

Strauss, A. 2005. 'Taking Democracy Global: Assessing the Benefits and Challenges of a Global Parliamentary Assembly', *One World Trust Pamphlet Series*. London: One World Trust.

Subedi, S. 2003. 'The Road from Doha: The Issues for the Development Round of the WTO and the Future of International Trade', *International and Comparative Law Quarterly* 52(2): 425–46.

tran-Nguyen, A. and Zampetti, A. (eds.) 2004. *Trade and Gender: Opportunities and Challenges for Developing Countries*. New York: United Nations.

Upadhya, C. 2004. 'A New Testament Capitalist Class? Capital Flows, Business Networks and Entrepreneurs in the Indian Software Industry', *Economic and Political Weekly* 27 November.

VENRO. 2004. *Trade: A Driving Force in Combating Poverty?* Bonn: Verband Entwicklungspolitik deutscher Nichtregierungsorganisationen (VENRO).

Weiss, F. 2002. 'WTO Decision Making: Is it Reformable?', in Kennedy, D. and Southwick, J. (eds.), *The Political Economy of International Trade Law: Essays in Honor of Robert E. Hudec*. Cambridge University Press.

WTO (World Trade Organization). 1994. *The Results of the Uruguay Round of Multilateral Trade Negotiations*. Geneva: WTO.

1998. *Appellate Body Report, United States – Import Prohibition of Certain Shrimp and Shrimp Products*. WT/DS58/AB/R. 12 October. Geneva: WTO.

2004. *European Communities – Conditions for the Granting of Tariff Preferences to Developing Countries*. WT/DS246/AB/R. 7 April. Geneva: WTO.

Zimmerman, T. 2005. 'A WTO Dispute Settlement at Ten: Evolution, Experiences, and Evaluation', *Aussenwirtschaft – The Swiss Review of International Economic Relations* 60(1): 27–61.

11

Reclaiming development in the world trading system (revisited): proposals for reform of WTO governance

YONG-SHIK LEE

In a world where the vast majority of nations are developing countries and a significant portion of the world population still suffers from crushing poverty, economic development is one of the most important global issues. The importance of international trade for successful economic development, as shown in the cases of South Korea, Taiwan, Singapore, Hong Kong, and, more recently, China, has been well documented (World Bank 1993; Findlay 1984; Krueger 1984; Helleiner 1992 and Srinivasan 2001),[1] and it is essential that the international governance and regulatory framework for international trade is structured in a way that facilitates, rather than hampers, the economic development of developing countries.

The World Trade Organization (WTO) is the most comprehensive international governance and regulatory framework for international trade.[2] Currently, the WTO's 153 Members include all major economies and trading nations, except perhaps Russia. WTO rules outline the fundamental legal principles that govern conduct on international trade and all WTO legal disciplines are mandatory for Members.[3] The WTO dispute settlement body adjudicates trade dispute cases brought up by a Member State and rule

Yong-Shik Lee is Director and Professorial Fellow of the Law and Development Institute and Editor-in-Chief of the *Law and Development Review*. Earlier versions of this chapter were published in *Asper Review of International Business and Trade Law*, 2006 (6): 177–208; *Reclaiming Development in the World Trading System*, New York: Cambridge University Press, 2006, 2009; *Economic Development through World Trade: A Developing World Perspective*, The Hague: Kluwer Law International, 2008: pp. 3–32; *Developing Countries in the WTO Legal System*, New York: Oxford University Press, 2009: pp. 291–319.

1 Also see Amsden 1989, 2007 and Wade 2003.

2 The WTO was established in 1994 by the Marrakesh Agreement Establishing the World Trade Organization succeeding the earlier GATT regime, which had been evolving since 1947. See WTO 1994a (hereinafter referred to as the WTO Agreement).

3 The WTO Agreement, Articles 14:4–5.

violations alleged to be committed by another. Various report mechanisms of the WTO also monitor conduct of Member States on international trade and ensure their compliance with WTO disciplines. Thus, the WTO has become the 'United Nations' of international trade and its rules constitute an international law of trade that can be specifically enforced.[4]

This chapter reviews the current governance system in the WTO, as well as WTO disciplines, and assesses whether they are structured adequately to support and facilitate the economic development of developing countries. Given the significant impact that the rules on international trade have on economic development, relevant trade rules should facilitate, not inhibit, the adoption of effective economic development policies. This chapter offers a series of proposals to close gaps between the current arrangements and those needed to facilitate economic development. The WTO may not be a development institution per se: its primary objective is to create and maintain an integrated, more viable and durable multilateral trading system (WTO 1994a: Preamble, para. 5). The WTO also acknowledges the importance of international trade for the economic development of developing countries and recognizes the 'need for positive efforts designed to ensure that developing countries, especially the least developed among them, secure a share in the growth in international trade commensurate with the needs of their economic development' (WTO 1994a: para. 2). Also, the core agenda of the current WTO trade negotiation round, the Doha Round – also known as the Doha Development Agenda (DDA) – is the facilitation of development.[5]

1 Reclaiming development in WTO governance

1.1 The WTO's institutional arrangements for developing countries

The major organizational body with a mandate to address trade and development within the WTO is the Committee on Trade and Development (CTD), which reports to the General Council. The CTD is also mandated to address related issues, such as the implementation of preferential provisions for developing countries, guidelines for technical cooperation, increased participation of developing countries in the trading system,

[4] WTO disciplines are included in the WTO Agreement and its Annexes.

[5] For a detailed description of the DDA, see www.wto.org/english/tratop_e/dda_e/dda_e.htm [accessed in November 2010].

least developed countries (LDCs) issues, notifications of Generalized System of Preferences (GSP) programmes, and preferential trade arrangements among developing countries. In addition, a Subcommittee on Least Developed Countries is mandated to look specifically at issues of particular importance to LDCs. This Subcommittee also monitors the work of the Integrated Framework for Trade-Related Technical Assistance to Least Developed Countries.

At present, WTO assistance to developing countries focuses on capacity-building. In this area, the WTO Secretariat primarily offers assistance through its Training and Technical Cooperation Institute. Assistance includes legal advice to some developing countries, regular training sessions on trade policy in Geneva, and the organization of approximately 400 technical cooperation activities annually, compromising both seminars and workshops in developing countries and courses in Geneva.[6] These capacity-building activities are undoubtedly helpful to developing countries, but the scope of the WTO's activities for developing countries must go well beyond these efforts. Already, the WTO's initiative on Aid for Trade, launched in 2005, is an important step in the right direction. The initiative aims to help developing countries, and LDCs in particular, to develop trade-related skills and infrastructure needed to implement and benefit from the WTO agreements and to expand trade.[7] Beyond technical cooperation activities, the WTO needs to better address other essential issues for trade and development, such as technology transfer, financial mechanisms and debt relief.

However, the CTD's mandate is too limited to address these other key issues and has spurred calls for the WTO to take a more systematic

[6] For legal assistance, thirty-two WTO Members created an Advisory Centre on WTO Law in 2001. Its Members consist of countries contributing funding and those receiving legal advice. LDCs are automatically eligible for advice, while other developing countries and transition economies have to be fee-paying Members. For further information see http://www.acwl.ch/e/index.html/ [accessed in November 2010]. In addition, the WTO Reference Centres programme was initiated in 1997 with the objective of creating a network of computerized information centres in LDCs and developing countries. The International Trade Centre (ITC), a joint body with UNCTAD, also helps developing countries to expand exports and to improve their import operations. For more information on ITC and the WTO Reference Centres programme, see www.intracen.org/ [accessed in November 2010] and www.wto.org/english/tratop_e/devel_e/train_e/ref_centres_e.htm [accessed on 1 November 2010].

[7] For more information, see www.wto.org/english/tratop_e/devel_e/a4t_e/aid4trade_e.htm [accessed in November 2010].

approach to development, including the Doha Round. The developing countries' call for a new Round to address development resonated widely. A 2004 United Nations Report on the Implementation of the UN Millennium Declaration emphasized, for instance, the responsibility of developed countries to meet development goals, stating specifically that developed countries must fulfil their responsibilities 'by increasing and improving development assistance, concluding a new development-oriented trade round, embracing wider and deeper debt relief and fostering technology transfer' (UN 2004: para. 43). In response to this demand, the new DDA includes a series of development issues in its agenda. In addition, the DDA established two working groups: one on Trade, Debt and Finance, and the other on Trade and Transfer of Technology (WTO 2001).[8] It also calls for the CTD to meet in special sessions to handle negotiations related to special and differential treatment (SDT) under the DDA.

1.2 Case for a WTO Council for Trade and Development

The WTO's current organizational apparatus for development issues is insufficient to address complex and long-term development issues on trade and development. To strengthen the WTO's organizational apparatus, the Committee on Trade and Development should be elevated to full Council status.

The need for such an institutional elevation can be explained by comparison with the organizational arrangements for trade-related aspects of intellectual property rights, promoted by developed countries. While trade and development issues concern the vast majority of WTO Members, a relatively limited number of countries promoted intellectual property rights in the Uruguay Round negotiations. Nonetheless, the importance of intellectual property rights was emphasized during the negotiations, and a full Council (not a Committee) and a separate Agreement (the Agreement on Trade-Related Aspects of Intellectual Property Rights, or TRIPs) were established to address complex and long-term intellectual property issues in the WTO.[9]

As mentioned, trade and development issues are of concern to a vast number of developing countries and there is consensus in the WTO, as

[8] Including technical cooperation and capacity-building; LDCs; and special and differential treatment.

[9] The Council for Trade-Related Aspects of Intellectual Property Rights is organized under Article 4 of the WTO Agreement.

reflected in the current Round, that these issues should be addressed within the Organization. If these trade and development issues are considered as important as the TRIPs Agreement, which was promoted by a small number of developed countries, it is justified that they should be accorded the same institutional attention and weight by elevating the present Trade and Development Committee to full Council status. This proposed institutional reform would help resolve the long-standing concern that trade and development issues have not received due attention (WTO and International Institute for Sustainable Development 1999), and would make a statement about the essential importance of development issues. The suggested elevation would also address the practical need to upgrade the present working groups on trade, debt and finance, and trade and technology transfer. Separate committees, rather than limited subcommittees, will be necessary to incorporate these complex and important issues as part of the core working agenda of the WTO. To oversee the effective operation of these committees, a separate council would need to be established within the WTO.

In addition, given that individual developing countries face unique problems resulting from increased participation in the WTO and securing full benefits of Membership, an additional committee is necessary to bring more effective institutional attention to the needs of developing countries on an individual-country basis. The Advisory Centre on WTO Law, which is currently an independent intergovernmental organization, could be expanded, and incorporated into this Committee to render legal advice to developing country Members.

In summary, the inadequate organizational status has exacerbated both the problem of insufficient institutional attention at the WTO to development issues and widespread perception that the WTO represents the interests of developed countries and multinational corporations, rather than those of its majority members: developing countries. Establishing a new Council on Trade and Development could help address this problem by providing a more appropriate organizational apparatus for addressing development with a broader mandate for discussion of all necessary trade issues and measures relevant to the range of complex and long-term issues of development.

1.3 Role of the proposed Council for Trade and Development

The primary objective of the new Trade and Development Council would be to establish a development agenda for the WTO and promote development interests in the multilateral trading system. Its role could include:

- Promoting a development agenda and implementation of trade-related development assistance policies;
- Monitoring regulatory developments relevant to developing countries; and
- Establishing and supervising subcommittees to address specific development issues.

1.3.1 Implementation of development policies and assistance

The proposed Trade and Development Council should support a regulatory environment in the trading system that allows and facilitates the implementation of effective development policies by developing country Members. To this end, the Council should on a regular basis identify problems and gaps in the current trading system in facilitating development and, accordingly, set a trade and development agenda. This agenda may be discussed at the Ministerial Conferences and in trade negotiations to develop a more development-supportive regulatory system, including modifying relevant rules when necessary. In promoting a trade and development agenda, the Council may cooperate with relevant international bodies such as the United Nations Committee on Trade and Development (UNCTAD) and the United Nations Industrial Development Organization (UNIDO). Through such cooperation, the trade and development agenda set by the WTO would be promoted and coordinated more effectively and consistently.

In addition, a reporting mechanism should be devised for developed country Members and participating developing country Members to file a mandatory Trade-Related Development Assistance Report (TDAR) on a regular basis. This report would relay those Members' activities that are in compliance with the trade and development agenda set by the Council. The Council should examine TDARs regularly and consult with relevant Members to discuss their development assistance activities. The Council could agree on specific commitments to be fulfilled by the developed country WTO Members and participating developing country Members to promote the trade and development agenda, and the Council may further examine, within a certain time period, whether these commitments are being met.

Notably, at present, enforceability of developed country commitments to assist developing countries is weak. Not only are many of the provisions non-binding, few developing countries have the economic or political leverage to force compliance by developed countries. That said, since the creation of the WTO, developed country Members have complied with many of the specific obligations to assist developing countries, despite developing countries lacking the means, beyond exhortation, to impose pressures on them to do so. Thus, the Council's work would help developing countries create further pressure for progress in this respect.

1.3.2 Regulatory monitoring

The Trade and Development Council could also monitor compliance with WTO provisions on development assistance, including the existing provisions for special and differential treatment in favour of developing countries (SDT provisions),[10] GATT Articles[11] 36–38, and the pro-development provisions proposed in the following section of this chapter. A portion of this monitoring could be incorporated in the aforementioned Trade-Related Development Assistance Report. Violations of such provisions should be reported to the Council if the violations are detrimental to the trade interests of developing country Members. The Council may subsequently consult with the violating Member to seek a resolution.

The TDAR could also monitor the commitments of developed country Members to developing countries in GATT Article 37. Compliance with these commitments may require a broader policy adjustment by the developed country Member, which may necessitate monitoring by the Council. The Council should publish an annual report on compliance with these development assistance provisions and provide monitoring of any systematic compliance failure. The Council may also include issues of compliance failure in the trade and development agenda with an eye to possible modification of rules.

1.3.3 Establishing and supervising WTO committees

The Council may also establish standing or ad hoc committees to address specific issues of trade and development that require long-term attention, such as technological transfer among developed and developing country Members. There should be at least one committee specifically devoted to the problems of LDCs and another to assist with building the capacities of developing countries to participate fully in the trading system and realize

[10] See section 2.1.4 below.

[11] The old GATT Articles have been incorporated in the WTO Agreement in Annex 1A: Multilateral Trade Agreements in Goods.

its benefits (such as through Aid for Trade). Greater assistance should also be provided to developing country Members involved in costly and time-consuming trade disputes. As alluded to above, consideration should also be given to whether it would better serve the needs of developing country Members to assign the function of the existing WTO Advisory Centre to a committee under the proposed Council for Trade and Development. In either case, the current WTO Advisory Centre needs to be expanded with additional resources, which should be sufficient to assist every developing country Member in need of support with respect to the panel or Appellate Body proceedings.

2 Reclaiming development in WTO disciplines

2.1 Current WTO rules to aid developing countries and their limitations

Just as the current governance structure in the WTO is inadequate to address development, current WTO disciplines are also ineffective to promote development interests and, in some important areas, inhibit the adoption of effective development policies. This section examines the inadequacy of the current rules and makes proposals for reform.

The major development assistance provisions in WTO disciplines include GATT Articles XVIII, 36–38, the Enabling Clause, and SDT provisions in various WTO Agreements. Part IV of GATT (Articles 36–38), entitled 'Trade and Development', also provides a set of provisions attempting to assist economic development.

2.1.1 GATT Article 18

Article 18 of GATT, entitled 'Governmental Assistance to Economic Development',[12] facilitates the establishment of industries by authorizing relevant trade measures such as tariff protection to promote domestic industries in the early stages of development.[13] The Article gives developing countries space to pursue infant industry protection policies by authorizing them to maintain a flexible tariff structure (e.g. to

[12] See WTO 1994b (hereinafter referred to as the GATT).

[13] Friedrich List is widely known as the father of infant industry promotion, which was proposed in his famous work of 1841, *The National System of Political Economy*.

offer increased tariff protection for infant industries by modifying their Schedule of Concessions). Article 18 also acknowledges the need for trade measures for balance of payment (BOP) purposes.[14]

To modify the Schedule of Concessions, WTO Members are required to negotiate with those Members with which the relevant concession was initially negotiated (paragraph 7(a) of Section A). Such modifications may require a compensatory measure by the modifying Member. If an agreement is not reached within sixty days after the WTO is notified of the modification, the Member may still unilaterally modify the concession in question. This can occur only on the condition that WTO Members agree that the compensatory adjustment offered by the modifying Member is adequate and that every effort was made to reach an agreement (GATT Article 18.7(b)). In addition, the modifying Member must give effect to the compensatory adjustment at the same time as the modification (GATT Article 18.7(b)). However, if the WTO finds that the compensatory adjustment offer is not adequate, other Members with a considerable interest are free to adopt retaliatory measures by modifying or withdrawing substantially equivalent concessions against the modifying Member (GATT Article 18.7(b)).

However, the requirement of consultations and negotiations may cause considerable delays in implementing trade measures for development purposes. The requirement of reciprocal concessions (compensation) may also impose a burden on the economy of the modifying developing country. While the effectiveness of infant industry facilitation policies has been questioned in economic circles, the cases of recent development history indicate that the facilitation of industry by government has contributed to successful economic development.[15] In short, the provisions of Article 18 can play a positive role in assisting economic development, but the requirements of negotiations and compensation may diminish the effectiveness.

[14] Section B of GATT Article 18 authorizes BOP measures for development purposes. Paragraph 8 of the Article provides, 'The contracting parties recognize that contracting parties coming within the scope of paragraph 4(a) of this Article [i.e. developing countries in the early stages of development] tend, when they are in rapid process of development, to experience balance of payment difficulties arising mainly from efforts to expand their internal markets as well as from the instability in their terms of trade' (explanation added).

[15] For more discussion on this point, see Lee (2009).

2.1.2 GATT Articles 36–38

The provisions in GATT Articles 36–38 set out an array of measures, commitments, and collaborations on the part of developed countries and the WTO in support of economic development.

GATT Article 36 addresses the vital role of export earnings in economic development; the possible authorization of special measures to promote trade and development; the need for more favourable and acceptable conditions of access to world markets for primary products (on which many developing countries depend); the need to diversify the economic structure in developing countries and to avoid excessive dependence on the export of primary products; and the important relationship between trade and financial assistance for development (GATT Article 36). The Article also clarifies that there should be no expectation of reciprocity by developed countries for commitments made by them in trade negotiations to reduce or remove tariffs and other trade barriers for developing country WTO Members (GATT Article 36.8).

GATT Article 37[16] elaborates the commitment of developed country Members to assist developing countries with economic development, including according high priority to the reduction and elimination of import barriers to products of particular export interest to developing Members; refraining from introducing or increasing import barriers to such products (GATT Article 37.1(b)); and according high priority to the reduction and elimination of policies specifically applicable to primary products wholly or mainly produced in developing countries, which hamper the growth of consumption of those products (GATT Article 37.1(c)). When developed country governments directly or indirectly determine the resale price of products wholly or mainly produced in developing country Members, they are required to make efforts to maintain trade margins for developing countries at equitable levels (GATT Article 37.3(a)). Article 37 also obliges developed countries to adopt measures that provide a greater scope for the development of imports from those developing countries (GATT Article 37.3(b)). Special regard is also to be given to the trade interests of developing countries in the

[16] Also with respect to this commitment, Article 37.1 provides: 'The developed contracting parties shall to the fullest extent possible – that is, except when compelling reasons, which may include legal reasons, make it impossible – give effect to the following provisions.' This provision allows developed countries to avoid this commitment by, for instance, legislating for import restraints from developing countries.

application of trade measures against imports (paragraph 3). Article 38 calls for joint action and an institutional effort by the WTO to assist developing countries.

Critics have argued that the provisions of Articles 36–38 are declaratory rather than obligatory since they are not enforceable by effective sanctions. Article 37 excuses developed country Members from the various commitments set out in the Article for 'compelling reasons', which may include domestic legal obligations, thus further weakening the effectiveness of these provisions (GATT Article 37.1). Developed countries may, for example, avoid their 'commitments' by legislating against them. There is little evidence that the commitments under Articles 36–38 have affected the policies of developed countries in any significant way that accords more favourable treatment to developing countries.

2.1.3 Enabling clause

Provisions for assistance to developing countries were also included in the GATT Decision on *Differential and More Favourable Treatment, Reciprocity and Fuller Participation on Developing Countries*, referred to as the 'Enabling Clause' (GATT 1980). This Enabling Clause establishes the legal framework for the GSP, including the exchange of preferences among developing country Members (Para. 2(a)). It also provides for differential and preferential treatment for developing countries with respect to non-tariff measures (Para. 2(b)), as well as special treatment for LDCs (Para. 2(d)). The Enabling Clause states that developed countries should not expect reciprocity for the commitments made by them in trade concessions (Para. 5), and that they should exercise utmost restraint in seeking concessions from LDCs (Para. 6). As in the case of Articles 36–38 discussed above, the Enabling Clause is not mandatory in that there is no effective sanction against a violation of these commitments. The Enabling Clause *enables* developed countries to provide preference for developing countries, but it does not *oblige* them to do so.

2.1.4 Provisions for special and differential treatment

A number of provisions in the WTO agreements provide special and differential treatment in favour of developing countries.[17] One hundred and forty-five such provisions are scattered throughout several WTO

[17] For a review of the special and differential treatment provisions in the WTO Agreements, see WTO 2000.

agreements, understandings and GATT articles, among which twenty-two are exclusively for the benefit of LDCs. In general, kinds of special or differential treatment contained in these provisions either relax current discipline requirements for the benefit of developing countries, require special protection of the interests of developing countries, or give more compliance time for developing countries (transitional periods).

Currently, however, this special and differential treatment (SDT) is not sufficient to meet the development needs of developing countries for several reasons. First, protection is often not sufficient. For instance, Article 9.1 of the Agreement on Safeguards requires the exemption of imports originating in a developing country from safeguards where the portion of such imports does not exceed 3 per cent, provided that the collective share of imports from all such developing country Members (under 3 per cent) accounts for no more than 9 per cent (WTO 1994c). Article 9.2 of the Agreement on Safeguards allows developing country Members to apply safeguards for an additional two years beyond the maximum duration and to re-apply safeguards to the same product after shortened intervals. Critics have argued that the ceilings (the individual 3 per cent and collective 9 per cent) are too low, and the small extensions are not helpful for developing countries (Mah 2001). Similarly, these provisions do not substantially relieve developing countries of the requirements of WTO disciplines or give substantial protection in the areas where their trade interests are significantly affected, such as tariff bindings, subsidies and anti-dumping rules.

Transition periods for developing countries are not very helpful either. After a stipulated period for transition, this benefit is lost, while the need for development that may justify the SDT may remain. Where permanent exceptions are given, the number of beneficiary developing countries is often too limited – e.g. where exemptions are allowed in subsidy rules to permit export subsidies, only a handful of LDCs benefit from this exemption on a permanent basis.[18] In addition, current SDT does not provide differentiated treatment to developing countries of a widely different development status other than LDCs (Hart and Dymond 2003: 395–409).

[18] For instance, only LDCs are exempted from the prohibition of export subsidies. See section 2.2.3 below for a relevant discussion.

2.2 *Reform proposals*

2.2.1 An Agreement on Development Facilitation

As discussed in the preceding section, the current rules are inadequate to facilitate economic development. Substantively, permanent SDT should be given to developing countries in the areas that affect economic development such as tariff bindings, subsidies, anti-dumping, trade-related intellectual property rights and trade-related investment measures. In addition, provisions offering SDT to developing countries are scattered throughout various WTO disciplines without any coherent regulatory standard. A separate agreement, which provides a coherent standard to determine which developing country Members benefit from certain SDT and set out underlying principles providing it, will meet the need for a coherent structure. This agreement may be termed 'The Agreement on Development Facilitation'.

Under the current system, developing country status is self-declaratory and the absence of a definition for developing country Members seems to create regulatory ambiguity (Cui 2008). In addition, the current system provides the same level of SDT to developing country Members with widely different stages of development and economic needs. The Agreement on Development Facilitation should provide a definition for what constitutes a developing country Member, as well as differentiate SDT for developing country Members, with the treatment depending on the Member's state of development and economic needs, so as to enhance the clarity and rationality of the system.[19] The Agreement on Development Facilitation may also include substantive, permanent SDT provisions as suggested in the remainder of this section.[20]

[19] What standard can be adopted to determine developing country status? For one, individual income levels can be considered. The World Bank uses gross national income (GNI) per capita to categorize nations into different income groups. This economic indicator can be used as a primary determinant for the development status. Methods for differentiating SDT for different developing country members should also be sought, and the subcategorization of developing country Members, such as the one used by the World Bank, can be adopted for such differentiation. For instance, Article 9.2 of the Agreement on Safeguards authorizes a longer duration of a safeguard measure to be applied by a developing country Member. This additional duration can be differentiated in accordance with the developed status of the particular developing country Member (perhaps extended for poorer developing countries and shortened for richer ones) identified by the subcategorization discussed earlier.

[20] Developed country Members were rather reluctant to provide extensive SDT, while developing country Members insisted on such treatment. Some types of SDT simply buy

2.2.2 Adjustment to tariff bindings[21]

The WTO system requires Members to maintain their tariff commitments in the form of bindings stipulated in the Schedule of Concessions (GATT Article 2). While this principle provides essential stability to the international trading system, the tariff commitments remove the ability of developing countries to use trade protection to facilitate their industries at early stages of development (infant industries). There is considerable debate on the validity of infant industry promotion policies. Nonetheless, a recent study recognizes that fundamental economic restructuring seldom takes place in the absence of governmental intervention (Rodrik 2004: 15), and the case for state-supported industrial facilitation has already been made in certain literature (Lee 2004: 938–9). Regardless of the debate, a developing country should be allowed to choose policies that are best suited for its own development, fully considering the ramifications of the proposed tariff increases. If it determines that its industrial promotion policy demands tariff increases, its previous tariff commitments should not tie its hands. The provisions of GATT Article 18 allow modification of the schedule to aid the facilitation of infant industries, but these provisions require Members to undergo potentially time-consuming and complicated negotiations with other interested Members prior to the application of higher tariffs. Thus, more flexible treatment should be available to developing countries with respect to the possibility of modifying tariff commitments, to facilitate industries for economic development.[22]

developing country Members more time to comply with WTO obligations, while others provide permanent preferential treatment. The reluctance on the part of developed country Members to provide extensive SDT may represent their preference for 'one rule for all nations'. In other words, eventually one rule should apply to all trading nations, both developed and developing, and SDT that offers temporary preferences should not be extended in time. In addition, SDT that offers a permanent preference to a limited number of developing country Members, such as LDCs, should not be expanded to benefit more developing country Members. It would be necessary to reconsider whether this one-rule policy is justifiable. If the development needs of developing country Members justify preferential treatment in the first place, then this treatment *should not expire* until they attain developed status, and therefore, this one-rule policy is not tenable from the perspective of economic development.

[21] Proposal to adjust binding concessions to facilitate development was first made in Lee (2004).

[22] Arguably, the need for tariff protection should have been contemplated by developing countries when they agreed to specific tariff bindings in the multilateral trade negotiations. Nonetheless, their economic needs and national goals may have changed following political shifts (e.g. election of a new government, end of a dictatorship, etc.), and

This additional tariff applied for the purpose of infant industry promotion could be called a 'Development-Facilitation Tariff'.[23] In brief, the Development-Facilitation Tariff would allow a developing country to apply tariff rates above the scheduled commitments unilaterally when the country can demonstrate a development need for such a tariff and have a concrete plan for industrial facilitation. The application of a Development-Facilitation Tariff should require procedural safeguards to minimize the possibility of abuse. Safeguards could include a formal investigation and hearing requirement, notices to other interested Members, consultations, and a maximum duration for its application. The maximum applicable rate of the Development-Facilitation Tariff should also be systematically differentiated according to the development stage of a developing country, as determined by the level of its per capita income.[24] For example, the maximum Development-Facilitation Tariff rate applicable by wealthier developing countries should be lower than that of less affluent developing countries.[25]

Some may argue that the introduction of a Development-Facilitation Tariff in the world trading system will undermine the import concessions made by developing countries and disrupt the balance of concessions achieved through trade negotiations. While these concessions are important, the need for economic development should be given priority. The impact of a Development-Facilitation Tariff on world trade will be rather limited since the majority of world trade is conducted among developed economies and would thus not be subject to Development-Facilitation Tariff applications.[26] In addition, due to demands by developed countries with more powerful economies, developing countries with limited negotiating power are often compelled to make concessions beyond the levels that they are prepared to offer or accept.[27]

therefore, development initiatives may begin long after the conclusion of trade negotiations. If so, the developing country should not be prohibited from offering trade protection to its infant industry because of its previous import commitments, and it should be allowed to do so without prolonging negotiations and the burden of compensations or threat of retaliations.

23 For more details of the proposed Development-Facilitation Tariff, see Lee (2004).

24 Lee 2004: 946–7.

25 There will likely be some concern that this liberal treatment may lead to rampant protectionism by developing countries without either a genuine need or a constructive plan for infant industry promotion. The procedural safeguards introduced above counter this possibility of abuse.

26 Organization for Economic Co-operation and Development (OECD). Stats Extracts, available at: http://stats.oecd.org.

27 For developing countries and trade negotiations, see Krueger (1999).

Consequently, where there are clear development plans that demand import protection, it would be fair to allow import restraints to meet development needs.

2.2.3 Subsidy treatment[28]

Another essential element of industrial promotion policies for economic development is the use of government subsidies. Strategically planned government subsidization has contributed to the successful development of some developing countries, such as South Korea. Under the WTO Agreement on Subsidies and Countervailing Measures (SCM Agreement), export subsidies (subsidies that are provided contingent on export performance) and import-substitution subsidies (subsidies that are contingent on the use of domestic over-imported goods) are prohibited as they have adverse effects on international trade.[29] In addition, a subsidy is 'actionable' (i.e. another country may retaliate against the subsidy with countermeasures) when certain conditions are met.[30] Countervailing duties, which are additional tariffs imposed on imports to offset the effects of subsidies,[31] are also an applicable remedy where subsidization causes or threatens material injury to an established domestic industry or materially retards the establishment of a domestic industry (GATT Article 6.6).

These WTO subsidy provisions reduce the ability of developing countries to provide support to promote their industries in the early stages of development.[32] Infant industries in developing economies often need

[28] The proposals in this section were first offered in Lee (2004: 948–53).

[29] See WTO 1994d (hereinafter referred to as the SCM Agreement). Annex 1 of the SCM Agreement includes the illustrative list of prohibited export subsidies.

[30] These conditions are: i) the subsidy is specifically limited to an enterprise or group of enterprises, an industrial sector or group of industries, or a designed geographic region within the jurisdiction of the granting authority (specificity requirement); and ii) the subsidy causes adverse effects to the interests of other Members. Adverse effects include: a) injury (material injury) to the domestic industry of the importing country; b) nullification or impairment of benefits of bound tariff rates; or c) serious prejudice to the domestic industry. *SCM Agreement*. Ibid. Articles 2 and 5.

[31] Part 5 of the SCM Agreement (Articles 10–23) provides for substantive and procedural rules for the application of countervailing duties. According to Article 18, exporters can also avoid countervailing duties by undertaking to increase their export prices (price undertaking). This price undertaking is voluntary on the part of the exporters and the importing country may consider the acceptance of the undertaking impractical, for instance, where the number of actual or potential exporters is too great.

[32] Rodrik observes that the WTO's current subsidy rules have made 'a significant dent in the ability of developing countries to employ intelligently designed industrial policies'

export markets due to limited domestic markets. Government support is called upon to improve their competitiveness in the foreign market, as well as in their own. The SCM Agreement recognizes this and affirms, 'subsidies may play an important role in economic development programmes of developing country Members' (Article 27.1). The SCM Agreement also provides certain SDT to developing countries, i.e. LDC Members of the WTO are not prohibited from applying export subsidies (Article 27.2(a)),[33] and other developing countries are permitted to apply export subsidies for a period of eight years from the date of entry into force of the WTO Agreement in 1995, which has already expired (Article 27.2(b)). These prohibited or otherwise actionable subsidies should be allowed for developing countries if they demonstrate a need for such subsidies with a concrete development plan. Such a subsidy specially authorized to facilitate development could be called a 'Development-Facilitation Subsidy' (Lee 2004: 948–53).

As in the case of the Development-Facilitation Tariff, procedural safeguards should be provided to minimize the abuse of Development-Facilitation Subsidy applications. The maximum applicable Development-Facilitation Subsidy rate should also be differentiated in accordance with the per capita income level of developing countries. Questions may arise as to whether the availability of a Development-Facilitation Subsidy would lead to a subsidy race among developing countries, thus diminishing the effect of the subsidy for the industrial promotion of individual developing countries and causing only a distortion of resources. However, a developing country should be trusted with its own best judgement as to whether subsidization would be necessary. Many economic and political factors would affect a government decision to grant a subsidy and a prudent government would consider the existence of a subsidy and even the possibility of similar subsidies being applied by competing developing countries in the future. A developing country would subsidize those export industries that it believes have the best potential for success; the possibility of these competing subsidies will be part of that equation.

(2004: 34–5). Note that developed countries provided extensive subsidies during their development stages, which would have been either prohibited or actionable under the SCM Agreement (Chang 2002).

[33] This preference ceases to apply to any of these LDC Members when it reaches US$1,000 GNP per capita. See SCM Agreement, Annex 7.

2.2.4 The suspension of anti-dumping measures, the TRIMs Agreement and the TRIPs Agreement

Anti-dumping actions[34] that are applied against 'dumped imports' in the form of increased tariffs are the most frequently applied import measures; from 1995 to 2008, as many as 2,190 anti-dumping measures were applied (WTO 2009: 39–40). To support developing countries, the proposed Agreement on Development Facilitation could also include provisions that allow for the suspension of the use of anti-dumping measures and that authorize suspension of developing country commitments under the Trade-Related Investment Measures (TRIMs) and TRIPs Agreements.[35]

To date, developing countries have been the primary target of anti-dumping measures (WTO 2009: 30–40).[36] Economists widely question the economic justifications for anti-dumping measures. Further, the inherent complexity and arbitrariness in the determination of dumping[37] have created a breeding ground for abuse of anti-dumping actions.[38] For instance, national authorities can adopt a methodology

[34] For background on the specific determination of dumping margins and the imposition and collection of anti-dumping duties, see WTO 1994g: Articles 6.10 and 9. For the origin of anti-dumping measures, see Congressional Budget Office (1994: 18).

[35] An argument could be made that such provisions could instead be included directly in the corresponding agreements and not in the Agreement on Development Facilitation. Their regulatory placement requires further discussion. For the purpose of this chapter, the concepts are introduced to stimulate discussion of their substantive merits.

[36] However, anti-dumping measures are increasingly being applied by developing countries, notably India.

[37] Dumping is defined as the sale at a price under 'normal value' that needs to be first determined (ADP Agreement: Article 2.1). The complexity and arbitrariness in the determination of normal value are easily seen: e.g. there may not be a single home market price to compare and the complex adjusted average may have to be calculated to come up with a reference home price. The home country may not completely be a market economy (e.g. 'transitional economy'), and, therefore, the home price may not represent the true market price, or the product in question may not even be sold in the home market or too little of it is sold to be the basis of a valid home price. In all these cases, the price needs to be 'constructed' by an evaluation of cost (constructed cost) plus reasonable profit. Finding the 'export price' that is necessary to determine the existence of dumping by comparison with the home price can be equally complex since a number of adjustments to the transaction price may be necessary to keep the comparison with the home price fair. These adjustments may include complex calculations involving numerous items, such as warranty services and advertising costs (Lee 2009: 4).

[38] Depending upon the specific methodology adopted to calculate costs and average prices, the result can be vastly different, not to mention that the measure of 'reasonable profit' can also vary. In the case of the United States, for instance, the vast majority of national anti-dumping practices do not even actually identify either price discrimination or sales below cost (Lindsey 1999).

that will yield the least desirable result for foreign exporters[39] and produce finding of dumping.[40] Depending upon their choice of methodology and calculation, authorities can determine different dumping margins.

Anti-dumping measures targeting inexpensive products of developing countries pose critical impediments to the exports of many developing countries, because the competitiveness of their products is often based on low prices, reflecting lower labour costs. Although a lower price alone is not sufficient ground for the application of anti-dumping measures[41] current WTO provisions (such as those that permit the 'construction' of costs and reference prices) make it relatively easy for national authorities to find dumping and apply anti-dumping measures against low-cost exports from developing countries.

The scope for such arbitrariness in the current anti-dumping rules and its significant adverse effect on trade prompted the inclusion of anti-dumping rules as a topic for the Doha Round negotiations, with a possibility for rule modifications (WTO 2001: para. 28; Lindsey and Ikenson 2002).[42] Nonetheless, it is unlikely that the inherent arbitrariness in determining dumping will be reduced to a satisfactory level.[43] In light of the needs of developing countries, there should be the possibility for the suspension of the application of the WTO's anti-dumping provisions to developing countries. Importantly, as an alternative, safeguard measures[44] could be used where there are legitimate concerns about preda-

[39] Article 2 of the Anti-Dumping Agreement authorizes such leeway in the determination of dumping.

[40] Although the provisions of the Anti-Dumping Agreement attempt to provide disciplines on anti-dumping actions, 'in common parlance, it is usual to designate all low-cost imports as dumped imports' (International Trade Centre UNCTAD/WTO and Commonwealth Secretariat 1995: 181).

[41] Dumping should also *cause* or *threaten* material injury to the domestic industry for the application of an anti-dumping measure (GATT, Article 6.6). Unlike the serious injury standard required for the application of a safeguard measure (Agreement on Safeguards, Article 4), the threshold for material injury is not considered high.

[42] Reform proposals have been made to reduce the abuse and arbitrariness in the application of anti-dumping measures.

[43] It is because the very attempt to determine the 'normalcy' of a price in a market economy, in which prices are determined by market forces and not by any normative rules, is inherently arbitrary no matter what standard is applied. It was pointed out that '[t]he primary justification for the antidumping law is really more political than economic. The guiding precept is *legitimacy* rather than *efficiency*' (emphasis in original) (Lindsey 1999: 3).

[44] Article 2.1 of the Agreement on Safeguards sets out the general requirement for the application of a safeguard measure.

tory dumping by developing countries that results in the displacement of domestic products.[45]

Another area of WTO law that has significant relevance to the economic development and trade of developing countries is the WTO Agreement on TRIMs.[46] Foreign direct investment (FDI) may provide developing countries with resources necessary for development that they typically lack, including financial capital, technological resources, production facilities and managerial expertise. FDI can also offer employment opportunities for local populations. In accepting FDI, host developing countries may be inclined to set a series of conditions to steer FDI to maximize its contribution to their development objectives. Such measures can also have significant implications for trade. For instance, a host country may require the foreign investor to ensure that a certain portion of its exports contain domestically produced goods or services (in an attempt to promote domestic exports and reduce competition with other domestic producers). Similarly, if investment measures require foreign investors to purchase domestic products, this may reduce imports that may have occurred in the absence of such measures.

As mentioned, TRIMs are often adopted in pursuing development objectives. Although there remains some doubt as to the industrial promotion effects of TRIMs,[47] governments frequently hope to use them to promote exports and encourage the use of domestic products as one means for facilitating the growth of infant domestic industries. Notably, all of today's developed countries adopted investment measures during their own development processes (Chang and Green 2003: 33).[48] The

[45] For more discussion, see Lee (2005: section 14.2).

[46] See WTO 1994e (hereinafter referred to as the TRIMS Agreement).

[47] The criticism includes: TRIMs are economically inefficient since investment terms are controlled by investment measures rather than by market forces; the governments of the hosting countries may abuse TRIMs politically, for instance, to serve the interests of select producers that are not necessarily relevant to the needs for development; and the restrictive terms of TRIMs may also discourage investors from making investments in developing countries adopting these measures and thereby deprive the host developing countries of the opportunities to benefit from the investment that can provide necessary resources for their development. See also Lee 2009: chapter 3.1.

[48] TRIMs can be either effective or counter-effective to the development interest of a particular developing country depending upon the economic conditions and the development stage that the individual developing country is in. For instance, an imposition of a local content requirement may be unnecessary and economically inefficient at a time when the domestic industry can compete with imports. On the other hand, this particular investment measure may be useful and facilitate domestic infant industries in the initial stages of development where domestic industries require some protection. This suggests that TRIMs can be a means to facilitate development.

TRIMs Agreement seems to mainly target the investment regulations of developing countries, but there is no clear need for such multilateral control on investment. For instance, major investors are often in a position to negotiate the terms of their investment with the host developing country directly. In addition, over 2,600 bilateral investment treaties (BITs) around the world already require national treatment in favour of foreign investors and prohibit a wider range of TRIMs than those restrained by the Agreement. If a developing country is ready to give up certain TRIMs, it will do so bilaterally or unilaterally, even without any treaty obligations. However, if a developing country considers the adoption of TRIMs as necessary to meet its development objectives, then mandatory trade rules should not prohibit their adoption. The multilateral control on TRIMs should thus be removed (WTO 1999b).[49]

Lastly, the application of the TRIPs Agreement (WTO 1994f) in developing countries should be reconsidered. Access to advanced knowledge, such as new technology and production techniques, is essential to facilitating industrial development. Historically, the ability to copy technologies developed in advanced countries has been one of the most essential elements in determining the ability of developing countries to catch up (Nelson 2004). The enforcement of IPRs (intellectual property rights) in developing countries can, however, impede their capacity to acquire advanced technology. The introduction of the TRIPs Agreement into trade disciplines was one of the most important attempts to enforce IPRs around the world.

The TRIPs Agreement establishes mandatory standards for the protection of various IPRs, including copyrights, trademarks, geographical indications, industrial designs, patents and layout designs of integrated circuits, providing substantial minimum terms of protection. In addition to providing effective enforcement procedures under their own laws (Article 41), the TRIPs Agreement also requires Members to apply national treatment and most favoured nation (MFN) provisions to protect foreign IPRs (Articles 3 and 4). Rules of other major IPR conventions are also incorporated by reference in the relevant provisions of the TRIPs Agreement (Article 1).[50]

[49] Reflecting this concern, twelve countries proposed to change the text of the TRIMs Agreement to make commitments under the Agreement optional and not mandatory.

[50] The Paris Convention (1967), the Berne Convention (1971), the Rome Convention (1961) and the Treaty on Intellectual Property in Respect of Integrated Circuits (1989) are incorporated by reference.

The inclusion of the TRIPs Agreement within the international trade regime raises important concerns for developing countries and is not a desirable precedent. First, the TRIPs Agreement imposes requirements to establish a regulatory regime to protect IPRs within all WTO Member States, even those where economic and social developments do not yet embrace the concept of IPRs and whose judicial systems have not yet developed sufficiently to recognize and enforce IPRs (Chang 2002: 83–5).

Second, the imposition of an IPR regime that is too stringent may prematurely set economic and legal barriers to acquiring advanced technology for development (e.g. TRIPs requires long durations for IPR protection) and thus impede the development prospects of developing countries.[51] While the protection of IPRs can provide incentives for creativity and innovation that may contribute to economic development, developing countries cannot close the vast technological gap between their economies and those of developed countries by relying on their own 'creativity' alone[52]; they need access to advance knowledge and technology. In this respect, developing countries today face a much more stringent international IPR regime than developed countries when they were at similar phases of economic development.

That said, the trade effect of IPR violations may need to be addressed, and the need for developing countries to have access to advanced knowledge and technology does not mean that developed countries have to give up their IPR interests entirely. Rather than attempting through TRIPs to establish a uniform IPR regime throughout the world, WTO Members should limit the scope of the TRIPs Agreement to enabling developed countries to seek a trade remedy or apply trade measures where they can demonstrate that a violation of their IPR has led to significant and demonstrable injury to their trade.[53] In the meantime, the application of the

[51] In addition, concern was raised that compliance with the TRIPs Agreement will impose a considerable financial burden on developing countries, particularly LDCs. According to a study, implementing the TRIPs obligations would require 'the least developed countries to invest in buildings, equipment, training, and so forth that would cost each of them US$150 million — for many of the least developed countries this represents a full year's development budget' (Finger 2000).

[52] On the other hand, if a developing country considers that the extensive protection of IPRs is in their own interest, this country, rather than the WTO, should be trusted to set its own standards for protection in their own laws and regulations (Lee 2009).

[53] The general exceptions of GATT Article 20 already allow trade sanctions to protect IPRs. What seems necessary is to set detailed rules for the substantive and procedural requirements for the application of a trade measure to remedy injury caused by an IPR violation. A Member should be authorized to apply trade measures only where a violation of its

TRIPs Agreement to developing countries should be suspended to the extent that it imposes the establishment of an IPR regime for which they are not ready.

2.2.5 Extension of special treatment for LDCs

Some developed countries have offered preferential treatment to LDCs greater than that provided under existing GSP schemes. For instance, the European Union has introduced the 'Everything But Arms' (EBA) initiative, offering duty-free and quota-free treatment to products currently exported by LDCs.[54] Other countries, such as the United States and Canada, offer similar preferential treatment to LDCs, although less comprehensive and more limited in scope than the EBA initiative.[55] Considering the dire economic need of LDCs, an EBA-type of duty-free and quota-free treatment needs to be implemented by developed countries and participating developing countries in the WTO. A transitional period can be established for the complete removal of trade barriers to sensitive products.[56] Members would also have to ensure that non-tariff measures do not undermine the trade benefit of these preferences for LDCs.[57]

3 Conclusion

To facilitate economic development effectively in trade disciplines, it is important to examine the current institutional apparatus and

IPRs *causes injury* to its domestic industry through trade. An injury test, such as the one found in Article 4.2(a) of the Agreement on Safeguards, should be required to ensure that the measure is applied based on a reasonable assessment of injury caused by IPR violations and not on an arbitrary determination by national authorities. This way, developed countries will be able to protect their own IPR interests by applying their own laws, as well as the rules of relevant international IPR conventions, without imposing a regulatory burden on developing countries such as the one currently imposed by the TRIPs Agreement (Lee 2009).

[54] For an initial evaluation of the EBA initiative, see Brenton (2003).

[55] For instance, the United States established the *Africa Growth and Opportunity Act*, which offers improved access to certain African, but not Asian, LDCs (Brenton 2003: 644–5).

[56] In the EBA initiative, three products were exempt from liberalization: fresh bananas, rice and sugar, where tariffs will be gradually reduced to zero (in 2006 for bananas and 2009 for rice and sugar).

[57] Non-tariff measures, as well as stringent rules of origin, continue to limit exports from LDCs significantly (Inama 2002: 115). Applications of administered protection, such as anti-dumping measures, countervailing duties and safeguards, can also diminish the beneficial effect of preference for LDCs.

regulatory structure in the WTO. The current Committee on Trade and Development and the development assistance provisions scattered throughout the GATT/WTO disciplines are not sufficient to meet this objective. Regulatory and organizational reforms are thus necessary to effectively meet the development agenda and implement development assistance policies. This reform should include the elevation of the CTD to the new Council for Trade and Development and the establishment of a coherent body of rules that facilitates development (in the form of an Agreement on Development Facilitation).

On the logistical front, the proposed expansion of the WTO's current organizational apparatus would mean an expansion of staff and an increase in resources available to assist developing countries, as well as some procedural improvements. It is widely known that the limited financial and human resources of developing countries often prevent them from participating in the trade organization fully. The lack of participation by developing countries in WTO processes has often been pointed out as a reason for the poor representation of the interests of developing countries. WTO meetings and negotiation schedules should also be set to allow maximum participation of developing countries.[58] The use of modern technology, such as web technology, should be adopted to increase participation of developing countries, which cannot afford to station experts in Geneva to participate in these meetings, without having to travel from their home countries.

Financial assistance from some Members has allowed trade ministers and representatives from developing countries to participate in WTO meetings and negotiations. The financial assistance necessary to enable the participation of developing countries should not be left to the generosity of individual Members, but should rather be provided systematically through the WTO's regular budget. The Advisory Centre on WTO Law should also be supported by the WTO budget. The WTO budget allocation to the activities and functions of trade and development should be significantly increased to meet these needs.

Finally, a monitoring and enforcement mechanism for the proposed development assistance provisions should also be devised and the creation of an annual Trade-Related Development Assistance Report should

[58] Renato Ruggiero, the former Director-General of the WTO, acknowledged that some developing and least developed countries had difficulty in participating fully in the organization, mainly due to too many meetings. He believed that it was an objective problem, but not the result of a deliberate policy of exclusion (WTO and International Institute for Sustainable Development 1999).

be considered. Developed country members should be required to report regularly to the Council for Trade and Development on the development assistance they provide. The proposed organizational and regulatory reform, as well as this suggested improvement of practical logistics, would help to turn what many have doubted as merely 'rhetoric for development assistance' into real and effective actions to assist developing countries.

References

Amsden, A. 1989. *Asia's Next Giant: South Korea and Late Industrialization*. New York: Oxford University Press.

2007. *Escape from Empire: The Developing World's Journey through Heaven and Hell*. Cambridge, MA: MIT Press.

Brenton, P. 2003. 'Integrating the Least Developed Countries into the World Trading System: The Current Impact of European Union Preferences Under "Everything But Arms" ', *Journal of World Trade* 37(3): 623–46.

Chang, H. 2002. *Kicking Away the Ladder: Development Strategy in Historical Perspective*. London: Anthem Press.

Chang, H. and Green, D. 2003. *The Northern WTO Agenda on Investment: Do As We Say, Not As We Did*. South Centre/CAFOD.

Congressional Budget Office. 1994. *How the GATT Affects U.S. Antidumping and Countervailing-duty Policy*. www.cbo.gov/doc.cfm?index=4848&type=0 [Accessed in September 2010].

Cui, F. 2008. 'Who Are the Developing Countries in the WTO?' *The Law and Development Review* 1(1). www.bepress.com/ldr/vol1/iss1/art7 [Accessed in November 2010].

Findlay, R. 1984. 'Growth and Development in Trade Models', in Jones, R. and Kenen, P. (eds.), *Handbook of International Economics, Vol. I*, New York: North Holland, pp. 185–236.

Finger, J. 2000. 'The WTO's Special Burden on Less Developed Countries', *Cato Journal* 19(3): 425–37.

GATT. 1980. *Differential and More Favourable Treatment, Reciprocity and Fuller Participation on Developing Countries*, C.P. Nov. L/4903, 26th Supp. B.I.S.D.: 203.

Hart, M. and Dymond, B. 2003. 'Special and Differential Treatment and the Doha "Development" Round', *Journal of World Trade* 37(2): 395–415.

Helleiner, G. K. (ed.) 1992. *Trade Policy, Industrialization, and Development*. Oxford University Press.

Inama, S. 2002. 'Market Access for LDCs: Issues to Be Addressed', *Journal of World Trade* 36(1): 85–116.

International Trade Centre UNCTAD/WTO and Commonwealth Secretariat. 1995. *Business Guide to the Uruguay Round*. Geneva: ITC/CS.

Jones, R. and Kenen, P. (eds.) 1984. *Handbook of International Economics, Vol. I.* New York: North Holland.

Krueger, A. 1984. 'Trade Policies in Developing Countries', in Jones, R. and Kenen, P. (eds.), *Handbook of International Economics, Vol. I*, New York: North Holland, pp. 519–69.

1999. 'The Developing Countries and the Next Round of Multilateral Trade Negotiations', *The World Economy* 22(7): 909–32.

Lee, Y. 2004. 'Facilitating Development in the World Trading System: A Proposal for Development Facilitation Tariff and Development Facilitating Subsidy', *Journal of World Trade* 38(6): 935–54.

2005. *Safeguard Measures in World Trade: The Legal Analysis*, 2nd edn. The Hague: Kluwer Law International.

2009. *Reclaiming Development in the World Trading System*. New York: Cambridge University Press.

Lindsey, B. 1999. 'The U.S. Antidumping Law: Rhetoric versus Reality', *Cato Institute Trade Policy Analysis No. 7*: 16 August. www.cato.org/pub_display.php?pub_id=3650 [Accessed in September 2010].

and Ikenson, D. 2002. 'Reforming the Antidumping Agreement: A Road Map for WTO Negotiations', *Cato Institute Trade Policy Analysis No. 21*. www.cato.org/pub_display.php?pub_id=3636 [Accessed in September 2010].

List, F. 1841. *The National System of Political Economy*, trans. by Sampson S. Lloyd. London: Longmans, Green, and Co.

Mah, J. S. 2001. 'Injury and Causation in the WTO Agreement on Safeguards', *Journal of World Intellectual Property* 4(3): 380–2.

Nelson, R. 2004. 'The Changing Institutional Requirements for Technological and Economic Catch Up.' Paper presented at the DRUID Summer Conference, Industrial Dynamics, Innovation and Development. Elsinore, Denmark, 14–16 June.

Rodrik, D. 2004. *Industrial Policy for the Twenty-First Century.* Paper prepared for UNIDO, September. www.hks.harvard.edu/fs/drodrik/Research%20papers/UNIDOSep.pdf [Accessed in November 2010].

Srinivasan, T. 2001. 'Trade, Development, and Growth', *Princeton Essays in International Economics No. 225*. December.

United Nations. 2004. *Implementation of the United Nations Millennium Declaration*. UN 59th Sess., UN Doc. A/59/282 (2004). New York: United Nations.

Wade, R. 2003. *Governing the Market: Economic Theory and the Role of Government in East Asian Industrialization*. Princeton University Press.

World Bank. 1993. *The East Asian Miracle*. Oxford University Press.

World Trade Organization (WTO). 1994a. *Marrakesh Agreement Establishing the World Trade Organization*. Geneva: WTO.

1994b. *General Agreement on Tariffs and Trade*. Geneva: WTO.

1994c. *Agreement on Safeguards*. Geneva: WTO. www.wto.org/english/docs_e/legal_e/25-safeg.pdf. [Accessed in November 2010].

1994d. *The Agreement on Subsidies and Countervailing Measures*. Geneva: WTO.

1994e. *Agreement on Trade-Related Investment Measures*. Geneva: WTO. www.wto.org/english/docs_e/legal_e/18-trims.pdf [Accessed in November 2010].

1994f. *Agreement on Trade-Related Aspects of Intellectual Property Rights*. Geneva: WTO.

1994g. *Agreement on Implementation of Article 6 of the General Agreement on Tariffs and Trade*. Geneva: WTO.

1999a. *The Legal Texts: The Results of the Uruguay Round of Multilateral Trade Agreements*. Geneva: WTO.

1999b. *Preparations for the 1999 Ministerial Conference*. WT/GC/W/354. Geneva: WTO.

2000. *Implementation of Special and Differential Treatment Provisions in WTO Agreements and Decisions — Note by Secretariat*, WT/COMTD/W/77. 25 October. Geneva: WTO.

2001. Doha *Ministerial Declaration*, WT/MIN(01)/DEC/1. 20 November. Geneva: WTO.

2007. *World Trade 2006, Prospects For 2007: Risks Lie Ahead Following Stronger Trade in 2006, WTO Reports*. WTO Press Release. www.wto.org/english/news_e/pres07_e/pr472_e.htm [Accessed in September 2010].

2009. *Annual Report 2009*. Geneva: WTO.

WTO and International Institute for Sustainable Development. 1999. *Report on the WTO's High-Level Symposium on Trade and Development, 17–18 March 1999*. www.wto.org/english/tratop_e/devel_e/summhl_e.htm. [Accessed in September 2010].

12

Fostering developing country engagement in the WTO dispute settlement system: outstanding challenges and governance implications

NIALL MEAGHER

Since its inception in 1995, the dispute settlement system of the World Trade Organization (WTO) has provided WTO Members with a successful system of third-party adjudication of intergovernmental disputes. However, the success of the system is not unqualified, especially with respect to the engagement of developing and least developed countries in the system.

There is considerable debate as to whether developing countries are maximizing the opportunities to advance their trade interests provided by the system. This chapter will briefly explain the system and discuss how developing countries have made increasing use of it. It begins by describing the main features of the WTO system, how it applies to developing countries and what special treatment is available to developing countries under the system. It reviews the participation of developing countries in the system since 1995 and discusses the role the Advisory Centre on WTO Law (ACWL) has played in fostering developing and least developed country engagement in the system. The chapter summarizes the ongoing challenges facing developing countries in WTO dispute settlement proceedings, including the complexity of the process, their lack of resources, the lack of public–private sector partnerships, the disuse of alternative mechanisms and the fear of retaliation. Finally, the chapter evaluates some of the alternative mechanisms and proposals to assist developing countries in utilizing the dispute settlement system to the full

Niall Meagher is Senior Counsel at the Advisory Centre on WTO Law (ACWL), Geneva.
The views expressed in this chapter, and especially any errors, are those of the author alone. The author would like to thank Chad Bown, Carolyn Deere Birkbeck, Bonnie Galvin, Tom Prusa, Frieder Roessler and three anonymous reviewers for their comments on a draft of this chapter.

and concludes that improvements can be made both in streamlining the system itself and in increasing the capacity of developing countries to engage in the system.

1 Overview of the WTO dispute settlement system

The WTO's dispute settlement system was, like the WTO itself, created in 1995.[1] The system is the successor of the dispute settlement process of the WTO's predecessor, the General Agreement on Tariffs and Trade (GATT). Beginning in 1948, the GATT had always used a process of resolving trade disputes among its contracting parties.[2] The GATT's process emphasized diplomacy over law: it was initially referred to as a process of 'conciliation', not arbitration, and was administered by panels of experts that tended to be diplomats, not lawyers. The WTO dispute settlement process still retains some of these features, despite the 'legalization' of the process.

The main weakness of the GATT dispute settlement process was that the GATT could proceed only on the basis of consensus of all of those parties. Any contracting party could effectively block either a request by another contracting party for the establishment of a GATT panel to address a dispute, or the adoption of a report of a GATT panel resolving the dispute. The GATT's procedural rules evolved over time, but by the completion of the Uruguay Round of multilateral trade negotiations in 1994, the GATT process was not yet a fully binding or effective legal system.

The Uruguay Round led to the creation of the WTO and the adoption of, inter alia, the 'Understanding on Rules and Procedures Governing the Settlement of Disputes', more commonly known as the 'Dispute Settlement Understanding' or the 'DSU'. The DSU created the Dispute Settlement Body (referred to as the 'DSB') – consisting of a representative of each WTO Member – to administer the dispute settlement system. Under the DSU, defending Members may no longer block the establishment of a WTO dispute settlement panel or the adoption of a report of a WTO panel unless there is a 'reverse' or 'negative consensus' *not* to adopt

[1] This overview of the WTO dispute settlement system is based on that in Palmeter and Meagher (2009). A similar description may be found in Davey (2007), while a more detailed description can be found in Palmeter and Mavroidis (2004).

[2] Since the GATT was a multilateral agreement rather than an international organization, it consisted of 'contracting parties' rather than 'Members'.

the report.[3] Thus far, this 'reverse consensus' has meant the automatic establishment of panels and adoption of reports.

The other major change under the DSU was the establishment of a standing Appellate Body to which decisions of WTO panels may be appealed. WTO panels are appointed on an ad hoc basis and consist of three individuals, one of whom serves as chair. These individuals are normally present or former officials of delegations of WTO Members that are not party to the dispute, other government officials, lawyers or academics, all of whom serve in their personal capacities. In contrast, the WTO Appellate Body consists of seven individuals appointed by the DSB for four-year terms, which may be renewed once. Appellate Body members must be persons of recognized authority and demonstrated expertise in law, international trade and the subject matter of the WTO agreements. In practice, the composition of the Appellate Body has come to be determined by geography: there is always one member from the United States, one from the European Union, one from Africa, etc.

The WTO dispute settlement process is relatively complex and time-consuming. The first mandatory step consists of formal consultations between the complainant and defendant parties (although there are also usually informal consultations between the parties beforehand). The consultations phase is intended to provide the parties with a forum to resolve the dispute without recourse to a panel and, on occasion, it accomplishes this purpose (Davey 2007: 104–6). If consultations do not resolve the matter, the complaining party may, after sixty days, request the establishment of a panel. The request for the establishment of a panel is incorporated into the panel's terms of reference and sets its subject matter jurisdiction.

Although Article 12.8 of the DSU provides that the panel should normally complete its work within six months, in practice, the process takes much longer. The parties make two rounds of written submissions to the panel and participate in two meetings with the panel in a question-and-answer format, with written answers and comments submitted after each meeting. Third-party WTO Members that indicate an interest in the dispute are also entitled to present a written submission to the panel and to participate in a session of the panel's first meeting with the parties. After all the evidence and arguments have been presented, the panel issues an interim report to the parties, who may request review or revision of aspects

[3] DSU Articles 6.1 and 16.4. In a vestige of the GATT process, a defending Member may block the establishment of a WTO dispute settlement panel for one month until the next monthly meeting of the DSB at which the panel is automatically established.

of the report that they consider incorrect. With only a few exceptions, panels have not revised their substantive findings at this stage. The final panel report is issued to the parties a few weeks after the comments on the interim review are submitted. The report is then translated into the three official WTO languages (English, French and Spanish) before being circulated to all WTO Members and issued to the public. Notwithstanding the six-month deadline, the average time between the establishment of a panel and the issuance of the final report is almost twelve months.[4]

The Appellate Body process is much more efficient. Panel reports are adopted by the DSB within sixty days of circulation unless either party gives notice of an appeal. Under the DSU, the Appellate Body must normally complete the entire appeal process in ninety days or less and the Appellate Body has adhered to this deadline (although the parties have agreed to short extensions in some cases). The process before the Appellate Body consists of a single round of initial and response written submissions, followed by a hearing before the three-member division of the Appellate Body responsible for the case; Appellate Body reports are normally adopted by the DSB within thirty days of circulation of the report.

The major difficulties with the dispute settlement process arise *after* the adoption of the panel and Appellate Body reports. The defending Member is entitled to a 'reasonable period of time' to bring itself into compliance with its WTO obligations with respect to any aspects of its measures that were found to be inconsistent with WTO law. This period is either agreed by the parties or determined by a WTO arbitrator (normally a current or former member of the Appellate Body) in a separate arbitration process. The average period of time agreed by the parties is approximately nine months; the arbitrators, on average, determine eleven and a half months.

The overall record of WTO Members in implementing adverse panel and Appellate Body reports is quite good. Indeed, implementation took place in 83 per cent of panel reports that found violations issued up to September 2005 (Davey 2007: 109). Nevertheless, in some cases, at the end of the reasonable period of time, questions frequently arise as to whether the defending Member has implemented an adverse ruling properly. In these circumstances, Article 21.5 of the DSU permits the matter to be referred back to the original panel to examine whether the

[4] The statistics regarding the time taken in the WTO dispute settlement system used in this chapter are taken from the www.worldtradelaw.net research and data service (subscription required).

actions taken by the implementing Member have brought it into compliance with its WTO obligations. These Article 21.5 proceedings consist of a truncated version of the original panel process, with only one meeting of the panel with the relevant parties. The proceedings are supposed to be completed within ninety days; the average, however, is approximately eight months.

When a defending Member fails to implement properly an adverse ruling, Article 22 of the DSU provides for additional remedies in the form of *compensation* or *suspension of concessions*. Compensation normally refers to a reduction in the defending Member's tariffs or other trade barriers in order to offset the trade harm caused by the WTO-inconsistent measure, rather than to a cash payment. Suspension of concessions, also referred to as retaliation, refers to the imposition by the complaining Member of additional tariffs or other trade barriers against imports from the defending Member.

In both cases, the amount of the compensation or retaliation is supposed to be 'equivalent' to the harm caused by the WTO-inconsistent measure. This amount can be difficult both to quantify and for the parties to agree on. Accordingly, Article 22.6 of the DSU provides for the possibility of arbitration by the original panel on the permissible amount of compensation or retaliation. This arbitration process normally takes sixty days.

There are many concerns with these remedies. The possibility of compensation as a remedy means, in effect, that Members are *not* obliged to get rid of measures that have been found to be inconsistent with WTO law and, therefore, the precise form of compliance is ultimately left to the discretion of the defending Member. This is an important limitation on the relief available under the WTO dispute settlement system even though, in practice, compensation is rarely used.

Another important limitation is that neither compensation nor retaliation necessarily directly benefits the complaining Member's exporting industry on whose behalf the dispute was originally initiated. For example, if the complaining Member's exports of beef to the defending Member are harmed by a WTO-inconsistent measure, neither the defending Member offering reduced tariffs on the complaining Member's other exports, nor the complaining Member increasing tariffs on imports from the defending Member would directly benefit the complaining Member's beef exports or rectify the original problem that precipitated the dispute.

Practical challenges also arise in implementing these remedies. The complaining Member may find it difficult to select a product imported from the defending Member on which to impose retaliatory measures: either imports from the defending Member may not be large enough for retaliation to impose any pressure on the defending Member; or, the consumers and importers of the product on which retaliatory measures in the complaining Member country are imposed may object to bearing the cost of the retaliation in the form of increased duties and prices.

A further difficulty is that the DSU provides that retaliation must be in the same sector of trade as the violation of WTO law unless it is not practical or effective to do so. This means that if the defending Member's violation affected the complaining Member's trade in goods, the retaliation should be applied against the defending Member's trade in goods rather than, for example, its trade in services. Developing countries have been particularly concerned that the difficulty in 'cross-retaliating' against trade in sectors that may be more important to developed countries – such as services or intellectual property – limits their ability to retaliate effectively. The extent to which complaining Members should be permitted to cross-retaliate against other sectors has become an important topic in negotiations on the reform of the WTO dispute settlement system.

In practice, the right to retaliate has been obtained and exercised relatively infrequently in the WTO dispute settlement system. There have been less than twenty instances (out of almost 400 disputes up to 2010) in which the right to retaliate has been granted by the DSB and in at least some of those instances, the complaining Member never actually exercised the right to retaliate. This reflects both the relatively good rate of implementation by defending Members of adverse panel and Appellate Body rulings and the limitations of retaliation just described.

The DSU contains several provisions providing for special treatment for developing countries in dispute settlement proceedings. For example, Article 4.10 of the DSU provides that during consultations, Members should give 'special attention to the particular problems and interests of developing country Members'. In a dispute between a developing country Member and a developed country Member, the former has the right to have at least one member of the panel be from another developing country. In a case against a developing country, Article 12.10 of the DSU provides that panels must 'accord sufficient time for the developing country to prepare and present its argumentation'.

These provisions refer to the participation of developing countries in the process and are designed to ensure that developing countries are not at a disadvantage *procedurally* in a dispute settlement proceeding. However, they do not address how the panel is to make its substantive assessment of the case. Under Article 11 of the DSU, however, a panel's duty is to make an objective assessment of the case before it, regardless of whether the parties include developing countries: justice must be blind with respect to the evaluation of the case. Many of the WTO agreements contain substantive provisions on differential and more-favourable treatment for developing countries. In cases in which developing countries rely on any of these provisions, the panel's report must explicitly address how the panel has taken account of these provisions in evaluating the case.

2 Developments in the dispute settlement system since its inception

The dispute settlement system has evolved considerably since its inception in 1995. Many of the changes have been organic, in that panels and the Appellate Body have developed procedures to deal with issues such as their ability to accept *amicus curiae* submissions, the selection of experts in technically complicated cases, the development of procedures for handling business confidential information, and, more recently, the opening to the public (on a relatively limited basis[5]) of panel and Appellate Body hearings. These issues all relate to a system that is becoming increasingly legalistic and complex.[6] This increased complexity naturally poses additional problems for developing countries with less resources that seek to participate in the system.

In addition to these organic changes, negotiations have been under way since the inception of the system to reform the process. These negotiations were originally initiated pursuant to a WTO Ministerial Decision taken at the time of the creation of the WTO that called for a review of the DSU by 1999. This deadline has since been extended and these negotiations are proceeding in tandem with the Doha Round negotiations (although the negotiations on DSU reform are technically separate from the Doha Round).

These negotiations cover both technical issues relating to the operation of the system as well as more fundamental issues regarding the scope of the system. The latter issues include the proposed creation of a permanent

[5] In several recent cases, members of the public have been permitted to watch panel and Appellate Body hearings on closed circuit broadcasts to an adjoining room at the WTO.

[6] A recent document circulated by the WTO Appellate Body regarding proposed changes to its working procedures noted that the *average* length of an appellant's written submission to the Appellate Body is now 120 pages. See *Working Procedures for Appellate Review* WT/AB/WP/W/10 (12 January 2010).

roster of panellists (in effect, professionalizing the panel process), the nature of the remedies available (one proposal would provide for monetary compensation to developing country Members) and a proposal whereby Members could propose that certain sections of panel reports would not be adopted by the DSB (potentially undermining the binding nature of the process).[7] Other proposals include making cross-retaliation available to developing country complainants without requiring them to show that retaliation in the same sector is not feasible.

3 Developing country participation in the dispute settlement system

Many factors affect the use of the WTO dispute settlement system, including the size of the countries involved, how much and with whom they trade, etc. It is difficult, therefore, to evaluate empirically whether developing countries are fully participating in the system. It is also worth noting at the outset that the term 'developing countries' does not denote a homogeneous group of countries: WTO Members are free to elect whether they wish to be considered as developing countries. The category therefore includes countries as disparate as China and Cameroon. It is not realistic to treat these countries as part of the same category in assessing developing country participation in the system. As noted below, the larger developing countries, such as China, Brazil and Mexico, have participated extensively in the system and can, therefore, be considered separately in assessing its effectiveness. However, it is harder to distinguish between the smaller developing countries in assessing their participation in the system.

Overall, the WTO dispute settlement system has been a success, at least in terms of the volume of disputes. In the first fourteen years of the system, 1995–2008, there were 388 disputes initiated, which is almost 50 per cent greater than the total number of disputes in the forty-seven years of the GATT era (Bown 2009: 64). However, the rate of initiation of disputes dropped considerably after the first five years: during the period

[7] A full description of the issues under negotiation may be found in WTO document JOB(08)/81 and a summary in the report of the Chairman of the negotiations, *Special Session of the Dispute Settlement*, 22 March 2010 (TN/DS/24). The technical issues in the negotiations include the rights of third parties, the ability of the Appellate Body to 'remand' a case to the panel for further proceedings, the 'sequencing' of compliance panel proceedings under Article 21.5 of the DSU and requests for the right to retaliate under Article 22, and the transparency of the process.

1995–2000, an average of forty-one disputes were initiated each year. In contrast, in the period 2001–8, an average of only twenty-one new disputes were initiated each year (Bown 2009: 65). The higher level of activity in the first years of the system may be explained by Members delaying the initiation of proceedings regarding several longstanding disputes pending the establishment of the new system, as well as by a desire on the part of Members to clarify new provisions of the WTO agreements and to test the new system itself.

Developing countries' use of the system has been increasing. These countries initiated seventy-eight disputes, or 32 per cent of the total, in the period 1995–2000. In the period 2001–8, developing countries initiated eighty-six disputes, which, in light of the decrease in overall activity noted above, accounted for 51 per cent of the total in that period (Bown 2009: 69–72). During the earlier period, developing countries grew concerned that the increasing legalization of the system and the frequently prohibitive cost of private legal counsel were impeding their access to the system. This concern led to the establishment in 2001 of the ACWL, an intergovernmental organization in Geneva mandated to provide legal advice on WTO law, including assistance in dispute settlement proceedings, and training to developing and least developed countries. The ACWL's role is discussed in more detail below.

Three additional points regarding developing country participation are worth noting. First, six developing countries (Argentina, Brazil, Chile, Korea, India and Mexico) accounted for 60 per cent of disputes initiated by developing countries in 1995–2008. These countries also accounted for more than half of the disputes initiated *against* developing countries during this period. These countries' participation in the system is, therefore, comparable to that of developed countries: only the United States (116), the European Union (89) and Canada (31) initiated more disputes than Brazil (24), and each of these six countries initiated more disputes than Australia and New Zealand (7 each) in this period. China also presents a special case. Since its accession to the WTO in December 2001, China has initiated seven disputes and has been the defending Member in seventeen disputes. These seven countries' proven ability to participate effectively in the system means that any discussion of fostering developing country engagement in the system should focus on the participation of developing countries other than these seven.

Second, developing countries are increasingly initiating WTO disputes against each other rather than against developed countries, suggesting that these countries' trade with each other is becoming as important as their trade with the developed countries. It may also reflect the fact, discussed below, that much of the developing countries' trade with the developed countries is subject to preferential market access that is not enforceable under WTO law. Thus, the developing countries may have more rights under WTO law with respect to their trade with each other than with respect to their trade with the developed countries. It also indicates that the question of developing country access to and use of the WTO dispute settlement system cannot be viewed solely as a 'north–south' issue – it is also a 'south–south' issue. This has some practical consequences: as developing countries are increasingly defendants, and not just complainants, in WTO dispute settlement proceedings, their views on issues such as implementation obligations and other remedies become more nuanced.

Finally, the participation of least developed countries (LDCs) in the system has been very limited. Only one LDC, Bangladesh, has initiated a dispute settlement proceeding since 1995. In that case, Bangladesh initiated a dispute with India regarding India's anti-dumping measures against batteries from Bangladesh. The matter was resolved in consultations without the need for recourse to a panel.[8] In addition, LDCs have occasionally participated in dispute settlement proceedings as third parties, notably in the disputes concerning US cotton subsidies (Benin and Chad[9]) and the European Union's sugar regime, in which several LDCs participated as part of the ACP (African, Caribbean and Pacific) group of countries.[10]

The cotton case illustrates some of the problems faced by these countries in participating in the system. At the time of writing, Brazil has obtained the right to retaliate against the United States for the latter's failure to implement properly the panel and Appellate Body rulings in the case. Brazil has indicated that it does not intend to exercise the right to retaliate and is reported to be negotiating a compensation arrangement with the United States that would provide funding for projects to develop the Brazilian cotton industry. Had Benin, Chad and the other African cotton-producing countries participated as co-complainants with Brazil

[8] See *India – Anti-dumping Measures on Batteries from Bangladesh* (WT/DS52), Notification of Mutually Satisfactory Solution, WT/DS306/3, G/L/669/Add.1, G/ADP/D52/2 (23 February 2006).

[9] See www.wto.org/english/tratop_e/dispu_e/cases_e/ds267_e.htm [accessed in November 2010].

[10] See www.wto.org/english/tratop_e/dispu_e/cases_e/ds283_e.htm [accessed in November 2010].

in the dispute, they would now enjoy rights to retaliate corresponding to Brazil's and would be in a position to negotiate a similar arrangement with the United States. As third parties, however, Benin and Chad have no rights to retaliate.

The participation of LDCs may also be affected by the fact that so much of their trade is under preferential agreements not enforceable under WTO law (Abbott 2007: 13; Nottage 2009: 498–500). This is likely to continue if these countries benefit in the future from the 'duty-free quota-free' access to developed country markets currently being discussed as part of the Doha Development Round of multilateral trade negotiations. Whether these preferential schemes are beneficial in the long run is the subject of much debate, in terms of their impact both on the recipients of the preferences and on the multilateral trading system as a whole. Regardless of the economic or legal merits of these schemes, however, it seems clear that they reduce the likelihood of dispute settlement proceedings arising out of the large percentage of trade by developing and least developed countries covered by these schemes.

4 The role of the ACWL

In 2001, the ACWL was established to provide developing and least developed countries with the legal resources necessary to participate effectively in the WTO dispute settlement system. As noted above, a perception had emerged in the first five years of the operation of the WTO dispute settlement system that developing and least developed countries did not have equal access to the system. At the initiative primarily of diplomats from Colombia and the Netherlands, the ACWL was created to redress this problem of access. Thus, the ACWL's basic mission is to ensure that these countries have a full understanding of their rights and obligations under WTO law and an equal opportunity to defend their interests in WTO dispute settlement proceedings. The ACWL's experience in assisting developing and least developed countries in dispute settlement proceedings and providing them with legal advice on issues of WTO law even where these do not give rise to dispute settlement proceedings yields some interesting lessons regarding these countries' engagement in the WTO legal system.

Membership in the ACWL is open to all developing country Members of the WTO, thirty of whom have thus far chosen to join. In addition, all LDCs that are either members of, or in the process of acceding to, the WTO (forty-four LDCs at present) are automatically entitled to the

ACWL's services. Thus, seventy-four countries, or almost half the membership of the WTO, are currently entitled to the ACWL's services.

At its inception, it was anticipated that the ACWL's primary role would be to assist developing and least developed countries in WTO dispute settlement proceedings. The ACWL has fulfilled that role, assisting these countries in thirty-four disputes since its establishment:

> During the first seven years of its existence, the ACWL has worked on behalf of the complainant country in more disputes than all other WTO members except for the United States and the EC. Put differently, if the ACWL were not an intergovernmental organization but itself were a WTO member country, it would be considered as the third most frequently active complainant litigant in the Dispute Settlement Understanding (DSU) system during this time period.
>
> (Bown 2009: 138)

When assisting one of these countries in dispute settlement proceedings, the ACWL's lawyers collect evidence, draft submissions and statements, and appear as part of the country's delegation at panel and Appellate Body meetings to answer questions, in much the same manner as private lawyers would represent countries in these disputes.

The countries that have benefitted from the ACWL's assistance in WTO dispute settlement proceedings are developing countries that participate occasionally in the process, but not regularly enough to develop sufficient expertise in the process to do so without legal assistance. Of the six most frequent developing country participants in the system discussed above, only India has become a member of the ACWL. The other frequent participants, such as Brazil and Korea, appear to have sufficient in-house capacity or are able to afford private counsel.[11] Of the twenty-three other developing countries that participated as complainants or defendants in WTO disputes since the ACWL was established, all have joined the ACWL except Antigua, which was the complainant in the *US – Gambling* dispute, and South Africa, which has participated in consultations but never in a panel proceeding (ACWL 2010: 21).

LDCs have also benefitted from the ACWL's assistance in dispute settlement proceedings. Bangladesh, which, as noted, is the only LDC to have initiated dispute settlement proceedings, was assisted by the ACWL in that

[11] By the same token, India, which used the ACWL's assistance in several WTO disputes after the ACWL's inception, now relies on in-house and Delhi-based counsel for assistance in these disputes.

case (Bown 2009: 156). The ACWL also assisted Chad as a third party in the *US – Upland Cotton (Article 21.5 –* Brazil*)* proceeding (Bown 2009: 157).

Despite this record, the ACWL's role has evolved somewhat differently than originally expected. The ACWL now provides almost 200 legal opinions on WTO law each year in response to requests from its members and the LDCs (ACWL 2010: 4). These legal opinions, which are provided free of charge, cover a wide range of topics. The largest category consists of opinions on legal issues relating to WTO decision-making and legal issues arising in the WTO negotiations. The second largest category consists of legal opinions regarding the requesting country's own measures and implementation of its WTO obligations. The third and smallest category consists of legal opinions regarding *other* countries' measures. Consistent with the trend in dispute settlement proceedings discussed above, approximately half of these legal opinions involve measures of other *developing* countries. This again illustrates that developing countries attach increasing importance to access to each other's markets.

This growth in the ACWL's legal advisory function means that the ACWL has come to serve, in effect, as an in-house legal advisory service for countries that could otherwise not afford to develop such a resource. The extent to which developing and least developed countries have taken advantage of this resource suggests several conclusions regarding their participation in the WTO dispute settlement system. First, developing countries that participate only occasionally in WTO dispute settlement continue to need legal assistance in determining whether and when to do so. Second, developing countries' participation in, and ability to benefit from, the WTO legal system cannot properly be measured purely by reference to their participation in dispute settlement proceedings. Third, developing countries need legal assistance in participating in the WTO system more generally, separate and apart from their participation in dispute settlement proceedings.

5 Ongoing challenges facing developing countries in participating in the dispute settlement system

Notwithstanding the assistance available to developing and least developed countries through the ACWL, and other resources, these countries continue to face considerable challenges in participating in the dispute settlement system. We will now discuss these challenges, many of which arise from the process itself.

5.1 Complexity of the process

As discussed above, the WTO's dispute settlement process is time-consuming and burdensome, and also slow to yield results. Initiating a proceeding requires a commitment of resources for a period of roughly two to three years in a typical case, including the preparation of the case and the panel proceeding (which takes approximately one year) and the implementation period (which also averages almost one year). This is no small commitment for developing or least developed countries that are rarely involved in international dispute settlement proceedings and that do not have in-house resources to handle proceedings. The sheer complexity of the proceedings can have a deterrent effect on developing and least developed countries considering whether to initiate dispute settlement proceedings.

5.2 Lack of resources

There are also significant resource issues – apart from the necessary expertise in WTO law – that affect developing countries' ability to pursue dispute settlement proceedings. For example, the United States and the European Commission have large legal bureaus with experts in every facet of WTO law. These and other more experienced WTO Members have well-established internal processes for deciding whether to initiate a dispute, including interdepartmental committees, a clear hierarchy for reviewing recommendations from the staff level on whether to initiate a dispute, and an established process for obtaining budget approval for any expenses that might be incurred in pursuing the dispute.

In contrast, many developing countries do not have similar internal decision-making procedures. This means that when potential disputes arise, these decisions must be taken on an ad hoc basis, which can lead to delay or even inaction. This problem may be exacerbated in smaller countries with smaller government departments where institutional knowledge may be lost and decisions delayed due to turnover in government officials. And while the ACWL can provide legal expertise to developing countries, it cannot exactly replicate the internal political role played by the developed countries' in-house legal offices. In addition to the ACWL, developing countries have access to pro bono assistance from academics, law firms and non-governmental organizations. Also, some of the larger developing countries, such as Brazil, are working to bridge this gap successfully through frequent participation in disputes and the development of in-house expertise and systems for handling these disputes.[12]

Similarly, while more frequent participants in dispute settlement are likely to have funds allocated to dispute settlement activity on a contingent basis, less frequent participants may not have such funds and may have to go through a budget appropriation and allocation process before acting.[13] On a more basic level, a simple lack of familiarity with the process is also a disincentive to act. More frequent actors in the process will recognize that they may not be successful in all of the disputes; less frequent actors may require more assurance of likely success before going through the difficult process of obtaining approval to initiate a dispute. Put simply, it may be easier to be a repeat participant in the system than an occasional participant. As the system becomes more complex and legalistic, the resource gap continues to increase between developed countries that participate more frequently in the system and developing countries that do not.

5.3 *Limitations of the remedies available*

As noted above, there are problems with the remedies available under WTO law. The normal remedy is that the measure found to be WTO-inconsistent must be brought into compliance with the WTO. In practical terms, this may not necessarily be worth much to the complainant. For example, assume a developing country successfully challenges an anti-dumping duty in the amount of 15 per cent *ad valorem* against its exports in dispute settlement proceedings.[14] After implementation, the defending Member may be able to comply with the panel rulings by revising, but not removing, its measure, resulting in a reduced anti-dumping duty (for example, of 5 per cent). Whether this 'success' is worthwhile must be evaluated on a case-by-case basis, depending on how much the reduced duty improves the exporter's market access. Even in a 'successful' case,

[12] Brazil, among other larger developing countries active in WTO dispute settlement, has established an in-house unit of government lawyers focused solely on WTO dispute settlement. See Shaffer *et al.* (2006).

[13] Informal estimates of the cost of private legal counsel for a typical WTO dispute settlement proceeding range from US$500,000 to US$1,000,000.

[14] Anti-dumping duties are additional duties that may be imposed by a WTO Member on imports that are found to be sold at less than 'fair value' and that are causing, or threatening to cause, injury to a domestic industry in the importing Member, following an investigation conducted in accordance with the procedures of the WTO Anti-Dumping Agreement.

therefore, the tangible benefits of dispute settlement proceedings may not be worth the time and trouble involved in proceeding with the dispute.

Moreover, the benefit of winning a 'successful' case becomes more attenuated when the defending Member fails to implement properly. In these circumstances, the subsequent right to compensation or retaliation may not provide the complaining Member with any benefit for the industry on behalf of which it first initiated the dispute settlement proceedings, even when authority is granted to cross-retaliate against trade in other sectors. This is a disincentive to initiate the proceeding in the first place.

5.4 *Lack of public–private partnerships*

A further resource issue affecting participation in dispute settlement proceedings is that the private and public sectors do not coordinate to defend their commercial interests in developing countries as well as they do in developed countries. In many countries, there are well-developed systems whereby governments and private industry work together to ensure that a country's commercial rights are fully defended at the WTO. Shaffer has described in detail how these partnerships between the public and private sector improve the ability of major WTO Members, such as the United States and the European Union, to defend their rights at the WTO (Shaffer 2003). Bown has explained how developing countries do not have similar systems for coordination between the private and public sectors (Bown 2009). In the author's experience, government officials in developing countries are frequently not informed as to the difficulties faced by their commercial sectors, while the commercial sector may not be aware that the government may be able to protect their trade by asserting its rights at the WTO. Moreover, the more involved developing countries become in the WTO legal system – not merely through participation in dispute settlement but also by raising concerns in the various WTO committees and resolving trade problems informally with their fellow WTO Members – the more aware their private sector officials become of the possibility of defending their trade interests through the WTO legal system.

5.5 *Infrequent use of alternative mechanisms*

The DSU provides for various alternative dispute settlement mechanisms that would seem ideally suited to developing countries' needs. However, these mechanisms have been used very rarely. Article 5 of the DSU provides that parties to a dispute may use 'good offices, conciliation and mediation' of, inter alia, the Director-General of the WTO, as a means to resolve the dispute. In addition, Article 25 of the DSU provides for an arbitration process upon mutual agreement of the parties. In effect, the parties are free to agree on their own procedures, although they are bound to abide by the arbitration award. Some other WTO agreements, including the Agreement on Subsidies and Countervailing Measures and the General Agreement on Trade in Services, also contain provisions for arbitration on technical issues arising under those agreements.

Why these mechanisms are so rarely used is a matter of speculation. They appear to provide a less complicated and less expensive means of resolving disputes than the normal process. As such, they should be ideally suited for use in disputes between peer developing countries that may normally have good relations and would mutually benefit from a simpler process. In practice, however, this has not proved to be the case. Perhaps potential disputes, especially between developing countries, can be divided into two categories: those that can be resolved relatively easily and those that cannot. It may be that the disputes that can be resolved relatively easily are in fact being resolved by means of informal consultations between the parties, without recourse even to simplified alternative dispute resolution mechanisms. In this manner, based on anecdotal evidence, the ACWL's legal advice has been used to facilitate the informal resolution of less intractable disputes.

Many disputes, cannot, however, be so easily resolved. For example, trade remedies (anti-dumping, countervailing duty and safeguard measures) now account for about 40 per cent of the WTO dispute settlement caseload.[15] It is frequently very difficult, if not impossible, to resolve disputes arising out of these measures informally, both because of the importance of these measures to the domestic industry of the imposing Member, and because of the complexities of domestic law governing them.[16] This means that alternative simplified mechanisms may not be of use in these cases.

[15] In relative terms, developing countries are much more likely to initiate disputes over agriculture, beverages and seafood and the apparels and textile sector than developed countries (Bown 2009: 73). Bown also finds that developing and developed countries tend to initiate WTO dispute settlement proceedings with respect to violations of different WTO agreements. Developing countries are relatively more likely to focus disputes on allegations of violations of the rules regarding so-called 'trade remedy' measures – anti-dumping and countervailing duties and safeguard measures (Bown 2009: 78–9).

[16] For example, US law provides that US trade remedy measures may be revised only following the issuance of a WTO panel report that finds a measure to be WTO-inconsistent

5.6 *Fear of retaliation*

A more sensitive issue that may affect developing country and LDC participation in dispute settlement proceedings is the fear of possible reprisal by a respondent developed country. One recent study conducted a regression analysis that suggested that developing countries' dependence on foreign aid was a disciplining factor on their initiation of WTO disputes (Francois *et al.* 2008: 23). However, it is difficult to know how significant this concern really is in practice: the evidence that threats to withhold foreign aid have discouraged developing countries from initiating dispute settlement proceedings appears to be anecdotal, not empirical, and inconclusive (Nottage 2009: 497). Further, as noted above, developing and, in particular, least developed countries are much less likely to challenge developed countries in WTO dispute settlement proceedings in part because so much of their trade is covered by preferential access conferred at the discretion of developed countries that cannot be enforced under WTO law. This seems a more likely explanation for these countries' lack of participation in dispute settlement proceedings than their fear of losing foreign aid. In addition, while developing countries are increasingly bringing disputes against other developing countries rather than against developed countries, it cannot be assumed in the latter case that this is because they are inhibited by a fear of reprisal by developed countries.

6 Possible approaches to improving the process

There have been several proposals to overcome these problems and facilitate developing countries' engagement in the WTO dispute settlement process. However, there are no easy solutions. All of these proposals must be considered in light of the relatively delicate balance on which the current dispute settlement system is premised. As noted above, the WTO system, unlike its predecessor under the GATT, provides for more or less binding dispute settlement with respect to the establishment of panels and the adoption of panel and Appellate Body reports. The binding nature of this system raised important sovereignty concerns in many countries and, therefore, came at a price: the remedies available are qualified and include the right to offer compensation rather than removing a measure that has been found to be WTO-inconsistent. In these circumstances, any

and not following consultations between the United States and its trading partners (see section 129 of the 1994 Uruguay Round Agreements Act).

discussion of proposals to strengthen the system generally or, in particular, the remedies available, must bear in mind that the commitment of all WTO Members to a binding system of dispute settlement cannot be taken for granted.

One means of making the process more attractive to developing countries would be to make it less time-consuming. This may be easier said than done. While the time normally taken by WTO panels to complete their work is well in excess of the six months envisaged under the DSU, as a practitioner, this author can attest that this is not time idly spent. As the disputes become more and more factually complex, it becomes correspondingly more difficult for ad hoc panels to complete the process in a timely manner. A permanent roster of panellists, which has been proposed by the European Union, may lead to a streamlining of the panel process through the development of stricter rules of evidence and other more efficient procedures.

With respect to the remedies available, there have been many proposals to make cross-sectoral retaliation more readily available. It is thought that it would be easier for developing countries to use the right to retaliate if they could retaliate against, for example, trade in services or intellectual property rights of a developed country where a measure of the developed country affecting the developing country's trade in goods was found to be WTO-inconsistent. It is important to bear in mind, however, that by the time the question of retaliation arises, the defending Member has made a decision – probably on the basis of important domestic policy considerations – not to implement fully the adverse ruling against it. It cannot be assumed that an increase in the right to retaliate or increased flexibility in how retaliation is imposed will necessarily outweigh the domestic considerations compelling the defending Member not to implement.

A more practical avenue to improve the remedies available may be to consider more specific remedies for particular violations. For example, there have been proposals to make cash payments available as a remedy for some violations. However, this may strain the commitment of some Members to the system. A better example may be the trade remedies area (i.e. cases involving safeguards, anti-dumping and countervailing duty measures), which currently accounts for approximately 40 per cent of all WTO disputes. There may be some scope to provide for more specific remedies in these cases, including the suspension of duties for the duration of the reasonable period of time for implementation, thereby temporarily removing the contested barrier to trade. However, these proposals implicate the WTO's long-standing rule against retroactive remedies: normally defending Members are required to bring their measures into compliance only as of the end of the reasonable period of time to comply with the panel or Appellate Body rulings. The availability of retroactive remedies in the form of suspension or re-payment of duties on imports prior to that date would likely be strongly opposed by several Members. At a minimum, panels might make greater use of their existing authority under Article 19.1 of the DSU to provide more and clearer suggestions as to how their rulings should be implemented.

There are also several possible approaches to improving WTO dispute settlement procedures by means that would supplement the existing provisions of the DSU. For example, Nordstrom and Shaffer have proposed an additional 'small claims' dispute settlement procedure that would provide an accelerated and less cumbersome means of resolving certain disputes (Nordstrom and Shaffer 2008). This procedure would, presumably, be more attractive to developing countries with less resources. The use of this process, as proposed by Nordstrom and Shaffer, could be limited to those countries. This idea may be worth pursuing as a means of providing developing countries with a lower-cost alternative to the current, increasingly complex process. However, it remains to be seen what demand there actually would be in practice for such a procedure. As noted above, developing countries have made almost no use of the existing alternative dispute settlement procedures in the DSU, suggesting there is little demand for such mechanisms. It may be that the main factor that leads to cases coming before the dispute settlement system is not the size of the dispute, but the inability of the defending Member to resolve the situation without an adverse ruling from a WTO panel. In those circumstances, it may be that an alternative or small claims procedure may not carry sufficient weight to influence the defending Member's domestic policy considerations sufficiently to bring about compliance, thereby achieving the complaining Member's goal.

Another avenue that might be worthwhile for developing countries would be to develop more effective dispute settlement procedures under regional trade agreements (RTAs). The multilateral approach to trade relations has taken something of a backseat to the spread of RTAs in recent years. While these RTAs generally include some form of dispute settlement procedures, they have not been as widely used as the DSU procedures. Again, it would seem that resolving disputes in a regional system, without the expense of going to Geneva, would be more attractive to developing countries than the WTO system. However, the same reasons why a small claims procedure may not be successful may also apply to procedures under RTAs: they may not carry as much weight with defending Members as the more formal and more recognized WTO dispute settlement process.

A final avenue to fostering developing country engagement in the dispute settlement system may be to increase the resources available to developing and least developed countries, such as through the ACWL. In this regard, WTO Director-General Pascal Lamy has stated that 'a boost to the ACWL [to enable it to continue its work] would surely be welcome' (Lamy 2009).

In addition, notwithstanding the work of the ACWL and non-governmental organizations, developing country industries and their government officials still lack information about the underlying causes of their lost foreign market access (Abbott 2007:12–13; Bown 2009: 208). To remedy this, Bown has proposed a new independent organization to be called the Institute for Assessing WTO Commitments (IAWC) that would actively monitor countries' compliance with their WTO obligations and maintain a database of potential WTO violations, with a special focus on potential violations of interest to developing country exporters and previously underanalysed areas of market access. In this way, the IAWC would provide a more detailed analysis of possible trade barriers than the Global Trade Alert, a recent independent initiative that provides internet bulletins on trade measures taken around the world that may improperly affect trade.[17] This proposal emphasizes the need to inform both developing country commercial interests and their governments of measures affecting their market access for which there may be a remedy under WTO law. The IAWC would, therefore, address the public–private partnership deficit discussed above by making available to the private sectors in these countries expert evaluations of trade policies and measures that may affect their trade. However, it would leave it to others – the governments themselves, the ACWL or private sector lawyers – to provide the legal expertise necessary to enforce the WTO rights at issue.

7 Implications for global trade governance

Notwithstanding the overall success of the WTO dispute settlement system, the issue of developing country engagement in the system remains important. The main changes to the system itself that would foster this

[17] See www.globaltradealert.org [accessed in November 2010].

engagement are those that would simplify and reduce the cost of the system. While there is also room for improvement in the area of remedies, only limited changes in this area may be feasible if WTO Members' commitment to a system of binding dispute settlement is to be preserved.

One means of increasing developing countries' capacity and familiarity with the process is for those countries to participate more frequently as third parties. Some developed countries, such as the United States, the European Union and Japan, routinely participate as third parties in disputes to ensure that they benefit fully from the system. China, among other countries, has used third country participation as a means of increasing its understanding of the system and equipping itself to participate as a complainant or defendant. As noted above with respect to the cotton case, however, third-party participation is not necessarily sufficient to guarantee that developing countries obtain the same redress as they would as complainants.

Also, developing and least developed countries are increasingly participating more effectively in the WTO by pooling their resources in coalitions such as the LDC Group and the Africa Group. The coordination of common interests in these groups is a valuable means for these countries of sharing their experience and resources and participating more effectively in the system.

Developing and least developed countries continue to need increased legal capacity to engage fully in the WTO dispute settlement system. While the ACWL provides some of their capacity needs, these countries continue to face internal capacity constraints – both in their public and private sectors – that limit their ability to engage in the system. In considering means of overcoming these constraints, it is important to recall that how these countries benefit from the system cannot be measured solely in terms of their participation in formal dispute settlement proceedings. These countries also engage in and benefit from the WTO legal system when they are able to use their Membership in the WTO to make informed choices on how to achieve their trade policy goals. Thus, efforts to increase these countries' capacity should focus on their ability not just to participate in dispute settlement proceedings, but to benefit more broadly from their membership in the WTO's legal system.

The effectiveness of the rules-based multilateral trading system depends on the ability of WTO Members to participate fully in the system. This, in turn, depends on the existence of an effective dispute resolution process by which all WTO Members, including the weakest among them, can give effect to their rights and obligations under the system. As we have discussed, developing and least developed countries are increasingly participating in the WTO legal system, either directly by direct participation in WTO dispute settlement proceedings or indirectly by using the legal services of the ACWL. However, both the system itself and the level of developing and least developed country participation could and should be improved. It is important to note that many obligations under the WTO Agreements provide for transparent, rules-based administration of the laws governing trade. Fostering developing and least developed country participation in this system therefore also fosters the spread of the rule of law and improved governance in those countries.

References

Abbott, R. 2007. *Are Developing Countries Deterred from Using the WTO Dispute Settlement System?: Participation of Developing Countries in the DSM in the Years 1995–2005*, ECIPE Working Paper No. 01/2007. Brussels: ECIPE.

Advisory Centre on WTO Law (ACWL). 2010. *Report on Operations 2009*. Geneva: ACWL.

Bethlehem, D., McRae, D., Neufeld, R. and van Damme, I. (eds.) 2009. *The Oxford Handbook of International Trade Law*. Oxford University Press.

Bown, C. P. 2009. *Self-Enforcing Trade: Developing Countries and WTO Dispute Settlement*. Washington, DC: Brookings Institution Press.

Davey, W. J. 2007. 'Evaluating WTO Dispute Settlement: What Results Have Been Achieved Through Consultations and Implementation of Panel Reports?', in Taniguchi, Y. Yanovich, A. and Bohanes, J. (eds.), *The WTO in the Twenty-first Century: Dispute Settlement, Negotiations, and Regionalism in Asia*, Cambridge University Press, pp. 98–140.

Francois, J., Horn, H. and Kaunitz, N. 2008. *Trading Profiles and Developing Country Participation in the WTO Dispute Settlement System*, ICTSD Issue Paper No. 6. Geneva: ICTSD.

Lamy, P. 2009. 'Looking Ahead at the WTO General Council Meeting on 29 April 2009'. www.wto.org/english/news_e/news09_e/tnc_chair_report_29apr09_e.htm [Accessed in November 2010].

Nordstrom, H. and Shaffer, G. 2008. 'Access to Justice in the World Trade Organization: A Case for a Small Claims Procedure?', *World Trade Review* 7(4): 587–640.

Nottage, H. 2009. 'Trade and Development', in Bethlehem, D., McRae, D., Neufeld, R. and van Damme, I. (eds.), *The Oxford Handbook of International Trade Law*, Oxford University Press, pp. 481–504.

Palmeter, D. and Mavroidis, P. 2004. *Dispute Settlement in the World Trade Organization*, 2nd edn. Cambridge University Press.

Palmeter, D. and Meagher, N. 2009. 'World Trade Organization Dispute Settlement', in Reinert, K. and Rajan, R. (eds.), *The Princeton Encyclopedia of the World Economy*, Princeton University Press, pp. 1192–1202.

Reinert, K. and Rajan, R. (eds.) 2009. *The Princeton Encyclopedia of the World Economy*. Princeton University Press.

Shaffer, G. 2003. *Defending Interests: Public-Private Partnerships in WTO Litigation*. Washington, DC: Brookings Institution Press.

Shaffer, G., Ratton Sanchez, M. and Rosenberg, B. 2006. *Strengthening the State though Diffusing Expertise: Brazil's Response to the Judicialized WTO Regime*, ICTSD Issue Paper. Geneva: ICTSD. http://ictsd.org/i/publications/11326/ [Accessed in November 2010].

Taniguchi, Y., Yanovich, A. and Bohanes, J. (eds.) 2007. *The WTO in the Twenty-first Century: Dispute Settlement, Negotiations, and Regionalism in Asia*. Cambridge University Press.

13

Rethinking the governance of Aid for Trade

DAVID LUKE AND LUISA BERNAL

Aid for Trade is an important development initiative. It gives concrete expression to the objective of securing greater developing country participation in international trade, which is vital for promoting the global public good of a rules-based international trading system. Yet the complicated arrangements for the 'governance' and implementation of the Aid for Trade initiative make it challenging for developing countries to access the available resources. In its current form, Aid for Trade governance is at best ambivalent when it comes to the declared mission of supporting developing countries to build trade capacity, overcome supply side constraints and profit more fully from the international trading system. Moreover, there is a deficit in the institutional arrangements regarding access to and predictability of Aid for Trade resources. This is reflected in the skewed distribution of Aid for Trade across countries: in 2008, out of over a hundred eligible countries, the top twenty recipients captured 70 per cent of all Aid for Trade commitments (OECD 2010a).

The objectives of this chapter are twofold. First, it outlines the institutional arrangements for the governance and implementation of Aid for Trade. Second, it argues that as Aid for Trade has evolved, the key governance principle guiding implementation has become the mutual accountability of donors and beneficiaries, whereas equally important principles of access to and predictability of resources are much less prominent.

This chapter is divided into four main sections. The first section sets out the importance of Aid for Trade as a critical development-centred initiative. Section 2 outlines an analytical framework centred on the principles of mutual accountability, access to and predictability of resources,

David Luke and Luisa Bernal are, respectively, Senior Adviser and Policy Specialist, Trade and Human Development Unit, United Nations Development Programme (UNDP), Geneva Office. The views expressed in this chapter do not necessarily reflect the position of the UNDP or any UN Member State. The authors are grateful to Carolyn Deere Birkbeck, Sheila Page and Ambassador Shree Servansing of Mauritius (past Chair of the WTO Committee on Trade and Development) for very helpful comments on the initial draft.

which is then used to assess the governance arrangements of the Aid for Trade initiative. Section 3 presents three case studies that explore how three other initiatives designed to support the provision of global public goods have embedded these principles in their governance architecture (i.e. the Global Environment Facility (GEF), the Global Fund to Fight AIDS, Tuberculosis and Malaria (the Global Fund) and the Enhanced Integrated Framework for Trade-Related Technical Assistance to Least Developed Countries (EIF)).

Section 4 argues that institutional innovation is required to overcome the current deficit in the implementation arrangements with respect to access and predictability of resources. It makes the case for dedicated Aid for Trade regional financial facilities for funding both national and regional trade capacity priorities and outlines practical considerations for their successful operation.

1 Aid for Trade: a vital development-centred initiative

While globalization has been a key driver of economic growth, its benefits have not been shared equitably either between or within countries (UNDP 2005). Moreover, the shocks associated with the 2008–9 global economic and financial crisis, including significant reversals in key economic indicators in the poorest countries, has provided a timely reminder that well-formulated domestic policies are not effective without opportunities for more balanced growth in the global economy. A clear lesson from almost thirty continuous years of trade expansion before the 2008–9 global financial crisis is that the ability of countries to translate participation in international trade into rising incomes depends significantly on whether they are successful in adding value to both exports and production for domestic markets.[1] A review of effective development experiences and evidence confirms that countries which become successful traders are also able to raise living standards, achieve higher levels of human development and generate more sustainable economic growth (UNDP 2005).

To date, however, while many poor countries have benefitted from favourable market access conditions in major markets, including through preferential schemes, the majority has neither been able to integrate

[1] Value addition refers to the process of increasing the value of products and services through transformation and quality improvement, from the primary stage until it reaches the final consumer. (See UNIDO 2009 for a discussion on value chain analysis and value addition throughout the chain.)

higher value-added into their exports nor to effectively utilize trade preferences. Indeed, as global average tariff levels fell in the wake of multilateral trade liberalization negotiated in the Uruguay Round, preferences have proved to be inadequate to expand market shares in traditional markets. Moreover, many elements in multilateral and other trade agreements have limited the 'policy space' of late developers challenged with export diversification and value addition.

These concerns – supply-side constraints and the need for development-friendly flexibilities in trade agreements – were at the forefront of developing country priorities when the Doha 'Development' Round was launched in 2001 (Njinkeu and Cameron 2008). The Declaration of the WTO Doha Ministerial Conference recognized these concerns, even if only in a hortatory way (WTO 2001). Among other provisions, paragraph 2 recalled the Preamble to the Marrakesh Agreement, and the commiments WTO Members made to make positive efforts 'to ensure that developing countries, and especially the least-developed among them, secure a share in the growth of world trade commensurate to the needs of their economic development'. Paragraph 38 of the Declaration emphasized 'that technical cooperation and capacity-building are core elements of the development dimension of the multilateral trading system … ', highlighting the need to support domestic efforts for trade mainstreaming into national development plans and poverty reduction strategies, enhance the coordinated delivery of aid and ensure predictability of funding.

As the Doha negotiations progressed – or regressed – with many development demands in gridlock, concerns emerged among low-income countries about the impacts of preference erosion and adjustment costs if the Round was successfully completed.[2] Another concern was the need to scale up support for trade capacity development, particularly given the limited ambition of the Integrated Framework and its focus only on least developed countries (LDCs). Together, these concerns triggered a new effort to devise an appropriate mechanism to provide some comfort to low income countries on adjustment and trade capacity development.

[2] Adjustment costs in this context refer to the costs to communities and the country as a whole arising from the reallocation of resources, as a result of trade reform. As noted by the OECD: 'Freer trade and investment can lead to firm closures and job losses in some sectors, while creating new opportunities in others. The adjustment costs resulting from job displacement reduce the short-term efficiency gains from structural changes and place the burden on a narrow segment of the population, raising equity concerns and potentially eroding political support for trade liberalisation and, more generally efficiency-enhancing structural change' (2005b).

The Declaration of the 2005 WTO Ministerial Conference in Hong Kong addressed these issues by endorsing proposals both to 'enhance' the Integrated Framework and to launch an Aid for Trade initiative. In particular, paragraph 57 of the Declaration provided that 'Aid for Trade should aim to help developing countries, particularly LDCs, to build the supply-side capacity and trade-related infrastructure that they need to assist them to implement and benefit from WTO Agreements and more broadly to expand their trade' (WTO 2005). The Declaration called for the establishment of a Task Force to provide recommendations on how to operationalize Aid for Trade, and explore how it could best contribute to the development dimension of the Doha Round of multilateral trade negotiations (although it was also agreed from the outset that further progress on the initiative was not dependent on movement in the Round itself).

The potential of Aid for Trade and its importance as a vital development-centred initiative is clear. By providing assistance to help developing countries build their productive capacities, and their physical and institutional infrastructures, Aid for Trade can help assist low income nations to take advantage of market access opportunities. Aid for Trade can also usefully bolster the ability of developing countries to meet the costs of trade adjustments.

2 Aid for Trade governance and implementation arrangements

Following several months of deliberations, the WTO General Council adopted the recommendations of the Task Force on the operationalization of Aid for Trade in October 2006 (WTO 2006a).[3] These recommendations provided the foundations for Aid for Trade's governance architecture and implementation arrangements at country, regional and global levels (WTO 2006a).

The Task Force proposed that the scope of Aid for Trade 'be defined broad enough to reflect the diverse needs identified by countries' (WTO 2006a) and recommended six categories of Aid for Trade: 1) trade policy and regulations; 2) trade development; 3) trade-related infrastructure; 4)

[3] The Task Force was composed of thirteen WTO Members: Barbados, Brazil, Canada, China, Colombia, the European Union, Japan, India, Thailand and the United States, and the coordinators of the African, Caribbean and Pacific States (ACP), the African Group and the least developed country (LDC) groups. The Task Force was chaired by the Permanent Representative of Sweden, Ambassador Mia Horn Af Rantzien.

building productive capacity; 5) trade-related adjustment; and 6) other trade-related needs.

The Task Force articulated the rationale for Aid for Trade as the need to assist developing countries in expanding their trade, exploiting market access opportunities for goods and services, and better integrating into the multilateral trading system. It recommended that Aid for Trade be guided by the Paris Declaration on Aid Effectiveness (OECD 2005a) (which was complemented in 2008 by the Accra Agenda for Action (OECD 2008)). The Paris Declaration emphasizes principles of country ownership; mutual accountability; alignment of aid and support to national development strategies; effective donor coordination and harmonization of donor procedures; use of programme-based modalities; transparency; and managing for results, as well as predictable and multi-year commitments. It also recommended that Aid for Trade projects and programmes be identified as trade-related development priorities in the recipient country's national development strategy or the equivalent at the regional level.

In rethinking the Aid for Trade governance arrangements, this chapter employs an analytical framework that is centred on three key principles that were at the core of the deliberations of the Aid for Trade Taskforce, namely: 1) the mutual accountability of donors and beneficiaries to ensure that the objectives of the Aid for Trade initiative are met; 2) access to Aid for Trade resources by the beneficiaries through existing official development assistance channels; and 3) predictability in the flow of Aid for Trade resources.

How were these principles derived? How are they reflected in Aid for Trade governance and implementation arrangements? How have these principles played out in practice?

2.1 Analytical framework

Drawing on the Paris Declaration on Aid Effectiveness, the Task Force incorporated the principle of *mutual accountability* into its recommendations for the governance arrangements for Aid for Trade. Mutual accountability refers to the joint responsibility of donors and beneficiaries to work towards development and represents conventional wisdom on what works in the management of development assistance resources (OECD 2005a). The principle embodies the idea that mutual accountability also implies that the beneficiary country is responsible for the prioritization of objectives, programmes and projects – in short, the beneficiary has autonomy and ownership in deciding how Aid for Trade should be allocated. For donors, mutual accountability means that their assistance must be in line with the beneficiaries' prioritization and objectives. Furthermore, mutual accountability requires coordination between donors and beneficiary countries in providing support and harmonizing management procedures for the resources provided.

The principle of ensuring *access* to Aid for Trade resources through the existing channels of official development assistance (ODA) was derived from the Task Force's own deliberations. Although some developing countries argued for a new Aid for Trade 'global fund', the Task Force recommended in favour of using existing channels for ODA.

The principle of *predictability* of Aid for Trade resources was also derived from the Task Force's discussions. The Task Force proposed that resources made available by donors should be in addition to existing ODA levels, as one way to assure the predictability of resource flows.

Together, these three principles constitute the analytical framework that we deploy in this chapter for assessing the Aid for Trade governance arrangements. A discussion of how effectively each of these principles is reflected in the Aid for Trade governance architecture follows. To begin, we outline the formal governance architecture.

2.2 Aid for Trade governance architecture

The organigram on the next page (Figure 13.1) presents the Aid for Trade governance architecture as it operates in practice. The institutional arrangements for Aid for Trade governance assigned the WTO Committee on Trade and Development an oversight role of implementation. Following a specific recommendation of the Task Force, the role of the WTO Trade Policy Review Mechanism, which periodically reviews Member States' trade policies, was expanded to include an assessment of the effectiveness of donor support for Aid for Trade, as well as any progress in developing trade capacity in beneficiary countries. It was expected that this reporting would help enhance the monitoring of Aid for Trade flows.

The Task Force further recommended that the WTO Director-General create an Advisory Group composed of key development agencies and development banks to advise on implementation issues on the ground. In addition, Aid for Trade reviews emerged as an innovation. Hosted by the WTO Secretariat, these fora shine the spotlight on the initiative's progress at global and regional levels.

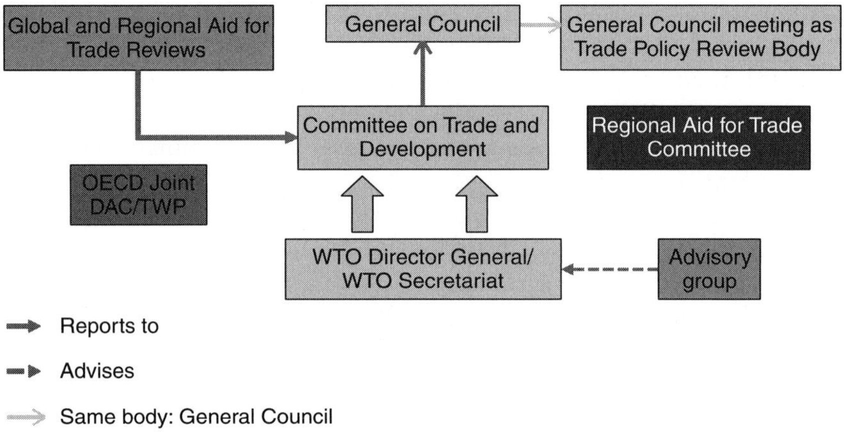

Figure 13.1 The Aid for Trade governance architecture

In order to consider the regional dimension of Aid for Trade, the Task Force recommended exploring 'the merits of establishing a Regional Aid-for-Trade Committee, comprising sub-regional and regional organizations and financial institutions, to oversee the implementation of the sub-regional and regional dimensions of Aid for Trade, to report on needs, responses and impacts, and to oversee monitoring and evaluation' (WTO 2006a).

However, the establishment of this Regional Committee has not yet been taken up in the governance arrangements of Aid for Trade. On the other hand, although not a Task Force recommendation, the OECD's Working Party of the Trade Committee has been active in providing guidance on reporting Aid for Trade financial flows and other information.

2.2.1 WTO Committee on Trade and Development

The Committee on Trade and Development (CTD), composed of all WTO Members, provides a forum for oversight of the overall orientation of the Aid for Trade initiative. The CTD formally approves the annual Aid for Trade work plan and road map, which includes a regular listing of upcoming activities, including global and regional reviews. Between 2006 and 2009, the CTD held thirteen dedicated Aid for Trade sessions and a number of informal meetings covering various aspects of implementation.

At first, the CTD was particularly interested in what was happening on the ground with respect to projects and programmes in the main Aid for Trade categories. Accordingly, bilateral and multilateral donor agencies were invited to CTD meetings to provide briefings. Issues such as trade-related infrastructure (WTO 2007c), building productive capacity, trade facilitation, sanitary and phytosanitary standards (WTO 2007b, 2007d) and adjustment (WTO 2007d) were each covered at dedicated CTD Aid for Trade sessions. In 2008, the CTD sponsored a symposium on monitoring and evaluation (WTO 2008) and the CTD invited the UNDP to present the findings of its study of trade mainstreaming at the national level in beneficiary countries (WTO 2009a). In addition, the CTD hosted briefings by the regional development banks regarding their activities in support of the Aid for Trade initiative, including in particular, preparatory work for the regional reviews that were organized by the Inter-American Development Bank (IADB), the African Development Bank (AfDB) and the Asian Development Bank (ADB) in their respective regions.

Although individual developing country WTO Members have raised issues regarding *access* to Aid for Trade funds at the CTD, proposing that 'real time' information flows were required, the prevailing focus of discussion has been on monitoring activities on the ground and sharing experiences – that is, on issues related to mutual accountability.

2.2.2 The Trade Policy Review Mechanism (TPRM)

The Trade Policy Review Mechanism (TPRM) is the WTO's surveillance arm. It undertakes periodic reviews of Members' trade policies and provides an opportunity for them to examine the implementation of WTO commitments. As noted above, the Aid for Trade Task Force proposed that the work of the TPRM be expanded to include regular assessments of the effectiveness of donor support for Aid for Trade and progress in developing trade capacity among beneficiaries.

At the time of writing, a number of WTO Members agreed to be the first pilots to include Aid for Trade assessments in their TPRM surveillance reviews.[4] Following a review of these tests, Members will further consider the inclusion of Aid for Trade assessments in trade policy reviews on a regular basis.[5] This expansion of the TPRM's surveillance mandate further illustrates the weight given to mutual accountability in Aid for Trade governance arrangements.

[4] These WTO Members are Belize, China, Honduras, Malawi, the United States and Benin, as well as Burkina Faso and Mali, which will do a joint review. See WTO (2009b).

[5] A related recommendation by the Task Force regarding strengthening Aid for Trade monitoring through the adoption of notification requirements for WTO Members has not been implemented so far.

2.2.3 The Advisory Group

In response to the Aid for Trade Task Force's recommendation to create 'an *ad hoc* consultative group to take forward the practical follow up of [its] recommendations' (WTO 2006a), the WTO Director-General established an Advisory Group on Aid for Trade composed of agencies and development banks.[6] The role of this group is to draw upon the development expertise of its Members to provide advice on various aspects of the implementation of the Aid for Trade initiative. In particular, the Advisory Group is called upon to review the annual Aid for Trade work plan and road map, as well as to provide updates on Aid for Trade implementation on the ground. Given that the WTO itself has no field offices and is not a development agency per se, the perspective of the Advisory Group is particularly important.

2.2.4 OECD Working Party of the Trade Committee on Aid for Trade

As Aid for Trade is a component of ODA, it falls within the purview of the OECD's Development Assistance Committee (DAC), composed of twenty-four OECD Members,[7] which monitors the flow of ODA funds as well as other qualitative issues in donor-beneficiary relations surrounding the aid effectiveness agenda. In addition, the OECD's Trade Committee follows trade-related issues of interest to OECD Member States, including Aid for Trade.

Shortly after the Aid for Trade initiative was launched, the OECD's Trade Committee established a Working Party to review various aspects of Aid for Trade from an OECD perspective. The Working Party of the

[6] The following institutions are Members of the Advisory Group: African Development Bank, Asian Development Bank, European Bank for Reconstruction and Development, International Monetary Fund (IMF), Inter-American Development Bank, Islamic Development Bank, International Trade Centre (ITC), Organisation for Economic Co-operation and Development (OECD), United Nations Conference on Trade and Development (UNCTAD), United Nations Development Programme (UNDP), United Nations Economic Commission for Africa (UNECA), United Nations Industrial Development Organization (UNIDO) and the World Bank.

[7] The following countries are Members of the OECD Development Assistance Committee: Australia, Austria, Belgium, Canada, Denmark, Finland, France, Germany, Greece, Ireland, Italy, Japan, Republic of Korea, Luxembourg, Netherlands, New Zealand, Norway, Portugal, Spain, Sweden, Switzerland, United Kingdom, United States and the European Commission. The World Bank, the IMF and the UNDP participate as observers. For more information on the DAC, see OECD (2010b).

Trade Committee (WPTC) includes DAC representation and draws upon development agencies and banks as well as beneficiary countries as needed. The Working Party therefore operates outside the framework of the WTO but it has a strong influence in the implementation of the Aid for Trade initiative through its analytical input and as a platform for coordination among donors (which in turn gives them an edge in terms of preparation for CTD meetings and other WTO discussions). Through the activities of the WPTC, the WTO has in effect conceded 'space' outside its own institutional framework for important inputs to the Aid for Trade initiative by its OECD Membership and, accordingly, outside the formal framework for oversight by the WTO Membership as a whole. The OECD's inputs have overwhelmingly been concerned with ensuring beneficiary countries' engagement and compliance with the mutual accountability agenda.

The Working Party has focused 'on creating an aid-for-trade performance assessment framework consisting of guidance on how to evaluate Aid for Trade, and [how to] apply the Paris Declaration management for results principles to Aid for Trade' (OECD 2009c). Issues tackled to date include how to identify and address binding constraints to trade (OECD 2009b), and how to evaluate Aid for Trade (OECD 2009a). Future work by the WPTC is expected to centre on the monitoring of Aid for Trade implementation and strengthening linkages between Aid for Trade and the wider development agenda (OECD 2009c).

In pursuit of beneficiary countries' engagement with the mutual accountability agenda, the Working Party has also sought to facilitate dialogue with and outreach to them. It organized Aid for Trade dialogues in 2006 and 2008, and has planned another for 2011. The thematic focus of these dialogues has varied. In 2006, the Aid for Trade dialogue was structured around sharing of experiences and information among stakeholders supporting trade development in beneficiary countries. The meeting also provided an opportunity for the OECD Secretariat to receive feedback on its proposed Aid for Trade work programme. In 2008, the dialogue reviewed tools and instruments to deliver Aid for Trade more effectively and created a platform for exchange of experiences and information regarding South–South initiatives in support of trade capacity development in low-income countries.[8] The dialogue in 2011 is expected

[8] For more information on the OECD Aid for Trade dialogues, see www.oecd.org [accessed in November 2010].

to focus its discussion 'on what works best in Aid for Trade and to ensure that all key stakeholders involved are aware of the good practices' (OECD 2009c).

2.2.5 Aid for Trade reviews

Aid for Trade reviews are an innovation of the WTO Secretariat. Their purpose is 'to shine a spotlight' on the progress of Aid for Trade on the ground. Although no binding commitments on access and predictability of Aid for Trade resources were proposed, the Task Force did envisage that the WTO would over time become a 'clearing house' for monitoring Aid for Trade flows and impact. The 'spotlight effect' of the WTO's reviews has been the main innovation in the governance arrangements for Aid for Trade. The reviews create awareness among governments, regional organizations, donor agencies, and development and financial institutions on the main elements of the initiative and generate incentives for improvement on delivery and use of aid through peer pressure and scrutiny.

This 'spotlight effect' was achieved through two main pillars, which reinforce the weight of mutual accountability in its implementation and governance architecture. The first pillar combines the ongoing development of a joint WTO and OECD framework for monitoring progress and results as reported by donors and developing countries through self-assessment questionnaires, as well as the effort to track financial flows through the Creditor Reporting System (CRS).

The second pillar is the hosting of global and regional reviews, which review the information gathered through the first pillar and provide a space for discussion of concrete steps and commitments required to achieve Aid for Trade objectives. To date, two global reviews and several regional and subregional reviews (though not fully covering all the major developing regions) have been held. The latter were led by regional development banks. Regional Economic Communities (RECs) responsible for regional integration schemes have been less prominent. Generally, discussions have focused on local specificities and needs as well as showcasing programmes and projects for which financial pledges from development partners are sought. Taken together, the two pillars help 'to promote dialogue and encourage all key actors to honour commitments, meet local needs, improve effectiveness and reinforce mutual accountability' (OECD and WTO 2009: 18).

2.3 *Aid for Trade governance architecture: an assessment*

The Aid for Trade governance arrangements place considerable importance on mutual accountability, with great hope placed in the prospect that peer pressure on donors and beneficiaries through monitoring and surveillance activities at the CTD, TPRM and Aid for Trade reviews, as well as the OECD's WPTC, will promote effectiveness. Less emphasis, however, is placed on issues of access and predictability of resources that address Aid for Trade needs. Indeed, in the current institutional arrangements, there is no single point of access, criteria or process for beneficiaries to follow in order to tap into the Aid for Trade commitments from bilateral and multilateral donors. As previously noted, the Task Force failed to offer significant guidance on the question of access, agreeing only that existing channels of ODA be used. Yet, the Task Force did recognize that there were major gaps in the development finance architecture especially regarding trade-related infrastructure, adjustment support, cross-border constraints and other trade-related public goods. Accordingly, while the Task Force emphasized the fundamental importance of '[a]dditional, predictable, sustainable and effective financing' (WTO 2006a) as critical for the effectiveness of the implementation arrangements and instructed that a baseline of existing resources for Aid for Trade be established to measure additionality, mechanisms for ensuring contributions from donor Members and the additionality of these funds do not exist. The Task Force merely urged the WTO Director-General to confirm the pledges made at Hong Kong and other high-level events.

It remains unclear to what extent peer pressure and monitoring of overall Aid for Trade flows can ensure improved country allocations of aid or address coordination challenges related to its delivery, particularly for regional or cross-border needs. Limitations in the CRS data used for monitoring Aid for Trade further hinder transparency and mutual accountability (see Box 13.1). In sum, the Aid for Trade arrangements are designed to encourage change through increased awareness and understanding between donors and beneficiary countries. They are not, however, specifically designed to match demand and supply of Aid for Trade. To this extent, the institutional arrangements are fundamentally concerned with mutual accountability rather than access and predictability.

BOX 13.1: TRACKING AID FOR TRADE FLOWS: THE CREDITOR REPORTING SYSTEM

There are several concerns about the transparency of the CRS as a reliable source of data on Aid for Trade trends. These include:

- Reliance on proxies for deriving baseline data and subsequent trends for five of the six Aid for Trade categories (trade policy and regulations; trade development; trade-related infrastructure; building productive capacity; and trade-related adjustment).
- Insufficient differentiation between Aid for Trade commitments and aid for other purposes, which can lead to significant overestimation of actual Aid for Trade volumes (OECD and WTO 2007: 20). In only a few cases, for instance, are donors able to distil trade-related infrastructure from overall support to economic infrastructure.[9]
- Incomplete donor coverage (non-OECD or 'emerging' donors are not included), which leads to underestimating Aid for Trade commitments. Emerging donors are generally wary that their support should be counted as aid.
- Incomplete reporting on support for trade adjustment (which is expected to become more important over time). In 2007, only two donors reported under this category, making it difficult to assess any trends.
- Lack of clear alignment between what donors report to the CRS and the developing countries' own records of what assistance they have received (OECD 2010a). The cross-cutting nature of Aid for Trade makes it difficult to track assistance that is not channelled through a national finance or aid coordination entity in developing countries. The lag between Aid for Trade commitments and disbursements make efforts to match CRS data with national data even more difficult.
- Confusion regarding Task Force-defined Aid for Trade categories and how they relate to the flow of assistance on the ground.
- Lack of consensus on the definition of additionality. The Aid for Trade (AFI) monitoring framework sees additionality as the share of AfT that comes out of total sector allocable ODA. Most developing countries, on the other hand, understand additionality to mean Aid for Trade flows that represent fresh funding over and above total ODA.

Arguments in favour of using the CRS data, despite its shortcomings, are the following:

- Comprehensive coverage, which extends to 90 per cent of ODA activities (OECD and WTO 2009: 52).

[9] The World Bank and the United States' own monitoring systems allow for a distinction between the trade-related capacity-building programmes and trade-related infrastructure. See OECD and WTO (2007: 7).

BOX 13.1 (CONT.)

- Better coverage of the Aid for Trade categories than in the joint OECD/WTO database, which had previously been used to track flows of resources for trade-related assistance. The latter provided a more detailed tracking of trade-related technical assistance programmes but lacked information on infrastructure and other categories important for the monitoring of Aid for Trade (WTO 2007a).
- The CRS tracks ODA disbursements as well as commitments.
- Facilitates comparisons between donors and between beneficiaries and over time.

2.4 Access and predictability in practice

In the Task Force deliberations, developing countries argued in favour of a new fund or multilateral financial arrangement to ensure predictability and accessibility of Aid for Trade (WTO 2006c, 2006d, 2006e).[10] There was no appetite among donor countries, however, for establishing a global or vertical Aid for Trade fund mechanism.[11] Instead, it was agreed that Aid for Trade should use existing bilateral and multilateral procedures for accessing ODA resources. Still, the Task Force viewed principles of predictability and additionality[12] as critical for the viability of Aid for Trade and thus requested that a baseline of existing resources be established to measure additionality and the adequacy of funding available to meet Aid for Trade needs (WTO 2006a).

How have the predictability and access principles played out in practice? The tracking of Aid for Trade flows is led by the OECD Secretariat using data from the OECD's CRS. The adoption of the CRS as the main tool for measuring Aid for Trade flows has introduced a number of challenges in terms of transparency and reliability of the data used for ensuring accurate accounting and assessing additionality of Aid for Trade flows

[10] Developing countries argued for donors to mainly provide grants (supplemented by concessional loans limited to specific interventions) and other non-debt creating commitments.

[11] Some international agencies such as the IMF and the Inter-American Development Bank also argued against the creation of a new fund in their submissions to the Task Force.

[12] The Task Force did not provide a definition of additionality. However, by calling for the establishment of a baseline of Aid for Trade flows, the Task Force suggested that increasing volumes of Aid for Trade above the baseline effectively implied additionality. But it should be noted that there is no common understanding among WTO Members of what is meant by additionality. See Box 13.1 for further discussion of this issue.

as recommended by the Task Force (see Box 13.1). These difficulties have prompted developing country calls for better 'real time' information on Aid for Trade flows.

Based on the CRS data, the WTO's 2007 Aid for Trade global review established a baseline of annual Aid for Trade global commitments of nearly US$21 billion on average between 2002 and 2005, in constant 2005 prices (OECD and WTO 2007: 9). The WTO's 2009 Global Aid for Trade Review observed a 10 per cent year-on-year increase in Aid for Trade commitments in 2006 and 2007, giving a total of US$25.4 billion in 2007 (OECD and WTO 2009: 53). Aid for Trade further increased in 2008 to US$41.7 billion (OECD 2010a) in line with the overall increase of ODA, which attained the highest dollar value so far that year: US$119 billion. Data on Aid for Trade beyond 2008 was not available at the time of writing. However, the OECD notes that '[w]hile ODA flows in 2009 were stable, the outlook for 2010 and 2011 is less promising' (OECD 2010a). The global economic and financial crisis has the potential to negatively affect Aid for Trade flows in the future through a decline in ODA commitments resulting from both lower growth rates and budgetary constraints on ODA in the aftermath of stimulus packages enacted to respond to the crisis.

CRS data on the sectoral distribution of Aid for Trade in 2007 showed strong growth in support for trade-related infrastructure and productive capacity, with increases of 21 per cent each in real terms above the 2002–5 baseline (OECD and WTO 2009: 57) (see Figure 13.2). Support to both these categories increased further in 2008 reaching US$23 billion and US$17 billion, respectively (OECD 2010a).

The CRS data shows that global, regional and multi-country programmes increased from US$2.1 billion in 2002–5 to US$4.3 billion in 2007 (OECD and WTO 2009: 61), and then rose by a further US$900 million in 2008 (OECD 2010a). In 2007, the cross-country distribution of Aid for Trade showed that 54 per cent of Aid for Trade flows were allocated to low-income countries (OECD and WTO 2009: 60), mainly in the form of support to infrastructure, whereas Aid for Trade for building productive capacity was more important for middle-income countries.

In 2007, Asia was the region that attracted the greatest share of Aid for Trade, receiving 42 per cent of the total (see Figure 13.3). Africa was second, with 38 per cent. Most of the support committed to sub-Saharan Africa was financed by international financial institutions (OECD and WTO 2009: 59). Together, these institutions allocated almost half of their Aid for Trade to Africa (and 60 per cent of their total support to economic infrastructure projects). Data for 2008 shows that Asia (44 per cent)

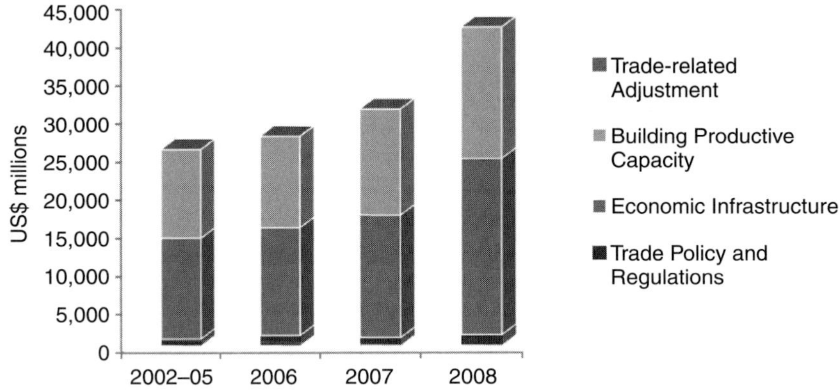

Figure 13.2 Global Aid for Trade commitments
Source: OECD/CRS.

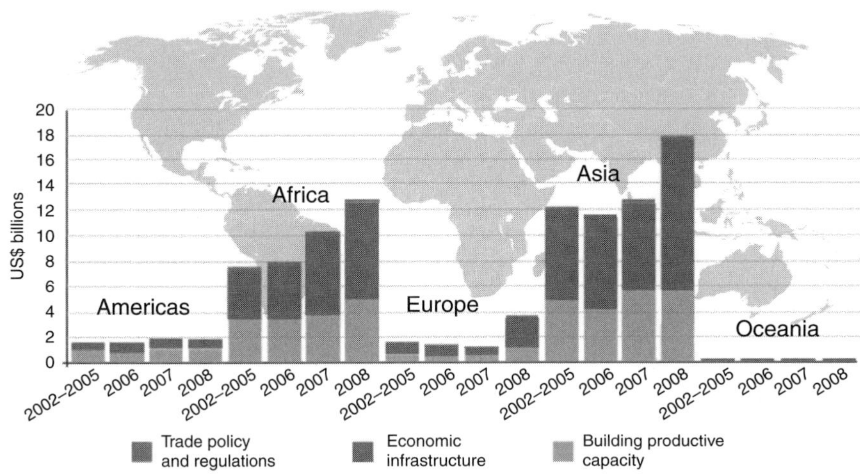

Figure 13.3 Aid for Trade allocation by region
Source: OECD/CRS.

and Africa (37 per cent) continue to lead global Aid for Trade allocation (OECD 2010a).

Strikingly, Aid for Trade is highly concentrated in a few countries. In 2007 only four countries – India, Vietnam, Afghanistan and Iraq – captured 20 per cent of all commitments (OECD and WTO 2009: 61) (see Figure 13.4). Similarly, in 2008 three countries – India, Iraq and

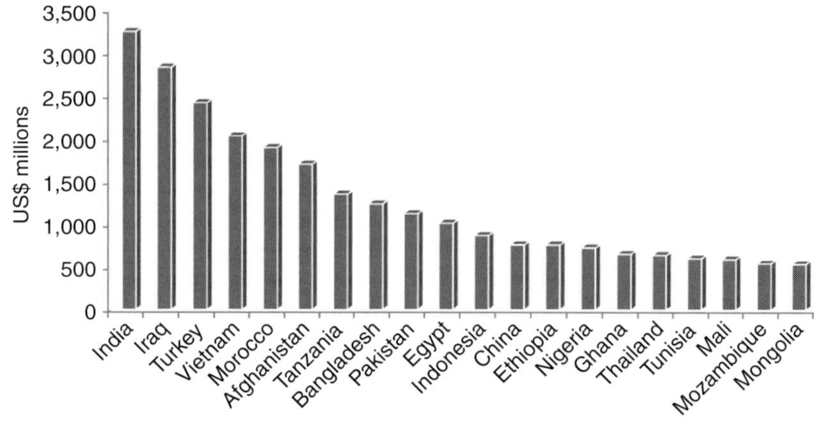

Figure 13.4 Top Aid for Trade recipients in 2008
Source: OECD/CRS.

Turkey – captured 20 per cent of total Aid for Trade (OECD 2010a). Country-specific analysis of Aid for Trade flows to Africa by the United Nations Economic Commission for Africa (UNECA 2009) also suggests high volatility of Aid for Trade allocations per country and subregions over time (see Figure 13.5). Further, in per capita terms, the allocation of Aid for Trade to African countries varies widely. The UNECA estimates that the weighted average per capita Aid for Trade allocation in 2006 was US$10.7. However, twenty-eight of the fifty-four African countries considered scored below that average, most of which were LDCs (UNECA 2009: 4).

This analysis of flows suggests that certain categories of Aid for Trade that did not receive sufficient support at the outset – such as infrastructure, building productive capacity and regional programmes – now attract more attention. Nevertheless, the caveats about the CRS data noted above are serious and will need to be addressed in the future for better tracking of Aid for Trade. In particular, the fact that developing countries are unable to relate the CRS data to their own information regarding trade-related support makes it difficult to ascertain whether needs at the individual country level are adequately addressed. Further, the data does not yet provide a clear picture of the support provided to developing countries under the trade-related adjustment category of Aid for Trade.

Our analysis underlined that the uneven country coverage of Aid for Trade, which emerged as an important concern in the Task Force

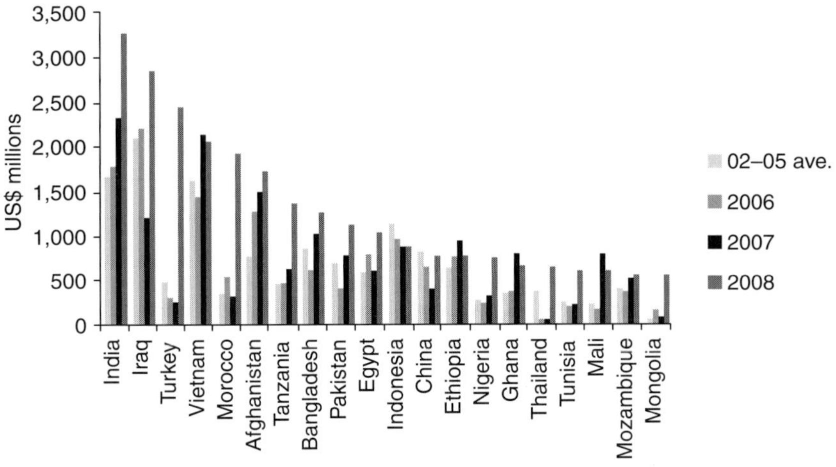

Figure 13.5 Aid for Trade volatility
Source: OECD/CRS.

deliberations on predictability and access, remains an issue. As noted by the OECD, '[T]racking aid for trade flows on a country-by-country basis clearly shows that in some cases objectives other than building trade capacities are driving aid flows' (OECD and WTO 2009: 61). In reality, Aid for Trade allocations are influenced by the same factors that determine general ODA. According to analytical work by the OECD, 'almost half the predicted value of aid is determined by donor-specific factors, one-third by needs, a sixth by self-interest and only 2% by performance' (OECD 2009d).

2.5 *Mutual accountability in practice*

Self-assessment questionnaires completed by donors and beneficiary countries in preparation for the 2007 and 2009 Aid for Trade global reviews shed further light on how mutual accountability has played out in practice. For the WTO's 2009 Aid for Trade global review, eighty-five developing countries responded to the self-assessment questionnaire as compared to only seven in 2007, indicating an increase in awareness about, and interest in, the initiative. Virtually all donor countries responded to both surveys.

Donors were required to report on the extent to which they had taken action to mainstream Aid for Trade in their development assistance programmes, to align their assistance with national processes, and to harmonize and coordinate their interventions with other donors. In parallel, beneficiary countries were required to report on the extent to which trade is mainstreamed in their national development strategies and on their prioritization of trade capacity development.

Most donors reported the adoption of specific Aid for Trade strategies or integration of Aid for Trade components in their development assistance instruments. Many donors reported they had taken measures to enhance institutional and human resources capacity to respond to demand for Aid for Trade and also to improve systems for the monitoring and evaluation of Aid for Trade projects and programmes.

In terms of the operational alignment of donors' assistance to country systems,[13] the outcome was less clear-cut: a significant proportion of donors (37 per cent) were not able to specify the degree of alignment to beneficiary country systems. Here however, it is also important to note that the degree of alignment depends partly on the effective prioritization of trade-related support by beneficiaries in their dialogue with donors, as well as the capacities of the institutions and systems in beneficiary countries.

With regard to the extent of harmonization or coordination among donors, questionnaires revealed limited participation of donors in joint initiatives such as joint assessments, programming, monitoring and evaluation, etc. For United Nations agencies, there were some steps forward. As part of the broader 'One UN' reform agenda, a new Trade and Productive Capacity Cluster reported progress in terms of both alignment to partner country systems and harmonization.[14]

Responses of beneficiary countries to the WTO's 2009 global review questionnaires suggest that developing countries are increasingly mainstreaming trade in their national development plans and poverty reduction strategies,[15] but that policy statements are not necessarily translated

[13] 'Country systems' is used here in the sense of the Paris Declaration on Aid Effectiveness. It refers to the use of processes and procedures of partner countries for the delivery of aid such as financial management and procurement systems.

[14] The Chief Executive Board Inter-agency Cluster on Trade and Productive Capacity coordinates the support of UN agencies, raises awareness among UN country teams about the importance of trade for economic growth and development, and coordinates Aid for Trade interventions by UN agencies through joint programming. In addition to the eight pilot countries originally identified for launching the Delivering as One programme (including Albania, Cape Verde, Mozambique, Rwanda, Tanzania, Uruguay and Vietnam), a number of countries have requested UN support in the trade area under the 'Delivering as One' modality.

[15] This conclusion has also been reached by a UNDP assessment of the trade content of PRSPs. For more details, see UNDP (2009).

into operational strategies with concrete outcomes and budgets. This makes dialogue between beneficiaries and donors around specific priorities difficult. Similarly, with regard to monitoring and evaluation systems for Aid for Trade, only fifteen beneficiary countries affirmed that they have the necessary systems in place. There is no evidence, however, of how effective these systems are. Further, several beneficiary countries report initiatives to improve the institutional framework at the national level for the coordination of Aid for Trade and trade policy more broadly (the specific arrangements vary by country).

Beneficiary countries also report that there is a need for more coordinated initiatives among donors. The core priorities they outline for improving the effectiveness of Aid for Trade included a stronger focus by donors on trade capacity development; increased beneficiary ownership in the design of programmes; more predictable funding; and increased provision of budget support and coordinated sector-wide approaches.[16]

In addition, a number of beneficiary countries identify support for regional integration as a priority in their national trade strategies (OECD and WTO 2009: 84). To advance this regional integration agenda, these countries propose trade facilitation, infrastructure, competitiveness, export diversification and capacity for regional trade negotiations as priorities. For landlocked countries (many of which are located in Africa) and Small Island Developing States (SIDS), infrastructure and trade facilitation are noted as particularly important areas for support. To date, developing countries reported receiving regional Aid for Trade 'mainly for infrastructure and for trade negotiations capacity building' (OECD and WTO 2009: 86).

For their part, donor countries noted a number of challenges for Aid for Trade implementation at the regional level including: 'high co-ordination costs for multi-country programmes; the lack of credit standing among many regional entities; and the absence of lending and aid disbursement instruments suited to regional contexts' (OECD and WTO 2009: 88).

The human and institutional capacities of regional interlocutors vary significantly. Some RECs, for instance, are not able to meet the challenge of leading their Members' engagement with the Aid for Trade initiative on regional integration issues. In the case of African countries, for instance, 'capacity building – especially support for

[16] A sector-wide approach refers to situations where 'all significant donor funding supports a single, comprehensive sector policy and independent programme, consistent with a sound macro-economic framework, under government leadership' (OECD 2007).

RECs (e.g. ECOWAS, WAEMU, COMESA, SACU) – is typically considered as the starting point for regional assistance' (OECD and WTO 2009: 86).

The self-assessment questionnaires reveal that awareness about the importance of trade-related support for growth and development is increasing in both donors and beneficiary countries, and that the Aid for Trade initiative is contributing to this progress. Increased awareness creates a platform for improvement. The adoption of Aid for Trade strategies by donors as well as the establishment of coordination entities by developing countries to identify trade-related needs and liaise with development partners is important. Nevertheless, both donors and developing countries noted important challenges, including difficulties matching Aid for Trade demand and supply at the country and regional level. Further, the limited involvement of the RECs in the Aid for Trade initiative remains an important missing link in its governance architecture.

The following section reviews the governance architecture of three other prominent international initiatives designed to support the achievement of global public goods. By highlighting alternative arrangements for access, predictability and mutual accountability, the core studies shed light on the options and lessons that could be learned for Aid for Trade governance.

3 Case studies of governance arrangements for providing global public goods: lessons for Aid for Trade

Three case studies of alternative governance arrangements for providing global public goods are reviewed in this section: the Global Environment Facility (GEF); the Global Fund to Fight AIDS, Tuberculosis and Malaria (the Global Fund); and the Enhanced Integrated Framework for Trade-Related Technical Assistance to Least Developed Countries (EIF).[17]

3.1 The Global Environment Facility (GEF)

The GEF is a partnership of 182 Member governments, international organizations, non-governmental organizations (NGOs) and the private sector that provides financial resources to developing countries and economies in transition to support the implementation of several international environmental conventions, such as the Convention

[17] For a review of past financing arrangements relevant to Aid for Trade, see ILEAP (2006).

on Biological Diversity; Stockholm Convention on Persistent Organic Pollutants; United Nations Framework Convention on Climate Change; UN Convention to Combat Desertification; and the Montreal Protocol on Substances that Deplete the Ozone Layer.

The GEF was launched in 1991 as a US$1 billion pilot programme managed by the World Bank, which serves as its trustee. Since its creation, the organization has undergone several institutional adjustments to adapt to the evolving requirements of international environmental conventions, for which it serves as a financial mechanism, and to take on board major changes in the overall aid architecture reflected in the Paris Declaration on Aid Effectiveness adopted in 2005.[18]

Replenishment of the GEF is carried out every four years. As of February 2009, the GEF had allocated US$8.8 billion supplemented by more than US$38.7 billion in co-financing arrangements.[19]

GEF governance combines an assembly, a political body composed of representatives of participating countries, and a council, which serves as its executive decision-making body. There are thirty-two seats on the council – fourteen allocated to the donor constituency and eighteen to beneficiary countries (GEF 2008a: 40).

Decision-making by the assembly and the council is based on consensus. If consensus cannot be reached at the council, a formal vote is taken, weighted according to financial contribution to the facility. This means that donors, especially the larger ones, have more say. Donors often also attach conditions to their contributions during replenishment negotiations (e.g. regarding the size of the envelope for climate mitigation versus adaptation, and other thematic areas of funding), which significantly influence both the 'strategic objectives and programme priorities decided by the GEF Council' (GEF 2009: 174). During the fifth replenishment negotiations (for the period July 2010 to June 2014), Members decided 'to allow the participation of four representatives of recipient countries as well as two representatives of civil society in its meetings' (GEF 2009: 174).

Although the international environmental conventions provide the framework for GEF operations, coordination and communication with their secretariats are considered to be weak. The 'limited role and voice'

[18] Although the GEF has reviewed its policies and processes with a view to adapt to the Paris Declaration Principles, it has not formally adhered to the Declaration.

[19] See www.thegef.org [accessed in November 2010]. Co-funding for GEF projects can be provided by a number of sources: beneficiary government; concerned agency; other multilateral or bilateral donors; and the private sector, etc.

of the conventions in the governance of the GEF (GEF 2009: 179) undermines accountability.

Coordination at the country level and alignment with national priorities is also generally regarded to be weak (GEF 2009). In this context, the Fourth Overall Performance Study of the GEF recommended that the organization support 'the creation of GEF National Committees ... ' (GEF 2009: 58) or other mechanisms that would allow interaction between government entities, GEF agencies and other donors involved in supporting environment-related interventions for better aligning and responding to national priorities.

Against these weaknesses, the GEF has a robust monitoring and evaluation system in place. A Scientific and Technical Advisory Panel provides independent advice to the GEF on scientific and technical aspects of programmes and policies, which helps to ensure that initiatives are approved on the basis of their technical merits. Finally, embedded within the organization is an independent evaluation office that reports directly to the Council. The evaluation office undertakes performance audits and provides other information for replenishment negotiations (GEF 2006).

In terms of access and predictability, the GEF has faced several important challenges. First, although it has mobilized significant resources for environmental programmes, it is widely acknowledged that funding remains below what is required to tackle the increasing cost of overcoming global environmental problems and meeting the extended mandate of the international environmental conventions that it serves. The Fourth Overall Performance Study of the GEF prepared by its Evaluation Office to inform the fifth replenishment discussions suggested that a significant increase in resources was needed (GEF 2009). The negotiations concluded in May 2010 with a total of US$4.25 billion pledged by thirty donors.

Second, the GEF operational guidelines specify that project approval is dependent on the extent to which additional funding is leveraged by beneficiary countries.[20] This co-financing requirement has limited the ability of developing countries to access GEF funding because in practice it means acquiring loans through the World Bank or a regional development bank usually subject to specific additional conditions (South Centre 2008).

[20] For more information on the GEF policy on co-financing, see GEF (2002).

Third, the United Nations Development Programme (UNDP), the United Nations Environment Programme (UNEP) and the World Bank act as implementing agencies in cooperation with seven regional banks and international organizations to assist governments and other stakeholders eligible for GEF funding to develop, implement and manage projects. Projects are submitted for funding through the implementing agencies only, with local stakeholders including governments, civil society, private sector and indigenous peoples participating through implementing initiatives. Developing countries have criticized the lack of direct government access to the GEF as a deficit in its operational arrangements (Third World Network (TWN) 2009).

Fourth, the GEF has been criticized for a tardy process of review and approval of projects (GEF 2009: 1). On average, it takes twelve months to prepare projects, with particular bottlenecks concentrated in the GEF's project identification phase (TWN 2009).

3.2 The Global Fund to Fight AIDS, Tuberculosis and Malaria

The Global Fund was created in 2002 to mobilize additional resources to support efforts by low-income countries to fight and treat HIV/AIDS, tuberculosis and malaria. As in the case of the GEF, the World Bank serves as the trustee of the Global Fund.

In relation to mutual accountability, the Global Fund's main decision-making body is its Board of Directors, which meets twice a year and is responsible for defining policies and strategies, mobilizing funding and making funding decisions. The Board is composed of thirty individuals, representing donors and recipient governments, civil society, private sector, philanthropic foundations and communities directly affected by the diseases. It has twenty voting Members and six non-voting Members. The voting Members include eight donors, seven recipient countries and five stakeholders. Board decisions are made on the basis of consensus.[21] In terms of global governance arrangements, the Global Fund's formal incorporation of stakeholders into its decision-making structures represents a major innovation.

[21] In case it is not possible, a motion will pass with a two-thirds majority of those present of both the group encompassing the eight donors and the two private sector seats; and the group encompassing the seven developing country representatives, the two seats of NGOs and the representative of communities affected by HIV/AIDS. For more details see The Global Fund to Fight Aids, Tuberculosis and Malaria By-laws as amended 5 May 2009, available at www.theglobalfund.org [accessed in November 2010].

A further aspect of the Global Fund's governance arrangement that enhances accountability is the Country Coordinating Mechanisms (CCMs), comprised of governmental entities, NGOs, private business and communities directly affected by the diseases. The CCMs decide at the national level which programmes will be presented for funding to the Global Fund in alignment with national health strategies and priorities. The CCMs also decide on the principal recipient entities to carry out the programmes and, once the grants are approved, oversee programme implementation. In this regard, the CCMs are central for realizing the principles of country ownership and participatory decision-making in Global Fund operations. Although the CCMs are perceived as one of the most positive contributions of the Global Fund in terms of promoting partnerships among a wide range of stakeholders, the first independent evaluation of the Global Fund (The Global Fund 2009a) recommended that the CCMs should be better integrated into broader schemes for the coordination of the health and social sectors at the national level to ensure stronger alignment and harmonization in line with the Paris Declaration and Accra Agenda principles.

The mutual accountability framework of the Global Fund includes a performance-based system. The Global Fund's overall performance is assessed on the basis of indicators that include resource mobilization, administrative effectiveness, portfolio management, and special initiatives.[22] The independent evaluation of the Global Fund highlighted that the results orientation of its grant process has helped foster an accountability culture. However, it highlighted that inadequate capacities and weaknesses in the information systems of recipient countries limits 'the feasibility of the performance based funding approach espoused by the Global Fund' (The Global Fund 2009a: 10).

The governance architecture of the Global Fund includes a Reference Group that advises the Secretariat on evaluation approaches and practices, and reporting procedures, as well as an Office of the Inspector General, whose function is to provide independent advice about the effectiveness of controls in place to manage risks associated with programmes and operations. The Inspector General Office reports directly to the Board.

In terms of access and predictability, the Global Fund's Board has approved US$19.2 billion of support for 572 programmes in 144 countries since 2002 (The Global Fund 2010: 3). Grants are provided for five years.

[22] For more details on the performance-based system of the Global Fund, see www.theglobalfund.org [accessed in November 2010].

The Global Fund was conceived and functions as a network of partners and entities that implement the programmes that it funds. In particular, the Global Fund engages principal recipients in developing countries (i.e. beneficiary governments, civil society, private sector, foundations, representatives of communities living with the disease, etc.) that can either implement programmes directly, or subcontract others to do so. A Local Fund Agent (LFA) – usually an established accounting firm – assesses the capacities of the principal recipient entities. Around 50 per cent of grants are channelled through government entities as principal recipients. The Board has adopted guidelines for a dual-track approach to actively encourage the designation of non-governmental entities as principal recipients. This policy was introduced as a means to improve the absorptive capacity of beneficiaries (The Global Fund 2007).

After eighteen months of the life of a project, the LFA assesses programme performance and makes a recommendation to the Global Fund Board as to whether the programme should be 'continued, terminated, or adjusted after two years' (Ooman *et al.* 2007).

All low-income and lower-middle-income countries (according to the World Bank system of Country Income Classification) are eligible to apply for funding to the Global Fund. Upper-middle-income economies are also eligible to apply if they have a high disease burden based on information provided by UNAIDS and WHO. A Technical Review Panel (TRP) composed of forty health and development experts is responsible for reviewing projects on their technical merits and making funding recommendations. This ensures that projects are approved on the basis of merit, thus enhancing transparency and equity in access by beneficiary countries.

There have, however, been some challenges with the disbursement of Global Fund resources, including bottlenecks 'primarily caused by challenges faced by ROs [recipient organizations] in managing resources' (Ooman *et al.* 2007: 42) and uncertainties about whether assessments adequately identify the capacity challenges faced by prospective recipients and whether the Global Fund is effective at addressing them.

Although contributions from governments continue to be the main source of the Global Fund's resources, individuals, businesses and private foundations also contribute. In 2004, the Global Fund Board decided to substitute the system of ad hoc voluntary contributions by regular replenishment cycles with a view to ensuring more sustained and predictable funding. At the time of writing, negotiations for the third replenishment to cover the period 2011–13 were in progress. While the Global Fund has had considerable success in mobilizing additional resources, the independent evaluation (The Global Fund 2009a) highlighted the importance raised by the issue of sustainability, particularly given that beneficiary countries rely mainly on external funding to fight the three diseases. The mobilization of in-country resources was identified as an area for improvement. Investments in long-term capacity development and greater alignment of Global Fund activities with national health systems were also considered critical for ensuring the sustainability of the programme's achievements.

3.3 *The Enhanced Integrated Framework (EIF)*

The EIF was launched following a decision at the 2005 WTO Hong Kong Ministerial Conference to enhance the Integrated Framework, which had operated since 1997. The Integrated Framework began as an inter-agency programme supported by six agencies (the International Monetary Fund (IMF), International Trade Centre (ITC), United Nations Conference on Trade and Development (UNCTAD), UNDP, World Bank and WTO), coordinated through an Inter-Agency Working Group. In 2000, the Integrated Framework was reformed to better emphasize mainstreaming trade in the national development and poverty reduction initiatives of the beneficiary countries and to better coordinate assistance and support (WTO 2006b). A multi-donor Trust Fund was also created, managed by UNDP, to which seventeen donors had contributed over US$60 million by 2008. Funding was available under two windows (WTO 2006b). Window I financed trade diagnostic studies with allocations of up to US$300,000 per country and to strengthen in-country structures' capacities with allocations of up to US$38,000 per country. Window II financed priority capacity-building projects arising from the diagnostic study and action matrix, with allocations of up to US$1 million per country.

In 2003, an independent evaluation of the Integrated Framework (WTO 2003) concluded that although progress had been made in a number of areas as a result of the 2000 restructuring, results varied significantly across LDCs. In particular, the evaluation observed that the Integrated Framework had 'failed to mainstream trade into the PRSP process and has not provided adequate financial and human resources to the LDCs to deliver the intended outcomes' (WTO 2006b: 3). The evaluation also found that 'priorities identified [through the diagnostic studies] are not being picked up in mainstream investments', that country ownership is weak, and that the IF is still often seen by both the donor community and the LDCs as a stand-alone process (WTO 2006b: 3).

Following the WTO Hong Kong Ministerial Conference, an IF Task Force was established to look into three main elements to 'enhance' the programme: 1) increased, predictable and additional funding; 2) strengthened capacities in-country; and 3) improved IF management to effectively steward increased financial resources and programme delivery (WTO 2005).

The enhanced IF became fully operational in July 2009. The EIF is more broadly conceived as a partnership between donors, LDCs and international organizations with two clear objectives: first, to assist LDCs to mainstream trade in their national development strategies and second, to facilitate the coordinated delivery of trade-related development assistance to LDC beneficiaries. All LDCs are eligible to become beneficiaries following a technical review of their preparedness to participate in the programme.

In terms of governance arrangements, EIF governance comprises a Steering Committee and a Board. The Steering Committee is the assembly of all the main stakeholders and has oversight responsibility. It includes all forty-nine LDCs, the bilateral donors that have contributed to the EIF Trust Fund and the six core IF agencies (IMF, ITC, UNCTAD, UNDP, World Bank and WTO). The Board, which is the main decision-making forum, brings together three representatives of the donor and the LDC constituencies, and a representative of each of the six core agencies. The United Nations Industrial Development Organization (UNIDO) has been invited to participate at the Board as an observer. Decision-making is by consensus. If consensus is unattainable, a vote is held, with three donors and three LDC representatives having one vote each. The Chair has a casting vote in case of deadlock. The Board is responsible for funding allocations, monitoring implementation, periodic reviews and evaluation of activities.

The EIF replaced the IF Inter-Agency Working Group with an Executive Secretariat led by an Executive Director. The Secretariat is responsible for the day-to-day management of the programme and, together with the trust fund manager, provides guidance to LDCs in the implementation of the programme. The Secretariat is independent, although administratively hosted by the WTO, and reports directly to the Board.

At the country level, the EIF strengthened provisions for mutual accountability. A national IF focal point (usually from the trade ministry), and a donor facilitator (usually from the resident donor community), collaborate to oversee project implementation arrangements. A national implementation unit supports the IF focal point. The unit is responsible for coordination, trade mainstreaming in national development strategies, project development and monitoring implementation.

Provisions are made for stakeholders from across governments, the private sector, civil society and the donor community to be represented in a National Steering Committee responsible for the oversight of national trade capacity development initiatives. The National Steering Committee has a formal role in the in-country approval process for IF-funded projects as well. A variety of national stakeholders as well as international partners can also directly access the trust fund and be involved in the implementation of EIF projects in so far as the trust fund manager and the EIF Secretariat assess their implementation capacities to be adequate.

It is anticipated that this country level institutional framework will also be used to mobilize Aid for Trade resources and meet reporting requirements. Indeed, the self-assessment reports of LDCs and donors to the Aid for Trade Global Review have highlighted the value stakeholders place on the EIF structures to increase resource mobilization, and to improve alignment and harmonization processes. To this extent, the EIF has meant that LDCs are better equipped to engage with the Aid for Trade initiative than many other developing countries.

The EIF has further emphasized mutual accountability by placing considerable emphasis on integrating a results-based approach to its interventions. A monitoring and evaluation framework is under development and being piloted in several countries.

In terms of access, a multi-donor trust fund managed by the United Nations Office for Project Services (UNOPS) has been established to support EIF interventions, with an overall funding target of US$250 million over five years to 2013. In 2007, bilateral donors committed US$170 million to the programme at a pledging conference, of which US$94 million had been contributed to the Trust Fund as of 31 March 2010 with commitments up to 2013 reaching US$182 million (UNOPS 2010). Funding has significantly increased as compared to the 'old' IF, although predictability may become an issue in the future as no process for regular replenishment of the trust fund has been established. The trust fund manager maintains fiduciary responsibility for the management of the trust fund and is accountable to the Board for resource use, activities, outputs and results achieved based on reports by implementing entities drawing upon log-frames developed for each project.

The first step in the EIF process (as was the case in the 'old' IF) is the completion of a Diagnostic Trade Integration Study (DTIS). This DTIS identifies the main constraints on the country's trade expansion and priorities, and captures these in a matrix. The matrix facilitates dialogue between LDCs and donors on trade-related needs within the context of broader development programming. The DTIS has also become the main point of reference for integrating trade and productive capacity concerns in assistance provided by UN agencies in the countries concerned. The DTIS and its periodic updates – introduced as part of the enhanced programme – are financed through the trust fund.

Under a Tier 1 funding window, beneficiary countries have access to funding for projects aimed at supporting national in-country implementation arrangements to enhance trade mainstreaming, institutional capacities and dialogue among stakeholders. Specific guidelines have been developed to define the scope and operational requirements for these types of projects. A second funding window, Tier 2, is available for funding priority needs identified in the DTIS action matrix; no fixed allocation per country has been established. Grants available from the trust fund are considered subsidiary or complementary to resources mobilized with other development partners. Major infrastructure projects are excluded from eligibility from the trust fund, as are adjustment costs. The scope of funding available under the EIF is thus limited as compared to the much broader Aid for Trade categories.

3.4 Assessment

The three case studies illustrated above shed light on different options that have been pursued to govern resource flows from developed to developing countries to aid the provision of global public goods. The impact of these different governance arrangements on mutual accountability, predictability and access vary.

Regarding access and predictability, the three case studies highlight the benefits of approaches that ensure beneficiaries have a clear point of access for resources, with criteria for funding linked to programmatic and operational considerations that are made clear to beneficiaries in advance. Regular replenishments – for the GEF and the Global Fund – ensure that funding is available to meet needs over the agreed period of time. Ultimately, however, commitment by development partners remains the *sine qua non* condition to ensure that funding available is commensurate to needs. As shown in the case of the GEF, the replenishment process has not always been successful in mobilizing sufficient funding for meeting the increasing needs of beneficiaries and the global environmental conventions. The technical criteria used for the assessment of funding proposals in the three initiatives indicates that all beneficiaries have, in principle, a fair chance to access available resources. The EIF's main strength in this regard is the explicit emphasis on building capacities of local stakeholders to be able to manage the programme and the overall trade agenda. In the case of the Global Fund, the CCMs are expected to play a similar role, but their capacities are weak, and Fund support for building local capacities is not clearly outlined or systematized.

Each of the cases reviewed has governance structures that allow donors and beneficiary countries to participate in decision-making, including on matters affecting funding allocation. That said, deficiencies are identified in the case of the GEF, for instance, due to the unequal weight in decision-making by donors and beneficiaries. The three facilities also place emphasis on measuring results. The GEF and the Global Fund have mechanisms for monitoring the results and, to some extent, the impact of the projects and the programme as a whole. The EIF is in the process of establishing a monitoring and evaluation framework. The independent evaluation facilities in the GEF and the Global Fund further underscore the importance of mutual accountability in the implementation and governance architecture of these facilities.

In the case of the Aid for Trade initiative, the spotlight effect provided by the global and regional reviews, in addition to the oversight activities of the WTO Committee on Trade and Development, the Trade Policy Review Mechanism, the WTO Director-General's Advisory Group and the OECD Working Party of the Trade Committee significantly reinforce mutual accountability principles in the governance arrangements. Awareness raising and peer pressure is expected to create incentives for improving effectiveness in the delivery and use of Aid for Trade resources at the country level over time. However, the governance arrangements do too little to harness regional processes for Aid for Trade delivery and use. And in the absence of well-established funding arrangements, the initiative faces important challenges with respect to access and predictability. As already seen, the distribution of Aid for Trade flows is skewed across countries. Further, analytical work by the UNECA and others highlights the volatility of Aid for Trade resources (UNECA 2009).

Accordingly, the main challenge for governance of the Aid for Trade initiative is to respond to the deficit in the arrangements for access and predictability. There are several ways through which this could be achieved. One option advocated by developing countries during the Aid for Trade Task Force deliberations is the establishment of a vertical or global fund to respond to underfunded needs related to regional integration

Table 13.1. *Aid for Trade governance arrangements compared*

	Global Environment Facility (GEF)	The Global Fund	Enhanced Integrated Framework (EIF)	Aid for Trade
Mutual accountability	*Medium*	*Medium*	*Medium*	*Medium*
Access and predictability	*Medium*	*High*	*Medium*	*Low*

commitments and intra-regional trade development. Another option is the creation of regional Aid for Trade funds.

Based on the information and evidence reviewed in this section, Table 13.1 compares the Aid for Trade governance to those for the three case studies.

4 Overcoming the deficit in Aid for Trade governance: the case for regional facilities

This section makes the case for Aid for Trade regional financial facilities to complement the current global arrangements. While such regional facilities may not necessarily fully resolve the institutional deficit on access and predictability in Aid for Trade governance, our recommendation is in line with developing countries' own call for greater support for their regional integration efforts (as expressed in their 2009 Aid for Trade global review self-assessment questionnaires). It will also help give expression to the as yet unimplemented Aid for Trade Task Force recommendation for the establishment of a Regional Aid for Trade Committee.

Intra-regional trade represents a significant proportion of total trade for developing countries. Average intra-regional merchandise exports in developing country regions accounted for 23.5 per cent of their total trade in 2008.[23] The multilateral trading system provides important disciplines for trade activities at global, regional and indeed bilateral levels; but regional integration can also generate dynamic gains in investment,

[23] Calculated by the authors based on WTO data (WTO 2009c). Africa, with 9.3 per cent, registered the lowest proportion of intra-regional trade and Asia, with 50 per cent, showed the highest.

production and trade. Accordingly, almost all developing countries are engaged in regional integration arrangements. At the national level, they prioritize regional cooperation and integration objectives. However, the RECs charged with implementing regional trade agreements and supporting cross-border integration initiatives have thus far been somewhat marginal in the Aid for Trade initiative. In the 2009 self-assessment questionnaires, donor countries reported that a key challenge for increasing funding for cross-border activities was the weak articulation between national and regional priorities and inadequate institutional capacity in many regional integration schemes.

In contrast to RECs, regional development banks have been more active in the Aid for Trade initiative by leading regional Aid for Trade reviews. Regional banks have also made major investment commitments associated with the initiative, such as the financing of the North–South Corridor in Southern Africa by the Southern Africa Development Bank and the African Development Bank; the Asian Development Bank's support to the Greater Mekong Sub-Region Economic Cooperation Programme (GMS); and the Central Asia Regional Economic Cooperation (CAREC) Programme, which is a partnership of eight countries and six multilateral institutions, which include regional development banks.[24]

More systematic and direct involvement by RECs in the Aid for Trade initiative could help address its shortcomings with regard to access and predictability of resources. Specifically, RECs could be empowered with financial facilities to fund national and regional Aid for Trade projects. A number of RECs have already taken steps to establish a regional financial facility for channelling resources to finance trade-related support activities.[25] The COMESA Fund (see Box 13.2) has, for instance, one window

[24] The partners are the eight CAREC countries of Afghanistan, Azerbaijan, the People's Republic of China, Kazakhstan, the Kyrgryz Republic, Mongolia, Tajikistan and Uzbekistan. The Programme's six multilateral partners are the Asian Development Bank (ADB), European Bank for Reconstruction and Development (EBRD), International Monetary Fund (IMF), Islamic Development Bank (IsDB), United Nations Development Programme (UNDP) and the World Bank. For further background, see www.adb.org/carec/ [accessed in November 2010].

[25] In 2010, a group of bilateral donors, led by the UK Department of International Development (DFID) and including Belgium, Canada, Denmark and the Netherlands, announced their plans to launch TradeMark East Africa (TMEA) to focus on building East African regional integration capacity and as a platform for scaling up Aid for Trade. For information on the launch of the initiative, see www.dfid.gov.uk/Media-Room/News-Stories/2011/UK-launches-trade-initiative-to-pull-millions-of-Africans-out-of-poverty/ [accessed in February 2011].

BOX 13.2: FUND FOR COOPERATION, COMPENSATION AND DEVELOPMENT OF THE COMMON MARKET FOR EASTERN AND SOUTHERN AFRICA

Article 150 of the 1994 Treaty establishing the Common Market for Eastern and Southern Africa (COMESA) provided for the creation of a special fund for cooperation, compensation and development (including trade) to address the problems of underdeveloped areas and other disadvantages arising from the integration process. It also mandated the adoption of a protocol for the operationalization of this article. The protocol was adopted during the Seventh Summit of COMESA Heads of State and Government.

According to the protocol, the Fund would be used to: 1) provide grants or loans for financing research and development activities and feasibility studies promoting regional integration; 2) provide means to facilitate mobilization of financial resources for development activities in Member States; and 3) promote regional integration through development initiatives in Member States, as well as the objectives of Chapter XXII of the Treaty, which relates to specific measures in favour of LDCs and economically depressed areas.

The COMESA Fund includes a capital base composed of contributions by COMESA Member States that ratify the protocol, as well as the general fund composed of contributions by cooperating development partners. It is managed by a Committee comprised of representatives of COMESA Members and development partners that have contributed to the COMESA Fund. The protocol foresaw the establishment of a Special Facility, open to contributions by development partners, to provide budgetary support to assist with adjustment costs arising out of COMESA's trade liberalization programmes. This window of the Fund is known as the COMESA Adjustment Facility. It became fully operational in 2009, providing support to Rwanda and Burundi to cover anticipated revenue losses resulting from the alignment of their tariffs to the East Africa Community common external tariff. The EU provides financial support to the Adjustment Facility.

A second window is the COMESA Infrastructure Fund, which is conceived as a revolving loan facility to finance regional infrastructure projects through a number of financial modalities. The Infrastructure Fund is expected to leverage donor funding by encouraging private financing of infrastructure projects, and exploring private–public partnerships. The Infrastructure Fund is not yet operational.

At the programmatic level, a master plan of priority programmes to enhance regional integration is to be formulated by the COMESA Secretariat with the COMESA Fund facilitating financing for projects. An Aid for Trade Unit within the COMESA Secretariat was established in October 2008 to develop a regional strategy and Aid for Trade projects.

Source: See www.comesa.int; COMESA Fund Protocol.

for funding infrastructure investments and another window to support adjustment to regional integration agreements (the former is not yet operational).

Regional Aid for Trade financial facilities that have dedicated trust funds (with provision for multi-donor and multi-annual commitments) could offer the following advantages:

1. Empowering the RECs to fund interventions at national and regional levels will significantly enhance their own credibility, help them build capacity to manage regional integration initiatives, and breathe new life into regional integration schemes.
2. Responding to challenges related to access and predictability, in addition to providing a vehicle for donor coordination and alignment.
3. Providing a vehicle to attract transfers from the emerging economies to developing countries for trade capacity development. Discussions at the WTO Committee on Trade and Development reveal that emerging economies have thus far viewed Aid for Trade as an OECD initiative and are wary of the inclusion of South–South transfers in ODA flows. The possibility of direct contributions by emerging economies to a regional trade programme could help overcome this concern.

However, for these gains to be fully achieved, the following general principles should govern the operation of the proposed facilities.

1. Satisfactory fiduciary arrangements will be required. A widely utilized model in trust fund management is to assign programmatic and fiduciary responsibilities to different entities. In this case, the REC can assume responsibility for the implementation of the medium-term programme and partner with a regional development bank or a professional fund manager who will serve as trust fund manager with fiduciary responsibility. In the COMESA example provided in Box 13.2, the Secretariat is responsible for programmatic activities with a professional fund manager accountable for management of the COMESA Fund, both reporting to a Committee of Member States and participating development partners.
2. The facility should be constructed around a medium-term programme cycle that reflects the resource requirements to fully finance projects and details the successive replenishments envisaged for subsequent cycles.
3. The activities in the medium-term programme should fall under the broad categories identified by the WTO Aid for Trade Task Force: that

is, trade policy and regulations, trade development, trade-related infrastructure, building productive capacity, trade-related adjustment, and other trade-related needs. Strong emphasis should be placed on trade capacity development and in-country support, critical for ensuring long-term sustainability.

4. The facility's architecture should have different windows for disbursements to fund national and regional interventions using appropriate criteria. Grants should be the main financial instrument, but adequate provision should be envisaged for leveraging private investments and loans in view of the growing importance of public–private partnerships in areas critical for integration and trade development, such as infrastructure and energy.
5. The facility should be open for contributions from all interested development partners, including emerging economies, to realize the full benefits of reduced transaction costs and coordination. The possibility for engagement at the regional level may help overcome the reluctance on the part of some emerging economies to participate in the Aid for Trade initiative as donors.
6. The facility's governance arrangements should involve Member States and donors in the joint development of guidelines for funding allocation, project support and other operational requirements, as well as mutual accountability. Involvement of the private sector and civil society in the governance structure should also be considered.

Robust monitoring, evaluation and reporting arrangements would provide incentives for enhanced effectiveness and confidence-building, and thereby further support the goals of mutual accountability.

The organigram (Figure 13.6) on the next page provides an illustration of Aid for Trade governance with the introduction of regional facilities. While an assessment of the suitability of developing country RECs (Table 13.2 provides an illustrative list of RECs) to host and lead the establishment of regional Aid for Trade facilities is beyond the scope of this chapter, we note that several RECs, notably COMESA and the East African Economic Community (EAC), have already taken steps towards adopting regional Aid for Trade facilities.

5 Conclusions

Since the launch of the Aid for Trade initiative in 2005, both donor and beneficiary countries have taken considerable action to engage with it. As

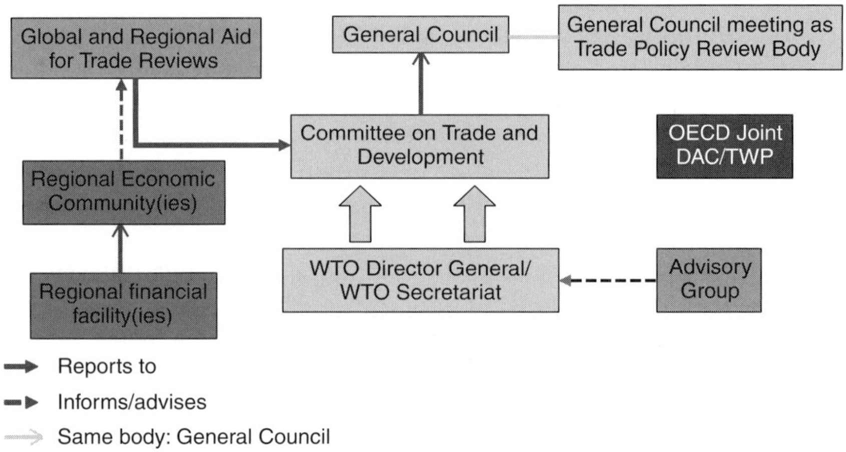

Figure 13.6 Aid for Trade governance revised

the initiative has evolved, the mutual accountability of donors and beneficiaries has emerged as the main governance principle in its implementation arrangements – most notably through the 'spotlight effect' of global and regional reviews and through dialogue in fora such as the WTO Committee on Trade and Development, which has focused on identifying what is required from all partners to make the initiative work. Attention to equally important issues of access and predictability of Aid for Trade resources has been less prominent. As a result, developing countries' access to the available resources remains challenging. There is no single point of access or identified process and criteria for beneficiaries to tap into the Aid for Trade resources committed by bilateral and multilateral donors.

Given the fairly weak recovery of the main donor countries from the 2008–9 economic and financial crisis, ODA flows in general and Aid for Trade resources in particular can be expected to decline. Against this background, there is an even stronger need to enhance the current Aid for Trade governance arrangements to overcome the deficit with respect to the intermediation between supply and demand of Aid for Trade resources. There are various ways in which this could be done. The three case studies presented in this chapter illustrated how, compared to the Aid for Trade initiative, other international arrangements to provide global public goods have been more comprehensive in incorporating the aid effectiveness agenda of the Paris Declaration and Accra Agenda, in

Table 13.2. *Illustrative list of regional integration schemes in developing country regions*

Regional integration schemes				
Africa	Latin America and the Caribbean	Central Asia	Asia Pacific	Middle-East
Common Market for Eastern and Southern Africa (COMESA)	Central American Common Market (CACM)	Special Programme for the Economies of Central Asia (SPECA)	South Asian Association for Regional Cooperation (SAARC)	Arab Maghreb Union (AMU)
Eastern African Community (EAC)	The Caribbean Community (CARICOM)	Central Asia Regional Economic Cooperation (CAREC)	Pacific Islands Forum (PIF)	Gulf Cooperation Council (GCC)
Southern Africa Development Community (SADC)	Andean Community			
The Economic Community of West African States (ECOWAS)	Southern Common Market (MERCOSUR)			
Mano River Union (MRU)				
West African Economic and Monetary Union (WAEMU)				
Economic Community of Central African States (ECCAS)				
Southern African Customs Union (SACU)				

particular by giving greater prominence to issues of access and predictability of resources.

To stimulate rethinking of Aid for Trade governance, this chapter has made the case for the establishment of regional Aid for Trade financial facilities firmly grounded in the Paris and Accra principles to channel funding to national and regional priorities. The establishment of such regional facilities will require political will from donors. For their part, RECs will need to build their own capacity to take on this intermediation role. The potential benefits of this approach are several: it would give regional integration efforts much-needed momentum and, if appropriately designed, provide national stakeholders with more transparent and responsive vehicles to access financial support. Further, regional Aid for Trade facilities could be complemented by national Aid for Trade basket funds as vehicles for managing, coordinating and reporting on bilateral and other support received for trade capacity development initiatives. Additional reforms for consideration include refining the CRS to better capture the flows of support in all of the Aid for Trade categories[26] and specific efforts to boost the capacity of beneficiary countries to monitor general ODA and Aid for Trade flows.

References

Cali, M. 2007. *Scale and Types of Funds for Aid for Trade*. Negotiation Advisory Brief No.15, Toronto: International Lawyers and Economists Against Poverty.

Duval, A. 2009. 'Experts Want African Aid Funds Channeled Away from HIV', *The Observer*, 25 October.

Global Environment Facility (GEF). 2002. *Policy on Co-financing*. GEF/C.20/6. Washington, DC: Global Environment Facility.

2006. *The GEF Monitoring and Evaluation Policy*. Evaluation Document No.1, Evaluation Office. Washington, DC: Global Environment Facility.

2008a. *Instrument for the Establishment of the Restructured Global Environment Facility*. Washington, DC: Global Environment Facility.

2008b. *From Projects to Programs: Clarifying the Programmatic Approach in the GEF Portfolio*. GEF/C.33/6. Washington, DC: Global Environment Facility.

2009. *Fourth Overall Performance Study of the GEF*. Washington, DC: GEF Evaluation Office.

2010. GEF-5 Programming Document. *Sixth Meeting for the Fifth Replenish ment of the GEF Trust Fund*. GEF/R.5/31. Washington, DC: Global Environment Facility.

[26] See WTO (2010) for plans in this area by the OECD and WTO Secretariats.

International Lawyers and Economists Against Poverty (ILEAP). 2006. *Financing International Public Goods: A Framework to Address Aid for Trade*. Negotiation Advisory Brief No.14. Toronto: ILEAP.

Njinkeu, D. and Cameron, H. (eds.) 2008. *Aid for Trade and Development*. Cambridge University Press.

OECD. 2005a. *Paris Declaration on Aid Effectiveness*. Paris: OECD.

2005b. *Trade and Structural Adjustment*. Paris: OECD.

2007. *Glossary of Statistical Terms*. Paris: OECD.

2008. *Accra Agenda for Action*. Endorsed at the 3rd High Level Forum on Aid Effectiveness. Paris: OECD.

2009a. *How to Evaluate Aid for Trade. A Scoping Note*. Development Co-operation Directorate and Agriculture Directorate. COM/DCD/TAD(2009)3. Paris: OECD.

2009b. *Binding Constraints to Trade Expansion. Aid for Trade Objectives and Diagnostic Tools*. OECD Trade Policy Working Paper No.94. Development Co-operation Directorate and Agriculture Directorate. COM/DCD/TAD(2009)5/FINAL. Paris: OECD.

2009c. *Aid for Trade Proposal for the Joint 2010–2012 DAC-TC PWB on Aid for Trade*. Development Co-operation Directorate and Agriculture Directorate. COM/DCD/TAD (2009)8. Paris: OECD.

2009d. *Aid Orphans: Whose Responsibility?* Development Brief, Issue 1. Paris: OECD.

2010a. *Aid for Trade Flows: 2008*. Development Co-operation Directorate and Trade and Agriculture Directorate. COM/DCD/TAD/RD(2010)4/RD1. Paris: OECD.

2010b. *Inside the DAC: A Guide to the OECD Development Assistance Committee. 2009–2010*. Paris: OECD.

OECD and WTO. 2007. *Aid for Trade at a Glance: 1st Global Review*. OECD/WTO. Paris: OECD.

2009. *Aid for Trade at a Glance –Maintaining Momentum*. OECD/WTO. Paris: OECD.

Ooman, N., Bernstein, M. and Rosenzweig, S. 2007. *A Comparative Analysis of the Funding Practices of PEPFAR, the Global Fund and World Bank MAP in Mozambique, Uganda and Zambia*. HIV/AIDS Monitor Analysis. Washington, DC: Centre for Global Development.

South Centre. 2008. *Financing the Global Climate Change Response: Suggestions for a Climate Change Fund (CCF)*. Geneva: South Centre.

The Global Fund. 2007. *Report of the Policy and Strategy Committee*. Fifteen Board Meeting, The Global Fund, GF/B15/6 – Revision 1. Geneva: The Global Fund.

2009a. *The Global Fund Five Year Evaluation. Synthesis Report*. Technical Evaluation Reference Group Synthesis Report. Geneva: The Global Fund.

2009b. *Progress Report on Aid Effectiveness*. Geneva: The Global Fund.
2010. *Innovation and Impact*. Geneva: The Global Fund.
Third World Network (TWN). 2009. *TWN Copenhagen News Update 6*. Third World Network. www.twnside.org.sg [Accessed in August 2010].
United Nations Development Programme (UNDP). 2005. *International Cooperation at a Cross Roads: Aid, Trade and Security in an Unequal World*. New York: UNDP.
2009. *Trade for Poverty Reduction: The Role of Trade in Poverty Reduction Strategy Papers*. New York: UNDP.
United Nations Economic Commission for Africa (UNECA). 2009. *Global Review on Aid for Trade 2009: Issues and State of Implementation in Africa*. Addis Ababa: UNECA.
United Nations Industrial Development Organization (UNIDO). 2009. *Value Chain Diagnostics for Industrial Development*. UNIDO Working Paper. Vienna: UNIDO.
United Nations Office for Project Services (UNOPS). 2010. *Financial Progress Report. 31 March 2010*. Geneva: UNOPS.
WTO. 2001. *Doha Ministerial Declaration*. Adopted on 14 November at the Doha Ministerial Conference. WT/MIN(01)/DEC/1.
2003. *Final Report of the Evaluation of the Integrated Framework*. Integrated Framework Steering Committee. WT/IFSC/6/Rev.2. Geneva: WTO.
2005. *Hong Kong Ministerial Declaration*. Adopted on 18 December at the Hong Kong Ministerial Conference, WT/MIN(05)/DEC, Doha Work Programme.
2006a. *Recommendations of the Task Force on Aid for Trade*. Aid for Trade Task Force, WT/AID FOR TRADE/1. Geneva: WTO.
2006b. An Enhanced Integrated Framework. *Report by the Chairman of the Task Force on an Enhanced Integrated Framework, Including Recommendations*. Integrated Framework Steering Committee. WT/IFSC/W/15. Geneva: WTO.
2006c. *Communications from Mauritius on Behalf of the ACP Group*. Aid for Trade Task Force, WT/AFT/W/8. Geneva: WTO.
2006d. *Communications from Benin on Behalf of the African Group*. Aid for Trade Task Force, WT/AFT/W/21. Geneva: WTO.
2006e. *Communications from Zambia on Behalf of the LDC Group*. Aid for Trade Task Force, WT/AFT/W/22. Geneva: WTO.
2007a. *Note on the Meeting of 18 May 2007*. Committee on Trade and Development, Second Session on Aid for Trade, WT/COMTD/AID FOR TRADE/M1. Geneva: WTO.
2007b. *Note on the Meeting of 19 June 2007*. Committee on Trade and Development, Second Session on Aid for Trade, WT/COMTD/AID FOR TRADE/M2. Geneva: WTO.

2007c. *Note on the Meeting of 9 July 2007.* Committee on Trade and Development, Third Session on Aid for Trade, WT/COMTD/AID FOR TRADE/M3. Geneva: WTO.

2007d. *Note on the Meeting of 11 October 2007.* Committee on Trade and Development, Fourth Session on Aid for Trade, WT/COMTD/AID FOR TRADE/M4. Geneva: WTO.

2008. *WTO Work Programme on Aid for Trade: Results of the Symposium on Monitoring and Evaluation. 15–16 September 2008.* Committee on Trade and Development, Aid for Trade, WT/COMTD/AID FOR TRADE/W9. Geneva: WTO.

2009a. *Note on the Meeting of 11 June 2009.* Committee on Trade and Development, Eleventh Session on Aid for Trade, WT/COMTD/AID FOR TRADE/M11. Geneva: WTO.

2009b. *Aid-for-Trade Work Programme 2010–2011.* Committee on Trade and Development, WT/COMTD/AID FOR TRADE/W/16. Geneva: WTO.

2009c. *International Trade Statistics 2009: World Trade Developments in 2008.* Geneva: WTO.

2010. *Monitoring Aid for Trade at the Global Level.* Committee on Aid for Trade. JOB/DEV/3. Geneva: WTO.

14

Strengthening WTO surveillance: making transparency work for developing countries

ARUNABHA GHOSH

Trade governance is moving higher on the World Trade Organization (WTO) agenda – and monitoring and transparency are integral parts of it. On 15 October 2009, eighteen WTO Members (including the largest trading powers) submitted a brief text calling for a 'deliberative process to review the organization's functioning, efficiency *and transparency* and consider possible improvements' (WTO 2009b, emphasis added). A month later Pascal Lamy, the Director-General, explained that the Geneva Ministerial meeting (30 November to 2 December 2009) would offer 'a platform for ministers to review the functioning of this house' (Lamy 2009). At the conclusion of the meeting, the Chair noted that Members believed that WTO monitoring had helped to 'stave off protectionist responses to the [economic] crisis' but notifications, data collection, analysis, and dissemination needed further improvement (WTO 2009a).[1] As

Arunabha Ghosh is Chief Executive Officer at the Council on Energy, Environment and Water (CEEW) and was previously Oxford-Princeton Global Leaders Fellow at the Woodrow Wilson School of Public and International Affairs, Princeton. The author would like to thank trade delegates from Argentina, Australia, Brazil, Chile, China, Colombia, the European Union, Ghana, Hong Kong, India, Japan, Rep. of Korea, Lesotho, Mexico, Namibia, Pakistan, Singapore, South Africa, Swaziland, Chinese Taipei, Tanzania, Thailand, Turkey, Uganda, the United States and Uruguay for sharing their insights on and experiences with the Trade Policy Review Mechanism and monitoring in the WTO more generally. Officials from the UNCTAD and WTO, and from ICTSD and ODI, London, also provided very useful insights. The author also greatly benefitted from his time as a researcher at the Trade Policies Review Division in the WTO during January–February 2008, which allowed him to observe the review process from close quarters. Many thanks to Carolyn Deere Birkbeck and Robert Wolfe for very helpful comments and suggestions on earlier drafts of this chapter. Thanks also to Ngaire Woods, John Odell, Walter Mattli and Richard Steinberg for useful feedback on some parts of this research. Any errors or omissions are solely the author's own.

[1] During 2009, the most extensive discussions on how to improve notifications occurred in the committees on agriculture and standards for food products and goods, bodies that were already committed to the notifications process. See Collins-Williams and Wolfe 2010.

the Doha Round of trade negotiations stumbles on, WTO Members and the Secretariat are taking increasing interest in the governance and effectiveness of the multilateral trade regime (Deere 2009; Deere Birkbeck and Cherneva 2010). Against this background, this chapter examines WTO monitoring to ask how it has responded to calls for improved transparency and whether it meets developing countries' information needs in the trade regime.

At the outset, it is useful to clarify some conceptual terms. Information is a crucial ingredient for promoting and maintaining international cooperation (Keohane 1982). Its value is found at all stages of a regime (Abbott and Snidal 2009: 93–5).[2] During agenda-setting and negotiations, information is useful for States keen to assess each other's preferences and in *reducing uncertainties over complex issues*. But it is in the implementation, monitoring and enforcement phases that information assumes its role in making sure that States are adhering to their commitments. Here, information systems serve a vital role in *reducing hidden/inaccurate information* about Members' behaviour. They are also needed to help poorer countries *overcome information barriers arising from resource constraints*. And multilateral transparency mechanisms ensure that countries do not have to rely on their own resources to monitor every other regime Member. For developing countries, resource constraints are the dominant information gap, since it affects their ability to invest in additional research to reduce issue uncertainties or to monitor other States to discover hidden/inaccurate information.

Information systems in international regimes are sets of institutions, actors and procedures involved in collecting, analysing and disseminating information about the actions of States and the regime's effectiveness. There can be several *types of information systems* ranging from self-reporting by Members, reporting on other States' behaviour, non-State actor reporting and institutional reporting by regime Secretariats.[3] In practice, a regime can use a combination of these reporting procedures and the design of information systems can change over time to reflect growing Membership, shifting interests and rising demands on monitoring capacity.

In turn, information systems can be expected to perform three kinds of functions (Mavroidis 1991–2: 408–9; Ghosh 2008: 77–87; Ghosh 2010:

[2] For a conceptualization of different kinds of information gaps, see Ghosh 2010: 424–6.

[3] For an exposition of the factors affecting the design of information systems, see Ghosh 2010: 426–7.

436–7). They *disseminate information* about Members' policies and actions in response to hidden information problems as well as to overcome the resource constraints faced by individual Members. They also *promote compliance* via peer pressure among Member States, explicit sanctions or by pressure from non-State actors. Independently collected information, say by regime secretariats or non-State actors, can counter deliberate deception by Member States. Information systems also *evaluate regimes* and their impact on Members as a whole in response to issue uncertainty and resource constraints. Other scholars offer a slightly different conceptual framework, which distinguishes between 'three generations' of the evolution of transparency: an initial focus on the 'right to know'; 'targeted transparency' to promote greater consistency with the rules of the trading system; and 'collaborative transparency' or more user-friendly formats for information that the public can understand (Collins-Williams and Wolfe 2010). In fact, the first two generations of transparency are consistent with the information dissemination and compliance promotion roles, respectively. Again, the mandates to perform these functions vary across regimes and over time.

With monitoring activities accounting for half of its budget (Lamy 2007), the WTO has an extensive information system. It has formal review mechanisms, particularly the Trade Policy Review Mechanism (TPRM), which has been operating since 1989, and new mechanisms that have emerged more recently. The WTO also relies on notifications by Member States to reduce information gaps. In 1979, the Tokyo Round concluded with an Understanding Regarding Notification, Consultation, Dispute Settlement, and Surveillance, providing for special GATT Council meetings to review developments in the trading system. Notifications and discussions within individual WTO Committees continue to be an important part of the WTO's activities. This chapter, however, will focus primarily on the TPRM and new monitoring mechanisms. This is because these processes are among the most institutionalized parts of the WTO's information system, are extensive in the scope of countries and issues covered, and have budgets dedicated to monitoring and reviewing the policies of Member States.

The rest of the chapter proceeds as follows. Section 1 begins with a brief history of the evolution of surveillance in the multilateral trade regime. It then critically examines the TPRM's mandate and the content- and process-related challenges that it has faced so far, with particular consideration of the needs and interests of developing countries. Section 2 outlines the minimal reforms that have been made to the TPRM thus far and explores why developing countries have not pushed for further changes. Sections 3, 4 and 5 then focus on three more recent transparency mechanisms for regional trade agreements (RTAs), sanitary and phytosanitary standards (SPS) and Aid for Trade (AFT). These developed thanks to changing demands for information from Member States even as they wrestled with questions of giving greater authority to the WTO Secretariat or making review procedures more effective. Further, developing countries participated actively in these debates, so the designs of these mechanisms reflect how far developing countries' needs have been addressed. Section 6 concludes by suggesting ways to make the WTO's monitoring activities more agile and responsive to changing information needs in the context of a larger, growing Membership with diverse interests.

1 TPRM – comprehensive but losing relevance

Trade surveillance dates back to the early General Agreement on Tariffs and Trade (GATT) days when ad hoc reviews were conducted into quantitative restrictions, customs administration and restrictions on agricultural trade (GATT 1987c: para. 4; Blackhurst 1988: 135). By the 1960s and 1970s, Members had to report and notify on changes in policies related to textiles (under the Multi Fibre Agreement), balance of payments restrictions and multinational trade negotiation codes. Large trading powers (the USA and the EU) also started reporting on the policies of their major trading partners. Growing Membership and a broader scope of trade issues meant that by the early 1980s there was increasing demand for more institutional reporting. Special Council sessions were held twice a year to report on non-tariff barriers. By 1983, the Council was examining the consistency of trade policies with GATT principles. Developing countries, now 70 per cent of the GATT Membership, also demanded that the Committee on Trade and Development (CTD) examine policies that restricted access to rich countries' markets, policies that affected least developed countries (LDCs), and how the special circumstances of poor nations were being handled under GATT (GATT 1987a: paras. 7, 9–11, 12–15).

However, sovereignty concerns were responsible for the GATT Secretariat not getting a full mandate for institutional monitoring until 1989. In 1985 an expert group called for the Secretariat to act as a 'watchdog' for the trading system (Leutwiler *et al.* 1985: 42). On one hand, rich countries wanted surveillance to act as an early warning system and to promote compliance. On the other hand, developing countries were worried that an 'unwarranted asymmetry' had crept into trade surveillance where their trade policies were reviewed but rich nations were not (GATT 1987b: para. 7). They wanted surveillance to target rich countries but were careful to demand that no legal procedures be established. Eventually, in 1989 the TPRM was established as the WTO's most institutionalized monitoring mechanism. Each Member would be reviewed periodically. The frequency of reviews depended on a Member's share of world trade (the four largest traders are reviewed every two years, the next sixteen every four years, and the remaining every six years, with longer gaps for LDCs).

For the review, the WTO Secretariat prepares a report that examines the Member's domestic institutional structures for trade policy-making, the macroeconomic context and specific trade policies by measure and by sector. The government also prepares a shorter Statement of policy but it is the Secretariat's report that primarily serves as the basis for discussion. The reviews are held over two days, prior to which Member States submit advance questions to the country under review. The Member is expected to provide written answers to these questions at the start of the review meeting. The review meetings are also facilitated by comments from a discussant belonging to another Member State. During the meeting, Members raise additional questions orally, replies to which are given either at the meeting or afterwards in writing.

1.1 A weak mandate

When established, the TPRM's core aim was to promote 'improved adherence' to rules through 'regular collective appreciation and evaluation' of Members' policies and practices (GATT 1989a: A(i)).

There was a broader expectation that this multilateral form of surveillance would correct the existing asymmetries in monitoring, address poor countries' capacity constraints in reviewing trade policies and the implementation of agreements, send signals to the markets regarding a country's openness to trade and investment, and improve trade policy-making within countries (Francois 2001: 150–4; Ghosh 2010).

Within this broad remit, there have been disagreements among WTO Members about how to use the information generated in trade policy reviews (TPRs). At a basic level, Members agreed to disseminate information by distributing TPR reports to the public and interested stakeholders and to use the information as reference material in various WTO committees (GATT 1988c: para. 36; GATT 1989b: para. 10; WTO 1995: para. 7).

But no clear mandate was given for how the GATT/WTO would ensure that there was improved adherence with rules. Compliance promotion was an implicit aim of the TPRM, not an explicit mandate (Qureshi 1990). The expectation was that such information would help to reduce uncertainties in negotiations and also help poor countries overcome resource constraints that limited their ability to review trade policies. Members agreed that information from the TPRs could not be used for dispute settlement proceedings. Instead, Members would rely on moral suasion and peer pressure to urge changes in trade policies.

In other words, the TPRM was the first attempt to 'institutionalize peer pressure' in the trade regime (Curzon Price 1991: 231). The process would allow countries to carefully examine each other's policies and apply pressure to change. But GATT/WTO monitoring struck a balance between reporting, on one hand, and reviews, on the other. Reporting is primarily a technical process of collecting and analysing information. Reviews, by contrast, are essentially political and their effectiveness depends on how widely information is disseminated, the extent of consultations between State and non-State actors at the domestic level, and the degree of participation in multilateral fora. The problem was that peer pressure would, in turn, rely not only on the Secretariat's reports but also on the extent of participation in review meetings and the ability to raise difficult questions against one's more powerful trading partners. Further, since there were no structured follow-up procedures to promote compliance, the TPRM's purpose as a review mechanism was undercut at the very outset.

Nevertheless, the TPRM continues to be an important part of the WTO's work schedule. By the end of 2009, 136 of the 153 Members had been reviewed at least once; 27 of 32 LDCs had also been reviewed. Interviews with numerous trade delegates and WTO officials reveal that there are high expectations of the material contained in the reports.[4] The reports, by comprehensively covering a Member's trade policies, are a one-stop source of information. But delegates, especially from developing countries, also complain that the information is not user-friendly or that the reports are not analytical enough. They are also concerned about how information might be used against them during review meetings when they, in turn, are unable to apply pressure for developed countries to change their policies.

[4] Interviews with developed and developing country trade diplomats in Geneva, July 2007, January–February 2008.

1.2 Reports miss out on salient information

For the TPRs to be salient, Members must get information on trade issues most critical to them. In my analysis, I use disputes that a Member initiates as a proxy for which trade issues are most important to it. Filing a dispute is a costly affair, both monetarily and politically, and a Member would not choose this route unless the trade issue is absolutely critical.[5] Trade monitoring, on the other hand, comes one step before disputes. It is intended to increase transparency, so that potential protectionist tendencies are exposed/identified in advance, or so that a Member can be pressured not to adopt a controversial trade measure.[6] The point is not that TPRs can facilitate or prevent disputes by offering legal judgements – that is not the TPRM's mandate. The claim here is simply that, if TPRs actually fulfil their mandated task, we should observe that the reports would include a description or analysis of disputed measures since they are the most contentious trade issues.

I analysed 172 dispute-dyads where the complainants were all the developing, least developed and transition economies that had initiated a dispute until end-2007. I examined the TPRs of the respondents (that is, the Members with the contentious policies in place) both before and after the dispute had been initiated. Reports preceding disputes mentioned the policies in only 53 per cent of the cases and only 15 per cent of the reports had any analysis or criticism of them. Reports after disputes had begun increased coverage of disputed policies to 80 per cent but analysis or criticism remained low at 16 per cent of the cases. In recent years, the coverage of such issues in developed countries' reports dropped to under 50 per cent. Thus, even as TPR reports seek to present a comprehensive picture of a Member's policies, in many cases the most contentious policies barely get a mention and are not subject to detailed analysis. This partly explains why many delegates complain that, although voluminous, the reports leave something to be desired in terms of relevant information.

[5] To be sure, disputes are an imperfect proxy indicator for which trade issues are most important. Many factors may go into the decision to launch a dispute – cost of the case, prospects of success, whether a strong domestic lobby exists on the issues, whether there are other paths for resolving a dispute, whether ongoing negotiations might prove a channel for resolving the dispute, etc. In the absence of a common metric to judge the important issues to Member States, disputes are used as a useful, albeit imperfect, indicator.

[6] For a similar argument on the role of transparency, see Hoekman and Mavroidis (2000).

1.3 Poor participation means less peer pressure

While reports are not sufficiently analytical, the other reason why the reviews are less than satisfactory is how peer pressure operates in practice. TPRs have not been effective in applying pressure against the biggest trading powers. Again, using the launching of disputes as a proxy for what trade issues matter most intensely to particular Members, I examine if Members pose questions regarding these issues during TPR meetings. First of all, Members have submitted advance questions in TPRs prior to initiating disputes on the same issue in only one-quarter of all potential cases. Even after filing disputes, in only one-fifth of review meetings have complainants posed questions on the disputed issue to the respondents under review. There is still value in the TPR process because in more than half of the cases Members not party to a dispute posed advance questions on that issue during a respondent's TPR.

But peer pressure works unequally and has generally been applied against poorer countries. Let us assume that developing countries might be only interested in asking questions when their top trading partners are under review. Even then, comparing the number of questions Members submit when their biggest trading partners are under review with how many questions they get in return for their own reviews, I find that the direction of peer pressure is largely skewed against developing countries. Rich countries file far more questions against poorer ones, rather than the other way round.

Further, I examined all TPR meetings held between 1995 and 2007, using the available minutes, to analyse which Members raise questions or make Statements during the meetings. The analysis of 181 meetings covered 70 countries: the top 20 trading powers, additional Member States that have initiated disputes, leaders of negotiating coalitions and LDCs that have undergone a TPR.[7] The analysis shows that participation levels are very low. While Canada, the European Union, Japan and the United States[8] almost always attend TPRs and raise questions during the meetings (repeating advanced questions and also posing new ones), only a few other Members have actively participated in even half the meetings (Figure 14.1). For LDCs, participation is negligible with an average LDC having participated in only 3 per cent of eligible meetings.

[7] During this period 190 TPR meetings occurred but documents were missing for 9 random cases.

[8] These were historically the top four trading powers before China became one of the world's largest trading nations. China's low participation rate since its accession can be attributed to it choosing to first observe and learn the procedures before actively taking part. Interview with Chinese delegate, Geneva, 13 February 2008.

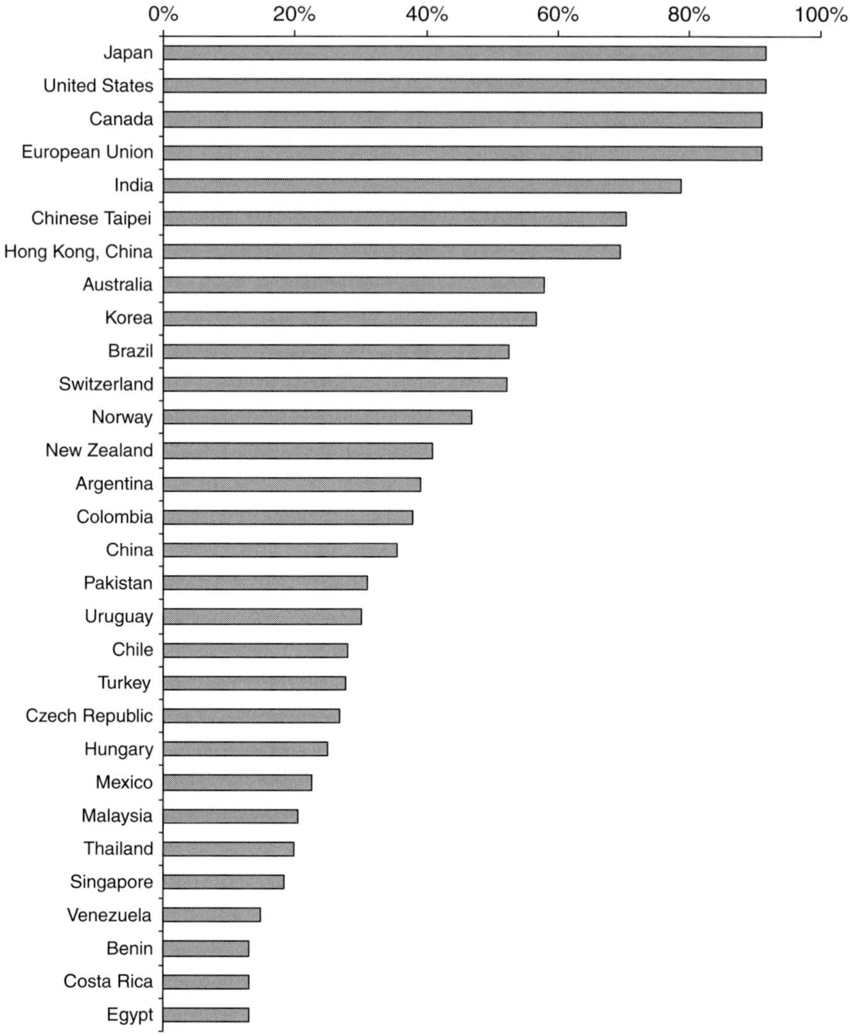

Figure 14.1 Rate of participation in TPR meetings since accession to the WTO, 1995–2007
Source: Author's analysis of 181 TPR meetings.

In other words, although TPRs were expected to serve as a forum for peer reviewing each other's trade policies, in practice the process has been used by a small proportion of the WTO's Membership. For the poorer

Members, which should benefit the most from a multilateral and cost-effective way of getting information on others' trade policies, the TPRM has fallen short of even its limited mandate. Both the content of reports and the process of meetings have not responded to demands for salient and timely information, or for the meetings to promote improved adherence with rules.

1.4 Participation depends on institutionalized domestic monitoring

We can find clues to poor participation rates at the multilateral level in the extent of domestic capacity for trade monitoring. I examine the domestic trade policy-making structures for seventy WTO Members along four dimensions: consultations among State actors (agencies involved, role of the legislature); consultations with non-State actors (formal agencies for consultations, legal/constitutional provisions for consultations); provisions for domestic transparency (including independent/statutory institutions for policy reviews); and provisions for monitoring external trade partners (collecting commercial intelligence, specialized agencies for trade monitoring, formal reports on external trade barriers).[9] For the analysis, I rely primarily on each country's TPR documents. Chapter 2 of each Secretariat report outlines the trade policy-making structure within each country. The reports are also vetted by governments and updated information is presented in subsequent documents, so we get a complete picture of the trade policy administrations within a country. I also rely on interviews with delegates of twenty-six major WTO Members to get deeper insights on the evolution of policy-making in their countries.[10]

All ten countries – five developed and five developing – with the highest rates of participation in TPR meetings (Japan, United States, Canada, European Union, India, Chinese Taipei, Hong Kong, Australia, Korea and Brazil) have institutional bodies to coordinate trade policy-making among State actors. In a majority of them, legislatures are also closely involved in approving and reviewing trade-related policies. Similarly, institutional bodies facilitate consultations with non-State actors. In half the cases,

[9] For a framework linking domestic institutional capacity and engagement in multilateral monitoring mechanisms, see Ghosh (2008: 244–57).

[10] Argentina, Australia, Brazil, Chile, China, Colombia, the European Union, Ghana, Hong Kong, India, Japan, Korea, Lesotho, Mexico, Namibia, Pakistan, Singapore, South Africa, Swaziland, Chinese Taipei, Tanzania, Thailand, Turkey, Uganda, the United States and Uruguay.

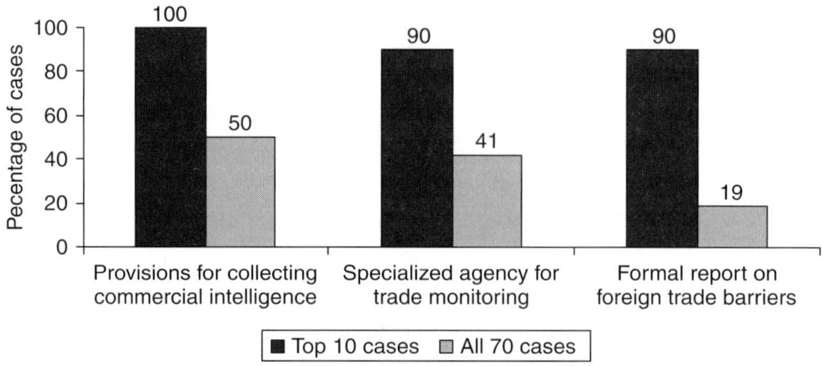

Figure 14.2 Provisions for external monitoring of participation in TPR meetings
Source: Author's analysis based on TPR documents and interviews.

domestic law mandates consultations. And half the countries have statutorily independent agencies to review domestic policies – a proportion that is double the average of the seventy countries examined.

But the monitoring of external trade partners sets the participative countries apart from the rest (Figure 14.2). Whereas just half of the seventy countries had provisions for regularly collecting commercial intelligence, all countries among the top ten do so. Also, nine of the top ten countries have specialized agencies to monitor foreign trade powers and publish their own reports.

Comparing the five most active developing countries (those that were in the list of ten most participative countries) with the next fifteen developing countries,[11] differences emerge on the more institutionalized features of trade policy-making. If informal consultations among State agencies occurred in all cases, policy coordination via formal bodies was found in all cases in the first group but only for two-thirds of the second group. Similarly, all twenty countries consulted with non-State actors, but formal structures were present in every case in the first group of five countries and in only three-quarters of the second group of fifteen. Finally, the top five developing countries were again much more involved in external trade monitoring. Only a minority of the next fifteen developing countries produced reports on foreign trade barriers.

[11] Argentina, Colombia, China, Pakistan, Uruguay, Chile, Turkey, Mexico, Malaysia, Thailand, Singapore, Venezuela, Benin, Costa Rica and Egypt.

The implications of this for the TPR process are that India, China and Brazil tap their official resources to monitor other countries and raise questions in TPR meetings. In fact, although domestic policy coordination and consultations and transparency have evolved considerably in these three countries, they have paid more attention to external trade monitoring.[12] Other countries, such as Chile, Hong Kong, Korea and Singapore, which also collect commercial intelligence, undertake specific investigations and publish trade barriers reports are also among the more participative countries in the TPRM. In other words, the TPRM seems to be serving those countries that already have the resources to monitor other Members. For the WTO's poorer Members, TPR reports and procedures have to provide more relevant information and improve domestic monitoring capacity as a step towards better multilateral participation.

2 Minimal reform, maintaining status quo

Despite the shortcomings, there have been few reforms of the TPRM. Three rounds of appraisals (in 1999, 2005 and 2008) yielded minimal decisions on TPRM reform. On the analytical content of reports, the coverage of sensitive trade topics/decisions that directly affect Members' welfare did not receive much attention. At the end of the first appraisal Members wanted 'fully informed' reviews but were unwilling to let the Secretariat identify and analyse contentious issues more thoroughly (WTO 1999a: para. 5).

The tension between the widening scope of issues covered by the reports and the limited analysis in them reflects a divide between developed and developing countries. On one hand, developing countries had/have a strong desire that reviews be conducted against the background of their development needs.[13] They want to ensure that monitoring does not circumscribe their ability to frame policies that used flexibilities in the WTO's rules. On the other hand, even as the Secretariat and some WTO Members now seek more analytical reports, developing countries remain

[12] For developments in domestic capacity and transparency in leading developing countries, see Ghosh (2008: 281–98). On India, also see Sen (2004); Aggarwal (2007); and Dhar and Kallummal (2007). On China, also see Gong (2005); Huang (2005); and Zeng and Mertha (2007). On Brazil, also see da Motta Veiga (2005); Marconini (2005); and da Motta Veiga (2007). There are more case studies in Gallagher *et al.* (2005); and Halle and Wolfe (2007).

[13] WT/MIN (05)/1(21/9/2005): para. 4.

wary that more analysis would mean more pressure against them, rather than against developed countries.

Small changes occurred on the procedural front. Since 2005, in order to give Members more time to analyse information and pose pertinent questions, TPR reports drafted by the Secretariat have to be submitted to the Members five weeks in advance (until then it had been four weeks) and advance questions have to be sent in by Members a fortnight ahead (rather than ten days). Developing countries have opposed sending in answers in advance as well, fearing that it would give rich nations more opportunity to increase pressure on them rather than vice versa.

Further, the role of discussants has also not been exploited fully. Acting in their personal capacity, discussants can facilitate critical and analytical debate by highlighting policies that are either contrary to a Member's stated trade policy objectives, or are of concern to a large section of the WTO Membership. They can also countervail pressures on poor countries by ensuring that the review takes full account of a Member's development context and the flexibilities available in WTO rules. In practice, more than half the time discussants have been from developed country governments. They have also been passive or 'surprisingly serene', even when contentious issues are being discussed (Tharakan 2006: 1305). They do not prepare detailed comments of their own due to time and resource constraints and instead rely almost entirely on Secretariat documents and advice. Discussants are also unwilling to be too critical of their diplomatic colleagues, with the result that the 'meetings tend to be very nice, too nice'.[14] The imbalance in representation has made developing countries resist a more proactive role for discussants. By and large the role of discussants remains circumscribed. Developed and developing countries alike prefer 'peer protectors' to peer reviewers.

Members have also been unwilling to establish any systematic procedure for following up on reviews at the international or domestic levels. Some recognize the usefulness of a periodic policy review that might suggest areas for future domestic reforms.[15] But Members in general do not want external reviews to force any reforms. On this issue there is no conflict between developed and developing countries. A developed country delegate argued that, 'For the "Quad", the TPR is work in progress, but

[14] Interview, Geneva, 6 July 2007.

[15] Some delegates also suggested having follow-up documents to highlight the measures taken by the country after its review. Interview, Geneva, 14 and 19 February 2008.

for other countries it is an event.' The implication is that since developed countries already had domestic policy review processes, there was no particular need to follow up on TPRs.[16] The ambassador of a major developing country also rejected any suggestion that TPRs could impact the speed or scope of domestic reforms. 'Our reform process … has its own dynamic … The tone of the TPR is to do a bit more here, a bit more there, as if [the] advice matters. It doesn't matter … '[17]

In sum, developing countries, including the more participative ones, have adopted largely defensive positions with regard to the TPRM. While privately calling (during interviews) for more analytical reports, delegates seem to be wary of how such reports might compromise their negotiating positions. They also reiterate their sovereign right to determine how to disseminate information and consult with domestic constituencies. Despite the growing influence of developing countries in key aspects of trade negotiations (due to the growing economic weight of some countries and also the expanding and strategic use of coalitions), they are of the view that the TPRM offers little chance of shifting rich countries' policies. Making the reviews more analytical and critical, they fear, would only undermine their position. Maintaining the status quo remains a preferred option (Table 14.1 highlights the limited reforms in the TPRM).

2.1 Information gaps remain for WTO surveillance

Based on the TPRM's performance to date and the limited reforms thus far, trade diplomats from developing countries observe that their countries face persisting information deficits in the WTO. To be sure, the TPRM might not even be able to address these deficits given its mandate. Although information gaps are recognized in the TPRM, they are also relevant to the work of other WTO committees. Interviews with delegates from large developing countries as well as LDCs reveal a pattern of demands for better information. These demands are subsets of the three types of information gaps described in the Introduction, namely due to hidden information, resource constraints and issue uncertainties.

First, developing countries demand improved *notifications and advance warning* of policy changes. Notifications have long been considered a principal way to improve transparency. During the Uruguay Round,

[16] Interview, Geneva, 6 July 2007.
[17] Interview, Geneva, 4 July 2007.

Table 14.1. *Limited reforms in the WTO's trade policy review mechanism*

Common challenges for WTO surveillance	Developing countries' demands	Observed outcomes	Role for WTO Secretariat
Hidden information	More timely information demanded	Reports to be circulated five weeks in advance; advance questions sent in fourteen days ahead	Secretariat has greater burden of completing reports sooner
Issue uncertainties	Reviews to be conducted in the context of economic development needs – maintain flexibilities in WTO rules	Persistent fear that monitoring could circumscribe developing countries' policy space – but TPR reports used as reference material in WTO committees	Secretariat's role primarily for transparency and not further analysis
Resource constraints	Calls for more comprehensive TPR reports and 'fully informed' reviews	No clear agreement	Unwilling to give Secretariat more authority to undertake critical analyses
Domestic capacity constraints	Calls for more technical assistance	LDCs complain about limited assistance; large developing countries build indigenous monitoring capacity	Secretariat includes technical assistance needs in LDC reviews

Table 14.1. *(cont.)*

Common challenges for WTO surveillance	Developing countries' demands	Observed outcomes	Role for WTO Secretariat
Lack of follow-up after reviews	Some countries want wider dissemination of reports and follow-up documents on measures taken	Limited role of discussants in TPR meetings No institutionalized follow-up procedures Deny influence of TPRs on domestic policy	Secretariat provides information to discussants; compiles advance questions and answers

Source: Author's analysis based on WTO documents.

notification procedures were wide-ranging but ad hoc.[18] For developing countries the administrative burden of submitting multiple notifications was a concern and they hoped a new review mechanism would rationalize the process (GATT 1987d: para. 5).[19] In June 1990, parties agreed to a general obligation to notify, a central registry of notifications and the provision to remind contracting parties that did not fulfil their commitments (GATT 1990c: 14–16). But gaps in the fulfilment of WTO notification requirements are now widely understood to be less an issue of administrative capacity, but more a reflection of deliberate strategies to withhold information.[20] The TPRM process is not well positioned to fill the notification gap. Given the long time lags between TPRs, sudden shifts in policies are not captured by the reports nor, delegates note, do

[18] Obligations related to, among others, tariffs, quantitative restrictions, subsidies, government procurement, customs unions and PTAs, trade and development linkages, differential treatment, technical barriers to trade, customs valuation, the Multi-Fibre Agreement and so forth (GATT 1988a).

[19] Also, GATT 1988b; GATT 1990a: paras. 27–8.

[20] For instance, by March 2008 only eleven WTO Members had fully complied with their notification obligations under the Agreement on Agriculture for the period 1995–2006, with many developed countries having not notified since 2002 or earlier. Under the Agreement on Subsidies and Countervailing Measures, only twelve of twenty-one major WTO countries had submitted complete notifications for 2005 on time; and the data is often inconsistent. See Collins-Williams and Wolfe (2010).

review meetings and advance questions always succeed in revealing such information. Thus, advance warning can be considered a specific subset of hidden/inaccurate information that poor countries want multilateral surveillance to capture.

Second, many delegates from developing countries want some degree of *impact analysis* of trade measures (both current and proposed) of other Members, especially for regulatory measures. During GATT negotiations, developing countries were unwilling to let the Secretariat assess the impact of any trade measure that had been notified (GATT 1990b: para. 6). Delegates now recognize, however, that without analysis, advance information would be effectively unusable. Thus, impact analysis of trade measures applied in other jurisdictions has emerged as a specific type of resource-constrained information gap, which Members expect multilateral bodies to fill.

Third, as the negotiating agenda expands there is growing demand for *compliance-oriented information*. Developing countries are keen to know how others have interpreted WTO rights and obligations and exploited the flexibilities in WTO rules. TPRs have seldom pointed out such flexibilities,[21] one reason why developing countries have resisted moves to increase peer pressure or use external discussants in meetings. Several delegates suggested that the TPRM or other monitoring mechanisms should provide information on 'best practices'. The underlying objective, however, is to identify policies that suit one's development context and priorities. Thus, compliance-oriented information can be a specific response to information gaps arising from issue uncertainties.

In the wake of the global economic crisis, the WTO Secretariat has tried to address some of these information problems. Especially regarding demands for early warning, the Secretariat has initiated regular monitoring of protectionist tendencies. The additional transparency has thrown light on the threat of protectionism during the crisis and the reports (three by the Secretariat and two jointly with the Organisation for Economic Cooperatiion and Development (OECD) and the United Nations Conference on Trade and Development (UNCTAD)) have

[21] For instance, on intellectual property rights, one commentator argues that TPRs put pressure on Members to showcase progress towards TRIPS implementation, thereby creating a 'policy climate in favour of compliance'. But the reports do not highlight differences in the nature of Members' WTO obligations (Deere 2009: 158, 236–40). Nor is there much discussion in the TPRs about the cost implications of building stronger IP regimes. See Ghosh (2008: 193).

been discussed in informal meetings of the Trade Policy Review Body (the equivalent of the General Council) (WTO 2009c; WTO, OECD and UNCTAD 2009; OECD and UNCTAD 2010; WTO, OECD and UNCTAD 2010).

Monitoring efforts outside the WTO have also emerged, such as the Global Trade Alert (GTA) initiative that focuses on measures taken during the crisis and their impact on other countries. One such study found that in the one year since the November 2008 G20 leaders' summit (when representatives of the world's leading economies promised not to raise protectionist barriers), 294 measures had been implemented that discriminated against foreign commercial interests. As of that date, there were more than 200 measures still to be implemented, most of which would also harm international trade (Evenett 2009a: 38, 2009b). Much of this kind of protectionism has been 'murky' in the sense that they might not violate WTO rules directly but are discretionary measures that discriminate against foreign goods, firms and workers (Baldwin and Evenett 2009: 4–5). In turn, trade experts from developed and developing countries recommend tougher 'real-time surveillance', especially of the hidden details in domestic support measures (Dhar *et al.* 2009: 69; Gallagher and Stoler 2009). Thus, these calls for greater surveillance also reflect the demand for advance warning and impact analyses and, to an extent, compliance-oriented information.

Notwithstanding these initiatives, spurred in no small part by the economic crisis, others argue that the independent exercise undertaken by periodic GTA reports might not have added much to the data that is already collected by international organizations like the OECD, UNCTAD and WTO (Wolfe 2010). Both sets of exercises have found that government interventions during the crisis seem to have been restricted to sectors that were already receiving high levels of protection prior to the crisis.

In fact, developing countries have increasingly turned to new transparency mechanisms *within* the WTO to get more issue-specific and timely information. Although developing countries have generally opposed linking monitoring with formal dispute procedures, they also complain about the lack of teeth in the WTO's monitoring system. The TPRM is inward-oriented (by design), focusing on a country's policies rather than the trade barriers it faces abroad. TPRs offer little analysis of how rich countries' policies restrict trade opportunities for developing countries. The poorest countries have also failed to see a clear link between resources the WTO Secretariat invests in monitoring and better access to markets or improved trade capacity at home.[22] Thus, calls for a strengthened role for the WTO Secretariat have grown, in the hope that strengthened surveillance by an international institution would increase the information available and in a format that enabled greater use of the information (Collins-Williams and Wolfe 2010: fn. 16).[23] The next three sections discuss how new transparency mechanisms for RTAs, SPS measures and Aid for Trade navigate these tensions and seek to fill some of the outstanding information gaps.

3 Transparency for RTAs – resisting close examination

In December 2006, a WTO Transparency Mechanism (TM) for regional trade agreements (RTAs) was established, reflecting an acknowledgement by WTO Members that better understanding of RTAs and their threat to the multilateral trading system was of 'systemic interest' and would benefit all Members (WTO 2006b). For developing countries, there is an additional concern that the proliferation of RTAs reduces their bargaining power. Moreover, there is the worry over increasingly complex rules of origin (the 'spaghetti bowl' effect) and the fear that trade would be diverted away from countries that are not party to the RTAs (Bhagwati *et al.* 1998). Given these concerns, sudden announcements of preferential arrangements further reduce the time available for non-Members of the RTA to adjust to new market realities.

Members were also concerned about the lack of information on systemic effects. Developing countries, with barely the resources to monitor the multilateral regime, were not in a position to analyse the impact of hundreds of RTAs. Although TPRs did examine each country's RTA Memberships, the analysis failed to assess the impact of a trade bloc on the multilateral trading system as a whole (Keesing 1998: 35). This section explains the reasons for developing the RTA Transparency Mechanism and examines the extent to which its provisions meet the information demands of developing countries.

[22] Although there have been efforts to link TPRs to technical assistance needs and provisions, a perception remains that despite the reviews, there is no guarantee of more assistance and, more importantly, of access to markets. Interviews with LDC delegates, Geneva, 4 July 2007, 22 October 2007, 31 January 2008 and 25 February 2008.

[23] The authors highlight a submission by the Indian delegation prior to the December 2009 Ministerial Conference, calling for better notifications, more discussion in committees and greater use of the 'specific trade concerns' procedures (WTO 2009d).

3.1 *Delayed notifications, limited impact analysis*

In the GATT era, RTAs were examined by ad hoc working parties of GATT Members. This process was formalized under the Committee on RTAs (CRTA) in February 1996 with an eye to evaluating their systemic implications (WTO 1996a). To that extent, it was a shift towards not only providing more information on RTAs but also understanding how they would affect the multilateral trading system. In practice, despite the Committee's work, Members continued to suffer from lack of advance information about RTAs. Despite proposals from developed and developing countries for early notifications of RTAs,[24] the EU opposed formalizing the process (WTO 1996e: paras. 7, 75). By 1997 some Members were demanding 'counter-notifications', whereby even if RTA Members did not submit information, other countries could report on the same.[25] But the proposals were not well developed and paid no attention to the capacity of other States or a small WTO Secretariat to monitor the proliferating number of RTAs on a regular basis. More fundamentally, the proposals were far too radical to overcome political sensitivities on the part of many Member States against ceding control of reporting authority to other countries or multilateral institutions (WTO 1997a: paras. 61–2).

In May 1997, the CRTA Chairman issued guidelines, on his own responsibility, to improve the RTA examination process under the committee (WTO 1997c: para. 1). Similar to the TPRM, the guidelines envisaged that written inputs would comprise factual presentations (i.e. brief reports) by the Secretariat, communications from Members and written replies to advance questions. The Committee's conclusions regarding the RTA's conformity with WTO rules would be recorded. The CRTA also requested the WTO Councils for trade in goods and services and the CTD to build in reporting requirements for RTAs and standardize the information that the Councils submitted to the CRTA. Parties would now have to submit additional information if the RTA underwent substantial changes; biennial reports from Members would provide updates.

However, by linking the Secretariat's factual presentations to CRTA examinations, proponents of greater transparency were stoking apprehensions among other Members. And some argued that in the absence of clear conclusions about the WTO-compatibility of RTAs, mere examination was a tacit 'toleration' of trade-diverting agreements (WTO

[24] See WTO 1996b; WTO 1996d: para. 46; WTO 1997a: paras. 18, 20, 25.

[25] See WTO 1996c: para. 97; WTO 1996e: paras. 5, 11, 14, 20; WTO 1997b: para. XVII.

2000: para. 21(a)). Compliance with biennial reporting by Member States remained low, the WTO Secretariat's attempts to survey RTAs was hampered by delays in notifications, and agreements in force for many years escaped scrutiny. As a result, no RTA examination report was finalized during 1996–2003.

3.2 Institutionalizing transparency, retaining flexibility

The Doha Ministerial Declaration initiated negotiations 'aimed at clarifying and improving disciplines and procedures' applicable to RTAs (paragraph 29). Taking the lead, Australia, Chile, Hong Kong, Korea and New Zealand proposed a two-stage notification process, once when an RTA was signed and once again before entry into force (WTO 2003a: paras. 5–6, 8, 9, 11). From September 2004, the WTO Secretariat was given the provisional task of preparing factual presentations of notified RTAs (WTO 2004b: para. 11). In 2006, negotiations on institutionalizing transparency for RTAs concluded by explicitly responding to the primary concern of hidden information on RTAs. As one Indian official put it, the mechanism would not straighten the spaghetti bowl of preferential arrangements, but it would 'definitely help unravel its mysteries' (Priya 2007).

The resulting 'Transparency Mechanism' was the result of converging interests over the need for information, on one hand, and compromise on more contentious ideas, on the other. The new mechanism demands early announcements when negotiations commence and conclude, as well as notifications of the RTA text, annexes and protocols *before* the agreement takes effect, notification of amendments and factual presentations by the Secretariat. The presentations, in turn, are discussed in review meetings that have to be completed within one year. This forces Members to submit relevant data on time (ten weeks for developed countries and twenty weeks for developing ones, from the date of notification). The provision is expected to overcome a key problem that had plagued earlier reviews, namely stalled examinations because of delayed notifications.

Unlike the TPRM, the mechanism also institutionalizes 'other reporting'. Any Member can now submit information that it considers ought to have been submitted under the Transparency Mechanism. It also gives other Members sufficient time to submit comments and questions to the Members of the RTA under examination. In order to make the information widely available, a new electronic database has been created and the Secretariat is tasked with updating it regularly.

While both developed and developing countries desired transparency, the latter were also concerned about retaining maximum flexibility over the application of WTO rules. Most developing countries feared that conducting reviews at the CRTA would dilute the Enabling Clause. The Clause, which pertains to RTAs between developing countries, applies a less stringent understanding of the provision of 'substantially all trade' (a hallmark of Article 24). For developing countries the worry was that information about preferential arrangements, if the RTA did not cover substantially all trade, could mean that pressure would be applied on them during the RTA's examination. Therefore, they argued that there was no legal obligation to provide such information (WTO 1998: paras. 21–3). Developed countries, by contrast, believed that the CRTA's transparency-promoting role extended even to agreements having waivers under the Clause.[26] Finally, all sides compromised: there would be a single TM process for all RTAs, but the CTD would retain its authority to review those RTAs that were covered by the Enabling Clause.[27]

The other compromise was on what would be the outcome of the RTA examinations. Many WTO Members feared that RTA examinations might be used against them to launch dispute proceedings. The transparency enthusiasts abandoned calls for more thorough examinations in return for the promise of greater compliance with RTA reporting rules. The compromise, however, has undercut the value of the TM. The Secretariat's mandate is even more limited than under the TPRM: whereas TPR reports sometimes have critical analyses of Members' policies, RTA factual presentations cannot criticize any RTA-related policy on the grounds that it might be inconsistent with WTO rules. Though the Secretariat can rely on data from non-official sources, it mostly depends on information from Members and governments have already found ways to submit incomplete information and to edit it in the reports (Langille 2008:107). In the absence of a mandate for a more thorough critical examination of RTAs and their impacts for other Members and the multilateral trade system, it is unlikely that adding a TPRM-style review meeting will make the RTA TM any more effective (Table 14.2).

[26] See WTO 1997d: para. XXXI; WTO 1997e: para. 77; WTO 2004a: paras. 3, 5.

[27] See WTO 2006a: para. 9; WTO 2006b: paras. 1, 18, 22.

Table 14.2. *RTA monitoring as response to Members' demand for information*

Common challenges for WTO surveillance	Demands of transparency supporters	Observed outcomes	Role for WTO Secretariat
Advance warning (hidden information)	Calls for early notifications of RTAs	Two-stage notification process; notify amendments; online databases	No opposition to principle of transparency
Impact analysis (resource constraints)	Calls for 'systemic' analysis of RTA impacts on multilateral regime	No clear agreement	Absence of examination procedures undermines impact analysis
Compliance-oriented information (issue uncertainties)	Want to preserve flexibilities under Enabling Clause	CTD remains forum for reviewing RTAs between developing countries	Compromise solution retains institutional reporting by Secretariat
Domestic capacity constraints	Burden of reporting RTA negotiations; lack of capacity to monitor other States	Other-reporting permitted – stronger provision than TPRM	Strengthened institutional reporting; self-reporting depends on domestic capacity
Lack of follow-up after reviews	Want thorough examination of RTAs	Compromise to establish transparency mechanism: Members cannot pass judgement	Secretariat prepares only factual presentations

Source: Author's analysis based on WTO documents.

4 Transparency for SPS measures – more information but voluntary requirements

On 30 May 2008, the WTO Committee on Sanitary and Phytosanitary Measures adopted revised recommendations on how governments should submit information on new or proposed measures with regard to food safety and animal and plant health. For many developing countries with an interest in agricultural exports, SPS measures and their abuse can impose severe barriers on access to key export markets. The new recommendations incorporate new procedures for notifications and were accompanied by provisions for online databases and improved access to electronic resources. Do these efforts satisfy developing countries' needs?

4.1 Improving notifications and analysis, maintaining flexibilities

The 2008 recommendations were the third round of revisions since SPS-related notification procedures and transparency requirements were introduced in 1996. Table 14.3 showcases the changes in transparency provisions that occurred over three phases. Earlier revisions were limited in the scope of notifications and analysis included in the submissions. They were also less clear about the notice period prior to introduction of new measures or the time given to react to notifications.

The 2008 round of revisions directly address the need for advance warning of new SPS measures. As discussed above, advance warning is important because sudden regulatory changes can significantly threaten Member States' access to export markets. The revisions are significant on two counts. First, Members are encouraged to notify not only changes related to new domestic regulations, but also those measures that reflect efforts to conform to international standards, if such measures are expected to have a significant impact on others' trade prospects.[28] Note, however, that this is a voluntary provision.

Second, the new procedures recommend (again on a voluntary basis) that Members notify 'expected modifications' (WTO 2008b: paras. 8 and 11). Developing countries argued that they needed more time to adjust their animal and plant exports to meet new standards. Mexico, for instance, had proposed annual publications of Members' SPS programmes, Egypt sought advance notifications and China demanded

[28] See WTO 2004c: para. 3(a)(ii); WTO 2004d: paras. 8–10; WTO 2004e: paras. 3–7; WTO 2004f: paras. 6–10; WTO 2005: para. 6.

Table 14.3. *Evolution of SPS-related transparency procedures*

	1996 recommendations	1st revision (1999)	2nd revision (2002)	3rd revision (2008)
Reporting by	Member State	Member State	Member State	Member State
Scope of notifications/ analysis	Products covered by new measures; Deviations from international standards	Also information on regions/ countries likely to be affected; Likely trade effects to be described	New procedures for addenda, corrigenda and revisions; Notification of recognition of equivalence of SPS measures of another Member(s)	Encouraged to notify even regulations conforming to international standards; Summary should enable assessment of trade impact; Provide information on expected modifications; 'Strongly encouraged' to use addenda to notify adoption of proposed regulation
Timing of notifications	Draft regulation 'when amendments can still be introduced'; May proceed with implementation after forty-five days	'Well before the entry into force'	Normally allow 'at least' sixty days for comments	Sixty-day comment period to begin with circulation of notification; Sixty-day comment period applies to addenda and revisions as well
Requests for information/ documents and dissemination	Response or acknowledgement within five days	Encouraged to publish SPS measures on the World Wide Web	'Strongly encouraged' to reply within five days	Provide website address or specific hyperlink when documents online; Unofficial translations to be submitted as supplements to original notification; Access to electronic resources – SPS IMS; FAO IPFSAPH

Follow-up	Explain how Member will take comments into account	Make available to other Members comments received and answers provided		
Special measures for developing countries		Extend time limit for comments by at least thirty days if notification of particular interest to developing countries		If possible allow more than sixty days for comments; Encouraged to use procedures to enhance transparency of SDT of developing countries

Source: Author's compilation based on WTO 1996f; WTO 1999b; WTO 2002c; WTO 2002d; WTO 2008g.

additional notifications when modifications were substantially different.[29] While the new provisions responded to developing countries' demand for early warning, developed countries were in favour as well.

The new procedures also partly respond to the resource constraints of developing countries. The notification guidelines recommend that the notifying Member offer summary analyses to help its main trading partners determine the impact on their exports.

For developing countries, however, it is not sufficient to be aware of new SPS measures in export markets. They also need information about how to comply with the new SPS measures and guidance on whether they can avail themselves of options and flexibilities in those new measures. For instance, in 2002 Egypt demanded that notifying Members should also clearly specify the special and differential treatment (SDT) in proposed regulations, such as special flexibilities for developing countries as well as information on technical assistance that the Member could offer them.[30] In 2004, the SPS Committee recommended various ways that governments could devise SPS measures to alleviate developing countries' concerns: modifying the measure in question, applying SDT to all developing countries, and giving technical assistance to the exporting country. It also asked Members to notify what kind of SDT they would provide and the rationale for rejecting requests for such treatment (WTO 2004g: paras. Steps 5–7). The revisions of 2008 call for a further review of SDT in SPS regulations to strengthen these obligations: more information on testing and inspections, and better treatment of the special needs of developing countries (WTO 2008d: paras. steps 4–6).

Developing countries have also been conscious of the difficulties they face in submitting notifications. LDCs account for less than 1 per cent of all SPS-related notifications submitted since 1995, highlighting the need for technical assistance to help them collect and submit data. To overcome some of the capacity constraints, the new guidelines promote the use of online databases and call for improved access to international electronic resources such as the WTO's SPS Information Management System and the Food and Agricultural Organization's (FAO) International Portal on Food Safety, Animal and Plant Health. They also encourage WTO Members to submit up-to-date information for inclusion on the WTO's SPS webpage. These provisions improve access to information and help Members track notifications and trade concerns raised in the

[29] See WTO 2003b: para. 1; WTO 2007a; WTO 2007b: para. 10; WTO 2008c.

[30] See WTO 2002a : paras. 2, 5–6; WTO 2002b: paras. 3–4, 7.

SPS Committee and other SPS-related documents. Although poor countries continue to need technical assistance to strengthen their notification apparatus, the databases could greatly reduce the burden of collecting information on other countries and also reduce some of the reporting burdens on national enquiry points.

4.2 Flaws remain – little institutional reporting; procedural hurdles for reviews

Despite the revised SPS notification guidelines, a major flaw is that they rely entirely on Members' self-reporting. Unlike the TPRM or RTA Transparency Mechanism, the WTO Secretariat has no role in collecting or analysing information on Members' policies. But the guidelines did give it a role in monitoring the harmonization of international SPS standards. The Secretariat was tasked with compiling an annual report of recently adopted measures. But it does not involve any independent reporting by the Secretariat. In the absence of institutional reporting, the implementation by governments of voluntary standards for notifications cannot be monitored, thus potentially undermining the effort to improve the transparency of SPS measures.

Another shortcoming relates to the procedures for raising trade-related concerns and following up on notifications. Noticing that the monitoring system was being used very sparsely, in 2003 the Secretariat proposed that the deadline for identifying specific issues could be shortened from thirty to ten days, so that more Members could raise their concerns (the SPS Committee accepted the proposal in 2004) (WTO 2003c: paras. 5–6). But the participation of developing countries in SPS-related debates remained low. Until 2006, they had brought only sixteen SPS standards-related issues before the SPS Committee. By contrast, developed countries have annually raised more than twenty specific trade concerns in most years since 1997 (WTO 2006c: paras. 2, 4).

Part of the reason for low participation in raising trade concerns is procedural. A Chinese study on SPS notifications found that only 22.2 per cent of 995 regular notifications in 2002–3 offered comment periods of more than 60 days. Also, only 6.5 per cent of the notifications allowed for adjustment periods of at least six months (WTO 2004h: paras. 8–10). China argued that, as a result, developing countries were neither able to comment on proposed regulations nor adjust their exports in time to comply with new standards. In response to demands from China, Mexico and Chinese Taipei, the new 2008 transparency guidelines provide more than sixty days for others to comment on proposed regulatory changes.[31]

The 2008 guidelines also made some tentative steps towards improved follow-up procedures. Responses to queries now have to be provided within five days. Specific trade concerns that arise from notifications are now discussed in Committee meetings. And the 'good offices' of the SPS Chairperson have been used in the capacity of a mediator to resolve a few disputes (WTO 2007c: paras. 17–20). But Members continue to express the same frustrations as they had with the TPRM, namely that transparency in itself is not sufficient to secure market access.

Table 14.4 summarizes the demands for SPS transparency and explains the institutional responses, including the limited role assigned to institutional reporting. For developing countries there continues to be a dual challenge: having to raise their SPS standards and also actively monitor policy changes elsewhere. The latest 2008 efforts to improve advance warning, offer analyses for the potential impact of new measures, and provide SDT and assistance to adjust to new measures had the support of developed and developing countries. These efforts should significantly improve transparency. Recent procedural changes should also give Members more time to analyse notifications. But whether these initiatives can substitute for the lack of domestic capacity in developing countries and increase faith in the efficacy of the review process remains, for now, an open question.

5 Reviews of Aid for Trade – demand for dedicated monitoring

Aid for Trade (AFT) is aimed at developing countries, particularly LDCs, to develop trade-related skills and infrastructure, which in turn could help them expand their trade and implement and benefit from WTO agreements. The AFT initiative was launched in 2005 and recent years have witnessed new commitments for AFT from donor countries.[32] While donors want AFT to be 'mainstreamed' in development planning, recipients are wary that such trade-related assistance might divert aid resources from other sectors. In February 2006 the WTO created an AFT Task Force with

[31] See WTO 2003b: para. 4; WTO 2004i: paras. 4–6; WTO 2007a: paras. 1–2.

[32] EU: US$2.54 billion per year by 2010 (at 2010 exchange rates); Canada: disbursed US$504 million during 2001–7; promised more than US$94 million from 2007 (at 2007 exchange rates); Australia: US$84–168 million each year during 2003–7 (at 2007 exchange rates); United States: US$6.5 billion since 1999. See WTO 2007d: paras. 12, 86–87, 98, 101.

Table 14.4. *SPS transparency as response to developing countries' needs*

Common challenges for WTO surveillance	Developing countries' demands	Observed outcomes	Role for WTO Secretariat and other organizations
Advance warning (hidden information)	Information on expected modifications	Voluntary self-reporting; information on measures taken to meet international standards as well	Members unwilling to cede responsibility to WTO Secretariat
Impact analysis (resource constraints)	Call for technical assistance to process information	Recommended summaries on expected impact	
Compliance-oriented information (issue uncertainties)	Information on SDT	Recommended provisions for SDT with technical assistance; rationale for rejecting SDT application required	
Domestic capacity constraints	Administrative burden of reporting	More transparency for information already available	Online databases in selected international organizations
Lack of follow-up after reviews	Longer comment period and quicker responses	Sixty days for comments; five days for responses	Members reluctant to give Secretariat reporting authority

Source: Author's analysis based on WTO documents.

the aim of 'operationalizing' AFT. By July that year it recommended that, 'Monitoring and evaluating progress is essential in building confidence that increased Aid for Trade will be delivered and effectively used' (WTO 2006d: 7). Once the WTO General Council accepted the recommendations in October, a three-level approach to monitoring AFT was developed: the OECD's Development Assistance Committee (DAC) would monitor global flows; donor agencies would undertake self-evaluations of their AFT activities; and recipients would prepare in-country assessments. The WTO would have overall charge of AFT surveillance, its newest monitoring responsibility (WTO 2006e: paras. 5–7; WTO 2006f).

For developing countries, a primary concern was the calculation of additional aid under AFT programmes. Several LDCs repeatedly demanded separate measurements for AFT disbursements and provisions to record, follow up and assess allocations of AFT.[33] A WTO–OECD Trade Capacity Building Database was established in 2002, with the remit to cover trade-related technical assistance (TRTA) and capacity-building projects. But there were different interpretations of what constituted AFT with no single framework for monitoring or agreed benchmarks (WTO 2007f: para. 22). Definitional uncertainties meant that submission of data and effectiveness of monitoring suffered.

5.1 WTO gets primary responsibility for institutional reporting

Given the importance of AFT for their trade interests, poor countries needed independent reporting, preferably by an international institution, to overcome their own resource constraints. But they also had to decide which institution to back for AFT monitoring.

With several multilateral and bilateral agencies responsible for delivering AFT, the AFT taskforce involved a long list of actors (including donors, recipient countries, regional bodies, multilateral agencies and even the private sector) and issued a number of recommendations for monitoring. National AFT committees would report to a global monitoring body. Further, country assessments of AFT could be included in the TPRs of both donors and recipients. As a new suggestion for modifying the content of TPR reports, this was a step towards including additional and more relevant information. Further, multilateral agencies like the World Bank and the Asian Development Bank (ADB) had already established independent departments for AFT project evaluation (WTO 2006h: para. 5).

Meanwhile, several larger developing countries, having also emerged as donors, wanted monitoring to highlight their own AFT contributions. But they were averse to creating additional bureaucracy or replicating the work of other agencies,[34] and argued that existing organizations could perform the monitoring task. Developed country donors were also

[33] See WTO 2006g: paras. 32, 60, 62; WTO 2007d: para. 29; WTO 2007e: paras. 21, 52.

[34] See WTO 2006i: 5; WTO 2007d: paras. 22–23, 60, 64, 69, 75–7, 105, 110, 147, 221–4.

against new institutional structures for AFT monitoring. They preferred the already existing OECD Creditor Reporting System (CRS). Operating since 1967, the CRS records more than 100,000 new grant and loan commitments by Members of the OECD–DAC and by multilateral development banks and some UN agencies. Since the data is also comparable, donors felt that the CRS could also gather information on AFT commitments and disbursals.[35]

So, why was the WTO given the overall responsibility of AFT surveillance? For poorer countries, monitoring through existing multilateral institutions could not substitute for a dedicated AFT monitoring scheme. Bangladesh argued against a single monitoring mechanism, anxious that the CRS would suffer from shortcomings as a facility for information-gathering, including mislabelling aid intended for other purposes as AFT and mistaking estimates of total resources (in particular by over-estimating the additionality of AFT) (WTO 2007d: paras. 245–6). The LDC Group wanted representatives from non-governmental organizations (NGOs), the private sector and development banks to be part of a biennial forum on AFT (WTO 2006g: para. 49). However, unlike the multilateral development banks or donor agencies, where LDCs had little say in governance and limited voting powers, the WTO offered a forum where LDCs could have equal voice. Barbados, for example, argued that a multilateral mechanism was necessary to improve the quality of information and assessments of AFT (WTO 2006j: para. 41). The ACP countries also wanted the WTO's CTD to exercise 'overall responsibility' for monitoring AFT flows (WTO 2006k: para. 21).

Eventually, Members gave the WTO the charge of AFT monitoring with a call for improved coordination with other institutions. A joint WTO–OECD working group started refining the CRS to provide appropriate data for global AFT reviews.[36] But the OECD also warned that a definition of AFT that is 'too scientific and too specific' might be problematic since donors had different AFT strategies and visions (WTO 2007e: paras. 38, 43, 63). Regional bodies (like the ADB, African Development Bank and Inter-American Development Bank) would also work with the WTO to conduct regional reviews. And annual global reviews would permit poor countries to participate and learn from the experiences of other Members and organizations.

[35] See WTO 2007e: para. 12; WTO 2008e: para. 63; WTO 2008f: para. 14.

[36] In 2008, the WTO Director-General reported that, in order to measure the full impact of AFT, the OECD would add a new category to the CRS, namely trade-related adjustment (WTO 2008f: paras. 6–7).

5.2 *Focusing on impact analysis and follow-up*

Having established the WTO as the AFT monitoring forum, attention turned to follow-up questions, a refreshing change from other monitoring debates. Monitoring could not be undertaken for its own sake: there had to be a link between recipients' demands and donors' responses (WTO 2008e: paras. 9, 12).

During AFT debates in 2006, there was also no consensus among Members on how to analyse AFT's impact. Information on impact was needed not only for static annual analyses, but also as inputs into future debates about how to improve AFT. The International Trade Centre argued that the WTO–OECD Trade Capacity Building database could not provide a 'clear picture of the world of TRTA' (WTO 2006l: para. 21). Other agencies, including UNCTAD, the United Nations Development Programme (UNDP) and the World Bank, acknowledged the role of databases but underscored the importance of measuring the development impacts of AFT activities.[37]

Meanwhile, the LDC Group wanted peer reviews of donors and recipients, under the auspices of the CTD, to measure aid delivery and impact. These countries recognized that they had limited capacity to monitor AFT or its impacts at the country level, which prompted their calls for 'analytical' AFT reports (WTO 2006g: paras. 64, 67–8). The African Group also wanted the monitoring mechanism to promote both transparency *and* accountability (WTO 2006p: 8, 12).

Larger developing countries as well as developed countries also supported the idea of a more rigorous and compliance-oriented monitoring mechanism for AFT. While recipient countries could increase their capacity to manage and monitor aid, in-country assessments would have to be ultimately subjected to international scrutiny (WTO 2007e: para. 47). India and China wanted the mechanism to measure coherence (between donors), additionality (of aid) and satisfaction of recipient countries (WTO 2007d: paras. 148, 225). Rich countries argued that unless monitoring was linked to better delivery of aid, developing countries would also not undertake necessary self-evaluations. In fact, there was a risk that AFT reviews would slip into a routine rather than a lively process (a reference perhaps to what had happened to the TPRM).[38]

Thus, on 25 February 2008, the CTD gave the 'green light' to the Director-General's proposed AFT 'road map', under which reviews would be 'more

[37] See WTO 2006m: paras. 21–2; WTO 2006n: para. 6; WTO 2006o: paras. 29, 31.

[38] See WTO 2007d: paras. 134–5, 151; WTO 2007e: para. 31; WTO 2008f: para. 19.

focused, technical and results-oriented', through monitoring of concrete national and especially subregional plans. Global reviews would be complemented with national and subregional reviews and the establishment of an AFT 'knowledge network' and new Regional AFT Networks (WTO 2008a). So far, two rounds of regional and global reviews have been conducted. Whereas the first set of regional reviews in 2007 were aimed at gathering the financial resources to be dedicated towards AFT, the second set in 2009 sought to showcase specific AFT activities. The second global review also paid particular attention to the impact of the economic crisis and on the impact of AFT, not just for increasing trade prospects but also for poverty reduction. But it recognized that many difficulties remained in monitoring AFT: accounting for cross-border, regional and subregional aspects of AFT activities; applying principles of ownership and mutual accountability to AFT programmes; and establishing links between the impact of individual projects on a country's overall trade capacity.[39]

Table 14.5 summarizes how AFT monitoring overcomes several of the problems with WTO transparency schemes outlined earlier in the chapter. The AFT monitoring mechanism adopts a mix of self-reporting by donors and recipients but the institutional role of the WTO is a prime position. In contrast to the TPRM and SPS mechanisms, the monitoring capacity of developing countries and regional institutions has been given special consideration in the design of the AFT monitoring process. The active participation of large numbers of poor countries in AFT monitoring debates and reviews is another encouraging sign. And by at least initiating a debate on accountability, follow-up and compliance with commitments, AFT monitoring has, in theory, succeeded in giving transparency a real purpose. The success of the AFT initiative will ultimately depend on the quality of the information collected and the sincerity with which commitments are met.

6 Conclusion – closing the information gaps

The main purpose of the WTO's transparency norm is to 'enhance the effectiveness of the WTO agreements'.[40] By providing information on Members' policies and measures, transparency mechanisms hope to fill

[39] See OECD and WTO 2009: 109; also OECD and WTO 2007.

[40] Collins-Williams and Wolfe (2010). The authors contrast this purpose of transparency with accountability and transparency of the WTO itself or transparency with regard to governments disclosing information to the public.

Table 14.5. *AFT monitoring in response to developing countries' demands*

Common challenges for WTO surveillance	Developing countries' demands	Observed outcomes	Role for WTO Secretariat and other organizations
Advance warning (hidden information)	Worried about double-counting aid flows	LDCs succeed in getting multiple agencies involved	OECD–CRS exists but poor countries do not trust it
Impact analysis (resource constraints)	Evaluation of AFT impact	World Bank, ADB, EBRD undertake project evaluation	Specialized agencies take on impact evaluation responsibility
Compliance-oriented information (issue uncertainties)	Call for agreeing on benchmarks for AFT	WTO takes the lead in monitoring AFT	WTO–OECD working group for defining AFT
Domestic capacity constraints	Administrative burden of national monitoring	AFT knowledge network and regional networks to be established	Technical assistance is country-specific but regional banks play important role
Lack of follow-up after reviews	WTO–CTD to have overall responsibility	WTO gives developing countries equal voice unlike in multilateral development banks	Annual global and regional reviews under WTO

Source: Author's analysis based on WTO documents.

various kinds of information gaps: issue uncertainties, when negotiators are unaware of their counterparts' (or their own) preferences; hidden/inaccurate information, when countries withhold information or submit incomplete data to the WTO; and gaps arising from resource constraints, when poorer countries are unable to monitor others. The promise of transparency is critical to a smoothly functioning trade system.

This chapter has explored the extent to which that promise is being fulfilled. The WTO has numerous transparency provisions (not least via its notifications process). The chapter has, however, focused on institutionalized surveillance mechanisms that not only disseminate information but have some role in promoting compliance and evaluating the impact of Members' policies on the trade regime as a whole. The most institutionalized format is the Trade Policy Review Mechanism but the chapter also analyses recent developments of three other mechanisms, targeting regional trade agreements, food safety standards and Aid for Trade.

The TPRM has the mandate to review the policies of all WTO Members, periodically. Despite its attempt at being comprehensive in scope, a detailed analysis of TPR reports and meetings reveals several deficiencies: the reports often do not describe or analyse the most contentious trade policies; the procedure of advance questions is used more by developed countries and the direction of peer pressure flows against developing countries; and participation in TPR meetings is dominated by a handful of WTO Members.

There has been little consensus on how to improve the content of TPR reports. Developing countries fear that more analytical reports would target their policies more than rich ones. They have also resisted moves to increase peer pressure because the pressures are applied asymmetrically. Realizing their limited influence over policies in rich countries, they have also opposed any institutionalized follow-up to the reviews. Larger developing countries, which are already using their own resources for external monitoring, want to maintain the status quo. Poorer countries, failing to see any benefit of the reviews, have disengaged from the process.

With minimal reform in the TPRM, several common information challenges remain. Poor nations need advance warning of changes in policies, analyses of the impact of those changes and information that can help them countervail pressures to overcomply with their commitments. Beyond the TPRM, developing countries have engaged in designing new surveillance mechanisms in areas of relevance to them. They demand that new mechanisms respond to their information needs and capacity constraints and also help promote compliance in rich countries. Hence, they increasingly demand a stronger role for surveillance, including at times giving greater authority to the Secretariat. The TPRM's experience in practice and the institutional design of new mechanisms point in the direction of further reform in the multilateral trade regime's information system.

6.1 *Improving timing of information*

Poor countries have secured early warning provisions in both the RTA and SPS monitoring initiatives. Compared with the TPRM's inability to identify critical issues in advance, this is a big achievement. But WTO Members have not taken the further step of converting these provisions into obligations; they remain voluntary codes of conduct.

As the recent efforts of the WTO Secretariat as well as transparency activities led by civil society show, regular monitoring and prompt notification of major shifts in trade policies are essential during a crisis. This chapter noted that information systems can have various designs and, in practice, regimes often use a mix of designs. The trade regime largely relied on self-reporting until the early 1980s. Institutional reporting has grown since then but the Secretariat is hampered by limited mandates. Looking beyond the latest financial crisis, the timing of information will continue to matter if trust in the trading system is to be maintained. If self-reporting and institutional reporting fail to deliver information on time, then reporting by non-State actors should also become part of the mix.

6.2 *Improving quality of information*

In designing the new monitoring mechanisms, developing countries also insisted on getting compliance-oriented information to ensure that their interests (including flexibilities) were maintained when they negotiated RTAs or when other Members introduced new standards. In order to ensure that the Enabling Clause, which gives more leeway to developing countries forming RTAs, was not threatened, the CTD rather than the CRTA was chosen for reviewing RTAs among developing countries. Similarly, the SDT for SPS measures got attention whereby countries are requested to inform how their new measures would offer special treatment and flexibilities to developing countries. Efforts are also under way to clarify definitions of AFT, so that it does not displace aid for other purposes. The purpose is to ensure that developed countries comply with their commitments to provide AFT and that credible information on their performance is available to all other Members.

In response to their resource constraints, developing countries also demanded more impact analysis. If transparency is to add value, then the information has to undergo more analysis than has been the case so far. However, there has been less progress on this front. At best (in SPS) notifying Members are expected to mention how their policies would affect others. At worst (in RTAs) there has been categorical opposition to evaluations of systemic impact.

Fulfilling demands for compliance-oriented information and impact analyses is not easy. The WTO Secretariat has to balance these against the constraints on its mandate. One option is to clarify definitions (say, on subsidies or what is considered AFT) and then leave it up to WTO Members to ask questions about impact and flexibilities during TPR or committee meetings (Collins-Williams and Wolfe 2010). Greater coordination will also be necessary between different WTO divisions and with the World Bank, International Monetary Fund (IMF), regional banks and national research institutions to incrementally increase policy analysis. The WTO Secretariat will also have to draw on sector- and country-specific expertise both during a country's TPR and for periodic reporting to identify sudden shifts in policies.

6.3 *Improving sources of information*

In addition to greater institutional coordination, another way to improve the quality of information is to tap into multiple sources of information. We have already seen the importance on reporting by non-State actors in offering timely information. But WTO Members have been reluctant generally to let non-State actors provide information or participate in review meetings as observers. Yet, they cannot be wished away. The availability of new technologies to disseminate information and growing constituencies of actors interested in trade developments mean that such reporting will grow. In fact, the debates on AFT monitoring suggest that developing countries are willing to let non-State actors contribute when the information generated directly benefits their trade interests.

The resistance to non-State actors is also partly due to poor domestic capacity. This issue of building capacity has been tackled only partially with the use of online databases to help countries get information on other countries. But developing countries' own reporting and reviewing capacities remain underdeveloped. In part, capacity will develop as countries grow and trade more (as some of the larger developing countries have done). But countries will be more willing to participate in policy reviews if capacity-building efforts focus not only on self-evaluations but also on monitoring foreign trade barriers.

6.4 *Improving uses of information*

The biggest stumbling block to improved surveillance in the multilateral trading system, however, has been the inability of Members to agree on follow-up procedures. Like the TPRM, procedural innovations – earlier submissions of factual presentations for RTAs; longer comment periods for SPS notifications – have been passed off as genuine reform and remain untested. The usefulness of these reforms will depend on Members' capacities to engage with review procedures. The choice of venue is one criterion: by opting for the WTO as the forum for AFT reviews, the poorest WTO Members have ensured they have greater voice than in multilateral development banks and donor agencies. But low participation rates in other review meetings (TPRM, SPS Committee) suggest that the value of participation is still unclear to many countries.

The value of monitoring mechanisms could be boosted with simple reforms: targeting Members' reporting behaviour and exposing laggards; increasing developing country representation among discussants; making high-level representation mandatory for review meetings; increasing media coverage of reviews; and requesting the Secretariat or non-State actors to publish follow-up documents to show how countries have responded to concerns raised in review meetings.

In theory, transparency increases confidence in a rules-based trade regime. In practice, Members often prefer that transparency works to shine the light on others but not on their own policies. For developing countries this feeling is strengthened when they face pressure but are unable to use transparency mechanisms to coax changes in policies in developed countries. But power asymmetries are a given in any international organization. Reforms in the WTO's extensive information system will have to deliver timely and quality information on issues of relevance to developing countries. If the reforms succeed in doing that, then reporting by multiple actors can enable developing countries to have greater leverage in policy reviews. In turn, such enhanced transparency can even begin to mitigate some of the existing power asymmetries in the trade regime.

References

Abbott, K. W. and Snidal, D. 2009. 'The Governance Triangle: Regulatory Standards Institutions and the Shadow of the State', in Mattli, W. and Woods, N. (eds.), *The Politics of Global Regulation*, Princeton and Oxford: Princeton University Press, pp. 72–134.

Aggarwal, A. 2007. 'Anti-Dumping Protection: Who Gets it? An Exploratory Analysis of Anti-Dumping Use in the Most Active User Countries', *Centre for Trade & Development Working Paper* 9 (November): 1–29.

Baldwin, R. (ed.) 2009. *The Great Trade Collapse: Causes, Consequences and Prospects.* Brussels: Centre for Economic Policy Research and VoxEU.org.

Baldwin, R. and Evenett, S. 2009. 'Introduction and Recommendations for the G20', in Baldwin, R. and Evenett, S. (eds.), *The Collapse of Global Trade, Murky Protectionism, and the Crisis: Recommendations for the G20*, London: Centre for Economic Policy Research and VoxEU.org, pp. 1–9.

Bhagwati, J., Greenaway, D. and Panagariya, A. 1998. 'Trading Preferentially: Theory and Policy', *The Economic Journal* 108(July): 1128–48.

Blackhurst, R. 1988. 'Strengthening GATT Surveillance of Trade-related Policies', in Hilf, M. and Petersmann, E.-U. (eds.), *The New GATT Round of Multilateral Trade Negotiations: Legal and Economic Aspects.* Deventer (The Netherlands): Kluwer Law and Taxation Publishers.

Collins-Williams, T. and Wolfe, R. 2010. 'Transparency as a Trade Policy Tool: The WTO's Cloudy Windows', *World Trade Review* 9(4): 551–81.

Curzon Price, V. 1991. 'GATT's New Trade Policy Review Mechanism', *The World Economy* 14(2): 227–38.

da Motta Veiga, P. 2005. 'Brazil and the G20 Group of Developing Countries', in Gallagher, P., Low, P., and Stoler, A.L. (eds.), *Managing the Challenge of WTO Participation: 45 Case Studies*, Cambridge University Press pp. 109–19.

2007. 'Trade Policy-Making in Brazil: Changing Patterns in State-Civil Society Relationship', in Halle, M. and Wolfe, R. (eds.), *Process Matters: Sustainable Development and Domestic Trade Transperency*, Winnipeg: International Institute for Sustainable Development, pp. 143–82.

Deere, C. 2009. *The Implementation Game: The TRIPS Agreement and the Global Politics of Intellectual Property Reform in Developing Countries.* Oxford University Press.

Deere Birkbeck, C. and Cherneva, I. 2010. 'The 2009 WTO Ministerial Conference: A Review of Outcomes and Proposals on the Functioning of the WTO', GEG Working Paper, Global Economic Governance Programme, University College, Oxford.

Dhar, B. and Kallummal, M. 2007. 'Trade Policy Off the Hook: The Making of Indian Trade Policy since the Uruguay Round', in Halle, M. and Wolfe, R. (eds.), *Process Matters: Sustainable Development and Domestic*

Trade Transparency, Winnipeg: International Institute for Sustainable Development, pp. 183–240.

Dhar, B., Evenett, S. J., Long, G. *et al.* 2009. 'Disavowing Protectionism: A Strengthened G20 Standstill and Surveillance', in Baldwin, R. and Evenett, S. (eds.), *The Collapse of Global Trade, Murky Protectionism, and the Crisis: Recommendations for the G20*, London: Centre for Economic Policy Research and VoxEU.org, pp. 69–74.

Evenett, S. 2009a. 'Crisis-era Protectionism One Year After the Washington G20 Meeting', in Baldwin, R. (ed.), *The Great Trade Collapse: Causes, Consequences and Prospects*, Brussels Centre for Economic Policy Research and Vox EU.org, pp. 37–45.

2009b. *Broken Promises: a G-20 Summit Report by Global Trade Alert*. London: Centre for Economic Policy Research and Global Trade Alert.

Francois, J. F. 2001. 'Maximising the Benefits of the Trade Policy Review Mechanism for Developing Countries', in Hoekman and Martin (eds.), *Developing Countries and the WTO: A Pro-Active Agenda*. Oxford: Blackwell, pp. 147–65.

Gallagher, P. and Stoler, A. 2009. 'G20 Surveillance of Harmful Trade Measures', in Baldwin, R. and Evenett, S. (eds.), *The Collapse of Global Trade, Murky Protectionism, and the Crisis: Recommendations for the G20*. London: Centre for Economic Policy Research and VoxEU.org, pp. 65–8.

Gallagher, P., Low, P. and Stoler, A. L. (eds.) 2005. *Managing the Challenges of WTO Participation: 45 Case Studies*. Cambridge University Press.

GATT. 1987a. 'Existing Surveillance Functions in the GATT – Note by the Secretariat', Negotiating Group on Functioning of the GATT System, MTN. GNG/NG14/W/3. 9 June.

1987b. 'Meeting of 23 June 1987 – Note by the Secretariat', Negotiating Group on Functioning of the GATT System, MTN.GNG/NG14/2. 26 June.

1987c. 'The 1954/55 Review Session – Note by the Secretariat', Negotiating Group on Functioning of the GATT System, MTN.GNG/NG14/W/12. 14 August.

1987d. 'Meeting of 3 and 4 November 1987 – Note by the Secretariat', Negotiating Group on Functioning of the GATT System, MTN.GNG/NG14/4. 30 November.

1988a. 'Notification Procedures in GATT – Note by the Secretariat', Negotiating Group on Functioning of the GATT System, MTN.GNG/NG14/W/18. 10 March.

1988b. 'Communication from the Delegation of Jamaica', Negotiating Group on Functioning of the GATT System, MTN.GNG/NG14/W/22. 16 May.

1988c. 'Meeting of 20 and 22 June 1988 – Note by the Secretariat', Negotiating Group on Functioning of the GATT System, MTN.GNG/NG14/8. 13 July.

1989a. 'Functioning of the GATT System: Decisions of 12 April 1989', Negotiating Group on Functioning of the GATT System, L/6490. 12 April.

1989b. 'Meeting of 19–20 June 1989 – Note by the Secretariat', Negotiating Group on Functioning of the GATT System, MTN.GNG/NG14/12. 30 June.

1990a. 'Meeting of 19 February 1990 – Note by the Secretariat', Negotiating Group on Functioning of the GATT System, MTN.GNG/NG14/15. 23 March.

1990b. 'Meeting of 22–23 May 1990 – Note by the Secretariat', Negotiating Group on Functioning of the GATT System, MTN.GNG/NG14/17. 19 June.

1990c. 'Meeting of 25–26 June 1990 – Note by the Secretariat', Negotiating Group on Functioning of the GATT System, MTN.GNG/NG14/18. 9 July.

Ghosh, A. 2008. *See No Evil, Speak No Evil?: The WTO, the Trade Policy Review Mechanism, and Developing Countries*. PhD dissertation. University of Oxford.

2010. 'Developing Countries in the WTO Trade Policy Review Mechanism', *World Trade Review* 9(3): 419–55.

Gong, B. 2005. 'Shanghai's WTO Affairs Consultation Center: Working Together to Take Advantage of WTO Membership', in Gallagher, P., Low, P. and Stoler, A.L. (eds.), *Managing the Challenges of WTO Participation: 45 Case Studies*, Cambridge University Press, pp. 167–77.

Halle, M. and Wolfe, R. (eds.) 2007. *Process Matters: Sustainable Development and Domestic Trade Transparency*. Winnipeg: International Institute for Sustainable Development.

Hoekman, B. M. and Mavroidis, P. C. 2000. 'WTO Dispute Settlement, Transparency and Surveillance', *The World Economy* 23(4): 527–42.

Huang, R. 2005. 'How has Accession to the WTO Changed Trade Policy Making in China?' *Paper Prepared for a Workshop on Trade Policymaking in Developing Countries*, 25 May: 1–19.

Keesing, D. B. 1998. *Improving Trade Policy Reviews in the World Trade Organization*. Washington, DC: Institute for International Economics.

Keohane, R. O. 1982. 'The Demand for International Regimes', *International Organization* 36(2): 325–55.

Lamy, P. 2007. 'Monitoring and Surveillance: The Rising Agenda of the WTO', *Address to Georgetown University Law Centre*. Washington, DC. 22 October.

2009. 'Geneva Ministerial a "Unique Occasion" to Send Strong Signals on WTO Issues', *Report to the General Council*. Geneva. 17 November. www.wto.org/english/news_e/news09_e/tnc_chair_report_17nov09_e.htm [Accessed in July 2010].

Langille, J. 2008. *Regulating Regionalism? The GATT, the WTO, and Regional Trade Agreements*. MPhil dissertation. University of Oxford.

Leutwiler, F., Bradley, B., Gyllenhammar, P. G. *et al.* 1985. *Trade Policies for a Better Future: Proposals for Action*. Geneva: GATT.

Marconini, M. 2005. *Trade Policy-Making Process in Brazil*, Mimeo. www6.miami.edu/hemispheric-policy/LSEWorkshopTradePolicy250505.pdf [Accessed in July 2010].

Mavroidis, P. C. 1991–2. 'Surveillance Schemes: The GATT's New Trade Policy Review Mechanism', *Michigan Journal of International Law* 13(2): 374–414.

OECD and UNCTAD. 2010. 'Third Report on G20 Investment Measures', Geneva and Paris. 14 June. www.wto.org/english/news_e/news10_e/report_oecd_unctad_june10_e.pdf [Accessed in August 2010].

OECD and WTO. 2007. Aid for Trade at a Glance 2007: 1st Global Review. www.wto.org/english/tratop_e/devel_e/a4t_e/a4t_at_a_glance07_e.pdf [Accessed in July 2010].

2009. Aid for Trade at a Glance 2009: Maintaining Momentum. www.wto.org/english/res_e/booksp_e/aid4trade09_e.pdf [Accessed in July 2010].

Priya, S. 2007. 'Making RTAs Transparent', *The Hindu Business Line*. 30 January.

Qureshi, A. H. 1990. 'The New GATT Trade Policy Review Mechanism: An Exercise in Transparency or "Enforcement"?', *Journal of World Trade* 24(3): 147–60.

Sen, J. 2004. 'Trade Policy Making in India: The Reality Below the Water Line', *CUTS International Paper* 0415: 1–28.

Tharakan, P. K. M. 2006. 'Storm Signals: An Analysis of the Trade Policy Review of the European Communities', *The World Economy* 29(10): 1301–10.

Wolfe, R. 2010. 'Did the Protectionist Dog Bark? Transparency, Accountability, and the WTO During the Global Crisis', *Paper Prepared for the Annual Meeting of ISA-Canada with the Canadian Political Science Association*. 1 June. www.cpsa-acsp.ca/papers-2010/Wolfe.pdf [Accessed in July 2010].

World Trade Organization (WTO). 1995. 'Procedural Improvements to the Trade Policy Review Mechanism – Note by the Chairman', Trade Policy Review Body, WT/TPR/13. 13 December. Geneva: WTO.

1996a. 'Committee on Regional Trade Agreements – Decision of 6 February 1996', WT/L/127. 7 February. Geneva: WTO.

1996b. 'Communication from the Delegations of Australia, Hong Kong and Korea', Committee on Regional Trade Agreements, WT/REG/W/5. 27 June. Geneva: WTO.

1996c. 'Second Session – Note on the Meeting of 2–3 July 1996', Committee on Regional Trade Agreements, WT/REG/M/2. 14 August. Geneva: WTO.

1996d. 'Third Session – Note on the Meeting of 29–31 July 1996', Committee on Regional Trade Agreements, WT/REG/M/3. 29 August. Geneva: WTO.

1996e. 'Fourth Session – Note on the Meeting of 17–20 September 1996', Committee on Regional Trade Agreements, WT/REG/M/4. 28 November. Geneva: WTO.

1996f. 'Recommended Notification Procedures', Committee on Sanitary and Phytosanitary Measures, G/SPS/7. 11 June. Geneva: WTO.

1997a. 'Eighth Session – Note on the Meetings of 19, 20, 21 and 24 February 1997', Committee on Regional Trade Agreements, WT/REG/M/8. 1 May. Geneva: WTO.

1997b. 'Ninth Session – Note on the Meetings of 17 and 18 March 1997', Committee on Regional Trade Agreements, WT/REG/M/9. 1 May. Geneva: WTO.

1997c. 'Guidelines on Procedures to Improve and Facilitate the Examination Process – Note by the Chairman', Committee on Regional Trade Agreements, WT/REG/W/15. 6 May. Geneva: WTO.

1997d. 'Tenth Session – Note on the Meetings of 28 April and 1–2 May 1997', Committee on Regional Trade Agreements, WT/REG/M/10. 9 June. Geneva: WTO.

1997e. 'Eleventh Session – Note on the Meetings of 19–20 June 1997', Committee on Regional Trade Agreements, WT/REG/M/11. 9 July. Geneva: WTO.

1998. 'Sixteenth Session – Note on the Meetings of 16–18 and 20 February', Committee on Regional Trade Agreements, WT/REG/M/16. 18 March. Geneva: WTO.

1999a. 'Appraisal of the Operation of the Trade Policy Review Mechanism – Report to Ministers', Ministerial Conference Third Session, Seattle, WT/MIN(99)/2. 8 October. Geneva: WTO.

1999b. 'Recommended Notification Procedures – Revision', Committee on Sanitary and Phytosanitary Measures, G/SPS/7/Rev.1. 26 November. Geneva: WTO.

2000. 'Synopsis of 'Systemic' Issues Related to Regional Trade Agreements – Note by the Secretariat', Committee on Regional Trade Agreements, WT/REG/W/37. 2 March. Geneva: WTO.

2002a. 'Enhancing Transparency of Special and Differential (S&D) Treatment within the SPS Agreement – Submission by Canada', Committee on Sanitary and Phytosanitary Measures, G/SPS/W/127. 30 October. Geneva: WTO.

2002b. 'Comments on the Canadian Proposal – Statement by Egypt at the Meeting of 7–8 November 2002', Committee on Sanitary and Phytosanitary Measures, G/SPS/GEN/358. 15 November. Geneva: WTO.

2002c. 'Recommended Procedures for Implementing the Transparency Obligations of the SPS Agreement (Article 7) – Revision', Committee on Sanitary and Phytosanitary Measures, G/SPS/7/Rev.2. 2 April. Geneva: WTO.

2002d. 'Notification of Determination of the Recognition of Equivalence of Sanitary and Phytosanitary Measures – Decision by the Committee, Addendum', Committee on Sanitary and Phytosanitary Measures, G/SPS/7/Rev.2/Add.1. 25 July. Geneva: WTO.

2003a. 'Submission on Regional Trade Agreements – Joint Communication from Australia; Chile; Hong Kong, China; Korea and New Zealand', Negotiating Group on Rules, TN/RL/W/117. 11 June. Geneva: WTO.

2003b. 'Transparency – Communication from Mexico', Committee on Sanitary and Phytosanitary Measures, G/SPS/W/136. 4 September. Geneva: WTO.

2003c. 'Review of the Provisional Procedure to Monitor the Process of International Harmonization – Note by the Secretariat', Committee on Sanitary and Phytosanitary Measures, G/SPS/W/134. 10 June. Geneva: WTO.

2004a. 'Submission on Regional Trade Agreements – Paper by Japan', Negotiating Group on Rules, TN/RL/W/165. 8 October. Geneva: WTO.

2004b. 'Report by the Chairman to the Trade Negotiations Committee', Negotiating Group on Rules, TN/RL/10. 3 December. Geneva: WTO.

2004c. 'Second Review of the Operation and Implementation of the SPS Agreement – Submission by New Zealand', Committee on Sanitary and Phytosanitary Measures, G/SPS/W/150. 8 September. Geneva: WTO.

2004d. 'The Second Review of the Operation and Implementation of the SPS Agreement – Further Elaboration of Issues for Consideration by New Zealand', Committee on Sanitary and Phytosanitary Measures, G/SPS/W/157. 12 October. Geneva: WTO.

2004e. 'Issues for Consideration as Part of the Second Review of the Operation and Implementation the SPS Agreement – Further Elaboration of Issues for Consideration by Canada', Committee on Sanitary and Phytosanitary Measures, G/SPS/W/158. 14 October. Geneva: WTO.

2004f. 'Review of the Operation and Implementation of the SPS Agreement – Submission by the European Communities', Committee on Sanitary and Phytosanitary Measures, G/SPS/W/159. 14 October. Geneva: WTO.

2004g. 'Procedure to Enhance Transparency of Special and Differential Treatment in Favour of Developing Country Members – Decision by the Committee 27 October 2004', Committee on Sanitary and Phytosanitary Measures, G/SPS/33. 2 November. Geneva: WTO.

2004h. 'Second Review of the Operation and Implementation of the SPS Agreement – Submission by China – Revision', Committee on Sanitary and Phytosanitary Measures, G/SPS/W/162/Rev.1. 21 December. Geneva: WTO.

2004i. 'Second Review of the Operation and Implementation of the SPS Agreement – Comments from the Separate Customs Territory of Taiwan, Penghu, Kinmen and Matsu on Monitoring the use of International Standards (Articles 3.5 and 12.4)', Committee on Sanitary and Phytosanitary Measures, G/SPS/W/161. 19 October. Geneva: WTO.

2005. 'Second Review of the Operation and Implementation of the SPS Agreement – Communication by Chile', Committee on Sanitary and Phytosanitary Measures, G/SPS/W/170. 23 February. Geneva: WTO.

2006a. 'Report by the Chairman to the Trade Negotiations Committee', Negotiating Group on Rules, TN/RL/16. 28 March. Geneva: WTO.

2006b. 'Transparency Mechanism for Regional Trade Agreements: Decision of 14 December 2006', WTO General Council, WT/L/671. 18 December.

2006c. 'Review of the Provisional Procedure to Monitor the Process of International Harmonization – Note by the Secretariat', Committee on Sanitary and Phytosanitary Measures, G/SPS/W/200. 16 June.

2006d. 'Recommendations of the Task Force on Aid for Trade', Aid for Trade Task Force, WT/AFT/1. 27 July.

2006e. 'Follow-Up to the Aid-for-Trade Task Force Recommendations (WT/AFT/1): WTO Monitoring and Evaluation – Report by the Director-General', JOB(06)/262. 12 December.

2006f. 'Agenda Item 8 – Aid for Trade – Follow-Up to Report and Recommendations of the Task Force – Statement by the Director-General', General Council, JOB(06)/267. 20 December.

2006g. 'Communication from Zambia on Behalf of the LDC Group', Aid for Trade Task Force, WT/AFT/W/22. 29 June.

2006h. 'Communication from the Asian Development Bank', Aid for Trade Task Force, WT/AFT/W/6. 27 April.

2006i. 'Communication from Brazil – Aid for Trade Non-Paper by Brazil', Aid for Trade Task Force, WT/AFT/W/10/Rev.1. 7 June.

2006j. 'Communication from Barbados', Aid for Trade Task Force, WT/AFT/W/18. 15 June.

2006k. 'Communication from Mauritius on Behalf of the ACP Group – ACP Concept Paper on Aid for Trade', Aid for Trade Task Force, WT/AFT/W/8. 4 May.

2006l. 'Communication from the International Trade Centre', Aid for Trade Task Force WT/AFT/W/3. 21 April.

2006m. 'Communication from the United Nations Conference on Trade and Development', Aid for Trade Task Force, WT/AFT/W/11. 19 May.

2006n. 'Communication from the United Nations Development Programme', Aid for Trade Task Force, WT/AFT/W/5. 26 April.

2006o. 'Communication from the World Bank', Aid for Trade Task Force, WT/AFT/W/2. 21 April.

2006p. 'Communication from Benin on Behalf of the African Group – Concept Paper African Perspectives on Aid for Trade: Scope and Gaps', Aid for Trade Task Force, WT/AFT/W/21. 21 June.

2007a. 'China's Proposal on the Amendment to "the Recommended Procedures for Implementing the Transparency Obligations of the SPS Agreement (Article 7)" – Submission by China', Committee on Sanitary and Phytosanitary Measures, G/SPS/W/212. 25 September.

2007b. 'Compilation of Proposals regarding the Revision of the "Recommended Procedures for Implementing the Transparency Obligations of the SPS Agreement (Article 7)" – Note by the Secretariat', Committee on Sanitary and Phytosanitary Measures. G/SPS/W/215. 8 October.

2007c. 'Ad Hoc Consultations and Resolution of Trade Concerns – Note by the Secretariat', Committee on Sanitary and Phytosanitary Measures, G/SPS/GEN/781. 15 June.

2007d. 'Annual Debate on Aid for Trade – Minutes of Meeting Held in the Centre William Rappard on 21 November 2007', General Council, WT/GC/M/111. 18 December.

2007e. 'First Session on Aid for Trade – Note on the Meeting of 2 April 2007', Committee on Trade and Development, WT/COMTD/AFT/M/1. 18 May.

2007f. 'Third Session on Aid for Trade – Note on the Meeting of 9 July 2007', Committee on Trade and Development, WT/COMTD/AFT/M/3. 19 September.

2008a. '2008 Aid-for-Trade Roadmap', Committee on Trade and Development, WT/COMTD/AFT/W/6. 16 June.

2008b. 'Recommended Procedures for Implementing the Transparency Obligations of the SPS Agreement (Article 7) – as of 1 December 2008 – Revision', Committee on Sanitary and Phytosanitary Measures, G/SPS/7/Rev.3. 20 June.

2008c. 'Compilation of Proposals regarding the Revision of the "Recommended Procedures for Implementing the Transparency Obligations of the SPS Agreement (Article 7)" – Note by the Secretariat, Revision', Committee on Sanitary and Phytosanitary Measures, G/SPS/W/215/Rev.1. 14 February.

2008d. 'Proposed Revision of the Procedure to Enhance Transparency of Special and Differential Treatment in Favour of Developing Country Members (G/SPS/33) – Note by the Secretariat', Committee on Sanitary and Phytosanitary Measures G/SPS/W/224. 6 June.

2008e. 'Fifth Session on Aid for Trade – Note on the Meeting of 16 November 2007', Committee on Trade and Development, WT/COMTD/AFT/M/5. 13 February.

2008f. 'Sixth Session on Aid for Trade – Note on the Meeting of 25 February 2008', Committee on Trade and Development, WT/COMTD/AFT/M/6. 20 March.

2008g. 'Recommended Procedures for Implementing the Transparency Obligations of the SPS Agreement (Article 7) – as of 1 December 2008 – Revision', Committee on Sanitary and Phytosanitary Measures, G/SPS/7/Rev.3. 20 June.

2009a. 'Seventh Ministerial Conference – Chairman's Summary', WT/MIN(09)/18. 2 December.

2009b. 'Strengthening the WTO: Communication from Australia, Brazil, Canada, China, Hong Kong China, European Communities, India, Japan, Korea, Malaysia, Mauritius, Mexico, Norway, South Africa, Switzerland, Turkey, United States and Uruguay', WT/MIN(09)/W/1. 16 October.

2009c. 'Report of the Trade Policy Review Body for 2009', WT/TPR/249. 29 October.

2009d. 'Strengthening the WTO: Communication from India', World Trade Organization, General Council, WT/GC/W/605. 3 July.

WTO, OECD and UNCTAD. 2009. 'Report on G20 Trade and Investment Measures', Geneva and Paris. 14 September. www.wto.org/english/news_e/news09_e/trdev_14sep09_e.htm [Accessed in March 2010].

2010. 'Report on G20 Trade and Investment Measures: September 2009 to February 2010', Geneva and Paris. 8 March. www.wto.org/english/news_e/archive_e/trdev_arc_e.htm [Accessed in March 2010].

Zeng, K. and Mertha, A. 2007. 'Introduction', in Zeng (ed.), *China's Foreign Trade Policy: The New Constituencies*. London: Routledge, pp. 1–19.

15

Why not an ombudsperson at the WTO? A proposal for debate

FÉLIX PEÑA

Transparency and accountability – and the participation of civil society representatives – were not the central concerns of governments when the General Agreement on Tariffs and Trade (GATT) was founded (Lacarte 2005: 447). Indeed, demands for transparency and accountability of international organizations, including non-governmental organizations, mostly emerged only in the 1990s as part of a larger debate on how to improve their performance (Blagescu *et al.* 2005; Coicaud and Heiskanen 2001; Dombrowski 2006; GAR 2003; Kovach *et al.* 2003; Lloyd 2005; Neligan 2003; Woods 2007; Woods 2008). The need for openness is now widely accepted as a way to improve not only the social legitimacy of international organizations, but also their efficacy, as measured by the capacity to fulfil their mandates. Whereas the work of GATT in its early days could be conducted at a distance from the people, this is no longer possible in this new era of the World Trade Organization (WTO).

After the experiences of the Seattle and Cancún WTO Ministerial Conferences (Aaronson 2001; Bertrand and Kalafatides 2002; Jawara and Kwa 2003), it is now difficult, if not impossible, to explain or justify either a lack of transparency or a refusal to increase accountability to citizens of the main institution of the global trading system. That said, do people have a right to know about and contribute to the work of a system that is mandated, among other goals, to contribute to the sustainable development of the country in which they live and to the preservation of the environment at the global level?

Today's challenges relate more to *how* to improve transparency and accountability – including the participation of civil society than to justifying the need for such improvements (Van den Bossche 2010). As such, rather than offering an in-depth study of the reasons for demanding or

Félix Peña is, at present, a Professor at Universidad Nacional de Tres de Febrero. The author thanks Julio Lacarte and Carolyn Deere Birkbeck for comments on this chapter.

expecting more transparency and accountability of the WTO, this chapter focuses on the development of a concrete proposal that could contribute to bringing the WTO closer to citizens in all countries. The further elaboration of such proposals should be undertaken after a broad process of consultations that involves WTO Member States as well as civil society representatives. In this way, transparency and accountability would rightfully be a critical part of the larger and necessary exercise of rethinking the WTO (Cottier 2010: 43; Deere Birkbeck 2010: 11; Ismail 2009; Orellana 2009: 671; Petersmann 2005; Porter *et al.* 2001; Steger 2010b: 3).

The core question addressed in this chapter is whether the creation of the figure of a WTO ombudsperson (Gottehrer and Hostina 1998)[1] would help improve its efficacy and positively impact on global economic governance. If so, how could it be created within the WTO's existing institutional structure and obtain the necessary support of the full Membership, particularly developing nations? What could be some of the main functions of the ombudsperson and what should be their modalities of operation? To what extent, and how, could a WTO ombudsperson contribute to strengthening the participation of developing nations and their people in the multilateral global trading system?

By exploring these questions, we aim to propose elements that could stimulate a further – and necessary – global debate about the desirability of creating an ombudsperson at the WTO (Loy 2001: 113). While recognizing that the WTO is a 'Member-driven' organization (Bacchus 2005: 429), the reality is that it is already evolving into a more open, transparent, accountable, efficient and participatory international organization. The establishment of an ombudsperson function at the WTO would be a small step among many others that could be undertaken. Other steps could include, for instance, improving the efficiency of the Trade Policy Review and of the Dispute Settlement Understanding, as has been already proposed (Consultative Board 2004; Deere Birkbeck 2010; De Mestral and Auerbach-Ziogas 2005; Sandford 2007; Warwick Commission 2007). The creation of an ombudsperson role at the WTO should then be a relatively modest step conceived as part of a complex, incremental and long-term process of shortening the distance between the WTO and citizens.

[1] World Bank, Law and Justice Institutions. 2010. *Ombudsman*. http://web.worldbank.org/WBSITE/EXTERNAL/TOPICS/EXTLAWJUSTINST/0,,contentMDK:20755184~menuPK:2035525~pagePK:210058~piPK:210062~theSitePK:1974062,00.html [accessed in November 2010].

The assumption underpinning this proposal is that a multilateral trading system that works, and is perceived to work, for the benefit of all the people of the world would also boost the stability of the international system (Ismail 2007, 2009; Woods 2007). The creation of a WTO ombudsperson role would also help achieve the larger goal of increasing the WTO's legitimacy by contributing more positively and concretely to the sustainable economic and social development of all nations and to fairer global economic governance (Steger 2010b: 3). Here, we should bear in mind that pressure for the empowerment of the people, both at the global and domestic levels, is a trend that will continue to intensify as a main characteristic of the international relations of the twenty-first century (Cooper Ramo 2009). International organizations such as the WTO cannot ignore this trend without affecting their efficacy and social legitimacy.

1 Factors contributing to greater WTO transparency, accountability and civil society participation

Although further progress remains necessary, there have already been improvements in the levels of transparency, accountability and of civil society participation at the WTO. Among other examples, the *Decision of the General Council on the Procedures for the Circulation and De-restriction of WTO Documents*; the *Guidelines for Arrangements on Relations with Non-Governmental Organizations* (NGOs), and the annual WTO Public Forum are steps in that direction (Bonzon 2010: 287–308; Van den Bossche 2010).

This positive trend is the outcome of at least three related factors:

1.1 Transparency

The first factor is the ongoing evolution of new information technologies coupled with an increasing public demand for easy access to relevant information. In the WTO's case, one outcome has been the development of a web page, which in general can be considered very high quality. Even if different limitations have been observed concerning the concrete impacts of the WTO's website on transparency (GAR 2003, 2006, 2008), it is possible to find an abundance of relevant information and analysis on the site – ranging from teaching materials, reports, a database for searching official documents and online video debates – delivered in a user-friendly way (Van den Bossche 2010: 325–7). The posting of online video debates and webcast coverage of large events, such as the WTO Public Forum, illustrate some of the ongoing adaptations to the new possibilities opened up by new information technologies as well as the political will on the part of the WTO Secretariat to take advantage of what is available.

For anyone outside Geneva or the negotiating processes – in other words the vast majority of citizens – who is interested in the evolution of global trade policies and rules, the WTO's website is a very useful working instrument. It is already a unique tool for trade experts and academic institutions and performs a valuable role decoding and explaining sometimes highly complex technical information in ways that make it easier to understand. As such, it becomes more useful for those operating at the country level in the private or social sector, as well as in academia or media. This is particularly true when it is complemented with similar quality instruments provided by national governments. The quality of those domestic instruments and the ability of people to access them are not, however, equal.

In the coming years, we can expect that citizens living across the diversity of the WTO's Member States will become increasingly forceful in their demand for transparency of trade negotiations and greater access to relevant information on trade rules. Indeed, access to information is considered a public good that people everywhere demand as a right related to their freedom of choice and as a critical factor for advancing sustainable social and economic development. This is particularly the case for trade policies, international agreements and rules, which have concrete impacts on the daily lives of citizens and in the development of nations.

Accurate and reliable information is today a crucial element in levelling the playing field of international economic competition. Decoding complex and highly dynamic information is now essential for the competitiveness of all nations. Competitors particularly need easy and quick access to data and trends that enables them to foresee evolving scenarios in world markets. This is one reason why access to information is conceived as a key factor for the democratization of international relations and global economic competition. Conversely, it could also be one of the reasons why there is still some resistance to transparency and accountability in the multilateral trading system.

The WTO's website makes a concrete contribution to greater transparency of the institution by facilitating the access of all stakeholders to the evolution of its work, including, for example, the Doha Round. While it is clear that any strong website should always be considered a work in progress, the fact is that the WTO has evolved, leaving aside the more medieval secrecy culture that dominated the previous GATT period and, in some ways, also the first years of the WTO. As a result, it is possible to argue that the distance between the multilateral global trading system of the WTO and global civil society has now become shorter.

1.2 Empowerment

The second factor that has produced increased transparency and accountability at the WTO is a deep cultural change, with significant political implications at the domestic and global level. Today, people everywhere either are, or are becoming conscious of their power as consumers, workers, intellectuals, investors and citizens to influence international affairs and the need to attempt to do so. Precisely because it is technologically possible, more people demand to be well informed and to participate in some way in the elaboration of new policies and rules that could have an impact on their lives, both at the global and domestic level. They are increasingly conscious that the decisions, performance and inadequacies of international organizations, such as the WTO, are important to their daily lives, as well as those of future generations (Charnovitz *et al.* 2005; Charnovitz 2005: 437). Institutions and rules at the global level are perceived, with good reason, as a critical factor in the development and international competitiveness strategy of all nations – large or small, developed or developing – and of their firms as well as for the prospects of improving the everyday lives of people.

As a result, more people are inclined to use their power and to seek vehicles and channels through which they can exercise that power to influence international decision-making. This trend is having a strong impact on how international relations is conceived and trade policies elaborated (Evans 2003). Already, this trend is observable at the international and regional level (Bonzon 2010), such as in the case of the European Union (Woolcock 2003: 211), the North American Free Trade Agreement (NAFTA) and other regional integration arrangements, such as the Association of South East Asian Nations (ASEAN) and Mercosur. In the case of Mercosur, for instance, every citizen of its Member countries has the name Mercosur imprinted in their passports and national documents. If Mercosur is presented as an element of identification for all of these citizens, why should we not expect them to be well informed about its development?

There are two key ways in which people exercise their power. First, through mediators, such as experts, the media and even politicians. Second, they exercise power through the many channels of information-sharing and communication opened up by the internet and the various activities of both international and national NGOs.

Compared to the world when the GATT was created, people now realize they can be active protagonists at the international level, and moreover, that this can be crucial to the prospect that their interests, whether as farmers, workers, investors or consumers, will be taken into account. For this reason, the expectations and demands for easy access to information and analysis about anything they consider could have an impact on their welfare and quality of life are growing day by day.

We can safely predict that the empowerment of civil society, even allowing for differences according to countries, is a trend that will advance in the future, thereby increasing demand for high-quality processed information, as well as for real participation in decision-making and rule production processes, mainly at the domestic level, but also globally and regionally.

1.3 *Accountability*

The third factor, which is also a result of the first two factors mentioned above, is the increasing demand for greater accountability of individuals and institutions with power and responsibilities that concern the livelihoods and future of its citizens. We should assume this demand for accountability will continue to grow (Goetz and Jenkins 2005). Power carries a responsibility to respond to the needs and interests of citizens. Not only is accountability increasingly considered an obligation, but the absence of such accountability reduces the efficacy, as well as the social legitimacy, of international organizations such as the WTO.

Even if we are still far from any kind of global citizenship or formal global supranational community that could substitute nation-states, the fact is that people now want to be (assuming the means provided by information technologies are not blocked in one way or another) active protagonists at the global and domestic levels, whether directly or through the mediation of actors they can trust. This means that they want to be both well informed and listened to by those with the power to shape the conditions of their lives.

1.4 *Implications for the WTO*

Across the world, people are increasingly aware of the influence of international trading rules and practices on their livelihoods. The global trade agenda thus has new constituencies that go well beyond Member countries and business interests to incorporate a growing diversity of citizens groups.

Obviously, Member States of the WTO will continue to be the main focal points of trade decision-making processes (Biukoviç 2010: 193; Halle and Wolfe 2007; Sapra 2010: 219; Wang 2010: 257; Wolfe and Helmer 2007; Ziegler and Bonzon 2007). As a result, the effort to increase the accountability, transparency, efficacy and social legitimacy of global trading rules will and should continue to have a concrete domestic focus. Parliaments, the media, various kinds of NGOs, businesses and labour organizations will continue to play a crucial role in improving transparency, accountability and civil society participation in the processes of defining national trade policy and national policy with respect to international trade rules and mechanisms.

Importantly, what is achieved in this respect within each Member country will have a strong impact on anything that could also be achieved at the global level. The inverse is also true. National governments can no longer be indifferent to the fact that an emergent global constituency of people now exists and will continue to enlarge in its scope, its connectivity and the intensity of its expectations with respect to values such as transparency and accountability.

In sum, the transparency and accountability demands of global civil society present a growing challenge for the efficacy and also social legitimacy of the multilateral global trading system. While the need to address these demands at the domestic level will continue to be the most important focus of attention, the growing global constituency will demand more transparency and accountability from the multilateral global trading system.

2 Tentative elements for a worldwide multi-stakeholder consultation about a WTO ombudsperson

This section sets out tentative elements of the proposed figure and office of a WTO ombudsperson. This role is proposed as a practical way, among other options, to contribute to improve transparency, accountability and the participation of citizens in the multilateral global trading system.

The main function of the ombudsperson should be to express an independent opinion with solid technical arguments concerning the efficacy of the multilateral trading system and its level of transparency. The criteria against which these two elements would be evaluated should include the impact of WTO rules, the WTO Secretariat's activities, and the efforts of Member States to implement WTO rules in light of the organization's main goals as defined in the Preamble of the Marrakesh Agreement Establishing the World Trade Organization, and in particular, the goals of: 1) optimal use of the world's resources in accordance with the objective of sustainable development, seeking both to protect and preserve the environment and to enhance the means for doing so in a manner consistent with their respective needs and concerns at different levels of economic development (WTO 1994: Preamble, para. 1); and 2) the 'need for positive efforts designed to ensure that developing countries, and especially the least developed among them, secure a share in the growth in international trade commensurate with the needs of their economic development' (WTO 1994: Preamble, para. 2).

A number of international organizations have established accountability mechanisms, including in some cases the appointment of an ombudsman figure. There are also examples at the regional and domestic level. While their modalities of operation differ,[2] the main functions are relatively similar: an ombudsperson and their associated mechanisms are conceived as channels for listening and eventually responding to the complaints of citizens in Member States. That said, ombuds mechanisms are also sometimes created to respond to concerns raised by the staff of an organization, as in the case of the World Bank's Ombuds Services.[3]

In the case of multilateral financial and development institutions, the citizen complaint mechanisms are designed to respond to problems originating in their operational policies and instruments, or in their concrete operations and projects. Examples of such mechanisms include the World Bank Inspection Panel; the Inter-American Development Bank's (IDB) Independent Investigation Mechanism; the Asian Development Bank (ADB) Accountability Mechanism; the International Finance Corporation (IFC)/ Multilateral Investment Guarantee Agency (MIGA) Compliance/Advisor Ombudsman (CAO); and the European Bank for Reconstruction and Development (EBRD) Independent Recourse Mechanism (Bissell and Nanwani 2009).

[2] For a description of these offices, see www.cao-ombudsman.org; www.ombudsman.europa.eu/home/en/default.htm; www8.cao.go.jp/kisei-kaikaku/oto/english/oto_about_e.html (accessed in November 2010).

[3] World Bank Website. 2010. *The World Bank's Ombuds Services*. See http://web.worldbank.org/WBSITE/EXTERNAL/EXTABOUTUS/ORGANIZATION/ORGUNITS/EXTCRS/EXTOMBUDSMAN/0,,menuPK:64166180~pagePK:64166170~piPK:64166175~theSitePK:468444,00.html [accessed in November 2010].

The functions of the proposed WTO's ombudsperson should be developed through a gradual process, rather than a more ambitious one-shot attempt. The WTO's ombudsperson functions could then be enlarged in the future in accordance with a learning process that concrete experiences will provide. The further elaboration or expansion of the office of the WTO ombudsperson would only be desirable if it is clear that it can really be a useful instrument in bringing the organization closer to citizens, listening to their views and expressing its technically based opinion.

To begin, the main function of the WTO ombudsperson should be to listen to complaints from citizens of Member States regarding the WTO's transparency and how the multilateral global trading system is performing in relation to the goals defined in the Marrakesh Agreement. The ombudsperson should then give their independent, technically based (i.e. not political) opinion on this matter. Having listened to citizen complaints, they should then analyse their arguments and the facts, and produce a report with technically based conclusions, including recommendations that could address any deficiencies or insufficiencies detected. The precise modalities for the accomplishment of this function should be defined through pertinent rules. A further important aspect that should be defined in those modalities concerns who should have access to the WTO ombudsperson and to their intervention, and under what conditions.

In our opinion, the creation of an ombudsperson figure, including the definition of the precise functions and modalities of operation, should emerge from intense interactive worldwide multi-stakeholder consultations. The consultation process should be carefully defined in advance to ensure the representative character of those consulted. It should be led and conducted by the WTO Director-General with all the interested parties – represented by recognized, transparent and previously identified organizations – of the Member countries. The consultative process could also include the use of the WTO's website as a mechanism for soliciting input. The consultation should, of course, also involve the WTO Member countries directly through, for example, the WTO General Council. Based on the results of the worldwide multi-stakeholder consultations, the Director-General should then put forward a concrete proposal for the consideration and eventual approval of the WTO General Council.

Some key elements that could be considered as part of the proposed global multi-stakeholder consultation process regarding the role, functions and modalities for operation of the ombudsperson figure follow:

- The office of the ombudsperson should be created, through a decision of the General Council, as an independent function within the WTO Secretariat. The ombudsperson should have a guarantee of complete independence within the Secretariat and report directly to the WTO Director-General and through him/her to the WTO General Council. The General Council should elect the ombudsperson for a three-year period from a shortlist proposed by the WTO Director-General that includes three prestigious, high-level personalities with strong global trade experience. They could eventually be re-elected for an additional three-year period. The description of the ombudsperson's main functions and the modalities of operation, including criteria for their intervention, as well as for those eligible to register a request for intervention, should be approved by the General Council also based on a proposal by the WTO Director-General.
- The office of the ombudsperson should have its own budget within the annual budget of the WTO Secretariat. This should include the resources necessary to analyse concrete cases with the participation of independent experts.
- The ombudsperson's investigations could originate either at the request of Member countries or of third parties, including, for instance, international or domestic NGOs, or individual citizens through them. The core criteria for the right of an NGO to submit a complaint and seek access to the ombudsperson should be the transparency of their membership and funding.
- Given that its creation would imply an innovation in the way the WTO operates, it may be useful to carefully circumscribe the ombudsperson's functions, at least in the initial phases. These functions should be limited to providing opinions in response to concrete complaints from citizens about the transparency of the WTO's activities and the development impact of the rules of the global system. In addition, the ombudsperson should also have the right to analyse different practices that could affect the WTO's efficacy, as well as insufficiencies in the multilateral global trading system that could frustrate the achievement of its main goals, particularly those related to sustainable development, the environment and the economic development of developing countries, especially the least developed countries and vulnerable groups within them.
- In terms of its reports, any opinions of the ombudsperson should be technically based and non-political. The ombudsperson's reports should include non-mandatory recommendations for Member States to solve the deficiencies detected – that is, the opinions offered would

not generate legal consequences for WTO Members. Further, recommendations should be seen as only one of many elements to consider in any eventual action or decision by Member States concerning the issue analysed by the WTO ombudsperson.

- All proceedings of the ombudsperson's meetings should be transparent and all reports made publicly available. This should include the creation of a dedicated section of the WTO's website, which would be open to comments from any interested and identified stakeholder.
- The ombudsperson should provide an annual report to the Director-General, who should make additional comments and recommendations, which then would be presented to the WTO General Council for its consideration.

The General Council should review the performance of the ombudsperson on a periodic basis. Following an independent appraisal every two years, the Council could introduce modifications of the functions and modalities of operation of the ombudsperson.

3 Preliminary conclusions

The main argument advanced in this chapter is that the creation of an ombudsperson within the institutional structure of the WTO could make a positive contribution to the improvement of the WTO's relations with global civil society by strengthening its transparency and accountability. At the same time, the creation of such a figure could contribute to increasing the participation of citizens of all WTO Member States – developed and developing – and to the achievement of the main goals of the organization, namely development and sustainable development.

To obtain the support of all WTO Member States for the creation of a WTO ombudsperson we have argued for a gradual approach that could begin with a process of broad, worldwide multi-stakeholder consultations. These discussions would include Member States and representatives of civil society via recognized and transparent domestic and transnational NGOs. Such consultations should include input on whether there is a need for such an ombudsperson, and the main functions and modalities of that figure and office. Based on the feedback received, the WTO Director-General would prepare a concrete proposal for the consideration and eventual approval of the WTO General Council.

We recommend a first phase of activity in which the WTO ombudsperson would have limited functions and would produce only non-mandatory technically based opinions about the issues which they have been asked to investigate and respond to. We have emphasized that submissions requesting the intervention of the ombudsperson could be made by highly transparent and recognized domestic civil society groups from any Member country or from international NGOs. The focus of complaints considered should relate to insufficiencies of the multilateral global trading system that could affect its efficacy in achieving its main goals, and those related to its transparency.

Based on an external independent appraisal of whether the ombudsperson has demonstrated their value and efficiency for strengthening the transparency and accountability of the multilateral global trading system, the Director-General could eventually propose to the General Council to improve its modalities of operation and possibly extend its functions as well.

To conclude, the proposal advanced in this chapter is intended to promote a debate about the idea of a WTO ombudsperson role and the needs and challenges it should address, its functions and its modalities of operation. Importantly, that debate could be, in itself, a way to bring the citizens nearer to *their* multilateral global trading system. It could also serve as an innovative example of the kinds of processes that, with the aid of new and constantly evolving information technologies, should now be an essential part of the decision-making of international organizations and governments in their international negotiations.

References

Aaronson, S. 2001. *Taking Trade to the Streets. The Lost History of Public Efforts to Shape Globalization*. Ann Arbor: University of Michigan Press.

Alvarez-Jiménez, A. 2010. 'Improvements to the WTO Decision-Making Process: Lessons from the IMF and the World Bank', in Steger, D. (ed.), *Redesigning the World Trade Organization for the Twenty-first Century*, Ottowa CIG–Wilfrid Laurier University Press, pp. 91–126.

Bacchus, J. 2005. 'A Few Thoughts on Legitimacy, Democracy, and the WTO', in Petersmann, E.U. (ed.), *Reforming the World Trading System. Legitimacy, Efficiency and Democratic Governance*, Oxford; New York: Oxford University Press, pp. 429–35.

Barton, J., Goldstein, J., Josling, T. and Steinberg, R. (eds.) 2006. *The Evolution of the Trade Regime: Politics, Law and Economics of the GATT and WTO*. Princeton University Press.

Bayne, N. and Woolcock, S. 2003. *The New Economic Diplomacy. Decision-Making and Negotiation in International Economic Relations*. Hampshire-Burlington: Ashgate.

Bertrand, A. and Kalafatides, L. 2002. *OMC, le Pouvoir Invisible*. Paris: Fayard.

Bethlehem, D., McRae, D., Neufeld, R. and Van Damme, I. (eds.) 2009. *The Oxford Handbook of International Trade Law*. Oxford; New York: Oxford University Press.

Bissell, R. and Nanwani, S. 2009. 'Multilateral Development Bank Accountability Mechanisms: Developments and Challenges', *Central European Journal of International and Security Studies* 3(2): 154–96.

Biukoviç, L. 2010. 'Selective Adaptation of WTO Transparency Norms and Local Practices in China and Japan', in Steger, D. (ed.), *Redesigning the World Trade Organization for the Twenty-first Century*, Ottowa: CIG–Wilfrid Laurier University Press, pp. 193–218.

Blagescu, M. 2004. *What Makes Global Organizations Accountable?* London: One World Trust.

Blagescu, M., de la Casas, L. and Lloyd, R. 2005. *Pathways to Accountability: The GAP Framework*. London: One World Trust.

Bonzon, Y. 2010. 'Options for Public Participation in the WTO: Experiences from Regional Trade Agreements', in Steger, D. (ed.), *Redesigning the World Trade Organization for the Twenty-first Century*, Ottowa: CIG–Wilfrid Laurier University Press, pp. 287–308.

Bradlow, D. 2005. 'Private Complainants and International Organizations: A Comparative Study of the Independent Inspection Mechanisms in International Financial Institutions', *Georgetown Journal of International Law* 36, Winter Issue.

Carin, B. and Wood, A. (eds.) 2005. *Accountability of the International Monetary Fund*, Ottawa: Ashgate.

Charnovitz, S. 2005. 'The WTO and Cosmopolitics', in Petersmann, E.U. (ed.), *Reforming the World Trading System Legitimacy, Efficiency and Democratic Governance*, Oxford; New York: Oxford University Press, pp. 429–45.

Charnovitz, S., Steger, D. and Van Den Bossche, P. (eds.) 2005. *Law in the Service of Human Dignity*. Cambridge; New York: Cambridge University Press.

Coicaud, J. and Heiskanen, V. (eds.) 2001. *The Legitimacy of International Organizations*. Tokyo; New York; Paris: United Nations University Press.

Consultative Board. 2004. *The Future of the WTO. Addressing Institutional Challenges in the New Millennium*. Geneva: WTO.

Cooper Ramo, J. 2009. *The Age of the Unthinkable*. New York; Boston; London: Little, Brown and Company.

Cottier, T. 2008. *The Legitimacy of WTO Law*. Bern: WTI.

2010. 'A Two Tier Approach to WTO Decision-Making', in Steger, D. (ed.), *Redesigning the World Trade Organization for the Twenty-first Century*, Ottowa: CIG–Wilfrid Laurier University Press, pp. 43–66.

Deere Birkbeck, C. 2010. 'Reinvigorating Debate on WTO Reform: The Contours of a Functional and Normative Approach to Analyzing the WTO System', in Steger, D. (ed.), *Redesigning the World Trade Organization for the Twenty-first Century*, Ottowa: CIG–Wilfrid Laurier University Press, pp. 11–40.

Deere Birkbeck, C. and Monagle, C. 2009. *Strengthening Multilateralism: A Mapping of Proposals on WTO Reform and Global Trade Governance*. Geneva; Oxford: ICTSD-University of Oxford, Global Economic Governance Programme.

De Las Casas, L. 2005. *Complaint and Redress Mechanisms in International Organizations*, London: One World Trust.

De Mestral, A. and Auerbach-Ziogas, M. 2005. 'A Proposal to Introduce an Advocate General's Position into WTO Dispute Settlement', in Charnovitz *et al.* (eds.), *Law in the Service of Human Dignity*, Cambridge; New York: Cambridge University Press, pp. 159–80.

Dombrowski, K. 2006. *Overview of Accountability Initiatives*. London: One World Trust.

El-Naggar, S. 2005. 'Developing Countries and the International Trading System', in Charnovitz *et al.* (eds.), *Law in the Service of Human Dignity*, Cambridge; New York: Cambridge University Press, pp. 58–75.

Evans, P. 2003. 'Is Trade Policy Democratic? And Should it Be?', in Bayne, N. and Woolcock, S. (eds.), *The New Economic Diplomacy. Decision-Making and Negotiation in International Economic Relations*, Hampshire Burlington: Ashgate pp. 147–59.

GAR. 2003. *Global Accountability Report*. London: One World Trust.

2006. *Global Accountability Report*. London: One World Trust.

2008. *Global Accountability Report*. London: One World Trust.

Goetz, A. M. and Jenkins, R. 2005. *Reinventing Accountability. Making Democracy Work for Human Development*. New York: Palgrave Macmillan.

Gottehrer, D. and Hostina, M. 1998. 'Essential Characteristics of a Classical Ombudsman'. www.usombudsman.org/documents/PDF/References/Essential.PDF [Accessed in November 2010].

Global Accountability Project. 2004. *Increasing Accountability Through Complaint and Redress Mechanisms: Workshop Report*. Workshop convened by the One World Trust.

Halle, M. and Wolfe, R. (eds.) 2007. *Process Matters. Sustainable Development and Domestic Trade Transparency*. Winnipeg, Manitoba: International Institute for Sustainable Development.

Herz, S. and Ebrahim, A. 2005. *A Call for Participatory Decision Making: Discussion Paper on World Bank–Civil Society Engagement*. Commissioned and presented by the Civil Society Members of World Bank–Civil Society Joint Facilitation Committee (JFC).

Hormats, R. 2001. 'Governance of the Global Trade System', in Porter *et al.* (eds.), *Efficiency/Equity/Legitimacy. The Multilateral Trading System at the Millennium*, Washington: Brooking Institution Press, pp. 392–418.

Howse, R. 2001. 'The Legitimacy of the WTO', in Coicaud, J. and Heiskanen, V. (eds.), *The Legitimacy of International Organizations*, Tokyo; New York; Paris: United Nations University Press, pp. 355–407.

Howse, R. and Nicolaïdis, K. 2001. 'Legitimacy and Global Governance: Why Constitutionalizing the WTO is a Step Too Far', in Porter *et al.* (eds.), *Efficiency/Equity/Legitimacy. The Multilateral Trading System at the Millenium*, Washington: Brooking Institution Press, pp. 227–63.

Ismail, F. 2007. *Mainstreaming Development in the WTO*. Jaipur: CUTS-Friedrich Ebert Stiftung.

Ismail, F.. 2009. *Reforming the World Trade Organization. Developing Countries in the Doha Round*. Jaipur: CUTS-Friedrich Ebert Stiftung.

Jawara, F. and Kwa, A. 2003. *Behind the Scenes at the WTO*. London; New York: Zed Books.

Keoane, R. and Nye Jr., J. 2001. 'The Club Model of Multilateral Cooperation and Problems of Democratic Legitimacy', in Porter *et al.* (eds.), *Efficiency/Equity/ Legitimacy. The Multilateral Trading System at the Millenium*, Washington: Brooking Institution Press, pp. 264–307.

Kovach, H., Neligan, C. and Burall, S. 2003. *Power Without Accountability. The Global Accountability Report 2003*. London: One World Trust.

Lacarte, J. 2005. 'Transparency, Public Debate, and Participation by NGOs in the WTO: a WTO Perspective', in Petersmann, E.U. (ed.), *Reforming the World Trading System. Legitimacy, Efficiency and Democratic Governance*, Oxford; New York: Oxford University Press, pp. 447–51.

Lamy, P. 2010. *Towards Shared Responsibility and Greater Coherence: Human Rights, Trade and Macroeconomic Policy*. Colloquium on Human Rights in the Global Economy, Co-organized by the International Council on Human Rights and Realizing Rights, 13 January. Geneva: WTO.

Lloyd, R. 2005. *Transparency in International Organisations: Background Research for the Transparency Dimension*. London: One World Trust.

Loy, F. 2001. 'Public Participation in the World Trade Organization', in Sampson, G. (ed.), *The Role of the World Trade Organization in Global Governance*, Tokyo; New York; Paris: United Nations University Press, pp. 113–35.

Moore, M. (ed.) 2004. *Doha and Beyond: The Future of the Multilateral Trading System*. Cambridge University Press.

Neligan, C. 2003. *Increasing Accountability through External Stakeholder Engagement*. London: One World Trust.

Orellana, M. 2009. 'WTO and Civil Society', in Bethlehem *et al.* (eds.), *The Oxford Handbook of International Trade Law*, Oxford; New York: Oxford University Press, pp. 671–94.

Ostry, S. 2004. 'External Transparency: The Policy Process at the National Level of the Two Level Game', in Moore, M. (ed.) *Doha and Beyond: The Future of the Multilateral Trading System*, Cambridge University Press, pp. 94–114.

Petersmann, E. U. (ed.) 2005. *Reforming the World Trading System. Legitimacy, Efficiency and Democratic Governance*. Oxford; New York: Oxford University Press.

Porter, R., Sauve, P., Subramanian, A. and Beriglia Zampetti, M. 2001. *Efficiency/Equity/Legitimacy. The Multilateral Trading System at the Millennium*. Washington: Brooking Institution Press.

Sampson, G. (ed.) 2001. *The Role of the World Trade Organization in Global Governance*. Tokyo; New York; Paris: United Nations University Press.

Sandford, I. 2007. *The Importance of Transparency in WTO Dispute Settlement*. Sydney: International Trade Group. www.minterellison.com/public/resources/file/eb9805448f03134/RG-transparencyWTO.pdf [Accessed in November 2010].

Sapra, S. 2010. 'Domestic Politics and the Search for a New Social Purpose of Governance for the WTO', in Steger, D. (ed.), *Redesigning the World Trade Organization for the Twenty-first Century*, Ottowa: CIG–Wilfrid Laurier University Press, pp. 219–56.

Steger, D. 2005. 'The Challenges to the Legitimacy of the WTO', in Charnovitz *et al.* (eds.), *Law in the Service of Human Dignity*, Cambridge; New York: Cambridge University Press, pp. 202–21.

(ed.) 2010a. *Redesigning the World Trade Organization for the Twenty-first Century*. Ottawa: CIGI–Wilfrid Laurier University Press.

2010b. 'Why Institutional Reform of the WTO is Necessary', in Steger, D. (ed.), *Redesigning the World Trade Organization for the Twenty-first Century*, Ottowa: CIG–Wilfrid Laurier University Press, pp. 3–9.

Suzuki, E. and Nanwani, S. 2005. 'Responsibility of International Organizations: The Accountability Mechanisms of Multilateral Development Banks', *Michigan Journal of International Law* 27(1): 177–225. http://students.law.umich.edu/mjil/article-pdfs/v27n1-suzuki-nanwani.pdf [Accessed in November 2010].

Van den Bossche, P. 2010. 'Non-Governmental Organizations and the WTO: Limits to Involvement', in Steger, D. (ed.), *Redesigning the World Trade Organization for the Twenty-first Century*, Ottowa: CIG–Wilfrid Laurier University Press, pp. 309–59.

Wang, H. 2010. 'Enhancing Business Participation in Trade Policy-Making: Lessons from China', in Steger, D. (ed.), *Redesigning the World Trade Organization for the Twenty-first Century*, Ottowa: CIG–Wilfrid Laurier University Press, pp. 257–84.

Warwick Commission. 2007. *The Multilateral Trade Regime: Which Way Forward, The Report of the First Warwick Commission*. Coventry: The University of Warwick.

Wolfe, R. and Helmer, J. 2007. 'Trade Policy Begins at Home: Information and Consultation in the Trade Policy Process', in Halle, M. and Wolfe, R. (eds.),

Process Matters. Sustainable Development and Domestic Trade Transperency, Winnipeg, Manitoba International Institute for Sustainable Development, pp. 1–19.

Woods, N. 2007. *Power Shift. Do We Need Better Global Economic Institutions?* London: IPPR. www.ippr.org [Accessed in November 2010].

2008. *Governing the Global Economy: Strengthening Multilateral Institutions*. New York: International Peace Institute.

Woolcock, S. 2003. 'The Regional Dimension: European Economic Diplomacy', in Bayne, N. and Woolcock, S., *The New Economic Diplomacy. Decision-Making and Negotiation in International Economic Relations*, Hampshire-Burlington: Ashgate, pp. 197–213.

World Trade Organization (WTO) 1994. *Marrakesh Agreement Establishing the World Trade Organization*. Adopted on 15 April 1994 and entered into force on 1 January 1995. Geneva: WTO.

Ziegler, A. and Bonzon, Y. 2007. *How to Reform WTO Decision-Making? An Analysis of the Current Functioning of the Organization from the Perspectives of Efficiency and Legitimacy*. NCCR Trade Working Paper no. 2007/23. Bern: WTI.

PART IV

Making WTO negotiations and decision-making processes fairer

16

Towards fair and inclusive decision-making in WTO negotiations

FAIZEL ISMAIL AND BRENDAN VICKERS

Negotiating new market access and rules in the World Trade Organization (WTO) has become increasingly complex and difficult. The WTO's maiden trade round, the Doha Development Agenda (DDA), is today the longest running trade round in the history of multilateral trade negotiations. Prior to the DDA's launch in November 2001, WTO rule-making was restricted to a handful of plurilateral agreements negotiated among the leading exporters of information technology, telecommunications and financial services. In contrast to the lethargy of the multilateral process, there has been a rapid proliferation of regional trade agreements (RTAs), which undermine the multilateral regime's non-discriminatory norms.

Several factors, past and present, explain the WTO's negotiating drift and the deadlock that thwarts the conclusion of the DDA. The history of the General Agreement on Tariffs and Trade (GATT) reflects the marginalization of developing country interests; the assertion by the major economic powers of their own market access interests in foreign markets (a mercantilist approach); and trade protectionism in the major developed country markets (Wilkinson 2006a; Finger 2007). This has resulted in an 'asymmetry of economic opportunity' against developing countries and the persistence of unbalanced negotiating texts in favour of developed countries in the GATT up to the Uruguay Round (Wilkinson 2006b). In the current Doha Round, the collapse of several ministerial meetings

Faizel Ismail is the Permanent Representative of South Africa to the World Trade Organization based in Geneva. Dr Brendan Vickers is the Chief Director of Research and Policy in the International Trade and Economic Division of South Africa's Department of Trade and Industry. This research was undertaken when he was Director of the Multilateral Programme at the Institute for Global Dialogue (IGD) in South Africa. The authors are indebted to Professor Rorden Wilkinson and Carolyn Deere Birkbeck for detailed comments on an earlier draft of this chapter. The normal caveats apply.

can be partly attributed to the continuation of this protectionist tendency (Ismail 2009a).

The persistence of the 'principal supplier' approach to the negotiations, whereby a few of the major players are brought together in informal processes to make a breakthrough in the negotiations (such as the G4,[1] G5/FIPS,[2] G6[3] and G7[4]), has also contributed to the successive failures of ministerial meetings (Ismail 2009a). The role of the chairs of WTO negotiating processes has also sometimes been a contributory factor in biasing the outcomes of the negotiations and creating further delays (Ismail 2009b). In sum, the WTO's negotiating process is today more politicized and complex, reflecting the growing weight, diversity and expectations of the WTO's 153-country Membership. New international dynamics – particularly the rise of the emerging economies of Brazil, China and India, as well as the assertive role of developing country coalitions in the WTO – portends a more multipolar/multicultural world economy, further complicating the prospects for collective global action (Narlikar and Vickers 2009).

While these factors all impact on the efficiency of the multilateral process, some scholars argue that there is a more fundamental flaw in the procedural aspects of the WTO negotiations. They argue that the WTO's established rules, principles and practices of decision-making are simply ill-suited to respond to the fast-changing needs of the trading system and an increasingly globalized world. This perspective is most succinctly expressed by Cottier and Elsig (2009). They argue that the GATT/WTO's 'golden' triangle of decision-making – i.e. the dominance of contracting parties, the consensus principle and the logic of the single undertaking – is incompatible with the requirements and realities of modern global trade governance. They argue that the WTO's current negotiating methodology leads to lowest common denominator deals that do not generate either new trade flows or new rules for dynamic markets. While there have been salutary institutional innovations to the WTO's litigation apparatus, the legislative branch of the system (i.e. the negotiation platform) has stalled, thus creating a de facto imbalance between rule-making and rule-implementation (Elsig 2009), and also between the WTO's

[1] The G4 consists of the EU, US, Brazil and India.

[2] The Five Interested Parties (FIPS) in agriculture comprised the EU, US, Brazil and India (representing the G20) and Australia (representing the Cairns Group).

[3] The G6 consists of the EU, US, Japan, Australia, Brazil and India.

[4] The G7 consists of the EU, US, Brazil, India, China, Australia and Japan.

negotiation function and its dispute settlement function (Steinberg and Goldstein 2009).

Frustration with the status quo has led to a raft of reform proposals that seek to make the WTO a more effective and efficient negotiating institution (Deere Birkbeck and Monagle 2009). These proposals range from relaxing the single undertaking in favour of variable geometry, to weighted voting as an alternative to the organization's consensus-based approach to decision-making. Unfortunately the bulk of these proposals place too much emphasis on the formal processes of decision-making, privileging efficiency over other principles, such as inclusiveness and legitimacy. Few proposals address the representation problem in the WTO, namely the inclusion of developing countries at the 'High Table' of the negotiations. The reality is that developing countries now constitute the bulk of the WTO's membership. For this reason, this chapter makes the case for more inclusive decision-making, so that trade opportunities can be made available to all Members on a more equitable basis and trade rules do not subvert their development prospects. In addition, more inclusive negotiations are vital for developing countries, because the process of negotiating comprises not only *bargaining* over known interests but also *learning* through arguing and deliberation. Through a process of learning, negotiators are able to better understand complex issues (e.g. services, intellectual property rights or the Singapore issues: investment, competition, government procurement and trade facilitation), identify their countries' interests and contribute towards shaping the negotiating agenda (Wolfe 2008). Since participation in negotiations provides the primary conduit for such learning on WTO matters – and consequently for empowerment in the negotiation process – the WTO must fully accommodate developing and least developed countries in multilateral decision-making processes.[5]

By 'decision-making' our primary focus in this chapter is thus on the WTO's multilateral negotiation process, and not decisions related to the organization's regular business or general legal-institutional functioning (e.g. appointment of the Director-General, management and internal administration, etc). We draw a key distinction between the WTO's *formal* and *informal* negotiation procedures and practices. Formal processes include WTO Ministerial Conferences, WTO Committees and subsidiary negotiating bodies (e.g. the Trade Negotiations Committee established by

[5] Following Amartya Sen's conceptualization of 'development as freedom' (Sen 1999), Ismail (2005) similarly argues that *participation* by developing countries in WTO decision-making constitutes an essential element of the development process.

the Doha Declaration). Informal mechanisms include mini-ministerial gatherings, small groups of ministers meeting among themselves (e.g. G4, G5/FIPS, G6 and G7) and larger groups of ministers (often thirty-plus) convened as the 'Green Room'.

Our starting point is that modern global trade governance requires a careful balance between three competing demands, namely greater efficiency, legitimacy and inclusiveness. These objectives are not incompatible, but require transforming the WTO from an ad hoc mercantilist institution to an organization that promotes the objective of 'sustainable development' as set out in the Preamble to the 1994 Marrakesh Agreement Establishing the WTO. The chapter proceeds in three steps. In the first section, we review the WTO's decision-making practices and evaluate current reform proposals against the normative benchmarks of fair and inclusive decision-making. The second section argues that the WTO needs to shift from the traditional mercantilist approach established under the GATT and adopt development as its broader overall *goal or objective* (contrasted to its main *functions* of opening trade and creating rules). This shift will require changes to formal and informal WTO negotiation processes to ensure greater inclusiveness of developing countries in decision-making. We make three recommendations to this end, namely strengthening the WTO's consensus principle and culture, avoiding decision-making through informal small groups and adopting a code of conduct for WTO chairs. The chapter concludes with a review of the argument.

1 Current proposals for reform

In this section, we outline the two cornerstone principles of WTO decision-making – consensus and the single undertaking – and contrast these to existing proposals for reform, namely weighted voting and variable geometry of rights and obligations.

1.1 The consensus principle

Consensus-based decision-making has historically been the hallmark of the multilateral trading system and has distinguished the GATT/WTO as a more formally democratic forum than its Bretton Woods counterparts. The consensus principle was one of the few victories developing countries achieved in the negotiations on the proposed International Trade Organization (ITO), where the major Allied powers had sought a system of weighted voting (Wilkinson and Scott 2008).[6] This consensus-based approach was carried into the GATT, where consensus diplomacy underpinned by bargaining and consultation became the norm rather than the rule. Upon its establishment in 1995, the WTO further internalized this consensual model for decision-making, as spelt out in Article IX of the Marrakesh Agreement: 'The WTO shall continue the practice of decision-making by consensus followed under GATT 1947.' Importantly, consensus and unanimity are not the same. In actual GATT/WTO practice, consensus is assumed when no party present at the meeting when a decision is taken overtly objects to the decision, rather than that all the parties must agree. This amounts to a default rule of consensus when Members are not able to participate in meetings or abstain; of course, this arrangement prejudices smaller developing countries that have limited representation and negotiating capacity in Geneva to cover the full WTO agenda. In the absence of consensus, the GATT and the WTO prescribe voting for particular circumstances, each requiring specified majority thresholds ranging from unanimity to a two-thirds majority. The latter rarely happened in the GATT era, apart from sanctioning new accessions and waivers.

Building consensus in multilateral trade negotiations has historically been a slow process, even when the issues were less complex than they are today. Under a bipolar system dominated by the European Union (EU) and the United States (USA), the GATT membership concluded eight trade rounds over fifty years, but was not immune to episodic crises (Wilkinson 2006a). With the shift towards systemic multipolarity and a more complex trade agenda, there are greater tensions between the demands of efficiency and constructing consensus.

Theoretically, the consensus and sovereign equality principles assign each Member State equal veto status to block decisions. However, in today's multipolar trading system, blocking is best orchestrated by coalitions, rather than Members acting in their own right (Cottier 2009). Moreover, in practice, the power asymmetries among Members of the

[6] For decision-making in the ITO, the US delegation proposed the same method of weighted voting that was used in the then recently created International Monetary Fund (IMF). A similar proposal was made by Britain, to take into account the economic size of the country in its share of the vote – a system of weighted voting. Developing countries voiced their opposition to such a system of voting as they feared that this would institutionalize their secondary status. A number of developing countries (such as Czechoslovakia, Turkey, Lebanon, Iraq, El Salvador, Venezuela and Mexico) voiced strong opposition to weighted voting, and came out in favour of consensus. As a consequence, the ITO did not adopt a system of weighted voting (Ismail 2009c).

WTO constitute a de facto system of weighted voting that favours the stronger economic powers. This 'shadow of power' (Steinberg 2002) has tempered nay-saying by smaller countries, since efforts to block the decisions of interest to the rich and powerful may come at a high political cost for these countries. Stated otherwise, the larger Members of the WTO are able to withstand the pressure to join the consensus more easily than the smaller Members. Critics therefore argue that the GATT/WTO's consensus arrangements mask a system of 'managed hypocrisy': it produces a false sense of equal participation, erodes procedural transparency and accountability,[7] and leads to frequent frustration among parties excluded from small group negotiations (Steinberg 2002; Cottier and Elsig 2009; Low 2009).

Compared to the alternative proposition of weighted voting (discussed below), the consensus principle remains the preferable instrument for building more inclusive multilateral trade architecture. Although consensus-based bargaining may be a slower and more complex process than some proposed alternatives (and carries the risk of disaffected parties turning to regional or bilateral agreements), it is more sustainable and fairer in the long term. That is, the search for consensus forces WTO Members to learn about their respective circumstances, build convergences in their positions, and make compromises in the interests of the trading system as a whole. Moreover, since negotiations facilitate social learning through arguing and deliberation, countries are able to better understand complex issues (e.g. services, intellectual property rights or the Singapore issues) and identify their specific interests in the multilateral trading regime (Wolfe 2008). In reality, the recurrent failure to reach consensus in the Doha Round may have less to do with procedural design and more to do with domestic politics and the skewed outcomes of earlier Rounds. From this perspective, developed countries share some blame for frustrating the consensus-building process. Indeed, it is disconcerting that critics of the consensus principle appear to raise efficiency concerns only when smaller developing countries and larger emerging economies (e.g. Brazil, China, India and South Africa) refuse to join the consensus of the developed countries.

[7] At the domestic level, the consensus principle may weaken a government's positions vis-à-vis particular interests among their constituencies. As Cottier and Elsig (2009) argue, a government that faces well-organized domestic groups is under constant pressure to accommodate the calls of vested interests and use its veto powers on specific issues. The consensus principle thus undermines their credibility at home and at the WTO.

1.2 Voting: an alternative to consensus?

The failure to reach consensus in the Doha Round has sparked debate about the merits of introducing a voting system in the WTO. Critics argue that voting need not replace consensus; instead, it could be used as a supplementary instrument of decision-making within rounds and in between rounds, or for conducting the WTO's regular business (Cottier and Takenoshita 2008). In the simplest terms, there are two possible voting systems: simple majority voting, already spelt out by the GATT/WTO, or a system of weighted voting that better reflects the trading regime's underlying power dynamics. However, there is good reason to be cautious about introducing this mode of decision-making into an organization that regards voting as 'counter-cultural' (Consultative Board 2004: 29). Voting has been used less than twice in the existence of the GATT/WTO, so it sits awkwardly with the organization's institutional culture and history. A simple majority voting system would be unacceptable to the major developed countries, particularly the USA and the EU. Their position is entirely understandable: developed countries account for the largest shares of world trade (and budgetary contributions to the WTO), but would have the least voice in the organization. Since developing countries constitute more than two-thirds of the WTO's membership, a majority voting scenario would favour developing country interests in every North–South issue in the organization. This arrangement would alienate the largest and most powerful Members, precipitating their disengagement from the organization.

The converse proposition involves a system of weighted voting similar to the evolving arrangements of the EU (i.e. the Lisbon Treaty reform process)[8] or existing practices in the IMF.[9] Proponents argue that weighted votes could be allocated on the basis of Members' trade shares, Gross Domestic Product (GDP), openness of markets and population size in a manner that would approximate a fair balance of rights and powers

[8] In December 2007, EU leaders signed the Lisbon Treaty, which seeks to reform the EU's governing institutions and decision-making processes to enable a larger EU to operate more effectively. The new Treaty introduces a 'double majority' qualified voting system. Under this system, a minimum of 55 per cent of Member States (currently fifteen of twenty-seven countries) representing at least 65 per cent of the EU's population must vote in favour of new legislation for it to pass.

[9] In the IMF, each Member country is assigned a quota, based broadly on its relative size in the world economy. A Member's quota determines its maximum financial commitment to the IMF and its voting power, and has a bearing on its access to IMF financing. For a detailed discussion on IMF decision-making, see Alvarerez-Jimenez (2009).

among industrialized, emerging and developing countries (Cottier and Takenoshita 2008).

A related but more nuanced arrangement proposes a 'two-tier' approach in the WTO, with different models of decision-making for the organization's primary and secondary rules (Cottier 2009). In this scenario, the WTO's 'primary' or 'constitutional rules'[10] could continue to operate under the consensus principle – or even 'consensus-minus' as happens in the Dispute Settlement Body (DSB)[11] – or weighted voting with a particular quorum required. By contrast, there may be greater flexibility (including variable geometry of rights and obligations) for the WTO's 'secondary rules', such as those related to implementation of a Member's agreed schedules for liberalization and plurilateral agreements. Cottier (2009) argues that this model would provide a more appropriate pairing of substance and decision-making structure and it would allow a distinction between work within and beyond trade rounds. In sum, this two-tier model would reduce high-level political negotiations to core elements and issues within a package deal, while leaving secondary issues and implementation-related matters to subsequent negotiations.

Given their formal equality but practical inequality in the WTO, developing countries are unlikely to accept any weighted voting that is based on economic power, particularly for negotiations of 'primary rules'. For 'secondary rules', greater flexibility in decision-making could indeed facilitate plurilateral accords, but the risk is that some of these may be welfare diminishing for smaller developing countries (see later discussion).

In sum, weighted voting would formally and structurally institutionalize developing countries' secondary status in an organization that has distinguished itself as relatively more democratic and inclusive than the international financial institutions. The changing patterns of global trade and the increasing share of China and other emerging economies in total trade flows will result in a reduced weighting of the major developed economies in total trade, making the possibility of even a weighted voting system disadvantageous to Europe and the United States as it would

[10] The primary or constitutional rules of the WTO set out the fundamental rights and obligations of the Members, and provide a binding framework for the trading regime. Today, they comprise the Agreement Establishing the WTO, the GATT 1994, the General Agreement on Trade in Services (GATS) and the Agreement on Trade Related Aspects of Intellectual Property Rights (TRIPS).

[11] When the DSB establishes panels, adopts panel and Appellate Body reports and when it authorizes retaliation, decisions are approved unless there is a consensus against them. This special decision-making procedure is commonly referred to as a 'negative' or 'reverse' consensus.

yield the prospect of the rest of the WTO membership being able to vote against them. These two major players are thus also unlikely to support a weighted voting system in preference to the consensus method of decision-making.

1.3 *The single undertaking*

The second cornerstone of the modern multilateral trading system is the principle of the single undertaking. Similar to the WTO's 'internalized norm of consensus' (Cottier and Elsig 2009), the single undertaking has achieved paradigmatic status in the organization. Established at the beginning of the Uruguay Round in 1986, the single undertaking introduced the procedural notion that 'nothing is agreed until everything is agreed' in order to maximize cross-linkages and trade-off possibilities within a 'grand bargain' package deal. The single undertaking initially served a distinct function, namely to discourage parties from 'cherry-picking' results as had happened during the Kennedy (1963–7) and Tokyo (1973–9) Rounds. The Tokyo Round had produced nine agreements covering largely non-tariff measures,[12] to which GATT parties could subscribe on a voluntary à la carte basis. This arrangement had established an asymmetry of rights and obligations among the GATT's growing membership.

With the establishment of the WTO in 1995, the single undertaking required that the organization's founding Members adopt obligations across the board. The Tokyo codes were thereby updated and multilateralized and the single undertaking ensured that all Members accepted the new behind-the-border obligations for trade in services, intellectual property protection and investment (among others), with some caveats at the margins for developing countries. However, many of these obligations have been inappropriate for the circumstances or stages of development of many WTO Members,[13] hence developing country calls for greater 'policy space' (Chang 2002; Gallagher 2005). In 2001, the single undertaking was

[12] The Tokyo codes included agreements on issues such as technical barriers to trade, anti-dumping measures, subsidies and countervailing measures, government procurement, import licensing, customs valuation and so on.

[13] The costs of implementing the Uruguay Round agreements were estimated to be onerous for many developing countries. World Bank estimates were that in three areas of implementation alone – i.e. TRIPS, sanitary and phytosanitary measures, and customs valuation – the cost to a developing country could amount to about US$150 million, which is more than a full year's development assistance budget in many least developed countries (Finger and Schuler 2000).

again carried into the new trade round launched at Doha. A broad round was seen as necessary to break out of the deadlock of the unsuccessful single-issue negotiations on agriculture and services that were part of the Uruguay Round's built-in agenda (Harbinson 2009). The latter experience is instructive. Although there may be scope for resolving specific minor issues through single-track negotiations, the failure of WTO Members to make progress on the built-in agenda items raises doubts about the efficacy and utility of this approach where political sensitivities and economic stakes are high.

In our view, it is not the concept of broad trade rounds or the single undertaking per se that cause developing countries to be disadvantaged or the negotiations to be so protracted. Rather the challenge is that each round of negotiations is based on the inequities of previous rounds. This generates repeated stand-offs whereby developing countries seek to remedy past anomalies and injustices, while developed countries seek to protect sectors of decreasing competitiveness and to open up new areas of economic opportunity (Wilkinson 2009).

That said, it is often the case that most of the issues included in large rounds are areas of greater interest to the more powerful players, creating an imbalance in the negotiating agenda. This was the case with the so-called Singapore issues (i.e. investment, competition, government procurement and trade facilitation). However, developing country resistance allowed only one of these issues – trade facilitation – to remain on the Doha Round's agenda. Future negotiators will hence be reluctant to entertain large rounds with too many issues, since these make the negotiations more complex and difficult to manage, particularly for smaller developing countries. Nonetheless, the single undertaking does create the basis for a single (rather than a two-tier) system, and a more durable and inclusive rules-based multilateral trading scheme, provided that the agreements are balanced, fair and development-friendly. A round of negotiations based on the principle of the single undertaking could still conceivably offer the possibility of trade-offs and an exchange of concessions that recognizes the various capabilities of the different stakeholders and results in a fair and balanced outcome allowing all the players to make gains.

1.4 Variable geometry: an alternative to the single undertaking?

To enhance the WTO's negotiating efficiency, there have been proposals to replace or relax the single undertaking principle with the concept of 'variable geometry' and 'less-than-full-consensus' decision-making (e.g.

Warwick Commission 2007; Cottier and Elsig 2009; Low 2009). The latter would allow a subset of able and willing Members to negotiate secondary rules in areas of mutual interest. For critics of the WTO's established decision-making practices, a two-speed system has obvious attractions: 1) advancing a progressive and responsive WTO agenda; 2) blunting the diversion of liberalization initiatives to RTAs; 3) allowing for more efficient differentiation in the levels of rights and obligations among a community of highly diverse economies; and 4) serving as a mechanism for promoting greater efficiency at lower cost in WTO negotiations (Low 2009).

The practice of variable geometry is hardly new to the trading system, which already accommodates considerable flexibility in terms of the rights and obligations of the membership. The Tokyo Round codes were a prime example. In the 1990s there were plurilateral negotiations among the leading exporters of information technology, telecommunications and financial services. Special and differential treatment (SDT) for developing countries and least developed countries (LDCs) is another case in point, although the latter is largely limited to longer implementation periods and some ineffectual substantive provisions.[14] Further, the 'endless cycling' (Elsig 2009) of negotiating proposals in the Doha Round has resulted in draft texts being riddled with exceptions and provisions for special treatment and non-reciprocity. A case in point is agriculture, where negotiations have largely followed a bottom-up process that accommodates a diversity of interests.

A number of different proposals have therefore been floated for introducing variable speed in the WTO. The two most common modes are plurilateral and critical mass agreements, discussed below.

1.5 Plurilateral agreements

Plurilateral agreements are separate or optional agreements contracted only among Members that agree with their provisions. Several proposals have emerged for making greater use of plurilateral agreements at the WTO (Low 2009; Draper 2010; World Economic Forum (WEF) 2010). Lawrence (2006) has proposed restructuring the WTO into a 'club of clubs', allowing for a set of plurilateral agreements among subsets of WTO Members.

[14] At the Doha Ministerial Conference in 2001, developing countries argued that the existing SDT provisions in the GATT/WTO were ineffective and thus called for these provisions to be made more 'precise, mandatory and operational'. For a fuller discussion on this issue, see Ismail (2006).

The ostensible benefit of such small group negotiations is that pioneering Members could deepen liberalization or rule-making in selected sectors. Membership of these agreements could then gradually be extended to a larger group of countries (e.g. China and the USA have agreed to pursue China's inclusion in the WTO's Government Procurement Agreement). At the Doha Round, WTO Members are already experimenting with elements of this model, especially for deepening services liberalization and for forging zero-for-zero tariff deals in the non-agricultural market access (NAMA) negotiations.

However, since plurilateral agreements do not require a critical threshold of Members, the risk is that they will perforate the trading regime by discriminating against non-signatories. Further, since plurilateral negotiations are club-like arrangements that widen asymmetric rights and obligations, they may even be welfare-diminishing, particularly for smaller developing countries. And, plurilateral market access negotiations could have a negative and disadvantageous impact on those countries that are excluded from them. For example, deeper liberalization among the major trading nations in the NAMA sectoral negotiations will erode the existing preferences enjoyed by the LDCs and other small vulnerable economies.

In addition to concerns about how plurilateral negotiations may advance unwelcome trade liberalization in some areas, there are even greater concerns among many developing countries that in the case of the rules negotiations, plurilateral agreements could create a two-track or two-tier system, marginalizing those that are excluded from the benefits in procedural terms of the rules-based system. Only two plurilateral agreements are currently in force, namely those covering government procurement and trade in civil aircraft. It may also be difficult to add more plurilateral agreements to the WTO's institutional architecture, since expansion of such so-called 'Annex 4 instruments' requires a consensus decision by WTO Members (as outlined in Article X(9) of the Marrakesh Agreement). That said, this provision also gives developing countries considerable bargaining leverage, since they can secure their own interests in exchange for sanctioning new Annex 4 plurilateral instruments.

1.6 Critical mass agreements

Critical mass agreements are an alternative plurilateral approach to multilateral cooperation in the WTO. Theoretically, it is possible to negotiate agreements that are consistent with the WTO's most favoured nation (MFN) clause, whereby the benefits of an agreement apply to all non-participants, but the obligations fall only on the signatories. Yet critical mass decision-making is also fraught with challenges for both developed and developing countries. The definition of 'critical mass' is likely to be disputed. Market power, including shares of global trade, production and consumption, may not be a sufficient proxy for delineating the requisite participatory threshold. Not all WTO Members would participate in these initiatives, whereas other Members might see an opportunity for free-riding on the outcomes without undertaking any obligations. There are other concerns too: would non-participants that later sign up to an agreement negotiated among a critical mass of Members be required to accept the latter as a fait accompli (or would there be flexibility?); or would Members that simply observe critical mass negotiations to share their country positions and perspectives prejudice their intended non-participation right from the outset (Harbinson 2009)?

Although critical mass decision-making could settle demands for greater efficiency, the latter would be meaningless unless sanctioned as legitimate, notably by non-participating 'outsiders'. Critical mass therefore has two dimensions: 'A bargain must satisfy Members whose market weight is sufficient to give effect to the deal, but it must also satisfy Members whose acquiescence is sufficient to give the deal legitimacy' (Wolfe 2008: 295). For example, all participants in the trading system – not just the major powers – must accept new rules as appropriate and legitimate (Wolfe 2008). Such acceptance will not emerge if critical mass decisions impose negative welfare outcomes on a subset of WTO Members. One approach to addressing negative outcomes would be to require compensatory transfers or mechanisms for the losers, but this would steer the WTO into hitherto uncharted waters and the political plausibility is low (Low 2009).

Moreover, the variable geometry introduced by the Kennedy and Tokyo Rounds provides a sober reminder that plurilateral processes may be divisive and discriminatory, or may also pre-empt the broader multilateral agenda. The reason for adopting the single undertaking during the Uruguay Round was precisely to stem fragmentation and restore symmetry to the rules-based system. From a systemic perspective, there is thus good reason to be cautious about club models of decision-making. From a developing country perspective, there is concern that the proposals for variable geometry seek to further raise the level of ambition beyond their interests, whether for existing or new areas of WTO law. They are suspicious that this decision-making design would create a two-speed and two-track system, compromising the principle of inclusiveness. Here, we concur with Wolfe: 'If developing countries are exempted from participation in clubs, they will forever be trying to catch up, they will not be playing their part in the continual evolution of the system and in the development of consensual knowledge about the system, and they will continue to complain about having to implement rules they had no part in drafting' (Wolfe 2008: 308).

For these reasons, the Sutherland Report (2004) adopted a cautious approach to variable geometry. The Commissioners expressed concerns that a differentiated process would enshrine a 'multiclass membership structure' that takes the multilateral trading system backwards rather than forwards.

With judicious consideration, plurilateral or critical mass approaches may have merit for resolving special cases. But the latter modes are second-best to genuinely multilateral processes, particularly for the major issues of concern to WTO Members (e.g. subsidies, anti-dumping, trade facilitation and TRIPS). Moreover, plurilateral or critical mass decision-making may also not settle the demands for greater efficiency. There is a misleading assumption that a broad mass of Members, mostly smaller developing countries, are stalling the multilateral process, hence progress would be quicker if Members with a greater or more immediate commercial interest were allowed to proceed on their own. By contrast, the reality is that small group bargaining – i.e. among and within the G4, G5/FIPS, G6 and G7 – and substantive differences over complex issues among the major players (and associated domestic political constraints) are the core issues that have bogged down the negotiations. As Harbinson (2009) reminds us, the suspension of the Doha Round in 2006 resulted mainly from deadlock among the bigger players with the greatest commercial interest, while small developing countries expressed disappointment with the impasse. In 2008, it was a disagreement among the G7[15] – specifically the USA, China and India – which frustrated the process of consensus formation. The small players had no seat at the 'High Table' of the negotiations; moreover, their interests were simply discarded during the negotiating endgame (Ismail 2009a). What then can be done to improve the WTO's decision-making? In the next section, we advance some proposals for designing a fairer and more inclusive multilateral process.

[15] The G7 in the WTO context consists of the EU, USA, Brazil, India, China, Australia and Japan.

2 Towards fair and inclusive decision-making

The WTO's decision-making processes must reflect and support the organization's overall objectives. Since developing countries today constitute more than two-thirds of the WTO's membership, there are two issues at stake for modern global trade governance. The first is for the WTO to clarify the higher level or overall objectives of the organization. Since the onset of the Doha Round, there have been increasing pressures and demands from developing country delegations, non-governmental organizations (NGOs) and academics for the development dimension of the WTO to be recognized (Qureshi 2009) and indeed mainstreamed into the WTO (Ismail 2005). The Preamble to the 1994 Marrakesh Agreement Establishing the WTO set out the objective of 'sustainable development' and expressly referred to the need for 'positive efforts to ensure that developing countries secure a share in the growth of international trade commensurate with the needs of their economic development'. However, the WTO still lacks clarity as to its main goals and objectives, which are often confused with its main functions of trade opening and rules creation. Given its historical failure to address the concerns of developing countries and the fact that developing countries now constitute the overwhelming majority of its membership, the WTO needs to declare its mission to be that of advancing the development interests and concerns of the majority of its Members. This will not turn the WTO into a 'development agency or institution', as some critics of this argument suggest. Rather, it will clarify the overall high-level principles and objectives that should guide the WTO in executing its functions.

Clearly, the adoption of the developmental objective as the overall high-level goal of the WTO is not sufficient. Consequent reforms to the organization's formal and informal negotiation procedures and practices are called for to ensure that decision-making actually supports development. A second broad challenge for the WTO is therefore to ensure greater inclusiveness of developing countries in decision-making, so that trade opportunities are made available to all Members on a more equitable basis and that trade rules do not subvert their development prospects. Below, we outline three propositions to ensure inclusive decision-making, namely to strengthen the consensus principle, avoid decision-making through informal small groups and adopt a code of conduct for WTO chairs.

2.1 *Strengthen the consensus principle*

The importance of the WTO's consensus principle has been addressed at length above. Notwithstanding the practical inequality of Members, it is worth recalling that the consensus principle was one of the few victories of developing countries in the ITO that was carried into the GATT and has since distinguished the WTO as a more democratic organization than its Bretton Woods counterparts. The challenge for the WTO is thus to improve the functioning of the consensus principle by reducing its weaknesses and building on its strengths.

As a first step, WTO Members should adopt the Sutherland Report's recommendation to strengthen the consensus principle. In an attempt to reduce the resort to blocking measures by some countries, the Sutherland Report rightly proposed that there should be a responsibility by the country seeking to block a decision to declare in writing that the matter is one of vital national interest to it. This recommendation, if implemented, could help the WTO to strengthen the consensus approach to decision-making and neutralize the efforts of large Members to block consensus, where the underlying reasons are extraneous to trade issues. While consensus-building is more complex and challenging than a simple majority or weighted voting system, this form of decision-making is more sustainable and efficient in the long term. It is inclusive on multiple fronts. Not only does consensus force WTO Members to build convergences in their positions and make compromises in the interests of the system as a whole, but arguing and deliberation in search of a negotiated consensus furthermore facilitates social learning about complex issues and countries' interests (Wolfe 2008).

2.2 Rethink the approach to informal small group negotiations

The WTO has formal Ministerial Conferences that are required to take place at least every two years. However, there are other informal ministerial gatherings of the WTO that have taken different forms, including the so-called mini-ministerial meetings held to discuss the launch of the Doha Round; small groups of ministers meeting among themselves (e.g. G4, G5/FIPS, G6 and G7); and larger groups of ministers (approximately thirty) convened by the Director-General to negotiate breakthroughs in the negotiations, sometimes referred to as the 'Green Room'. These smaller informal ministerial meetings have no legal status and any 'breakthroughs' arrived at in these must be taken to the broader membership for decision. In recent years, increased recourse to informal processes of decision-making has trumped more genuine and inclusive multilateral processes.

The small group approach to negotiations – i.e. Green Rooms or mini-ministerial gatherings, a form of critical mass – harks back to the 'principal supplier' approach adopted by the USA and the EU during the earlier GATT period. The main players insisted on this method of negotiation, which included the main economic powers only and thus marginalized the developing countries from the 'High Table' of the negotiations. A country could only be asked to make tariff cuts on a particular product by the principal supplier of that product to that country. This meant that for any particular product the importing country negotiated its tariff rate with its principal supplier and not with all suppliers of the same product. Developing countries at the time were seldom principal suppliers of any product, except raw materials that entered industrialized countries duty-free. Only at the fourth Geneva Round of the GATT in 1956 was the principal supplier approach modified to allow developing countries to negotiate collectively in requesting concessions. However, developing countries were still effectively prevented from requesting concessions in any products that they did not produce in large quantities. Thus the principal supplier rule had the effect of locking developing countries out of the tariff-cutting negotiations.

The current debate in the WTO on the formation of small informal groups that become the main decision-making fora or that shape the main content of proposed deals has significant resonance with debates in the GATT since its inception. The 'pressure cooker' mode of negotiations continues in the WTO and has evolved through the emergence of new informal forms, such as through the formation of the G4, G5/FIPS, G6 and recently the G7. Not only do such arrangements lead to frustration among the 'outsiders' left waiting in the corridors (literally), but these groups are also found wanting in their efficiency. Almost all past 'G efforts' have resulted in collapse or failure. The continuation of this approach to negotiation in its present form thus requires urgent review in favour of more inclusive, democratic and genuinely multilateral methods.

In particular, the WTO should carefully consider how it constitutes small groups to advance negotiations. China, India, the USA and the EU can claim to be part of any small group that is created to broker a deal because of their size. However, to promote inclusiveness and transparency, the interests of the rest of the membership should also be represented in any negotiating group. The model of small groups that includes Members simply on the basis of their economic and political weight – a perpetuation of the 'principal supplier approach' – is not suited to the diversity of economic interests and the political expectations of Members to be represented and included at every stage of the negotiating process.

In the current Doha Round, the role of developing countries has been unprecedented, most notably through the building of powerful developing country groupings or alliances such as the G20, G33, NAMA-11 and African, Caribbean and Pacific Group (ACP), LDC and Africa Group, among others. These coalitions can play an important role in building joint negotiating positions and convergence among the membership. In his former role as EU Trade Commissioner, current WTO Director-General Pascal Lamy acknowledged the positive role of developing country groups in the WTO: post-Cancún, he compared the G20 to a trade union legitimately representing its Members' interests. Subsequently, at the Hong Kong WTO Ministerial, he observed that the negotiating process was genuinely multilateral since the Green Room included representatives of the different developing country groupings (Ismail 2008). The bruising experience of the Geneva negotiations in July 2008[16] suggests that for future negotiations, Green Room processes and small group bargaining must include the mandated representatives of recognized developing country groups. There should also be sufficient time and space for subordinate negotiations within coalitions and intra-coalitional caucusing and deal-making. Coalitions thus need to strengthen their own internal mechanisms concerning representation and accountability by their designated spokespersons.

A related proposal is for the formalization of coalitions or specific issue-based platforms as the bargaining principals in a two-step negotiation process (Narlikar 2009; see Jones 2010). The first step would involve the constitution of coalitions – comprising developed or developing countries – that would then become the principals for the actual multilateral trade negotiation in the second step. Importantly, countries would need to credibly demonstrate the unity of the coalition. According to Narlikar (2009), formal recognition of these collective entities as principals could potentially empower even small developing countries by elevating them into the role of principal suppliers as members of coalitions. To strengthen coalition unity and permit greater flexibility to negotiate concessions, there should be a restriction on side-deals (e.g. an outright moratorium

[16] During the July 2008 negotiations, not one African representative was included in the inner locus of bargaining. This meant that the continent's agenda – cotton, bananas and duty-free quota-free market access for LDCs, among others – was simply discarded and not resolved.

on efforts to split coalitions through the use of rewards/punishments or through an extension of such deals to all coalition members on an MFN basis).

Together, these two solutions may resolve the WTO's efficiency, inclusiveness and legitimacy conundrums. They offer greater empowerment to developing countries via the coalitions that they have already developed, and thereby also improvements in perceptions of fairness of the multilateral trading system. Simultaneously, they are likely to improve the ability of the system to deliver results, and hence its efficiency, resulting in greater buy-in and engagement from the developed world.

2.3 *Adopt a code of conduct for WTO chairs*

In WTO decision-making and negotiating processes, chairs have limited, but significant, capacity to influence the efficiency of consensus-building and the resulting distribution of gains and losses, and the legitimacy of these outcomes (Odell 2005; Tallberg 2010). The Director-General of the WTO acts as the chair of the Trade Negotiations Committee (TNC), which gives him (as it has so far always been a 'him') overall responsibility for the DDA negotiations. During the previous Uruguay Round, the Director-General of the GATT was tasked with similar responsibilities. In addition, Member States give special influence to ministers and ambassadors who temporarily chair the organization's ministerial conferences and subsidiary negotiating bodies. WTO chairs clearly occupy asymmetric positions in the negotiations by virtue of their privileged access to information about the real preferences of Members, the back-up they receive from the WTO Secretariat and their control over the negotiating process.

While the WTO's decision-making system (generally by consensus) and the institutional design of decision-making (election and appointment of chairs by Members) creates more controls and less discretion for chairs to influence decisions towards their own preferences, there still exists significant room for chairs to influence, intentionally or inadvertently, the negotiations towards inefficient outcomes that result in imbalanced and unfair agreements or the collapse of the negotiations.

Outcomes are also inefficient if the overwhelming majority of Members are dissatisfied with the results, expect to make more losses than gains from the results, and developing countries perceive that they will make a greater contribution than developed countries. In addition, outcomes that lead to breakdowns of the negotiations only serve to delay the process further and can be deemed to be inefficient.

A study of the role of chairs in the agriculture and NAMA modalities negotiations in the period before the July 2008 Ministerial Meetings reveals significant differences in style and strategy and a number of weaknesses in the WTO system of chairing negotiations (Ismail 2009b).[17] The WTO does not have clear rules or guidelines regarding the role of chairs. Odell (2005: 429) observes that the only set of guidelines that have been formulated are that 'chairpersons should continue the tradition of being impartial and objective, ensuring transparency and inclusiveness in decision-making and consultative processes; and aiming to facilitate consensus' (WTO 2003). We thus recommend strengthening the selection process with the use of a code of conduct for the selection of prospective chairs. The code of conduct should pay attention to the attributes of a prospective chair and their willingness to work for the common good of the organization, with due regard for the broader goals of the WTO and the agreed mandates of the negotiations.

There are a number of attributes that a chair requires to be competent to contribute to efficient outcomes in the WTO negotiations. These include, first, the willingness to rise above their national interests and provide a fair and unbiased judgement of the compromises that would be required to build convergence in the negotiations, with due regard to the development dimensions and mandate of the negotiations. Second, the chair must be capable of building confidence and ownership of a bottom-up process among the Members, and of listening carefully to the Members, without being unduly influenced by more powerful groups (usually the major developed countries), Third, the chair must be capable of offering solutions to blockages in the negotiations in a step-by-step manner using a variety of negotiating tools (i.e. tools of brokerage) available to the chair.

The code of conduct should require chairs to make an explicit undertaking to subordinate their national interests to that of the general good of the organization and to exercise a fierce independence from the influence of the major developed or developing country groups. The development of such a code of conduct would raise awareness of the role of the chair,

[17] In this study, Ismail compares the role of the Chair of NAMA, Ambassador Don Stephenson of Canada, with that of the Chair of Agriculture, Ambassador Crawford Falconer of New Zealand. The study concludes that Stephenson failed to provide efficient formal leadership. By contrast, Falconer displayed a capacity to listen carefully to the views of different Members, to act in an objective manner, to make judicious use of the tools of brokerage (i.e. providing alternative options, single texts, etc.) and appropriate timing of single texts, and a fierce independence from the influence of any of the major developed or developing country groups in the WTO.

create greater pressure on chairs to be objective and fair, and empower the membership to seek greater commitments from prospective chairs during the selection process to abide by such a code of conduct. This would reduce the tendency of chairs to be influenced by the *realpolitik* of the negotiations – that is, the dominant interests of the major powers and the tendency of the system to strike a compromise in their favour.

The WTO Members should also consider the use of supranational chairs drawn from the ranks of the Secretariat where a suitable chair is unavailable from among the Members. It is often the case that WTO Members have to choose from a limited number of available candidates. Developing countries are often unable to field candidates due to their limited capacity and staff levels. Thus the Members are bound to choose from a small pool of Members that may not satisfy all the criteria for a suitable chair discussed above. In this context, the WTO Secretariat itself must build greater confidence among the membership about its own capacity and objectivity to play an efficient role in the chair.

3 Conclusion

There is no shortage of proposals for making the WTO a more effective and efficient negotiating institution. Irrespective of whether the DDA is concluded or not, a post-Doha reform agenda looms large. Importantly, there is no 'procedural panacea' that will magically resolve substantive differences over complex issues. Harbinson (2009: 12) is correct that: 'Constitutional and procedural refinements at best could ease the path to making decisions and concluding negotiations.' The litmus test for reform must be how well the WTO balances the competing demands for greater efficiency, inclusiveness and legitimacy.

Thus far, the debate has been characterized by a disproportionate focus and emphasis on the formal processes of decision-making. Critics have proposed reviewing the principles of consensus and the single undertaking, and moving towards some form of variable geometry of rights and obligations (i.e. plurilateral and critical mass decision-making), or weighted voting to overcome the WTO's consensus conundrum. However, WTO Members are still divided on many of these issues. And it remains unclear to what extent the proposed alternatives will address the challenges of efficiency, and rarely is sufficient attention paid by their proponents to issues of inclusiveness. Moreover, the call for change often emerges from a misdiagnosis of the underlying tensions thwarting progress in the Doha Round, most notably the hangover of previous asymmetries in negotiating outcomes, substantive differences of interests and the challenges of domestic politics within major players. The reality is that developing countries constitute the bulk of the WTO's membership. The resulting need for a more inclusive approach to decision-making means that the WTO should not deviate or abandon the consensus method in favour of other concepts. Instead, the consensus principle should be strengthened as the Sutherland Report has recommended. Although this may be a slower and more difficult process that risks both frustration with the system and greater recourse to RTAs for new market access and rules, it is more sustainable and fairer in the long term. Not only does consensus force WTO Members to build convergences in their positions and make compromises in the interests of the system as a whole, but it also creates learning opportunities and empowerment for developing and least developed countries.

By contrast, to date, little attention has focused on the WTO's informal negotiating methods. In recent years, small informal groups have emerged as the decision-making fora that shape the main content of proposed WTO deals. These exclusive conclaves have trumped more genuine and inclusive multilateral processes, often shifting the negotiations away from Geneva to national capitals. The continuation of this form of negotiation in its present form requires an urgent review in favour of more inclusive, democratic and genuinely multilateral methods.

We have argued that the rich tapestry of developing country (and developed country) coalitions created during the Doha Round should be better represented in the decision-making processes of the WTO. This should be supplemented by the development of a code of conduct by WTO Members to provide clearer guidance to the selection and behaviour of the chairs of WTO negotiations. With judicious consideration, there may even be merit in strengthening some aspects of the role-agency of the WTO Secretariat in the negotiating process. If properly implemented, these reforms could contribute to transforming the WTO from a mercantilist institution that serves narrow commercial interests into a global public good, or, in the words of WTO Director-General Pascal Lamy, into an institution that is 'more development-friendly, more user-friendly, so that its benefits are felt by all, large and small, rich and poor, strong and weak' (WTO 2009).

References

Alvarez-Jimenez, A. 2009. 'Improvements to the WTO Decision-making Process: Lessons from the International Monetary Fund and the World Bank', in

Steger, D. (ed.), *Redesigning the World Trade Organization for the Twenty-first Century.* Waterloo, Ont.: Wilfred Laurier University Press, CIGI and IDRC, pp. 91–128.

Chang, H.-J. 2002. *Kicking Away the Ladder. Development Strategy in Historical Perspective.* London: Anthem Press.

Consultative Board. 2004. *The Future of the WTO: Addressing Institutional Challenges in the New Millennium.* Geneva: WTO.

Cottier, T. 2009. 'A Two-Tier Approach to WTO Decision Making', NCCR Working Paper 2009/06 (March).

Cottier, T. and Elsig, M. 2009. 'Reforming the WTO: the Decision-Making Triangle Re-Assessed'. Paper presented at the World Trade Forum, World Trade Institute, University of Bern, 25–6 September.

Cottier, T. and Takenoshita, S. 2008. 'Decision-making and the Balance of Powers in WTO Negotiations: Towards Supplementary Weighted Voting', in Griller, S. (ed.), *At the Crossroads: The World Trading System and the Doha Round.* Austria: Springer-Verlag Wein, pp. 181–229.

Deere Birkbeck, C. and Monagle, C. 2009. *Strengthening Multilateralism: A Mapping of Proposals on WTO Reform and Global Trade Governance,* Geneva/Oxford: ICTSD and the Global Economic Governance Programme.

Draper, P. 2010. 'Whither the Multilateral Trading System? A Case for Plurilaterals', IDEAS Centre Information Note, Geneva: IDEAS Centre.

Elsig, M. 2009. 'WTO Decision-Making: Can We Get a Little Help From the Secretariat and the Critical Mass?', in Steger, D. (ed.), *Redesigning the World Trade Organization for the Twenty-first Century.* Waterloo, Ont.: Wilfred Laurier University Press, CIGI and IDRC, pp. 67–90.

Finger, M. 2007. 'Implementation and the Imbalance: Dealing with Hangover from the Uruguay Round', *Oxford Review of Economic Policy* 23(3): 440–60.

Finger, M. and Schuler, P. 2000. 'Implementation of Uruguay Round Commitments: The Development Challenge', *The World Economy* 24(4): 511–25.

Gallagher, K. (ed.) 2005. *Putting Development First. The Importance of Policy Space in the WTO and International Financial Institutions.* London: Zed Books.

Harbinson, S. 2009. 'The Doha Round: "Death-Defying Agenda" or "Don't Do it Again?"', European Centre for International Political Economy (ECIPE), Working Paper 10.

Ismail, F. 2005. 'Mainstreaming Development in the World Trade Organization', *Journal of World Trade* 39(1): 11–21.

2006. 'How Can Small, Weak and Vulnerable Countries also Gain from the WTO Doha Development Round?' *Journal of World Trade* 40(1): 37–68.

2008. 'An Assessment of the Sixth WTO Hong Kong Ministerial Conference from a Development Perspective', in Hohmann, H. (ed.), *Agreeing and Implementing the Doha Round of the WTO.* Cambridge University Press, pp. 98–110.

2009a. 'An Assessment of the WTO Doha Round July–December 2008 Collapse', *World Trade Review* 8(4): 579–605.

2009b. 'The Role of the Chair in the WTO Negotiations: From the Potsdam Collapse in June 2007 to July 2008', *Journal of World Trade* 43(6): 1145–71.

2009c. 'Reforming the World Trade Organization', *World Economics* 10(4): 109–46.

Jones, K. 2010. *The Doha Blues. Institutional Crisis and Reform in the WTO*. Oxford University Press.

Lawrence, R. 2006. 'Rulemaking Amidst Growing Diversity: A Club-of-Club Approach to WTO Reform and New Issue Selection', *Journal of World Trade* 35(4): 575–602.

Low, P. 2009. 'WTO Decision-Making for the Future', background paper prepared for the Inaugural Conference of Thinking Ahead on International Trade (TAIT), Geneva, 17–18 September.

Narlikar, A. 2009. 'A Theory of Bargaining Coalitions in the WTO', in Narlikar, A. and Vickers, B. (eds.), *Leadership and Change in the Multilateral Trading System*, Dordrecht: Republic of Letters Publishing/Martinus Nijhoff, pp. 183–201.

Narlikar, A. and Vickers, B. (eds.) 2009. *Leadership and Change in the Multilateral Trading System*. Dordrecht: Republic of Letters Publishing/Martinus Nijhoff.

Odell, J. 2005. 'Chairing a WTO Negotiation', *Journal of International Economic Law* 8(2): 425–48.

Qureshi, A. 2009. 'International Trade For Development: The WTO as a Development Institution?', *Journal of World Trade* 43(1): 173–88.

Sen, A. 1999. *Development as Freedom*. New York: Anchor Books.

Steinberg, R. 2002. 'In the Shadow of Law or Power? Consensus-Based Bargaining and Outcomes in the GATT/WTO', *International Organization* 56(2): 339–74.

Steinberg, R. and Goldstein, J. 2009. 'Regulatory Shift: The Rise of Judicial Liberalization at the WTO', in Mattli, W. and Woods, N. (eds.), *The Politics of Global Regulation*, Princeton University Press, pp. 211–41.

Tallberg, J. 2010. 'The Power of the Chair: Formal Leadership in International Cooperation', *International Studies Quarterly* 54(1): 241–65.

Warwick Commission. 2007. *The Multilateral Trade Regime: Which Way Forward?* Coventry: University of Warwick.

Wilkinson, R. 2006a. *The WTO: Crisis and the Governance of Global Trade*. London: Routledge.

2006b. 'The WTO in Hong Kong: What it Really Means for the Doha Development Agenda', *New Political Economy* 11(2): 291–304.

2009. 'Barriers to WTO Reform. Intellectual Narrowness and the Production of Path Dependent Thinking' (mimeo).

Wilkinson, R. and Scott, J. 2008. 'Developing Country Participation in the GATT: A Reassessment', *World Trade Review* 7(3): 473–510.

Wolfe, R. 2008. 'Can the Trading System be Governed? Institutional Implications of the WTO's Suspended Animation', in Alexandroff, A., (ed.), *Can the World Be Governed? Possibilities for Effective Multilateralism*. Waterloo, Ont.: Wilfrid Laurier University Press, pp. 289–344.

World Economic Forum (WEF). 2010. *Everybody's Business: Strengthening International Cooperation in a More Interdependent World – Report of the Global Redesign Initiative*. www.weforum.org/pdf/grs2010/GRI_Report_2010.pdf [Accessed in November 2010].

World Trade Organization (WTO). 2003. *Guidelines for Appointment of Officers to WTO Bodies*. Adopted by the General Council on 11 December–21 January. Geneva: WTO.

2009. *Appointment of the Director-General. Statement of the Director-General*. General Council, Job (09)/39, 29 April. Geneva: WTO.

17

Revisiting the single undertaking: towards a more balanced approach to WTO negotiations

MIGUEL RODRÍGUEZ MENDOZA AND MARIE WILKE

The idea of a 'single undertaking' was first introduced as a procedural device in the Punta del Este Declaration, which formally launched the Uruguay Round of multilateral trade negotiations in 1986.[1] Since then, the scope, function and impact of the single undertaking have evolved considerably.

While the single undertaking was originally constructed as a mechanism for preventing negotiations from advancing in areas that may be of interest to some countries but not others, by the end of the Uruguay Round it was used to secure the final package deal that enabled the establishment of the World Trade Organization (WTO). Later on, with the launch of the Doha Round in 2001, the meaning and role of the single undertaking changed further as it acquired the status of an almost immutable 'principle' whereby *nothing can be agreed, until everything is agreed.*

In this chapter, we argue that while the single undertaking was initially introduced to level the playing field, it now artificially limits the flexibilities of WTO Members in their negotiations. Moreover, and more importantly, the single undertaking currently serves as a tool for those that aim to block negotiations until certain concessions in their favour

Miguel Rodríguez Mendoza is Senior Fellow at the International Centre for Trade and Sustainable Development (ICTSD). Marie Wilke also works at ICTSD as Programme Officer for International Trade Law in the Programme on Dispute Settlement and Legal Aspects of International Trade. The authors are indebted to the insightful comments provided by Alejandro Jara, Pedro Roffe, Carolyn Deere Birkbeck and Trineesh Biswas. The views expressed in the present article are exclusively those of the authors, and do not necessarily represent the views of ICTSD.

1 Part I:B (ii) reads as follows: 'The launching, the conduct, and the implementation of the outcome of the negotiations shall be treated as a single undertaking. However, agreements reached at an early stage may be implemented on a provisional or a definitive basis by agreement prior to the formal conclusion of the negotiations.'

have been made. The objectives of the Doha Development Agenda to improve the fairness and responsiveness of WTO agreements to development concerns are prejudiced by this lack of progress, which causes disproportional harm to developing countries. The single undertaking is not responsible for the current deadlock in the Doha Round of negotiations; ultimately, it is the divergence or convergence of the interests of WTO Members that force a particular outcome in negotiations. However, the single undertaking facilitates the position of those countries that hold negotiations hostage.

On this basis, we argue that the single undertaking should be set aside in the post-Doha environment, if not before. By analysing past experiences we attempt to deconstruct how the single undertaking works in practice and to elaborate an alternative approach to multilateral trade negotiations that accounts for today's realities. This redesign must include moving away from all encompassing 'rounds' of negotiations on an ever increasing number of subjects to more à la carte negotiations on subjects that are more likely to produce significant and faster results.

This chapter begins by describing the emergence of the single undertaking as a procedural device during the Uruguay Round. The second section then analyses the evolution of the various forms, functions and meanings the single undertaking has assumed over time, including during the Doha negotiations. Finally, we will discuss alternative approaches to conduct WTO negotiations without recourse to the single undertaking and suggest possible ways forward. This chapter aims to supplement the existing scholarly literature on the WTO negotiation process, with insights drawn from the practical experience of the authors in international trade negotiations.

1 The emergence of the 'single undertaking'

While the Tokyo Round of multilateral trade negotiations was not guided by the single undertaking, the results of those negotiations – limited and rejected by many countries, particularly developing ones – were critical for the later inclusion of the single undertaking as a negotiating principle in the Uruguay Round (Lanoszka 2008: 663–4). The seventy-seven countries that were members of the General Agreements on Tariff and Trade (GATT) at that time were joined by around forty non-Member countries (mainly developing ones) that had been invited to participate in the negotiations in an attempt to make the GATT a stronger and more universal organization by ensuring greater participation of developing countries

(McRae and Thomas 1983: 60, 77).[2] However, when the Tokyo Round was concluded in 1979, after more than six years of intense negotiations to reduce tariffs and regulate the use of non-tariff measures, less than half of its participants signed a *procès-verbal* in Geneva (Wilkinson 2006).[3] Moreover, only one developing country accepted the suite of codes that emerged to regulate 'new issues', namely subsidies and countervailing measures, technical barriers to trade, government procurement, customs valuation, import licensing and anti-dumping measures (Farless 1981).

As a consequence, the GATT emerged from the Tokyo Round negotiations as a fragmented and debilitated mechanism. Most importantly, disillusionment among developing countries was widespread, as the issues of interest to them had been neglected in the negotiations in favour of the concerns of industrialized countries. For instance, the most pressing issues that developing countries faced, such as 'orderly marketing arrangements' and 'voluntary export restraints' and the frequent recourse to quantitative restrictions, which affected their exports of textiles, footwear, steel and televisions, among other products, were left without disciplines at the end of the Tokyo Round. Moreover, attempts to reach an agreement on issues of importance to developing countries, such as 'safeguards',[4] were fruitless. In addition, talks on agriculture – the most important trade issue for most developing countries – were almost non-existent during the Tokyo Round (McRae and Thomas 1983).

The results of the Tokyo Round had a number of significant consequences for the multilateral trading system. Neither developing nor developed countries were completely satisfied with the outcomes of the

[2] Previous GATT rounds had seen a participation of a maximum of twenty to forty countries. The increase to over one hundred participating countries meant an extreme challenge for the Tokyo Round process, particularly as it was mainly developing countries that had joined the GATT or the negotiations since the previous round. For further discussion, see Sampson (2005: 206–7) and Wilkinson (2006).

[3] Of the almost one hundred negotiating parties, only forty-one signed the *procès-verbal*, and of these only twenty-three countries – mainly industrialized ones – accepted the full range of agreements crafted during the talks. Among the developing countries, only Argentina decided to accept all the agreements.

[4] A WTO Member may take a 'safeguard' action (i.e. restrict imports of a product temporarily) to protect a specific domestic industry from an increase in imports of any product which is causing, or which is threatening to cause, serious injury to the industry. Safeguard measures were always available under the GATT (Article XIX), however, they were infrequently used; some governments preferred to protect their industries through 'grey area' measures ('voluntary' export restraint arrangements on products such as cars, steel and semiconductors). The WTO Safeguards Agreement broke new ground in prohibiting 'grey area' measures and setting time limits ('sunset clause') on all safeguard actions (www.wto.org).

Tokyo Round and there was considerable discomfort among all GATT Members about the fragmentation of the multilateral trading system caused by the six codes (McRae and Thomas 1983: 60). Because the codes were not applied on a most favoured nation (MFN) basis and most developing countries chose not to join them, they created a duality of rights and obligations among the GATT Members. Countries that had accepted the code on subsidies and countervailing measures (SCMA), for instance, denied non-Members treatment agreed in the code, which dictated that duties could only be imposed if the subsidies harmed the importing country's economy (Croome 1995: 78). The unease was exacerbated by the fact that the codes had emerged from negotiations conducted mainly among industrialized countries, a dynamic that was reflected in the content of the codes.

This discomfort was compounded by concerns in the 1980s about a deteriorating global economic situation, rising protectionism, acute differences between developing and developed countries on where the multilateral trading system should go, and a push, mainly from the United States, to further expand the coverage of the GATT to include issues such as trade in services, investment and intellectual property (later called the 'new issues') (Croome 1995: 6–27). It is against this background that the emergence of the single undertaking needs to be examined.

1.1 Launching of the Uruguay Round

The Uruguay Round of negotiations started with a large set of diverse interests, objectives and ideas. Yet there was general agreement on the need for greater coherence, and to redesign the fragmented system that had emerged from the Tokyo Round codes to restore the multilateral nature of the GATT system (Lanoszka 2008: 664). In particular, the European Communities (EC) insisted that all negotiations be linked and have a multilateral character in order to introduce a greater degree of reciprocity and to prevent 'free-riding'.[5] Moreover, developing countries and the newly formed Cairns Group[6] insisted that they would not

[5] The lack or limited level of commitments to the GATT negotiations by developing countries was usually described as meaning that they benefitted from the rights conferred to them by being Members of the GATT without matching those rights with comparable obligations.

[6] The Cairns Group is an interest group established by nineteen agricultural exporting countries, composed of Argentina, Australia, Bolivia, Brazil, Canada, Chile, Colombia, Costa Rica, Guatemala, Indonesia, Malaysia, New Zealand, Pakistan, Paraguay, Peru, the Philippines, South Africa, Thailand and Uruguay. It was founded a few weeks prior to the

agree on any new trade rules that disregarded their interests by once again ignoring, or insufficiently addressing, controversial issues such as agriculture, textiles, tariff escalation and safeguards. That is, they sought a greater balance in the subject matter and outcomes of negotiations (Croome 1995: 31, 34).

These priorities were clearly reflected in the Punta del Este Declaration that launched the Uruguay Round of negotiations in 1986 as it states that 'the launching, the conduct and the implementation of the outcome of the negotiations shall be treated as parts of a single undertaking' (Punta del Este Declaration, Part I:B (ii)). Consequentially, *all agreements* needed to be negotiated, adopted and implemented by *all negotiating parties* at the *same time* – we thus speak of the three characteristics of the single undertaking. Yet this novel approach came with two important caveats.

First, the single undertaking was to cover only the negotiations on goods: that is, those subjects included in Part I of the Punta del Este Declaration. Until the very last minute, the request to include the new issue of trade in services was hotly debated. A prolonged, closed meeting with the United States, Brazil and India as the central actors eventually resulted in a compromise that allowed the negotiations to proceed on two different tracks: one covering the traditional areas of the GATT plus two of the new issues, namely trade-related aspects of intellectual property rights (TRIPS) and trade-related investment measures (TRIMS); and a second track covering trade in services included in Part II. To make this distinction clearer, the GATT negotiations were launched by the contracting parties acting collectively, whereas the negotiations on services were launched by the Ministers present at Punta del Este acting as representatives of their own governments rather than as GATT signatories (Stewart 1993). This distinction was progressively blurred, but in 1986 two distinct sets of negotiations were initiated and only one subset was covered by the single undertaking. In this manner, developing countries, including those that agreed to include services in the negotiations, wanted to avoid a repetition of their experience during the Tokyo Round and prevent negotiations from concentrating on trade in services – a

launch of the Uruguay Round with the aim of pressing for a significant agreement on agriculture and played a critical role in those negotiations. It continues to do so in the Doha negotiations although less effectively due to the emergence of the G20, which also seeks to influence the negotiations on agriculture.

subject that was perceived at that time as being mainly in the interest of industrialized countries.

The second caveat concerning the application of the single undertaking was included in the text of the single undertaking clause itself. The use of the single undertaking was to be limited in the sense that: 'agreements reached at an early stage may be implemented on a provisional or a definitive basis by agreement prior to the formal conclusion of the overall round of negotiations. Early agreement shall be taken into account in assessing the overall balance of the negotiations' (Punta del Este Declaration, Part I:B (ii)).

This construct thus introduced the single undertaking as a new procedural device to be applied to the Uruguay Round negotiations on goods, intellectual property and investment. As the renegotiation of the Tokyo codes was included in this mandate, the single undertaking approach was likely to end the fragmentation of the GATT system. Moreover, by covering the full spectrum of GATT issues (including issues of great importance to developing countries, such as agriculture), the approach assured developing countries that their concerns would be included in a final package as no agreement was possible without their consensus.

1.2 The conduct of the negotiations

The single undertaking as a procedural device started to pay off for developing countries early on when negotiations on issues of interest to developing countries, such as agriculture, ran into difficulties. Agriculture was, and continues to be, one of the most complicated and sensitive issues in multilateral trade negotiations, and discussions during the Uruguay Round – as in the Doha negotiations – often faced a near breakdown. In that context, the availability of the 'nothing is agreed until everything is agreed' argument was of great help to developing countries in their continuous push for movement in this sector. It provided them with a 'legal basis' that supported their firm position, and the continuous reference to this rule as a prerequisite for the negotiations, in the long run, changed the dynamics of the negotiations.

For instance, during the 1988 Montreal GATT Ministerial Meeting, the conflict between the USA and the EC over agricultural liberalization accelerated and no solution to their differences seemed in sight. Rather than continuing the negotiations, the two parties proposed to adopt what was already on the table and to proceed with other negotiations, including agriculture, at a later stage. The Latin American Members of the Cairns Group outright rejected this proposal and brought the negotiations to a sudden halt. They made clear that any agreement was only possible when substantial commitments were made in the area of agriculture. It was the first time in GATT negotiating history that developing countries, acting in a group, were so firm and insistent with their position, accepting the possible consequence of the Round collapsing as a whole (Croome 1995: 173). Again, in Brussels two years later, the same countries managed to stop the Uruguay Round negotiations altogether after concluding that the EC's offer on agriculture was unacceptable. The single undertaking, prescribing that negotiations would be conducted and finalized as a whole, was an important factor for enabling the countries to enforce these halts until agreement on agriculture was reached; such a request was considered 'legitimate' due to the agreement of all parties to proceed on the basis of a single undertaking – consequentially a naming and shaming of the blocking countries was not possible.

Despite these instances of success for developing countries, the new interlinkages between negotiating issues also proved difficult at times as negotiating parties started to view the interlinkages cautiously and feared the consequences of revealing their negotiating positions too quickly. However, assuming that the GATT negotiations would have been launched not as a single undertaking but on the premise that sector agreements or codes were no longer available, presumably similar linkages would have emerged. In fact, the interlinkages were the result of the broad set of topics covered by one single round (compared to the scope and coverage of negotiations during previous rounds) and not of the single undertaking as such (Rolland 2010). These two issues have to be carefully distinguished: the single undertaking only shaped the form of interlinkages but did not create them. That is, the single undertaking was critical in shaping the dynamics that characterized this round of negotiations. This occurred mainly due to the participants' understanding that they had a legitimate right to linkage and that they could halt negotiations or insist on their right to improvements in one area before making commitments in another without risking being left behind (as had happened during the Tokyo Round).

The linkages as such, however, were the consequence of the large set of topics covered by the round. Moreover, as consensus was required for the adoption of any package, countries could not be left behind by other negotiating parties deciding to set aside issues of particular interest to them or to conclude sector or code agreements (Lanoszka 2008: 670).

1.3 *The establishment of the World Trade Organization*

As the Uruguay Round negotiations continued, the various negotiating groups started to face critical questions regarding rules on dispute settlement. Should separate mechanisms and rules on dispute settlement be developed for TRIPS and the future agreement on trade in services? Or, should the GATT dispute settlement mechanism apply in order to prevent internal forum-shopping? This and other institutional issues were discussed in a parallel negotiating group on the Functioning of the GATT System, better known as the FOGS group. After the Brussels Ministerial, this issue was effectively moved to the FOGS group and shortly thereafter an understanding emerged that one single, integrated dispute settlement mechanism was to be preferred to deal with all matters that would be included in the final Uruguay Round agreements (Croome 1995).

That decision, however, resulted in a new question: did an integrated dispute settlement system require a united institutional framework? Was there a need for a new multilateral trade organization that would cover all future agreements including the GATT (as modified during the negotiations), as well as new rules on trade-related intellectual property measures, trade-related investment measures and trade in services? Moreover, if participation in this single institution was required, was it still possible to allow countries to pick and choose which agreements to join?[7] In early 1990, Canada submitted the first proposals for a new multilateral trade organization, which were further developed during the following years in the FOGS negotiating group (Wilkinson 2000: 29).

Though delegates were confident that all negotiating countries would eventually accede to a new multilateral organization at the close of the Uruguay Round, consensus was far from being secured. There was a justifiable concern that a negative decision on some of the agreements by some countries would not only risk the successful conclusion of the Uruguay Round, but also imperil the effort to institutionalize and strengthen the multilateral trading system (Croome 1995). To insist that all agreements belonged in one 'take it or leave it' package seemed to be the solution. It was also a clever device to ensure that a large number of developing countries and thus 'new markets' would accede to all agreements, including

[7] The decision to establish such a multilateral organization – the WTO – was certainly not undisputed. In fact, the USA largely rejected that idea and only towards the end of the round agreed to its establishment.

the GATT, TRIPS, TRIMS and the various new agreements based on the former Tokyo codes.[8]

Eventually all the Uruguay Round agreements, as well as a framework agreement establishing the WTO, were presented as a single undertaking, transforming the latter from a procedural device into a negotiating tool and, through its inclusion in the final text, a legal principle. This allowed Members to link all the agreements negotiated during the Uruguay Round, including those where negotiations took place with little or no participation from the developing countries (in particular, the negotiations on the revision and updating of the various Tokyo Round codes). This outcome was consistently criticized in later debates, which in turn significantly shaped discussions leading up to the launch of the Doha Round.

Finally, it should be noted that the single undertaking did not deprive negotiating parties of all flexibilities during the Uruguay Round as countries made use of its explicit endorsement to adopt early harvest agreements. In that regard, a number of agreements related to the GATT dispute settlement mechanism were adopted on a provisional basis during the mid-term review of the negotiations that took place in Montreal in 1988.[9] Moreover, at the end of the Uruguay Round, countries decided to incorporate as part of the Marrakesh Agreement some 'plurilateral' trade agreements that only signatory countries were to enforce (WTO 1994: Article 2:3).[10] Finally, some agreements were left unfinished and were completed only after the closing of the negotiations.

In summary, despite the aforementioned criticism of the Round's general outcome, it can be said that the single undertaking played a critical role during the Uruguay Round. First, it helped GATT Members avoid a repetition of the Tokyo Round (albeit with mixed results).[11] Second, it

[8] Indeed, the single undertaking is often seen as the prime reason for developing countries' accession to TRIPS and TRIMS and thus is often understood as *development unfriendly*.

[9] Decisions by the Contracting Parties to the General Agreement on Tariffs and Trade on Improvements to the GATT Dispute Settlement Rules and Procedures, adopted 12 April 1989, BISP 36S/61–67.

[10] At the end of the round, two plurilateral agreements were adopted: one on Civil Aircraft and one on Government Procurement. Both were based on former Tokyo codes. Unlike the other Tokyo codes, they were neither multilateral (and thus included in the WTO package) nor ceased to exist. Rather, they were renegotiated and continued to exist as plurilateral agreements. This means that they apply only to WTO Members that have accepted the agreements; neither obligations, nor rights apply to third countries. However, they are integrated in the WTO system in the sense that special provisions in the Agreement Establishing the WTO administer their application. Moreover, the Understanding on the Rules and Procedures Governing the Settlement of Disputes is applicable to these agreements.

[11] The outcome of the Uruguay Round has often been criticized for its unbalanced and non-development-friendly outcome. In particular, TRIPS and the agreements resulting

contributed to a more reciprocal multilateral trading system. Finally, the single undertaking facilitated the establishment of the WTO and thereby the bolstering and further institutionalization of the multilateral trading system.

2 The single undertaking since 1994

At the conclusion of the Uruguay Round, the single undertaking was introduced as a guiding principle of the WTO, with the aim of ensuring the unity and coherent application of the different WTO agreements and the integrity of the multilateral trading system as such. In that regard, Article 2:2 of the Agreement Establishing the World Trade Organization (the Marrakesh Agreement) accordingly states that 'the agreements and associated legal instruments ... are integral parts of this Agreement, binding on all Members' (WTO 1994).[12]

Since then, the single undertaking has developed along two paths. First, it has gained acceptance as a legal principle through Article 2:2 of the Marrakesh Agreement, which informed a series of decisions by WTO dispute settlement panels and by the WTO Appellate Body (WTO 1994). Second, it was re-introduced as a negotiation device in the 2001 Doha Ministerial Declaration, which launched the current round of multilateral trade negotiations: the Doha Development Agenda (DDA) (WTO 2001a).

Both developments cannot be viewed separately. Moreover, in order to assess the main question of this chapter – whether the single undertaking as a negotiation device continues to be supportive of the negotiation process and, most importantly, whether it is 'development friendly' – it is important to first explore the differences of these two versions of the single undertaking.

2.1 WTO dispute settlement and the single undertaking

Legal certainty is of utmost importance for any rules-based system. Only if countries have assurance regarding their rights and obligations and,

from the 'multilateralization' of the former Tokyo codes, including the Anti-Dumping Agreement (Agreement on Implementation of Article VI of the General Agreement on Tariffs and Trade 1994) and the Customs Valuation Agreement (Agreement on Implementation of Article VII of the GATT 1994), have been heavily criticized. Moreover, agreement on certain issues of interest to developing countries, such as restriction on agricultural subsidies, has arguably not reached far enough.

12 Note that Article 2:2 refers to the 'multilateral' trade agreements only, i.e. not to the 'plurilateral' agreements.

where necessary, have access to a judicial dispute settlement system can a multilateral organization such as the WTO be successful. Article II: 2 of the Marrakesh Agreement plays a central role in ensuring this certainty – and thus stability – of the WTO by safeguarding the coherent and consistent application of WTO rules. It has done so by serving as a guiding principle that informs and shapes the interrelation of the different WTO agreements, its Members and institutions and provides guidance on how the rights and obligations of Members should be interpreted.

The meaning and function of this important provision was clarified in a series of rulings. In 1998, for instance, the Appellate Body found in the *Korea-Dairy* case that 'the WTO Agreement is a *single undertaking* and therefore all WTO obligations are generally cumulative and WTO members must comply with all of them simultaneously' (WTO 1999a: 21, emphasis added). This reading was further clarified by the WTO Appellate Body in the 1999 *Argentina-Footwear* case (WTO 1999b: para. 89), by WTO panels established for the *US-Lamb* case in 2000 (WTO 2000: para. 7.11) and the *US-Steel Safeguards* case in 2003 (WTO 2003). By ruling in *Argentina-Footwear* (WTO 1999b: para. 89) that all WTO agreements referred to in Article II:2 of the Marrakesh Agreement 'apply equally and are equally binding on all WTO Members' and that 'a treaty interpreter must read all applicable provisions of a treaty in a way that gives meaning to all of them, harmoniously', while 'an appropriate reading of this "inseparable package of rights and disciplines" must, accordingly, be one that gives meaning to *all* the relevant provisions of these … equally binding agreements', the Appellate Body ensured that any provisions would be read harmoniously thus ensuring the internal integrity of the system (WTO 1999b).

However, despite this series of rulings and the language chosen by both the WTO Appellate Body and various dispute settlement panels, one has to carefully distinguish between the single undertaking as a legal principle and as a negotiating device. While the adoption of the Uruguay Round agreements as a single undertaking had considerable impact on the nature of the WTO by ensuring that all agreements would be applied cumulatively, the fact that the Appellate Body and the panels have chosen to refer to Article II: 2 as a 'single undertaking' does not imply that it *as a negotiating device* (as discussed above) is a legal principle that WTO Members cannot depart from in future negotiations. To the contrary, neither the Appellate Body nor the panels have ever addressed the modus operandi for negotiations – rather, any rulings that addressed the *single undertaking* concerned the legal interrelation of already existing agreements. In *argumentum e contrario*,[13] WTO Members are generally free to choose the modus operandi for future negotiations as long as the integrity of the framework agreement is preserved.[14]

Thus, while institutional improvements, such as the reform of the Dispute Settlement Understanding (DSU), or changes in the existing general rules that apply to all WTO agreements can only be undertaken if all WTO Members agree,[15] this is not necessarily the case for new rules and/or future trade liberalization.

2.2 *The single undertaking in the Doha negotiations*

When WTO Members agreed on the Doha Development Agenda, they aimed to conclude the new round of negotiations by January 2005. Since then, negotiations have dragged on and now, at the time of writing, a successful conclusion looks more unlikely than ever before.

Importantly, contrary to popular misperception, it is not the case that WTO Members have been unable to agree on anything since the conclusion of the Uruguay Round. Indeed, since 1994, a number of new, individual agreements on different issues have emerged. Moreover, when the opportunity has presented itself Members have not hesitated to undertake new commitments, including on issues that were supposed to have been settled during the Uruguay Round.

For instance, shortly after the entry into force of the WTO, a significant number of countries agreed to craft new agreements on financial and basic telecommunication services, which resulted in one full agreement in 1997 and one reference paper in 1996, respectively.[16] Moreover, the Ministerial Declaration on Trade in Information Technology Products (ITA) agreed in 1996, can be considered a further post-Uruguay Round success. The ITA now has seventy signatories and regulates around 97

[13] That is, it permits the converse conclusion.

[14] This, however, needs to take account of the decision-making procedures outlined in Article IX of the Agreement Establishing the WTO.

[15] Strictly speaking, depending on the nature of the provisions concerned, amendments to WTO agreements can also be adopted through approval by a two-thirds majority. However, such amendments only take effect for those WTO Members that accepted them (Article X of the Agreement Establishing the WTO). It is beyond the scope of this chapter to outline and consider the numerous rules for the different provisions and agreements. Thus, when addressing amendments to existing agreements, we assume for the purposes of this chapter a situation where all Members take a decision by consensus.

[16] Agreement on Financial Services, 15 December 1997; Reference Paper on Basic Telecommunication Services, 24 April 1996.

per cent of global trade in information technology products.[17] Moreover, the preparatory process of the Doha negotiations resulted in the 2001 Ministerial Declaration on the TRIPS Agreement and Public Health, providing important guidance on the interpretation and application of some of the most critical TRIPS provisions (WTO 2001b). More recently – and thus after the launch of the Doha Round – Members agreed to the establishment of a mechanism to channel financial resources that help poorer countries increase their participation in international trade. This Aid for Trade mechanism was put into place after an intensive process of consultations that differed only in name from a negotiating exercise (WTO 2005). Finally, in 2006, the General Council adopted a Decision on the Transparency Mechanism for Regional Trade Agreements (RTAs) (WTO 2006).

Interestingly, some of these agreements were not, *strictu senso*, multilateral agreements, as not all WTO Members adopted them. This is particularly true for the agreement on financial services, the declaration on basic telecommunication services and the ITA, where only a subset of interested WTO Members conducted the negotiations and joined the final agreements (Gallagher and Stoler 2009). Importantly, however, all of these agreements are applied on a MFN basis, and thus their benefits are extended to all WTO Members. The inclusion of the MFN principle was critical for ensuring that the decision to initiate such 'group negotiations' would strengthen, rather than debilitate, the multilateral trading system, as had been the case with the plurilateral Tokyo Round codes. The Declaration on TRIPS and Public Health, on the other hand, was a multilateral undertaking. All WTO Members at that time negotiated, accepted and implemented the declaration on a multilateral basis, which constitutes the only amendment to the WTO agreements to date as well as the only WTO rules that have been crafted completely outside a negotiating round.

Similar stories, however, are missing in the context of the Doha Round. This is despite the fact that the Doha Ministerial Declaration, which almost identically reproduced the concept of the single undertaking of Part I of the Punta del Este Declaration,[18] also allows early harvest

[17] For information on the WTO ITA Gateway, see www.wto.org/english/tratop_e/inftec_e/inftec_e.htm [Accessed in November 2010].

[18] The single undertaking in the Doha Development Agenda reads: 'With the exception of the improvements and clarifications of the Dispute Settlement Understanding, the conduct, conclusion and entry into force of the outcome of the negotiations shall be treated as parts of a single undertaking. However, agreements reached at an early stage may be

agreements to be adopted on a temporary or definite basis. During the Doha Round, the single undertaking has been repeatedly presented as an immutable principle under which *nothing can be agreed until everything is agreed*. This argument, coupled with the highly confrontational nature of the negotiations, has to a great extent prevented countries from putting in place potential 'interim' agreements (with the exception of the Aid for Trade and RTA transparency decisions mentioned above). The ongoing review of the DSU, where there seems to be a very high degree of convergence among WTO Members, and which has been explicitly excluded from the scope of the single undertaking, comes to mind. The outstanding implementation of at least some of the agreements reached so far in the area of trade facilitation is another example. Lastly, issues of critical importance to the poorest economies, such as the 'cotton conflict' and the agreement on 'duty free, quota free' market access for exports from least developed countries (LDCs) are, with reference to the single undertaking, left in limbo until the end of the negotiations.

Naturally, the single undertaking as such cannot be blamed for the failure of the Doha negotiations. Rather, changes in WTO Membership, including the rise in Membership, the emergence of new economic powers, increased differences in size and level of development, and the great variety of economic priorities among the WTO Members, have resulted in negotiating dynamics that differ considerably from the Uruguay Round experience and lend themselves more easily to deadlocks (Narlikar and Vickers 2009).[19] Yet, the single undertaking exacerbates this situation by providing countries with a blocking tool to hold the negotiations captive from those least willing to enter into new agreements. This reflects the confrontational nature of the Doha negotiations, where participating countries seem to believe that only when all their particular objectives and aspirations are met, negotiations may be concluded.

3 Revisiting the single undertaking: the next steps

After sixty years of periodical and mostly successful rounds of trade negotiations, the time has come to change the general approach to negotiations. The diversity among WTO Members makes it extremely difficult

implemented on a provisional or a definitive basis. Early agreements shall be taken into account in assessing the overall balance of the negotiations.'

[19] This statement, however, does not simply refer to the nominal increase in Membership. For a comprehensive analysis on the issue view Harbinson (2009: 7).

to reach agreement, simultaneously, on the highly complex sets of issues included in rounds of negotiations (Narlikar and Vickers 2009). To move beyond deadlocks, such as the one facing the Doha Round, we suggest an alternative approach. Our suggestions are predicated on the need for the WTO to move away from the confrontational character and rhetoric of the current negotiations towards a more cooperative approach. Such a new approach, in our view, needs to allow for negotiations to be undertaken by groups of interested countries as long as certain conditions are met and the multilateral nature and integrity of the WTO is preserved.

The idea outlined here is not a completely novel approach; many scholars over the last few years have researched and written on these issues (in addition to the ones below see e.g. Consultative Board 2004; Wolfe 2009; MacMillan 2010). Among others, ideas on critical mass (Gallagher and Stoler 2009), variable geometry (VanGrasstek and Sauvé 2006; Low 2009), weighted voting approaches (Cottier and Takenoshita 2008) and less than full consensus (Warwick Commission 2007; Cottier and Elsig 2009) have been discussed and suggested in various forms and designs. Rather than providing a 'final' proposal we aim to outline what we believe need to be the 'cornerstones' of any reform approach based on the analysis presented above and practical experience.

Based on the assumption that any approach needs to ensure the greatest inclusiveness, we propose the following three components:

3.1 Abandon the idea that WTO negotiations can only be conducted in all encompassing rounds of negotiations

As indicated above, since the establishment of the WTO, only partial, sector agreements have been concluded. These are the agreements on basic telecommunication services (formally a reference paper), financial services and trade in information technology products, the 2001 WTO Declaration on TRIPS and Public Health, and the agreement on the Aid for Trade mechanism.[20] There are several lessons from these various experiences that can and should guide a possible alternative approach to WTO negotiations. These include the fact that in most cases the initiative for these agreements came from groups of interested countries, the negotiations were open to all WTO Members and the results were applied on a MFN basis, i.e. its benefits were extended to all WTO Members, including those that undertook no commitments and/or decided not to participate

[20] Not included here is the RTA transparency mechanism as it did not concern new financial or market access obligations and rights but a procedural measure.

in the respective negotiations. Another characteristic of each of these agreements mentioned above is that they cover areas not previously regulated by the WTO. The only exception is the agreement on TRIPS and Public Health, which offers another lesson: on matters already regulated by the WTO, negotiations have to be undertaken and agreements concluded among the entire WTO Membership.

It is important to note that 'no rounds' does not mean 'no packages' per se. To the contrary, we assert that the practice to move towards large, all encompassing rounds, supported by the use of the single undertaking, has hurt the system while interlinkages as such cannot and must not be avoided.

3.2 *Recognize that WTO Members are bound by the existing rules and regulations, the* acquis multilateral, *and that these can only be modified and implemented by all Members*

The WTO embodies a set of rights and obligations that bind all its Members – that is, the *acquis multilateral*. It is only natural that any change to this set of rights and obligations be subject to a collective engagement by all Members. This is precisely the value of the declaration on TRIPS and Public Health, which was debated first by the TRIPS Council, then negotiated by all WTO Members, and finally implemented by a declaration adopted during the Doha Ministerial Conference. The TRIPS agreement could only be modified by a collective decision by WTO Members and the same applies *mutatis mutandis* to all core provisions contained in existing WTO agreements.[21]

Thus we consider that all negotiations on changes to existing WTO rules and regulations can only be initiated, conducted and finalized by agreement among all WTO Members. This would preserve the WTO's multilateral character and ensure the inclusiveness of the system, which is of utmost importance for ensuring the efficiency, approval and, above all, legitimacy of the WTO.

3.3 *Develop and adopt some specific procedures to tackle new issues using the 'critical mass' approach linked with an opt-out procedure*

For crafting new rules or negotiating on new issues, negotiations among groups of interested WTO Members should be allowed. However,

[21] See note 13 above.

the launching of these negotiations should be undertaken by all WTO Members – through a Ministerial or General Council decision – and be open to their participation at any moment during the negotiations. The results of the negotiations should be applied on a MFN basis and kept open for later acceptance by WTO Members.

This is not completely different to the 'critical mass' approach to negotiations in its simplest form. Critical mass requirements were not alien to the GATT negotiations; the negotiations of the Tokyo Round codes were arguably conducted on such a basis and during the Uruguay Round the (unsuccessful) zero-to-zero negotiations on a number of issues were based on the same. Some authors have even asserted that 'successful negotiating outcomes in the GATT/WTO system have been based not on a single undertaking approach, but rather on what has come to be called the critical mass approach' (Gallagher and Stoler 2009: 383). However, in order to make the critical mass approach operational and responsive to today's challenges, the approach needs to be designed in a way that does not prejudice the multilateral character of the WTO and that ensures its inclusiveness.

The idea to base the critical mass approach on the representation of a certain share in world trade would not do justice to this. Small countries, for instance, may not have a great share in a particular sector in world trade, yet that sector may account for a significant portion of their Gross Domestic Product (GDP). Furthermore, rules on certain sectors can affect public policies of countries that neither account for considerable world trade or GDP shares in that sector. This includes, for instance, strategies on food security, nutrition, public health and access to water and essential services. It is our view that these legitimate interests need to be fully taken into account when determining the *characteristics* of a critical mass approach, in order to make it workable as well as legitimate (Wolfe 2008; Low 2009). This, however, should be determined prior to the launch of negotiations on a case-by-case basis according to the sector or interests at stake. For instance, tariff reduction negotiations would require a fundamentally different 'critical mass' approach than negotiations on a possible side agreement addressing the relation of climate change and multilateral trading rules. The first would create rights but no obligations for third parties whereas the second may have far-reaching implications for all WTO Members.

It is important that the decision to undertake sector negotiations is taken by consensus by all WTO Members, irrespective of whether they all subsequently actively join in the negotiations, and eventually the agreement. In other words, all countries should participate in the process of determining the requirements for WTO negotiations that might be based on the critical mass approach. Moreover, outlining the appropriate critical mass – i.e. its definition and purpose – should be taken together with other decisions pivotal to the process. This includes the general agenda-setting, decisions on interlinkages and rules for 'opt out' rights.

All these issues are closely linked to a fundamental premise that we suggest for the adoption of a critical mass approach: it would need to provide an 'opt out' option. Moreover, WTO Members must be involved in the decision to launch new negotiations, as well as the deliberations on the procedural rules regarding how the talks are conducted. If they participate initially, they can then at a later stage decide to 'opt out' (Rolland 2010). This differs fundamentally from the classical approach whereby a critical mass of countries can decide to launch negotiations that are thereafter open for other countries to 'opt in' (Warwick Commission 2007; Gallagher and Stoler 2009). Equally importantly, rights established on the basis of a critical mass approach should be applied unconditionally to all WTO Members and incorporated in the multilateral set of rules and regulations as plurilateral agreements in the sense of Article 30 of the Marrakesh Agreement (WTO 1994).

Such a dual approach – the 'opt out' mechanism and the application on MFN basis – would have several advantages and it would help countries overcome numerous procedural difficulties. First, all countries would be entitled to participate in the negotiations if they so chose, thus preserving their multilateral nature. Second, countries may decide to withdraw from the negotiations or not to join the concluded agreements if they considered themselves better off by doing so. The multilateral dimension would be further strengthened by the application of the agreements on a MFN basis, thus avoiding the 'fragmentation' of the system, as happened with the Tokyo Round codes.

Furthermore, every decision on the procedural requirements should take account of the individual position of developing countries. That is, in order to ensure both the success and legitimacy of the process, sufficient procedural special and differential treatment for developing countries, particularly LDCs and small and vulnerable economies, needs to be provided. For instance, the 'opt out' requirements for specific negotiations and countries should be designed according to the country's role in that specific sector, the nature of the concessions concerned, available resources for the implementation process, and other relevant factors.

Finally, the success of this approach would critically depend on the ability of countries to sufficiently account for the sensitivity of certain issues.

Only if Members find a way to finally consider the *real value* of issues and commitments at stake for each country can such an approach be successful for the WTO and, ultimately, its Member countries. The proposals made above can support such a process, yet it will eventually rest with WTO Members to reshape the process by viewing offers and individual engagements in a different light (Rolland 2010).

4 Conclusion

In sum, for future negotiations, including on new issues that are not yet within the purview of the multilateral trading system, we believe that the *critical mass* approach suggested by a number of analysts offers a constructive way out. We do not, however, agree that it is sufficient to assemble countries as a predetermined percentage of trade in the sector concerned for negotiations to proceed, as suggested by some (drawing on the experience of the zero-to-zero negotiations during the Uruguay Round). As mentioned earlier, if this approach is applied too rigidly it risks leaving out countries for which a particular sector is significant in its economy but the country itself is too small to be relevant at the global level. In addition, when new rules are proposed to be negotiated on issues such as, for instance, climate change, it would be extremely difficult to draw the line between countries that are relevant and those that are not.

Thus, rather than quantitative criteria for using the *critical mass* approach, we believe that each negotiation needs to be evaluated by its merits. Consistency with multilateralism would be ensured by: 1) requiring the WTO Ministerial Conference or the General Council to launch the negotiations, thereby implying a collective decision by all WTO Members; 2) establishing criteria on the determination of what constitutes a critical mass on a case-by-case basis, taking into account the political and economic position of individual countries; 3) providing for particular 'opt out' options for WTO Members in negotiation clauses; and 4) applying all agreements on an MFN basis.

A new approach to WTO negotiations is possible and would help to preserve the integrity of the multilateral trading system. It is difficult to see how a continuation of the current deadlocks in the Doha Round or a repetition of the same approach to trade negotiations in the future would be in the interest of WTO countries, particularly developing countries. The successes of the past cannot serve as an excuse to continue with an approach that has clear limitations. Although it would not be practical or feasible to apply this new approach to the Doha negotiations, we think that the matter should be given serious consideration – the sooner the better. Alternative approaches to negotiations will also be of critical importance for the multilateral trading system beyond Doha. Currently, the single undertaking coupled with observable dynamics not only block the Doha talks, but moreover delay the WTO's capacity to tackle new issues, such as climate change, and to better reflect the realities of today's global economy while supporting sustainable development.

References

Consultative Board. 2004. *The Future of the WTO: Addressing Institutional Challenges in the New Millennium*. Geneva: WTO.

Cottier, T. and Elsig, M. 2009. *A Two Tier Approach to WTO Decision Making*. NCCR Working Paper 06 (March) 2009. Bern: National Centres of Competence in Research.

Cottier, T. and Takenoshita, S. 2008. 'Decision-making and the Balance of Powers in WTO Negotiations: Towards Supplementary Weighted Voting', in Griller, S. (ed.) *At the Crossroads: The World Trading System and the Doha Round*. Austria: Springer-Verlag Wein.

Croome, J. 1995. *Reshaping the World Trading System*. Geneva: WTO.

Farless, N. J. 1981. 'GATT and the Tokyo Round: Legal Implications of the New Agreement', *California Western International Law Journal* 11: 302–25.

Gallagher, P. and Stoler, A. 2009. 'Critical Mass as an Alternative Framework for Multilateral Trade Negotiations', *Global Governance* 15: 375–92.

Harbinson, S. 2009. *The Doha Round: 'Death-Defying Agenda' or 'Don't Do it Again'?* ECIPE Working Paper No. 10. Brussels: European Centre for International Political Economy (ECIPE).

Lanoszka, A. 2008. 'The Promises of Multilateralism and the Hazards of "Single Undertaking": The Breakdown of Decision Making within the WTO', *Michigan State Journal of International Law* 16: 654–75.

Low, P. 2009. 'Potential Future Functions of the World Trade Organization', *Global Governance* 15: 327–34.

MacMillan, E. 2010. 'Doha Decision-Making: Implications of the Consensus and Single-Undertaking Principles for Developing Countries', *Commonwealth Trade Hot Topics* 71.

McRae, D. M. and Thomas, J. C. 1983. 'The GATT and Multilateral Treaty Making: The Tokyo Round', *American Journal of International Law* 77: 51–83.

Narlikar, A. and Vickers, B. (eds.) 2009. *Leadership and Change in the Multilateral Trading System*. Dordrecht: Martinus Nijhoff.

Rolland, S. E. 2010. 'Redesigning the Negotiation Process at the WTO', *Journal of International Economic Law* 13: 65–110.

Sampson, G. P. 2005. *The WTO and Sustainable Development*. Tokyo: United Nations University Press.

Stewart, T. P. (ed.) 1993. *The GATT Uruguay Round: A Negotiating History Vol. I Part 1*. Dordrecht: Kluwer Academic Publishers.

VanGrasstek, C. and Sauvé, P. 2006. 'The Consistency of WTO Rules: Can the Single Undertaking be Squared with Viable Geometry?', *Journal of International Economic Law* 9: 837–64.

Warwick Commission. 2007. *The Multilateral Trade Regime: Which Way Forward?*. Coventry: University of Warwick.

Wilkinson, R. 2000. *Multilateralism and the World Trade Organization*. London: Routledge.

2006. *The WTO: Crisis and the Governance of Global Trade*. London: Routledge.

Wolfe, R. 2008. 'Can the Trading System be Governed? Institutional Implications of the WTO's Suspended Animation', in Alexandroff, A. (ed.) *Can the World be Governed? Possibilities for Effective Multilateralism*. Waterloo, Ont.: Wilfrid Laurier University Press, pp. 289–344.

2009. 'The WTO Single Undertaking as Negotiating Technique and Constitutive Metaphor', *Journal of International Economic Law* 12: 835–57.

World Trade Organization (WTO). 1994. *Marrakesh Agreement Establishing the World Trade Organization*. Adopted on 15 April 1994 and entered into force on 1 January 1995. Geneva: WTO.

1999a. *Korea – Definitive Safeguard Measure on Imports of Certain Dairy Products*. WT/DS98/AB/R. 14 December. Geneva: WTO.

1999b. *Argentina – Safeguard Measures on Imports of Footwear*. WT DS121/AB/R. 14 December. Geneva: WTO.

2000. *United States – Safeguard Measures on Imports of Fresh, Chilled or Frozen Lamb Meat from New Zealand and Australia*. WT/DS177/R and WT/DS178/R. 21 December. Geneva: WTO.

2001a. *Doha Ministerial Declaration*. WT/Min(01)/Dec/1. November 20. Geneva: WTO.

2001b. *WTO Declaration on the TRIPS Agreement and Public Health*. WT/MIN(01)/DEC/2. 20 November. Geneva: WTO.

2003. *United States – Definitive Safeguard Measures on Imports of Certain Steel Products*. WT/DS248–59/R. 11 July. Geneva: WTO.

2005. WTO Declaration Hong Kong Ministerial 2005. WT/MIN(05)/DEC. 22 December. Ministerial Conference, Final Session. Geneva: WTO.

2006. *WTO General Council Decision on the Transparency Mechanism for Regional Trade Agreements*. WT/L/671, 18 December 2006. Geneva: WTO.

18

Enhancing developing country participation in global trade governance through South–South coalitions in the WTO

VICENTE PAOLO B. YU III

For much of the post-Second World War era, maintaining global trade governance has largely been the responsibility of developed countries, particularly under the 1947 General Agreement on Tariffs and Trade (GATT 1947). With the launch of the Uruguay Round, developing countries began to play a more active and consistent role in global trade governance. However, developing countries had and continue to struggle with how to ensure that their concerns and interests are reflected in global trade policy outcomes.

Today, the need for collective action by developing countries is greater and more urgent than ever, for several reasons. First, the world economy has an ever greater importance for developing countries' national development, economic policy, environmental space and sovereignty. Second, the development process is increasingly complex and not conducive to sectoral or narrow approaches. Third, developed countries continue to dominate multilateral processes, institutions and outcomes in ways that impact developing countries' political and economic space, as well as their opportunities to use their economic, social and environmental endowments.

This chapter will discuss how developing countries seek to enhance their engagement and effectiveness in global trade governance. In particular, it examines how developing countries have used ad hoc South–South

Vicente Paolo B. Yu III is the Programme Coordinator of the South Centre's Global Governance for Development Programme. The contents of this paper are personal to the author and do not reflect the official views or positions of the South Centre, its Member States or other developing countries. The usual disclaimers apply. This is a short version of Yu 2008. Observations made in this paper draw from the author's experience of observing and assisting developing countries involved in negotiations on WTO issues in Geneva.

coalitions as innovations to ensure their development concerns and trade interests are projected and reflected in World Trade Organization (WTO) negotiations. It argues that the use of such coalitions has resulted in a positive qualitative improvement in the engagement of developing countries in the WTO.

1 Developing countries in the global economy

The economic and geopolitical map of the world is rapidly changing. In this new context, a number of international legal regimes and institutional architectures have an impact on developing countries'[1] development policies and prospects. These include, for instance, the institutional architecture for global trade policy represented by the WTO, and its comprehensive set of binding trade rules. These in turn influence and are influenced by other existing trade-related global institutions such as the UN Conference on Trade and Development (UNCTAD) (Boutros-Ghali 2006).

A second aspect of the current global context is developing countries' growing economic weight in the global economy. Consequently, developing countries have sought to have a greater and more effective influence on global policy discourse and outcomes, as evidenced in, for example, the WTO.

The first decade of the twenty-first century was marked by a significant shift in the global economic environment. Developing countries as a group achieved an average of 5–6 per cent growth between 2002 and 2007, although 'not all countries or segments of the population [were] beneficiaries of this growth' (UNCTAD 2007). Still, some large developing countries, such as China and India, evolved so much that they are now considered 'engines of growth for the world economy'. Further, the South–South share of global trade has been increasing, thereby making inter-South trade a 'veritable locomotive of growth' (UNCTAD 2007: para. 8).[2]

[1] For the purposes of this paper, the phrase 'developed countries' refers to States that are Member States of the Organisation for Economic Co-operation and Development (OECD) or the European Union (EU). 'Developing countries' refers to those States that are members of the Group of 77, and may be used interchangeably with the term 'South'. States that do not fall into either category would be the 'economies in transition', composed mostly of the non-EU Member States of Eastern Europe and the successor States of the former Soviet Union.

[2] South–South trade in goods is estimated to have increased from US$577 billion in 1995 to US$1.7 trillion in 2005, resulting in a rise of the South–South share of global trade in

Developing countries' increasing economic share in the global economy was an integral part of the world's economic recovery between 2001 and 2008, stimulated to a large degree by the rapid growth of developing country exports.[3] The fast-growing economies of China, India and Brazil, among others, helped create new trade opportunities for both developed and developing countries, especially in terms of increased demand in these economies for primary commodities and intermediary inputs (UNCTAD 2006). The relative success of these big developing country economies even in the wake of the global financial crisis of 2008–9 suggests that these countries have – and will continue to – play a major role in shaping the global economic policy environment.

This chapter will examine the continuing challenges facing developing country participation in global economic governance and, more specifically, the WTO. Section 2 explores the pursuit of a development agenda through coalition-building, and proposes suggestions to enhance the effectiveness of South–South coalitions. Finally, the use of coalitions in the global trade governance regime will be evaluated as an essential element in strengthening developing country participation and improving imbalances of economic and political power.

1.1 The continuing challenge of the widening development gap

Within this new context, the development gap (as measured in terms of income inequality) between developed and developing countries continues to widen, even as some developing countries are putting in place sustained, economic growth strategies. The persistence of global income inequality matters not only because it fuels global economic and social instability, but also because it affects how existing global economic governance structures function. As noted in a 2006 UN report: '[E]conomic power and political power tend to be reinforcing. The rules governing global markets are likely to be less advantageous for developing countries, as these countries tend to have less of a voice in the negotiation processes leading to the establishment of those rules' (UN DESA 2006: 2).

goods from 11 per cent in 1995 to 15 per cent in 2005. Overall, the share of developing countries in global trade has increased from 29 per cent in 1996 to 34 per cent in 2006 (UNCTAD 2007: paras. 15–16).

[3] Developing country exports 'nearly tripled between 1996 and 2006, whereas those from the G-7 only rose by some 75 percent. In this area, Asia clearly dominated the picture, with transition economies and Latin America coming in second, and Africa showing exactly the same increase as the G-7.' Asia's imports rose by 170 per cent in the same time, while those of transition economies grew by 150 per cent (UNCTAD 2007: para. 15).

Unfortunately, systemic global economic inequality is likely to persist in the medium and long term. Many developing countries in Africa, South Asia and the Pacific, and Central and South America continue to languish with low levels of economic development and may take decades or even centuries to 'catch up' (UNDP 2005). In fact, with the exception of some countries in Asia, most developing countries are falling behind, rather than catching up to developed countries in terms of income growth (UNCTAD 2007: para. 15).[4] Indeed, Africa's share of the world's income poor is projected to increase. While income levels have steadily risen in developed countries over the past half-century, they have not done so in most developing countries, especially over the past twenty-five years (UN DESA 2006).

1.2 Imbalances in developing country participation in global economic governance

Economic inequities often reflect political inequities and vice versa. The current global trading system reflects both 'historical and structural inequities' with the result that it is 'less advantageous for developing countries' (UNDP 2003). Changing the rules of the trading game to make them more equitable and supportive of developing countries' development interests requires attention to flaws in the institutional architecture for trade, as we see in the terms and implementation of international trade agreements. This endeavour calls for a renewal of how well trade institutions proactively support rules that reflect and promote the needs of the disadvantaged in their constituency.

Cognizant of the difficulties they face in participating effectively and fully in various global institutions, developing countries have long called for governance reforms to boost their representation in such institutions. These demands have been made in the context of, for example, the World Bank and the International Monetary Fund (IMF) vis-à-vis voice and quota reforms; the UN Security Council with respect to its permanent Membership; international financial institutions, such as the Bank of International Settlements (BIS); international standards-setting organizations such as the Codex Alimentarius and the International Standards Organization (ISO); and, in the WTO itself (G24 2003a, 2003b; G77 2010;

[4] See also World Bank (2007: 42) where the World Bank projects that '[t]here would be a further falling behind in sub-Saharan Africa with its modest per capita growth below the high-income average, and Latin America would see little if any convergence on average'.

G77 and NAM 2007). Parallel to these initiatives, developing countries have also been active in establishing mechanisms to improve their cooperation and coordination with each other in these international institutions and to bolster their substantive capacity to participate.

Across international fora, developing countries have also consistently emphasized that development should be the main priority for international economic cooperation and global action. The past few years of robust (although unequal) growth in many developing countries, especially among the big emerging economies, have spurred an increasing sense of confidence, self-reliance and optimism not only in terms of national prospects for development, but also with respect to enhanced South–South cooperation, solidarity and the usefulness of working together in international institutions such as the WTO.

Unfortunately, however, effective developing country participation in and influence over most international economic institutions remains limited. Institutional problems with global governance have been consistently highlighted by developing countries through the collective statements of the G77 and China (G77 2005), especially with respect to the World Bank, IMF (G24 2007; G77 2006a, 2006b; G77 2007), WTO (G77 2005; G77 2006a: para. 14), United Nations (G77 2005: para. 22; G77 2007: para. 8) and with respect to international standards setting (G77 2005: para. 15(ix)).

Often, the problem of unequal levels of participation is deeply rooted in the architecture of these institutions, which in turn reflects the power balance that existed at the time the organizations were created (Barnett and Duvall 2005).[5] While the official mandates of many international organizations stress the need to promote the interests of their weaker Members, their policy orientation and agenda too often favour the interests of more powerful Members over others. Moreover, their decision-making processes often limit the ability of weaker Members to effectively participate in both agenda-setting and decision-making (Barnett and Duvall 2005: 58[6]).

[5] As the authors have pointed out: '[l]ong-standing institutions represent frozen configurations of privilege and bias that can continue to shape the future choices of actors' within that institution. In this article, the authors defined 'power' as 'the production, in and through social relations, of effects that shape the capacities of actors to determine their circumstances and fate' (Barnett and Duvall 2005: 58).

[6] See p. 58, which states that 'the institutional rules that establish a particular focal point also serve to generate unequal leverage or influence in determining collective outcomes ... the institutions that are established to help actors achieve pareto-superior outcomes also create "winners" and "losers", to the extent that the ability to use the institution

2 Developing country participation in the WTO

2.1 *Participation in the WTO*

The WTO is now the most prominent institution in the trade arena in terms of policy setting and implementation. It serves as the framework through which multilateral rules and disciplines are discussed, designed, implemented, enforced and managed, in order to ensure a smooth interface between different national systems. Given the WTO's key role in shaping global trade rules, effective developing country participation in its decision-making is particularly important.

Concerns about the transparency, inclusiveness, participation and efficiency of the WTO's internal mechanisms and decision-making processes have long been on the WTO agenda (WTO 1996, para. 6; WTO 1998, para. 4; WTO 2001: para. 10; Narlikar 2001; Steinberg 2002; South Centre 2003).[7] Here, two major issues have a bearing on developing countries' ability to participate effectively in negotiations: 1) the decision-making process; and 2) the capacity to participate.

The WTO's decision-making processes are important because of the impact they can have on actual outcomes. For example, difficulties in meeting the WTO's requirement for formal consensus as the basis for decision-making has pushed the WTO to engage in and increasingly rely on informal processes for building consensus (UNDP 2003). These processes have in turn tended to reflect, in terms of both process and outcome, the differential power relations among the Members of the organization.

The difficulties developing countries face in the WTO's decision-making processes are well recognized as a core institutional problem for the organization. This concern was succinctly expressed in the following statement from UNCTAD's 2006 Trade and Development Report:

> WTO negotiation procedures have often given the impression of less than full transparency and participation, so that some countries appear to have stronger influence than others. Decisions taken in so-called 'green room' meetings or in other gatherings of a limited number of members are often presented to the entire membership as fait accompli. These procedures

and, accordingly, collective rewards are unevenly distributed. This institutional context, moreover, lingers into the future, thus constraining action in ways that might not have been intended but nevertheless limit choice and shape action.' They went on to state that 'great powers' have the ability 'to establish international institutions and arrangements to further or preserve their interests and positions of advantage into the future, even as they do not directly or fully control those future arrangements'.

7 For an in-depth account of power politics in the WTO, see e.g. Jawara and Kwa 2003.

> may have resulted from well-intentioned attempts to preserve practicality and efficiency in complex decision-making. However, they have prompted concerns about unequal influence and unequal representation of national priorities in processes the results of which affect all participants.
>
> (UNCTAD 2006)

This does not mean, however, that power relations among Members predetermine WTO negotiating outcomes. The ability of developed country Members to agree on the terms of a deal and expect it to be ratified by the rest of the Membership is now fast diminishing as developing country Members, even the smallest among them, are becoming more able and willing, individually and collectively, to assert and defend their own perspectives and opinions (Patel 2007; Jones *et al.* 2010).

In addition to how processes affect the quality of individual developing country participation in WTO decision-making, there is also an issue of capacity. Effective participation is a function of the size and expertise of the Member's delegation in Geneva and the extent to which delegations receive adequate technical and policy support from their capital (South Centre 2003),[8] and can benefit from organized processes for public input and analytical capacity at the national level.

In sum, the WTO's institutional decision-making process, limitations in the capacity and information asymmetries constrain the effectiveness and mode of developing countries in WTO decision-making. Developing countries recognize that negotiating success in the WTO calls for more effective and active participation in the institution's decision-making process. In response, developing countries have worked to strengthen existing groupings with other developing countries and to create new ones. This response has been particularly evident since the launch of the WTO's Doha Round of multilateral trade negotiations in late 2001.

2.2 Governance adaptation by developing countries in the WTO: coalition-building in pursuit of a development agenda

Following the Seattle Ministerial Conference in 1999, and especially the launch of the Doha negotiations in 2001, a fundamental ideational shift

[8] The UN has noted for instance, that '[i]n practice … developing countries find it difficult to follow negotiations or invest in studies that evaluate the implications of the trade reforms for their economies, or they simply have no resources even for sending delegates to the negotiations … the role played by developing countries is limited and changing the rules of the game in their favour is hard, making asymmetries difficult to redress' (UN DESA 2006: 26).

has taken place in how developing countries view the WTO, its role in their respective development processes and their role in its governance. This ideational shift is clearly seen in the development-oriented negotiating positions of developing country coalitions that seek to ensure that scope for development policy choices is adequately reflected in operational terms in the outcomes of negotiations. Such efforts are reflected, for example, in references to 'less than full reciprocity' in the non-agricultural market access (NAMA) negotiations championed by the NAMA-11; 'paragraph 6 flexibilities' championed by the Paragraph 6 countries; 'special products' and the 'special safeguard mechanism' in the agriculture negotiations being promoted by the G33; the more than thirty-five references to 'development' in the Doha Ministerial Declaration itself; least developed Countries (LDC) positions relating to the provision of special and differential treatment; and proposals by the Core Group on Trade Facilitation together with the African Group, ACP and LDC groups to link new disciplines on trade facilitation to binding commitments on technical assistance, capacity-building and special and differential treatment. Simultaneously, developing countries that participate in the Doha Round both directly as individual Members and indirectly as Members of various groups or coalitions. This trend is most evident for major negotiating issues, such as agriculture, non-agricultural market access and trade facilitation (but less so in the services negotiations where the bilateral request-offer format of negotiations offers less scope for group-based negotiations).

Rather than seeing the WTO as simply a forum where trade concessions may be negotiated and exchanged, developing country coalitions view it as a forum in which the development implications of trade concessions should be considered as part and parcel of the philosophical moorings and values underlying the multilateral trading system.[9] Across the major groupings (including the G20, the G33, the NAMA-11, the Core Group on Trade Facilitation, the African Group, the African, Caribbean and Pacific (ACP) Group, the least developed countries (LDC) Group and the small vulnerable economies (SVE) Group) developing countries have

[9] Importantly, in other fora, such as in the context of the UN Conference on Trade and Development (UNCTAD), the UN discussions relating to the New International Economic Order during the late 1960s and early 1970s, and even, to some extent, in the GATT in the run-up to the launch of the Uruguay Round, developing countries stressed that they view development to be their first and overriding priority. However, in terms of actively articulating this view as an element that needs to be reflected at the technical level in multilateral trade negotiations, it has only been since the launch of the Doha negotiations in 2001 that developing countries, through their various coalitions, have sought to do this.

clearly and distinctly linked their negotiating positions to their respective longer-term strategic development objectives and ideas (see Table 18.1).[10] This developing country insistence on seeing the WTO as a trade *and* development institution has been evident in all of the Ministerial Conferences since Seattle in 1999, and was instrumental in ensuring that the mandate of the Doha negotiations was contextualized within a broader development discourse.

For developing countries, working together and forming coalitions is a rational response to the governance challenges they face at the WTO, their individual negotiating constraints and the desire to better advance their development agendas. In theory, strategic use of coalitions should enable developing countries to pool resources, find strength in numbers, be better represented (directly or indirectly) in various negotiating formats and have a vehicle through which they can influence negotiating agenda and outcome (Odell 2000; Narlikar 2003; Bernal *et al.* 2004; Draper and Sally 2005; Wolfe 2006).

In practice, despite the complexity of the issues and the political dynamics that occur in the negotiations, coalitions do indeed help developing countries to increase their power in the WTO and consequently their ability to influence outcomes (Narlikar 2004; Narlikar and Tussie 2004). Learning from their collective negotiating efforts in the Uruguay Round (such as from the activities of the G10 and the Café au Lait group[11]), and their disappointment with the results of negotiations undertaken individually, developing countries now increasingly negotiate in the WTO on the basis of voluntary developing-country-only coalitions, organized along regional, cross-regional and/or issue-based lines.

[10] See G33 (2007a), which states that the group's commitment is to 'secure a more balanced outcome that addresses the development dimensions of the Doha Development Agenda as well as the genuine concerns of small, poor and vulnerable farmers worldwide'. See also G20 *et al.* 2007, which states that 'the WTO negotiations' outcome must be one that delivers on the development dimension of the Round within the shortest period of time possible'. The Joint Statement (G20 *et al.* 2007) reads that 'the full integration of developing countries into the multilateral trading system will only be achieved if the WTO reflects their development needs and concerns'. See also, Small Vulnerable Economies (SVEs) Statement, 18 December 2007, available at www.tradeobservatory.org/library.cfm?refID=101175 [accessed in November 2010].

[11] The original G10 was a group of developing countries (Argentina, Brazil, Cuba, Egypt, India, Nicaragua, Nigeria, Peru, Tanzania and Yugoslavia) that opposed the inclusion of negotiations on trade in services, intellectual property and investment, within the scope of the Uruguay Round. The G10 were often seen to be 'hardliners' in the GATT negotiations. The Café au Lait group was a coalition of developed and developing countries that proposed a compromise text, which eventually became the basis for the GATT Ministerial Declaration that launched the Uruguay Round.

Table 18.1. *South–South coalitions in the WTO as of 2008*

A. Regional groups or coalitions	B. Issue-based coalitions	C. Groups or coalitions based on common characteristics
• African Group • African, Caribbean, Pacific (ACP) Group • Association of South East Asian Nations (ASEAN) • Caribbean Community (CARICOM) • Pacific Islands Forum (PIF)	• Cotton-4 (composed of four cotton-producing African countries pressing for elimination of cotton subsidies in developed countries; formed in 2003) • Core Group in Trade Facilitation (CGTF) (group focused on ensuring special and differential treatment for developing countries in trade facilitation; formed in 2005) • G20 (group of developing countries that push for increased market access and elimination of agricultural subsidies; formed in 2003) • G33 (group of developing countries that push for special products and special safeguard mechanisms for developing countries in agriculture; formed in 2003) • NAMA-11 (group of developing countries that push for special and differential treatment for developing countries in the NAMA negotiations; formed in 2004) • Paragraph 6 NAMA countries (group of developing countries with low bound NAMA tariffs of below 35 per cent pushing to not be required to undertake further NAMA tariff liberalization in the NAMA negotiations; formed in 2005)	• Least developed countries (LDCs) • Landlocked developing countries (LLDCs) • Small vulnerable economies (SVEs)

Existing studies on the different kinds of collective action and coalition-building by developing countries at the WTO (Narlikar 2003; Bernal *et al.* 2004; Draper and Sally 2005; Wolfe 2006) have examined their mechanics, internal dynamics and role in WTO decision-making. These studies concur that developing country coalitions are, per se, becoming an integral and important part of WTO decision-making. They have become the de facto preferred response of developing countries to imbalances in power, processes and participation at the WTO. Coalitions help countries to harness the power of numbers in favour of those who join the group and to improve their negotiating ability and influence by enabling them to take more proactive and defensive negotiating positions. As the ability of developing countries to establish and maintain coalitions and cooperation improves, so too is there strategic use of such coalitions.[12]

Of the 112 WTO Members who are commonly recognized as, or who describe themselves as, 'developing countries', 99 (or, 87.61 per cent) are Members of one or more developing country-only groups or coalitions. While region-based groups (such as the African or ACP groups) or common characteristic-based groups (such as the LDC Group) continue to be major vehicles for coalition-based action by many developing countries, informal issue-based groups or coalitions (such as the G20, the G33 and the NAMA-11) are also becoming a key means for group-based action by developing countries. Of the coalitions in place in late 2009, some sixty-seven developing countries (or 58.77 per cent of developing WTO Members) have joined one or more informal *issue-based* developing country coalitions and sixty-one developing countries are Members of a *regional* group (including thirty-five that are also Members of one or more issue-based groups, and thirty-seven that are Members of one or more *common characteristic* groups). Furthermore, fifty-one developing countries have joined one or more common characteristic groups and nineteen countries have Membership in all three types of developing country groups or coalitions.

[12] See, for instance, former Indian Trade Minister Kamal Nath's response to a question about the role of the developing country negotiating blocs. He explained that 'India's responsibilities as a leader of the G20 bloc of countries did not constrain it in negotiations. Rather, representing the G20 has guaranteed that India pursues a balanced deal because the G20 itself groups together a broad range of offensive and defensive interests across different sectors. The positions taken by the G20 already represent a compromise between the interests of many developing countries.' See www.carnegieendowment.org/events/index.cfm?fa=eventDetail&id=1016&&prog=zgp&proj=zted [accessed in November 2010].

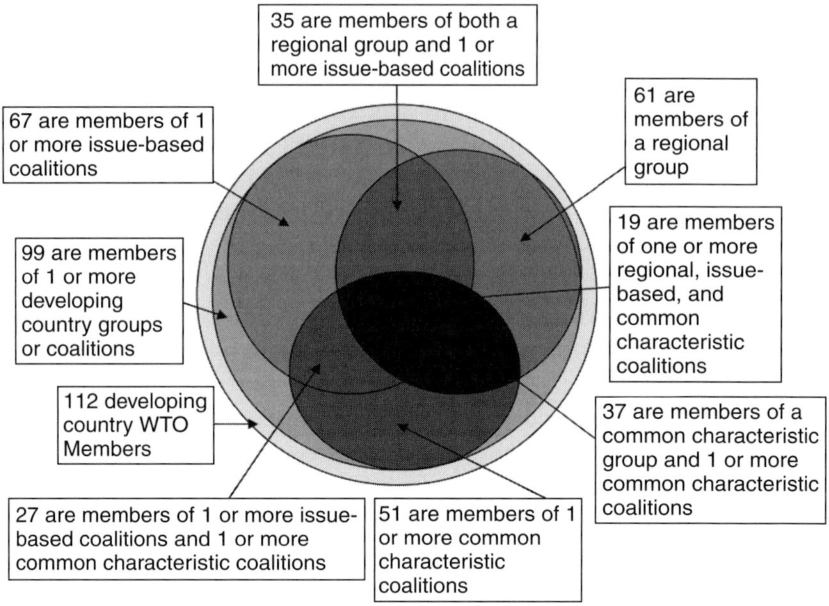

Figure 18.1 Developing countries in the WTO: groups and overlapping Memberships

The use of both formal and informal coalitions by developing countries as vehicles for their participation in the negotiations naturally leads to overlapping Memberships. For example, all Members of the African Group and CARICOM are Members of the ACP Group; all thirty-two LDC WTO Members – except for Bangladesh, Cambodia, Haiti, Maldives and Nepal – are also Members of the ACP Group. The extent of overlapping Memberships among the various developing country coalitions is illustrated above (see Figure 18.1).

Overlapping Memberships can both be a source of weakness and of strength for developing country coalitions. For the most part, however, over the course of the Doha negotiations, developing countries have managed to maximize the strengths that overlapping Memberships give to their respective groups. Countries that are Members of two or more coalitions often play key roles in ensuring that intercoalition dynamics remain positive and mutually complementary to the maximum extent possible. One example concerns the roles that India, Indonesia and the Philippines have played, individually at various times, in ensuring intergroup cohesion between the G20 and the G33.

From observing the work of South–South coalitions in the context of the WTO negotiations in Geneva, coalitions with a diverse and large constituency – whether cross-regional or intergroup – are most actively used to advocate on issues for which a previous general common understanding exists while abstaining from sensitive issue-specific negotiations where consensus is harder to reach. An example is the joint statement made by the 'G110' during the 2003 Cancún WTO Ministerial Conference in which countries insisted on a development content to the Doha negotiations and opposed the inclusion of negotiations on investment, government procurement, competition policy and trade facilitation. The G110 was an ad hoc group composed of virtually all developing countries in the WTO, including all G20 members and all members of the 'G90' group, made up of the African Group, LDC Group and ACP Group. At the same time, several regional coalitions now show greater cohesiveness across virtually all negotiating areas in the WTO, which suggests that similarities among Members of the group (such as those shaped by many – but not all – countries within regional groups) can enhance engagement, coordination and negotiating strength.

Since 2001, developing countries have placed greater emphasis on mechanisms for establishing and maintaining stable and sustainable intra-group coordination, whether through a system of rotating responsibility or by delegating responsibilities to a group member; group cohesiveness has become a key priority in coalition-building.

2.3 *Enhancing the effectiveness of South–South coalitions*

The effectiveness of South–South coalitions in the context of the WTO negotiations depends on many factors. These include, for example, the choice of the type of coalition to use (e.g. formal institutions or ad hoc formations); the effectiveness and continuity of leadership and coordination of individual coalitions; the relationships among coalitions; the role of individuals; the degree of internal group cohesion; the identification of specific communications and research strategies; and the nature of collaboration with external actors, such as the media, non-governmental organizations (NGOs) and other institutions.

The approach developing country groups take to leadership and coordination vary. In the African, ACP and LDC groups, for instance, the task of coordinating the overall actions and positions of members is rotated among group Members who are both willing and able to provide the necessary human, administrative and logistical resources in their missions in

Geneva. Typically, group organization is handled by the ambassador of the country acting as the coordinator, who is then supported by their Geneva-based staff. By selecting 'issue focal points', coordination is enhanced and simplified; here, another Member of the group who is willing and able to take the lead on specific negotiating issues assigns one of their technical-level experts or delegates in the Geneva missions to take charge of suggesting, formulating and organizing group positions and actions. For example, in the trade facilitation negotiations, while the overall African Group coordinator for 2007 was Uganda, the focal point was Morocco. For the LDC Group, the overall coordinator was Bangladesh, while the focal point was Nepal.

An alternative approach used by some coalitions, particularly issue-based groups, is to give specific Members both coordination and leadership functions. In this case, the success of groups relies upon a combination of strong leadership with willing acceptance of such leadership on the basis of perceived commonalities of interest by other group members. For example, the leadership roles of Brazil and India in merging the offensive and defensive agricultural interests of G20 Members into a coherence negotiating position, while proactively countering pressures on Members to leave the group, ensured that the group did not collapse after the 2003 Cancún Ministerial Conference. In the case of the G33 (the Special Products/Special Safeguard Mechanism (SP/SSM) group), leadership by Indonesia and the Philippines in terms of providing intellectual input and technical support continues to be instrumental in keeping the group together.

Developing countries are now more conscious about effective communication and engagement across groups in order to form mutually supportive ad hoc inter-group alliances. For example, the G90 (composed of the African, ACP and LDC groups) has become the vehicle of choice for many developing country Members to express common views, as it can give them numerical strength at critical times of the WTO negotiations. At critical moments, during negotiations, for instance, the G90 has joined with members of the G20, SVEs and G33 to become the G110.

Where developing countries share common and clearly articulated perspectives on *specific* issues, they now form strategic issue-based coalitions. These coalitions are increasingly strategic in articulating both defensive (in the sense of responding to perceived negotiating pressure from other Members) and proactive (in the sense of seeking to advance a specific negotiating agenda) positions in their areas of interest. The G20, for instance, has a clearly defined agenda that contains defensive and proactive elements with respect to the WTO agriculture negotiations (Aggarwal 2005).

Finally, the working relationship between individual delegates has an important impact on developing country coalition-building and cohesion, while the decision to join a particular group – especially an issue-based one – is a political choice made by capital-based decision-makers (e.g. the trade minister). Typically such decisions follow the recommendations of Geneva delegations. In this regard, personal, working relationships and contacts among delegates and missions play an important role in shaping the decision to join a coalition or not. Shared personal perspectives and experiences on certain issues can also significantly affect how well delegations work together.

In many cases, developing country delegates find it easier to relate to each other on a personal and working level than with their developed country counterparts, whether because of common negotiating experiences or shared perspectives. This engenders mutual confidence and positive interpersonal dynamics, which helps to ensure smooth intra-group and intergroup relations. This is not to say that differences do not exist among developing country delegations, or that intra- and intergroup developing country dynamics are free of friction. But resolving or surmounting differences is often made easier for delegates when they come from the same region or when they perceive that they share common interests with respect to certain development issues (such as special and differential treatment).

Developing countries are increasingly aware of the need to ensure that their negotiating positions are supported by arguments grounded in a solid body of research and data analysis, whether undertaken by their Members or provided by external institutions supportive of their positions. This research and analysis, complemented by intra-group information sharing, is the basis for more strategic approaches to negotiations.

Many developing country coalitions now also have a more proactive approach to engaging external actors that can help them promote their agenda, including international organizations, civil society and the media. The G33 and the G20 have become more media-savvy, issuing press releases and making their spokespersons available when needed. Developing country coalitions have also become more open to the support of civil society advocacy and campaigning organizations on specific issues. In addition, technical-level assistance in negotiations and policy research such as that available from developing country intergovernmental organizations, like the South Centre, is used more frequently by coalitions.[13] The Geneva-based missions of regional organizations, like the African Union and the ACP Group of States, also play important roles in supporting the work of developing country groups in WTO negotiations. Such support, from organizing workshops to substantive input on negotiations, is also provided by organizations such as UNCTAD, the United Nations Development Programme (UNDP), the Commonwealth Secretariat and the UN Economic Commission for Africa (UNECA). Civil society organizations with offices in Geneva, such as the International Centre for Trade and Sustainable Development (ICTSD) and Third World Network (TWN), have also become resources, to varying degrees, which developing country groups tap for technical and political input.

While external input and support are important for developing country groups, they are conscious of the need to ensure such assistance is demand-driven and, on the basis of their assessment, consistent with their own negotiating interests and positions. The most useful form of technical policy input and support is iterative and undertaken in close consultation with the group concerned to ensure its needs are met. For example, the use of technical policy input provided by the South Centre to various developing country groups such as the African Group, LDC Group, ACP Group, G33, NAMA-11 and the Core Group of Developing Countries on Trade Facilitation, is completely at the discretion of the group concerned. The recipient may choose to accept, amend, revise or disregard the input provided. For organizations providing such support, a consultative process with the intended group partner is therefore necessary.

In sum, there has been a distinct change in the negotiating dynamics among WTO Members. Since the 1999 Seattle WTO Ministerial took place, developing countries have learned to work together in cohesive groups or coalitions based on their self-identified interests in a much more coordinated manner. The development of more cohesive regional,

[13] The South Centre is the only intergovernmental organization composed solely of developing countries that provides policy research and analysis and technical negotiating support to developing countries in, inter alia, the WTO. It also supports developing country groups and coalitions in other international fora such as the World Intellectual Property Organization (WIPO) and UNCTAD. In the WTO negotiations, the South Centre has provided direct negotiating assistance and technical policy research and support to the African Group, ACP Group, LDC Group, SVEs, Paragraph 6 NAMA Group, NAMA-11, G33 and the Core Group on Trade Facilitation.

cross-regional, common characteristic and issue-based groupings of developing countries in the run-up to the 2003 Cancún Ministerial Conference was followed by more consistent efforts to work in a more coordinated fashion both internally and with other groups. This trend is clearly reflected in a 2007 joint statement by the various major developing country-only groups in the WTO as follows:

> The Ministers and Senior Officials of the G20 and the coordinators of the G33, the NAMA-11, the ACP Group, the Least Developed Countries (LDCs), the African Group, the Small, Vulnerable Economies (SVEs) and the Cotton-4 met in Geneva on 15 November 2007 to review the situation in the Doha Round and to discuss ways to enhance coordination among developing country groups on issues of mutual interest.
>
> They welcomed the engagement and solidarity demonstrated by developing country groups. They noted that developing-country coordination and contribution increased the efficiency and legitimacy of the negotiating process. Developing countries have shown an unprecedented level of participation in this Round. They are ready to continue playing an active role in the WTO commensurate with the growing importance of developing countries in international trade.
>
> The Groups pledged to maintain the unity and cooperation among developing country groups. They reasserted their readiness to engage with other WTO Members with a view to achieving an outcome acceptable to all in the shortest possible time.[14]

The result of this emphasis on collective action has been a marked improvement in the extent of overall developing country participation in, and influence on, WTO negotiations. This influence is demonstrated by the fact that developing country issues now form part of the core WTO negotiating agenda. Examples include the emphasis on the elimination of agricultural subsidies in the agriculture negotiations (as a result of pressure from the G20); the presence on the negotiating agenda of proposals regarding developing country special products and a special safeguard mechanism (as a result of pressure from the G33); and the reflection of the principle of special and differential treatment in the NAMA and trade facilitation negotiations (as a result of pressure from the NAMA-11 and the Core Group of Developing Countries on Trade Facilitation).

[14] See the Joint Statement of the G-20, the G-33, the NAMA-11, the ACP Group, the LDCs, the African Group, the Small, Vulnerable Economies (SVEs), and the Cotton-4, 15 November 2007. Available at www.tradeobservatory.org/library.cfm?refID=100810 [accessed in November 2010].

3 Conclusion: developing country coalitions as an essential component in global trade governance

The way developing countries now participate in the governance of the WTO reflects their adaptation to perceived and real imbalances of economic and political power, both in terms of the bigger international economic system, as well as with respect to the organization's existing institutional mechanisms for decision-making.

The experiences of developing countries in the WTO to date shows that in the face of power imbalances, further enhancing developing country participation and influence in global trade policy-making and governance will require:

- *Clear policy issue and agenda articulation.* Strong group action can only take place on the basis of a perception among group Members that share a common agenda they are willing to promote. Prominence of issue-based developing country coalitions, and the success of developing country efforts to work together across different group issues to pursue common development-oriented negotiation outcomes clearly illustrate this.

An important trigger for such collective group action in the WTO by developing countries has been a generally shared perception of the imbalances that exist in the WTO's legal and institutional framework. Such mutual understanding is an essential foundation for group action, and is especially important given the need to continuously update, fine-tune and articulate a clear policy framework, a set of well-articulated policy objectives and a clearly defined action agenda. This shared foundation is also vital for overcoming the intellectual and conceptual dependence vis-à-vis the North in which the developing countries have been entrapped. Looking ahead, the South faces the challenge of 'intellectual liberation': a challenge that has to be tackled collectively by developing countries in a serious, systematic and sustained effort.

- *Effective internal coordination and leadership.* Institutionalized coordination and group leadership mechanisms are vital to the long-term survival and strength of coalitions. Recognition of this point has spurred all developing country groups to establish internal coordination mechanisms that allow them to designate individual Members to be the focal point or lead for the group with respect to specific issues, to report back to the group and to suggest the actions that need to be taken. This is particularly visible in the regional or cross-regional coalitions in the WTO such as the African Group, the ACP Group and the LDC Group.

Leadership patterns have been more complex. Developing country groups often tend to not have a single identified 'leader'. Instead, 'leadership' is often linked to the internal coordination mechanism of each group, especially for the regional and cross-regional coalitions. Issue-based groups, on the other hand, tend to have de facto recognized 'leaders' – i.e. those countries that are most active and provide significant input and influence into internal group dynamics, such as Brazil and India for the G20, Indonesia for the G33 and South Africa for NAMA-11.

- *Building effective working relationships.* Given the role that human resource constraints play in determining the extent of developing country participation, the working relationships that individual delegates have with other developing country delegates within groups are important factors in ensuring smooth intra- and intergroup coordination and action. Since most of the WTO's developing country groups are ad hoc formations, the establishment of such working relationships – which in turn often depend on the personal skills of the delegates concerned – provide the basis for internal group trust and coordination.
- *Institutional support.* Full and continuous institutional support of the highest professional quality is essential for any multilateral endeavour, especially in a multilateral setting such as the WTO, where developing countries are confronted by a complex, overlapping and interrelated agenda. Creating, financing, staffing and operating such institutional support remains one of the weakest links in the effort to strengthen collective action by developing countries. Institutional support for group action at the WTO is very much dependent on the willingness and resources of individual countries – especially those coordinating the groups – and a few organizations (such as the South Centre). Developing country institutions such as the South Centre, the African Union and the ACP Group (all of which have small offices in Geneva) try to fill the gap in institutional support to developing country groups in the WTO, but are themselves hampered by a lack of sufficient human and financial resources.

The experience of developing countries, individually and collectively, confirms that they need to be consistent and united in promoting their views and interests. To succeed in that effort, developing countries need to join forces and pursue group action in most domains of the development agenda, including trade.

Bolstered by the important strides in development and economic growth achieved by China, India and Brazil, the collective economic weight that the South can mobilize today is significant and should be put to good use, both for launching major policy initiatives, as well as to counter the systemic economic and political imbalances in global trade policy and trade governance that favour developed countries.

References

Aggarwal, R. 2005. 'Dynamics of Agriculture Negotiations in the World Trade Organization', *Journal of World Trade* 39(4): 741–61.

Barnett, M. and Duvall, R. 2005. 'Power in International Politics', *International Organization* 59(1): 39–75.

Bernal, L., Kaukab, R., Musungu, S. and Yu, V. 2004. *South–South Cooperation in the Multilateral Trading System: Cancún and Beyond*. South Centre TRADE Working Paper No. 21, May. Geneva: South Centre.

Boutros-Ghali, B. 2006. *Reinventing UNCTAD*. South Centre Research Paper 7, Geneva: South Centre.

Draper, P. and Sally, R. 2005. *Developing-Country Coalitions in Multilateral Trade Negotiations. SAIIA Trade Report No. 8*. South African Institute of International Affairs.

Group of 20 (G20) *et al.*, 2007. The Joint Statement of the G-20, the G-33, the NAMA-11, the ACP Group, the LDCs, the African Group, the Small, Vulnerable Economies (SVEs), and the Cotton-4, 15 November. www.tradeobservatory.org/library.cfm?refID=100810 [Accessed in November 2010].

Group of 24 (G24). 2003a. *Reforming the Governance of the IMF*. G24 Briefing Paper No. 1, March. www.g24.org/rgover.pdf [Accessed in November 2010].

2003b. *Adjustment of European Quotas to Enhance the Voice and Participation of Developing and Transition Countries*. G24 Briefing Paper No. 2, August. www.g24.org/adjeuq.pdf [Accessed in November 2010].

2007. Communiqué from April 2007. www.imf.org/external/np/cm/2007/041307.htm [Accessed in November 2010].

Group of 33 (G33). 2007a. Ministerial/Senior Officials Coordination Meeting Statement, 15 November. www.tradeobservatory.org/library.cfm?refID=100807 [Accessed in November 2010].

2007b. Statement on 17 December. www.tradeobservatory.org/library.cfm?refID=101176 [Accessed in November 2010].

Group of 77 (G77). 2005. Doha Declaration of the Second South Summit. Document No. G77/SS/2005/1, 15 June. www.g77.org/southsummit2/doc/Doha%20Declaration(English).pdf [Accessed in November 2010].

2006a. Special Ministerial Statement, May. www.g77.org/Speeches/052906.htm [Accessed in November 2010].

2006b. Ministerial Statement, September. www.g77.org/ammfa/30/conclusion.html [Accessed in November 2010].

2007. Final Communiqué of the 41st Meeting of the Chairmen/ Coordinators of the G77 Chapters. www.g77.org/chmeeting/0702/communique.php [Accessed in November 2010].

2010. Position Paper of the Group of 77 and China on the Reform of the International Financial and Economic System. 26 May. www.un.org/esa/ffd/events/2010GAWGFC/6/Stmt_G77.pdf [Accessed in November 2010].

Group of 77 (G77) and Non-Aligned Movement (NAM). 2007. *Joint G77-NAM Letter on UN Coherence on 28 March 2007.* www.g77.org/statement/getstatement.php?id=070913 [Accessed in November 2010].

Jawara, F. and Kwa, A. 2003. *Behind the Scenes at the WTO: The Real World of International Trade Negotiations.* London: Zed Books.

Jones, E., Deere Birkbeck, C. and Woods, N. 2010. *Manoeuvring at the Margins: Constraints Faced by Small States in International Trade Negotiations.* London: Commonwealth Secretariat.

Narlikar, A. 2001. *WTO Decision-Making and Developing Countries.* TRADE Working Paper No. 11. Geneva: South Centre.

2003. *International Trade and Developing Countries: Coalitions in the GATT and WTO.* London: Routledge.

2004. *International Trade and Developing Countries: Coalitions in the GATT and WTO.* London: Routledge.

Narlikar, A. and Tussie, D. 2004. 'The G-20 at the Cancún Ministerial: Developing Countries and their Evolving Coalitions at the WTO', *The World Economy* 27(7): 947–66.

Odell, J. 2000. *Negotiating the World Economy.* Ithaca and London: Cornell University Press.

Patel, M. 2007. *New Faces in the Green Room: Developing Country Coalitions and Decision-Making in the WTO.* Oxford University College, GEG Working Paper 2007/33, September.

South Centre. 2003. *Institutional Governance and Decision-Making Processes in the WTO* (SC/TADP/AN/IG/7). Geneva: South Centre.

2004. *The Group of 77 at Forty: Championing Multilateralism, A Democratic and Equitable World Order, South–South Cooperation, and Development.* Geneva: South Centre.

Steinberg, R. 2002. 'In the Shadow of Law or Power? Consensus-Based Bargaining and Outcomes in the GATT/WTO', *International Organization* 56(2): 339–74.

UNCTAD. 2006. *Trade and Development Report 2006: Global Partnership and National Policies for Development.* Geneva: UNCTAD.

2007. *Report of the Secretary-General of UNCTAD to UNCTAD XII – Globalization for Development: Opportunities and Challenges*. TD/413. Geneva: UNCTAD.

UN DESA. 2006. *World Economic and Social Survey 2006: Diverging Growth and Development*. New York: UN DESA.

UNDP. 2003. *Making Global Trade Work for People*. New York: UNDP.

2005. *Human Development Report 2005: International Cooperation at a Crossroads – Aid, Trade and Security in an Unequal World*. New York: UNDP.

Walters, R. 1971. 'International Organization and Political Communications: The Use of UNCTAD by Less Developed Countries', *International Organization* 25(4): 818–35.

Wolfe, R. 2006. *New Groups in the WTO Agricultural Trade Negotiations: Power, Learning and Institutional Design*. CATPRN Commissioned Paper CP 2006–2. www.uoguelph.ca/catprn/PDF-CP/commissioned_paper_2006-2.pdf [Accessed in November 2010].

World Bank. 2007. *Global Economic Prospects: Managing the Next Wave of Globalisation*. Washington: The World Bank.

World Trade Organization (WTO). 1996. *Singapore Ministerial Declaration*. WT/MIN(96)/DEC. 18 December. Geneva: WTO.

1998. *Geneva Ministerial Declaration*. WT/MIN(98)/DEC. 20 May. Geneva: WTO.

2001. *Doha Ministerial Declaration*. WT/MIN/01/. 20 November. Geneva: WTO.

Yu, V. 2008. *Unity in Diversity: Governance Adaptation in Multilateral Trade Institutions through South–South Coalition-Building*. South Centre Research Paper No. 17, July 2008. www.southcentre.org/index.php?option=com_content&task=view&id=682&Itemid=67 [Accessed in November 2010].

19

Inclusive trade governance: participation of stakeholders from the national to the multilateral level

RASHID S. KAUKAB

National trade policy is an important determinant of the production and trade structure of any country. In turn, national trade policy development and implementation take place within the context of international trade-related agreements (i.e. bilateral, regional and multilateral). The scope of these agreements, and hence trade policy, nowadays goes far beyond issues of customs duties at the border. As trade agreements cover an increasing diversity of 'behind the border' aspects of trade regulation, they now impact the economic choices available to all groups of producers and consumers in the country, whether directly engaged in international trade or not. This chapter argues that it is critically important that the instruments of trade governance – national trade policy as well as international trade agreements – are developed through an inclusive process that ensures the participation of all relevant stakeholders.

The analysis presented in this chapter draws on the author's work on trade-related issues over fifteen years. This experience has encompassed working with a range of stakeholders from developing countries to build their capacity for development-oriented national trade policy-making

Rashid S. Kaukab is Deputy Director and Research Coordinator, CUTS Geneva Resource Centre, Geneva, Switzerland. This paper has been written in a personal capacity and does not reflect the views of CUTS. The author is grateful to E. B. Manyara (Principal Counsellor Trade, Permanent Mission of Kenya to the UN and Other International Organizations in Geneva, Switzerland) and Mr Vicente Paulo B. Yu III, at the South Centre, for their useful comments on an earlier draft of the paper, and to Dr Carolyn Deere Birkbeck for her guidance, support and useful suggestions throughout the process. The author's special thanks are also due to Carolyn's wonderful team of assistants for their help in editing the draft and to his daughter Faiza Kaukab for providing research assistance. However, he remains solely responsible for any remaining omissions and mistakes.

as well as more effective participation in the World Trade Organization (WTO) negotiations.

The need for the inclusiveness of trade governance processes can be argued on several grounds.[1] First, it supports the process of democratization and improves accountability of governments to their citizens. Inclusiveness also contributes to the 'legitimization' and public acceptance of the outcomes of trade policy. In addition, inclusiveness can lead to better policies and outcomes that are more aligned with national development objectives (Ndulu 2001: 155).[2]

Elaborating on a comprehensive definition of inclusiveness is beyond the scope of this chapter: it generally follows the approach developed by Koening-Archibugi and Zürn (Koening-Archibugi and Zürn 2006). Accordingly, inclusiveness here refers to the extent to which the actors affected by the resulting policies and rules share decision-making power. This definition has two dimensions: access and influence. What share of the actors bound by a rule, or directly affected by a policy, participate actively in determining its content? And, how equally is influence distributed among participants? The focus of this chapter is on the access dimension while fully acknowledging the importance of influence.

The chapter starts with a categorization and description of stakeholders in trade governance in section 1. Section 2 takes a closer look at evidence regarding the participation of stakeholders in trade policy-making at the national level in a number of developing countries. This section also includes an analytical table juxtaposing various groups of stakeholders against their participation and influence in trade-related consultations and decision-making. Section 3 is devoted to the examination of stakeholder participation at the multilateral level of trade governance; that is, at the WTO. Finally, section 4 offers some recommendations to improve the inclusiveness of trade governance. The evidence and analysis provided in the chapter focus exclusively on developing countries, particularly African ones.

[1] There is a growing body of literature on this issue indicating the interest of both academics and practitioners. This interest is often based on a realization that inclusive processes can create national ownership of trade policy measures. Such an ownership is important to facilitate the required adjustments often inherent in trade policy measures. This literature also looks at the constraints to inclusiveness as well as possible ways to overcome these constraints. See, for example, Gallagher *et al.* (2005); Halle and Wolfe (2007); Deere Birkbeck and Meléndez-Ortiz (2009); and Saner (2010).

[2] 'Better performance, where inclusiveness in national policy choice is applied, is corroborated by evidence of differential growth performance across political regimes in Africa exercising different degrees of participation in decision-making at the macro level and restraint against predatory behaviour' (Ndulu 2001: 155).

1 Stakeholders in trade governance: categorizations

Given the broad remit and impact of trade governance instruments, the group of relevant stakeholders is broad. From a management perspective, the International Organization for Standardization (ISO) offers a useful functional categorization of all stakeholders, which is commonly used in analysis of stakeholder engagement at both the national and international levels (ISO 2005). This categorization includes consumers, government, industry, labour and non-governmental organizations (NGOs), among others, and the categories are largely based on the specific interests of the various groups of stakeholders. However, in relation to trade governance, this categorization needs further disaggregation. First, government stakeholders can be divided into two categories, i.e. executive and parliament. This distinction is important in developing countries where international negotiations and approval of international trade agreements, as well as formulation of trade policy, are generally constitutionally defined as the prerogative of the executive branch. Parliaments only come into the picture when these agreements and related policies require budgetary approvals and/or legislative actions. Second, executive stakeholders of the government can also be viewed as consisting of at least two distinct groups: the ministry responsible for trade policy and trade negotiations, and other line ministries and government agencies responsible for issues that have trade dimensions (e.g. ministries of agriculture, environment, science and technology, revenue authorities, bureaus of standards, etc). This distinction is relevant because ministries responsible for trade generally view trade policy and negotiations from a purely trade promotion angle. Yet, at the same time, national trade policies and negotiating positions can substantially impact all sectors of the economy whether directly related to trade or not. By contrast, other government ministries and agencies often treat trade and trade policies as an exogenous though important issue relative to their primary mandates. Moreover, they also have responsibility for the implementation of the relevant parts of trade policy and agreements, even if they are not often involved in their formulation.

Third, the industry category needs to distinguish between larger industrial enterprises and the small and medium-sized enterprises (SMEs), as well as between national- or foreign-owned industry (i.e. multinational corporations). These distinctions are important as the interests and concerns of larger and smaller enterprises can be quite different. In addition, the interests of a foreign-owned enterprise or a multinational corporation (MNC) may be based on its global business strategy and hence different from a nationally owned enterprise.

Fourth, the ISO categorization, like most stakeholder categorizations, does not include those who are not organized in some way. Unorganized stakeholders are either lumped together in the category of 'others' or assumed to be represented by other more organized groups of stakeholders, for example NGOs. This can be a critical gap as it most often leaves out significant groups such as farmers and the informal sector, which are neither well organized nor can be fully represented by other groups of stakeholders.

Finally, the media should be considered an additional category of stakeholder. The media often plays an important role in informing public opinion on trade governance issues and also in shaping, to some extent, national trade policy and positions in international trade negotiations.

Accordingly, a more comprehensive functional categorization of stakeholders for trade governance should at minimum include the government ministry responsible for trade, other government ministries and agencies, parliaments, large industry, SMEs, MNCs, labour, consumers, farmers, NGOs, the informal sector and media.

Broad groups of stakeholders can also be categorized in at least two thematic ways. For example, stakeholders can be categorized according to the degree of impact the policy has on them. This leads to five broad categories of stakeholders: personally impacted, administratively impacted, generally concerned, process concerned and the remainder of the public (Love *et al.* 2008). In addition, stakeholders can also be categorized in terms of their level of involvement in the decision-making process. Here, it is useful to divide them into four broad categories: those involved only as informants (i.e. as sources of information to the government), those consulted, those directly involved in decision-making and those involved as co-actors (Dick 1997).

All these groups of stakeholders are recognized to varying degrees in developing countries and may have some opportunity to participate in the consultative process related to trade governance. Drawing on this analytical foundation, the following section reviews the evidence on trade-related consultative processes in a range of developing countries.

2 Stakeholder participation at the national level

For almost all developing countries, the process of stakeholder participation in trade policy discussion has evolved considerably in the last two decades. While governments of developing countries often held consultations with affected/interested industries on specific trade policy measures, these were generally on an ad hoc basis – that is, without any regular, formal mechanism. The usual practice was to invite comments from, and hold informal meetings with, the umbrella association of relevant industry/exporters when a specific trade policy measure affecting that industry/exporters was being initiated. Alternatively, the industry/exporters' associations would also approach the government to lobby for the adoption of specific trade policy measures in their favour.

Most developing country governments have now however established formal consultative fora at the national level to consult multiple groups of stakeholders including private sector, civil society organizations, relevant government ministries and agencies on a broad range of issues in the area of trade.[3] Several developments have contributed to this evolution. The establishment of the WTO on 1 January 1995, and the reach and impact of WTO agreements and negotiations, generated public interest and demand for inclusiveness through trade-related consultations. In addition, the move towards greater consultation was boosted by the strengthening of democratic processes in many countries that emerged from dictatorships and quasi-dictatorships, proliferation of free trade agreements and interest of donors in funding and supporting inclusive consultations on trade policy issues in developing countries (CUTS 2009a).

These consultative fora are the primary means for stakeholders to provide formal inputs on trade-related issues. Data compiled from a recent study of such consultative fora in five African countries (Kenya, Malawi, Tanzania, Uganda and Zambia) is presented in Table 19.1 (CUTS 2009b).

Several conclusions can be drawn from Table 19.1. First and most important, all of the formal consultative fora presented lack a legal mandate to take decisions and make binding recommendations to government. They can only offer suggestions and advice that the government may or may not accept. That said, it was expected that the government would normally follow the advice if the relevant consultative forum unanimously proposed a course of action. Moreover, and since such fora are formal and expected to function on a regular basis, one could expect that a consistent disregard by the government of the views expressed by

[3] For examples of these fora, see the Diagnostic Trade Integration Studies (DTIS) in respect of LDCs developed under the Integrated Framework (IF), in available at www.enhancedif.org/ [accessed in November 2010], the Trade Policy Review (TPR) reports by the WTO Secretariat and TPR reports by developing country governments at www.wto.org/english/tratop_e/tpr_e/tp_rep_e.htm#bycountry [accessed in November 2010]. These reports provide information about the consultative processes, including the functioning of formal consultative mechanisms in LDCs and other developing countries.

Table 19.1. *Multi-stakeholder trade-related consultative fora in five African countries*

Consultative forum	Mandate	Composition	Role
National Committee on the WTO (NCWTO), Kenya	Convened by Ministry of Trade (MoT) to develop national positions on WTO issues	Representatives of other government ministries, private sector, NGOs and research institutions and academia	Advisory
National Development and Trade Policy Forum (NDTPF), Kenya	Convened by Ministry of Trade (MoT) to facilitate Kenyan preparations for EPA negotiations with the EU	Representatives of other government ministries, private sector, NGOs and research institutions and academia	Advisory (also disseminates information related to EPA)
National Working Group on Trade Policy (NWGTP), Malawi	Convened by Ministry of Industry, Trade, and Private Sector Development (MITPSD) to advise the government on trade-related issues, including regulatory provisions and policy reform	Representatives of other government ministries, private sector, NGOs and research institutions	Advisory
Malawi National Development and Trade Policy Forum (MNDTPF)	Convened by Ministry of Industry, Trade, and Private Sector Development (MITPSD) to organize and coordinate Malawi participation in EPA negotiations	Representatives of other government ministries, private sector, NGOs and research institutions	Advisory

National EPA Technical Team (NETT), Tanzania	Convened by Ministry of Industry, Trade and Marketing (MITM) to discuss and coordinate Tanzanian participation in EPA negotiations	Representatives of eighteen public sector organizations, two private sector umbrella organizations, one NGO umbrella organization, and one research institution	Advisory
Inter-Institutional Trade Committee (IITC), Uganda	Convened by the Ministry of Trade, Tourism and Industry (MTTI) to ensure interministerial coordination and consultation with stakeholders on trade-related issues	Fifty-five representatives of other government ministries, private sector, NGOs and research institutions	Advisory
National Development and Trade Policy Forum (NDTPF), Uganda	Convened by the Ministry of Trade, Tourism and Industry (MTTI) to discuss and coordinate Ugandan participation in EPA negotiations	Representatives of other government ministries, private sector, NGOs and research institutions	Advisory
National Working Group on Trade (NWGT), Zambia	Established by Ministry of Commerce, Trade and Industry (MTTI) to consult stakeholders on all trade issues	Headed by a private sector representative and includes representatives of other government ministries, private sector and NGOs	Advisory
Trade Expansion Working Group (TEWG), Zambia	Established by Ministry of Commerce, Trade and Industry (MTTI) to provide a platform for public–private sector consultations on export-related issues	Headed by a private sector representative and includes representatives of only public and private sectors	Advisory

Source: Compiled by author based on information in CUTS 2009a.

the majority of stakeholders would stir objections and hence be raised in subsequent meetings, creating pressure on the government to show some accommodation. Unfortunately, this has not been the case as evidenced during a recent study of the functioning of these consultative fora in five African countries (CUTS 2009a). Interviews with non-state stakeholders for this study showed a general dissatisfaction among them as the government had not often taken their suggestions into account. This has led to a decreased interest among some non-state stakeholders in regular participation in the formal consultative fora (CUTS 2009a). Second, several important stakeholders are not included in the consultative fora. For example, parliamentarians, farmers, the informal sector and media are generally absent. Similarly, representation of SMEs, consumers and labour is not assured in all the consultative fora. It is often expected that other stakeholders will represent the interests of groups of stakeholders that are not directly represented. For example, industry associations are assumed to represent the SMEs and the informal sector; and NGOs to represent consumers, farmers and labour. This can be a false assumption. For example, many NGOs work only in capitals and other big cities of the country and have only limited direct connection with farmers. Similarly, industry umbrella associations usually only represent the interests of their members and are often considered to tilt more towards the interests of their bigger members. Third, all the countries covered in Table 19.1 have dedicated consultative fora for consultations on Economic Partnership Agreement (EPA) negotiations. However, these fora were established as one of the requirements of EPA negotiations as agreed between the European Union (EU) and African, Caribbean and Pacific (ACP) countries and the EU provided funding support for the establishment and initial functioning of these fora.[4]

Formal consultative fora are not the only vehicles for providing input into national trade governance. Anecdotal evidence abounds regarding the role that informal processes – ranging from breakfast meetings with policy-makers to industry gala dinners – can play in the formulation of specific trade policy measures. In addition, while parliamentarians are not part of the formal consultative fora, they can still attempt to influence national trade governance by holding parliamentary hearings: every developing country parliament has a parliamentary committee

[4] While EPA negotiations are still under way between most ACP countries and the EU, the funding for such consultative efforts is dwindling, putting the continued functioning of these fora into question.

that deals with trade either exclusively or as part of a larger portfolio that also includes industry, finance, economic affairs, etc.

The following examples illustrate how the various aspects of access and influence of different groups of stakeholders play out on the ground.

Malawi is negotiating an EPA with the EU. However, it is among those countries that refused to initial an EPA with the EU at the end of 2007 – a rather bold decision for a small least developed country (LDC).[5] The author's interviews with several NGO and government representatives in Malawi revealed interesting and rather different views regarding the basis for this decision by the government. On the one hand, the NGOs claimed that their research-based advocacy and coordinated lobbying successfully influenced the decision. On the other hand, government officials asserted that the decision was made based on a careful analysis of the pros and cons of the decision and that the NGO campaign did not play a role. The truth is perhaps somewhere in between: this was a case where NGO research and advocacy supported and strengthened governmental analysis, leading to a decision where all could claim credit.

Other anecdotes from Uganda and Kenya described quite the opposite.[6] NGOs in both countries complained that their governments had made up their minds in favour of the EPA with the EU and did not listen to their well-argued case against the EPAs.[7] Some Kenyan NGOs even alleged that due to their consistent and vocal opposition to the EPA, they were excluded from the formal consultative fora for some time. When contacted by the author, the relevant government officials contested this assertion and emphasized that the NGOs concerned did not attend some consultations despite being invited.

The political situation in Malawi in 2007–8 had an interesting impact on the involvement of parliamentarians in national trade governance. Due

[5] The initial deadline to conclude EPA negotiations was the end of 2007, i.e. two years after the scheduled completion of the WTO Doha Round negotiations. Since EPA negotiations were far from completion at that time, the EU insisted that the available draft agreements could be initialled by the parties at the end of 2007 while continuing the negotiations to complete the agreements. The EU also made the continuation of ACP countries' preferential access to its market contingent upon this initialling. While some ACP countries agreed, several others refused as they felt that initialling an incomplete agreement would put them in a straightjacket and give an unfair negotiating advantage to the EU.

[6] Author's interviews with NGOs in Kenya and Uganda in October 2008.

[7] These NGOs also pointed out that since they are critical towards the neo-liberal economic policies, they are often marginalized by their governments who are following such policies on the advice of the World Bank/IMF/WTO as well as other key bilateral donors.

to a particular political development (i.e. midway through his term, the elected President left his party, which had the majority in parliament, and formed another political party with minority status in the parliament) opposing parties controlled the parliament and the executive during this time. Being in the majority, the opposition members of parliament also controlled the parliamentary subcommittee dealing with trade. This was the time when this subcommittee became more active through organizing regular hearings on trade issues where government officials were regularly interrogated on national trade policy and international trade negotiations.

Finally, there are also instances where the interests of a single enterprise had a large influence on governmental decisions. In Zambia, for example, Zambia Sugar Ilovo reportedly plays a key role in the Sugar Protocol negotiations with the EU.[8]

Table 19.2 on the next page presents a general picture of the role of various stakeholders at the national level under the two thematic categorizations described in section 1.

This analysis of inclusiveness of trade governance at the national level, while very generalized, yields several important findings. First, almost all stakeholders at the national level play some role in trade governance, but their role is limited to that of informing government either directly or through indirect means such as media, survey and opinion polls. Second, many stakeholders are consulted on issues related to trade policy and trade negotiations, either through formal consultative fora, parliamentary hearings or more informal means. Third, actual decision-making on trade rests mostly in the domain of the executive branch of the government albeit with some role played by large, directly affected enterprises. Fourth, implementation of trade policy lies in the hands of the executive branch of government, with the parliament playing a role where budgetary/legislative action is required.

The space for national trade policy-making and implementation is determined by legal commitments under international trade agreements, such as those undertaken by Members of the WTO. The next section is devoted to a brief discussion of the inclusiveness of the WTO for the broad spectrum of national stakeholders described above.

[8] The Sugar Protocol has been an important component of ACP countries' preferential market access to the EU under Lomé (see http://ec.europa.eu/development/geographical/lomegen_en.cfm) and Cotonou Conventions (see http://ec.europa.eu/development/geographical/cotonouintro_en.cfm) [accessed in November 2010].

Table 19.2. *Stakeholder categorization and participation at the national level*

	Involved only as informants	Consulted	Involved in decision-making	Co-actors in implementation
Directly impacted	Industry, Ministry responsible for trade, other government ministries/ agencies, SMEs, farmers, labour, consumers	Industry, other government ministries/ agencies, SMEs, farmers, labour, consumers	Ministry responsible for trade, other government ministries/agencies, selected enterprises	Ministry responsible for trade, other government ministries/agencies, selected enterprises
Administratively impacted	Other government ministries/ agencies, industry, SMEs, labour, farmers	Other government ministries/ agencies, industry, SMEs, labour, farmers	Ministry responsible for trade, other government ministries/agencies	Ministry responsible for trade, other government ministries/agencies
Generally concerned	Parliamentarians, NGOs, media	Parliamentarians, NGOs	None	Parliamentarians (where budgetary/ legislative action is required)
Process concerned	Parliamentarians, NGOs, media	Parliamentarians, NGOs	None	Parliamentarians (where budgetary/ legislative action is required)
Remainder of public	Through surveys/ opinion polls, etc.	Through public comments	None	None

3 Stakeholders and participation at the WTO

The WTO is at the centre of global trade governance. Its agreements cover not only various aspects of trade in goods (e.g. tariffs, standards, agriculture support, subsidies, etc.) but also trade in services, intellectual property and aspects of investment. These agreements are binding on WTO Members and can be enforced through its dispute settlement mechanism that provides for trade sanctions by the winning party against the losing party if the latter does not comply with the decision of the dispute settlement panel. The WTO is also a forum for global trade-related negotiations that aim to broaden and deepen the scope of existing agreements, as well as to conclude new trade-related agreements among Members.

Importantly, the WTO's agreements provide the framework within which Member States can develop and implement their national trade-related policies, and compliance with the WTO agreements is often the primary objective of trade-related measures adopted by developing countries. Through their implementation at the national level, WTO agreements impact the economic choices of all the categories of national stakeholders enumerated in section 1 above. It is therefore important to examine whether and how these stakeholders participate in the WTO discussions and negotiations.

WTO discussions and negotiations take place at two levels. At the top is the WTO Ministerial Conference where each Member has the right to be represented by a minister. The Ministerial Conference is the highest decision-making forum and is mandated to meet at least once every two years. The Ministerial Conference can take any decision regarding the WTO and its activities. More importantly, the WTO Ministerial Conference has the responsibility to launch new negotiations (e.g. the launch of the Doha Round of multilateral trade negotiations at the fourth WTO Ministerial Conference held in December 2001 in Doha, Qatar); to take stock of the progress in these negotiations and resolve outstanding issues related to the negotiations (e.g. at the fifth and sixth Ministerial Conferences held in Cancún and Hong Kong, China, in 2003 and 2005 respectively); and to conclude negotiations and approve their outcome in the form of new agreements. It can also examine broader strategic questions and the functioning of the organization (e.g. as was the case at the second and seventh Ministerial Conferences both held in Geneva, Switzerland in 1998 and 2009 respectively). The second level of WTO deliberations occurs through various other WTO bodies – both standing committees that monitor the implementation of the existing agreements and functioning of the WTO, and special bodies, such as those that have been established to conduct the negotiations under the Doha Round.[9] Each of these bodies meets at the WTO headquarters in Geneva, Switzerland several times a year. Member States have the right to be represented in these bodies through nominated officials, normally ambassadors and other staff in the Missions of these countries established in Geneva.

Most of the regular work of the WTO, as well as the negotiations, takes place at the second level, i.e. through a number of WTO councils, committees and working groups in Geneva. This is a continuous activity demanding regular participation by Members. Therefore, most of the WTO Members and observes have established permanent missions in Geneva. (However, it is important to note that there are still more than twenty WTO developing country Members and observers that do not have a permanent mission in Geneva and hence are unable to participate regularly in the discussions and negotiations taking place in the WTO bodies there, far less provide opportunity for broad-based stakeholder input.) These permanent missions are normally headed by an ambassador and include technical staff. Almost all the developing country missions in Geneva are staffed by experts from their ministries dealing with trade and foreign affairs and, in some cases, agriculture. The accountability of Geneva-based delegations to national governments and citizens, as well as the participation of other stakeholders, is assumed to be secured through indirect means (Woods and Narlikar 2001). The permanent missions report to and get instructions from relevant ministries (i.e. ministries responsible for trade and foreign affairs) in the capitals. These ministries in the capitals are in turn expected to ensure consultations with national stakeholders – both State and non-State – and channel that input to permanent missions in Geneva. Unfortunately, this does not always happen. The communication between Geneva missions and capitals of smaller developing countries is often weak,[10] and multi-stakeholder consultative mechanisms may not function well in many developing countries (CUTS

[9] For a graphic presentation of all WTO Bodies – both regular as well as those entrusted with the negotiations under the Doha Round – please see www.wto.org/english/thewto_e/whatis_e/tif_e/org2_e.htm [accessed in November 2010]. Two of these bodies are worth mentioning: the General Council, which has the mandate to perform all functions assigned to the WTO Ministerial Conference in between the Ministerial Conference sessions, and the Trade Negotiations Committee that is entrusted with the supervision of negotiations under the Doha Round.

[10] The weak communication between Geneva missions of developing countries and their capitals has been acknowledged as a serious issue. See, for example, Michalopoulos (2001).

2009a and 2009b; Jones *et al.* 2010). No developing country mission has any non-State stakeholders working as a staff member.[11]

The only instances where other national stakeholders have been directly engaged in Geneva-based WTO activities relate to dispute settlement cases. Relevant private sector representatives, including from developing countries, often travel to Geneva to assist their permanent missions and participate in the dispute hearings as part of the governmental delegation when their countries are involved in a dispute settlement process at the WTO.

In terms of stakeholder participation in day-to-day WTO activities, three levels can be identified. At the bottom are the media and some Geneva-based NGOs that have been accredited to the WTO.[12] They have access to the WTO building and are regularly briefed by the WTO Secretariat on important meetings. However, they cannot attend any formal meeting of any WTO body. Observers to the WTO bodies make up the next level, which includes delegations of countries that are not Members and those intergovernmental organizations that have been granted observer status at the WTO.[13] Delegates in this category have better access and can attend the formal meetings of those WTO bodies where they have been granted observer status. Since most of the meaningful WTO negotiations are conducted in informal meetings, the participation of observers is more symbolic than real. Moreover, observers are not allowed any role in decision-making, which is the prerogative of Members. At the highest level is the right to participate in all formal meetings and decision-making, which is reserved for the official delegations of Member countries generally consisting of the staff of the permanent missions.[14]

[11] Weak national consultative fora and lack of non-State stakeholders' representation in Geneva missions may in fact work in favour of dominant industries in the country which are regularly consulted by their governments for WTO negotiations related to those industries, e.g. banana companies in the case of some Latin American and Caribbean countries, and textiles and clothing industry in the case of some Asian countries.

[12] For discussion of issues related to NGO participation, or the lack thereof, in the WTO, please see Hernandez-Lopez (2001); Howse (2003); Lacarte-Muró (2004); and Van den Bosche (2009).

[13] Observer status has been granted to most organizations in the UN system but only a few of the regional and other intergovernmental organizations.

[14] However, many Members, particularly LDCs and smaller developing countries, have consistently complained that they are marginalized in the organization and its decision-making. They point out the practices such as Green Rooms, smaller informal meetings where participation is only by invitation, non-transparent consultations by chairs of various WTO bodies including the so-called confessionals, and the role of the WTO Secretariat, that constrain their participation. The limited human and technical capacity

While the WTO is an intergovernmental organization and all decisions are taken by governmental representatives, its rules allow Member governments to nominate anyone, including non-State actors, as its representatives to the WTO meetings. Developing country Members have, however, seldom used this opportunity.[15]

The obvious conclusion from this description is that most non-State stakeholders in developing countries participate in WTO discussions and negotiations only through their inputs at the national level. Hence their 'participation' at the multilateral level is based on the assumption that such mechanisms exist and are working properly at the national level. It is also obvious that stakeholders that are not part of the national consultative mechanisms have no other means of direct or active participation at the WTO.[16]

The lack of national stakeholders' participation in the day-to-day activities of the WTO could be mitigated to some extent if they were given greater opportunity to participate in the WTO Ministerial Conferences. The WTO Ministerial Conference draws its comprehensive legal powers from Article IV.1 of the WTO Agreement, which has invested the Ministerial Conference with the power to take any action necessary to carry out the functions of the WTO.[17] This legal foundation and the lack of clear limits to the remit of the WTO Ministerial Conference means that the Ministerial Conferences are neither ordinary gatherings of ministers nor events where deliberations and decisions are limited to matters of administrative oversight and functioning of the organization. This reflects a desire to involve the Ministerial Conferences with important decision-making that is related to crucial issues of agenda-setting, as well as conduct and conclusion of negotiations.

of these countries has also been widely reported as a hindrance to their full and effective engagement in WTO discussions and negotiations. Literature and reports on these issues abound (e.g. Kwa 2002; South Centre 2003; UNDP 2003; Kaukab *et al.* 2004; Jones *et al.* 2010).

15 Recorded examples include only some dispute settlement panel hearings and the WTO Ministerial Conferences, which are discussed later in this section.

16 It is acknowledged that opportunities for 'direct but passive' participation of non-State actors in some activities have increased over the years. For example, they are encouraged to attend and organize events during the annual WTO Public Forums, can observe selected Dispute Settlement proceedings, and can access a vast array of information through the WTO website.

17 'There shall be a Ministerial Conference composed of representatives of all the Members, which shall meet at least once every two years. The Ministerial Conference shall carry out the functions of the WTO and take actions necessary to this effect … ' (Article IV:1 of the WTO Agreement).

The records of the seven WTO Ministerial Conferences hosted since 1995 provide a useful data set for examining the extent of participation by national stakeholders from developing countries in these meetings, particularly those that are not represented in the day-to-day WTO discussions and negotiations. While fully acknowledging the particular problems that Ministerial Conference processes pose for smaller developing countries, concerns developing countries voice with regard to WTO processes in general (as given in footnote 14) are equally relevant for the Ministerial Conferences. Here, the focus of analysis is on the composition of official delegations of some developing countries and the level of access of various categories of stakeholders to the actual Ministerial Conference negotiations.[18]

The fifth WTO Ministerial Conference (MC), held in Cancún, Mexico in September 2003 provides a useful example for several reasons. First, it did not have constraining restrictions on the size of the delegations, which was the case for the fourth Ministerial Conference held in Doha in 2001. It hence gave the opportunity to all Members to bring larger delegations consisting of various groups of stakeholders. Second, it was a critical meeting in the context of the Doha Round of negotiations. Officially, the fifth Ministerial Conference was responsible for taking stock of the progress in the negotiations and making decisions on a number of items, including the set of development issues presented by developing countries, as well as the modalities for agriculture negotiations considered to be at the centre of the Doha Round. Third, it witnessed intense negotiations with very active and effective participation by developing countries. In fact, several of the developing country alliances and coalitions that have played an important role in the Doha negotiations emerged around the time of the Cancún Ministerial Conference (e.g. G20, G33 and G110 (South Centre 2003)). Fourth, the Cancún Ministerial Conference failed to reach any decision, an outcome that was partly attributed to active participation by developing countries and their strong resistance to pressure exerted by developed countries. All these factors together would imply that the Cancún Ministerial was a 'high point' of developing country participation in the WTO Ministerial Conferences and hence a fitting example to examine the composition of their participation.

[18] It is acknowledged that the WTO Secretariat establishes a well-equipped NGO Centre including free meetings facilities for each Ministerial Conference for use by the accredited NGOs, in addition to arranging regular briefings for them on the proceedings of the Ministerial Conference.

Table 19.3. *Stakeholder composition of selected developing countries' official delegations to the fourth WTO MC, at Cancún, Mexico in 2003*

	Bangladesh	Benin	Brazil	Egypt	Haiti	Namibia	South Africa	Zambia
Ministry of Agriculture	0	1	6	0	0	1	7	2
Parliamentarians	0	1	0	0	0	0	2	0
Public interest NGOs	2	3	0	0	0	0	6	0
Private sector	2	1	0	0	0	0	2	0
Other government ministries and departments including ministries dealing with trade and foreign affairs	10	9	28	5	7	9	35	13
Total no. of delegates	14	15	34	5	7	10	52	15

Notes: This table is based on data contained in the WTO Official List of Representatives, WT/MIN(03)/INF/14, 10 September 2003. However, the categories have been determined by the author based on the affiliations of delegates as given in the WTO document. Some errors in this tabulation cannot be ruled out, as the designation of all delegates is not always clearly indicated in the WTO source document.

Table 19.3 surveys delegations from eight countries including five LDCs as well as five African countries. It also includes two countries each from Asia and Latin America as well as some middle-income developing countries. In this sample, five of the eight developing countries included in their official delegations to the MC representatives from the agriculture ministries (not surprising given the importance of agriculture for these countries as well as for the Doha Round negotiations, particularly at the time of Cancún); three each had representatives from the private sector and public interest NGOs; and only two had parliamentarians. Only South Africa and Benin had representatives from all these categories of stakeholders included in the official delegations.

It must be emphasized that the actual situation is even more disappointing as inclusion in an official delegation does not entitle all delegates equal access to the negotiations at the MC, and even within the same delegation there are varying degrees of access. Participation in small meetings where actual hard bargaining takes place is usually restricted to only a few invited ministers, who are normally allowed to bring one additional delegate. This delegate is often a country's ambassador to the WTO or a high-level trade expert needed to assist the minister in technical aspects of the negotiations. Moreover, strategic planning and confidential feedback within the delegation is often limited to a select few who are responsible for trade policy-making. Hence official delegations seem to comprise two overlapping circles. The inner circle consists of a small number of trade policy experts in the national bureaucracy and diplomats. They attend and advise the ministers in the meetings where real negotiations take place. The outer circle comprises the rest of the delegation, including representatives of other ministries, the private sector, NGOs and parliamentarians. The latter normally attend only the formal sessions of the Ministerial Conference meetings, such as the opening and closing plenaries (like the delegates of observer countries, intergovernmental organizations and accredited NGOs) and the occasional briefings by the minister or his/her representative to learn about the progress in negotiations.

This brief description and analysis leads to certain conclusions. First and most important, national non-State stakeholders cannot participate in any WTO discussion/negotiations whether in the WTO bodies in Geneva or in the WTO Ministerial Conference without being part of the official delegations of their countries. Second, the official delegations to the WTO Ministerial Conferences, unlike Geneva permanent missions, do include some representatives of national stakeholders other than the ministries responsible for trade and foreign affairs. However, their number is quite limited and not all categories of national stakeholders are represented in all official delegations of developing countries. Third, the inclusion in the official delegations does not entitle these representatives to actually participate in the negotiations. One can therefore argue that the inclusiveness deficit at the multilateral level is greater than at the national level where most groups of stakeholders do have some access to consultative mechanisms established for stakeholders' consultations on trade issues.

4 Recommendations

Despite the growing acknowledgement of the need for inclusive processes for global trade governance – not least due to the ever-increasing scope and impact of trade policy measures and international trade agreements on all segments of the population in a country – there remains an inclusiveness deficit in trade policy-making processes at the national level and multilateral level. This finding remains true, even in the wake of important efforts to improve inclusiveness in recent years. For example, most developing countries now have established one or more consultative fora at the national level for multi-stakeholders' consultations on trade-related issues, and the WTO has made efforts to provide better opportunities to non-State actors mainly through greater access to information and improved transparency. However, much more remains to be done both at the national and multilateral levels. The following recommendations are offered to improve the inclusiveness of trade governance at both these levels.

At the national level, five interrelated actions should be undertaken to improve inclusiveness. These include: 1) enlarging the composition of the national consultation fora to include representatives of all groups of stakeholders – i.e. government ministry responsible for trade, other government ministries and agencies, industry minus SMEs, MNCs, labour, consumers, farmers, NGOs, the informal sector and media; 2) strengthening the mandate of the consultative fora by making it obligatory for the ministry responsible for trade to follow the advice offered by them; 3) ensuring the regular functioning of consultative fora by providing adequate human and financial resources to organize and service their meetings and to gather/finance participation of stakeholders; 4) organizing regular briefings on trade issues for parliamentarians and seeking their inputs; and 5) undertaking broad capacity-building of stakeholders on trade issues so that they are able to make effective use of the improved opportunities for inclusiveness through informed participation (Halle and Wolfe 2007).

Another set of actions by national authorities should address the gap between national and multilateral levels of trade governance. These include arranging regular briefings by staff of Geneva missions for the national consultative fora and for the parliamentarians; organizing periodic visits of representatives of groups of stakeholders to Geneva during important negotiations; including representatives of all groups of stakeholders in the official delegations to the WTO Ministerial Conferences; and including some non-State stakeholders and parliamentarians in the smaller delegations that attend informal, smaller meetings during the Ministerial Conferences.

Action at the domestic level by national authorities must be supplemented by action at the multilateral level; WTO and its membership cannot continue to hide behind its 'Member driven' and 'intergovernmental only' mantra. There are examples of greater stakeholder participation in other intergovernmental organizations, for example the International Labour Organization (ILO) that has a tripartite structure including representation by the governments, employers and employees.[19] Similarly, the environment-related negotiations in the UN system are much more open and provide greater access for non-State stakeholders.[20] In fact, organizations in the UN system have well-established mechanisms for the accreditation of non-State stakeholders, which provides them with greater access to information and meetings than is currently available at the WTO.[21] Improving inclusiveness at the WTO without changing its basic intergovernmental structure is possible and the following should be considered in this regard:

First, transparency of discussions and negotiations at the WTO should be improved both for its smaller Members and for the larger group of other stakeholders. Summary records of all meetings and the key points of negotiating drafts can be placed on the website without delay. This would enable the larger group of stakeholders at the national levels to approach their own governments to seek explanations and offer suggestions.

Second, like all the other international organizations, the WTO should establish clear criteria and procedures for the accreditation of other intergovernmental organizations and NGOs to observe its regular work.[22] This accreditation should allow access to formal meetings and documents and should be supplemented by creating a trust fund to support the participation of accredited NGOs from developing countries so that they have equitable access to the WTO.

[19] See www.ilo.org/global/About_the_ILO/Structure/lang – en/index.htm [accessed in November 2010].

[20] For example, see Guidelines for NGO participation in the meetings under the United Nations Framework Convention on Climate Change (UNFCCC) at http://unfccc.int/files/parties_and_observers/ngo/application/pdf/coc_guide.pdf [accessed in November 2010].

[21] For example, see information at www.un.org/esa/coordination/ngo/ [accessed in November 2010] regarding NGO accreditation and participation in the UN and compare it with the information regarding NGOs on the WTO website at www.wto.org/english/forums_e/ngo_e/ngo_e.htm [accessed in November 2010]. The key difference is that while the UN organizations provide for accreditation of NGOs and establish procedures for their participation, the WTO does not have any such system.

[22] WTO currently offers two mechanisms for NGO access: 1) they can apply and if accepted be accredited to the Ministerial Conference, which entitles them to access the NGO Centre and to attend the opening and closing plenaries; and 2) some Geneva-based NGOs active on trade and development issues have been issued entry badges to the WTO building and are invited to the briefings for NGOs by the WTO External Relations Division.

Third, taking into account the competence, expertise and grassroots connections of many international and national NGOs, the WTO Secretariat should better involve them in its outreach and capacity-building activities. Notably, some regional and international organizations have established parallel processes for business and civil society organizations (CSOs).[23] The WTO, too, should consider establishing a WTO Business and Labour Council (where representatives of business and labour organizations are represented) and a WTO CSO Council (to accommodate the representatives of public-interest NGOs). These parallel fora can develop their own recommendations for the consideration of the WTO Membership as represented by governments.

Finally, a WTO Parliamentary Assembly should be established where at least two parliamentarians from each Member – one from the ruling and the other from an opposition party – are included. This Assembly could deliberate on issues related to the WTO and offer its recommendations to the WTO Membership for its consideration.

All the above recommendations require further refinement and appropriate sequencing. The objective is not to offer a set menu but rather a blueprint for action.[24] This chapter has demonstrated that there is now enough experience to enable us to explore new approaches to improve the inclusiveness of global trade governance. Lack of response to the call for greater inclusiveness will only increase the gap between aspirations and concerns at the local level and the policies and actions at the national and multilateral levels. An increasingly interdependent world can little afford the resulting breakdown of legitimacy. Improving inclusiveness of global trade governance can counter some of the discontent with globalization and enable stakeholders as partners in the march towards a better future. What is needed is political will: without it no action is possible, and with it much can be done.

[23] For example, both the Asia-Pacific Economic Cooperation (APEC) and the Association of South East Asian Nations (ASEAN) have Business Advisory Councils (see www.abaconline.org/v4/index.php [accessed in November 2010]) whereas the Commonwealth Secretariat has quite elaborate arrangements to engage the CSOs as part of the Commonwealth Family (see www.thecommonwealth.org/Internal/174739/142018/civil_society/ [accessed in November 2010]).

[24] For a summary of existing proposals for WTO reform, see Deere Birkbeck and Monagle (2009).

References

CUTS International. 2009a. *Towards More Inclusive Trade Policy Making: Process and Role of Stakeholders in Select African Countries*. Jaipur, India: Consumer Unity & Trust Society (CUTS) International.

2009b. *Improving Ownership through Inclusive Trade Policy Making Processes: Lessons from Africa*. Jaipur, India: Consumer Unity & Trust Society (CUTS) International.

Deere Birkbeck, C. and Meléndez-Ortiz, R. (eds.) 2009. *Rebuilding Global Trade: Proposals for a Fairer, More Sustainable Future*. Geneva and Oxford: International Centre for Trade and Sustainable Development (ICTSD), and Global Economic Governance Programme, University College, Oxford.

Deere Birkbeck, C. and Monagle, C. 2009. *Strengthening Multilateralism: A Mapping of Proposals on WTO Reform and Global Trade Governance*. Geneva and Oxford: International Centre for Trade and Sustainable Development (ICTSD), and Global Economic Governance Programme, University College, Oxford.

Dick, B. 1997. *Stakeholder Analysis*. Southern Cross University Online. www.scu.edu.au/schools/gcm/ar/arp/stake.html [Accessed in November 2010].

Fatoumata, J. and Kwa, A. 2003. *Behind the Scenes at the WTO: The Real World of International Trade Negotiations*. London: Zed Books.

Gallagher, P., Low, P. and Stoler, A. L. (eds.) 2005. *Managing the Challenges of WTO Participation – 45 Case Studies*. Geneva: World Trade Organization.

Grynberg, R. (ed.) 2006. *WTO at the Margins: Small States and the Multilateral Trading System*. Cambridge University Press.

Halle, M. and Wolfe, R. (eds.) 2007. *Process Matters: Sustainable Development and Domestic Trade Transparency*. Geneva: International Institute for Sustainable Development.

Hernandez-Lopez, E. 2001. 'Recent Trends and Perspectives For Non-State Actor Participation in World Trade Organization Disputes', *Journal of World Trade* 35(3): 469–98.

Howse, R. 2003. 'Membership and its Privileges: the WTO, Civil Society, and the Amicus Brief Controversy', *European Law Journal* 9(4): 496–510.

International Organization for Standardization (ISO). 2005. *Guidance on Stakeholder Categories in the ISO/TMB/WG SR*. International Organization for Standardization Technical Management Board. ISO/TMB/WG SR N 48 rev. 1. 30 September 2005. www.econsense.de/_csr_info_pool/_managementsysteme/images/ISO%20Guidance%20WG%20SR.pdf [Accessed in November 2010].

Jones, E., Deere Birkbeck, C. and Woods, N. 2010. *Manoeuvring at the Margins: Constraints Faced by Small States in International Trade Relations*. London: Commonwealth Secretariat.

Kaukab, R. S., La Vina, A. and Yu III, V. P. B. 2004. *From Cancún to Hong Kong: Lessons from the Fifth Ministerial Conference of the World Trade Organization*, T.R.A.D.E. Working Paper No. 20, Geneva: South Centre.

Koening-Archibugi, M. and Zürn, M. 2006. *New Modes of Governance in the Global System: Exploring Publicness, Delegation and Inclusiveness.* New York: Palgrave Macmillan.

Kwa, A. 2002. 'Power Politics in the WTO: Developing Countries' Perspectives on Decision-Making Processes in Trade Negotiations', *Focus on the Global South Seminar*, Geneva.

Lacarte-Muró, J. 2004. 'Transparency, Public Debate and Participation by NGOs in the WTO: A WTO Perspective', *Journal of International Economic Law* 7(3): 683–86.

Love, B. R., Straja, S. R., Streeter, J. R., Jones, S. D. and Alan, M. A. 2008. 'Stakeholder Participation: A New Process and Its Application to Environmental Decisions', *Technology* 11(2): 61–74.

Michalopoulos, C. 2001. *Developing Countries in the WTO.* Basingstoke: Palgrave.

Ndulu, B. J. 2001. 'Partnership, Inclusiveness and Aid Effectiveness in Africa', in V. FitzGerald (ed.), *Social Institutions and Economic Development: A Tribute to Kurt Martin.* Oxford: Kluwer Academic Publishers, pp. 143–67.

Saner, R. 2010. *Trade Policy Governance through Inter-ministerial Coordination: A Source Book for Trade Officials and Trade & Development Experts.* Dodrecht: RoL Publications.

South Centre. 2003. 'Institutional Governance and Decision-Making Processes in the WTO', *South Centre Analytical Note*, SC/TADP/AN/IG/7. Geneva: South Centre.

UNDP. 2003. *Making Global Trade Work for People.* London: Earthscan.

Van den Bosche, P. 2009. 'Non-Governmental Organizations and the WTO: Limits to Involvement?' in Steger, D. (ed.), *World Trade Organization for the Twenty-first Century.* International Development Research Centre (IDRC) and the Centre for International Governance Innovation (CIGI): Wilfrid Laurier University Press.

Woods, N. and Narlikar, A. 2001. 'Governance and Accountability: the WTO, the IMF and the World Bank', *International Social Science Journal* 53(170): 569–83.

World Trade Organization (WTO). 1995. Agreement to Establish the World Trade Organization. 1 January 1995.

2003. Ministerial Conference Fifth Session: Official List of Representatives. WT/MIN(03)/INF/14. 10 September 2003.

20

Global trade governance and development: the WTO accession conundrum

CARLOS PRIMO BRAGA AND
OLIVIER CATTANEO

The set of non-discriminatory trading rules embedded in World Trade Organization (WTO) agreements has the characteristics of a global public good, and the WTO, as the main institutional framework for global trade governance, has a key role in facilitating an open international trading system.[1] In the United Nations Millennium Declaration the international community committed to 'develop further an open trading and financial system that is rule-based, predictable, and non discriminatory' with a view 'to ensure that globalization becomes a positive force for all the world's people' (Millennium Development Goal (MDG) No. 8).[2] Acceding to the WTO implies sharing responsibility in the governance of this global public good. Hence, universal membership of the WTO seems, prima facie, a worthwhile goal.

The WTO, however, faces a dilemma. On one hand, it inherits the old tradition of the General Agreement on Tariffs and Trade (GATT), whereby countries contribute to the objective of promoting trade 'by entering into reciprocal and mutually advantageous arrangements

Carlos Primo Braga is Special Representative and Director, External Affairs, Europe of the World Bank Group. Olivier Cattaneo is currently Adjunct Professor and Research Associate with the Groupe d'Economie Mondiale de SciencesPo, Paris. This chapter relies extensively on Primo Braga and Cattaneo (2009a). Comments and assistance from C. Deere Birkbeck, S. Evenett, N. Imboden and C. Osakwe are gratefully acknowledged. All the views expressed here are those of the authors. They do not necessarily express the view of the World Bank, its Executive Directors or the countries they represent.

[1] The market, for its proper functioning, depends upon global public goods that it cannot itself provide. Without a mechanism for collective action, these goods can be underproduced. The WTO system (and its rules) fosters global efficiency by facilitating international trade, curbing discrimination and promoting a level playing field for competitive firms across nations (Birdsall and Lawrence 1999).

[2] See UN (2000, 2001).

directed to the substantial reduction of tariffs and other barriers to trade and to the elimination of discriminatory treatment in international commerce' (Preamble of the GATT 1947 and 1994). In other words, accession to the WTO implies 'reciprocity'. At the same time, the central position of the WTO in the world trading system and the objective of universal Membership suggests that the 'cost' of accession should be kept as low as possible, so as to not exclude the poorest countries. In practice, however, tensions between the WTO's mercantilist heritage and its role as the institutional vessel for a global public good produce a number of challenges with respect to accession procedures.

A further complication is that almost all the remaining candidates for WTO accession are developing or transition countries.[3] WTO accession is therefore, de facto, a development issue. This is an important consideration because the faults of the accession process will necessarily affect – and remedies would benefit – developing or transition economies.[4] At the same time, developing countries represent a large majority of the incumbent Members; thus, the reform of the WTO accession process is not only a North–South debate, but also an issue between incumbent and acceding Members. Newly acceded countries have rarely been offered the same benefits as incumbent Members with comparable levels of development. In turn, those who have paid a high price to gain Membership have little incentive to discount the entry cost for the next in line. The solidarity that often prevails among WTO Members with the same level of development has not extended, so far, to non-Members.

From a strictly economic perspective, the larger the membership of an organization, the more costly the exclusion from the system and the more valuable the accession becomes.[5] Conversely, the larger the membership, the less benefits incumbent WTO Members will expect from new accessions – unless the country is a sizeable trading partner like China or Russia. In other words, the price of the entry ticket is more likely to increase than to decrease over time, against the original objective of universal membership.

[3] The only exception is Andorra.

[4] See, for example, the Communication from the Informal Group of Developing Countries (WTO 2009) in favour of improvements in the existing mechanisms for acceding developing countries to make their views on the accession process better known to WTO Members.

[5] For a discussion of strategic behaviour in the context of 'clubs', as exemplified by trade agreements, see Hallett and Primo Braga (1994).

For these reasons, reform of the WTO accession process is probably one of the most challenging issues facing global trade governance. Yet, its importance should not be underestimated. The conditions attached to a country's accession affect the whole experience of that country as a WTO Member and its ability to enjoy its benefits.

The experience of the twenty-five WTO accessions that occurred between January 1996 and July 2010 provides a solid evidence base for reviewing the functioning – and dysfunctions – of the accession process.[6] The dynamics of the negotiations and their results have significantly varied from country to country. For example, it took China more than fifteen years to complete the WTO accession process, compared to less than three years for the Kyrgyz Republic. Whereas the Chinese accession protocol consisted of a main text of 11 pages and 9 annexes, including 143 paragraphs that incorporated by reference the 77-page Working Party Report, for some other countries the accession protocol consisted of a main text of no more than 2 pages of standardized provisions. However, some common features and trends have emerged. According to Evenett and Primo Braga (2006), for example: 1) the WTO accession process is becoming more demanding in terms of market access commitments; 2) there is growing concern that the price of joining the WTO now includes commitments that go beyond the GATT/WTO agreements; and 3) the accession process takes limited account of the specific circumstances of applicant countries or their needs for special and differential treatment.[7]

Focusing on the governance dimension of WTO accession, this chapter will address two questions. First, has the price to pay for acceding to the WTO become too high, in particular with regard to the role of the WTO in the management of a global public good and to the objective of universal Membership? Second, have accession protocols created a 'second class' of citizens in the WTO and contradicted the core WTO principles of non-discrimination and single undertaking? Particular attention will be paid to the development dimension of these governance issues, with the underlying question of whether the WTO accession process ignores

[6] The twenty-fifth country to join the WTO under Article 12 accession procedures was Cape Verde on 23 July 2008.

[7] These authors also note, however, that the 'need to calibrate the process by level of development has been partially recognized by the WTO membership and was manifested in the WTO General Council's guidelines for the accession of least developed countries in December 2002' (WT/COMTD/LDC/12).

the specific needs of developing countries or not, and how the process of accession negotiations influences their outcomes.[8]

1 The accession process: too long, too complex and too costly for developing countries?

Governance starts at the WTO doorstep: if the price of WTO Membership is too high, a number of the poorest candidates for accession will be excluded and unable to participate effectively in global trade governance. From an historical perspective, the GATT/WTO accession process has allowed a growing participation of developing countries in the multilateral trade system. However, recent trends reveal an increase in the cost, complexity and length of the accession process. This section reviews the new challenges these trends pose for developing countries in the accession pipeline, and makes the case for both reforms to the accession process and improved assistance for accession countries.

1.1 From an historical perspective: a success story

If the size of Membership were taken as the relevant parameter for measuring success, the history of the GATT and then the WTO, could be characterized as a successful one. On 1 January 1948, the GATT was signed by 23 countries[9]; in the following years, the number of contracting parties increased, reaching 50 in the early 1960s, 100 in the early 1970s and 150 in 2005. First considered as a 'Club of the Rich', the GATT's Membership quickly became more diversified. Since 1960, the majority of its Members have been developing countries and the accession of many transition economies after the collapse of the Soviet Union further diversified GATT Membership. Over six decades, the number of contracting parties to the GATT increased by 130, and as of July 2010 there are 30 additional countries with observer status to the WTO, which are in the process of negotiating accession.[10]

[8] For a more complete analysis of WTO accession and its challenges, refer to Primo Braga and Cattaneo (2009b).

[9] Australia, Belgium, Brazil, Burma, Canada, Ceylon, Chile, China, Cuba, the Czechoslovak Republic, France, India, Lebanon, Luxembourg, the Netherlands, New Zealand, Norway, Pakistan, Southern Rhodesia, Syria, South Africa, the United Kingdom and the United States.

[10] See the summary table of ongoing accessions at www.wto.org [accessed in November 2010].

Not all WTO Members have, however, been through the same accession process. In particular, as pointed out by Van Grasstek (2001), the majority of developing countries that joined the GATT did not actually accede, but rather succeeded to GATT status. In the post-Second World War period, many countries that gained independence from colonial powers had the option of entering the GATT under the special terms of GATT Article 26.5(c), and acquired de facto GATT status, before converting this into full contracting party status by succession – a process that was much less stringent than the ordinary accession process under GATT Article 33. In total, sixty-four countries benefitted from this 'fast-track' accession process.[11]

Changes in the practices of accession also occurred with the establishment of the WTO in 1995. At that time, 128 GATT contracting parties became original Members of the WTO and a further 25 additional countries have joined the organization since, using the provisions contained in Article 12 of the WTO Agreement.[12] After fifteen years of practice, Article 12 is now the subject of increasing criticism, both for its brevity and general content, especially with regards to its section on the terms of accession 'to be agreed' between the acceding country and the WTO. While the WTO Secretariat, in consultation with its Members, established a set of procedures for accession, these guidelines dealt only with procedural aspects of the process and no general agreement was reached on what would constitute appropriate terms.[13]

1.2 An increasingly complex and lengthy process

Back in 1965, Curzon (1965: 36) wrote that the GATT's accession arrangements were biased in favour of newcomers and that incumbent Members did not normally 'try to drive too hard a bargain' in payment of

[11] Article 26.5(c) of GATT 1947 reads as follows: 'If any of the customs territories, in respect of which a contracting party has accepted this Agreement, possesses or acquires full autonomy in the conduct of its external commercial relations and of the other matters provided for in this Agreement, such territory shall, upon sponsorship through a declaration by the responsible contracting party establishing the above-mentioned fact, be deemed to be a contracting party.'

[12] Article 12 of the WTO Agreement provides that 'any State or separate customs territory possessing full autonomy in the conduct of its external commercial relations and of the other matters provided for in this Agreement and the Multilateral Trade Agreements may accede to this Agreement, on terms to be agreed between it and the WTO'. Although the article provides for a two-thirds majority vote, in practice, the unanimity rule prevails.

[13] For a detailed analysis of the accession procedures, see WTO (2005) and WTO (2008).

concessions they had made to third parties many years before. One could write the exact opposite today. Indeed, some commentators and countries have questioned the benefits of joining the WTO when the price is perceived to be excessive (Oxfam 2004). In one instance, a country (Vanuatu) suspended the procedures to finalize its accession bid after about ten years of negotiations (Gay 2005).[14] A number of circumstances explain this reversal in the bargaining over accession.

First, the scope of disciplines contained in the suite of WTO agreements that countries must join upon accession vastly exceeds those of the GATT 1947. They do not only apply to border measures, but also to a wide range of domestic policies such as standards, services regulation or intellectual property protection. The collection of relevant information and the review of existing (or under-reform) legislation across all of these areas, which is required in the fact-finding phase of the accession process, is more time consuming than the simple review of tariff lines. Existing Members can also delay the admission of a candidate until it has adopted (or implemented) the regulations/laws that make it fully compliant with WTO disciplines. The process of domestic regulatory/legislative reform can prove unpredictable and lengthy, often considerably more so than the process of tariff line adjustments.

Second, on market access, the level of commitments required from new entrants is much higher than it was in the early years of the GATT. This is due to a combination of three factors: 1) the level of tariffs bound/applied by incumbent Members has dramatically dropped as a result of successive rounds of multilateral trade negotiations (i.e. the standard of admission is higher); 2) WTO agreements extended the coverage of the GATT to encompass in a substantive manner agriculture, textiles, etc., which are particularly sensitive sectors in most countries; and 3) the WTO's General Agreement on Trade in Services (GATS) extended market access commitments to the services sector.

Third, the conjunction of bilateral and multilateral negotiations in the accession process compounds its length and complexity (see Appendix 1 for an overview of the accession process); the larger the WTO Membership, the more specific requests a candidate country will receive, and the longer the process is likely to be. With an increasing diversity of interests in the WTO, more topics are under scrutiny than ever before during accession.

[14] In 2008, Vanuatu indicated that it was ready to re-engage in its accession negotiations. Technical work to update the original accession package negotiated in 2001 is expected to resume. See WTO (2010).

Fourth, the remaining candidates for WTO accession are countries that have been (and in some cases still are) facing serious political distress, extreme poverty, geographical isolation or transition from centrally planned to market economies. Not only do these countries face more challenges to adjust to WTO disciplines, but their efforts also occur in a more difficult context (e.g. fragile domestic political environment), not to mention the fact that they often are constrained by limited resources (both human and financial).

1.3 Challenges facing candidate countries

The characteristics of the WTO accession process make it particularly demanding on candidate countries. In 2005, for instance, Saudi Arabia joined the WTO after 10 years of negotiations, 365 bilateral and 14 multilateral rounds of negotiation, answering 3,500 questions about its trading regime and system of business regulation, and submitting 7,600 pages of documentation. Saudi Arabia also prepared implementation of its commitments by issuing twenty-eight Royal Orders and forty-two laws and regulations (Evenett 2006). From an administrative perspective alone, a country must have the resources to sustain its engagement in such a demanding process.

Developing and transition acceding countries have limited human and budgetary resources. For example, in the case of Vanuatu (Gay 2005), only around five staff members from the Departments of Trade and Customs were available to deal with accession, none of whom had prior experience of the GATT or the WTO. The country had no permanent representation in Geneva and the cost of the long trips necessary for negotiating Membership were too difficult to finance (estimated to represent roughly one full year of the budget of the Department of Trade). A further constraint is that even when fully trained, trade officials working on accession often move jobs within governments and expertise then needs to be rebuilt.

Moreover, securing sufficient ownership of WTO accession (and its commitments) is a major issue, particularly in countries where political instability prevails and/or the decision/rule-making process remains opaque. In the case of Vanuatu, the length of the negotiations saw the succession of nine governments, most of which were not in power for long enough to become aware of (let alone familiar with) the details of the accession package and to fully understand the role of the WTO. In the case of Cambodia (Chea and Sok 2005), political turmoil also delayed accession. On the transparency and ownership front, Cambodia accession negotiations were conducted with limited participation of stakeholders. It is estimated that only 40 per cent of the Cambodian workers and 50 per cent of the Cambodian small and medium-sized enterprises (SMEs) had heard of the WTO at the time of the country's accession.

With a view to facilitating the accession process, and based on the experience of previous entrant countries, some authors have proposed accession strategies or tips for candidate countries (see for example, Michalopoulos 2002). These include the following:

- Analyse the possible implications of the various WTO agreements and link domestic reform and development plans to the WTO accession process;
- Define a negotiation strategy and position, including with regard to 'WTO-plus' concessions that incumbent Members might try to impose;
- Establish a central coordination point to provide direction and manage the multiplicity of legislative and regulatory changes in trade regimes that are necessary for accession;
- Seek and maintain strong public support for the accession process, including through transparency, information and continuous consultation with civil society, non-governmental organizations (NGOs), stakeholders and the media;
- Identify and focus on areas of WTO agreements where weaknesses in the country's institutional infrastructure require delays in the WTO provisions' implementation; and
- Seek technical assistance for these areas and prepare realistic implementation plans.

1.4 The need to increase flexibility and assistance to developing countries

In recognition of the special needs of least developed countries (LDCs), the 2001 Doha WTO Ministerial Declaration called for the facilitation and acceleration of accession negotiations with LDCs and, in December 2002, the WTO General Council adopted 'Guidelines on the Accession of LDCs'. According to these guidelines, WTO Members should give more consideration to the specific needs of acceding LDCs, particularly in the following areas: market access (restraint in seeking concessions and commitments from acceding LDCs); WTO rules (special and differential treatment, transition periods and plurilateral trade agreements); process (streamlined accession procedures); and technical assistance (priority attention to acceding LDCs) (WTO 2003).

In practice, however, Members have not necessarily followed the spirit or letter of these guidelines. Cambodia and Nepal – both recently acceded LDCs – were expected to commit three to four times more services sectors than the average WTO Member (Adlung 2007). Some analysts have suggested improving upon the guidelines. Gay (2005), for example, presents a set of basic rules and disciplines that would help some candidate countries overcome capacity limitations and would include fixed transition periods for the most demanding agreements (such as on intellectual property) and guidelines on market access commitments (including on tariff reductions and service sector reforms).

Flexibilities, such as extended transition periods, are not, however, sufficient; technical assistance and capacity-building (TACB) are also required. This is true both at the time of accession negotiations (upstream) and when countries are implementing their commitments (downstream). Primo Braga *et al.* (2004) analysed the different forms of TACB that had been provided to acceding countries and reached the following conclusions:

- General consensus-building and awareness-raising activities seem to be over-emphasized at the expense of supporting country-specific and sector-specific analysis;
- Appropriate timing and targeting of TACB is fundamentally important; and
- Parallel support by more than one donor agency is sometimes perceived to lead to a duplication of efforts, if not even wasteful competition among agencies, stressing the continuous need for donor coordination.

The conclusions incorporated the following proposals:

- The effectiveness of assistance must be addressed by multilateral and bilateral organizations;
- TACB should be available for countries to comply with WTO rules, in particular in the areas of tax treatment, pricing policies and trading rights;
- Initiatives to build research capacity should be promoted from the beginning of a country's accession;
- So-called 'South–South learning' initiatives should be promoted since they offer a forum for the exchange of experiences among acceding and recently acceded developing and transition countries; and

- Long-term institution-building should be integrated into accession-related TACB (road map to be developed at the beginning of the accession process).

In summary, more attention needs to be given to ensuring TACB is designed to help in the implementation of a country's obligations both during and post accession. Only through the successful implementation of its obligations will a country truly benefit from WTO accession.

2 The accession deals: towards a two-tier WTO membership?

Just as the *process* of WTO accession has been criticized, the results of the process (i.e. the content of accession protocols) have also been the subject of concern. Studies that emphasize the cost of accession often fail to recognize the benefits of WTO Membership that entice countries to join. Here, it is important to recall that WTO accession remains a voluntary process and no country has been forced into the Organization.

In order to draw lessons for the improvement of global trade governance, an analysis of accession deals is essential. This analysis is vital for assessing the real 'cost' of accession and hence the accessibility of the WTO to poor countries, but also to determine the extent to which recently acceded countries can effectively participate in global trade governance.

2.1 Between diversity and uniformity

The common legal framework and the consistent engagement of some WTO Members in accession negotiations ensures a certain uniformity of the process and a minimum degree of consistency across the various accession deals that emerge. For instance, the United States (USA), the European Union (EU), Japan, Australia and Switzerland participate in all accession working parties. Positions in WTO accession negotiations are closely linked to domestic trade policy considerations. As discussed by Lacey (2007), most WTO Members have 'pet' issues on which they will take a firm stance, irrespective of the level of development of the candidate country and even if no concrete or specific export interest exists in that area for each particular accession. In such cases, the 'demandeur' countries use the concessions obtained in accession negotiations as evidence to key domestic economic and/or political constituents of their commitment to promoting their interests.

Accession negotiations are driven by issues that are country-specific and the final terms of accession are tailor-made to each candidate. That said, the force of precedent should also not be ignored. A common mistake is to use the China accession protocol as a reference for analysing WTO accessions. As pointed out by Michalopoulos (2002: 68), 'China's accession is very unique, both for political and economic reasons, and lessons from it have to be drawn with extreme care'. Nonetheless, some provisions that China had to accept and that had been qualified as 'unique' at the time (e.g. on special treatment with respect to trade remedies) have since been reproduced in other countries' accession protocols (namely Vietnam, five years later).

The adoption of different negotiation strategies has produced diverse outcomes for accession candidates. Mongolia, for example, took an 'easy' approach to the accession negotiations and accepted far-reaching concessions without securing sufficient transition periods and exceptions (Tsogtbaatar 2005). By contrast, Nepal took a 'tough' stance to the negotiations and refused a number of concessions on market access and rules. The Nepalese negotiators convinced WTO Members to bind their country's tariffs on sensitive agricultural products at 51 per cent during the transition period (then at 42 per cent), while the prevailing applied tariff rate stood at 10 per cent. They also refused pressures to join the International Union for the Protection of New Varieties of Plants (UPOV), which some countries had requested as one way of fulfilling their commitment to minimum standards of plant variety protection in the Trade-Related Aspects of Intellectual Property Rights (TRIPS) Agreement. Instead, Nepal committed only to 'look at' major intellectual property conventions administered by the World Intellectual Property Organization (WIPO), and to 'explore the possibility of joining them in the future, as appropriate' (Rajkarnikar 2005). This example highlights that a country can resist requests that do not serve their interests and influence the outcome of the negotiations.

2.2 *Commitments on market access: goods and services*

Commitments on market access (e.g. binding or reduction of tariffs on imports) are probably the most visible and anticipated outcome of WTO accessions. Market access commitments (such as tariff levels) are more tangible and quantifiable than commitments on rules, and their impact on other Members' exports is more direct and immediate. However, the level of commitment demanded of new WTO entrants has attracted considerable debate.

At one end of the spectrum, after comparison of the levels of *applied* tariffs (as opposed to *bound* tariffs) before and after accession, some analysts find that acceding countries have not been exposed to unreasonable pressures to open up their markets.

> Many acceding (transition) countries have liberalized their trade regimes unilaterally and have been able to negotiate the terms of their WTO accession within the scope of measures already taken. As a result, their WTO commitments are less 'liberal' than the measures actually applied. … The only exceptions were the Czech Republic, Hungary, Poland and Slovakia which essentially bound the rates at their actual levels.
>
> (Drabek and Bacchetta 2004: 1092–3)

At the other end of the spectrum, after comparison of the levels of *bound* tariffs (as opposed to *applied* tariffs) before and after accession, some authors observe that those countries that acceded later had to make more concessions than earlier ones; they argue that the average level of negotiated tariff bindings has fallen over time (Kennett *et al.* 2005).

There are also important variations in the experience of acceding countries in terms of their market access commitments. Martin (2006: 27–8) observes that:

> [M]any acceding members were not required to make any cuts in their agricultural tariffs, and the average reduction from initial tariffs was only 14.3 percent for the members for which a calculation was feasible. However, some accessions, such as those of China, Albania, Panama and Croatia, appear to have involved very substantial reductions in average tariffs. … The reductions in average non-agricultural tariffs show some interesting patterns. In most accessions after Panama's in 1997, acceding countries have been expected to introduce a bound tariff averaging 10 percent or less, with exceptions made for Jordan, and for the LDCs of Nepal and Cambodia. The consequent reductions in average applied tariffs ranged from almost 60 percent in Albania and China to zero in Ecuador and Cambodia, with an average percentage cut of 21 percent.

Importantly, these 'before and after' tariff comparisons raise serious methodological concerns. For example, Ianchovichina and Martin (2001) observed that, in the case of China, most liberalization efforts were undertaken between 1995 and 2001 in preparation for accession, whereas tariff cuts undertaken after 2001 to meet China's WTO accession commitments were less substantial. What should then be the reference period for measuring the impact of WTO accession on market access? It would be erroneous to suggest that a country made little effort on market access by comparing tariffs before and after the date of accession if most efforts had already been made in preparation for accession.

Further, market access does not only concern tariffs. WTO Members may raise a number of so-called 'real' market access issues while negotiating with an acceding country. For example, the accession deal may include provisions pertaining to the use, allocations or phasing-out of tariff-rate quotas (Lacey 2007).

Accession negotiations have also yielded more significant commitments in the services sector from new entrant countries than those made by founding WTO Members. Evenett and Primo Braga (2006) observed that LDCs, developing and developed country founding Members of the WTO, respectively, committed on average 20, 44 and 108 services subsectors (of the 160 subsectors identified in the WTO's General Agreement on Trade in Services (GATS)). By contrast, countries in all categories that have acceded to the WTO since 1995 committed an average of 104 subsectors. In other words, countries that went through the WTO accession process typically committed a much higher number of services subsectors than did GATT contracting parties at a similar level of development in the Uruguay Round negotiations (1986–94). The number of GATS commitments is a poor indicator, however, of the depth and nature of reforms implemented. Indeed, Eschenbach and Hoekman (2006) observe a negative correlation between the level of GATS commitments of recently acceded transition economies and the quality of actual national policies on services. In the same vein, Mattoo (2003) characterizes China's commitments on services as 'the most radical reform of trade in services ever undertaken in the WTO', but observes that China's commitments were more frequently subject to qualifications or reservations than those of other countries. Finally, as has been the case for tariffs, a number of acceding countries had already unilaterally opened their services sector as part of a domestic development strategy before their WTO accession negotiations. As such, a high level of commitment on services in accession deals could just reflect the status quo in the country at hand, as was the case for Tonga ('Ofa 2007).

2.3 *Commitments on rules*

Beyond market access commitments, acceding WTO Members also commit to bringing their laws, regulations and other standards or practices into conformity with WTO law. These commitments should be straightforward (i.e. implementing WTO agreements). In practice, however, incumbent Members often see accession negotiations as an opportunity to prescribe obligations exceeding the existing requirements of the WTO agreements – the so-called 'WTO-plus' obligations and 'WTO-minus' rights. This attitude has spurred a number of criticisms of the accession process as 'power-based' and 'unfair', as well as concerns that it could lead to a 'multi-tier membership'.

A distinction is often made between so-called 'WTO-plus' and 'WTO-minus' commitments, where the former refers to commitments that go beyond those agreed during the Uruguay Round, and the latter refers to commitments where the acceding country forgoes rights available to other Members. Charnovitz (2008) disputes this classification and suggests a new typology of WTO-plus and WTO-minus commitments. Similarly, Evenett and Primo Braga (2006: 235) observe that 'whether an accession commitment goes beyond an existing WTO agreement depends in large part on how the latter is interpreted, and so it should not be surprising that disagreement is rife on the extent of WTO-plus commitments'. Acceding to the WTO means transferring some sovereignty to an international body. In some accessions, the 'power-based' nature of the accession process already exacerbates some hard feelings against this transfer of sovereignty. WTO-plus or WTO-minus commitments are seen as additional losses of sovereignty that could be interpreted as a breach of the principle of 'sovereign equality of nations' (Article 2.1 of the Charter of the United Nations). However, this debate should be placed in a broader context. First, all Members, not just accession countries, carefully guard their sovereignty. Indeed, the debate on 'policy space' perfectly illustrates that tensions about sovereignty are not confined to the context of accession. Second, if one believes that WTO disciplines help governments adopt more efficient economic policies, then 'more WTO' commitments should not necessarily be perceived as a bad thing (Cattaneo 2005). In short, the passions surrounding the perceived costs of accession should be contrasted with the rationale for, and benefits of, WTO Membership.

Intellectual property provisions that go beyond the TRIPS disciplines are commonly cited as examples of 'WTO-plus' measures. In addition, a number of acceding countries have been asked to ratify plurilateral agreements (e.g. the WTO Agreement on Government Procurement; or the WTO Information Technology Agreement) that were not necessarily universally adhered to by other WTO Members.

Special safeguards, in turn, are an example of 'WTO-minus' rights. In the same vein, shorter transition periods are often characterized as WTO-minus rights. Acceding countries typically stress the challenges they face in adopting the numerous new technical standards or regulations required of WTO Members and point to the transition arrangements that were available to the original Members (e.g. one year, five years and eleven years, respectively, for developed, developing and least developed countries to implement the TRIPS Agreement). Others, however, question the need for transitional arrangements. According to the WTO Secretariat, for instance:

> [T]hroughout the accession process, conformity with the WTO agreements is the standard against which acceding governments' trade policies are measured. In addition, maintaining a standstill on WTO-inconsistent measures, as well as on tariff increases, is a generally agreed principle in WTO accession negotiations. Therefore, governments coming through the accession process after years of negotiations are generally well-equipped to participate as full and effective players in the WTO from the day of accession, thus strengthening the rules-based multilateral trading system.
>
> (WTO 2005)

In practice, some transitional arrangements have been granted for a limited number of areas and for specific periods of time, but the applicant has had to demonstrate that it has done as much as possible to bring its system in line with WTO requirements and to present a plan and timetable for the next steps before making the request. Transition periods have also been extended more readily to accession countries that are LDCs, in accordance with the WTO Guidelines on accession of LDCs (WTO 2003).

While there is much focus on 'WTO-plus' accession commitments, WTO-minus rights merit special attention. As an example, safeguards against Chinese imports or more lenient anti-dumping rules, for instance, not only affected China's market access rights, but also introduced additional inefficiencies in the trade regimes of incumbent Members. As summarized by Martin:

> [T]here seems to be a strong case, on equity and efficiency grounds, to strongly restrict the right of existing members to introduce additional distortions into their own trade regimes. … The right to develop additional, discriminatory measures against exports from new members reduces the economic gains to both the new member and the existing member and was surely not envisaged in the design of the WTO agreement, which provided for non-application of the agreement only under tightly restricted circumstances.
>
> (Martin 2006: 22)

3 Consequences for global trade governance: a WTO à la carte?

The inclusion of WTO-plus provisions in accession protocols has raised concerns that they set precedents for a systemic trend towards higher standards in terms of WTO disciplines and an expansion of the trade liberalization agenda (to new areas such as investment). It remains unclear, however, whether these fears will be realized. In the case of China, for instance, Paragraph 9 of the Working Party Report clearly stipulated that all commitments made by China 'were solely those of China and would prejudice neither existing rights and obligations of members under the WTO Agreement nor on-going and future WTO obligations and any other process of accession' (WTO 2001). Still, it is true that accession deals have imposed obligations on new Members on a case-by-case (and discriminatory) basis – a trend that is at odds with the basic WTO principle of non-discrimination. Even if these à la carte accession deals do not lead to systemic changes in WTO agreements, they may still have significant implications for the WTO legal system (Ya Qin 2003).

Here, it is key to recall the evolution of the multilateral trading system and the importance placed on uniformity. After the Tokyo Round (1974–9), a 'GATT à la carte' developed, whereby contracting parties had obligations that varied according to the number of plurilateral trade agreements they had signed (Hudec 1988). In lieu of a single dispute settlement mechanism, individual agreements contained specific rules regarding disputes. This 'balkanization' of the system and the related uncertainty about applicable rules and disciplines became a threat to the GATT objectives of security and predictability of commercial transactions. The creation of the WTO in 1994 remedied this situation and restored a principle of uniform commitments. The 'single undertaking' meant that all countries committed to the same set of multilateral rules and governments agreed to a dispute settlement mechanism that applied across all WTO disciplines. However, Article 12 of the Marrakesh Agreement (Accession) introduced a loophole, making it possible for WTO Members to depart from the principle of uniformity and non-discrimination. The risk is then to create a 'multi-tier' Membership that may challenge some of the fundamental principles of the Organization.

The à la carte approach to WTO accessions has three further concrete implications (Ya Qin 2003). First, the ad hoc rule-making in WTO accession negotiations does not lend itself well to careful formulation of rules of conduct. Numerous ambiguities, gaps and inconsistencies can be found in the protocols provisions and many of these try to modify or expand existing WTO rules. Second, the negotiation of WTO-plus obligations on a Member-specific basis can lead to deals that contain the most stringent rules possible, without due regard to practical implications. The imposition of rules that are unlikely to be followed and enforced can only reduce the effectiveness of WTO law. Third, it is difficult for the public (including exporters and investors) to identify and keep track of all the special provisions that apply to trade relations with specific acceding countries detracting from the uniformity and transparency of WTO law.

In addition, the emergence of a 'law of WTO accession' has created new challenges and strains on the dispute settlement system. In 2006, Canada, the EU and the USA brought a case against China, which for the first time raised the issue of the implementation of accession commitments.[15] This dispute raised a number of legal questions, including whether protocols of accession were enforceable in WTO dispute settlement, whether the protocols were integral parts of (or amendments to) the WTO agreements, and what should be the proper approach to interpreting accession commitments within the context of WTO law (Charnovitz 2008). The absence of clear answers to these questions is a source of tension that could affect the legitimacy of the WTO dispute settlement system. At stake is the interpretation of the obligations contracted by all recent acceding countries. A new chapter of WTO jurisprudence is therefore poised to emerge, making the accession process a more central concern for all WTO Members whether or not they are actively involved in accession negotiations.

4 Accession as a critical trade governance concern

To what extent does the accession issue warrant the attention of those interested in global trade governance? While China's accession prompted great interest in the topic, since its completion the attention of the media and scholars alike has been much less intense. Further, with the growing number of preferential and regional trade agreements and the troubles of the Doha Round, it is possible that WTO accession may become less attractive to remaining outsiders. And with the completion of major accessions in the pipeline (e.g. Russia) only a few countries with relatively

[15] *China-Measures affecting imports of automobile parts*, WTO disputes WT/DS 339, 340, and 342, initiated on 30 March and 13 April 2006.

little economic weight would still remain out of the system.[16] In other words, we could be close to 'the end of history' in terms of reaching a truly 'global' multilateral trade system.

The authors of this chapter, however, take the opposite view. Accession is just the beginning of the story. All recently acceded countries are in the phase of implementation of the commitments made in the course of accession. This phase is very demanding of new entrants and tests the credibility of their commitments. The implementation phase is also the time when the impact of WTO accession deals can be observed and measured, thereby providing answers to the fundamental questions raised earlier on the rationale and effects of WTO accession. There is also a risk that the 'WTO-plus' conditions that form part of WTO accession deals could create a 'two-tier' Membership, challenging the principle of non-discrimination on which the GATT was originally founded. In addition, as noted above, recent WTO accessions have had major systemic effects on the WTO, which are still to be fully captured. Already, 'WTO accession law' (and soon jurisprudence) has emerged, which challenges the grounds of accession protocols and traditional WTO law, such as the principle of uniformity of WTO law inherited from the Uruguay Round. The considerable economic and political weight of some new WTO Members is also likely to affect strategies and alliances in future rounds of multilateral trade negotiations. A new chapter of history is open.

The accession process is also having impacts on ongoing multilateral trade negotiations. The perception among many recently acceded Members that a high 'price' was paid for accession has provoked the adoption of a conservative negotiating stance in the Doha Round negotiations that could add to the obstacles it already faces. That is, these countries believe that they have already undertaken 'too much' in terms of WTO commitments and that a pause in the liberalization process is necessary. Frustrated by the pace of progress, older WTO Members ready to deepen their commitments could look for alternative fora, such as regional trade agreements, to move their agendas forward. An unintended consequence of so-called WTO-plus commitments could thus be the expansion of discrimination in the world trading system.

The ultimate test of the fairness and adequacy of the terms of accession is the capacity of acceding developing countries to fully implement their

[16] The current 153 WTO Members account for more than 95 per cent of world trade. If all twenty-nine countries currently involved in negotiations complete their accession procedures, the WTO coverage of global trade would rise to 99.9 per cent of world trade (WTO 2010).

commitments. Here, it appears that a number of commitments by some countries were unrealistic with regards to their implementation capacities. Delays in certain reforms or inappropriate sequencing of reforms could hamper the realization of benefits of WTO accession. These implementation challenges present risks to the credibility of the system: the absence of full implementation of WTO commitments by recently acceded countries could incite older Members to seek further disciplines through bilateral/regional treaties. The use of the WTO dispute settlement system to enforce accession deals could exacerbate hard feelings of new entrants about the multilateral trade system.

These challenges – the difficulties accession countries face with implementation, the lengthy and complex accession process, and the prospect that accession deals may undermine perceptions about the fairness of the WTO system – underscore the need for greater support for accession countries and for improving the accession process. With the rising 'price' of accession, efforts to provide technical assistance and capacity-building to accession countries are more necessary than ever before. This support should be available at all stages of the accession process, from early negotiations to implementation. Moreover, as suggested by the WTO (2009), efforts to improve the transparency of the process via '(i) enhanced institutional mechanisms to provide acceding countries with the opportunity to express their views on the process; and (ii) periodic progress reports on accessions to the General Council' (WTO 2010: 11) are steps in the right direction. In sum, it is crucial that new entrants fully participate in the WTO governance process and contribute to shaping the rules of tomorrow's multilateral trading system. This will help to make the multilateral trading system more inclusive and sustainable.

Appendix 1: the accession process

Article XII of the Marrakesh Agreement establishes guidelines for the accession to the WTO. Document WT/ACC/1 (WTO 1995) reviews the different stages in the accession process, including: 1) the application for and the creation of a Working Party (WP); 2) the examination of the Foreign Trade Regime of the state or separate customs territory; 3) the establishment and negotiation of a schedule of concessions and commitments on goods (GATT 1994) and a schedule of commitments on services (GATS 1994); 4) the agreement on the report of the Working Party; and 5) the Protocol setting out the terms of accession.

A1.1 Establishment of the Working Party

Theoretically the establishment of the WP is a simple step. It involves a formal request to the Director-General who, in turn, submits it to the General Council. However, the establishment of the WP requires consensus and can be affected by non-economic considerations. Usually, Membership of the WP is open to all WTO Members, although only the most interested parties (either for political or trade-related reasons) generally participate actively.

A1.2 Examination of the trade regime (fact-finding)

'Fact-finding' is the first stage of interaction between the acceding country and WTO Members. In order to give Members an understanding of their economic and trade systems, acceding countries submit a detailed Memorandum of Foreign Trade Regime (MFTR) which includes a description of their trade policies, copies of the relevant legislation, data on agricultural domestic support and export subsidies, and information on services. The information requirements can be quite substantial even in this preliminary stage. Often, laws and regulations are supplied to the WTO only after the Memorandum has been distributed. This may occur because acceding countries are undertaking a parallel process of legislative reform and/or do not have adequate institutional and administrative capacity to provide and translate the required information.

Once an adequate documentary basis has been collected, the Secretariat will call the first WP for an in-depth discussion of the fact-finding stage. This includes a question and answer phase, which though formally part of the fact-finding phase, often includes negotiations on the 'facts' provided therein. As work proceeds and negotiations start, the Factual Summary of Points Raised evolves into a Draft Report of the Working Party.

A1.3 The negotiation phase

Once the fact-finding process is at fairly advanced stage, acceding countries start the real negotiation process, both at the multilateral and bilateral level. Multilateral negotiations relate to three main areas: rules for goods, TRIPS and services. Since they address different issues, each are treated as separate topics of negotiation. The bilateral negotiations, in turn, focus on market access concessions in goods and commitments in the services sector.

Multilateral negotiations. The acceding countries' regime must conform to WTO rules (including choices about Membership in plurilaterals, like the government procurement agreement that is optional for existing Members). Moreover, the acceding country must address how its national legislation is to be brought into conformity in case of deviations from WTO disciplines. In order to establish a formal execution path, representatives of the acceding country present a plan and a timetable for each of the subjects treated during the different sessions of the WP. Such documents indicate the current state of play, as well as the steps and commitments to be taken in the future. Once negotiated and accepted by WTO Members, they will become part of the Protocols of Accession. These negotiations can even cover the derogations allowed to existing Members, such as the imposition of textile quotas and product-specific safeguards on China.

Bilateral negotiations. (I) *Market access concessions in goods*: Concessions consist mainly of reductions in and bindings of import tariffs as well as of agricultural commitments. They are negotiated with the main trading partners of the acceding country. After an agreement has been reached, these concessions are extended on an unconditional most favoured nation (MFN) basis to all other WTO Members. Negotiations typically evolve as follows: either interested Members submit requests and the acceding country provides initial offers or alternatively, as a means of expediting the work, the acceding country tables its draft schedule of concessions and commitments to provide the basis for negotiation. The proposed agricultural commitments, namely in domestic support and export subsidies, are first negotiated bilaterally with interested parties and then negotiated plurilaterally, if necessary; (II) *Services schedule*: The negotiation process for services is very similar to that of market access negotiations in goods. It is often initiated once the WP has undertaken some form of multilateral examination of the services trade regime. Recently acceded Members, despite the difficulties encountered (mainly due to lack of technical expertise and available information), have adopted commitments in a large number of sectors.

A1.4 The adoption process

The final stage of a country's accession is the adoption process:

> The entire package of Report, Protocol of Accession and Schedules of Concessions and Commitments in Goods and Services constitute the

> conditions under which the acceding government is permitted to join the WTO Agreement ... They are presented to the WTO General Council or the Ministerial Conference. If a two-thirds majority of WTO members vote in favour, the applicant is free to sign the protocol and to accede to the organization. In many cases, the country's own parliament or legislature has to ratify the agreement before membership is complete.
>
> (WTO 1995, 2003)

Despite the apparent simplicity of the bureaucratic steps outlined above, the accession process proves to be a hard task for many countries and governments. The literature available on accession issues often mentions that the process is lengthy and difficult and that it should be shortened and simplified, especially for LDCs (Doha Declaration).

Sources: Michalopoulos 2002; Primo Braga *et al.* 2004; Kennett *et al.* 2005; Evenett and Primo Braga 2006.

References

Adlung, R. 2007. 'The Contribution of Services Liberalization to Poverty Reduction: What Role for the GATS?', *The Journal of World Investment and Trade* 8(4): 1–19.

Birdsall, N. and Lawrence, R. 1999. 'Deep Integration and Trade Agreements: Good for Developing Countries?', in Kaul, I., Grunberg, I. and Stern. M. (eds.), *Global Public Goods: International Cooperation in the 21st Century*, New York: Oxford University Press for the United Nations Development Programme, pp. 128–51.

Cattaneo, O. 2005. 'Has the WTO Gone Too Far or Not Far Enough? Some Reflections on the Concept of Policy Space', in Mitchell, A. (ed.), *Challenges and Prospects for the WTO*, London: Cameron May Publications, pp. 55–84.

Charnovitz, S. 2008. 'Mapping the Law of WTO Accession', in Janow, M., Donaldson, V. and Yanovich, A. (eds.), *The WTO: Dispute Settlement, Governance, and Developing Countries*, Huntington: Juris Publishing, pp. 855–920.

Chea, S. and Sok, H. 2005. 'Cambodia's Accession to the WTO: "Fast Track" Accession by a Least Developed Country', in Gallagher, P., Low, P. and Stoler, A.L. (eds.), *Managing the Challenges of WTO Participation, 45 Case Studies*, Cambridge University Press and WTO, pp. 120–34.

Curzon, G. 1965. *Multilateral Commercial Diplomacy, The GATT and its Impact on National Commercial Policies and Techniques*. London: Michael Joseph Ltd.

Drabek, Z. and Bacchetta, M. 2004. 'Tracing the Effects of WTO Accession on Policy-making in Sovereign States: Preliminary Lessons from the Recent Experience of Transition Countries', *The World Economy* 27(7): 1083–125.

Eschenbach, F. and Hoekman, B. 2006. 'Services Policies in Transition Economies: On the EU and the WTO as Commitment Mechanisms', *World Trade Review* 5(3): 415–43.

Evenett, S. 2006. *A Summary Report of the Discussion on Improving the Accession Process in the 21st Century.* Session organized by the International Development Center (IDRC) at the WTO Public Forum in 2006 at the WTO in Geneva, Switzerland.

Evenett, S. and Primo Braga, C. A. 2006. 'WTO Accession: Moving the Goalposts?', in Newfarmer, R. (ed.), *Trade, Doha, and Development: A Window into the Issues*, Washington, DC: World Bank, pp. 231–45.

Gallagher, P., Low, P. and Stoler, A. L. (eds.) 2005. *Managing the Challenges of WTO Participation, 45 Case Studies.* Cambridge University Press and WTO.

Gay, D. 2005. 'Vanuatu's Suspended Accession Bid: Second Thoughts?', in Gallagher, P., Low, P. and Stoler, A.L. (eds.), *Managing the Challenges of WTO Participation 45 Case Studies*, Cambridge University Press and WTO, pp. 590–606.

Hallett, A. and Primo Braga, C. 1994. 'The New Regionalism and the Threat of Protectionism', *Journal of the Japanese and International Economies* 8(4): 388–421.

Hudec, R. 1988. *Developing Countries in the GATT Legal System.* London: Trade Policy Research Centre.

Ianchovichina, E. and Martin, W. 2001. 'Trade Liberalization in China's Accession to the WTO', *Journal of Economic Integration* 16(4): 421–46.

Kennett, M., Evenett, S. and Gage, J. 2005. *Evaluating WTO Accessions: Legal and Economic Perspectives.* Draft manuscript.

Lacey, S. 2007. 'The View from the Other Side of the Table: WTO Accession from the Perspective of WTO Members', in Streatfeild, J. and Lacey, L. (eds.), *New Reflections on International Trade*, London: Cameron May, pp. 75–98.

Martin, W. 2006. 'Some Development Implications of WTO Accession', *Working Paper.* Washington, DC: World Bank.

Mattoo, A. 2003. 'China's Accession to the WTO: The Services Dimension', *Journal of International Economic Law* 6(2): 299–339.

Michalopoulos, C. 2002. 'WTO Accession', in Hoekman, B., English, P. and Mattoo, A. (eds.), *Development, Trade, and the WTO: A Handbook*, Washington, DC: The World Bank, pp. 61–70.

'Ofa, S. V. 2007. 'General Agreement on Trade in Services (GATS) and WTO Accession Process and Commitments – The Experience of Tonga', in Streatfeild, J. and Lacey, L. (eds.), *New Reflections on International Trade*, London: Cameron May, pp. 335–67.

Oxfam International. 2004. *Extortion at the Gate*. Oxfam Briefing Paper 67. www.oxfam.org [Accessed in November 2010].

Primo Braga, C. A. and Cattaneo, O. 2009a. 'Introduction', in Primo Braga, C.A. and Cattaneo, O. (eds.), *The WTO and Accession Countries*, Cheltenham, UK and Northampton, USA: Edward Elgar Publishing.

Primo Braga, C. A. and Cattaneo, O. (eds.) 2009b. *The WTO and Accession Countries*, Cheltenham, UK and Northampton, USA: Edward Elgar Publishing.

Primo Braga, C. A., Fink, C., Lucenti, K. and Zarcone, F. 2004. *Technical Assistance and WTO Accession: Lessons from Experience*. Draft manuscript prepared after a joint World Bank-GTZ workshop on WTO accession matters, Berlin (updated in 2009).

Rajkarnikar, P. 2005. 'Nepal: The Role of an NGO in Support of Accession', in Gallagher, P., Low, P. and Stoler, A.L. (eds.), *Managing the Challenges of WTO Participation, 45 Case Studies*, Cambridge University Press and WTO, pp. 420–9.

Streatfeild, J. and Lacey, L. (eds.) 2007. *New Reflections on International Trade*. London: Cameron May.

Tsogtbaatar, D. 2005. 'Mongolia's WTO Accession: Expectations and Realities of WTO Membership', in Gallagher, P., Low, P. and Stoler, A.L. (eds.), *Managing the Challenges of WTO Participation 45 Case Studies*, Cambridge University Press and WTO, pp. 409–20.

United Nations. 2000. General Assembly Resolution 55/2. *United Nations Millennium Declaration*. A/RES/55/2. New York: UN.

2001. *Road Map Towards the Implementation of the United Nations Millennium Declaration*. A/56/326. New York: UN.

Van Grasstek, C. 2001. 'Why Demands on Acceding Countries Increase Over Time: A Three-Dimensional Analysis of Multilateral Trade Diplomacy', in *WTO Accessions and Development Policies*, UNCTAD. Geneva: UNCTAD, pp. 78–95.

World Trade Organization (WTO). 1995. *Accession to the World Trade Organization, Procedures for Negotiations under Article 12. Note by the Secretariat*. WT/ACC/1. Geneva: WTO.

2001. *Report of the Working Party on the Accession of China*. WT/ACC/CHN/49. Geneva: WTO.

2003. *Accession of Least Developed Countries (Guidelines)*. WT/L/508. Geneva: WTO.

2005. *Technical Note on the Accession Process*. WT/ACC/10/Rev.3. Geneva: WTO.

2008. *A Handbook on Accession to the WTO*. Cambridge University Press and WTO.

2009. *Accession of Developing Countries – Communication from Gabon on Behalf of the Informal Group of Developing Countries.* General Council 20–21 October. WT/GC/119. Geneva: WTO.

2010. *WTO Accessions: 2009 Annual Report by the Director-General.* WT/ACC/13. Geneva: WTO.

Ya Qin, J. 2003. 'WTO-plus Obligations and their Implications for the World Trade Organization Legal System', *Journal of World Trade* 37(3): 483–522.

PART V

Conclusion

21

Development-oriented perspectives on global trade governance: a summary of proposals for making global trade governance work for development

CAROLYN DEERE BIRKBECK

Demand for global trade governance that supports development is high. Developing countries have long called for a greater role in governing the global economy and its trading system. As the importance of developing countries in global trade rises and South–South trade among them grows (UNCTAD 2010), they have stepped up calls for a stronger say in the decision-making processes and institutions that impact how global trade is conducted and the way its rules are made, implemented and enforced.

This book shows that the way global trade is governed can facilitate or hinder the prospects for reaching rules and arrangements that benefit developing countries. Yet, to date, the visibility of development perspectives in the scholarly debates on global trade governance has been weak. The unique contribution of this volume is its compilation of a broad geographical spectrum of development-oriented views and proposals, and its engagement of scholars and practitioners from government, international organizations and stakeholder groups. The volume builds on a large body of literature and many years of policy discussion on global trade governance, the future of the global trading system and how to make trade fairer for developing countries.[1]

Together, the contributors to this book provide concrete guidance on what a development agenda for global trade governance might include. They both reinforce and supplement development-oriented proposals

The author is a Senior Researcher at Oxford's Global Economic Governance Programme.
She is grateful to Meg Harbourd for editorial and research assistance for this chapter.

[1] Recent works include, for instance, Akyüz (2009); Cottier and Elsig (2011); Deere Birkbeck and Monagle (2009); Deere Birkbeck and Meléndez-Ortiz (2009); Lee and Wilkinson (2007); Lehmann and Lehmann (2010); Petersmann (2005b); Steger (2009a); and Taniguchi *et al.* (2007).

already on the table. For the purposes of this book, governance is broadly defined to include the suite of processes, principles and norms as well as the institutional architecture through which rules and practices for managing global trade are made, implemented and enforced.

In this concluding chapter, I draw together the priorities and proposals set forth in this book and place them in the context of policy debates and the scholarly literature.

The chapter begins with a review of the policy context for discussion of global trade governance and institutional reform of the WTO, noting the rise of debates on development and trade governance. It then outlines the scope of the broader literature on global trade governance and WTO reform, of which the development dimension is one part. It also reviews the main contours of debates on trade and development, observing that these debates have a considerable impact on the thrust of development agendas for trade governance reform.

The heart of the chapter draws together development-oriented proposals from across the book, showing where and how they build on or diverge from existing proposals. It highlights four thematic areas where clear development priorities and proposals for improved global trade governance exist.

The first theme places global trade governance in the context of global economic governance more broadly. It draws attention to the many components of trade governance, highlighting a range of relevant multilateral, bilateral and regional arrangements, as well as the relevance to trade governance of the many international economic, social and environmental regimes that impact development.

The second theme addresses expectations about the roles and responsibilities of developing countries in trade governance, the diversity of developing country priorities and strategies, their efforts to organize themselves collectively, and relationships with national stakeholders . The third theme identifies proposals for strengthening multilateralism in global trade and WTO reforms that would benefit developing countries. In light of the practical challenges of integrating development priorities into WTO negotiations and the subsequent implementation process,[2] proposals in this area relate to the goals and principles underpinning the WTO, the scope of the WTO agenda, its functions (such as dispute settlement, monitoring and capacity-building, among others) and the role of the Secretariat.

[2] See, for instance, Alavi (2008); Alessandrini (2010); Bhaumik (2006); Debroy and Chakraborty (2007); Hohmann (2008); Khan and Chakraborty (2008); and Ismail (2007, 2009d).

A fourth theme is devoted to proposals for improving the fairness of processes of trade negotiations at the bilateral, regional and multilateral level. The chapter concludes with the question of political strategy for making global trade governance work for development.

1 The state of debate on global trade governance and development

1.1 The trade governance debate: the policy context

Over the past two decades, the call for developing countries to have a greater influence on global economic governance has steadily intensified. Debates on globalization have fuelled pressures for fairer arrangements that would promote greater benefits for developing countries and protect them from globalization's pernicious aspects (ILO 2001; Rodrik 1997; Stiglitz 2003). Building on developing country efforts since the 1950s at the UN, the Bretton Woods Institutions and the General Agreement on Tariffs and Trade (GATT) to forge a more equitable international economic order (Cutajar 1985; Krasner 1985), this push regularly resurfaces wherever the governing bodies of international organizations meet, whether at the United Nations (UN 2009a), the UN Conference on Trade and Development (UNCTAD), the Organisation for Economic Co-operation and Development (OECD), annual meetings of the World Bank and the International Monetary Fund, or WTO Ministerial Conferences (Das 2000; OECD 2005, 2008; Woods 2010).

On the trade front, developing countries have long argued that global trade arrangements favour the needs of richer, developed countries that dominate decision-making. The complaints have not been completely ignored. In 2001, the WTO Ministerial Conference in Doha made 'development' a guiding objective of the round of trade negotiations it launched.[3] And, in the UN Millennium Development Goals (MDGs), the international community hailed the importance of a rule-based, predictable, non-discriminatory and open trading system to ensuring that 'globalization becomes a positive force for *all* the world's people' (emphasis added) (UN 2000, 2001). The MDGs' call for a 'partnership for development' highlighted the special trade needs of least developed countries.

[3] This decision was taken to make fresh negotiations more palatable to unenthusiastic developing countries whose priority was to rebalance the unequal outcomes of the Uruguay Round (Finger 2007; Safardi and Laird 1996; TWN 2001). For analysis of the Uruguay Round, see Croome (1999) and on the earlier days of the GATT, see Curzon (1965). For the texts of the Uruguay Round's outcomes, see WTO (1999).

Further, the quadrennial meetings of the United Nations Conference on Trade and Development (UNCTAD) have consistently taken up the challenges of developing country engagement in the international trade architecture.

Yet, by 2005, the UN Millennium Taskforce on Trade concluded that the international trading system remained 'stacked against developing countries' (UN Millennium Project 2005). And in 2009, a UN Commission on Reforms of the International Monetary and Financial System (UN 2009b) highlighted the outstanding need for coherence between policies and international organizations relevant to trade, development and finance. In 2009, the Geneva Ministerial Conference of the World Trade Organization (WTO) illustrated the enduring need more systematic attention to improving how the multilateral trading system addresses development (Deere Birkbeck and Cherneva 2011; WTO 2009e).

The publication of this book coincides with a time of uncertainty in trade and trade policy-making. The 2008–9 global financial and economic crisis saw trade flows and finance collapse, and protectionist pressures rise. As the G20 Leaders' Summits have unfolded as a new mechanism in global governance, albeit with limited legitimacy, commentators debate how the G20 Leaders should engage in the realm of global trade and whether the rise of their political meetings undermines or complements the role of the WTO.[4] Fatigue and exasperation with the lethargy of the Doha Round negotiations – now the longest-running round in the history of multilateral trade negotiations – has renewed concern about the WTO decision-making process and the search for Doha 'Plan B' has begun, particularly as regional and bilateral agreements proliferate (Baldwin 2009; Narlikar and Vickers 2009).[5] As developing countries' collective share of international trade grows, the shifting power balance in multilateral trade negotiations has prompted interest in the appropriate role

[4] While a more inclusive grouping than the G8, the scope of the G20's ambition remains unclear. In the meantime, the uneven representation of developing countries and ad hoc approach to membership continues to undermine its legitimacy in the eyes of many commentators and countries not represented in the grouping. For views on the G20, particularly in relation to trade, see Baldwin and Evenett (2009); Deere Birkbeck and Meléndez-Ortiz (2009); Higgott (2009); UN (2009b); and Woods (2010).

[5] While such arrangements do little by way of rule-making or subsidy reform, countries continue to forge them both for market access benefits and for foreign policy motivations, in spite of the challenges they pose to the multilateral regime's non-discriminatory norms. Notably, for instance, the USA estimates greater economic benefits from the market access negotiations in its pending bilateral deal with Korea, than from the entire Doha package. The bilateral arrangement does not, however, address trade rules.

of emerging powers and their responsibilities to the smallest and poorest developing countries, particularly those in Africa (Njinkeu 2009; Oyejide 2009). Meanwhile, debate on how the trade regime can address sustainable development objectives has intensified in light of the challenges of climate change (Cosbey 2009; Najam *et al.* 2007). As countries begin to grapple with the question of a post-Doha agenda for the multilateral trading system, even the process for discerning that agenda remains unclear.[6]

To date, much of the debate on global trade governance has focused on the WTO, the leading multilateral institution for global trade. In the fifteen years since the WTO was established, the issue of institutional reform – whether it is needed, in what form and through what kind of process – has been an ever-present issue for the organization and its Member States. Calls from Member States[7] and scholars for institutional reform of the WTO have been most acute at specific junctures in its relatively short history – most notably following the Seattle, Cancún and Hong Kong WTO Ministerial Conferences.[8] Civil society groups, business groups and parliaments have also expressed a wide range of concerns about the WTO's functioning, transparency and effectiveness, as well as on the representation of developing country interests.[9]

In 2004, WTO Director-General, Dr Supachai Panitchpakdi, responded by commissioning a Consultative Board of experts, led by Peter Sutherland (a former head of the GATT, to present proposals for institutional reform (Consultative Board 2004).[10] The Sutherland

[6] GEG and ICTSD (2010); Khor (2002); Mattoo and Subramanian (2009); Wilkinson (2009a).

[7] See, for instance, WTO Doc T/GC/M91, General Council – Minutes of Meeting – 26 January 2005; WT/MIN (03)/ST/58, Ministerial Conference – Fifth Session Cancún, 10–14 September 2003 – Honduras – Statement by H.E. Mr Norman García, Secretary of State, Department of Industry and Commerce; WT/GC/W/477, General Council – Preparatory Process in Geneva and Negotiating Process at Ministerial Conferences – Communication from Australia, Canada, Hong Kong, China, New Zealand, Singapore, Switzerland; WT/MIN(01)/ST/110, Ministerial Conference – Fourth Session – Doha, 9–13 November 2001 – Republic of the Fiji Islands – Statement by H.E. Mr Isikeli Mataitoga, Ambassador, Permanent Representative to the WTO; WT/GC/M/57, General Council – Minutes of Meeting – 17 and 19 July 2000.

[8] See, for instance, Bhagwati (2001), Baldwin (2006); Blackhurst (2001); Cho (2004); EC Directorate-General for Trade (2003), ETUC (2006); Moore (2003); and Schott (2000).

[9] See, for instance, CAFOD *et al.* (2002); Consumers International (2000); Kaukab *et al.* (2004); Khor (2006): Ismail (2008), (2009d); UK Parliament (2003); and Wilkinson (2006b).

[10] This initiative was preceded by earlier efforts within the GATT system, such as the Leutwiler Report (Leutwiler *et al.* 1985). The Sutherland Report spurred two journal special issues where scholars debated the analysis and recommendations of the report. See for instance Pauwelyn (2005), Wolfe (2005). Two former WTO Directors-General have also published articles or books with their reflections (e.g. Moore 2003, 2004 and Sutherland 2005).

Report was followed in 2007 by an independent commission supported by Warwick University on 'the Future of the WTO' (Warwick Commission 2007).[11] Both initiatives affirmed the political imperative of finding ways to assuage the concerns of developing countries. The launch of the 'Aid for Trade' initiative in 2005 as a new component of global trade governance was driven by the political need to address many developing countries' difficulties in deriving benefits from their participation in the international trade system.[12] The political salience of development concerns was also in clear view in 2009 when WTO Director-General Pascal Lamy called for transforming the WTO into an institution that is 'more development-friendly [and] more user-friendly, so that its benefits are felt by all, large and small, rich and poor, strong and weak' (WTO 2009a).

Neither the global trading system, nor the debate about its reform, is static. As the intensity of public debate on globalization waxes and wanes, and the salience of specific trade challenges shifts and evolves, so too has the debate on global trade governance.[13] Further, the record to date shows that some reform is possible.

At the WTO, for instance, a number of administrative and informal changes were made to how the organization works over its first fifteen years (see Box 21.1 later in this chapter) (P. Gallagher 2005; WTO 2007).[14] There have also been several formal decisions of the WTO's General Council, trade Ministers or the WTO Secretariat. Views differ on whether such changes have been sufficient, as do perspectives on the feasibility, desirability and necessity of further reform. Despite the recurrent stalling of the Doha Round negotiations and concern about threats to multilateralism in trade, the WTO's current Director-General maintains, for instance, that the organization is essentially in tact and working. While he once lambasted the WTO as a 'medieval institution', Lamy now insists that compared to other international economic organizations, the WTO faces no fundamental challenges in the realm of governance (Lamy 2009). Views also diverge on whether such reform should be incremental or if a

[11] The Warwick Commission proposed a number of institutional changes at the WTO, including increasing the size of the WTO Secretariat, expanding the powers of the Director-General, and revising the process for reaching new trade deals.

[12] See Njinkeu and Cameron (2008); Page (2003); Prowse (2002, 2005); and WTO (2006a, (2010a).

[13] Compare, for instance, the table of contents of the volume edited by Krueger in 1998 to those that of Steger in 2009a.

[14] Also see Deere Birkbeck and Monagle (2009).

more radical, structural overhaul is in order, and whether such processes should be essentially political or technical undertakings.[15]

Meanwhile, proposals for reform continue to be generated by governments, scholars, civil society and industry groups. Indeed, interest in more effective governance spurred governments to resume in 2009 the practice of holding biennial Ministerial Conferences as called for in the WTO's mandate and to consider ways to strengthen the multilateral trading system (Deere Birkbeck 2009b; WTO 2001, 2009c, 2009d).[16]

1.2 Development in the trade governance debate

Development-oriented proposals on trade governance can be found across the international policy arena. At the UN and the WTO, developing countries have emphasized the shortcomings of the structure and processes of trade governance, calling for greater participation and representation in decision-making (African Group 2000; G77 1999; G77 and China 2003).[17]

Informing such policy efforts is a growing body of research on trade governance from developing country scholars, research centres, think tanks and universities,[18] as well as from developing country negotiators and senior international officials.[19] Governance concerns also arise in developing country research on specific trade and development issues. In general, however, developing country scholarship on trade governance is less prominent than that on trade and development issues, and considerably less than that of developed country scholarship on governance.

A number of developed country researchers also offer development perspectives on governance challenges.[20] In parallel, many international non-governmental organizations (NGOs) have advocated in favour of

[15] For varying perspectives on this issue, see Bello (2002, 2002a); Ostry (2002); TWN (2001), TWN *et al.* (2003); and Wolfe (2008).

[16] These were each communications from WTO Member States regarding the Geneva WTO Ministerial Conference held in 2009. The statements were from India, Australia, Brazil, Canada, China, Hong Kong China, European Communities, India, Japan, Korea, Malaysia, Mauritius, Mexico, Norway, South Africa, Switzerland, Turkey, United States and Uruguay (WTO 2009c, 2009d).

[17] For a compilation and review of political statements on reform of the WTO, see Deere Birkbeck and Monagle (2009).

[18] See, for example, Aggarwal (2001); Draper (2010); Kumar (2002, 2007); RIS (2003); Srinivasan (1998); and Stewart (1993).

[19] See, for example, Ismail (2009d); Davies (2009); de la Calle (2000); and Ricupero (2001).

[20] See, for example, Alavi (2008); Alessandrini (2010); Hoekman (2001, 2005); and Stiglitz and Charlton (2005).

trade governance reforms they believe would better enable attention to development concerns.[21] Further, a good portion of the research and proposals on trade governance that self-describe as development-oriented emanates from international organizations, such as UNCTAD, the World Bank and various UN agencies. Questions of trade governance have been prominent themes at UNCTAD's regular conferences and in its flagship reports on trade and development (e.g. UNCTAD 2003a, 2007), as well as in UNDP-sponsored studies, notably its 2003 report on *Making Global Trade Work for People* (UNDP 2003; Rodrik 2001; TWN 2001) and its agenda-setting *Human Development Reports* (UNDP 2005). The South Centre, an intergovernmental think tank of developing countries, has also been a consistent source of proposals on trade governance reform to assist developing countries (see, for instance, 2003, 2008, 2009). In addition, the UK's Department for International Development (DFID) also supported a multi-year research project on the Architecture for Trade and Development (GTFA 2005) that engaged developed and developing country experts.

As noted above, debate on global trade governance extends far beyond development concerns. While the interest of leading international trade scholars in the development dimension of trade governance is growing,[22] it has not often been the core concern of their scholarship. (To date, scholars of international relations and North–South politics who frequently debate global economic governance have devoted surprisingly little detailed attention to global trade.) For some developed country researchers, the motivation for understanding developing country perspectives on governance is not one of advancing development, but rather a frustration with the languishing Doha Round and a concern for managing the competitive threats posed by emerging developing countries (see, for instance, the debate on China's entrance into the WTO). Indeed, the call for greater attention to developing country priorities has spurred sceptics to question the extent to which the WTO should be considered a 'development' institution.

[21] Action Aid *et al.* (2000); Das (1998, 2002, 2007); Oxfam (2000); Oxfam International *et al.* (2001); TWN (1999, 2001); and TWN *et al.* (2003). In 2000, for instance, ActionAid, CAFOD, Christian Aid, Consumers International, FIELD, Oxfam, the World Development Movement and the Royal Society for the Protection of Birds (RSPB) issued a joint set of proposals on WTO reform (Action Aid *et al.* 2000).

[22] See Cottier and Elsig (2011); Petersmann (2005b); and Steger (2009a).

1.3 Key contours of the trade governance debate: putting development debates in context

To place the development dimension in context, the following discussion outlines the contours of five core themes of the broader scholarly literature and policy discussions on global trade governance.

A first set of literature explores the political economy of the global trading system. It analyses the dynamics of negotiations among states, their relationships with non-state actors (e.g. industry and NGOs) and the interaction among the numerous institutions, rules and processes that comprise trade governance.[23] Here, key themes addressed include the intersection of the WTO with proliferating bilateral and regional trade and investment agreements; the implications of bilateralism and regionalism for multilateralism in trade (Baldwin and Low 2009; Bhagwati 2008; Zedillo 2009); and the WTO's role in global governance, including its interaction with other international institutions (Jackson 1999), most notably the United Nations family (Sampson 2001, 2004, 2005a, 2009) and international financial institutions (Auboin 2004, 2007; Cohn 2003; Siegel 2002; Vines 1998).

A second theme of the literature on global trade governance explores the interface of trade rules and other areas of international law (Pauwelyn 2003) (such as on the environment, human rights and labour rights),[24] voluntary standards (Kirton and Trebilcock 2004) and international declarations and commitments (such as the Millennium Development Goals). A core issue of debate has been the extent to which so-called 'non-trade' issues should be incorporated within trade agreements, subject to side-agreements, or dealt with through complementary action in other international fora or at the national level. In addition, concern about 'trade-and' issues has stimulated proposals for incorporating assessment and evaluation of sustainable development, environment, poverty and gender impacts into trade governance.[25]

A third preoccupation of scholars of trade governance has been processes of trade negotiation, decision-making and dispute settlement.[26]

[23] See, for instance, Barton *et al.* (2006); Bluestein (2009); Higgott (2009); Hudec (1975, 1987); Odell (2000); and Steinberg (2002).

[24] See Alvarez (2002); Beukel (2001); Cohn (2003); Conca (2000); Deere (2004); Esty (1994); Petersmann (2004, 2005a); Sampson (2001, 2009); Trachtman (2002); and WWF (1999b).

[25] Deere Birkbeck (2009a); Gehring and Segger (2005); IISD (1999, 2000); Konz *et al.* (2000); Schorr (2004); Turner *et al.* (2008); and von Moltke (2010).

[26] See Cottier (2007, 2009); Cottier and Takenoshita (2003, 2008); de Bievre (2002); Dunning (2002); Ehlermann and Ehring (2005); Elsig (2009); Evian Group (2007); Footer (2006);

Frustration with the failure to seal a Doha Round deal has prompted a raft of proposals to make the WTO a more effective and efficient negotiating institution. Other proposals to improve trade negotiations are motivated by goals of greater fairness and of transforming trade agreements from mercantilist instruments serving multinational commercial interests to ones that respond to sustainable development imperatives.[27] For some, the focus is on the transparency of trade negotiations, decision-making and dispute settlement processes, and their implications for national sovereignty and democratic processes.[28] A further subset of the literature on trade governance examines the legitimacy of the WTO and its accountability to citizens, and assesses opportunities for participation and oversight by civil society groups, labour unions, social movements and parliaments.[29]

In the WTO context, concerns about decision-making have yielded debate on the merits of the use of the concept of a 'single undertaking' in WTO negotiations and mini-Ministerials (Wolfe 2004, 2009), as well as alternative approaches to decision-making, including 'critical-mass', variable geometry and plurilateral agreements.[30] To facilitate progress in negotiations, researchers have explored issues such as how to make better use of Chairs in WTO negotiations (Odell 2005), options for differentiating among developing countries in the negotiation and application of WTO rules, and possibilities for the 'graduation' of some countries from 'developing' status (Hoekman 2005; Keck and Low 2004; Mitchell and Voon 2009). There has also been considerable attention to the political economy of engaging developing countries in new Rounds of negotiations and strategies for incorporating new issues (such as competition, investment and services) on the trade negotiating agenda (Krueger 1999; Lawrence 2006).

Jackson (1997); McGinnis and Movsesian (2000); Ostry (2002); Rolland (2010); Steger (2009b); van Dijck and Faber (1996); and Ziegler and Bonzon (2007).

27 Deere Birkbeck (2009a); Eagleton (2006); Gehring and Segger (2005); IISD (2000); ICTSD and IISD (2004); Meléndez-Ortiz and Delhavi (2000); Sampson (2005b); and von Moltke (1996).

28 On national sovereignty and democracy, see Bacchus (2004); Barfield (2001); Nader and Wallach (1996); Public Citizen (1999); and Wallach and Sforza (1999).

29 On legitimacy and accountability, see Bellmann and Gester (1996); and Esty (1998). On participation of non-state actors, see Charnovitz (2000, 2002); Halle (2007); Hilf (2003); Lacarte (2004); Marceau and Pedersen (1999); Marceau and Stilwell (2001); Shell (1996); van den Bossche (2009); Wilkinson (2002a, 2002b). For engagement of parliaments in trade policy-making, see Chutikul (2003); and Shaffer (2004a). On corporate influence, see Eagleton (2006).

30 See Gallagher and Stoler (2009); Low (2009b); McMillan (2010); van Grasstek and Sauvé (2006); and WEF (2010).

Fourth, as alluded to above, the WTO has been a focal point of governance debate. Beyond the WTO negotiation process, reform proposals have also been advanced for several more of the WTO's functions (Deere Birkbeck and Monagle 2009),[31] as well as its internal administration.[32] On the latter issue, analyses have covered the role and responsibilities of the Secretariat and the Director-General; the appropriate selection process for the Director-General; the Secretariat's management, staffing and culture; the appropriate scale and allocation of Secretariat resources; the sources of the WTO's budget (including trust funds and contributions to the regular budget); internal transparency within the Secretariat (such as the de-restriction of documents); and appropriate arrangements for the Secretariat's relationship with Member States and stakeholders. Scholars have also debated proposals for the creation of a WTO Executive Board (Blackhurst 1998; Steger 2009a), bolstering the WTO's 'missing middle' of policy deliberation (Deere Birkbeck 2009a; Evenett 2008; Low 2009a), and greater 'constitutionalization' of the WTO.[33]

In terms of the WTO's functions, analysis of the WTO's dispute settlement system and its negotiation function dominates the scene.[34] There is also growing interest in improving WTO surveillance and monitoring mechanisms to address the failures of compliance with the WTO's notification system, and more recently to address rising protectionist pressures in the wake of the latest global financial crisis.[35]

[31] Using the analytical framework advanced in Deere Birkbeck (2009a), which proposes a functional approach as a complement to existing approaches, Deere Birkbeck and Monagle (2009) review a diversity of proposals for WTO reform.

[32] Key contributions in these areas include: Alvarez-Jiménez 2009; Blackhurst 1998; Blackhurst and Hartridge (2004); Bohne (2010); Elsig (2007); Steger (2007, 2009b); and Steger and Shpilkovskaya (2009).

[33] See, for instance, Cass (2005); Howse (2003); Howse and Nicolaidis (2003); Joerges and Petersmann (2006) ; and Petersmann (2005a).

[34] This literature touches a vast range of issues related to improving the efficiency and transparency of the WTO dispute settlement process, as well as but also on matters such as judicial activism at the WTO (Bacchus 2004), the role of the Secretariat in dispute proceedings, and the balance between the WTO's legislative and dispute settlement functions (Barton *et al.* 2006; Steinberg and Goldstein 2009); opportunities for the public to observe and input into proceedings; the role of the Appellate Body and the panels; and the appropriate role for the Secretariat in the dispute settlement process, as well as the appropriate role of international organizations in WTO proceedings; the relationship between WTO dispute settlement processes and other international judicial bodies; as well as the relationship between WTO law and other sources of international law.

[35] Baldwin and Evenett (2009); Collins-Williams and Wolfe (2010); Lamy (2007); Mavroidis (1991–1992); and Wolfe (2010).

Finally, the development dimensions of trade governance is both a discrete issue and one that arises in each of the four areas discussed above.

To understand the origins and motivations of develoment-oriented proposals, it is helpful first to review the key contours of debates on trade and development. The development dimensions of the trade governance debate – and the contributions of this book to it – are then the focus of the remainder of this chapter.

1.4 The challenges of trade and development

The interactions between trade and development have inspired contributions from economists, development analysts and political scientists on a vast array of social, economic and political issues, many of which have links to governance debates. Indeed, this literature sets the scene for much of the debate on how better to govern global trade for development. This section thus briefly reviews some of the key aspects of the trade and development debate over the past five years to provide context for the governance proposals set forth in this book.[36]

A first subset of the literature studies the relationships between trade, trade agreements and trade liberalization, on the one hand, and growth, development and poverty alleviation on the other.[37] Here, there have been disagreements between critics opposed to globalization (Dunkley 2000), who are sceptical of the relationship between openness, trade and growth, and those who argue that freer, more open markets are a prerequisite to the trade expansion they believe will drive growth. In between these two positions are a vast range of nuanced views on questions of what kind of openness, at what pace openness should proceed, and what kinds of supportive institutions might facilitate development. Many critics call for rejecting the so-called 'Washington Consensus' on trade liberalization (Raghavan 2000b; Rodrik 2009), which they consider part of a discredited neo-liberal policy package. Among these, some argue in favour of 'bottom-up' and nationally oriented approaches to development as well as 'fair trade' initiatives,[38] while others work to improve the rules, promote a rules-based system and devise a development-friendly approach to open trade. This debate has in turn spurred a vast literature on the impacts of

[36] For a broad overview of literature on trade and development, see Irwin (2003).

[37] See, for instance, Cline (2004); Guha-Khasnobis (2004); Hertel and Winters (2005); McCulloch *et al.* (2001); Trachtman (2003); Turner *et al.* (2008); UNDP (2009).

[38] On fair trade movements and activities, and the challenges of transforming global trade in this direction, see Raynolds *et al.* (2007).

trade flows, rules and liberalization on social policies, regulation and services, food security and rural poverty (Burnett and Manji 2007; Rodrik 2001; WTO and ILO 2009),[39] as well as on particular segments of the population, such as urban and rural communities, informal labourers and women (Nadakavukaren Schefer 2010; Williams 2002). This literature also draws attention to the persistent marginalization of the smallest, poorest and most vulnerable countries from the benefits of participation in the global trading system.[40]

A second theme of scholarly debate on trade and development analyses specific trade issues of concern to developing countries, including market access to developed countries' markets; the obstacles imposed by discriminatory tariff escalation; preference erosion; trade rules deemed to favour developed countries (such as the WTO's Agreement on Trade-related Intellectual Property Rights (TRIPS)); the control of international supply chains by major developed country multinationals; developed country agricultural policies and subsidies; and the abuse of anti-dumping rules. A considerable part of this literature has focused on the links between trade reforms, industrial policy and investment (Kumar 2002; Laird and de Cordoba 2006; Shadlen 2005); the need to dismantle discrimination against developing countries (Hoekman 2004); the appropriate nature of development strategy in a globalized economy; and the importance of flexibilities in trade rules (K. Gallagher 2005).

A third area of the trade and development literature takes up legal dimensions of the WTO and its development obligations (Ezeani 2010). It includes studies on the participation of developing countries in the WTO legal system (Thomas and Trachtman 2009); the role of WTO law in developing countries (Bermann and Mavroidis 2007; Nottage 2008); and understanding what provisions are most used by and against developing countries (Horn and Mavroidis 2003).

A fourth area of attention focuses on devising specific proposals to help developing countries better advance their interests in the negotiation and implementation of multilateral, regional and bilateral trade arrangements. Central to this effort have been initiatives to devise a positive developing

[39] On developed country agricultural policies, food security and trade negotiations, see Diao *et al.* (2003); Diaz-Bonilla *et al.* (2003a, 2003b); Dowlah (2004); Hoda and Gulati (2008); Rosset (2006); Stevens *et al.* (2000). Analysis of impacts includes many national case studies. See, for instance, Aggarwal and Lee (2010); Ingco (2003); Mattoo and Stern (2003).

[40] See Bora *et al.* (2005); Centre for Policy Dialogue (2003); Commonwealth Secretariat and World Bank (2000); Grynberg (2006); Jones *et al.* (2010); UNCTAD (2004); and Wang (1997).

country agenda for trade negotiations (UNCTAD 2000, 2003b and 2007), including developing country options on individual topics of trade negotiation (Hoekman and Martin 2001; Jha and Vossenaar 1999). Amidst the Doha Round of trade negotiations, this work has focused on what the Doha deal needs to include to fulfil the development mandate of the negotiations.[41] This has included specific works on operationalizing the principle of special and differential treatment (SDT) and the concept of policy space for developing countries (Corrales-Leal 2007; K. Gallagher 2005; Stevens 2003a, 2003b); as well as on implementing WTO rules in ways that advance their development (Correa 2000; Deere 2008; Finger 2007; Shaffer 2006). Researchers have also proposed elements needed to make the overall package of trade arrangements more development-friendly, including, for instance, more attention to issues of migration, commodities trade and technology transfer (Hoekman *et al.* 2003; Mattoo and Subramanian 2003; TWN *et al.* 2003).

A final area of analysis takes up institutional and strategic issues relevant to how developing countries participate in trade (Page 1994). Here, scholars have debated the local conditions under which deeper economic integration can support development (Birdsall and Lawrence 1999) and the relationship between national institutions, trade policy reforms and the development outcomes of trade (Rodrik 2002, 2007). The literature here includes studies of the limited supply-side capacities of developing countries to profit from trade opportunities where they emerge, and the institutional constraints to managing the socio-economic impacts and trade-offs that accompany adaptation to new trade rules. The launch of the 'Aid for Trade' initiative in 2005 (WTO 2006b) has spurred numerous works on how best to boost those capacities as well as on what kinds of assistance would be most helpful. Scholars have also debated the economic and political merits of regional economic integration efforts among developing countries and of boosted South–South trade cooperation, and set forth detailed agendas in each area (RIS 2003; 2007).

2 Putting global trade governance in context: sustainable development challenges in the global economy

The remainder of this chapter reviews the proposals presented in this book, placing them in the context of existing contributions on improving the development-orientation of global trade governance. Notably, in each

[41] See, for instance, Anderson *et al.* (2005); Stiglitz and Charlton (2005); TWN *et al.* (2003), and van Dijck and Faber (2006).

area, there is not necessarily a unified or single view. The priorities and emphasis of different regions and subsets of countries (e.g. small states, least developed countries (LDCs), emerging powers), as well as stakeholders within them, can vary widely. Where this book is otherwise silent on some issues that have featured significantly in policy debates, I refer the reader to relevant sources and proposals.

The first priority advanced in this book is that of placing global trade governance in the context of broader global governance challenges and priorities in the area of social and sustainable development.

To set the scene, Ocampo opens the book by exploring what greater fairness means in the global economy.[42] He observes that the power asymmetries that characterize the global economic system largely determine divergence of income levels among countries.[43] He also observes a second asymmetry 'between the rapid globalization of (some) markets and the relative weakness of the international social agenda', which he regards as essential to overcoming worsening inequalities within countries.

Ocampo joins other contributors to this book in his emphasis on values. Together, they present the pursuit of an effective and inclusive global trading system as a global public good, both for the purposes of legitimacy but also for producing fair outcomes.[44] They emphasize that the credibility of international agreements is undermined when capacity to implement them is weak or absent. In the face of mercantilist pressures on the global trading system, the book emphasizes the importance of values of solidarity, fairness, human rights, environmental sustainability, and of social justice within and between countries for the pursuit of governance that is more responsive to developing countries. Alongside the policy work of integrating development principles and equity goals, Puri argues in Chapter 2, is the political challenge of fostering the global solidarity needed for the WTO to reinvent itself as a global 'development' good.

Interest in stronger alignment of international economic arrangements and policy-making with development goals has been a long-standing theme of development-oriented scholarship and policy advocacy, as have calls for greater coherence between policies for managing intersecting macroeconomic issues (i.e. trade, finance, debt and development

[42] On concepts of fairness and justice in international trade, see Barry (2006); Brown and Stern (2007); Moellendorf (2005); Moore (2010); and Risse (2007).

[43] For scholarly discussions of the various dimensions of power in international trade, see Eagleton-Pierce (2007); and Shaffer (2004b).

[44] For more on global public goods and international trade, see Bach (2007) and Mendoza (2003).

policy).[45] These concerns have spurred efforts to enshrine the principles of 'policy space' for development strategy and special and differential treatment in the governance arrangements that impact global trade, whether at the bilateral, regional or multilateral level (Rodrik 2001; RIS 2007). In addition, the impact of the global financial crisis on trade has spurred new emphasis on the importance of global cooperation to ensure predictable financing for developing country exports, whether through commercial banks, bilateral export credit and risk management facilities, or multilateral organizations (Abreu 2009).

Several contributors to this book reiterate the need for interactions among the WTO, international financial institutions, regional development banks and other international regimes for global governance to focus on development priorities. They call for greater deference to the United Nations as the most representative forum for global economic decision-making, boosting the status of other international organizations in WTO processes, and improving the WTO's cooperation with other international organizations, particularly UN agencies.

In Chapter 2, for instance, Puri argues that:

> Member States at the UN, the WTO, the International Monetary Fund (IMF) and the World Bank, as well as participants in emerging global economic fora such as the G20, need to take a holistic view that integrates the development perspective into trade, financial, monetary, environmental and technology governance systems. They need to balance the needs of liberalization with those of transparency, good regulation and oversight, while increasing the voice and participation of developing countries in decision-making. Greater coherence, less fragmentation and the elimination of asymmetries, including in the trading system, are critical.

In Chapter 10, Chimni also emphasizes the importance of properly placing the WTO in the context of 'other international institutions that collectively impinge on the ability of the Third World to pursue independent economic and social policies'. In Chapter 3, Nadal calls for better integrating debates on global trade governance with those on institutions responsible for macroeconomic policy and analysing what their joint impact on sustainable development may be.

In her chapter, Puri also emphasises the importance of bolstering the role of the UN and UNCTAD in efforts to achieve more effective, coherent and development-enhancing coordination of global economic policy.

[45] Akyüz (2004, 2009); Khor (2001); Raghavan (2000b); Rodrik (2001); Puri (2008); South Centre (2009; UN (2009b).

She calls for the UN to be given greater recognition as the repository of development-focused knowledge and experience. In particular, she proposes that a UN Global Economic Coordination Council, established at a level equivalent to the UN Security Council, be charged with independent international analysis, supported intellectually through contributions and participation from all the relevant global institutions and members of the UN Secretariat and the WTO. She argues that this Council would serve as a more democratic alternative to the G20 Leaders' Summits for promoting development and coherence as central policy goals of major international organizations.

There has also been considerable interest among development advocates in the linkages between global trade governance and the suite of international arrangements and commitments to address social issues, human rights, cultural diversity and environmental challenges, including those with major economic implications such as climate change (Stilwell 2009). Views vary on how best to govern this intersection. In Chapter 1, Ocampo draws attention to the idea that improved monitoring is a vital, albeit often overlooked, prerequisite for stronger coherence and accountability of the international community to objectives agreed upon at world conferences and summits. He argues for the regular production, dissemination and analysis of information on the situation of economic, social and cultural rights, and on the provision of both 'global public goods' and 'goods of social value'. He argues that such 'evaluations should be discussed at representative national fora, with active participation by parliaments and civil society'.

In Chapter 4, Meléndez-Ortiz and Biswas highlight the challenges to constructive, coherent interaction and coordination among trade arrangements and between them and the multiplicity of other institutions and rules affecting trade and sustainable development.[46] They caution that coordination efforts may be slow to yield results and advise governments to work for 'institutional subsidiarity', meaning that 'issues should be discussed wherever relevant, but with specific decisions to be negotiated in the institution most appropriate to do so'. Observing that efforts to boost the coherence of trade and other regimes around sustainable development goals may rely on progress at different levels, whether at the national level (e.g. natural resource management),[47] or through

46 Stilwell (2009), among other analysts, highlights the importance of mutual observerships among secretariats of international regimes at their respective negotiations as a prerequisite for coordination.

47 See, for instance, Deere and Esty (2001).

international action (e.g. on carbon pricing or on liberalization of trade in environmental goods and services),[48] Meléndez-Ortiz and Biswas warn that the utility of 'subsidiarity is contingent on sustainable development-friendly outcomes in each forum'.

In Chapter 3, Nadal also takes up environmental sustainability objectives, arguing that we must examine global trade and its governance in light of their interaction with other components of macroeconomic policy that condition trade dynamics, impact the environment and affect people's livelihoods. He uses examples from Latin America to demonstrate how trade is one component of a bigger policy package in which monetary and fiscal policies, financial deregulation and income policies can play a much more important role than trade in shaping the economic forces that affect the environment. On this basis, he proposes reforms to the international monetary system, stronger regulations for international finance and capital flows, a new approach to debt management and cancellation, and overhauling how development and global environmental stewardship are financed, as well as reforms to the international trade regime. On trade, he argues for greater attention to responsible use of balance of payments provisions when countries face crises; a new approach to agricultural trade that more directly addresses food security, livelihood and sustainability concerns; addressing concentrations of market power; and for a new generation of international commodity agreements (ICAs) to help stabilize commodity markets, promote value-added activities in developing countries and boost the terms of trade for those reliant on primary commodity exports.

A further challenge taken up by contributors to this book is that of managing the relationships between the multilateral trading system, regional integration and bilateralism.[49]

On the one hand, there is strong concern about the impacts of regional and bilateral trade agreements on the integrity of the multilateral trading system and on trade flows (e.g. concerns about trade diversion). The asymmetries of North–South Free Trade Agreements (FTAs) are cited as

[48] Meléndez-Ortiz and Biswas provide several examples of how this might be possible. They suggest that 'if a group of governments got together and cooperated on these other factors – for instance, by harmonizing standards or making them interoperable, and establishing incentives for the sharing of trade secrets linked to green technology – it would substantially expand the market for environmental goods'. In addition, they propose that 'WIPO could focus on an instrument to protect folklore and traditional cultural expressions, while also serving as a repository for best practices on the protection of genetic resources'.

[49] See, for instance, Bhagwati (2008); Low *et al.* (1999); and Taniguchi *et al.* (2007).

examples of the unfairness of global trade arrangements and the pressures that developing countries face to sign trade deals that may undermine their ability to promote development. (For instance, while developing countries successfully negotiated concessions in the Doha Declaration on TRIPS and Public Health, many have found that bilateral FTAs undermine their ability to use such flexibilities (Abbott 2004)) (Heidrich and Tussie 2009). Negotiations between the European Union and African, Caribbean and Pacific (ACP) countries to conclude Economic Partnership Agreements (EPAs) have also spurred considerable controversy, not only due to concerns about the relationship between such preferential arrangements and WTO rules, but also due to concerns that negotiations go beyond market access to include regulatory measures (Bilal and Grynberg 2007; Erasmus 2009; Faber and Orbie 2009). Preferential market access programmes (such as the US General System of Preferences and the African Growth and African Opportunity Act (AGOA)) also attract criticism, such as of their complex rules of origin, which in practice diminishes the level of market access actually achieved. In the case of North-South arrangements, many developing countries concede to deals that they acknowledge are unfair, arguing on strategic grounds that the economic costs may be offset by the benefits of stronger political relations with particular trading partners and boosted development and military assistance. In this book, contributors argue for reform of rules of origin requirements, greater transparency of bilateral and regional negotiation processes (see section 5), restraint on the part of developed countries, and deference to multilateral negotiation processes and principles (such as SDT).

On the other hand, there are numerous bilateral trade agreements as well as regional cooperative arrangements (such as ASEAN) and economic unions among developing countries. Indeed, the number of such arrangements has been growing. The South African Customs Union (SACU), among the oldest of trade agreements among developing countries, and Mercosur in South America have been joined, for instance, by trade integration agreements in the context of the West African Economic and Monetary Union (WAEMU), the Common Market for Eastern and Southern Africa (COMESA) and the South Asian Association for Regional Cooperation (SAARC). Although they have achieved varying degrees of success and institutionalization, many developing countries express support for regional economic integration as a complement or alternative to multilateral cooperation (Drabek 2010; Schiff and Winters 2003).

Several authors in this book take up the importance of improving governance arrangements for regional economic communities and integration initiatives as well as for their intersection with international regimes. Ocampo (Chapter 1) argues that 'the international order should offer ample room for the functioning of strong regional institutions respectful of a rules-based global order; in other words, a system of "open regionalism"'. In fact, he argues that building a strong network of regional institutions could be the best way to gradually build a better international order. To this end, Luke and Bernal (Chapter 13) recommend greater attention to providing Aid for Trade through regional economic communities as one way to boost their effectiveness.

A further priority for several analysts in this book is to continue improving arrangements for South–South trade cooperation (Bernal *et al.* 2004). In light of the growth of South–South trade, Puri highlights in Chapter 2 the importance of UNCTAD's Global System of Trade Preferences among Developing Countries (GSTP) as an integral part of global trade governance. She calls for strengthening UNCTAD's role in facilitating arrangements and negotiations for the promotion of South–South trade through the GSTP.

3 Improving how developing countries participate in global trade governance

Among the many studies of the political economy of the global trading system,[50] a growing number explore the evolution of developing countries' roles and concerns within the global trading system.[51] As the prominence of developing country coalitions and of several emerging developing countries in international trade negotiations mounts, their strategies and performance are a rising topic of interest as well.[52] Moreover, scholars and experts have set forth lessons for developing countries, as well as proposals on how to bolster the impact of their coalitions.[53]

In this book, discussion of developing country participation in global trade governance focuses on four areas: 1) analysing the implications of the rise of emerging developing countries; 2) boosting the role and impact

[50] See Helleiner (1992); Hoekman and Kostecki (1996); Khor (2001, 2002); Krueger (1984); Srinivasan (2001); TWN (2001); and World Bank (1993).

[51] See Hudec (1987); Jones (2009); Kim (2010); Michalopolous (2001); Raghavan (1990, 1997); Tussie (1987); and Wilkinson and Scott (2008).

[52] See Deere Birkbeck and Harbourd (2011); Kahler and Odell (1989); Narlikar (2003); Narlikar and Odell (2006); Patel (2007); and Yu (2008).

[53] See Das (2002); Odell and Ortiz Mena (2005); Odell (2006); Tussie and Glover (1993); Tussie and Lengyel (2002); and Wilkinson (2006a).

of developing country coalitions; 3) addressing the specific challenges that small and poor countries face in trade negotiations; and 4) improving how developing countries organize themselves at the national level to devise and advance their international trade policy objectives.

3.1 The rise of emerging developing countries

The rise of emerging developing countries over the past decade has reconfigured the power matrix of international economic relations. China, India and Brazil are now frequently present in the 'inner circle' of global economic decision-making, including in the trade arena. At the WTO, they have taken leadership in forming key developing country coalitions, most notably the G20 countries on agricultural trade (da Motta Veiga 2005; Narlikar and Tussie 2004).

Among analysts of the trade relations of developing countries, there is considerable debate about the strategic role, expectations and responsibilities of emerging powers in the global trading system (da Motta Veiga 2007; Hurrell and Narlikar 2006; Narlikar and Vickers 2009). At the regional level too, questions arise about the role of the new powers in regional integration initiatives, their responsibilities and roles vis-à-vis regional neighbours, and expectations of regional powers on the global stage, including the extent to which they can or should carry with them any regional mandate.[54]

A further question is how the rise of certain developing countries as 'middle' powers impacts WTO negotiations and the prospects for developing country coalitions. The rise of key developing countries certainly complicates cooperation among heterogenous developing countries with diverse interests. It has also reignited debate on whether some developing countries should be 'graduated' out of that category. Many developed countries loathe the idea of allocating special and differential treatment equally, calling for an approach that would enable greater differentiation within the developing country group. In practice, the draft texts of the Doha Round reflect that some differentiation is already happening either on an individual country basis for specific issues or for groups of countries, such as Small, Vulnerable economies (SVES), landlocked countries

[54] These questions were a major theme of regional dialogues co-hosted by the Global Economic Governance Programme with international partners and developing country research institutes in Brazil, India and China in 2007 and 2008. See Deere Birkbeck (2009a).

and LDCs. Most developing countries still appear to affirm the relevance and benefits of collective solidarity among developing countries on broad overarching issues of development, but some fear that the insistence on treating all countries similarly undermines their ability to achieve concessions from developed countries fearful of competitive threats from middle powers (Bradlow 2010). A growing number of individual developing countries now openly suggest that countries such as China, Brazil and India should be treated differently to other developing countries in order to open the way for weaker developing countries to secure much-needed flexibility in the content and application of trade rules. There is also considerable debate about the degree to which emerging powers represent, and are perceived to represent, other developing countries in the trading system as a whole.

As the biggest emerging power in the international trade arena, China's trade policies and its objectives with respect to the governance of trade are intensely debated. Alongside China's expanding share of global trade, investment and development aid, are criticisms of human rights practices, labour standards and environmental performance, as well as product safety. On the political front, China faces pressures to alter exchange rate policies considered to undermine the competitiveness of other economic powers already threatened by Chinese productivity and export growth.

In this book, Gao proposes that as China takes up its seat alongside other major powers at the heart of trade decision-making, its increasingly active role should be welcomed with mutual understanding and accommodation, not fear or suspicion (Chapter 6). Given its diverse interests, he argues that China's degree and style of engagement on different aspects of global trade governance will probably vary. Gao predicts that China's recent pursuit of bilateral and regional trade agreements across the world will slow. On the WTO front, he suggests that it is unlikely that China will propose any sweeping changes to its governing structure. Instead, Gao proposes that China will most likely be a system 'maintainer' with a focus on refining technical rules to fine-tune the system, mostly targeting those rules that it finds discriminatory against itself (rather than general WTO rules). He also predicts more WTO disputes involving China as either respondent or complainant, observing that these will likely reflect the tensions between the economic and political systems of China and the fundamental principles of the WTO, which were designed by and for economies that operate in vastly different environments.

Several contributors take up questions about the implications of the rising role of emerging powers for efforts to improve the fairness and efficiency of WTO decision-making. In Chapter 5, Narlikar argues that the WTO's efforts to accommodate the new developing country powers at the heart of its decision-making has produced new inefficiencies, heightened its proclivity to deadlock, and exacerbated disengagement and disillusionment among all its stakeholders. While she observes that very little can be done to alter the balance of power itself, she argues that appropriate institutional reform could help the multilateral trading system retain the advances it has made in terms of fairness while addressing the concerns of efficiency (for elaboration of her proposals, see Section 5 below). In Chapter 9, Bernal cautions against placing too much hope on the emerging developing countries to advance the diversity of developing country interests. He warns that we should not assume such countries are the logical or accepted spokespersons of all developing countries or that the problem of participation in negotiations has been solved. Indeed, he cautions that the elevation of some developing countries to new leadership positions 'should not be mistaken for change in the governance process', warning that their presence at the WTO's 'High Table' may make governance reform less urgent for achieving their interests.

3.2 *The role of coalitions*

Financial and human resource constraints regularly restrict the effective participation of developing countries in international trade decision-making. This book highlights the need and potential for more effective use of coalitions among developing countries, and with developed countries, to promote trade agreements that reflect their interests and to maximize the benefits of their participation in the international trading system. Already, the growth of developing country coalitions has been the subject of considerable analysis.[55] This book highlights some of the key current issues and debates on the prospects for developing country coalitions in trade governance and advances proposals for boosting their effectiveness.

In Chapter 18, Yu outlines three kinds of groupings among countries in the WTO context: 1) issue-based coalitions (e.g. the G20, the G33, the NAMA-11, the Core Group on Trade Facilitation); 2) characteristic-based groupings (e.g. the least developed countries (LDC) Group, the small vulnerable economies (SVE) Group and the G77/China); and 3) region-based groupings (e.g. the African Group, the African, Caribbean, and Pacific (ACP) Group and the Group of Latin American countries

[55] See, for example, Page (2003); Patel (2003a); Patel (2007); Rolland (2007); and Yu (2008).

(GRULAC)). Notably, there are also groupings that combine developed and developing countries (e.g. the Cairns Group, the Friends of Fish).

The analysis in this book identifies several reasons that coalitions can be useful to developing countries. First, coalitions can help countries build negotiating positions where their understanding of issues might otherwise be weak. Second, participation in coalitions can expand the representation of countries as their interests can be represented in multiple places. In some instances, countries have joined coalitions simply to ensure that their specific interests are heard by that coalition (Deere Birkbeck and Harbourd 2011). Third, coalitions can help build convergence among the WTO membership (Ismail and Vickers, Chapter 16 in this book). Fourth, the growing use of coalitions has significantly transformed the WTO's 'Green Room' process. Previously, closed-consultations included only a handful of developing countries on an individual basis. As coalitions have improved their communication strategies and information dissemination, the internal transparency of the Green Room has increased (Patel 2007). In addition, the composition of the Green Room has been expanded such that key players plus relevant coalitions are more often represented, making for a more legitimate and effective consultation process. However, important obstacles to effective developing country participation still remain (see section 5 below).

The analysis in this book instructs us that purpose, characteristics, internal functioning (e.g. internal leadership and coordination) and degree of formality of developing country groupings and evolve. After their early beginnings as mostly informal information-based exchanges, many of today's developing country groupings both share technical capacity and develop common negotiating platforms (Patel 2007). Of the 112 WTO Members who are commonly recognized as, or who describe themselves as, 'developing countries', 99 (or, 87.61 per cent) are Members of one or more developing country-only groups or coalitions (Yu, Chapter 18 in this book). Moreover, overlapping Memberships occur across these coalitions.

Across coalitions, effectiveness in negotiations varies. Indeed, in some cases, the purpose of particular groupings is not to advance specific issues in negotiations, but rather to defend broad principles or to provide a regional view on particular issues (such as the choice of Chairs for WTO negotiating groups). There is a commonly held view that issue-specific coalitions are most effective in the tussle of negotiations, whereas regional groupings often struggle to find sufficient commonality of interest to present a compelling position to negotiating partners. Among characteristic-based coalitions, the LDC group is considered to have a sufficiently specific goal to be effective, while the effectiveness of even broader coalitions such as the G77/China, the G90 and the G110 is considered highest when they focus on political statements and advocacy on broad principles, such as the importance of addressing development priorities in the Doha Round. Yu observes that strong group action occurs best where there is a shared perception by the group Members of having a common agenda to promote on a given issue. Even for issue-specific coalitions, however, it remains to be seen whether effectiveness will continue in the end-game of negotiations as countries come closer to having to make binding, individual trade commitments.

Recommendations set forth in this book focus on improving the internal organization negotiating strategy and tactics of coalitions. Yu emphasizes the need to improve the internal workings and management of coalitions to boost their sustainability, including developing clear principles for representation of coalition members and internal transparency. He highlights that: 'Institutionalized coordination and group leadership mechanisms are vital to the long-term survival and strength of coalitions', and notes the importance of investing in working relationships among developing country delegates for smooth intra- and inter-group coordination. Yu recommends that members that represent coalitions in WTO Green Room meetings need to be sure that they carefully listen to all views beforehand, follow the mandate given by the group, and faithfully report back on discussions to interested members in a timely fashion. He also underlines the need for greater institutional support for coalitions (including for research, analysis, coordination, staffing, web presence, etc.) (also see Laurent in Chapter 8, and Deere Birkbeck and Harbourd 2011). (Several further recommendations on coalition-building to boost the influence of the smallest and poorest countries on the global trading system are set out in section 3.3 below.)

3.3 Improving the participation of the poorest and smallest countries

Small states and very poor countries face well-known structural economic constraints and power asymmetries that heavily circumscribe their room for manoeuvre in international trade negotiations (Jones *et al.* 2010). The limited economic weight of such states often produces pessimism about their prospects for influence on the global trading system.

African countries face particular challenges in their efforts to generate greater benefits from the international trading system. In this book, several contributors offer views on the key constraints that the smallest and poorest developing countries face and explore what can be done to improve their engagement in international trade.

In Chapters 8 and 9, Bernal and Laurent emphasize the importance of international trade to small states. Given the vulnerability of small countries to asymmetric bilateral trade deals, they affirm the importance of a rules-based multilateral trading system to protect and advance small countries' interests. Whereas some commentators suggest that small states have too little at stake to warrant greater attention to engagement at the WTO, Bernal and Laurent insist that even where only a small proportion of the trade of small states is conducted under WTO rules, and even where their main trade activities are limited to a few exports, they nonetheless have a strong interest in clear, predictable multilateral rules and in contributing to the negotiation of new rules, particularly those which may be important to them in the future or which may present implementation challenges. In sum, they insist that exerting greater influence on the formation, application and enforcement of WTO agreements is a key imperative for small states.

The quest for greater small state influence demands attention to more effective participation, including through more consistent attendance at WTO meetings, giving sufficient national priority to trade policy, and more effectively mobilizing available resources, capabilities and tactics. Noting that the resources required for such improvements are beyond those available to individual small states, Bernal calls for greater political cooperation, technical collaboration and collective advocacy among small developing economies as well as greater external support to provide resources unavailable to them.

In Chapter 9, Bernal also reiterates the importance of democratizing WTO decision-making processes. In Bernal's view, the rise of some developing countries to the inner circle of WTO decision-making is 'no substitute for a concerted and persistently prosecuted campaign by SDEs [small developing economies] to reform governance in a way that allows for their adequate participation'. He contends that small developing economies 'cannot take for granted the support of other developing countries' in advancing their particular interests (also see Grynberg and Remy 2003). Bernal proposes that to 'break or dilute the stranglehold of the developed countries and large emerging economies on WTO governance, the various streams of disenchantment' with the status quo need to coalesce, including not only small states but also those that share some or many of their concerns and vulnerabilities.

In addition, Bernal also offers specific proposals for how the group of SVEs at the WTO could improve its effectiveness, notably by establishing clearer criteria for membership and by encouraging those WTO Members that do suffer extreme problems of smallness to become more active in the group and its agenda-setting. He also proposes that better briefing of the SVE representative before restricted group meetings and insisting on accountability to the wider group would boost the representation of the interests of group members. Alongside efforts to better define and strengthen the SVE coalition, Laurent (Chapter 8) emphasizes the importance of reinforcing practices that de-emphasize power in WTO negotiations (such as growing transparency of negotiations and greater openness of the Green Room).

The challenge of how to facilitate improved representation in Geneva of small and poor countries, including those without missions in Geneva, remains a critical issue (Nordström 2002; Weekes *et al.* 2001). In Chapter 11, Lee argues that participation of developing countries should not be left to the financial generosity of individual Members, but should rather be provided systematically through the WTO's regular budget.[56] To address challenges of limited individual capacity and the high financial cost of establishing or boosting representation in Geneva, some regional groups, including the African Union, the ACP group, the Organization of Eastern Caribbean States and the Pacific Islands Forum, have established offices or secretariats in Geneva, sometimes with the support of developed country donors. The Commonwealth Secretariat has also supported a Geneva representative and researchers to support the work of developing country members of the Commonwealth, and is preparing to support office space for Member countries in need of greater representation in Geneva.

This book underlines the need for specific improvements in global trade governance to support LDCs.[57] In Chapter 7, Kaushik and Mukiibi call on LDCs to exert greater ownership and leadership of efforts to integrate them into the trading system. They observe that the common positions taken by the LDC group at the WTO are a positive step. At present, the LDC group draws on support from the secretariats of other groupings

[56] This point has also been made by Alejandro Jara, WTO Deputy Director-General (Deere *et al.* 2007).

[57] Bhattacharya (2009); Brenton (2003); Centre for Policy Dialogue (2003); and Mattoo and Subramanian (2004).

they belong to (such as the ACP group), organizational support from the WTO Secretariat, and technical advice and support from Geneva-based organizations such as UNCTAD, AITIC (now closed), the International Centre for Trade and Sustainable Development (ICTSD) and the IDEAS Centre. To supplement such support, and in addition to strengthening SDT for LDCs in trade rules, Kaushik and Mukiibi propose the creation of a Geneva-based institution, the focus of which would be to ensure better representation of LDC interests in the Doha Round negotiations and the WTO's regular Committee work, as well as broader debates on global trade governance. As proposed, the institution would be created by LDCs, with additional resources from international donors, and would undertake activities such as examining and summarizing for national officials the suite of reports and submissions from Member states, Secretariat studies and WTO notifications.

Regrettably, this book does not include a dedicated chapter on the particular challenges African countries face in the global trading system. Existing studies of African participation in trade decision-making offer proposals on strategy for participation at the WTO[58] and its Ministerial meetings (SEATINI 2003), lessons from the Cotton Initiative (Anderson and Valenzuela 2007), and analysis of the dynamics of the ACP–EU negotiations for Economic Partnership Agreements (Faber and Orbie 2009).

The process by which four small West African countries successfully propelled the issue of cotton subsidies onto the Doha Round agenda has also been well analysed. The reality, however, is that beyond provisions of adjustment assistance, and assurances of more to come, the 'Cotton 4' countries have not yet secured any concessions from the United States in terms of reduced subsidies. Two key questions remain. Are the successful aspects of the 'cotton case' replicable by other African countries? How can success in agenda-setting be translated to success in securing actual commercial benefits from more powerful trading partners?

In considering options for more effective African engagement in trade, it is important to acknowledge that the specific trade interests of African countries can vary widely as do their national economic circumstances and priorities. The region includes rising economies, developing countries and LDCs. Few African countries expect or rely

[58] Anderson *et al.* (2006); Blackhurst *et al.* (2000); Ohiorhenuan (2005); Oyejide and Lyakura (2005); and Wang (1997).

on the more economically powerful countries of their region, such as South Africa and Nigeria, to reflect their interests. Those African countries not classified as LDCs frequently express frustration with the special treatment given to neighbours with whom they share many of the same development challenges and express concerns about the implications for their competitiveness of the special treatment given to their poorer neighbours.

Many African trade officials complain of a lack of detailed understanding within their countries of the implications of different trade proposals, which in turn undermines their participation negotiations and their ability to form effective coalitions. The prospects for effective collective action by African countries are also frustrated by the multiplicity of intersecting trade negotiations under way. The countries of the region are divided into several separate regional economic communities (e.g. for West Africa, East Africa and Southern Africa), but rarely organize their participation in WTO negotiations along these lines. Further, many African countries are simultaneously engaged in negotiations with the European Union, for which they are required to organize themselves subregionally in groupings that do not coincide with the regional economic communities to which they belong.

Beyond concerns about participation in trade negotiations, African countries also have distinct substantive priorities for improvements in the governance of global trade. In the wake of the global financial crisis, for instance, African analysts emphasized the enduring importance of debt relief to the economic and trade prospects of Africa, as well as the urgency of providing Aid for Trade and of addressing fluctuations in commodity prices and trade finance. There were also calls for an additional special Africa-led stimulus package to boost trade and economic recovery. Njinkeu (2009), for instance, argues for a Vulnerability Fund for Africa that would integrate trade, monetary and fiscal measures to facilitate economic adjustment, nurture investment in human capital and physical infrastructure, support appropriate safety nets, and assist small and medium sized enterprises (SMEs) vital to economic recovery in the region. African analysts also emphasize the importance of strengthening regional arrangements for trade and addressing the challenges of rules of origin in the preferential trading agreements upon which many countries rely (Oyejide 2009). Indeed, for most African countries, more trade is conducted under regional and preferential bilateral trade arrangements than multilateral trade agreements (Oyejide 2009).

3.4 *Bolstering national trade policy-making processes and negotiation capacity*

Contributors to this book offer several proposals for improving how developing countries make trade policy and building national negotiating capacity. There is wide recognition of the importance of stakeholder participation and inter-ministerial consultations to the prospect of development-oriented national trade policies and beneficial outcomes from international negotiations. A number of studies offer options and best-practices for greater transparency and opportunities for public participation in national trade policy-making and negotiating teams (Bonzon 2009; Brock and McGee 2004; CUTS International 2009a, 2009b; Gallagher *et al.* 2005; Jones *et al.* 2010; Halle and Wolfe 2007; Ostry 2004; Saner 2010; Sapra 2009).[59]

In Chapter 1 of this volume, Ocampo underlines the development rationale for national institutional capacities and arrangements that reflect democratic goals. He argues that because the nation-state remains the main space for the expression of political citizenry, national processes of representation and participation must be allowed to determine economic and social development strategies. He highlights their importance for mediating the tensions that globalization, and global trade arrangements, create in the context of international economic asymmetries.

Also in this book, Kaukab (Chapter 19) presents new empirical evidence showing that despite the growing acknowledgement of the need for inclusive processes of global trade governance – and important steps in the right direction – there remains an inclusiveness deficit in trade policy-making processes at the national level and multilateral level. Along with Meléndez-Ortiz and Biswas (Chapter 4), he recommends that developing countries bolster their efforts to establish and use multi-stakeholder consultative fora on trade-related issues at the national level. Meléndez-Ortiz and Biswas also highlight that stronger coherence of positions governments take in different trade-related international fora, a step vital for making trade more supportive of sustainable development, also requires

[59] Further case studies of practices at the national level can be found in da Motta Veiga (2007), Sen (2004); and Zeng and Mertha (2007). Alongside this work, there have also been studies that explore other aspects of the 'domestic' governance of trade, such as the transparency of national trade administration and customs regimes (Marconini 2005).

that governments use consultative mechanisms that engage all relevant ministries and civil society.

Kaukab proposes four interrelated actions to improve inclusiveness at the national level: 1) enlarging the composition of the national consultation fora to include representatives of all groups of stakeholders – i.e. the government ministry responsible for trade, other government ministries and agencies, parliaments, industry, small and medium-sized enterprises, multinational companies, labour, consumers, farmers, NGOs, informal sector and media; 2) strengthening the mandate of consultative fora by obliging the ministry responsible for trade to follow the advice offered by them; 3) ensuring the effective functioning of consultative fora by providing adequate human and financial resources to organize and service their meetings and to finance the participation of stakeholders; and 4) undertaking broad capacity-building of stakeholders on trade issues so that they are for informed participation and can make effective use of the improved opportunities for inclusiveness.

The ability of many states to leverage what bargaining power they do have is thwarted by in regard to negotiating strategies, tactics, accountability, and incentives facing negotiators, as well as by psychological factors and poor leadership (Jones *et al.* 2010). To complement proposals for using coalitions to bolster their negotiating leverage (see section 3.2 above), authors in this book underline the need to address the challenges of building effective negotiating teams which include deficits in human resources, access to information and expertise as well as in institutional coordination and communication. In Chapter 19, Kaukab calls for greater efforts to bridge the gap between national and multilateral levels of trade governance; regular briefings by staff of Geneva Missions for the national consultative fora and for the parliamentarians; periodic visits of representatives of groups of stakeholders to Geneva during important negotiations; inclusion of representatives of all groups of stakeholders in official delegations to the WTO Ministerial Conferences; and the incorporation of some non-State stakeholders and parliamentarians in the smaller delegations that attend informal meetings during the Ministerial Conferences.

Several contributors to this volume also highlight outstanding needs for more effective, development-oriented legal and regulatory advice, and technical training on trade negotiations and the implementation of trade agreements. They highlight the importance of the quality and independence of such advice. They also call for greater support for the representation of developing countries in Geneva (see above on proposals to boost support for developing country coalitions and for missions not represented in Geneva) and for travel to relevant negotiations. Importantly, while Aid for Trade includes negotiation and most attention focuses on supply-side capacity-building and trade-adjustment. As with Aid for Trade, other programmes and initiatives such as the Enhanced Integrated Framework (WTO 2006b) too rarely invest in negotiating capacity in ways that would boost developing country power. In Chapter 8, Laurent recommends, for instance, that existing donor programmes to build trade negotiating capacity in developing countries should be critically reviewed with an eye to making them more results-orientated and to grant the beneficiaries a fuller role in their planning and management.

Finally, Laurent draws attention to the neglected issue of the use by developing countries, particularly small countries, of paid lobbyists and public relations experts to assist them in their negotiations and interactions with trading partners. He notes that lobbyists 'can be useful where small States do not have permanent or effective diplomatic presence in the target city and, even where they do, these experts can help them organize professional information and conduct outreach campaigns'. He cautions, however, that lobbyists are expensive, meaning that there is competition for the best talent. To ensure lobbyists are used effectively, he highlights the need to define their terms of reference precisely, with measurable and clearly identifiable outputs and results, and to incorporate into contracts adequate provisions for effective oversight by designated government representatives. Most importantly, he argues that small States should view lobbyists not as a substitute for their own diplomatic engagement, but as a supplement to their outreach and representation to host governments, media, NGOs and other centres of influence.

4 Strengthening WTO governance to respond to developing countries

A third area of debate on development and global trade governance concentrates on WTO reform. The debate on how much the WTO can do for developing countries has been under way since its creation and many of the issues date from the earlier GATT years (Finger and Winters 1998). Since the launch of the Doha Development Agenda in 2001, the discussion of options for mainstreaming development concerns has intensified (Ismail 2005, 2009c; Lee 2007; Qureshi 2009), as has the scepticism in some quarters that the WTO should or can become more of a 'development institution'. Importantly, the WTO is not a static institution. Box 21.1 illustrates a number of the improvements, refinements and reforms made to WTO governance over the past fifteen years.[60]

This section begins with a review of debates on how development should feature in the mandate and core principles of the WTO, which in turn inform the organization's governance (and thereby its activities and agreements). It also notes how proposals on the appropriate scope of the WTO feature as part of the development and trade governance debate. It then summarizes proposals for improving the responsiveness to developing countries of the WTO's functions in the following areas: dispute settlement, monitoring, capacity-building and Aid for Trade, and public outreach, as well as evaluation and research. The section concludes with a summary of proposals for reforming WTO's institutional structure and internal management to work better for developing countries. The WTO's negotiation function is dealt with separately in section 5 of this chapter. (Note that recommendations related to the WTO's interaction with other regimes were discussed above in section 1 of this chapter).

4.1 The WTO's mandate, principles and scope

The contributors to this volume emphasize the importance of a rule-based, multilateral approach to trade. Their analysis confirms, however, enduring tensions over the underlying purpose, mandate and strategic direction of the WTO, the core multilateral trade institution.

In their chapter, Ismail and Vickers argue that the WTO needs to shift away from the traditional mercantilist approach established under the GATT (Chapter 16). They argue that the core purpose of the WTO is too often misconstrued as one of opening trade and creating new trade rules, whereas its broader overall goal should in fact be development. In her chapter, Puri similarly argues that the core mission of the WTO must be to promote development alongside the 'global public good' of a rules-based multilateral trading system. Further, for several analysts in this book, the heart of WTO reform must be systemic questions about how it addresses goals of sustainable development, and the challenge of coordination with other actors in the international system in pursuit of these goals. In Chapter 4, for instance, Meléndez-Ortiz and Biswas argue

[60] For further analysis of reforms thus far and outstanding recommendations, see Deere Birkbeck and Monagle (2009); P. Gallagher (2005); and WTO (2007).

BOX 21.1: SELECTED EXAMPLES OF WTO REFORMS AND EVOLUTION SINCE 1995

Following are selected examples of WTO reforms undertaken since 1995 as well as some evolutions in practices and the functioning of the multilateral trading system. In each case, there are many more examples that could be listed. The point here is simply to highlight that the multilateral trading system has not been static in the face of demands to adapt and change – though there are diverging perspectives on the desirability and impact of some of these changes, and on whether they go far enough or too far.

- *WTO Management and Internal Administration*: The WTO Secretariat has adopted performance-based management tools, and the internal organization of the Secretariat and the structure of its senior management have evolved. Members adopted guidelines regarding the process for selecting the organization's Director-General.
- *Strategic Direction, Policy Deliberation and Problem-Solving*: Examples of reform-related efforts include the commissioning of the Sutherland Report; the recent decision to regularize the holding of Ministerial Conferences; the creation of new working groups such as the WTO Working Group on Debt, Trade and Finance at the 2001 Doha Ministerial as well as a WTO Working Group on Technology Transfer; and the Director-General's leadership of new initiatives on Aid for Trade and on the cotton issue.
- *Negotiation Function*: Members agreed to the creation of a Trade Negotiations Committee for the Doha Round. The nature of the informal processes of negotiations has also consistently evolved (including how Green Rooms are conducted as well as the roles of Chairs and facilitators) as has the process for generating draft negotiating texts. WTO Members adopted a decision regarding the process of Accession for LDCs (2002) and Members have made increasing use of a variety of coalitions in the negotiation process.
- *Monitoring, Assessment and Evaluation Function*: WTO Members established a new transparency mechanism for monitoring regional trade agreements, an independent assessment of the WTO's technical assistance was commissioned, and the WTO Secretariat is monitoring trade policies introduced by governments struggling to cope with financial and economic crisis.
- *Dispute Settlement Function*: Amicus briefs have been received by a number of WTO panels and by the Appellate Body (although these have received varying responses from the relevant WTO adjudicating bodies and from Member States); some dispute settlement proceedings have been made open to the public; the good offices of the Director-General have been used in an effort to resolve at least one dispute; and a number of WTO Members collaborated to establish in 2001 an Advisory Centre on WTO Law (ACWL) that provides legal advice to developing countries.

BOX 21.1 (CONT.)

- *International Cooperation and Coordination Function*: Actions undertaken include an agreement between the World Intellectual Property Organization (WIPO) and WTO Secretariats on the provision of intellectual property-related capacity-building; joint publications with some international organizations on trade-related issues (e.g. with the World Health Organization, the International Labour Organization and the UN Environment Programme); partnerships with other international organizations in the creation of the International Trade Centre; collaborations in the hosting of joint seminars and workshops; and the participation of the Director-General in the G20 Leaders' meetings.
- *Outreach Function*: The WTO now undertakes an annual WTO Public Forum, provision is made for an NGO Centre at WTO Ministerial Conferences and NGO briefings take place in Geneva. The WTO's internet site has been enhanced considerably, and decisions regarding document de-restriction have been made. In addition, the General Council adopted Guidelines for Arrangements on Relations with Non-Governmental Organizations, the Secretariat has made a series of ad hoc informal arrangements for NGO and media participation in some of its events and activities, and the WTO Secretariat collaborates with the Inter-Parliamentary Union for its periodic Conferences on the WTO.
- *Capacity-building Function and Aid for Trade*: A Doha Development Agenda Global Trust Fund was established to facilitate Member support for capacity-building, and the Integrated Framework (IF) was created to facilitate a coordinated effort among providers of capacity-building and technical assistance. Subsequent reforms were undertaken to transform the IF into an Enhanced Integrated Framework and the Aid for Trade initiative was launched.
- *Research Function*: The resources allocated for the WTO's internal research have grown over time. There has also been increasing emphasis on collaborations with external researchers and with developing country research centres. The WTO has also initiated its own annual World Trade Reports since 2003 and has launched its own scholarly journal, the *World Trade Review*.

Source: Deere Birkbeck and Monagle (2009).

that sustainable development should be the yardstick by which the WTO is measured, setting out existing WTO mechanisms and provisions that could be fairly easily modified or elaborated to address sustainable development concerns. Chimni, on the other hand, argues in Chapter 10 that employment should be reinforced as the key goal of the WTO.

Contributors to this volume also offer views on the principles that should underpin the WTO. No contributor to this book challenges the core WTO principles of national treatment and most favoured nation treatment, but many call for greater attention to the importance of SDT as a foundation principle for multilateral rule-making. Their analysis highlights the dissatisfaction among developing countries with the operationalization of SDT in existing trade agreements (Stevens 2003a, 2003b) (developed countries also have concerns, see section 1.3 above). Whereas some analysts argue elsewhere that SDT should simply be a matter of further delaying the extended deadlines for developing countries to implement WTO Agreements (Srinivasan 1998, 2002, 2004), authors in this book insist on a more substantive approach. Notwithstanding ongoing negotiations as part of the Doha Round on SDT, authors in this book offer several concrete proposals. In Chapter 10, Chimni calls for recasting the SDT principle in the language of 'hard law', and advocates concrete steps to implement the 'right to development' in international law, including at the WTO. In Chapter 7, Kaushik and Mukiibi argue that SDT for LDCs should be locked into the commitments of WTO Members so that they are 'legally enforceable, predictable and therefore more beneficial to the LDCs'. In Chapter 11, Lee also calls for preserving the principle of non-reciprocal obligations for LDCs as a component of SDT. In addition, Meléndez-Ortiz and Biswas (Chapter 4) propose that WTO Members could use the emergence of developing country subgroups (such as SVEs, landlocked developing countries and specific issue-based coalitions) 'to experiment with new, deepened SDT provisions that would restore to beneficiaries an expanded policy toolkit through which to pursue sustainable development goals like food security and the creation of productive industrial capacity'.

A further development dimension of debate on WTO governance concerns the appropriate scope of the WTO agenda and its agreements. Indeed, for some experts, the 'meat' of building a more development-friendly architecture at the WTO is less about institutional considerations and more about the scope and content of the WTO negotiating agenda (Mattoo and Subramanian 2003). Here, critics highlight the challenges faced by developing countries in the implementation of existing WTO Agreements. They also debate the question of whether and how the WTO should take up 'non-trade' issues (such as labour and the environment). While Chimni argues that international trade should not be used as a tool for pursuing 'non-trade values', others see WTO attention to issues of sustainable development and human rights as vital (see chapters by Meléndez-Ortiz and Biswas, and Nadal). In reality, many issues of environmental sustainability are already integrated into WTO negotiations and dispute settlemen rulings. The Secretariat has also taken the initiative to jointly produce reports with other international organizations on the intersection of trade and climate (WTO and UNEP 2009), the environment (WTO 2000) and health (WTO and WHO 2002) although not yet on development.

In addition to calls for greater market access for developing countries exports, several authors in this book make concrete suggestions for changes in rules and the scope of the WTO that could form part of a post-Doha agenda.[61] In Chapter 11, Lee calls for rules that would allow the imposition of a 'Development Facilitation Tariff' aimed at infant industry protection, and for a reform of the TRIPs, TRIMS and GATS Agreements to benefit developing countries. In Chapter 3, Nadal echoes many of Lee's recommendations for specific changes to WTO Agreements that would increase the policy space available to developing countries. In Chapters 1, 2 and 10, authors call for greater attention to rules on migration at the WTO and for rules that allow greater movement of natural persons among WTO Members (UNCTAD 2003b; Winters *et al.* 2003). Authors also highlight the importance to developing countries of progress in the area of trade facilitation (see Puri, Chapter 2), greater support for Aid for Trade (see Luke and Bernal in Chapter 13) (including adjustment assistance when the reduction of trade barriers exacerbates unemployment (see Chimni, Chapter 10)), and attention to addressing the problems facing the primary commodity exports of developing countries (see Nadal, Chapter 3). In Chapter 4, Meléndez-Ortiz and Biswas propose that WTO Members could work to anticipate potential challenges to trade governance that might arise from the pursuit of sustainable development. They call for a deeper conversation on trade and climate in the WTO,[62] arguing for instance that the WTO Members could reinvent the 'Permanent Group of Experts' (PGE) set up by the WTO's Agreement on Subsidies and Countervailing Measures (SCM) to examine energy subsidies, including issues such as transparency in government support to the clean energy industry. While not addressed extensively by any author in this book, the challenge of better global management of trade imbalances and exchange rate policies has emerged as a critical trade-related concern after the most recent global economic crisis as has the question of the WTO's role in that broader global economic governance effort.

[61] For efforts to define a post-Doha agenda for the WTO, also see Hoekman (2001).

[62] They propose that this could include discussion of proposals for border carbon adjustments (BCA) – taxes or other charges on imports from carbon-unrestrained countries – to 'level the carbon playing field'.

4.2 *The WTO's dispute settlement function*

The challenges developing countries face in using and benefitting from the WTO dispute settlement system have attracted consistent concern since the creation of the WTO.[63]

This book affirms the view that the WTO's dispute system and the level of developing country participation in it could and should be improved. It highlights that financial, political and technical barriers to participation persist. In Chapter 12, Niall Meagher argues that developing and least developed countries continue to need increased legal capacity to engage fully in the WTO dispute settlement system. Drawing on experience of helping such countries engage in the system, he proposes that one means of increasing developing countries' capacity and familiarity with the process would be for them to participate more frequently as third parties. Additional countries, such as the United States, the European Union and Japan, for instance, routinely participate as third parties in disputes. Further measures that could be taken to boost awareness among developing countries what proceedings involve include continued efforts to open to the public aspects of WTO dispute proceedings, such as through webcasting. Further challenges facing developing countries include inadequate capacity to monitor where violations of WTO commitments that harm their economic interests have occurred (see Ghosh, Chapter 14). An important constraint here is the limited resources of developing country industries and small and medium-sized businesses to monitor and analyse overseas market conditions and draw problems to the attention of their governments.

To address the capacity gap, several authors in this volume propose greater financial contributions to the Advisory Centre on WTO Law (ACWL) (including from the WTO's regular budget) to boost its ability to respond to country requests for assistance, as well as an expansion of its mandate. One contributor recommends incorporating the ACWL into the WTO system through a new Council on Trade and Development (see Lee, Chapter 11). In Chapter 8, Laurent argues that a strengthened ACWL is not enough, noting that many developing countries want to build greater capacity within their borders. Moreover, he emphasizes that many of the WTO's small members do not belong to the ACWL. While LDCs

[63] Bown (2009); Bown and Hoekman (2005); Brewer and Young (1999); Busch and Reinhardt (2003); Chaytor (1998); Ching (1993); François *et al.* (2008); Lacarte and Gappah (2000); Nordström and Shaffer (2007); Oteng (1997); Raghavan (2000a); and van Grasstek (2001).

receive the ACWL's services free, other developing countries are expected to become members and/or pay for services provided, which in the case of smaller countries may dissuade them.

Beyond shortages of legal capacity in many developing countries, there are other explanations for their not making greater use of the WTO's Dispute Settlement Mechanism. Many of the poorest and smallest developing countries conduct most of their trade under preferential trading arrangements, rather than WTO rules, and so disputes on their trade practices are not likely to be brought to the WTO, but rather addressed (or set aside) through bilateral agreements (Nottage 2008).

This book also sets out proposals for reforms to the WTO Dispute Settlement Understanding (DSU) that could address constraints developing countries face in using the system.[64] In Chapter 10, Chimni recommends the adoption of a 'national deference principle' as the standard of review in disputes relating to developing countries. He also proposes that both the WTO and the WTO Appellate Body should take greater cognizance of Third World legal scholarship in their proceedings. To promote the consideration of sustainable development perspectives in disputes, Meléndez-Ortiz and Biswas (Chapter 4) propose that WTO panels could be empowered to invite input from the secretariats of multilateral environmental agreements (MEAs) if relevant environmental issues in a trade dispute are the subject of an MEA. In Chapters 8 and 9, Laurent and Bernal each draw attention to the challenges developing countries face in securing compliance with WTO decisions. Here, existing proposals to address this problem include calls for making greater use of mediation and alternative processes for resolving disputes; creating a 'small claims' procedure; and advancing the possibility of compensation as a remedy (Mercurio 2009). Laurent and Bernal each highlight the limited prospects of retaliation or cross-retaliation by small States. While neither dispute the significance of several WTO decisions that authorize developing countries to cross-retaliate (such as by reducing their commitment to protecting intellectual property rights held by nationals of the offending country), they note that except in very specific cases, the deterrent effects of potential threats to development assistance and fears of informal trade rebukes limit the feasibility of either retaliation or cross-retaliation.[65]

[64] Other suggestions of procedural improvements made in this book include a procedural suggestion by Meléndez-Ortiz and Biswas (Chapter 4) that WTO Members could adopt all panel proceedings by default, unless vetoed by a party to the dispute.

[65] On cross-retaliation, see Bown and Pauwelyn (2010).

4.3 *The WTO's monitoring function*

Monitoring is an integral part of trade governance. The 2008–9 global economic crisis spurred renewed interest in a strengthened WTO role in monitoring trade policies and imbalances as one way to avert protectionist pressures (Baldwin and Evenett 2009; Lamy 2007; Mavroidis 1991–1992; Wolfe 2010). Even before the crisis, however, there were concerns about the effectiveness of the multilateral trading system's mechanisms for promoting transparency of trade policies and measures (Collins-Williams and Wolfe 2010). Only a few studies, however, take up the issue from a development perspective (e.g. Ghosh 2008; Qureshi 1990).

There are several different monitoring processes and transparency provisions at the WTO, and their number has grown since the WTO was established. These include notification requirements embedded in many WTO Agreements (such as for subsidies); institutionalized surveillance mechanisms such as the Trade Policy Review (TPR) Mechanism (which has been operating since 1989 and periodically reviews the trade policies of all WTO Members); and monitoring work conducted by the WTO's regular committees. In recent years, further mechanisms have been created, most notably to monitor regional trade agreements, food safety standards and Aid for Trade.[66]

From an institutional perspective, the main purpose of the WTO's transparency norm (in terms of governments disclosing information to the public and each other) is to 'enhance the effectiveness of the WTO agreements' (Collins-Williams and Wolfe 2010). In this book, Ghosh highlights the implications of poor multilateral monitoring mechanisms for developing countries. For the poorest members of the trade regime monitoring mechanisms could help address challenges of limited resources and capacity for their own surveillance.[67] Ghosh observes that poorer nations need advance warning of changes in the trade policies or barriers of major trading partners, analyses of the impact of those changes, and information to help them counter pressures to overcomply with their commitments and to promote compliance by rich countries.

[66] In addition, a new SDT monitoring mechanism appears to be attracting consensus in the Doha negotiations. See http://ictsd.net/downloads/bridgesweekly/bridgesweekly10-13.pdf [accessed in November 2010].

[67] Ghosh observes that this capacity may grow as countries trade more, particularly if the emphasis of capacity-building shifts from not only self-evaluations but also monitoring foreign trade barriers.

Ghosh argues for improving the WTO TPR Mechanism to boost the participation of developing countries and its benefits to them. Drawing on a detailed analysis of TPR reports and meetings, Ghosh observes several deficiencies. The TPR reports often do not describe or analyse the most contentious trade policies; the procedure of advance questions is used more by developed countries such that the direction of peer pressure flows against developing countries; and participation in TPR meetings is dominated by a handful of WTO Members.

Among his recommendations, Ghosh proposes initiatives to target Members' reporting behaviour and expose laggards; increase developing country representation among discussants of the WTO's trade policy reviews; make high-level representation at TPRs mandatory; increase media coverage of reviews and publish follow-up documents to show how countries have responded to concerns raised in meetings (also see Ghosh 2008, 2010). Noting that WTO monitoring processes do not facilitate inputs or allow participation from non-State actors, Ghosh highlights that greater engagement by non-State actors could help boost the timeliness of information in the face of slow institutional and self-reporting, both within and outside the WTO's formal processes. Already, third-party efforts to provide information on trade rules, practices and policies are growing, including online databases.[68]

There are now many proposals for harnessing the TPR as a tool for integrating development and other dimensions into trade policy-making (ranging from environment to labour, gender and human rights considerations), and for stronger roles for other international organizations, experts and stakeholders in the TPR process. Meléndez-Ortiz and Biswas, for instance, propose that tweaking the Trade Policy Reviews to assess environmental and developmental factors would make the mechanism a useful tool for integrating sustainable development goals into trade policy-making (Chapter 4). There are also proposals to link the TPR process more closely to the assessment of adjustment costs arising from the implementation of WTO rules, the appropriate legal obligations for different members, and capacity-building needs (see Luke and Bernal, Chapter 13). There have also been calls to include in the TPR a review of national trade policy-making processes (Ostry 2002, 2004) and of developed countries'

[68] See, for instance, the work of the Global Subsidies Initiative (monitoring subsidies by WTO members) at www.globalsubsidies.org, and of the Global Trade Alert (monitoring protectionism) at www.globaltradealert.org [accessed in November 2010].

implementation of their commitments to provide trade-related capacity-building (see section 4.4 below).

To integrate an assessment of the impacts of WTO Agreements on development as part of the TPR, Ghosh proposes that greater coordination would be necessary between different WTO divisions and with the World Bank, IMF, regional banks and national research institutions to incrementally increase policy analysis. An alternative would be to boost the process of Trade Policy Reviews to see them as a tool for fostering input from and dialogue with researchers and stakeholders at the national level on the impacts of agreements (Deere Birkbeck 2009a). Meanwhile, the burden would remain with WTO Members to ask questions about impact during TPR or WTO committee meetings. On the SPS front, for instance, notifying members are already expected to mention how their policies would affect others (in the case of regional trade agreements (RTAs), however, there has been categorical opposition to evaluations of their impact on the WTO system). There are also questions about how well suited the WTO's TPR process is to expanded activities. Already, the TPR accounts for almost one-third of the WTO's regular budget. Sceptics argue that TPR reviews are too infrequent (every four years for developing countries, and less frequently for least developed countries) to serve as a dynamic tool for policy dialogue.

Importantly, there have been some changes in the WTO's monitoring function that benefit developing countries. Luke and Bernal (Chapter 13) note that the TPR's scope has already expanded to include some monitoring of Aid for Trade and some countries have nominated themselves as subjects for this expanded review (see section 4.4 on Aid for Trade below). Similarly, developing countries have successfully sought ways to boost other reporting mechanisms in ways that serve their interests.[69] At their insistence, the Committee on Trade and Development (CTD) rather than the Committee on RTAs (CRTA) is the forum for reviewing RTAs among developing countries. In regard to Sanitary and Phytosanitary Standards (SPS) measures, developing countries secured provisions calling on developed countries to advise how new standards they adopt would offer special and differential treatment to developing countries.

From a political perspective, the call for more timely, compliance-oriented information and impact analysis from the TPR will face several hurdles. First, the WTO Secretariat faces constraints on its mandate to

[69] Other procedural innovations include earlier submissions of factual presentations in the case of RTA monitoring and longer comment periods for SPS notifications.

investigate and evaluate the policies of its Members. Second, developing countries often argue that greater transparency and more analytical reports could target their policies more than those of the rich. They have also resisted proposals to increase peer pressure and institutionalize follow-up to the TPR for fear such initiatives may work against them as they may be less able to use transparency mechanisms to coax changes on the part of developed countries. Larger developing countries, some of which already use their own resources for external monitoring, may prefer to maintain the status quo. Poorer countries regrettably remain largely disengaged from the TPR process and these related debates.

4.4 Capacity-building and Aid for Trade

Several authors in this volume consider how improvements in the governance of Aid for Trade could enhance the effectiveness of trade-related technical assistance and capacity-building.[70] There are already many critical assessments of the content and flows of capacity-building for trade, now widely referred to as 'Aid for Trade'.[71] Key facts that emerge from these studies are that most developing countries struggle to coordinate the diversity of individual providers of trade-related assistance to their countries, that capacity-building received falls far short of international commitments, and that substantive tensions can arise between donors and recipients where assistance relates to the implementation of contentious WTO norms.

While few analysts refute the importance of Aid for Trade (Njinkeu and Cameron 2008), critical development advocates insist that the provision of such assistance must not be a quid pro quo to reward developing countries for agreeing to include new issues in trade negotiations or for accepting bad trade deals (Tandon 2004). They also caution that engagement in the Aid for Trade discussion should not so absorb developing country trade delegates that it distracts their limited resources from engaging in negotiations. In general, however, the governance of Aid for Trade has thus far received surprisingly little attention.[72] Among

[70] CUTS *et al.* (2006); Deere (2005); DFID (2001); Higgins and Prowse (2010); ICTSD and IISD (2003); OECD (2001); Prowse (2002, 2005, 2006); UNECA (2009); Urpelainen (2009); and WTO and OECD (2009).

[71] Aid for Trade has become shorthand for assistance to developing countries in the following areas: support for building supply-side capacity; adjustment assistance; technical assistance; legal advice and training.

[72] A review of the evolution of debate on these topics since 1999 highlights how much political acceptance of the need to invest aid for trade has grown. See for instance Moore (1999).

those governance-related proposals that have arisen are calls to enhance the monitoring and evaluation of technical assistance; boost the role of South–South cooperation in capacity-building; increase the accountability of donors for the overall level and quality of Aid for Trade; and establish stronger links between trade-related capacity-building and national development and poverty reduction strategies. There have also been specific reform proposals (and some action taken) for each of the main donor collaboratives, such as the Enhanced Integrated Framework (EIF), the Agency for International Trade Information and Cooperation (AITIC), the International Trade Centre (ITC) and the Joint Integrated Technical Assistance Program (JITAP) (the latter programme was closed in 2009). Other contributions include proposals for a new independent mechanism for capacity-building that would enable recipients to select their preferred providers of assistance from the 'marketplace' of potential donors; shifting emphasis from bilateral efforts to multilateral initiatives such as the EIF or the programmes of UNCTAD; and limiting the WTO's engagement in capacity-building to legal assistance for understanding WTO Agreements (Deere *et al.* 2007). Further proposals are to boost and/or more carefully define the appropriate role of the Bretton Woods Institutions, regional development banks and other international organizations in Aid for Trade. Finally, a number of proposals argue for a greater role for local, non-governmental actors with a durable presence in developing countries – such as civil society groups, research centres and industry groups – as independent providers and recipients of capacity-building.

In Chapter 13 of this book, Luke and Bernal present a critique of the governance arrangements for Aid for Trade. They argue that mutual accountability of donors and beneficiaries has emerged as the most prominent governance principle for Aid for Trade – most notably through the 'spotlight' effect of global and regional reviews and through dialogue in fora such as the WTO Committee on Trade and Development (which has focused on identifying what is required from all partners to make the Aid for Trade initiative work). In their view, attention to equally important issues of transparency, access to and predictability of resource flows has been less prominent in the Aid for Trade governance architecture. They note, for instance, that there is no single point of access, identified process or criteria for beneficiaries to follow in order to tap into the Aid for Trade commitments of bilateral and multilateral donors. They make the case for dedicated regional Aid for Trade financial facilities to support national and regional trade capacity-building priorities. Specifically, they argue for empowering regional economic communities (RECs) responsible for implementing regional trade agreements and other cross-border integration initiatives with such facilities, which in turn would be modelled on international aid effectiveness principles. While noting that RECs will need to build their own capacity to take on this intermediation role, the authors argue that these regional facilities would better ensure access to and predictability of resource flows. In addition, the use of regional facilities would give regional integration efforts much-needed momentum and, if appropriately designed, provide national stakeholders with more transparent and responsive vehicles to access financial support. Moreover, at the national level, they propose that the regional Aid for Trade facilities could be complemented by the establishment of a national Aid for Trade basket fund as a vehicle for managing, coordinating and reporting on bilateral and other support received for national trade capacity development initiatives.

In Chapter 7, Kaushik and Mukiibi argue that while initiatives such as the EIF are useful in identifying supply-side constraints, bringing in-country stakeholders on board, and mainstreaming trade in national development plans, countries should take greater ownership of efforts to mainstream trade into national development plans and rely less on donor funding. They advise LDCs to make better use of upfront assistance available through initiatives such as the European Development Fund, the EIF and the Aid for Trade initiative to more clearly identify their interests and address their constraints before taking on new commitments in trade agreements. They call for making greater and more focused financial assistance available to help countries meet new product standards that could otherwise impede market access, and for building trade and development issues into national university curricula in LDCs. They also make a specific recommendation for the creation of an LDC-specific institution in Geneva (see section 3.3 above).

Finally several contributors in this book call for better monitoring of the effectiveness of Aid for Trade (AFT) and the flows of assistance to ensure that developed countries comply with their commitments to provide resources and that credible information is available to all WTO Members.[73] Similarly, Lee recommends the creation of an annual Trade-Related Development Assistance Report, whereby developed country

[73] For the state of play in 2010 on this issue, see www.wto.org/english/tratop_e/devel_e/a4t_e/aid4trade_e.htm<http://www.wto.org/english/tratop_e/devel_e/a4t_e/aid4trade_e.htm> [accessed in November 2010].

Members should be required to report regularly to the Council for Trade and Development on the development assistance they provide (Chapter 11; also see Ghosh, Chapter 14).

4.5 *WTO public outreach and participation of non-State actors*

Developing countries have expressed a range of views on whether and how to expand the involvement of stakeholders, experts, parliamentarians and other international organizations in the work of the WTO. Key issues of debate have included the appropriate role for non-State actors and terms for public access to WTO processes, information and documentation (often referred to as 'external transparency' considerations). In this book, several contributors argue that improved interaction between the WTO, non-State actors and parliaments is vital to improving the organization's development outcomes (for the interaction of the WTO with other international organizations, see section 2 of this chapter above).

Debate often arises as to whether democratization at the international or national level would best promote the interests of developing countries. In the early days of the WTO, India promote a staunch position against stronger NGO participation at the WTO, fearing that better resourced NGOs from developed countries would most benefit from greater transparency and access, and would further reinforce the dominance of developed country priorities and perspectives on the international stage. Along with influential developing country commentators such as Bhagwati (2001) and Srinivasan (1998, 2002, 2004), India emphasized the national level as the appropriate locus for stakeholder engagement and democratic accountability. India also opposed, and continues to resist, proposals to allow the WTO dispute settlement system to receive and consider amicus briefs as part of its proceedings.[74]

More recently, however, the perspectives and practices of developing countries and their analysts have evolved. For instance, the debates at the WTO on TRIPS and Public Health, as well as on cotton subsidies, each involved considerable collaboration among national and international NGOs (including developed country NGOs) and developing country governments. Debates on monitoring of Aid for Trade also suggest that developing countries are willing to let non-State actors contribute when the information generated directly benefits their trade interests.

[74] The issue of amicus briefs was one of the first campaign agenda items of NGOs working on the WTO. See, for instance, WWF (1999a).

At present, however, poor domestic capacity of non-State actors in many developing countries continues to make their governments nervous about an expanded role for NGOs (both in negotiations and in WTO monitoring processes). As trade grows, however, so too may the interest and capacities of key constituencies in developing countries. Meanwhile, there have already been a number of changes that broaden opportunities for public engagement in the WTO (see Box 21.1). (Notably, the WTO Secretariat has taken an active interest in monitoring and analysing trends in civil society participation (Capling and Low 2010; Gallagher *et al.* 2005).)

In his contribution, Kaukab (Chapter 19) concurs that the WTO has made efforts to provide better entry to non-State actors mainly through greater access to information and improved transparency, but concludes that more is needed. He argues that the WTO and its Members cannot continue to hide behind their 'Member-driven' and 'intergovernmental only' mantra. Noting that almost all international organizations have well-established mechanisms for the accreditation of non-State stakeholders, which provides them with greater access to information and meetings than the WTO currently offers, he proposes a number of ways that the WTO could be more inclusive without changing its basic intergovernmental structure. To improve the participation by national stakeholders from developing countries, he calls for establishing clear criteria and procedures for the accreditation of other intergovernmental organizations and NGOs and for a trust fund to support the participation of accredited NGOs from developing countries so that they have an equitable access to the WTO. He also recommends the creation of a WTO Business and Labour Council (where representatives of business and labour organizations are present) and a WTO CSO (Civil Society Organizations) Council (to accommodate the representatives of public-interest NGOs), each of which could develop their own recommendations for consideration by WTO Members.

Kaukab also takes up the issue of parliamentary involvement in the WTO. He reiterates calls for a WTO Parliamentary Assembly, proposing that at least two parliamentarians from each Member – one from the ruling and the other from key opposition parties – be included. This Assembly would deliberate on WTO issues and offer its recommendations to the Membership for consideration. In his contribution to this volume, Chimni (Chapter 10) calls for assigning a greater mandatory role to national parliaments in the negotiation and ratification of WTO Agreements, as well as for changing the composition of negotiating teams to include more women delegates and greater representation for old and new social movements.

4.6 A WTO assessment and evaluation function

Contributors to this book offer several proposals for boosting the assessment and evaluation function of the WTO.

In Chapter 15, Peña sets out a proposal for the creation of a WTO ombudsperson, exploring the needs and challenges such an office should address, its functions and its modalities of operation. He recommends defining an ombudsperson function within the WTO's institutional structure that would receive complaints from stakeholders within WTO Members and initiate independent investigations of alleged negative impacts of WTO Agreements. He argues this function would strengthen WTO transparency and accountability; contribute to increasing the participation of the citizens of all WTO Member States; and facilitate the achievement of the organization's goal of sustainable development. He recommends a first phase of activity in which the WTO ombudsperson would have a limited mandate and would produce only non-mandatory, technically based opinions on the issues the office has been asked to investigate. Requests for such action could be made by civil society groups from any Member country or international NGO, so long as their own governance arrangements were transparent, and complaints could relate to any inadequacies of the multilateral trading system that could impact sustainable development and transparency. To elaborate the proposal, and build Member State support, he proposes a gradual approach through broad worldwide multi-stakeholder consultations. Based on the feedback received, the WTO Director-General would prepare a concrete proposal for the consideration and eventual approval of the WTO General Council. If, after an independent external appraisal the ombudsperson function has demonstrated its value and effectiveness, he proposes that the WTO General Council could agree to improve its modalities of operation and possibly extend its functions as well.

Several authors in this book call for the incorporation of greater assessment and evaluation of the impacts of existing and proposed WTO Agreements into the WTO's governance arrangements. The push for *ex ante* and *ex post* assessments of the impacts of trade liberalization and trade rules is not new. It has already spurred numerous efforts to devise methodologies and pilot studies of trade impact assessments on gender, poverty, human rights and labour (3D and FORUM-ASIA 2004; Dommen

2009). Indeed, many countries have now conducted assessments of the environmental impacts of trade agreements on particular sectors, and also of particular provisions, such as rules on intellectual property, on national public policy priorities, such as public health.[75] In this book, several authors affirm the need to properly understand different impacts of agreements on developing countries and specific groups within them. Meléndez-Ortiz and Biswas (Chapter 4), for instance, call for greater attention to the sustainable development impacts of agreements. In Chapter 10, Chimni emphasizes the importance of reviews of the negative impact of WTO Agreements on developing countries, as well as the impact of and links to IMF and World Bank conditionalities. He also calls for a social audit of WTO Agreements that maps their impact on subaltern classes.

4.7 WTO research and statistics function

Progress towards the kinds of impact analysis and evaluation described in section 4.6 above will rely on improvements in the WTO's capacity to gather, make available and analyse trade data and statistics. This in turn will demand support for countries to gather and report data, and also to rethink the methodologies for some aspects of data collection. A key practical challenge for negotiations is, for instance, how to determine and attribute the origins of products where they combine components from many countries.

Several development-oriented analysts of the global trading system highlight the need to address the information and research gaps facing developing countries (Tussie 2009; Tussie and Lengyel 2002; François 2001). It is widely known that many developing countries lack adequate detailed country-level research and practical, detailed negotiation-relevant analysis of their specific interests on particular subjects of WTO negotiations.

Two questions that arise are what the appropriate role and scale of the WTO Secretariat's research function in addressing these shortfalls should be, and how best to build research capacity beyond the Secretariat. While there appears to be at least implicit support or comfort with the WTO Secretariat's growing body of research, there is also a strong push

[75] For instance, among WTO Members, the European Union carries out sustainability impact assessments (SIAs) on trade negotiations; Canada has done environmental assessments (EAs) of the WTO negotiation; and the USA has conducted an environmental review (ER) of the Doha Development Agenda negotiations. See www.wto.org/english/tratop_e/envir_e/reviews_e.htm [Accessed in November 2010].

for building research and analytical capacity within universities, research institutes and NGOs in developing countries. Indeed, the WTO Secretariat has been involved in some such efforts. In addition, several contributors to this book emphasize the importance of developing country governments and researchers having a greater role in setting the WTO research agenda and process. In Chapter 2, Puri proposes greater investment in UN research on trade and development, such as the work of UNCTAD. In Chapter 10, Chimni proposes that the WTO Secretariat support a journal primarily devoted to publishing Third World writings on WTO reform. In Chapter 7, Kaushik and Mukiibi highlight the need for better incorporation of trade and development issues in local university curricula.

4.8 *The WTO's institutional structure and internal management*

A cross-cutting issue for the WTO is whether its institutional structure is adequate to the task of addressing development and of enabling strategic policy discussions and oversight of the trading system. There have been numerous proposals for new processes, structures and initiatives to strengthen the WTO's deliberative function and to provide a space for policy debate, problem-solving and thinking about the long-term strategic direction and challenges facing the multilateral trading system.[76] Some analysts also take up the question of whether the WTO should have some kind of management committee or executive board of members to guide negotiations and oversee, among other matters, the budget and management of the Secretariat (see Narlikar in Chapter 5).

In his chapter, Lee argues that the current institutional apparatus and regulatory structure in the WTO need to be revised in order to effectively integrate development into international trade disciplines. Among the reforms he proposes are the elevation of the WTO's Committee on Trade and Development to the status of a Council, and the establishment of a coherent body of WTO rules that facilitates development (in the form of an Agreement on Development Facilitation). There are also several proposals in this book for increasing the participation of developing countries in WTO bodies and for reinvigorating the work conducted in the WTO's regular Committees (also see WTO 2009a). In his chapter, Chimni calls

[76] Specific proposals include bolstering the regularity and purpose of the Ministerial Conference; boosting the role of Ministers and political leaders in the work of the WTO; reviewing the mandate of the Director-General and Secretariat; and reinforcing the role and operations of the General Council (see Deere Birkbeck and Monagle 2009).

for further development of global administrative law to increase transparency and accountability in the functioning of WTO and WTO-related bodies.

A further set of proposals address the role, management and resources of the WTO Secretariat. A key question in this area is whether a more development-oriented WTO will require more resources for the WTO Secretariat. Since the WTO's inception, some have called for the organization to have greater resources and staff (Blackhurst 1998; Steger 2009a), noting its relatively small size compared to other international organizations. Member States have, however, been reluctant to boost the role, budget and scope for initiative on the part of the Secretariat. This does not, however, mean that the Secretariat has been passive. On the contrary, it has taken numerous initiatives, several of which have ultimately received the consent or blessing of the Members (see Box 21.1). In Chapter 11, Lee argues that the WTO's budget allocation to the activities and functions of trade and development should be significantly increased,[77] noting that this in turn would demand an increase of WTO staff and resources. Other commentators propose that the case for more Secretariat resources should be reviewed on a function-by-function basis (Deere Birkbeck 2009a). In some instances, the desired function could be better performed by other actors within and outside the multilateral system (e.g. UNCTAD, NGOs and national universities might, for instance, be better vehicles for meeting many of the research needs of developing countries).

Several authors in this book also take up the relationship of the Secretariat with Member States, the importance of Secretariat neutrality and concerns about bias (such as bias in favour of greater trade liberalization or of more powerful Member States). Developing country concerns about the impartiality of the Secretariat have arisen in regard to many areas of the WTO's work, such as the trade policy review process, the dispute settlement process, the provision of technical assistance and training, and in its research agenda. One response from developing countries has been to take a close interest in the process for selection of the WTO's leadership (particularly its Director-General) (South Centre 2005) and in boosting developing country representation among the WTO's staff.

Notably, several contributors in this book see possibilities for rethinking the role of the WTO Secretariat in some areas. In

[77] Lee also argues that the WTO Advisory Centre on WTO Law should also be supported by the WTO budget (see section 3 above).

Chapter 16, for instance, Ismail and Vickers see potential for the WTO to be selectively involved in the chairing of negotiations. Ghosh's proposals for a more responsive TPR process also implies some expansion and intensification of the Secretariat's activities. Already, the WTO's work in promoting Aid for Trade has boosted confidence in selectively expanding the scope for Secretariat action. Despite initial reservations about the perceived lack of formal mandate from Member States for certain activities, most WTO Members concur that the WTO's initiative to provide regular monitoring on protectionist measures in the context of the financial crisis has been useful as has much of its expanded research output.

5 Improving trade negotiation processes

A fourth theme of this book is the fairness, transparency and inclusiveness of trade negotiation processes (Jawara and Kwa 2003; Narlikar 2001, 2002; Nordström 2002). Alongside studies on how to strengthen developing country coalitions and public participation in developing country trade policy-making (see section 3 above), there are numerous proposals for better managing the scope, complexity and asymmetric power dynamics of trade negotiation processes and agreements.

On the development front, a broad suite of studies have well documented the challenges of effective developing country representation in multilateral negotiations at the WTO (Ismail 2008, 2009a, 2009b; Wilkinson 2006a, 2009a, 2009b; Jawara and Kwa 2003) and in bilateral and regional processes (such as for Free Trade Agreements with the United States and Economic Partnership Agreements with the European Union) (Bilal and Grynberg 2007; Erasmus 2009), particularly for the smallest and poorest countries. In this book, the contributors focus predominantly on the WTO processes.

At the WTO, the ambit of concerns about trade negotiations encompasses the process for agenda-setting; the role of informal consultations; the role of coalitions and other negotiating groups; the role of Chairs in negotiations and the process of WTO Ministerial meetings; the role of the WTO Secretariat in negotiations; the regular work of WTO committees; and the WTO accession process.[78] Notably, there are a range of opinions on the costs and benefits of informal negotiating processes at the WTO,

[78] On the appropriate role of the WTO Secretariat, see South Centre (2008).

including whether and how these should be reformed and/or formalized. Concern about Green Rooms and mini-Ministerials[79] has yielded proposals for better guidelines and formal procedures for WTO negotiations, including at Ministerial Conferences, to ensure transparency and fairer representation (South Centre 2003).

Ismail and Vickers (Chapter 16) argue that the litmus test for proposals to reform the WTO's negotiating processes must be how well they balance competing demands for greater efficiency, inclusiveness and legitimacy. Noting that small informal groups are now the decision-making fora that most shape the main content of proposed WTO deals, they call for greater analysis of the WTO's informal negotiating methods. In Chapter 19, Kaukab proposes measures to improve transparency of WTO negotiations (e.g. by publishing summary records of all meetings and key points of negotiating drafts on the WTO website without delay), which he argues would enable national stakeholders to approach their own governments for explanations and to offer suggestions. In Chapter 11, Lee also calls for procedural improvements, arguing that WTO meetings and negotiation schedules should be designed to allow maximum participation of developing countries and that greater use should be made of web technologies to increase the participation of those developing countries that cannot afford to station experts in Geneva (for other proposals on transparency, parliamentary engagement, and public participation in the negotiation process, see section 4 above).

Ismail and Vickers (Chapter 16) insist that there is no 'procedural panacea' that will magically resolve substantive differences over complex issues and divergent national interests, which in their view remain the core challenges blocking progress in multilateral negotiations. They argue against 'exclusive conclaves' that shift negotiations from Geneva to national capitals. Ismail and Vickers also adopt the view advanced in the Sutherland Report (Consultative Board 2004) that the WTO should *not* deviate from or abandon the consensus approach to decision-making, but rather strengthen it. In their view, calls for abandoning the single-undertaking and the consensus principle often emerge from a misdiagnosis of the underlying tensions thwarting progress in the Doha Round.[80]

[79] Drahos (2003); Ismail (2005, 2007, 2009c, 2009d); Jawara and Kwa (2003); Luke (2000); Narlikar (2004); Narlikar and Tussie (2004); Narlikar and Wilkinson (2004); South Centre (2003, 2008).

[80] Instead, they attribute the ongoing difficulties concluding the Doha Round to a combination of factors, including the hangover of previous asymmetries in negotiating

While recognizing that consensus may be a slower and more difficult process that risks both frustration with the system and greater recourse to RTAs, Ismail and Vickers argue in its favour, concluding that 'more inclusive, democratic and genuinely multilateral methods' produce more sustainable and fairer solutions in the long term. 'Not only does consensus force WTO Members to build convergences in their positions and make compromises in the interests of the system as a whole, but it also creates learning opportunities and empowerment for developing and least developed countries.' On the reform front, they propose that the rich tapestry of developing country (and developed country) coalitions should be better and more reliably represented in WTO decision-making and that WTO Members should develop a code of conduct to provide clearer guidance on the selection and conduct of the Chairs of WTO negotiations.[81] They propose that there may even be merit in strengthening some aspects of the role-agency of the WTO Secretariat in the negotiating process. On a more legal note and to rectify the structural problems in the area of democracy, Chimni (Chapter 10) proposes to amend the Vienna Convention on the Law of Treaties to eliminate the use of economic and political coercion in multilateral negotiations.

This book also takes up the debate on whether the WTO should move towards a more variable geometry of rights and obligations (through, for instance, plurilateral and critical mass decision-making, or weighted voting). To date, only a few contributions to this debate seriously consider the implications of such proposals for inclusiveness and development.[82] In this book, Chimni calls for exploring alternatives to the single undertaking (Chapter 10). In Chapter 17, Rodríguez Mendoza and Wilke call for a move away from all encompassing 'rounds' of negotiations on an ever increasing number of subjects to more à la carte negotiations, which they propose are more likely to produce significant and efficient results. They argue that a *critical mass* approach would have greater potential than the single undertaking, not only to close the current Doha Round of negotiations, but also to address new issues, such as climate change. To decide when to use the *critical mass* approach, they argue that each

outcomes, substantive divergences of interests among key trading partners, and the challenges of domestic politics within major players.

81 For more on how to improve the role of Chairs of WTO negotiation groups (both in ongoing Geneva negotiations and at Ministerial Conferences), see Ismail (2009b and 2009c).

82 Cornford (2004); Draper (2010); Lanoszka (2008); Low (2009b); and Patel (2003b).

negotiation should be evaluated by its merits (rather than by quantitative criteria such as that the countries involved must represent a certain percentage of trade in the sector concerned).[83] To ensure consistency with multilateralism, Rodríguez Mendoza and Wilke propose: 1) requiring the WTO Ministerial Conference or the General Council to launch such negotiations, thereby implying a collective decision by all WTO Members; 2) establishing criteria for the determination of what constitutes a critical mass on a case-by-case basis, taking into account the political and economic position of individual countries; 3) providing for particular 'opt out' options for WTO Members in negotiation clauses; and 4) applying all agreements on an MFN basis.

Contributors also take up the issue of voting. Laurent (Chapter 8) suggests that where one powerful country withholds consensus on a particular issue of negotiation, the option of taking a vote should be considered. In Chapter 5, Narlikar considers the options for revising the WTO's voting system to remove the inefficiencies of the consensus-based system while still according veto power to the entire Membership to ensure they have a meaningful say in the decision-making process. She suggests that one combination would be a critical mass approach together with a voting system that requires a super-majority. Narlikar also rejects proposals for the use of an executive board to resolve negotiation deadlocks, arguing that such a delegation of authority by WTO Member States would exacerbate complaints of disenfranchisement and perceptions of unfairness by formalizing 'the exclusion of the greater part of its Membership'.

A final aspect of trade negotiations addressed in this volume is the WTO's accession process. Concerns about the WTO's accession process have yielded a number of studies of the challenges for developing countries and recommendations for reform.[84] Importantly, broader geopolitics sometimes complicates the accession process and the potential for its reform. The Russian accession, for instance, is highly political, and the candidacy of Iran and Syria are both significantly influenced by political considerations.

[83] They note, for instance, that this approach could leave out countries for which 'a particular sector is significant in its economy but the country itself is too small to be relevant at the global level. In addition, when new rules are proposed to be negotiated on issues such as, for instance, climate change, it would be extremely difficult to draw the line between countries that are relevant or not' (Chapter 17).

[84] Adhikari and Dahal (2003); Charveriat and Kirkbride (2003); Oxfam International (2004, 2005); Primo Braga and Cattaneo (2009).

In this book, Primo Braga and Cattaneo propose several procedural improvements to the WTO accession process, highlighting three core challenges: the difficulties accession countries face with implementation of accession agreements; the length and complexity of asymmetric negotiations; and the prospect that accession deals may undermine perceptions about the fairness of the WTO system. They emphasize that commitments undertaken by some acceding countries are unrealistic, exposing them to pressures for further disciplines through bilateral/regional treaties and the use of the WTO dispute settlement system to enforce accession deals (which in turn could exacerbate hard feelings of new entrants about the multilateral trade system). They also observe that the 'WTO-plus' conditions that form part of most WTO accession deals could risk creating a 'two-tier' WTO Membership, which would not only challenge the GATT principle of non-discrimination but could add to the obstacles facing WTO negotiations as countries believe they have already undertaken 'too much' in their accession deals.

Primo Braga and Cattaneo underscore the need for greater technical support and capacity-building for accession countries at all stages of the WTO accession process. Noting two proposals submitted in 2009 by groups of developing countries (and some developed countries) to make the WTO accession process more transparent and less burdensome for LDCs (e.g. WTO 2009f, 2010b), they endorse recommendations for '1) enhanced institutional mechanisms to provide acceding countries with the opportunity to express their views on the process; and 2) periodic progress reports on accessions to the General Council' (WTO 2010b:11).[85]

6 Conclusion: political strategies for reform

This book shows that there is no shortage of development-oriented views and proposals on the question of how to improve the global governance of trade. It also highlights the diversity of views on political strategy for achieving global trade governance that works better for development. These in turn reflect broader debates on how to transform the global economy. Some commentators argue for placing the issue of global trade governance within a 'Bretton Woods II' type process that would undertake a systematic and complete reform of the global economic architecture.

[85] The shortcomings of the accession process was a recurring concern at the 2009 Geneva WTO Ministerial Conference. As of early 2010, the WTO Secretariat commenced regular meetings on the progress of LDCs in the accession process.

Others highlight the advantages of a step-by-step approach to targeted trade reforms (Ismail 2009d), while still others advocate a gradual and incremental process of evolution. For the latter, patience and realistic expectations are required.

Yet, some critics caution against what they characterize as mere 'tinkering' with the existing system, arguing that the real challenges are political (Wilkinson 2006a). In the spirit of more deliberative and democratic global governance (Higgott and Erman 2010), some experts call for building opportunities for greater political deliberation within WTO decision-making (Howse 2002; Pauwelyn 2005). Other critics emphasize the need for broader thinking about whether deep reforms and a dramatically different system for global trade regulation is a prerequisite for achieving significantly greater coherence on global development and sustainability challenges (South Centre 2009). For some critics, the emphasis on boosting the power of the governments of developing countries is inadequate, and sometimes misplaced. In the spirit of 'Another World is Possible', social movements critical of the economic paradigm underpinning the global trading system call for a more bottom-up approach to the transformation of global trade.[86] In Chapter 10 of this book, for instance, Chimni calls for civil society and social movements to organize mass mobilizations and resistance. He argues that only this will compel national parliaments to resist pressures from powerful states and capitalist classes that marginalize the needs of vulnerable and poor groups within societies.

At present, calls for 'strengthening' the WTO seem to have greater traction with WTO Member States than calls for 'reform'. At the 2009 WTO Ministerial Conference, Member States articulated a number of priorities for strengthening the WTO, including greater fairness and efficiency in the WTO's accession process; strengthening the WTO's monitoring process; reinvigorating the functioning of the WTO's regular committees; and improving the delivery of Aid for Trade (Deere Birkbeck and Cherneva 2010; WTO 2009a). Many WTO members also concurred on the need for processes – formal and informal – to discuss such proposals as well as the post-Doha agenda for the WTO (WTO 2009a).[87] While some reform advocates prefer to postpone such discussions for fear of distracting political attention from the Doha Round, others recommend that a systematic process of intergovernmental reflection could and

[86] Amin (2010); Anderson (2000); Bello (2002a); Dunkley (2000); Rajagopal (2003); Raynolds *et al.* (2007); and Rosset (2006).

[87] See, for instance, Dadush (2009), Deere Birkbeck (2009a); Draper (2010); and WEF (2010).

should be delinked from the substantive agenda and day-to-day processes of the WTO. In Chapter 4, for instance, Meléndez-Ortiz and Biswas recommend that WTO Members create a standing body to review the functioning of the multilateral trading system, in effect institutionalizing the process of thinking about the WTO's functioning.[88] Chimni, on the other hand, calls for national parliaments, civil society and social movements to be charged with sifting through various grievances against the WTO in terms of both process and outcome to determine which groups within the population are seriously hurt by the WTO's Agreements and what can be done to address this.

To conclude, this book shows that there is a distinct set of developing country priorities for global trade governance reform. Top among these include calls for greater focus on the coherence of trade governance and broader global economic governance arrangements in terms of development-orientation; support for initiatives to boost South–South trade cooperation; and improved governance of Aid for Trade. While some priorities are shared with developed countries (such as the call for improvements in the WTO's monitoring function and for better management of the interaction between regional and multilateral trade regimes), developing country perspectives remain too neglected in the scholarly literature on global trade governance. The book highlights that the challenges of WTO participation for developing countries, particularly the smallest and poorest, and the fairness of trade negotiations processes are still top priorities that demand attention.

References

3D and FORUM-ASIA. 2004. *Practical Guide to the WTO for Human Rights Advocates*. Bangkok and Geneva: 3D Trade, Human Rights, Equitable Economy and the Asian Forum for Human Rights and Development.

Abbott, F. 2004. *The Doha Declaration on the Trips Agreement and Public Health and the Contradictory Trend in Bilateral and Regional Free Trade Agreements*. Geneva: QUNO.

Abreu, M. de Paiva. 2009. 'The G20 Agenda, Trade and the Developing World', in Deere Birkbeck, C. and Meléndez-Ortiz, R. (eds.), *Rebuilding Global*

[88] Some analysts focus on the roles that trade delegates could play in such reflection, while others emphasize the importance of leadership from political leaders and trade ministers. Still others promote a process that engages academics and/or stakeholders, either in a formal advisory capacity to the WTO Members or that takes place completely outside the framework of the WTO.

Trade: Proposals for a Fairer, More Sustainable Future. Geneva and Oxford: International Centre for Trade and Sustainable Development and the Global Economic Governance Programme.

Action Aid, CAFOD, Christian Aid, Consumers International, FIELD, Oxfam, RSPB and WDM. 2000. *Recommendations for Ways Forward on Institutional Reform of the World Trade Organisation*. Available at http://trade.ec.europa.eu/doclib/docs/2005/april/tradoc_122163.pdf [Accessed in November 2010].

Adhikari, R. and Dahal, N. 2003. *LDCs' Accession to the WTO: Learning from the Cases of Nepal, Cambodia and Vanuatu*. Kathmandu: South Asia Watch on Trade, Economics and Environment (SAWTEE).

African Group. 2000. *The View of the African Group on Enhancing the Internal Transparency and the Effective Participation of all Members of the World Trade Organization*. Geneva: Office of the Organization of African Unity.

Aggarwal, V. 2001. 'Governance in International Trade: Lessons from Sectoralism, Regionalism and Globalism', in de Jonge Oudraat, C. and Simmons, P. (eds.), *Managing Global Issues: Lessons Learned*. Washington, DC: Carnegie Endowment for International Peace.

Aggarwal, G. and Lee, S. 2010. *Trade Policy in the Asia-Pacific: The Role of Ideas, Interests and Domestic Institutions*. New York: Springer.

Akyüz, Y. 2004. 'Some Observations on the Question of Coherence and Development', *TWN Briefing Paper 24*. Penang, Third World Network.

2009. *The Role of the United Nations in Global Economic Governance*. Geneva: South Centre.

Ala'i, P. 1999. 'Free Trade or Sustainable Development? An Analysis of the WTO Appellate Body's Shift to a More Balanced Approach to Trade Liberali zation', *American University International Law Review* 14(4): 1129–71.

Alavi, A. 2008. *Legalization of Development in the WTO: Between Law and Politics*. Leiden: Kluwer Law International.

Alessandrini, D. 2010. *Developing Countries and the Multilateral Trade Regime: The Failure and Promise of the WTO's Development Mission*. Oxford: Hart Publishing.

Alvarez, J. 2002. 'The WTO as Linkage Machine', *The American Journal of International Law* 96(1): 146–58.

Alvarez-Jiménez, A. 2009. 'Improvements to the WTO Decision-making Process: Lessons from the International Monetary Fund and the World Bank', in Steger, D. (ed.), *Redesigning the World Trade Organization for the Twenty-first Century*. International Development Research Centre (IDRC) and the Centre for International Governance Innovation (CIGI): Wilfrid Laurier University Press.

Amin, S. 2010. *Ending the Crisis of Capitalism or Ending Capitalism?* Oxford: Pambazuka Press.

Anderson, S. (ed.) 2000. *Views from the South: The Effects of Globalization and the WTO on Third World Countries*. San Francisco: Food First Books.

Anderson, K. and Valenzuela, E. 2007. 'The World Trade Organisation's Doha Cotton Initiative: A Tale of Two Issues', *The World Economy* 30(8): 1281–1304.

Anderson, K., Martin, W. and van der Mensbrugghe, D. 2005. 'Global Impacts of the Doha Scenarios on Poverty', in Hertel, T. and Winters, A. (eds.), *Poverty and the WTO: Impacts of the Doha Development Agenda*, Washington, DC: World Bank.

2006. 'Would Multilateral Trade Reform Benefit Sub-Saharan Africans?' *Journal of African Economies* 15(4): 626–70.

Auboin, M. 2004. 'The Trade, Debt and Finance Nexus: At the Crossroads of Micro and Macroeconomics', *WTO Discussion Paper No. 6*. Geneva: WTO.

2007. 'Fulfilling the Marrakesh Mandate on Coherence: Ten Years of Cooperation between the WTO, IMF and World Bank', *WTO Discussion Paper No. 13*. Geneva: WTO.

Bacchus, J. 2004. 'A Few Thoughts on Legitimacy, Democracy and the WTO', *Journal of International Economic Law* 7(3): 667–73.

Bach, C. 2007. 'The International Trade System', in Anderson, E. and Lindsnaes, B. (eds.), *Toward New Global Strategies: Public Goods and Human Rights*. Leiden/Boston: Martinus Nijhoff Publishers.

Baldwin, R. 2006. 'Failure of the WTO Ministerial Conference at Cancún: Reasons and Remedies', *The World Economy* 29(6): 677–96.

(ed.) 2009. *The Great Trade Collapse: Causes, Consequences and Prospects*. Brussels: Centre for Economic Policy Research and VoxEU.org.

Baldwin, R. and Evenett, S. (eds.) 2009. *The Collapse of Global Trade, Murky Protectionism, and the Crisis: Recommendations for the G20*, A VoxEU.org Publication, available at www.voxeu.org/reports/Murky_Protectionism.pdf [Accessed in November 2010].

Baldwin, R. and Low, P. (eds.) 2009. *Multilateralizing Regionalism Challenges for the Global Trading System*. Cambridge University Press.

Barfield, C. 2001. *Free Trade, Sovereignty, Democracy: The Future of the World Trade Organization*. Washington, DC: AEI Press.

Barry, C. 2006. 'Just Trade under Law: Do We Need a Theory of Justice for International Trade Relations?' *The American Society of International Law Proceedings* 100.

Barton, J., Goldstein, J., Josling, T. and Steinberg, R. 2006. *The Evolution of the Trade Regime: Politics, Law and the Economics of the GATT and the WTO*. Princeton University Press.

Bellmann, C. and Gester, R. 1996. 'Accountability of the World Trade Organization', *Journal of World Trade* 30(6): 31–74.

Bello, W. 2000. *Why Reform of the WTO is the Wrong Agenda. Four Essays on Four Institutions: WTO, UNCTAD, IMF and the World Bank*. Bangkok: Focus on the Global South.

2002a. *Deglobalization: Ideas for a New World Economy*. London: Zed Books.

2002b. 'Learning from Doha: A Civil Society Perspective from the South', *Global Governance* 8: 273–79.

Bermann, G. and Mavroidis, P. 2007. *WTO Law and Developing Countries*. Cambridge University Press.

Bernal, L., Kaukab, R., Musungu, S. and Yu, V. 2004. 'South–South Cooperation in the Multilateral Trading System: Cancún and Beyond', *TRADE Working Paper No. 21*. Geneva: South Centre.

Beukel, E. 2001. 'Greening the World Trade Organization Trading Regime? Towards a Structural Power Model', *Journal of International Relations and Development* 4(2): 138–56.

Bhagwati, J. 2001. 'After Seattle: Free Trade and the WTO', *International Affairs* 77(1): 15–30.

(ed.) 2002. *On Going Alone: The Case for Relaxed Reciprocity in Freeing Trade*. Cambridge: MIT Press.

2008. *Termites in the Trading System: How Preferential Trade Agreements Undermine Free Trade*. Oxford University Press.

Bhagwati, J., Greenaway, D. and Panagariya, A. 1998. 'Trading Preferentially: Theory and Policy', *The Economic Journal* 108(July): 1128–48.

Bhattacharya, D. 2009. 'Creeping Trade and Phantom Aid: LDCs in the Global Context and Priorities for Reform of Governance', paper presented as part of the Geneva Lectures on Global Economic Governance, Global Economic Governance Programme, Oxford University, January 2008.

Bhaumik, T. 2006. *The WTO: A Discordant Orchestra*. New Delhi: Sage Publications.

Bilal, S. and Grynberg, R. (eds.) 2007. *Navigating New Waters: A Reader on ACP-EU Trade Relations*. London: Commonwealth Secretariat.

Birdsall, N. and Lawrence, R. 1999. 'Deep Integration and Trade Agreements: Good for Developing Countries?' in Kaul, I., Grunberg I., and Stern. M.A. (eds.), *Global Public Goods: International Cooperation in the 21st Century*, New York: Oxford University Press for the United Nations Development Program, pp. 128–51.

Blackhurst, R. 1998. 'The Capacity of the WTO to Fulfil Its Mandate', in Krueger, A. (ed.), *The WTO as an International Organization*. Chicago University Press.

2001. 'Reforming WTO Decision Making: Lessons from Singapore and Seattle', in Gunter Deutsch, K. and Speyer, B. (eds.), *The World Trade Organization Millennium Round: Freer Trade in the Twenty-First Century*. London: Routledge.

Blackhurst, R. and Hartridge, D. 2004. 'Improving the Capacity of WTO Institutions to Fulfil their Mandate', *Journal of International Economic Law* 7(3): 705–16.

Blackhurst, R., Lyakurwa, B. and Oyejide, A. 2000. 'Options for Improving Africa's Participation in the WTO', *The World Economy* 23(4): 491–510.

Bluestein, P. 2009. *Misadventures of the Most Favored Nation: Clashing Egos, Inflated Ambitions and the Great Shambles of the World Trade System*. New York: Public Affairs.

Bohne, E. 2010. *The World Trade Organization: Institutional Development and Reform*. Basingstoke: Palgrave Macmillan.

Bonzon, Y. 2009. 'Options for Public Participation in the WTO: Experience from Regional Trade Agreements', in Steger, D. (ed.), *Redesigning the World Trade Organization for the Twenty-first Century*, International Development Research Centre (IDRC) and Centre for International Governance Innovation (CIGI): Wilfrid Laurier University Press.

Bora, B., Grynberg, R. and Razzaque, M. 2005. 'Marginalisation of LDCs and Small Vulnerable States in World Trade', *Economic Paper No. 71*. London: Commonwealth Secretariat.

Bown, C. 2009. *Self-enforcing Trade: Developing Countries and WTO Dispute Settlement*. Washington, DC: Brookings Institution Press.

Bown, C. and Hoekman, B. 2005. 'WTO Dispute Settlement and the Missing Developing Country Cases: Engaging the Private Sector', *Journal of International Economic Law* 8(4): 861–90.

Bown, C. and Pauwelyn, J. (eds.) 2010. *The Law, Economics and Politics of Retaliation in WTO Dispute Settlement*. Cambridge University Press.

Bradlow, D. 2010. 'Reforming Global Economic Governance: A Strategy for Middle Powers in the G20', paper prepared for the workshop on *Going Global: Australia, Brazil, Indonesia, Korea and South Africa in International Affairs* held in Jakarta, Indonesia, 25–26 May.

Brandi, C. 2009. 'We the Stakeholders. The Power of Representation Beyond Borders?' *Global Justice: Theory Practice Rhetoric* 2: 35–41.

Brenton, P. 2003. 'Integrating the Least Developed Countries into the World Trading System: The Current Impact of European Union Preferences under Everything But Arms', *Journal of World Trade* 37(3): 623–46.

Brewer, T. and Young, S. 1999. 'WTO Disputes and Developing Countries', *Journal of World Trade* 33(5): 169–82.

Brock, K. and McGee, R. 2004. 'Mapping Trade Policy: Understanding the Challenges of Civil Society Participation', *IDS Working Paper No. 225*, Brighton: Institute of Development Studies.

Brown, A. and Stern, R. 2007. 'Concepts of Fairness in the Global Trading System', *Pacific Economic Review* 12(3): 293–318.

Burnett, P. and Manji, F. 2007. *From the Slave Trade to 'Free' Trade: How Trade Undermines Democracy and Justice in Africa*. Oxford: Fahamu Press.

Busch, M. and Reinhardt, E. 2003. 'Developing Countries and GATT/WTO Dispute Settlement', *Journal of World Trade* 37(4): 719–35.

CAFOD *et al.* 2002. A Genuine Development Agenda for the Doha Round of WTO Negotiations, Joint Agency Statement on the Doha Development Round signed by CAFOD, Save the Children, Oxfam, Action Aid, World Vision, Christian Aid, The Fairtrade Foundation, Traidcraft, ITDG and World Development Movement. Available at www.ukabc.org/doha_dev_round.htm [Accessed in November 2010].

Cali, M. 2007. 'Scale and Types of Funds for Aid for Trade', *Negotiation Advisory Brief No. 15*, Ottawa: ILEAP.

Capling, A. and Low, P. 2010. *Governments, Non-State Actors and Trade Policy-Making: Negotiating Preferentially or Multilaterally.* Cambridge/Geneva: Cambridge University Press and the WTO.

Cass, D. 2005. *The Constitutionalization of the World Trade Organization: Legitimacy, Democracy, and Community in the International Trading System.* Oxford University Press.

Cattaneo, O. 2005. 'Has the WTO Gone Too Far or Not Far Enough? Some Reflections on the Concept of Policy Space', in Mitchell, A. (ed.), *Challenges and Prospects for the WTO*, London: Cameron May Publications, pp. 55–84.

Cattaneo, O. and Braga, A. 2009. 'Everything You Always Wanted to Know about WTO Accession (But Were Afraid to Ask)', *Policy Research Working Paper Series No. 5116*, the World Bank.

Centre for Policy Dialogue. 2003. 'LDC Priorities and Dhaka Declaration: International Civil Society Forum on Advancing LDC Interests in the Fifth WTO Ministerial', paper presented at conference organized by Consumers International, SEATINI, SAWTEE, Oxfam International and the EU-LDC Network, 29–30 May, Dhaka, Bangladesh.

Chandra, R. 2002. 'Movement of Natural Persons and the GATS Major Trade Policy Impediments', in Hoekman, B., Mattoo, A. and English, P. (eds.), *Development, Trade, and the WTO: A Handbook*. Washington DC: World Bank.

Chang, H.-J. 2002. *Kicking Away the Ladder. Development Strategy in Historical Perspective*. London: Anthem Press.

Charnovitz, S. 2000. 'Opening the WTO to Non-governmental Interests', *Fordham International Law Journal* 24: 173–216.

2002. 'Triangulating the World Trade Organization', *The American Journal of International Law* 96(1): 28–55.

Charveriat, C. and Kirkbride, M. 2003. *Cambodia's Accession to the WTO: How the Law of the Jungle is Applied to One of the World's Poorest Countries*. Oxford: Oxfam GB.

Chaytor, B. 1998. 'Dispute Settlement Under the GATT/WTO: The Experience of Developing Countries', in Cameron, J. and Campbell, K. (eds.), *Dispute Resolution in the World Trade Organization*. London: Cameron May.

Ching, M. 1993. 'Evaluating the Effectiveness of the GATT Dispute Settlement System for Developing Countries', *World Competition* 16: 105–111.

Cho, S. 2004. 'A Bridge Too Far: The Fall of the Fifth WTO Ministerial Conference in Cancún and the Future of Trade Constitution', *Journal of International Economic Law* 7(2): 219–44.

Chutikul, K. 2003. 'Options for a Parliamentary Dimension of the WTO', in *Parliamentary Conference on the WTO*. Geneva: Inter-Parliamentary Union and the European Parliament.

Cline, W. 2004. *Trade Policy and Global Poverty.* Washington, DC: Institute for International Economics.

Cohn, T. 2003. *Governing Global Trade: International Institutions in Conflict and Convergence.* Farnham: Ashgate Press.

Collins-Williams, T. and Wolfe, R. 2010. 'Transparency as a Trade Policy Tool: The WTO's Cloudy Windows', *World Trade Review* 9(4): 289–318.

Commonwealth Secretariat and World Bank. 2000. *Small States: Meeting Challenges in the Global Economy.* Report of the Commonwealth Secretariat/ World Bank Joint Task Force on Small States.

Conca, Ken. 2000. 'The WTO and the Undermining of Global Environmental Governance', *Review of International Political Economy* 7(3): 484–94.

Consultative Board. 2004. *The Future of the WTO: Addressing Institutional Changes in the New Millennium.* Geneva: World Trade Organization.

Consumers International. 2000. 'The Way Forward for the Multilateral Trading System', *Trade and Economics Briefing Paper No. 1.* London: Consumers International.

Corrales-Leal, W. 2007. 'Basic Concepts and Proposals on the Use of Policy Spaces in Trade-supported Strategies for Sustainable Development', *ICTSD Programme on Competitiveness and Sustainable Development Series Issue Paper No. 1.* Geneva: International Centre for Trade and Sustainable Development.

Correa, C. 2000. *Intellectual Property Rights, the WTO and Developing Countries: The TRIPS Agreement and Policy Options.* Penang: Third World Network (TWN).

Cornford, A. 2004. 'Variable Geometry for the WTO: Concept and Precedents', *UNCTAD Discussion Paper No. 171*, May. Geneva: UNCTAD. Available at www.unctad.org/en/docs/osgdp20045_en.pdf [Accessed in November 2010].

Cosbey, A. 2009. *A Sustainable Development Roadmap for the WTO.* Winnipeg: International Institute for Sustainable Development (IISD).

Cottier, T. 2007. 'Preparing for Structural Reform in the WTO', *Journal of International Economic Law* 10(3): 497–508.

2009. 'A Two Tier Approach to WTO Decision Making', in Steger, D. (ed.), *Redesigning the World Trade Organization for the Twenty-first Century*, International Development Research Centre (IDRC) and the centre for International Governance Innovation (CIGI) Wilfrid Laurier University Press.

Cottier, T. and Elsig, M. (eds.) 2011. *Governing the World Trade Organization: Past, Present and Beyond Doha.* Cambridge University Press.

Cottier, T. and Takenoshita, S. 2003. 'The Balance of Power in WTO Decision-Making: Towards Weighted Voting in Legislative Response', *Aussenwirtschaft* 58: 171–214.

2008. 'Decision-making and the Balance of Powers in WTO Negotiations: Towards Supplementary Weighted Voting', in Griller, S. (ed.), *At the Crossroads: The World Trading System and the Doha Round.* Vienna: Springer-Verlag.

Croome, J. 1999. *Reshaping the World Trading System: A History of the Uruguay Round*, 2nd edn. Geneva: World Trade Organization.

Curzon, G. 1965. *Multilateral Commercial Diplomacy, The GATT and its Impact on National Commercial Policies and Techniques.* London: Michael Joseph Ltd.

Curzon Price, V. 1991. 'GATT's New Trade Policy Review Mechanism', *The World Economy* 14(2): 227–38.

Cutajar, M. 1985. *UNCTAD and the South-North Dialogue: The First Twenty Years.* New York: Pergamon Press.

CUTS International. 2009a. *Towards More Inclusive Trade Policy Making: Process and Role of Stakeholders in Select African Countries.* Jaipur, India: Consumer Unity & Trust Society (CUTS) International.

2009b. *Improving Ownership Through Inclusive Trade Policy Making Processes: Lessons from Africa.* Jaipur, India: Consumer Unity & Trust Society (CUTS) International.

CUTS, FLACSO and NSI. 2006. *Strategic Review of WTO-provided TRTA Activities: Final Report.* Consumer Unity & Trust Society, Latin American School of Social Sciences (FLACSO), and the North-South Institute. Available at rii.flacso.org.ar/web/wp-content/uploads/2010/10/doc15.pdf [Accessed in November 2010].

Dadush, U. 2009. 'WTO Reform: The Time to Start Is Now'. *Policy Brief – September.* Washington, DC: Carnegie Endowment for International Peace (CEIP).

da Motta Veiga, P. 2005. 'Brazil and the G20 Group of Developing Countries', in Gallagher, P., Low, P. and Stoler, A. (eds.), *Managing the Challenges of WTO Participation 45 Case Studies*, Cambridge University Press, pp. 109–19.

2007. 'Trade Policy-Making in Brazil: Changing Patterns in State-Civil Society Relationship', in Halle, M. and Wolfe, R. (eds.), *Process Matters: Sustainable Development and Domestic Trade Transparency*, Geneva: International Institute for Sustainable Development, pp. 143–82.

Das, B. 1998. *The WTO Agreements: Deficiencies, Imbalances and Required Changes.* London and Penang: Zed Books and Third World Network.

2000. *Globalization and the South: Some Critical Issues.* Penang: Third World Network.

2002. *Strengthening Developing Countries in the WTO.* Penang: Third World Network.

2007. 'The Multilateral Trading System: The Need for Basic Reform', *TWN Briefing Paper No. 42.* Penang: Third World Network.

Davey, W. 2005. 'The WTO Dispute Settlement System: The First Ten Years', *Journal of International Economic Law* 8(1): 17–50.

Davies, R. 2009. 'Reclaiming the Development Dimension of the Multilateral Trading System', lecture presented as part of the Geneva Lectures on Global Economic Governance, Global Economic Governance Programme, Oxford University, March.

de Bievre, D. 2002. 'Redesigning the Virtuous Circle: Two Proposals for World Trade Organization Reform', *Journal of World Trade* 36(5): 1005–13.

Debroy, B. and Chakraborty, D. 2007. *The Trade Game: Negotiation Trends at WTO and Concerns of Developing Countries*. New Delhi: Academic Foundation.

Deere, C. 2004. 'Greening Trade in the Americas: An Agenda for Moving Beyond the North-South Impasse', *Journal of World Trade* 38(1): 137–153.

2005. 'International Trade Technical Assistance and Capacity Building', *Human Development Report Office Occasional Paper 2005/5*, New York: United Nations Development Program.

2008. *The Implementation Game: The TRIPS Agreement and the Global Politics of Intellectual Property Reform in Developing Countries*. Oxford University Press.

Deere, C. and Esty, D. 2001. *Greening the Americas: NAFTA's Lessons for Hemispheric Trade*. Cambridge: MIT Press.

Deere, C., Patel, M. and Ghosh, A. 2007. 'A Governance Audit of the WTO: Roundtable Discussion on Making Global Trade Work for Development', paper presented at WTO Public Forum, October, Geneva. Global Economic Governance Programme.

Deere Birkbeck, C. 2009a. 'Reinvigorating Debate on WTO Reform: The Contours of a Functional and Normative Approach to Analyzing the WTO System', in Steger, D. (ed.), *Redesigning the World Trade Organization for the Twenty-first Century*. International Development Research Centre (IDRC) and the Centre for International Governance Innovation (CIGI): Wilfrid Laurier University Press.

2009b. 'From Crisis Management to Sustainable Development: Why We Need a Ministerial Conference This Year', in Deere Birkbeck, C. and Meléndez-Ortiz, R. (eds.), *Rebuilding Global Trade: Proposals for a Fairer, More Sustainable Future*. Geneva and Oxford: International Centre for Trade and Sustainable Development and the Global Economic Governance Programme.

Deere Birkbeck, C. and Cherneva, I. 2011. 'The 2009 WTO Ministerial Conference: A Review of Outcomes and Proposals on the Functioning of the WTO', *GEG Working Paper*, Global Economic Governance Programme, University College, Oxford.

Deere Birkbeck, C. and Harbourd, M. 2011. 'Developing Country Coalitions at the WTO: Lessons on Effectiveness', *GEG Working Paper*. Global Economic Governance Programme, University College, Oxford.

Deere Birkbeck, C. and Meléndez-Ortiz, R. (eds.) 2009. *Rebuilding Global Trade: Proposals for a Fairer, More Sustainable Future*. Geneva and Oxford: International Centre for Trade and Sustainable Development and the Global Economic Governance Programme.

Deere Birkbeck, C. and Monagle, C. 2009. *Strengthening Multilateralism: A Mapping of Proposals on WTO Reform and Global Trade Governance*. Geneva and Oxford: International Centre for Trade and Sustainable Development (ICTSD), and Global Economic Governance Programme.

de la Calle, L. 2000. 'The Functioning of the World Trade Organization', paper presented at WTO Symposium at the WTO in Geneva, April.

DFID. 2001. 'Building Capacity for Trade', in *Trade Matters: Eliminating World Poverty*. London: Department for International Development.

Dhar, B., Evenett, S. J., Long, G. *et al.* 2009. 'Disavowing Protectionism: A Strengthened G20 Standstill and Surveillance', in Baldwin, R. and Evenett, S. (eds.), *The Collapse of Global Trade, Murky Protectionism, and the Crisis: Recommendations for the G20,* A VoxEu.org Publication, available at www.voxeu.org/reports/Murky–Protectionism.pdf [Acesses in November 2010]

Diao, X., Diaz-Bonilla, E. and Robinson, S. 2003. 'Tell Me Where It Hurts, an' I'll Tell You Who to Call: Industrialized Countries' Agricultural Policies and Developing Countries', Washington, DC: International Food Policy Research Institute.

Diaz-Bonilla, E., Robinson, S. and Gulati, A. 2003a. 'Heterogeneity, Convergences and Divergences: Developing Countries and the WTO Agricultural Negotiations', background paper prepared for *Trade for Development*. New York: UN Millennium Project.

Diaz-Bonilla, E., Thomas, M. and Robinson, S. 2003b. 'On Boxes, Contents and Users: Food Security and the WTO Negotiations', Washington, DC: International Food Policy Research Institute.

Dommen, C. 2009. 'Governance of Global Trade: How Human Rights Can Help Define Priorities', in Deere Birkbeck, C. and Mélendez-Ortiz, R. (eds.), *Rebuilding Global Trade: Proposals for a Fairer, More Sustainable Future*. Geneva and Oxford: International Centre for Trade and Sustainable Development and the Global Economic Governance Programme.

Dowlah, C. 2004. *Backwaters of Prosperity: How Forces of Globalization and GATT/WTO Trade Regimes Contribute to the Marginalization of the World's Poorest Nations*. Westport: Praeger Publishers.

Drabek, Z. 2010. *Is the World Trade Organization Attractive Enough for Emerging Economies? Critical Esssays on the Multilateral Trading System*. Melbourne: Palgrave Macmillan.

Drahos, P. 2003. 'When the Weak Bargain With the Strong: Negotiations in the World Trade Organisation', *International Negotiation* 8(1): 79–109.

Draper, P. 2010. 'Whither the Multilateral Trading System? Implications for (South) Africa', *SAIIA Occasional Paper No. 64*, July.

Drezner, D. 2007. *All Politics is Global: Explaining International Regulatory Regimes*. Princeton University Press.

Dunkley, G. 2000. *The Free Trade Adventure: The WTO, the Uruguay Round and Globalism – A Critique*. London: Zed Books.

Dunning, J. 2002. 'The Future of the WTO: A Socio-relational Challenge', *Review of International Political Economy* 7(3): 475–483.

Eagleton, D. 2006. *Under the Influence: Exposing Undue Corporate Influence Over Policymaking at the World Trade Organization*. London: ActionAid.

Eagleton-Pierce, M. 2007. 'Uncovering Symbolic Power: Power Analysis, Southern Countries, and the World Trade Organisation', doctoral thesis on file with the University of Oxford.

EC Directorate-General for Trade. 2003. *Reflection Paper on WTO Organisational Improvements*, 29 October. Brussels: European Commission.

Ehlermann, C.-D. and Ehring, L. 2005. 'Decision-Making in the World Trade Organization: Is the Consensus Practice of the World Trade Organization Adequate for Making, Revising and Implementing Rules on International Trade?' *Journal of International Economic Law* 8(1): 51–75.

Elsig, M. 2007. 'The World Trade Organization's Bureaucrats: Runaway Agents or Master's Servants', *NCCR Working Paper No. 2007/19* NCCR Trade Project.

2009. 'WTO Decision-Making: Can We Get a Little Help from the Secretariat and the Critical Mass?' in Steger, D. (ed.), *Redesigning the World Trade Organization for the Twenty-first Century*. International Development Research Centre (IDRC) and the Centre for International Governance Innovation (CIGI): Wilfrid Laurier University Press.

Erasmus, G. 2009. 'Accommodating Developing Countries in the WTO: From Mega-debates to Economic Partnership Agreements', in Steger, D. (ed.), *Redesigning the World Trade Organization for the Twenty-first Century*. International Development Research Centre (IDRC) and the Centre for International Governance Innovation (CIGI): Wilfrid Laurier University Press

Esty, D. 1994. *Greening the GATT: Trade, Environment and the Future*. Washington, DC: Institute for International Economics.

1998. 'Non-Governmental Organisations at the World Trade Organization: Cooperation, Competition or Exclusion', *Journal of International Economic Law* 1(1): 123–48.

2002. 'The World Trade Organization's Legitimacy Crisis', *World Trade Review* 1: 7–22.

2010. 'Economic Series Seminar: 'Reassessing the Trade-Environment Relationship', paper presented at WTO Economic Seminar Series at the WTO, Geneva, 3 June.

ETUC. 2006. 'Breakdown of the WTO Negotiations: The EU Must Use this Crisis to Reaffirm the Principles of Development', *European Trade Unions Federation (ETUC) Press Release*, 25 July. Available at www.etuc.org/a/2755 [Accessed in November 2010].

Evenett, S. 2005. 'Can the WTO Rise to the Challenge of Economic Development?' *Aussenwirtschaft* 3(60): 257–76.

2008. 'Aid-for-Trade and the "Missing Middle" of the WTO', *Working Paper 2008–25*. University of St. Gallen Law & Economics.

Evenett, S. and Baldwin, R. (eds.) 2009. *The Collapse of Global Trade, Murky Protectionism, and the Crisis: Recommendations for the G20*. London: Centre for Economic Policy Research and VoxEU.org, pp. 69–74.

Evian Group. 2007. *The Doha Round: Has the Unravelling Begun?* Lausanne: Evian Group.

Ezeani, E. 2010.*The WTO and its Development Obligations: Prospects for Global Trade*. London: Anthem Press.

Faber, G. and Orbie, J. 2009. *Beyond Market Access for Economic Development: EU-Africa Relations in Transition*. London: Routledge.

Finger, M. 2007. 'Implementation and the Imbalance: Dealing with Hangover from the Uruguay Round', *Oxford Review of Economic Policy* 23(3): 440–60.

Finger, M. and Winters, A. 1998. 'What Can the WTO Do For Developing Countries?' in Krueger, A. (ed.), *The WTO as an International Organization*, Chicago University Press, pp. 365–401.

Footer, M. 2006. *An Institutional and Normative Analysis of the World Trade Organization*. Leiden/Boston: Martinus Nijhoff Publishers.

François, J. 2001. 'Maximising the Benefits of the Trade Policy Review Mechanism for Developing Countries', in Hoekman, B. and Martin, W. (eds.), *Developing Countries and the WTO: A Pro-active Agenda*, Oxford and Malden: Blackwell, pp. 147–65.

François, J., Horn, H. and Kaunitz, N. 2008. 'Trading Profiles and Developing Country Participation in the WTO Dispute Settlement System', *ICTSD Project on Dispute Settlement Issue Paper No. 6*. Geneva: International Centre for Trade and Sustainable Development.

G20. 2010. 'The G-20 Toronto Summit Declaration, 26–27 June 2010', available at www.g20.org/Documents/g20_declaration_en.pdf [Accessed in November 2010].

Gallagher, K. (ed.) 2005. *Putting Development First: The Importance of Policy Space in the WTO and IFIs*. London and New York: Zed Books.

Gallagher, P. 2005. *The First Ten Years of the WTO: 1995–2005*. Cambridge University Press.

Gallagher, P. and Stoler, A. 2009. 'Critical Mass as an Alternative Framework for Multilateral Trade Negotiations', *Global Governance* 15(3): 375–92.

Gallagher, P., Low, P. and Stoler, A. (eds.) 2005. *Managing the Challenges of WTO Participation: 45 Case Studies*. Cambridge University Press.

GEG and ICTSD. 2010. 'Rebuilding Global Trade and a post-Doha Agenda for Sustainable Development: Priorities for Reform of WTO Governance', in *WTO Public Forum 2009: Global Problems, Global Solutions: Towards Better Global Governance*. Geneva: WTO, pp. 201–4.

Gehring, M. and Segger, M. (eds.) 2005. *Sustainable Development in World Trade Law*. The Hague: Kluwer Law International.

Gerhart, P. and Seema Kella, A. 2005. 'Power and Preferences: Developing Countries and the Role of the WTO Appellate Body', *North Carolina Journal of International and Comparative Law* 30: 515–76.

Ghosh, A. 2008. 'Information Gaps, Information Systems, and the WTO's Trade Policy Review Mechanism', *GEG Working Paper No. 2008/40*, Global Economic Governance Programme, University College, Oxford.

2010. 'Developing Countries in the WTO Trade Policy Review Mechanism', *World Trade Review* 9(3): 419–55.

Gibbs, M. 1998. 'Special and Differential Treatment in the Context of Globalization', paper presented at G15 Symposium on Special and Differential Treatment in the WTO Agreements, 10 December, New Delhi.

G77. 1999. *Message of the Ministers of the Group of 77: Preparations for the WTO Ministerial Conference Third Session*. 30 November – 3 December, WT/MIN(99)/3. Geneva: World Trade Organization.

G77 and China. 2003. *Declaration by the Group of 77 and China on the Fifth WTO Ministerial Conference, Cancún*.

Grynberg, R. (ed.) 2006. *WTO at the Margins: Small States and the Multilateral Trading System*. Cambridge University Press.

Grynberg, R. and Remy, J. 2003. 'Small Vulnerable Economy Issues and the WTO', in Mbirimi, I., Chilala, B. and Grynberg, R. (eds.), *From Doha to Cancún: Delivering a Development Round*. London: Commonwealth Secretariat.

GTFA (Global Trade and Financial Architecture). 2005. *Strengthening the Global Trade Architecture for Economic Development: An Agenda for Action*. London: DFID.

Guha-Khasnobis, B. 2004. *The WTO, Developing Countries and the Doha Development Agenda: Prospects and Challenges for Trade-Led Growth*. New York: Palgrave Macmillan.

Halle, M. 2007. 'Catching up with the Slowest: NGO Accreditation at the WTO', *Bridges Monthly* 11(3).

Halle, M. and Wolfe, R. 2007. *Process Matters: Sustainable Development and Domestic Trade Transparency*. Geneva: International Institute for Sustainable Development.

Harbinson, S. 2009. 'The Doha Round: "Death-Defying Agenda" or "Don't Do it Again"?' *ECIPE Working Paper No. 10*. Brussels: ECIPE.

Heidrich, P. and Tussie, D. 2009. 'Regional Trade Agreements and the WTO: The Gyrating Wheels of Interdependence', in Steger, D. (ed.), *Redesigning the World Trade Organization for the Twenty-first Century*. International Development Research Centre (IDRC) and the Centre for International Governance Innovation (CIGI): Wilfrid Laurier University Press.

Helleiner, G. 1992. *Trade Policy, Industrialization, and Development: New Perspectives*. Oxford University Press.

Hertel, T. and Winters, A. 2005. *Poverty and the WTO: Impacts of the Doha Development Agenda*. Washington, DC: World Bank.

Higgins, K. and Prowse, S. 2010. 'Trade, Growth and Poverty: Making Aid for Trade Work for Inclusive Growth and Poverty Reduction', *ODI Working Paper No. 313*, London: Overseas Development Institute.

Higgott, R. 2009. 'Not Just a "Second Order" Problem in a Wider Economic Crisis: Systemic Challenges for the Global Trading System,' *Business and Politics*, 11(3). Available at www.bepress.com/bap/vol11/iss3/art5 [Accessed in November 2010].

Higgott, R. and Erman, E. 2010. 'Deliberative Global Governance and the Question of Legitimacy: What Can We Learn from the WTO?' *Review of International Studies* 36(2): 449–70.

Hilf, M. 2003. *How Can Parliamentary Participation in WTO Rule-Making and Democratic Control be Made More Effective in the WTO?* University of Hamburg.

Hoda, A. and Gulati, A. 2003. 'Indian Agriculture, Food Security and the WTO Uruguay Round Agreement on Agriculture', paper presented at the ICRIER-ICAR-IFPRI Conference on 'Economic Reforms and Food Security: The Role of Trade and Technology,' 24–25 April, New Delhi.

2008. *WTO Negotiations on Agriculture and Developing Countries*. Baltimore: Johns Hopkins University Press.

Hoekman, B. 2001. 'Strengthening the Global Trade Architecture for Development: The Post Doha Agenda', *World Trade Review* 1: 23–46.

2004. 'Dismantling Discrimination against Developing Countries: Access, Rules and Differential Treatment', *CEPR Discussion Paper Series No. 4694*. London: Commission for Economic Policy Research (CEPR).

2005. 'Operationalizing the Concept of Policy Space in the WTO: Beyond Special and Differential Treatment', *Journal of International Economic Law* 8(2): 405–24.

Hoekman, B. and Kostecki, M. 1996. *The Political Economy of the World Trading System: From GATT to WTO*. Oxford University Press.

Hoeckman, B. and Martin, W. (eds.) 2001. *Developing Countries and the WTO: A Pro-active Agenda*. Oxford and Malden: Blackwell.

Hoekman, B. and Mavroidis, P. 2000. 'Enforcing WTO Commitments: Dispute Settlement and Developing Countries – Something Happened on the Way to Heaven', paper prepared for the World Bank Conference on the World Trading System Post-Seattle: Institutional Design, Governance and Ownership, 14–15 July, Brussels.

Hoekman, B., Mattoo, A. and English, P. (eds.) 2002. *Development, Trade, and the WTO: A Handbook*. Washington, DC: World Bank.

Hoekman, B., Michalopoulos, C. and Winters, A. 2003. 'More Favorable and Differential Treatment of Developing Countries: Towards a New Approach', *World Bank Working Paper No. 3107*, World Trade Organization.

Hohmann, H. 2008. *Agreeing and Implementing the Doha Round of the WTO*. Cambridge University Press.

Horn, H. and Mavroidis, P. 2003. 'Which WTO Provisions Are Invoked by and against Developing Countries?' background paper for *Trade for Development*. New York: UN Millennium Project.

Howse, R. 2002. 'From Politics to Technocracy-and Back Again: The Fate of the Multilateral Trading Regime', *The American Journal of International Law* 96(1): 94–117.

2003. 'How to Begin to Think About the Democratic Deficit at the WTO', in Griller, S. (ed.), *International Governance and Non-Economic Concerns. New Challenges for the International Legal Order.* Vienna and New York: Springer.

Howse, R. and Nicolaidis, K. 2003. 'Enhancing WTO Legitimacy: Constitutionalization or Global Subsidiarity?' *Governance: An International Journal of Policy, Administration and Institutions* 16(1): 73–94.

Hudec, R. 1975. *The GATT Legal System and World Trade Diplomacy*. Santa Barbara: Greenwood Publishing Group.

1987. *Developing Countries in the GATT Legal System*. London: Trade Policy Research Centre.

Hurrell, A. and Narlikar, A. 2006. 'The New Politics of Confrontation: Brazil and India in Multilateral Trade Negotiations', *Global Society* 20(4): 415–33.

ICTSD and IISD. 1999. 'Implementation Issues and Concerns', *Doha Round Briefings*. Geneva: International Centre for Trade and Sustainable Development and International Institute for Sustainable Development.

2003. 'Technical Assistance and Capacity-Building', *Doha Round Briefing Series* 1(12).

2004. *Lessons Learned on Trade and Sustainable Development: Distilling Six Years of Research from the Trade Knowledge Network*. Geneva: Trade Knowledge Network.

IISD. 1999. 'Six Easy Pieces: Five Things the WTO Should Do – And One it Should Not', working paper presented to the WTO High-Level Symposia on Environment and Development, Geneva.

2000. *IISD Statement on Trade and Sustainable Development*. Geneva: International Institute for Sustainable Development (IISD).

ILO. 2001. *The Social Dimensions of Globalization*. Geneva: International Labour Office.

Ingco, M. 2003. *Agriculture, Trade and the WTO in South Asia: Interests and Options for South Asia*. Washington, DC: World Bank.

Irwin, D. 2003. 'Trade and Development: A Review of the Debate', background paper for project on Trade for Development. UN Millennium Project, New York: United Nations.

Ismail, F. 2005. 'Mainstreaming Development in the World Trade Organization', *Journal of World Trade* 39(1): 11–21.

2007. *Mainstreaming Development in the WTO Developing Countries in the Doha Round*. Jaipur: CUTS International/FES.

2008. 'An Assessment of the Sixth WTO Hong Kong Ministerial Conference from a Development Perspective', in Hohmann, H. (ed.), *Agreeing and Implementing the Doha Round of the WTO*. Cambridge University Press.

2009a. 'An Assessment of the WTO Doha Round July-December 2008 Collapse', *World Trade Review* 8(4): 579–605.

2009b. 'The Role of the Chair in the WTO Negotiations. From the Potsdam Collapse in June 2007 to July 2008', *Journal of World Trade* 43(6): 1145–71.

2009c. 'Reforming the World Trade Organization', *World Economics* 10(4): 109–46.

2009d. *Reforming the World Trade Organization: Developing Countries in the Doha Round*. Geneva: CUTS/FES.

Jackson, J. 1997. *The World Trading System: Law and Policy of International Economic Relations*, 2nd edn. Cambridge, MA: MIT Press.

1999. 'Fragmentation or Unification Among International Institutions: The World Trade Organization', *International Law and Politics* 31: 823.

Jawara, F. and Kwa, A. 2003. *Behind the Scenes at the WTO: The Real World of International Trade Negotiations*. London: Zed Books.

Jha, V. and Vossenaar, R. 1999. 'Breaking the Deadlock: A Positive Agenda on Trade, Environment and Development', in Sampson, G. and Chambers B. (eds.), *Trade, Environment and the Millennium*. Tokyo: United Nations University Press.

Joerges, C. and Petersmann, E.-U. (eds.) 2006. *Constitutionalism, Multilevel Trade Governance and Social Regulation*. Oxford: Hart Publishers.

Jones, E., Deere Birkbeck, C. and Woods, N. 2010. *Manoeuvring at the Margins: Constraints Faced by Small States in International Trade Relations*. London: Commonwealth Secretariat.

Jones, K. 2009. *The Doha Blues: Institutional Crises and Reform at the WTO*. Oxford University Press.

Kaukab, R., La Vina, A. and Yu, V. 2004. 'From Cancún to Hong Kong: Lessons from the Fifth Ministerial Conference of the World Trade Organization', *TRADE Working Paper No. 20*, Geneva: South Centre.

Kahler, M. and Odell, J. 1989. 'Developing Country Coalition-Building and International Trade Negotiations', in Whalley, J. (ed.), *Trade Policy and the Developing World*. University of Michigan Press.

Katrak, H. and Strange, R. (eds.) 2004. *The WTO and Developing Countries*. Melbourne: Palgrave Macmillan.

Keck, A. and Low, P. 2004. 'Special and Differential Treatment in the WTO: Why, How and When', *WTO Working Paper No. 2004–03*. Geneva: World Trade Organization.

Khan, A. and Chakraborty, D. 2008. *The WTO Deadlocked: Understanding the Dynamics of International Trade*. New Delhi: Sage Publications India.

Khor, M. 2001. 'Present Problems and Future Shape of the Multilateral Trading System', *TWN Briefing Paper No. 2*. Penang: Third World Network.

2002. *The WTO, the Post-Doha Agenda and the Future of the Trade System: A Development Perspective*. Penang: Third World Network.

2006. 'An Assessment of the WTO's Hong Kong Ministerial, December 2005', *TWN Briefing Paper No. 29*. Penang: Third World Network.

Kim, S. 2010. *Power and the Governance of Global Trade: From the GATT to the WTO*. Ithaca: Cornell University Press.

Kirton, J. and Trebilcock, M. 2004. *Hard Choices, Soft Law: Voluntary Standards in Global Trade, Environment and Social Governance*. Aldershot: Ashgate Publishing Limited.

Kleen, P. and Page, S. 2004. 'Special and Differential Treatment of Developing Countries in the World Trade Organization', *Global Development Studies 2*, Swedish Ministry for Foreign Affairs.

Konz, P., Bellmann, C. and Meléndez-Ortiz, R. (eds.) 2000. *Trade, Environment and Sustainable Development: Views from sub-Saharan Africa and Latin America – A Reader*. Geneva: International Centre for Trade and Sustainable Development (ICTSD) and United Nations University Institute for Advanced Study (IAS).

Krasner, S. 1985. *Structural Power: The Third World Against Liberalism*. Berkeley: University of California Press.

Krueger, A. 1984. 'Trade Policies in Developing Countries', in Jones, R. and Kenen, P. (eds.), *Handbook of International Economics Volume 1*, Elsevier Science Publishers, pp. 519–69.

(ed.) 1998. *The WTO as an International Organization*. Chicago University Press.

1999. 'The Developing Countries and the Next Round of Multilateral Trade Negotiations', *World Bank Working Paper No. 2118*. Washington, DC: World Bank.

Kumar, N. 2002. *Foreign Direct Investment and the WTO: Policies for Growth and Industrialization*. Oxford University Press.

2007. 'Building a Development-friendly World Trading System', *BRIDGES* 11(5): 21–2.

Lacarte, J. 2004. 'Transparency, Public Debate and Participation by NGOs in the WTO: A WTO Perspective', *Journal of International Economic Law* 7(3): 683–6.

Lacarte, J. and Gappah, P. 2000. 'Developing Countries and the WTO Legal and Dispute Settlement System: A View from the Bench', *Journal of International Economic Law* 3(3): 395–401.

Laird, S. and Fernandez de Cordoba, S. 2006. *Coping with Trade Reforms: A Developing Country Perspective on the WTO Industrial Tariff Negotiations*. Basingstoke: Palgrave Macmillan.

Lamy, P. 2003. 'Message from the Director General: A World Trade System for the Benefit of All', Available at www.wto.org/english/thewto_e/dg_e/dg_e.htm [Accessed in November 2010].

2007. 'Monitoring and Surveillance: The Rising Agenda of the WTO', *Address to Georgetown University Law Centre*. Washington, DC. 22 October.

2008. '60 Years of the Multilateral Trading System', lecture presented as part of the Geneva Lectures on Global Economic Governance, Global Economic Governance Programme, Oxford University, February.

2009. 'A New Triangle of Global Governance Emerging', speech presented at University of Warwick, 15 July.

Lanoszka, A. 2008. 'The Promises of Multilateralism and the Hazards of "Single Undertaking": The Breakdown of Decision Making Within the WTO', *Michigan State Journal of International Law* 16: 654–75.

Lawrence, R. 2006. 'Rulemaking Amidst Growing Diversity: A Club-of-Club Approach to WTO Reform and New Issue Selection', *Journal of World Trade* 35(4): 575–602.

Lee, D. and Wilkinson, R. (eds.) 2007. *The WTO After Hong Kong: Progress in, and Prospects for, the Doha Development Agenda*. London: Routledge.

Lee, Y. 2007. 'Development and the World Trade Organization: Proposal for the Agreement on Development Facilitation and the Council for Trade and Development in the WTO', *Review of International Business and Trade Law* 6.

Lehmann, J. and Lehmann, F. 2010. *Peace and Prosperity Through World Trade: Achieving the 2019 Vision*. Cambridge University Press.

Leutwiler, F., Bradley, B., Gyllenhammar, P. *et al.* 1985. *Trade Policies for a Better Future: Proposals for Action*. Geneva: GATT.

Low, P. 2009a. 'Potential Future Functions of the World Trade Organization', *Global Governance* 15: 327–34.

2009b. 'WTO Decision Making for the Future', paper presented at Thinking Ahead on International Trade (TAIT) Inaugural Conference, 17–18 September, Geneva.

Low, P., Rodriguez Mendoza, M. and Kotschwar, B. (eds.) 1999. *Trade Rules in the Making: Multilateral and Regional Trade Arrangements*. Washington, DC: Brookings Institution Press.

Luke, D. 2000. 'OAU/AEC Member States, the Seattle Preparatory Process and Seattle: A Personal Reflection', *Journal of World Trade* 34(3): 39–46.

Marceau, G. and Pedersen, P. 1999. 'Is the WTO Open and Transparent? A Discussion of the Relationship of the WTO with Non-governmental Organisations and Civil Society's Claims for More Transparency and Public Participation', *Journal of World Trade* 33(1): 5–49.

Marceau, G. and Stilwell, M. 2001. 'Practical Suggestions for Amicus Curiae Briefs Before WTO Adjudicating Bodies', *Journal of International Economic Law* 4(1): 155–87.

Marconini, M. 2005. 'Trade Policy-Making Process in Brazil', mimeo. Available at www6.miami.edu/hemispheric-policy/LSEWorkshopTradePolicy250505.pdf [Accessed in November 2010].

Mattli, W. and Woods, N. (eds.) 2009. *The Politics of Global Regulation*. Princeton and Oxford: Princeton University Press, pp. 72–134.

Mattoo, A. and Stern, R. 2003. *India and the WTO*. Washington, DC: World Bank.

Mattoo, A. and Subramanian, A. 2003. 'What Would a Development-Friendly WTO Architecture Really Look Like?' *IMF Working Paper No. 03/153*, Washington, DC: International Monetary Fund.

2004. 'The WTO and the Poorest Countries: The Stark Reality', *IMF Working Paper No. 81*. Washington, DC: International Monetary Fund.

2009. 'From Doha to the Next Bretton Woods', *Foreign Affairs* January.

Mattoo, A., English, P. and Hoekman, B. 2005. *Development, Trade and the WTO: A Handbook*. New York: World Bank.

Mavroidis, P. 1991–1992. 'Surveillance Schemes: The GATT's New Trade Policy Review Mechanism', *Michigan Journal of International Law* 13(2): 374–414.

McCulloch, N., Winters, A and Cirera, X. 2001. *Trade Liberalization and Poverty: A Handbook*. London: Centre for Economic Policy Research.

McGinnis, J. and Movsesian, M. 2000. 'The World Trade Constitution', *Harvard Law Review* 114(2): 511–605.

McMillan, E. 2010. 'Doha Decision-Making: Implications of the Consensus and Single-Undertaking Principles for Developing Countries', *Commonwealth Trade Hot Topics* 71. London: Commonwealth Secretariat.

Meléndez-Ortiz, R. and Delhavi, A. 2000. 'Sustainable Development and Environmental Policy Objectives', in Konz, P., Bellmann, C. and Meléndez-Ortiz, R. (eds.), *Trade, Environment and Sustainable Development: Views from Sub-Saharas Africa and Latin America–A Reader*. Geneva: International Centre for Trade and Sustainable Development (ICTSD and United Nations University Institute for Advanced Study (IAS).

Meléndez-Ortiz, R., Bellmann, C. and Hepburn, J. (eds.) 2010. *Agricultural Subsidies in the WTO Green Box: Ensuring Coherence with Sustainable Development Goals*. Cambridge University Press.

Mendoza, R. 2003. 'The Multilateral Trade Regime: A Global Public Good for All?' in Kaul, I., Conceição, P., Le Goulven, K. and Mendoza, R. (eds.), *Providing Global Public Goods: Managing Globalization*. New York: Oxford University Press.

Mercurio, B. 2009. 'Why Compensation Cannot Replace Trade Retaliation in the WTO Dispute Settlement Understanding', *World Trade Review* 8(2): 315–38.

Messerlin, P. 2003. "Making the Doha Development Work for the Poorest Developing Countries", in Griffith, P. (ed.), *Rethinking Fair Trade*. London: The Foreign Policy Centre.

Michalopoulos, C. 2001. *Developing Countries in the WTO*. Basingstoke: Palgrave Macmillan.

Mitchell, A. and Voon, T. 2009. 'Operationalizing Special and Differential Treatment in the World Trade Organization', *Global Governance* 15(3): 343–57.

Moellendorf, D. 2005. 'The World Trade Organization and Egalitarian Justice', *Metaphilosophy* 36(1–2): 145–62.

Moore, G. (ed.) 2010. *Fairness in International Trade*. Dordrecht: Springer.

Moore, M. 1999. 'Efforts to Assist Poor Countries'. *Presidents & Prime Ministers* 8(4).

2003. *A World Without Walls: Freedom, Development, Free Trade and Global Governance.* Cambridge University Press.

(ed.) 2004. *Doha and Beyond: The Future of the Multilateral Trading System.* Cambridge University Press.

Nadakavukaren Schefer, K. 2010. *Social Regulation in the WTO: Trade Policy and International Legal Development.* Cheltenham: Edward Elgar Publishing Limited.

Nader, R. and Wallach, L. 1996. 'GATT, NAFTA, and the Subversion of the Democratic Process', in Mander, J. and Goldsmith, E. (eds.), *The Case Against the Global Economy.* San Francisco: Sierra Club Books, pp. 92–107.

Najam, A., Halle, M. and Meléndez-Ortiz, R. (eds.) 2007. *Envisioning a Sustainable Development Agenda for Trade and Environment.* New York: Palgrave Macmillan.

Narlikar, A. 2001. 'WTO Decision-Making Processes and Developing Countries', *TRADE Working Paper No. 11.* Geneva: South Centre.

2002. 'The Politics of Participation: Decision-Making Processes and Developing Countries in the World Trade Organisation', *Commonwealth Round Table* 364: 171–85.

2003. *International Trade and Developing Countries: Bargaining Coalitions in the GATT and WTO.* London: Routledge.

2004. 'The Ministerial Process and Power Dynamics in the World Trade Organization: Understanding Failure from Seattle to Cancún', *New Political Economy* 9(3): 413–28.

Narlikar, A. and Odell, J. 2006. 'The Strict Distributive Strategy for a Bargaining Coalition: The Like Minded Group in the World Trade Organisation, 1998–2001', in Odell, J. (ed.), *Negotiating Trade: Developing Countries in the WTO and NAFTA.* Cambridge University Press.

Narlikar, A. and Tussie, D. 2004. 'The G20 at the Cancún Ministerial: Developing Countries and their Evolving Coalitions in the WTO', *The World Economy* 27(7): 947–66.

Narlikar, A. and Vickers, B. (eds.) 2009. *Leadership and Change in the Multilateral Trading System.* Dordrecht: Martinus Nijhoff.

Narlikar, A. and Wilkinson, R. 2004. 'Collapse and the WTO: A Cancún Post-Mortem', *Third World Quarterly* 25(3): 447–60.

Njinkeu, D. 2009. 'Africa, Trade, and the Crisis: A Stimulus Package for Africa', in Deere Birkbeck, C. and Meléndez Ortiz, R. (eds.), *Rebuilding Global Trade: Proposals for a fairer, More Sustainable Future.* Geneva and Oxford: International Centre for Trade and Sustainable Development and the Global Economic Governance Programme.

Njinkeu, D. and Cameron, H. 2008. *Aid for Trade and Development.* Cambridge University Press.

Nordström, H. 2002. 'Participation of Developing Countries in the WTO – New Evidence Based on the 2003 Official Records', National Board of Trade, Sweden.

Nordström, H. and Shaffer, G. 2007. 'Justice in the WTO – the Case for Small Claims Procedures', *Issue Paper No 2*. Geneva: International Centre for Trade and Sustainable Development.

Nottage, H. 2008. 'Trade and Development', in Bethlehem, D., McRae, D., Neufeld, R. and Van Damme, I. (eds.), *Oxford Handbook of International Trade Law*. Oxford University Press.

Odell, J. 2000. *Negotiating the World Economy*. Ithaca: Cornell University Press.

2005. 'Chairing a WTO Negotiation', *Journal of International Economic Law* 8(2): 425–48.

(ed.) 2006. *Negotiating Trade: Developing Countries in the WTO and NAFTA*. Cambridge University Press.

Odell, J. and Ortiz Mena, A. 2005. 'How to Negotiate Over Trade: A Summary of New Research for Developing Countries', *Working Paper No. 113*. Centro de Investigación y Docencias Económicas, Mexico.

OECD. 2001. *The DAC Guidelines – Strengthening Trade Capacity for Development*. Paris: OECD.

2005. *Paris Declaration on Aid Effectiveness*. Paris: OECD.

2008. *Accra Agenda for Action*, endorsed at the 3rd High Level Forum on Aid Effectiveness. Paris: OECD.

Ohiorhenuan, J. 2005. 'Capacity Building Implications of Enhanced African Participation in Global Rules-Making and Arrangements', in Oyejide, A. and Lyakura, W. (eds.), *Africa and the World Trading System*. Trenton: Africa World Press.

Ostry, S. 2002. 'The World Trading System: In Dire Need of Reform' Presentation given at the Canadians in Europe Conference hosted by the Centre for European Studies, Brussels in August. Available at www.utoronto.ca/cis/ostry/docs_pdf/World_Trade_Reform.doc [Accessed in April 2009].

2004. 'External Transparency: The Policy Process at the National Level of the Two Level Game', in Moore, M. (ed.), *Doha and Beyond: The Future of the Multilateral Trading System*. Cambridge University Press.

Oteng, K. 1997. 'From GATT to the WTO – The Developing Countries and Reform of the Procedures for the Settlement of International Trade Disputes', *Journal of World Trade* 31(5): 117–45.

Oxfam. 2000. *Institutional Reform of the WTO*. Oxford: Oxfam Great Britain.

Oxfam International. 2002. *Rigged Rules and Double Standards: Trade, Globalisation, and the Fight Against Poverty*. Oxford: Oxfam International.

2004. 'Extortion at the Gate', *Oxfam Briefing Paper No. 67*. Oxford: Oxfam International.

2005. *Make Extortion History: The Case for Development-friendly WTO Accession for the World's Poorest Countries*. Oxford: Oxfam International.

Oxfam International, WWF, CIEL, IATP, ActionAid, Friends of the Earth. 2001. *Joint NGO Open Letter on Institutional Reforms in the WTO*. October. Available at www.ciel.org/Publications/Reform.pdf [Accessed in November 2010].

Oyejide, A. and Lyakura, W. (eds.) 2005. *Africa and the World Trading System*. Trenton: Africa World Press.

Oyejide, T. 2009. 'Global Economic Governance Priorities of G20 Leaders: An African Perspective', in Deere Birkbeck, C. and Meléndez-Ortiz, R. (eds.), *Rebuilding Global Trade: Proposals for a Fairer, More Sustainable Future*. Geneva and Oxford: International Centre for Trade and Sustainable Development and the Global Economic Governance Programme.

Page, S. 1994. *How Developing Countries Trade: The Institutional Constraints*. London: Overseas Development Institute.

2003. 'Developing Countries: Victims or Participants – Their Changing Roles in International Negotiations', *ODI Working Paper*, London: Overseas Development Institute.

2005. 'A Preference Erosion Compensation Fund', *ODI Opinions* 35. London: Overseas Development Institute (ODI).

Patel, C. 2003a. 'ACP and African Union Role in Cancún – Some Reflections', available at www.twnside.org.sg/title/5423a.htm [Accessed in November 2010].

2003b. 'Single Undertaking: A Straitjacket or Variable Geometry?' *TRADE Working Paper No. 15*. Geneva: South Centre.

Patel, M. 2007. 'New Faces in the Green Room: Developing Country Coalitions And Decision Making In The WTO', *Working Paper No. 2007/33*, University College, Oxford: Global Economic Governance Programme.

Pauwelyn, J. 2003. *Conflict of Norms in Public International Law: How WTO Law Relates to Other Rules of International Law*. Cambridge University Press.

2005. 'The Sutherland Report: A Missed Opportunity for Genuine Debate on Trade, Globalization and Reforming the WTO', *Journal of International Economic Law* 8(2): 329–46.

Peet, R. 2009. *Unholy Trinity: The IMF, the World Bank and the WTO*. London: Zed Books.

Petersmann, E. 2004. 'The Human Rights Approach advocated by the UN High Commissioner for Human Rights and by the International Labour Organization: Is It Relevant for WTO Law and Policy?' *Journal of International Economic Law* 7(3).

2005a. 'Addressing Institutional Challenges to the WTO in the New Millennium: A Longer-term Perspective', *Journal of International Economic Law* 8(3): 647–65.

(ed.) 2005b. *Reforming the World Trading System: Legitimacy, Efficiency, and Democratic Governance*. Oxford University Press.

Primo Braga, C. and Cattaneo, O. 2009. 'Introduction', in Primo Braga, C. and Cattaneo, O. (eds.), *The WTO and Accession Countries*. Cheltenham: Edward Elgar Publishing.

Prowse, S. 2002. 'The Role of International and National Agencies in Trade-Related Capacity Building', *The World Economy* 25(9): 1235–61.

2005. '"Aid for Trade": A Proposal for Increasing Support for Trade Adjustment and Assistance', in Evenett, S. and Hoekman, B. (eds.), *Multilateral Trade Cooperation and Development*. Basingstoke: Palgrave Macmillan.

2006. '"Aid for Trade": Increasing Support for Trade Adjustment and Integration – a Proposal', in Evenett, S. and Hoekman, B. (eds.), *Economic Development and Multilateral Trade Cooperation*. Basingstoke: Palgrave Macmillan.

Public Citizen. 1999. *A Citizen's Guide to the World Trade Organization: Everything You Need to Know to Fight for Fair Trade*. Washington, DC: Public Citizen.

Puri, L. 2008. 'Towards a New Trade "Marshall Plan" for Least Developed Countries: How to Deliver on the Doha Development Promise and Help Realize the UN Millennium Development Goals?' Available at SSRN: http://ssrn.com/abstract=1280887 [Accessed in November 2010].

Qureshi, A. 1990. 'The New GATT Trade Policy Review Mechanism: An Exercise in Transparency Or "Enforcement"?' *Journal of World Trade* 24(3): 147–60.

2009. 'International Trade for Development: The WTO as a Development Institution?' *Journal of World Trade* 43(1): 173–88.

Raghavan, C. 1990. *Recolonization: GATT, the Uruguay Round and the Third World*. Penang: Third World Network.

1997. 'A New Trade Order in a World of Disorder?' in Griesgraber, J. and Gunter, B. (eds.), *World Trade: Toward Fair and Free Trade in the Twenty-first Century*. Vol. V of Rethinking Bretton Woods Series. London and Chicago: Pluto Press.

2000a. *The World Trade Organization and its Dispute Settlement System: Tilting the Balance Against the South*. Penang: Third World Network.

2000b. 'UNCTAD X: The Spirit of Bangkok vs. The Washington Consensus?' *Third World Resurgence* 116, April.

Rajagopal, B. 2003. *International Law from Below: Development, Social Movements and Third World Resistance*. Cambridge University Press.

Raynolds, L., Murray, D. and Wilkinson, J. 2007. *Fair Trade: The Challenges of Transforming Globalization*. New York: Routledge.

Ricupero, R. 2001. 'Rebuilding Confidence in the Multilateral Trading System: Closing the "Legitimacy Gap', in Sampson, G. (ed.), *The Role of the World Trade Organization in Global Governance*. Tokyo: United Nations University Press.

RIS. 2003. *World Trade and Development Report 2002: Cancún and Beyond*. New Delhi: Research and Information System for Non-Aligned and Other Developing Countries (RIS).

2007. *World Trade and Development Report 2007: Building a Development-Friendly World Trading System*. New Delhi: Oxford University Press.

Risse, M. 2007. 'Review Essay: Economic Justice in an Unfair World', *World Trade Review* 6(1): 1–23.

Rodrik, D. 1997. *Has Globalization Gone Too Far?* Washington, DC: Institute for International Economics.

2001. 'The Global Governance of Trade – As If Development Really Mattered', background paper for Trade and Sustainable Human Development Project, New York: United Nations Development Program.

2002. 'Trade Policy Reform as Institutional Reform', in Hoekman, B. and Mattoo, A. (eds.), *Development, Trade, and the WTO: A Handbook*, Washington, DC: The World Bank, pp. 3–10.

2007. *One Economics, Many Recipes: Globalization, Institutions, and Economic Growth*, Princeton University Press.

2009. 'Let Developing Nations Rule', in Deere Birkbeck, C. and Meléndez-Ortiz, R. (eds.), *Rebuilding Global Trade: Proposals for a Fairer, More Sustainable Future*. Geneva and Oxford: International Centre for Trade and Sustainable Development and the Global Economic Governance Programme.

Rolland, S. 2007. 'Developing Country Coalitions at the WTO: In Search of Legal Support', *Harvard International Law Journal* 48(2): 483.

2010. 'Redesigning the Negotiation Process at the WTO', *Journal of International Economic Law* 13: 65–110.

Rosset, P. 2006. *Food is Different: Why the WTO Should Get out of Agriculture*. London: Zed Books.

Safardi, R., and Laird, S. 1996. 'The Uruguay Round Agreements: Impact on Developing Countries', *World Development* 24(7): 1223–42.

Sampson, G. (ed.) 2001. *The Role of the World Trade Organization in Global Governance*. Tokyo: United Nations University Press.

Sampson, G. (ed.) 2009. *The WTO and Global Governance: Future Directions*. Tokyo: United Nations University Press.

Sampson, G. 2004. 'Is There a Need for Restructuring the Collaboration among the WTO and UN Agencies so as to Harness their Complementarities?', in Petersmann, E-U. (ed.), *Preparing for the Doha Development Round: Challenges to the Legitimacy and Efficiency of the World Trading System*. Florence: Robert Schuman Centre for Advanced Studies, European University Institute.

2005a. 'Challenges Facing the WTO: Determining its Role in International Affairs', in Jayasuriva, S. (ed.), *Trade Policy Reforms and Development: Essays in Honour of Peter Lloyd*. Northampton: Edward Elgar Publishing.

2005b. *The WTO and Sustainable Development*. Tokyo: United Nations University Press.

Saner, R. 2010. *Trade Policy Governance Through Inter-ministerial Coordination: A Source Book for Trade Officials and Trade & Development Experts*. Dodrecht: RoL Publications.

Sapra, S. 2009. 'The WTO System of Trade Governance: The Stale NGO Debate and the Appropriate Role for Non-State Actors', *Oregon Review of International Law* 11: 71–107.

Schiff, M. and Winters, A. 2003. *Regional Integration and Development*. Washington, DC: Oxford University Press.

Schorr, D. 2004. 'Healthy Fisheries, Sustainable Trade: Crafting New Rules on Fishing Subsidies in the World Trade Organization', Washington, DC: World Wildlife Fund.

Schott, J. (ed.) 2000. *The WTO After Seattle*. Washington, DC: Institute for International Economics.

SEATINI. 2003. *Africa and the World Trade Organization: A Ministers Brief for the Cancún Conference*. Geneva: Southern and Eastern African Trade Information and Negotiations Institute.

Sen, J. 2004. 'Trade Policy Making in India: The Reality Below the Water Line', *CUTS International Paper No. 0415*, pp. 1–28.

Shadlen, K. 2005. 'Exchanging Development for Market Access? Deep Integration and Industrial Policy under Multilateral and Regional-Bilateral Trade Agreements', *Review of International Political Economy* 12(5): 750–75.

Shaffer, G. 2004a. 'Parliamentary Oversight of WTO Rule Making: the Political and Normative Contexts', *Journal of International Economic Law* 7(3): 629.

2004b. 'Power, Governance, and the WTO: A Comparative Institutional Approach', in Barnett, M. and Duvall, R. (eds.), *Power in Global Governance*. Cambridge University Press.

2006. 'The Challenges of WTO Law: Challenges for Developing Country Adaptation', *World Trade Review* 5(2): 177–98.

Shahin, M. 1996. *From Marrakesh to Singapore: The WTO and Developing Countries*. Malaysia: Third World Network (TWN).

Shell, G. 1996. 'The Trade Stakeholders Model and Participation by Non-state Parties in the World Trade Organization', *University of Pennsylvania Journal of International Economic Law* 17(1): 359.

Shi, M. 2005. 'China's Participation in the Doha Negotiations and Implementation of its Accession Commitments', in Gao, H. and Lewis, D. (eds.), *China's Participation in the WTO*, London: Cameron.

Siegel, D. 2002. 'Legal Aspects of the IMF/WTO Relationship: The Fund's Articles of Agreement and the WTO Agreements', *The American Journal of International Law*, 96(3): 561.

South Centre. 2002. 'Process Issues in the WTO: State of Play November 2002', *South Centre Analytical Note*. Geneva: South Centre.

2003. 'Suggestions on Procedural Options Based on the 1996 WTO Rules of Procedure for Sessions of the Ministerial Conference with Respect to Some Issues', *South Centre Analytical Note*. Geneva: South Centre.

2005. 'Selection of the WTO Director-General: Some Points to Consider', *South Centre Analytical Note*, Geneva: South Centre.

2008. 'Some Thoughts on Process of the On-Going WTO Mini-Ministerial Negotiations of July 2008', Geneva: South Centre.

2009. *South Perspectives – Trade and Finance Linkages for Promoting Development*. Geneva: South Centre.

Srinivasan, T. 1998. *Developing Countries and the Multilateral Trading System*. Boulder, CO: Westview.

2001. 'Trade, Development and Growth', Graham Memorial Lecture, *Essays in International Economics* 225. Princeton University Department of Economics.

2002. 'Developing Countries and the Multilateral Trading System After Doha', *Economic Growth Centre Discussion Paper No. 842*. February. Yale University.

2004. 'The Future of the Global Trading System: Doha Round, Cancún Ministerial and Beyond', unpublished paper, April. Available at www.econ.yale.edu/~srinivas/ [Accessed in November 2010].

Steger, D. 2007. 'The Culture of the WTO: Why it Needs to Change', *Journal of International Economic Law* 10(3): 483–95.

(ed.) 2009a. *Redesigning the World Trade Organization for the Twenty-first Century*. International Development Research Centre (IDRC) and the Centre for International Governance Innovation (CIGI): Wilfrid Laurier University Press.

2009b. 'Why Institutional Reform of the WTO is Necessary', in Steger, D. (ed.), *Redesigning the World Trade Organization for the Twenty-first Century*. International Development Research Centre (IDRC) and the Centre for International Governance Innovation (CIGI): Wilfrid Laurier University Press.

Steger, D. and Shpilkovskaya, N. 2009. 'Internal Management of the WTO: Room for Improvement', in Steger, D. (ed.), *Redesigning the World Trade Organisation for the Twenty-first Century*. International Development Research Centre (IDRC) and the Centre for International Governance Innovation (CIGI): Wilfrid Laurier University Press.

Steinberg, R. 2002. 'In the Shadow of Law or Power? Consensus-Based Bargaining and Outcomes in the GATT/WTO', *International Organization* 56(2): 339–74.

Steinberg, R. and Goldstein, J. 2009. 'Regulatory Shift: The Rise of Judicial Liberalization at the WTO', in Mattli, W. and Woods, N. (eds.), *The Politics of Global Regulation*. Princeton and Oxford: Princeton University Press.

Stevens, C. 2003a. 'The Future of Special and Differential Treatment (SDT) for Developing Countries in the WTO', *IDS Working Paper No. 163*. Brighton: Institute of Development Studies.

2003b. 'Recognising Reality: Balancing Prevision and Flexibility in WTO Rules', paper prepared for the joint ICTSD-GP International Dialogue on Making Special and Differential Treatment More Effective and Responsive to Development Needs, 6 –7 May, Chavannes-de-Bogis, Switzerland.

Stevens, C., Greenhill, R. and Kennan, J. 2000. *The WTO Agreement on Agriculture and Food Security*. London: Commonwealth Secretariat.

Stewart, T. (ed.) 1993. *The GATT Uruguay Round: A Negotiating History. Vol 1. Part 1*. Dordrecht: Kluwer Academic Publishers.

Stiglitz, J. 2003. *Globalization and its Discontents*. New York: W.W. Norton and Company.

Stiglitz, J. and Charlton, A. 2005. *Fair Trade for All*. Oxford University Press.

Stilwell, M. 2009. 'Improving Institutional Coherence: Managing Interplay Between Trade and Climate Change', *Working Paper No. 2009/49*, Global Economic Governance Programme, University College, Oxford.

Stoler, A., Redden, J. and Jackson, L. 2009. *Trade and Poverty Reductions in the Asia-Pacific Region: Case Studies and Lessons from Low-Income Countries*. Geneva: WTO and Cambridge University Press.

Subramanian, A. 2009. 'Developing Nations and the New Global Order', in Deere Birkbeck, C. and Meléndez-Ortiz, R. (eds.), *Rebuilding Global Trade: Proposals for a Fairer, More Sustainable Future*. Geneva and Oxford: International Centre for Trade and Sustainable Development and the Global Economic Governance Programme.

Sutherland, P. 2005. 'The World Trade Organization at Ten Years', *World Trade Review* 4: 341–54.

Tallberg, J. 2010. 'The Power of the Chair: Formal Leadership in International Cooperation', *International Studies Quarterly* 54(1): 241–65.

Tandon, Y. 2004. 'Technical Assistance as a Political Instrument', in Blouin, C. (ed.), *The Reality of Trade: The WTO and Developing Countries*. Ottawa: The North–South Institute, pp. 62–74.

Taniguchi, Y., Yanovich, A. and Bohanes, J. 2007. *The WTO in the 21st Century: Dispute Settlement, Negotiations and Regionalism in Asia*. Geneva/ Cambridge: WTO and Cambridge University Press.

te Velde, D. 2005. 'Revitalising Services Negotiations at the WTO: Can Technical Assistance Help?' London: Overseas Development Institute.

Third World Network (TWN). 1999. 'Transparency, Participation and Legitimacy of the WTO', Statement of the Third World Network at the WTO Symposium on Trade and Environment and Trade and Development, 15–18 March, Geneva.

2001. 'The Multilateral Trading System: A Development Perspective', background paper for Trade and Sustainable Human Development Project, Bureau for Development Policy. New York: United Nations Development Programme.

Third World Network, Oxfam International, Public Services International, WWF International, The Center for International Environmental Law, Focus on the Global South, The Institute for Agriculture and Trade Policy, The Africa Trade Network, the International Gender and Trade Network, and the Tebtebba International Centre for Indigenous Peoples' Rights 2003. 'Memorandum on the Need to Improve Internal Transparency and Participation in the WTO', 13 July. Available at www.twnside.org.sg/title2/ briefing.../need.for.trnsp.and.part.in.WTO.pdf.

Thomas, C. and Trachtman, J. 2009. *Developing Countries in the WTO Legal System*. Oxford University Press.

Trachtman, J. 2002. 'Institutional Linkage: Transcending "Trade and …"' *The American Journal of International Law* 96(1): 77.

2003. 'Legal Aspects of a Poverty Agenda at the WTO: Trade Law and "Global Apartheid"', *Journal of International Economic Law* 6(3).

Turner, L., Nguyen, N. and Bird, K. 2008. *An Overview of Ex Ante Tools for Assessing the Impact of Trade Liberalisation on the Poor.* Report Prepared for BMZ/GTZ. London: ODI.

Tussie, D. 1987. The Less Developed Countries and the World Trading System: A Challenge to the GATT. London: Frances Pinter.

Tussie, D. (ed.) 2009. *The Politics of Trade. The Role of Research in Trade Policy and Negotiation. Studies in International Institutional Dynamics.* The Netherlands: Republic of Letters Publishing.

Tussie, D. and Glover, D. 1993. *The Developing Countries in World Trade: Policies and Bargaining Strategies.* Boulder, CO: Lynne Rienner.

Tussie, D. and Lengyel, M. 2002. 'Developing Countries: Turning Participation into Influence', in Hoekman, B., Mattoo, A. and English, P. (eds.), Development, Trade, and the WTO: A Handbook. Washington, DC: World Bank.

UK Parliament. 2003. 'Trade and Development at the WTO: Learning the Lessons of Cancún to Revive a Genuine Development Round', International Development Committee Session 2003–4, First Report. London: UK Parliament.

UN. 2000. General Assembly Resolution 55/2. *United Nations Millennium Declaration.* A/RES/55/2, New York: United Nations.

2001. *Road Map Towards the Implementation of the United Nations Millennium Declaration.* A/56/326. New York: United Nations.

2009a. 'Outcome of the Conference on the World Financial and Economic Crisis and Its Impact on Development', General Assembly Resolution A/63/L.75, New York: United Nations.

2009b. *Recommendations by the Commission of Experts of the President of the United Nations General Assembly on Reforms of the International Monetary and Financial System*, 21 September. New York: United Nations.

UNCTAD. 2000. *Positive Agenda and Future Trade Negotiations.* Geneva: UNCTAD.

2003a. *Trade and Development Report 2003.* Geneva: UNCTAD.

2003b. 'Increasing the Participation of Developing Countries through Liberalization of Market Access in GATS Mode 4 for Movement of Natural Persons Supplying Services', Note by the UNCTAD Secretariat. Geneva.

2004. *The Least Developed Countries Report 2004: Linking International Trade to Poverty Reduction.* Geneva: UNCTAD.

2007. *Trade and Development Report 2007.* Geneva: UNCTAD.

2009. *The Global Economic Crisis: Systemic Failures and Multilateral Remedies*, UN Publication E.09.II.D.4, New York and Geneva: UNCTAD.

2010. *Trade and Development Report 2010.* Geneva: UNCTAD.

UNDP. 2003. *Making Global Trade Work For People.* New York: UNDP.

2005. *Human Development Report 2005. International Cooperation at a Cross Roads: Aid, Trade and Security in an Unequal World.* New York: UNDP.

2009. *Trade for Poverty Reduction: The Role of Trade in Poverty Reduction Strategy Papers.* New York: UNDP.

UNECA. 2009. *Global Review on Aid for Trade 2009: Issues and State of Implementation in Africa.* Addis Ababa: UNECA.

UN Millennium Project. 2005. 'Trade for Development: Achieving the Millennium Development Goals', *UN Task Force on Trade.* New York: UNDP.

Urpelainen, J. 2009. 'Political-Economic Problems in Trade Capacity Building', *The Review of International Organizations* 4(4): 329–59.

van den Bossche, P. 2008. 'NGO Involvement in the WTO: A Comparative Perspective', *Journal of International Economic Law* 11(4): 717–49.

2009. 'Non-Governmental Organizations and the WTO: Limits to Involvement?' in Steger, D. (ed.), *Redesigning the World Trade Organization for the Twenty-first Century.* International Development Research Centre (IDRC) and the Centre for International Governance Innovation (CIGI): Wilfrid Laurier University Press.

van Dijck, P. and Faber, G. (eds.) 1996. *Challenges to the New World Trade Organization.* The Hague: Kluwer Law International.

2006. *Developing Countries and the Doha Development Agenda.* London: Routledge.

van Grasstek, C. 2001. 'Why Demands on Acceding Countries Increase Over Time: A Three-Dimensional Analysis of Multilateral Trade Diplomacy', in *WTO Accessions and Development Policies*, Geneva: UNCTAD, pp. 78–95.

2008. *The Challenges of Trade Policymaking: Analysis, Communication and Representation*, Geneva and New York: UNCTAD.

van Grasstek, C. and Sauvé, P. 2006. 'The Consistency of WTO Rules: Can the Single Undertaking Be Squared With Viable Geometry?' *Journal of International Economic Law* 9: 837–64.

Veiga, P. 2009. 'Brazil's Trade Policy: Moving Away from Old Paradigms', in Brainard, L. and Martinez-Diaz, L. (eds.), *Brazil as an Economic Superpower? Understanding Brazil's Changing Role in the Global Economy.* Washington, DC: Brookings Institution Press.

Vines, D. 1998. 'The WTO in Relation to the Fund and the Bank: Competencies, Agendas and Linkages', in Krueger, A. (ed.), *The WTO as an International Organization.* Chicago University Press.

von Moltke, A. (ed.) 2010. *Fisheries Subsidies, Sustainable Development and the WTO.* London: Earthscan.

von Moltke, K. 1996. *WTO and Sustainable Development: An Independent Assessment.* Winnipeg: IISD.

Wallach, L. and Sforza, M. 1999. *Whose Trade Organization? Corporate Globalization and the Erosion of Democracy – An Assessment of the World Trade Organization.* Washington, DC: Public Citizen.

Wang, Z. 1997. *Africa's Role in Multilateral Trade Negotiations*. Washington, DC: World Bank.

Warwick Commission. 2007. *The Multilateral Trade Regime: Which Way Forward?* Coventry: The University of Warwick.

Weekes, J., Thompson, R. and Wang, A. 2001. *A Study on Assistance and Representation of the Developing Countries without WTO Permanent Representation in Geneva*. London: The Commonwealth Secretariat.

WEF. 2010. *WEF Global Redesign Summit Report*, Geneva: World Economic Forum.

Whalley, J. (ed.) *Trade Policy and the Developing World*. University of Michigan Press.

Wilkinson, R. 2002a. 'Peripheralising Labour: The ILO, WTO and the Completion of the Bretton Woods Project', in Harrod, J. and O'Brien, R. (eds.), *Globalized Unions? Theory and Strategies of Organized Labour in the Global Political Economy*. London: Routledge.

2002b. 'The Contours of Courtship: The WTO and Civil Society', in Wilkinson, R. and Hughes, S. (eds.), *Global Governance: Critical Perspectives*. London: Routledge.

2006a. *The WTO: Crisis and the Governance of Global Trade*. Oxford: Routledge.

2006b. 'The WTO in Hong Kong: What it Really Means for the Doha Development Agenda', *New Political Economy* 11(2): 291–304.

2009a. 'The Problematic of Trade and Development Beyond the Doha Round', *Journal of International Trade and Diplomacy* 3(1): 155–186.

2009b. 'Language, Power and Multilateral Trade Negotiations', *Review of International Political Economy* 16(4): 597–61.

2011. 'Barriers to WTO Reform: Intellectual Narrowness and the Production of Path-dependent Thinking', in Cottier, T. and Elsig, M. (eds.), *Governing the World Trade Organization Past, Present and Beyond Doha*. Cambridge University Press.

Wilkinson, R. and Scott, J. 2008. 'Developing Country Participation in the GATT: A Reassessment', *World Trade Review* 7(3): 473–510.

Williams, M. 2002. 'Gender and Governance in the Multilateral Trading System: Critical Areas of Decision-making and Global Responses', paper presented at GERA Mid-Term Review Workshop, 25–29 November, Accra, Ghana.

Winters, A., Walmsley, T., Wang, Z. and Grynberg, R. 2003. 'Liberalising Temporary Movement of Natural Persons: An Agenda for the Development Round', *The World Economy* 26(8): 1137–62.

Wolfe, R. 2004. 'Informal Political Engagement in the WTO: Are Mini-Ministerials a Good Idea?' in Curtis, J. and Ciuriak, D. (eds.), *Trade Policy Research 2004*. Ottawa: Canadian Department of Foreign Affairs and International Trade, pp. 27–91.

2005. 'Decision-Making and Transparency in the "Medieval" WTO: Does the Sutherland Report Have the Right Prescription?' *Journal of International Economic Law* 8(3): 631–45.

2008. 'Can the Trading System Be Governed? Institutional Implications of the WTO's Suspended Animation', in Alexandroff, A. (ed.), *Can the World be Governed? Possibilities for Effective Multilateralism*. Waterloo, Ont.: Wilfrid Laurier University Press, pp. 289–344.

2009. 'The WTO Single Undertaking as Negotiating Technique and Constitutive Metaphor', *Journal of International Economic Law* 12: 835–57.

2010. 'Did the Protectionist Dog Bark? Transparency, Accountability, and the WTO During the Global Crisis', paper prepared for the Annual Meeting of ISA-Canada with the Canadian Political Science Association. 1 June. Available at www.cpsa-acsp.ca/papers-2010/Wolfe.pdf [Accessed in November 2010].

Woods, N. 2010. 'The G20 Leaders and Global Governance', *GEG Working Paper No. 2010/59*. Oxford: Global Economic Governance Programme.

World Bank. 1993. *Global Economic Prospects and the Developing Countries*. Washington, DC: World Bank.

2004. 'Trade Facilitation: Using WTO Disciplines to Promote Development', *Trade Note*. Washington, DC: World Bank.

WTO. 1999. *The Legal Texts: The Results of the Uruguay Round of Multilateral Trade Negotiations*. Cambridge University Press.

2000. *Trade, Development and the Environment*. Geneva: WTO and Kluwer Law International.

2001. *Communication from India on Behalf of the Like-minded Group*. WT/GC/W/471. 24 April. Geneva: WTO.

2003a. *Guidelines for Appointment of Officers to WTO Bodies*. Adopted by the General Council on 11 December 2002, WT/L/510. Geneva: WTO.

2003b. *Final Report of the Evaluation of the Integrated Framework*. Integrated Framework Steering Committee. WT/IFSC/6/Rev.2. Geneva: WTO.

2005. *Hong Kong Ministerial Declaration*. Adopted on 18 December 2005 at the Hong Kong Ministerial Conference, WT/MIN(05)/DEC. Geneva: WTO.

2006a. *Recommendations of the Task Force on Aid for Trade*. WT/AID FOR TRADE/1. Geneva: WTO.

2006b. *An Enhanced Integrated Framework: Report by the Chairman of the Task Force on an Enhanced Integrated Framework, including recommendations*. Integrated Framework Steering Committee. WT/IFSC/W/15. Geneva: WTO.

2007. *World Trade Report: Sixty Years of the Multilateral Trading System: Achievements and Challenges*. Geneva: WTO.

2009a. 'Appointment of the Director-General. Statement of the Director-General', General Council, Job (09)/39, 29 April. Geneva: WTO.

2009b. 'Seventh Ministerial Conference – Chairman's Summary', WT/MIN(09)/18, 2 December. Geneva: WTO.

2009c. 'Strengthening the WTO: Communication from Australia, Brazil, Canada, China, Hong Kong China, European Communities, India, Japan, Korea, Malaysia, Mauritius, Mexico, Norway, South Africa, Switzerland,

Turkey, United States and Uruguay', WT/MIN(09)/W/1. 16 October. Geneva: WTO.

2009d. 'Strengthening the WTO: Communication from India', WT/GC/W/605. 3 July. Geneva: WTO.

2009e. 'Geneva Ministerial a "Unique Occasion" to Send Strong Signals on WTO Issues', *Report to the General Council*. 17 November. Geneva. Available at www.wto.org/english/news_e/news09_e/tnc_chair_report_17nov09_e.htm [Accessed in July 2010].

2009f. 'Accession of Developing Countries – Communication from Gabon on Behalf of the Informal Group of Developing Countries', WT/GC/119. Geneva: WTO.

2010a. *Monitoring Aid for Trade at the Global Level*. Committee on Aid for Trade. JOB/DEV/3. Geneva: WTO.

2010b. *WTO Accessions: 2009 Annual Report by the Director-General*. WT/ACC/13. Geneva: WTO.

WTO and ILO. 2009. *Globalization and Informal Jobs in Developing Countries*. Geneva: WTO and ILO.

WTO and OECD. 2009. *Aid for Trade at a Glance 2009: Maintaining Momentum*. Geneva/Paris: WTO and OECD.

WTO and UNEP. 2009. *Trade and Climate Change: WTO-UNEP Report*. Geneva: WTO and UNEP.

WTO and WHO. 2002. *WTO Agreements and Public Health*. Geneva: WTO and WHO.

WWF. 1999a. 'Reform of the WTO's Dispute Settlement Mechanism for Sustainable Development', *WWF International Discussion Paper*. July. Gland, Switzerland: World Wildlife Fund.

1999b. 'A Reform Agenda for the WTO, Seattle Ministerial Conference 30 November–3 December 1999', *WWF Position Paper*. Gland, Switzerland: World Wildlife Fund International.

Youssef, H. 1999. *Special and Differential Treatment for Developing Countries in the WTO*. Geneva: South Centre.

Yu, V. 2008. *Unity in Diversity: Governance Adaptation in Multilateral Trade Institutions Through South South Coalition-building*. Geneva: South Centre.

Zedillo, E. 2009. *The Multilateral Trading System: A Response to its Challengers*. Available at www.ycsg.yale.edu/focus/papers/globalTrade.pdf [Accessed in November 2010].

Zeng, K. and Mertha, A. 2007. 'Introduction', in Zeng, K. (ed.), *China's Foreign Trade Policy: The New Constituencies*. London: Routledge, pp. 1–19.

Ziegler, A. and Bonzon, Y. 2007. 'How to Reform WTO Decision-Making? An Analysis of the Current Functioning of the Organization from the Perspectives of Efficiency and Legitimacy', *Working Paper No. 2007/23*, NCCR Trade Regulation Project.

INDEX